T0214871

Communications in Computer and Information Science 1390

More information about this series at http://www.springer.com/series/7899

Guangtao Zhai · Jun Zhou ·
Hua Yang · Ping An · Xiaokang Yang (Eds.)

Digital TV and Wireless Multimedia Communication

17th International Forum, IFTC 2020
Shanghai, China, December 2, 2020
Revised Selected Papers

 Springer

Editors
Guangtao Zhai (iD)
Shanghai Jiao Tong University
Shanghai, China

Hua Yang
Shanghai Jiao Tong University
Shanghai, China

Xiaokang Yang
Shanghai Jiao Tong University
Shanghai, China

Jun Zhou (iD)
Shanghai Jiao Tong University
Shanghai, China

Ping An (iD)
Shanghai University
Shanghai, China

ISSN 1865-0929   ISSN 1865-0937   (electronic)
Communications in Computer and Information Science
ISBN 978-981-16-1193-3   ISBN 978-981-16-1194-0   (eBook)
https://doi.org/10.1007/978-981-16-1194-0

This Springer imprint is published by the registered company Springer Nature Singapore Pte Ltd.
The registered company address is: 152 Beach Road, #21-01/04 Gateway East, Singapore 189721, Singapore

Preface

The present book includes extended and revised versions of papers selected from the 17th International Forum on Multimedia Communication (IFTC 2020), held in Shanghai, China, on December 2, 2020.

IFTC is a summit forum in the field of digital media communication. The 2020 forum was co-hosted by Shanghai Image and Graphics Association (SIGA), the China International Industry Fair (CIIF 2020), and Shanghai Association for Science and Technology, and co-sponsored by Shanghai Jiao Tong University (SJTU), China Telecom Corporation Limited Shanghai Branch, Shanghai Institute for Advanced Communication and Data Science (SICS), and Shanghai Key Laboratory of Digital Media Processing and Transmission. The 17th IFTC serves as an international bridge for extensively exchanging the latest research advances of digital media communication around the world. The forum also aims to promote technology, equipment, and applications in the field of digital media by comparing their characteristics, framework, significant techniques, and maturity, analyzing the performance of various applications in terms of scalability, manageability, and portability, and discussing the interfaces among varieties of networks and platforms.

The conference program included invited talks delivered by 4 distinguished speakers from Sydney University (Australia), Ryerson University (Canada), Jilin University (China), and Shenzhen Institute of Advanced Technology of Chinese Acacemy of Sciences (China), as well as an oral session of 5 papers and a poster session of 32 papers. The topics of these papers ranged from audio/image processing to telecommunications as well as machine learning. This book contains 37 papers selected from IFTC 2020.

The proceeding editors wish to thank the authors for contributing their novel ideas and visions that are recorded in this book, and all the reviewers for their contributions. We also thank Springer for their trust and for publishing the proceedings of IFTC 2020.

December 2020

Guangtao Zhai
Jun Zhou
Hua Yang
Ping An
Xiaokang Yang

Organization

General Chairs

Xiaokang Yang   Shanghai Jiao Tong University, China
Ping An   Shanghai University, China
Guangtao Zhai   Shanghai Jiao Tong University, China

Program Chairs

Xiangyang Xue   Fudan University, China
Jun Zhou   Shanghai Jiao Tong University, China
Yue Lu   East China Normal University, China
Hua Yang   Shanghai Jiao Tong University, China

Tutorial Chairs

Yu-Gang Jiang   Fudan University, China
Yuming Fang   Jiangxi University of Finance and Economics, China
Jiantao Zhou   University of Macau, China

International Liaisons

Weisi Lin   Nanyang Technological University, Singapore
Patrick Le Callet   University of Nantes, France
Lu Zhang   INSA de Rennes, France

Finance Chairs

Yi Xu   Shanghai Jiao Tong University, China
Hao Liu   Donghua University, China
Beibei Li   Shanghai Polytechnic University, China
Xuefei Song   Shanghai 9th People's Hospital, China

Publications Chairs

Hong Lu   Fudan University, China
Feiniu Yuan   Shanghai Normal University, China
Xianming Liu   Harbin Institute of Technology, China
Liquan Shen   Shanghai University, China

Award Chairs

Zhijun Fang	Shanghai University of Engineering Science, China
Xiaolin Huang	Shanghai Jiao Tong University, China
Hanli Wang	Tongji University, China
Yu Zhu	East China University of Science and Technology, China

Publicity Chairs

Wenjun Zhang	Shanghai Jiao Tong University, China
Bo Yan	Fudan University, China
Gang Hou	Central Research Institute of INESA, China

Industrial Program Chairs

Yiyi Lu	China Telecom Shanghai Branch, China
Guozhong Wang	Shanghai University of Engineering Science, China
Chen Yao	The Third Research Institute Of MPS, China
Yan Zhou	Renji Hospital, China

Arrangements Chairs

Cheng Zhi	Secretary-General, SIGA, China
Yicong Peng	Shanghai Jiao Tong University, China

Contents

Machine Learning

Media Transfer

Quality Assessment

Virtual Reality

Image Processing

Recurrent Multi-column 3D Convolution Network for Video Super-Resolution

Junjie Lian[2], Yongfang Wang[1,2(✉)], and Yuan Shuai[2]

[1] Shanghai Institute for Advanced Communication and Data Science,
Shanghai University, Shanghai 200444, China
yfw@shu.edu.cn
[2] School of Communication and Information Engineering,
Shanghai University, Shanghai 200444, China

Abstract. Super-resolution (SR) aims to recover high resolution (HR) content from low resolution (LR) content, which is a hotspot in image and video processing. Since there is strong correlation between video sequence, how to effectively exploit spatio-temporal information among serial frames is significant for video super-resolution (VSR). In this paper, we propose a recurrent multi-column 3D convolution network to fuse inter-frame and intra-frame information for VSR. Specifically, we first introduce motion compensation by optical flow to align the reference frame and supporting frames. Different from the previous methods, our supporting frames is originated from the previous reconstructed SR frame, instead of front and back low resolution frames of reference frame. This is more conducive to generating visual consistent video sequence. Then, 3D multi-column block (3DMB), which is composed with different separable 3D convolutions by reducing the parameters without performance penalties, is performed to fuse spatio-temporal features and recover missing details of reference frame. Finally, consecutive HR video sequence is obtained by reconstruction module. Comparative experiments are carried out to demonstrate our proposed method outperforms other advanced methods.

Keywords: Video super-resolution · Optical flow estimation · Separable 3D convolution · Recurrent multi-column 3D convolution

1 Introduction

Super-resolution (SR) aims to recover high resolution (HR) content from low resolution (LR) content by complex nonlinear mapping. The rapid development of streaming media stimulates the continuous upgrading of display hardware and puts forward great demand on HR content. High cost acquisition, storage and transmission of HR content, as well as the demand to improve the previous content to higher resolution, put forward new challenges to SR research.

Compared with a single image, it exists strong inter-frame temporal correlation between video sequence [1, 2]. The HR video sequence obtained directly from single

G. Zhai et al. (Eds.): IFTC 2020, CCIS 1390, pp. 3–11, 2021.
https://doi.org/10.1007/978-981-16-1194-0_1

image super-resolution (SISR) method is often limited by finite information of independent frame and presents obvious artificial traces. Therefore, it is crucial for video super-resolution (VSR) to fully utilize spatial and temporal information among video frames. Numerous previous researches [3–9] have proved that effective use of temporal correlations among continuous frames can accurately infer HR content from reference frame.

Due to the movement of the camera, there are spatial differences between the front and back frames. Therefore, the front and back frames of the reference frame are usually implemented motion compensation first. Then the aligned frame feature is analyzed to complete the reconstruction of the reference frame. In this way, the spatial and temporal information between frames is used to enrich the detail information of reference frame. However, due to the weak correlation between reconstructed SR frames, the generated video sequences inevitably have visual inconsistencies. To address these issues, we propose a recurrent multi-column 3D convolution network to build dependence between constructed SR frame and 3D multi-column block (3DMB) for feature analysis and fusion. As shown in Fig. 1, the input is the reference LR frame, previous LR frame and previous reconstructed SR frame. The optical flow estimation comes from LR content and is applied to previous SR frame. We conduct sub-pixel deconvolution to generate subgraphs of SR frame to achieve dimensional unification and conduct motion compensation to each subgraph. By considering the previous reconstructed frame and current reference frame, a recurrent structure is formed to generate video sequence with continuous consistency. Since 3D convolution can capture both spatial and temporal features at the same time, it is very suitable for video tasks [5]. However, 3D convolution will introduce abundant parameters, which increases model burden. Inspired by [10], we split 3D convolution to reduce parameters without degrading the performance. In this way, we can utilize the complementary characteristics of different convolution kernels to construct 3DMB. The reduction of parameters allows us to use large separable 3D convolution kernel to expand the receptive field rapidly, and to fuse features on different receptive fields. Through this recurrent generation mechanism and 3DMB, our model can accurately reconstruct HR video sequence without obvious single frame stitching trace. The remainder of the paper is composed as follows. Section 2 briefly introduces related work of VSR. Section 3 introduces the proposed method. Experimental results and analysis are displayed in Sect. 4. Section 5 is the conclusion of the paper.

2   Related Work

VSR is mainly confronted with two challenges: one is how to accurately align the consecutive frames, either explicitly or implicitly, and the other is how to fully utilize complementary information of consecutive frames to complete SR task. In this section, we briefly review typical VSR model in recent years.

Kappler et al. [3] use optical flow algorithm from Drulea [11] to handle neighboring frames, and reconstruct HR frame through brief network structure. Guo et al. [12] employ bidirectional long short term memory (Bi-LSTM) module to fuse spatial and temporal component. Through Bi-LSTM, they avoid explicit motion compensation and construct an end-to-end network. Huang et al. [13] use recurrent neural network to expand along temporal dimension to capture long-term dependency among video sequence. Jo et al. [7] introduce dynamic upsampling filters to generate residual images from loacl spatio-temporal neighborhood of each pixel. Dynamic upsampling filter has the ability of adaptive deformation to capture features, so the network does not need explicit alignment to frames. Inspired by iterative back projection algorithm from traditional SR method, Haris et al. [8] propose RBPN method which adopts multiple groups encoder-decoder structure to repeatedly learn the relationship between up and down sampling.

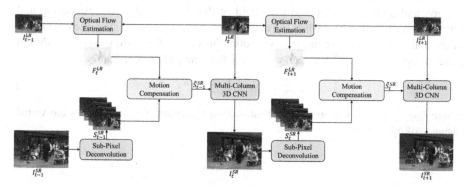

Fig. 1. The framework of proposed recurrent multi-column 3D convolution network.

3   Proposed Method

In this section, we introduce proposed recurrent multi-column 3D convolution network in details. The overall framework of our network is shown in Fig. 1. First, we predict the optical flow between previous and current LR frames. Then we handle previous reconstructed SR frame with sub-pixel deconvolution to get subgraphs and implement motion compensation. Because the previous SR frame has generous redundant sub-pixel information, it can complement the current frame and maintain good visual consistency. The compensated subgraphs and the current frame will be cascaded and be sent into 3D multi-column block to perform adequate feature extraction and analysis. Finally, the HR video sequence will be obtained through reconstructed module.

3.1   Motion Compensation on Previous SR Frame

Optical flow is the instantaneous velocity of the object pixel motion on the observation plane, represented as a velocity vector field, which is widely used in video processing. Previous works usually respectively predict optical flow of the front and back frame with the target frame, and then align them to compensate the detail information of the target frame. Although inter-frame tempo-spatial information is utilized, the correlation of reconstructed SR sequence is ignored, resulting in visual inconsistency. Therefore, the input of our model is the target LR frame I_t^{LR}, the previous LR frame I_{t-1}^{LR} and the previous reconstructed SR frame I_{t-1}^{SR}. Liu et al. [14] proposed a pyramid structure based optical flow algorithm, which can predict optical flow from coarse to fine, even if the motion of the observed object is large. As shown in Fig. 2, the under-processing images are first down-sampled under Gaussian blur at different multiples to obtain image pyramids. Then the optical flow method is used to estimate the motion of the image with small scale at the top of pyramid. Because of the small scale of the image, the motion of the object with higher speed is smaller at the small scale, satisfying the assumptions of the optical flow method. The calculated low level optical flow field is scaled up to the scale of next layer as the initial value of the next layer, inferring the corresponding incremental fraction and updating the optical flow field of that layer. And so on, estimating and refining layer by layer, and when the calculation reaches the final layer, the estimation of the optical flow field is complete. We adopt this optical flow estimation algorithm to generate optical flow F_t^{LR} between previous LR frame and current frame,

$$F_t^{LR} = f_{optical}\left(I_{t-1}^{LR}, I_t^{LR}\right) \tag{1}$$

where $f_{optical}$ denotes the optical flow estimation algorithm. Figure 3 shows the visual instance of optical flow.

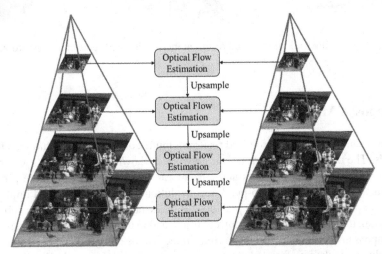

Fig. 2. Pyramid structure based optical flow algorithm framework.

In order to strengthen the correlation between previous frame and target frame reconstruction, we compensate not only the motion of the previous frame I_{t-1}^{LR}, but also the previous SR frame I_{t-1}^{SR}. Due to different size among I_t^{LR} and I_{t-1}^{SR}, we need to process I_{t-1}^{SR} with sub-pixel deconvolution. Sub-pixel deconvolution is the inverse operation of sub-pixel convolution, using scale conversion to channels to effectively preserve the sub-pixel information of the SR version. Compared with ordinary deconvolution, it does not need to lose pixel information,

$$[I_{t-1}^{SR}]^{sH \times sW \times C} \rightarrow [S_{t-1}^{SR}]^{s^2 \times H \times W \times C} \tag{2}$$

(a) The first frame   (b) The second frame   (c) Optical flow

Optical flow between the first and second frame of "walk"

(a) The first frame   (b) The second frame   (c) Optical flow

Optical flow between the first and second frame of "city"

Fig. 3. Visual instance of optical flow.

where H, W is length and width of the input LR frame, C denotes channel and s denotes upscale factor. We segment s^2 subgraphs S_{t-1}^{SR} from I_{t-1}^{SR} by sub-pixel deconvolution and conduct motion compensation on S_{t-1}^{SR} and I_{t-1}^{LR} to generate $\tilde{S}_{t-1}^{SR}$ and $\tilde{I}_{t-1}^{LR}$. Then we cascade $\tilde{S}_{t-1}^{SR}$, $\tilde{I}_{t-1}^{LR}$ with I_t^{LR} for fusion operations and feed them into the subsequent networks. Because previous SR frame is joined current frame reconstruction to establish relevance, it can effectively prevent the occurrence of visual discontinuity in the final reconstruction video sequence. This process can be expressed as follows,

$$\tilde{S}_{t-1}^{SR} = C(S_{t-1}^{SR}), \tilde{I}_{t-1}^{LR} = C(I_{t-1}^{LR})$$
$$F_t^{in} = f_{fuse}\left(\left[\tilde{S}_{t-1}^{SR}, \tilde{I}_{t-1}^{LR}, I_t^{LR}\right]\right) \tag{3}$$

where C denotes motion compensation, [] is cascading operation and f_{fuse} is fusion operation. F_t^{in} is the final input to the subsequent networks.

3.2 3D Multi-column Block (3DMB)

Due to unique structure, 3D convolution can capture spatio-temporal information at the same time. However, the usage of 3D convolution is accompanied by the sharp rise of parameters, which increases the computational burden. Therefore, most networks using 3D convolution cannot be designed too deep, which limits the network's performance. And the 3D convolution used in network is often only one $3 \times 3 \times 3$ choose. [10] proved that decomposing 3D convolution can greatly reduce the parameters without losing too much performance. We decompose the 3D convolution with dimension $k \times k \times k$ into one $1 \times k \times k$ and one $k \times 1 \times 1$. This means that for a $3 \times 3 \times 3$ convolution, parameter will reduce from 27 to 12 and for $5 \times 5 \times 5$ one, parameters will reduce from 125 to 30. Therefore, we can build a deeper network with various types of 3D convolution to increase the network's representation ability. As shown in Fig. 4, 3DMB takes advantages of the complementarity between different convolution types to construct three branches. At the end of each branch, we utilize $1 \times 1 \times 1$ convolution to perform fine adjustments, and fuse the features on different receptive fields. Through this multicolumn format, we construct feature pyramid from different receptive fields, enhancing the representation ability of the network. Features within the different channels can be fully integrated to enhance the performance of reconstruction. After multiple 3DMB, the spatio-temporal information between frames is fully fused, and the residual frame I_t^{Res} is obtained after upsampling. In the end, the reconstructed frame I_t^{SR} can be generated by adding I_t^{Res} and the bicubic LR reference frame I_t^{Bic}. This process can be presented as,

$$I_t^{Res} = f_{conv}(f_{deconv}(f_{3DMB} \cdots (f_{3DMB}(F_t^{in})))) \tag{4}$$

where f_{3DMB} is 3DMB, f_{deconv} is deconvolution operation to expand the scale, f_{conv} is a 3×3 convolution to make channel adjustments.

$$I_t^{SR} = I_t^{Res} + f_{bic}(I_t^{LR}) \tag{5}$$

where f_{bic} is bicubic interpolation, I_t^{SR} is the final reconstructed SR frame.

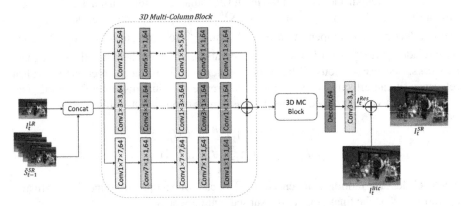

Fig. 4. 3D Multi-column Convolution Block (3DMB).

4 Experience

4.1 Datasets and Training Details

We adopt a public video dataset DAVIS [15] as training set and Vid4 [16] as testing set. The dataset contains 150 video sequence. During training, 10 consecutive frames are separated from video one time as a batch. When the scale factor is 2, we divide each frame into 82×82 blocks in 64 steps. When scale factor is 3, the step is 48 and the block size is 123×123. When scale factor is 4, the step is 32 and the block size is 164×164. We use random rotation, flipping and subsampling for data augmentation. Before training, we transform the images into YCbCr format. The training and testing are conducted on the Y channel (luminance channel). Due to the input requires previous frame, we assume the previous LR and SR frame of the first frame each sequence is pure black. Mean absolute error (MAE) is selected as loss function,

$$\mathcal{L}(\Theta) = \frac{1}{n} \sum_{i=1}^{n} \|I_t^{SR} - I_t^{HR}\| \tag{6}$$

We applied the Adam optimizer [17] with $\beta_1 = 0.9$, $\beta_2 = 0.999$. The training batch size is 16 and the learning rate is 1×10^{-5} which is reduced by half every 10 epochs. The network final converges at the 100th epoch. PyTorch platform in Ubuntu 16.04 is employed to train our network.

Table 1. Performance comparison with other methods on VID4 (PSNR/SSIM).

Scale	x 2	x 3	x 4
Bicubic	28.43/0.868	25.28/0.733	23.79/0.633
VSRNET [3]	31.30/0.928	26.79/0.810	24.81/0.702
VESPCN [18]	– /–	27.25/0.845	25.35/0.756
TDVSR [19]	– /–	– /–	25.34/0.745
DRVSR [20]	– /–	27.49/0.841	25.52/0.763
3DSRNet [5]	32.25/0.941	27.70/0.850	25.71/0.759
Ours	**32.91/0.941**	**28.23/0.869**	**26.01/0.771**

4.2 Comparison with Other Advanced Methods

We compare our algorithm with five advanced methods: VSRNet [3], VESPCN [18], TDVSR [19], DRVSR [20], 3DSRNet [5]. We evaluate the reconstructed SR results with peak signal to noise ratio (PSNR) and structural similarity index (SSIM). Quantitative evaluation results are shown in Table 1 for the scale factor of ×2, ×3, ×4. The best algorithm is blod. Our proposed method gets the best quantitative results over other state-of-the-art methods. Noted that 3DSRNet [5] also apply 3D convolution into network architecture, our model outperforms them with PSNR gain of 0.66 dB, 0.53 dB, 0.30 dB separately on the scale factor of ×2, ×3, ×4. It demonstrates the effectiveness of separable 3D convolutions in 3DMB which used less parameters. Moreover, we present visual qualitative comparison results for the scale factor of ×2 and ×4 in Fig. 5. Note that GT represents the original high resolution frame. Thus it can be seen that, our model can accurately reconstruct HR frames and have better visual details.

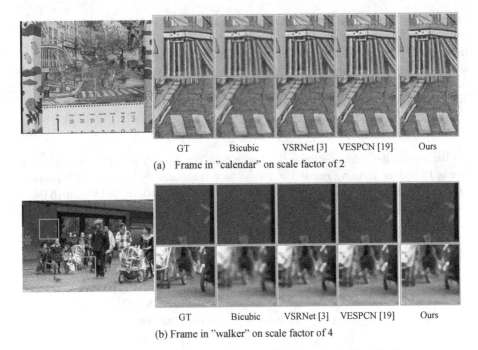

(a) Frame in "calendar" on scale factor of 2

(b) Frame in "walker" on scale factor of 4

Fig. 5. Visual qualitative comparisons with other advanced methods.

5 Conclusion

In this paper, we propose a recurrent multi-column 3D convolution network for VSR. We first speculate the optical flow between the target and previous LR frame. Then we conduct motion compensation to previous SR frame. By mixing the processed SR frame with current LR frame as input, the visual consistency of the reconstructed video is well maintained. 3DMB also enhances the interaction of features between different channels to accurately reconstruct HR frames. Quantitative and qualitative comparison with other advanced methods demonstrates the effectiveness of our proposed model.

Acknowledgment. This work was supported by Natural Science Foundation of China under Grant No. 61671283, 61301113.

References

1. Hayat, K.: Multimedia super-resolution via deep learning: a survey. Digit. Signal Process. **81**, 198–217 (2018)
2. Wang, Z., Chen, J., Hoi, S.C.H.: Deep learning for image super-resolution: a survey. IEEE Trans. Pattern Anal. Mach. Intell. **PP**(99), 1 (2020)
3. Kappeler, A., Yoo, S., Dai, Q., Katsaggelos, A.K.: Video super-resolution with convolutional neural networks. IEEE Trans. Comput. Imaging **2**(2), 109–122 (2016)

4. Wang, L., Guo, Y., Lin, Z., Deng, X., An, W.: Learning for video super-resolution through HR optical flow estimation. In: Jawahar, C.V., Li, H., Mori, G., Schindler, K. (eds.) Computer Vision – ACCV 2018, pp. 514–529. Springer, Cham (2019). https://doi.org/10.1007/978-3-030-20887-5_32

5. Kim, S.Y., Lim, J., Na, T., Kim, M.: 3DSRnet: Video Super-resolution Using 3D Convolutional Neural Networks, arXiv preprint arXiv:1812.09079 (2018)

6. Makansi, O., Ilg, E., Brox, T.: End-to-end learning of video super-resolution with motion compensation. In: Roth, V., Vetter, T. (eds.) Pattern Recognition, pp. 203–214. Springer, Cham (2017). https://doi.org/10.1007/978-3-319-66709-6_17

7. Jo, Y., Wug Oh, S., Kang, J., Joo Kim, S.: Deep video super-resolution network using dynamic upsampling filters without explicit motion compensation. In: Proceedings of the IEEE Conference on Computer Vision and Pattern Recognition, pp. 3224–3232 (2018)

8. Haris, M., Shakhnarovich, G., Ukita, N.: Recurrent back-projection network for video super-resolution. In: Proceedings of the IEEE Conference on Computer Vision and Pattern Recognition, pp. 3897–3906 (2019)

9. Li, S., He, F., Du, B., Zhang, L., Xu, Y., Tao, D.: Fast spatio-temporal residual network for video super-resolution. In: Proceedings of the IEEE Conference on Computer Vision and Pattern Recognition, pp. 10522–10531 (2019)

10. Ye, R., Liu, F., Zhang, L.: 3D depthwise convolution: reducing model parameters in 3D vision tasks. In: Meurs, M.-J., Rudzicz, F. (eds.) Advances in Artificial Intelligence - Canadian AI 2019, pp. 186–199. Springer, Cham (2019). https://doi.org/10.1007/978-3-030-18305-9_15

11. Drulea, M., Nedevschi, S.: Total variation regularization of local-global optical flow. In: 2011 14th International IEEE Conference on Intelligent Transportation Systems (ITSC), pp. 318–323. IEEE (2011)

12. Guo, J., Chao, H.: Building an end-to-end spatial-temporal convolutional network for video super-resolution. In: Thirty-First AAAI Conference on Artificial Intelligence (2017)

13. Huang, Y., Wang, W., Wang, L.: Video super-resolution via bidirectional recurrent convolutional networks. IEEE Trans. Pattern Anal. Mach. Intell. **40**(4), 1015–1028 (2017)

14. Liu, C.: Beyond pixels: exploring new representations and applications for motion analysis, Massachusetts Institute of Technology (2009)

15. Pont-Tuset, J., Perazzi, F., Caelles, S., Arbeláez, P., Sorkine-Hornung, A., Van Gool, L.: The 2017 davis challenge on video object segmentation, arXiv preprint arXiv:1704.00675 (2017)

16. Liu, C., Sun, D.: On Bayesian adaptive video super resolution. IEEE Trans. Pattern Anal. Mach. Intell. **36**(2), 346–360 (2013)

17. Kingma, D.P., Ba, J.: Adam: a method for stochastic optimization, arXiv preprint arXiv:1412.6980 (2014)

18. Caballero, J., et al.: Real-time video super-resolution with spatio-temporal networks and motion compensation. In: Proceedings of the IEEE Conference on Computer Vision and Pattern Recognition, pp. 4778–4787 (2017)

19. Liu, D., et al.: Robust video super-resolution with learned temporal dynamics. In: Proceedings of the IEEE International Conference on Computer Vision, pp. 2507–2515 (2017)

20. Tao, X., Gao, H., Liao, R., Wang, J., Jia, J.: Detail-revealing deep video super-resolution. In: Proceedings of the IEEE International Conference on Computer Vision, pp. 4472–4480 (2017)

The Generative Adversarial Network Based on Attention Mechanism for Image Defogging

Qingyi Zhang, Changhao Zhao, Xiangfen Zhang[✉], Feiniu Yuan[✉],
Chuanjiang Li, and Dawei Hao

The College of Information, Mechanical and Electrical Engineering,
Shanghai Normal University, Shanghai 200234, China
{xiangfen,yfn}@shnu.edu.cn

Abstract. The image collected under the haze weather conditions has
some obvious problems such as reduced contrast, reduced clarity and
color distortion, which seriously reduces the image quality. Combining with deep learning, this paper proposes a new end-to-end generative adversarial defogging network based on attention mechanism, which
transforms the problem of image defogging into the generation of fog-free
images based on foggy images. On the basis of generative adversarial
network, the attention mechanism was introduced into the generating
network to enhance the features of the foggy region and generate the
attention map. Then the attention map and the foggy image were input
into the auto-encoder for encoding and decoding the image and re-decode
the foggy. Finally, the fogless image was output. The attention map was
introduced into the discriminate network to discriminate the true and
false of the fogless image (the prediction fogless image and the real fogless image). A lot of experiments were carried out on the foggy images in
different scenes, and the various comparative analysis were carried out
with the evaluation index of image quality. The result shows that the
defogging network model proposed in this paper can not only be better
applied to all kinds of foggy scenes, but also generate fog-free images
that are more suitable for real scenes, and effectively improve the average gradient value, information entropy and NRSS of the image, and can
better restore edge information and color information of foggy images.

Keywords: Image defogging · Generative adversarial network ·
Attention in neural network · Structural similarity loss function ·
Induction loss function

1 Introduction

Image is one of the ways for humans to recognize the external environment
and obtain visual information. It is also an important part of the human visual

Supported by: National Natural Science Foundation of China (61862029) and Shanghai Normal University (Research on Automatic Focus Algorithm (209-AC9103-20-
368005221)). The corresponding authors: Zhang Xiangfen and Yuan Feiniu.

system. Foggy images are not only unfavorable for human eyes to observe, but also reduce the performance of the computer vision system [1]. Therefore, studying how to effectively solve the problem of image degradation caused by haze has important practical significance and practical value for restoring the characteristic information of foggy images and improving image recognition [2].

According to the implementation principles, the image defogging methods can be divided into two categories [3]: the first one is to enhance the information of the foggy images; the second one is to restore the images according to the foggy image models. The defog algorithms based on image enhancement, such as homomorphic filtering algorithm [4], multiscale Retinex algorithm [5], histogram equalization algorithm [6], wavelet transform algorithm [7], etc. are used to enhance the degraded image to improve the quality of the image, highlight the feature information in the image, and have the characteristics of high computing efficiency, but they can't fundamentally defog the images fundamentally [8]. The defogging algorithm based on the physical model considers the root cause of the deterioration of the quality of the foggy image, and establishes the atmospheric scattering model [9,10] to reverse the fog-free image. The representative algorithms are Tan [11], Fattal [12], Tarel [13], He [14], etc. Compared with the defog algorithm based on image enhancement, the physical model based defog algorithm can acquire more detailed image content. But due to the large amount of calculation, the defog timeliness of this kind of algorithm is slightly inferior to the defog algorithm based on image enhancement.

At present, the neural network defogging algorithm based on machine learning is widely adopted. It directly establishes an end-to-end network architecture to learn and optimize the information features between fog images and non-fog images, so as to obtain the mapping relationship between them to complete the model training. Input the foggy image to the model, and the defogged image can directly be output. Liu [15] established an end-to-end training model to estimate the transmission rate in the atmospheric degradation model using neural network, and recover the foggy image by the atmospheric imaging degradation model. A new end-to-end joint optimized demisting network is established by Lori [16]. The network adopts a dense coding and decoding network with edge preserving pyramid to accurately estimate the transmission mapping, and can estimate both transmission rate and atmospheric light value by combing the atmospheric degradation model. Lathed [17] uses the generative adversarial network to realize the end-to-end information recovery of the foggy image. The network structure does not rely on the prior theory, but learn and merge the feature information of different levels, and learn the weight of the features of different levels, and finally get the fused feature layer by weighting. The network can solve the problem of grid artifacts, greatly improve the objective index, and play a good role in most image restoration jobs. Berdan et al. [18] Designed a cyclic generation adversarial network (cycle-gan) to learn image style migration and used the unpaired images to train the network. For the cycle-gan architecture, perceptual consistency loss and cyclic consistency loss are added to enhance the single image. In this algorithm, non-fog image samples in the same scene are not needed, and the parameters of the atmospheric model need not to be estimated, which makes the network structure more universal and robust.

To some extent, the above researches improve the accuracy of image defogging, but there are still some shortcomings. Inspired by the single image raindrop removal work of Ruiqian [19], this paper designs the attention generation network structure to defog the images in different haze scenes. The process of image defogging in natural scene is transformed into the process of input foggy image to generate non foggy image in corresponding scene. The basic network is generate adversarial network, which is divided into two parts. In the first part, the attention neural network, which is composed of the depth residual network (RESNET), the long short-term memory neural network (LSTM) and the standard convolution neural network, is used to generate an attention map for the image, and the attention map is used to guide the network to focus on the target area of the foggy image; In the second part, the automatic encoding and decoding network and the partial convolution neural network are used to get more extensive image semantic information according to the input foggy image and the corresponding attention map, and finally the fogless image is generated according to the semantic information. The output of the convolution layer of the discrimination network is multiplied by the attention feature matrix to guide the discriminator network to focus on the area indicated by the attention map. In this network, we use a full connection layer to determine the true and false probability of the input image.

2   Deep Residual Network and Memory Neural Network

2.1   Deep Residual Network (RESNET)

The RESNET [20] has the ability to improve the gradient disappearance and network degradation. By introducing the identity mapping theory, the residual function is established to represent the data difference, and by optimizing the residual function to improve the learning efficiency, the network degradation problem is solved. The convolution structure of each layer is shown in Fig. 1.

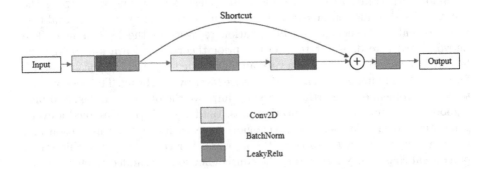

Fig. 1. Residual network layer structure.

In this paper, a five layers residual neural network is used, and the residual blocks are connected by an identity mapping shortcut. The residual value represents the target area of the foggy image, and the foggy area is located and restored by the iterative learning of the depth residual neural network. The fog can be removed accurately by extracting the semantic information through the neural network.

2.2   Long Short-Term Memory (LSTM)

The main structure of LSTM [21] follows the RNN network structure. Three modules, that is, output threshold, input threshold and forgetting threshold are added to make the network weight in a changing state, and the integration range can be dynamically adjusted at different times when the model parameters are unchanged. Thus, the problem of gradient disappearance or gradient expansion is avoided. The structure of LSTM is shown in Fig. 2.

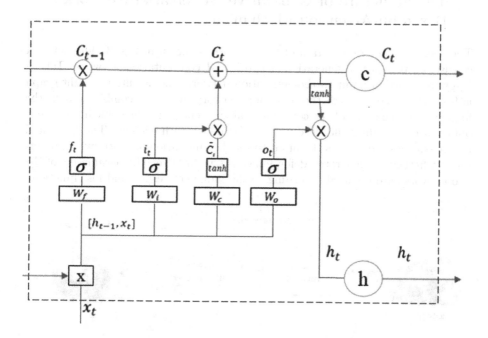

Fig. 2. The structure of LSTM.

In the LSTM network, the calculation formula of each LSTM unit [22] is as follows:

$$f_t = \sigma(W_f \cdot [h_{t-1}, x_t] + b_f) \tag{1}$$

$$i_t = \sigma(W_i \cdot [h_{t-1}, x_t] + b_i) \tag{2}$$

$$\tilde{C}_t = \tanh(W_c \cdot [h_{t-1}, x_t] + b_c) \tag{3}$$

$$C_t = f_t \cdot C_{t-1} + i_t * \widetilde{C_t} \tag{4}$$

$$\sigma_t = \sigma(W_o \cdot [h_{t-1}, x_t] + b_o) \tag{5}$$

$$h_t = o_t * \tanh(C_t) \tag{6}$$

Where f_t is the forget threshold, i_t is the input threshold, $\tilde{C}_t$ is the state of the LSTM unit at the previous time, C_t is the state of the unit where the current cycle occurs, o_t is the output threshold, h_t is the output of the current unit, h_{t-1} is the output of the previous time, x_t represents the input of the current cell. The input gate is used to control the entry of information into the cell, the forget gate is used to control the update of the information in the cell, and the output gate is used to control the output of the information in the cell, The state of each gate is controlled by the function f [22]. LSTM transfers the feature elements to the convolutional layer and generate a two-dimensional attention map.

3 The Structure of Generative Adversarial Network Based on Attention Mechanism

The overall schematic diagram of the network is shown in Fig. 3. The network consists of two parts: generation network and confrontation network. Take a foggy image as an input to the generation network, the attention weight graph is first generated through the attention network and then combined with the fog image as the input of the convolutional auto-encoder. The dehazing image is obtained by encoding and decoding the fog image with encoder. The generated fog-free images are used as the input to the discrimination network, which determines whether the generated defog image is true or false. The parameters of the two networks are updated according to the judgment results and loss function.

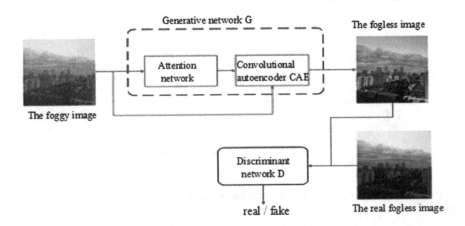

Fig. 3. Structure of dehazing network.

3.1 Generative Network

As shown in Fig. 4, the generating network consists of two sub-networks: attention network and convolutional auto-encoder. The attention neural network includes five layers residual neural network, which is mainly used to extract features between images. The following memory neural network (LSTM) and convolution layers are used to generate attention map. These attention areas are mainly the foggy areas in the image and the surrounding structures in the image. Then the attention map and foggy image are input into the self-encoder to encode and decode the foggy image and finally end up with the foggy image.

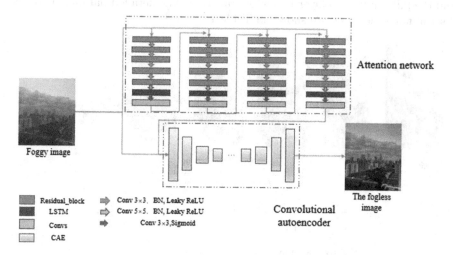

Fig. 4. Generative network structure diagram.

Convolutional auto-encoder composed of 16 convolutional modules and leakyrelu layer, and jump connection is added to prevent output image from blurring. Its network structure is shown in Fig. 5.

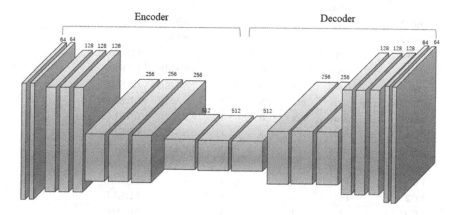

Fig. 5. Convolutional auto-encoder.

3.2 Discriminated Network

A fusion attention discriminator is proposed according to the attention graph obtained by the attention cycle network in the generated network. As shown in Fig. 6, the output of the convolution layer of the discriminator network is multiplied by the attention feature matrix to guide the discriminator network to focus the classified attention on the area indicated by the attention graph. Finally, a full connection layer is used to get the probability of the input image. Our network consists of nine convolution layers, with a full connection layer of 1024 dimensions. The activation function of convolution layer is LRELU function and the full connection layer is sigmoid function. The detailed parameters of the discriminated network are shown in Table 1.

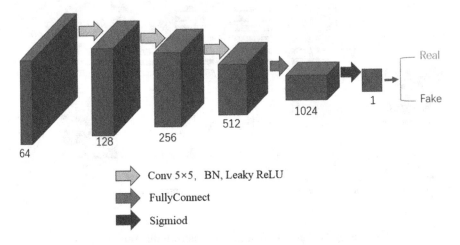

Fig. 6. Discriminated network structure diagram.

Table 1. Discriminated network structure parameter table.

Name	Type	Channel	Kernel	Stride	Padding	Activation Function
Input	Image					
conv1	conv	8	5	1	SAME	LRELU
conv2	conv	16	5	1	SAME	LRELU
conv3	conv	32	5	1	SAME	LRELU
conv4	conv	64	5	1	SAME	LRELU
conv5	conv	128	5	1	SAME	LRELU
attention map	conv	128	5	1	SAME	LRELU
conv6	conv	128	5	1	SAME	LRELU
conv7	conv	64	5	1	SAME	LRELU
conv8	conv	64	5	1	SAME	LRELU
conv9	conv	32	5	1	SAME	LRELU
FC1	FC	1024	1	1		LRELU
FC2	FC	1	1	1		LRELU
FC OUT	FC	1	1	1		SIGMOID

3.3   Loss Function

Content Loss Function. Generative network has two loss functions: structure loss function and perception loss function. The positions of these two loss functions in the generative network are shown in Fig. 7.

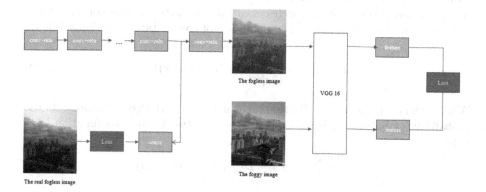

Fig. 7. The loss function in the network.

For the structure loss function, the output with different scale size is formed by extracting features from different convolutions of decoder, and the loss function is shown in formula (7).

$$L_{SSIM}(P) = \frac{1}{N} \sum_{c=1}^{c} \sum_{i=1}^{W} \sum_{j=1}^{H} (1 - SIMM(G(x), y)) \tag{7}$$

Where, C represents the number of color channels of the fog image (set to 3), W and H represent the width and height of the image, X represents the input fog image, P represents the generated network, G (x) represents the output fog free image of the generated network, Y represents the fog free image in the real scene, SSIM (x) represents the structural similarity function. L_{SSIM} represents the difference of structural similarity between the fog free image generated by the network model and the fog free image in the real scene.

The feature extraction auxiliary network model of perceptual loss function is vgg-16 network model, its formula is as follows:

$$L_{feature} = \frac{1}{CWH} \sum_{C=1}^{C} \sum_{W=1}^{W} \sum_{H=1}^{H} \left\| \phi(G(x^{c,w,h})) - \phi(y^{c,w,h}) \right\|_2^2 \tag{8}$$

Among them, C represents the number of color channels of foggy image (set to 3), G represents the generator network, $\phi(G(x))$ represents the feature map generated by the convolution of the generated fogless image, and $\phi(y)$ represents the feature map generated by the convolution of the real fogless image. The content loss difference $L_{content}$ in the training process is mainly composed of structure similarity loss L_{SSIM} and feature loss $L_{feature}$, as shown in Eq. (9).

$$L_{content} = L_{SSIM} + L_{feature} \qquad (9)$$

Counteraction Loss Function. In addition to calculating the content loss of the generated network, it is also necessary to calculate the loss content in the process of confrontation game. The definition of confrontation loss is as follows:

$$L_{adversarial} = \sum_{i=1}^{N} log(1 - D(G(x))) \qquad (10)$$

Where, $D(x)$ represents the discriminated network, and $D(g(x))$ represents the probability of judgment. In the discriminated network, the loss function is as follows:

$$L_D = \sum_{i=1}^{N}(log(1 - D(y)) + logD(G(x))) \qquad (11)$$

Therefore, the loss function of the generated network as a whole can be expressed as follows:

$$L_G = L_{content} + \gamma L_{adersarial} \qquad (12)$$

Among them, γ is the loss weight of the two loss functions, $L_{content}$ is to make the output image of the network more suitable for the real image, and $L_{adersarial}$ to make the game learning between the network and the discriminated network more accurate and faster convergence. In the experimental training process, we adjust the weight of the two loss functions to find a relatively balanced parameter by comparing the network iteratively.

3.4   Experimental Parameter Setting and Training Process

In this article the size of the generated sample buffer pool is set as 30. The network parameter optimization algorithm uses the Adam method, which sets the initial learning rate to 0.0002, and gradually shrinks during the training process until the maximum number of trainings reaches 10000. At the same time, during the training process, every 100 times the model is trained, and its variable file checkpoint is saved once. When initializing network parameters, a normal distribution with a mean of 0 and a standard deviation of 0.02 is used for network initialization. In addition, random deactivation is used to increase the randomness of neural network, reduce the over fitting, and the deactivation rate is 0.5.

4   Experiments and Result Analysis

The experimental data is composed of two data sets: the RESIDE data set and the VOC207 data set. These two data sets are specially designed for image defogging. The indoor fog image data set (ITS) and outdoor fog image data set

(OTS) in the RESIDE data set training set are both pairs of image sets. That is to say, each foggy image corresponds to the image without fog in the same scene. The test set selected is the real world task driven test set in the RESIDE. In order to increase the effectiveness and universality of the test, a more challenging and practical fog removal scenario is created for the test. In addition, the foggy image of the campus and the foggy image with dense fog or white scene are added.

4.1   Subjective Evaluation

(a)Orginal image (b)Foggy image   (c)DCP   (d)CAP   (e)NLID   (f)Ours

Fig. 8. Comparison of different defogging algorithms.

We test the model through the test data set, and we comparing the dehazed images abtained by different algorithms to illustrate the effectiveness of the demisting algorithm in this paper, which can more intuitively judge the demisting effect of the image. The (a)–(f) in Fig. 8 shows the demisting results of different algorithms in each scene and the comparison of the demisting images in the same scene.

Where (a) are the original images, (b) are the foggy images in the same scene, (c) are the defogging results obtained using the dark channel prior (DCP) method, (d) are the defogging results obtained by the color attenuation prior algorithm (CAP), (e) are the defogging results obtained by NLID method, and (f) are the fog-free images generated by the network model proposed in this paper.

From the perspective of subjective visual effect, the three algorithms DCP, CAP and NLID achieve some defogging effect. However, it can be seen from the figure that these three algorithms have more or less the problems of color distortion, distortion and edge halo. Dark channel defogging (DCP) can obtain clearer defogging images. However, for the image containing a large sky area, there will be halo phenomenon after defogging, such as the edge of the traffic sign and street lamp in Fig. 8 Traffic. The brightness and color saturation of the image will also decrease, resulting in information loss in the area with low pixel value in the image, for example, the building information is seriously distorted in Fig. 8 City. Color attenuation prior defogging (CAP) can obtain clear defogging image, but more bright areas in the image will produce color deviation after defogging, such as color distortion occurs in the upper right corner and the upper left corner in Fig. 8 Traffic and the overall image brightness in Fig. 8 City becomes lower, making the building information in the image difficult to recognize. In the process of defogging, the non local defogging algorithm recovers the edge information of the image well, and improves the brightness and color saturation of the image greatly, but the defogging is not complete. The image contrast after defogging is too high, and the image does not conform to the actual scene. As shown in Fig. 8 Road, there is still a lot of mist that has not been removed. In Fig. 8 Traffic, the color of the road is too bright, resulting in color deviation.

The defog image obtained by our algorithm is more similar to the non fog image in color and clarity, which also proves that the content loss function in the GAN has a good effect on the color constraints. The advantage of our defogging algorithm lies in its universality. From the experimental results, it can be concluded that the defogging ability of the proposed algorithm can reach the upper and middle levels for images of different scenes, The defogged image of the proposed defogging algorithm is better than that of the other algorithms in the sky regions. At the edge of the image, the other defogging algorithms appear edge halo. The algorithm used in this paper eliminates this phenomenon, makes the objects' color of the defogged image more consistent with that of the fog-free image and appears no color distortion.

4.2   Objective Evaluation

In order to objectively evaluate the effect of the proposed image defogging algorithm, the comprehensive quality evaluation indexes such as average gradient, information entropy [23] and structure clarity are used to evaluate the image quality in the experiment. The specific data is shown in Table 2.

From the comparison of evaluation indexes of different scene images in Table 2, we can see that the average gradient value, information entropy and NRSS value of the restored image obtained by the algorithm proposed in this paper are all the best. This shows that the visual clarity of the restored image obtained by our algorithm is improved more obviously, the edge details are kept better, the detail expression ability is stronger, the structural information is kept more completely, and the defogging effect is more in line with the subjective visual characteristics.

4.3   Dehazing Results Under Different Training Times

In order to intuitively show the influence of the training times, we will give the fog free image effect map generated under different training times, as shown

Table 2. Parameters comparison.

Image	City			Road		
index	$\bar{G}$	H(x)	NRSS	$\bar{G}$	H(x)	NRSS
Foggy image	4.52015	7.2306	0.9629	3.0236	7.1626	0.7921
Dark	5.0158	7.2231	0.9762	4.5728	7.429	0.8315
Color	4.2077	7.32	0.9812	7.1596	7.3684	0.8651
Nonlocal	6.1777	7.6019	0.9765	7.0095	7.4363	0.8217
Net	7.2512	7.7358	1.2143	7.8716	7.4684	0.8943

Image	House			Traffic		
index	$\bar{G}$	H(x)	NRSS	$\bar{G}$	H(x)	NRSS
Foggy image	3.6978	7.1757	0.9653	2.2145	6.6677	0.95621
Dark	5.9747	7.5424	0.9763	3.3462	7.1313	0.993
Color	5.9076	7.6054	0.9845	3.0057	7.0716	0.9458
Nonlocal	6.4762	7.547	1.0125	5.0057	7.4152	0.9528
Net	6.9629	7.6419	1.0197	6.0383	7.4163	1.0102

in Fig. 9. Among them, (a) is a fog image, (b) is the result after 100 times of training, (c) is the result after 300 times of training, (d) is the result after 500 times of training, and (e) is the result after 700 times of training.

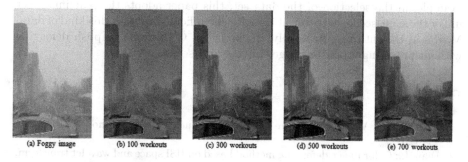

(a) Foggy image   (b) 100 workouts   (c) 300 workouts   (d) 500 workouts   (e) 700 workouts

Fig. 9. Effect of defogging under different training times.

In the model training process, as the number of network trainings continues to increase, the network will reach a learning balance point-the accuracy of the judgment of the network between the fog-free image generated by the network and the fog-free image in the real scene is 50. In the actual training process, our maximum number of training is 1000. We take the result of 1000 times training as the best defogging effect. As can be seen in Fig. 9, in our training range as the number of trainings increases, the fog on the buildings and the vehicles on the road in the image gradually disappears and finally achieves a clear effect.

And during the training process, the sky area in the image changes from dark to bright and the color contrast of the objects in the image gradually increases with the optimization of the training model.

4.4 Comprehensive Evaluation

In conclusion, the defogged image obtained by the proposed algorithm has better subjective visual effect, higher definition, and higher color fidelity of the scene in the image, which is more consistent with the real scene. Foggy image processing shows that the proposed algorithm has good generality, and it has an ideal defogging effect for foggy images in different scenes, and the defogging effect is better than other defogging algorithms.

5   Conclusion

In this paper, a deep learning defogging algorithm based on non physical model is proposed. Through the establishment of the generation adversarial network, the attention neural network is applied to the feature extraction in the foggy area. Also, the structure similarity loss function and the induction loss function are used. In this way, an image that is more close to the human vision and more close to the real image is obtained. The model proposed in this paper can effectively restore the foggy image, and get clear image. With the clarity effectively improved after the defog processing, the edge information of the scene is kept. However, there are some limitations in the proposed algorithm. For example, in the selection of the data set, this paper adopts the pair image set under the same scéne. However, it is relatively difficult to obtain this kind of data. Maybe in the future, we can rely on the cycle- GAN to accomplish defogging without providing a pair of images in the same scene.

References

1. Jun, C., Xin, W.: Digital image processing technology. Sci. Technol. **31**(31), 114–134 (2012)
2. Dian, L.: Color image defogging method based on HSI space and wavelet transform. Zhejiang University of Technology (2016)
3. Hautière, N., Tarel, J.P., Halmaoui, H., et al.: Enhanced fog detection and free-space segmentation for car navigation. Mach. Vis. Appl. **25**(3), 667–679 (2014)
4. Singh, D., Kumar, V.: Dehazing of remote sensing images using fourth-order partial differential equations based trilateral filter. IET Comput. Vis. **12**(2), 208–219 (2018)
5. Jobson, D.J., Rahman, Z., Woodell, G.A.: A multiscale retinex for bridging the gap between color images and the human observation of scenes. IEEE Trans. Image Process. **6**(7), 965–976 (1997)
6. Kim, J.Y., Kim, L.S., Hwang, S.H.: An advanced contrast enhancement using partially overlapped sub-block histogram equalization. IEEE Trans. Circ. Syst. Video Technol. **11**(4), 475–484 (2001)

7. Russo, F.: An image enhancement technique combining sharpening and noise reduction. IEEE Trans. Instrum. Measur. **51**(4), 824–828 (2001)
8. Wenfei, Z., Zhongsheng, M., Xiaolu, G.: A fast realization method of polarized optical defogging. J. Surv. Mapp. Sci. Technol. **28**(3), 182–185 (2011)
9. Narasimhan, S.G., Nayar, S.K.: Contrast restoration of weather degraded images. IEEE Trans. Pattern Anal. Mach. Intell. **25**(6), 713–724 (2003)
10. Hautière, N., Tarel, J.P., Lavenant, J., et al.: Automatic fog detection and estimation of visibility distance through use of an on board camera. Mach. Vis. Appl. **17**(1), 8–20 (2006)
11. Tan, R.T.: Visibility in bad weather from a single image. In: Proceedings of the IEEE Conference on Computer Vision and Pattern Recognition. IEEE Computer Society Press, Los Alamitos, vol. 1, pp. 1–8 (2008)
12. Fattal, R.: Single image dehazing. ACM Trans. Graph. **27**(3), Article No.72 (2008)
13. Tarel, J.P., Hautière, N.: Fast visibility restoration from a single color or gray level image. In: Proceedings of the 12th IEEE International Conference on Computer Vision. IEEE Computer Society Press, Los Alamitos, pp. 2201–2208 (2009)
14. He, K.M., Jian, S., Tang, X.O.: Single image haze removal using dark channel prior. In: Proceedings of the IEEE Conference on Computer Vision and Pattern Recognition, pp. 1956–1963. IEEE Computer Society Press, Los Alamitos (2009)
15. Garldran, A., Pardo, D., Picon, A., Alvarez-Gila, A.: Automatic red-channel underwater images restoration. J. Visual Commun. Image Represent. **26**, 132–145 (2015)
16. Gould, R.W., Arnone, R.A., Martinolich, P.M.: Spectral dependence of the scattering coefficient in case 1 and case 2 waters. Appl. Opt. **38**(12), 2377–2383 (1999)
17. Chen, D., Zhang ,W., Zhang, Z., et al.: Audio retrieval bas-ed on wavelet transform. In: 2017 IEEE/ACIS 16th International Conference on Computer and Information Science (ICIS). IEEE Computer Society (2017)
18. Russo, F.: An image enhancement technique combining sharpening and noise reduction (2002)
19. Qian, R., Tan, R.T., Yang, W., et al.: Attentive generative adversarial network for raindrop removal from a single image. In: Proceedings of the IEEE Conference on Computer Vision and Pattern Recognition, pp. 2482–2491 (2018)
20. Wu, Z., Shen, C., Van Den Hengel, A.: Wider or deeper: revisiting the ResNet model for visual recognition. Pattern Recogn. **90**, 119–133 (2019)
21. Jie, Z.: Research on stock price trend prediction based on LSTM neural network. Yunnan University (2019)
22. Ruiqi, S.: Research on the prediction model of US stock index price trend based on LSTM neural network. Capital University of Economics and Business (2015)
23. Kim, T.K., Paik, J.K., Kang, B.S.: Contrast enhancement system using spatially adaptive histogram equalization with temporal filtering. IEEE Trans. Consum. Electron. **44**(1), 82–87 (1998)

An Image Dehazing Algorithm Based on Adaptive Correction and Red Dark Channel Prior

Qingyi Zhang, Changhao Zhao, Xiangfen Zhang$^{(\boxtimes)}$, Feiniu Yuan$^{(\boxtimes)}$, Chuanjiang Li, and Dawei Hao

The College of Information, Mechanical and Electrical Engineering,
Shanghai Normal University, Shanghai 200234, China
{xiangfen,yfn}@shnu.edu.cn

Abstract. The dark channel prior defogging algorithm is one of the most representative image defogging algorithms. However, the restored images have problems such as halo effect, color distortion and so on. In view of the above problems, we proposes a method based on the red channel prior algorithm to estimate the transmission maps of different color channels. After defogging, it will reduce the brightness and contrast of the image, resulting in the loss of detail information. Therefore, this paper uses gamma function on the defogged image to performs color compensation and optimazes the detailed information of the image. The algorithm proposed in this article is used in the contrast experiment with other defogging algorithms, and the experimental results are evaluated objectively based on the information entropy and other parameters. Through experimental comparison, our algorithm compared to the dark channel prior defogging algorithm to obtain a clearer image defogging image, and the subjective vision is more consistent with the real scene.

Keywords: Image defogging · Dark channel prior · Red channel transmission · Gamma correction

1 Introduction

The premise for a computer vision system to work normally and efficiently is to get clear and meaningful images. However, computer vision imaging systems are particularly sensitive to weather conditions. Frequent haze weather is the main cause of image quality degradation. In the fog, many small suspended droplets and aerosols cause refraction and scattering of imaging light, resulting in a serious attenuation of the intensity of light transmission. Therefore, the contrast of the image is reduced, the sharpness is lowered, and the saturation is

Supported by: National Natural Science Foundation of China (61862029) and Shanghai Normal University (Research on Automatic Focus Algorithm (209-AC9103-20-368005221)). The corresponding authors: Zhang Xiangfen and Yuan Feiniu.

attenuated. This not only affects the visual effect of the image, but also affects the analysis and understanding of the image. As the foggy weather around the world becomes more and more serious, it poses a great challenge to the outdoor computer vision.

Last few years, image defogging methods have made significant progress. There are two categories about the image defogging algorithm: the first is the use of image enhancement technique to remove fogging image. Such as bilateral filtering [1], curved wave transform [2], morphological filtering [3] and Retinex [4] algorithm, etc. However, this kind of algorithm does not take into account the root cause of foggy image degradation, which will result in information loss. The other method is to consider the root cause of the reduced quality of images and establish atmospheric scattering model to reverse fogless images. Such method has good processing effect, and the information in the image will not be lost after restoration. Wang et al. [2] defogged the image by reflectance and transmittance of the scene, but the defogging speed was slow and the effect was not satisfactory. The article [5] performed white balance processing on the foggy image, then obtained the estimated value of the atmospheric surface layer. Then the image would be performed median filtering. The algorithm was faster, but the defogging effect was general. He et al. [6] proposed a defogging algorithm which can achieve better defogging effect. This algorithm is called the dark channel prior defogging algorithm However, in some bright background areas or in sky areas, the dark channel prior algorithm did not achieve the desired image restoration effect. In these areas, there would be color distortion or even distortion, halo and spot problems, and the image after the dark channel processing had a problem of dark color.

In order to solve the above problems, many improved algorithms have been proposed. Liu et al. [7] divided the image into two areas including sky and non-sky, and used gradient-guided filtering to correct the transmittance. Finally, the two areas of color-corrected were merged to complete the defogging process. Xiao et al. [8] combined dark channel priori with scene brightness constraints and used regularization method to defog a single image. The algorithm of the above paper improved the effect of the defogging algorithm. However, these methods were susceptible to noise during the dark channel acquisition process and these algorithms were prone to image color cast and a large number of stains when dealing with distant scenes.

According to the analysis of the above dehazing algorithm, this paper proposed a priori algorithm which through red dark channel prior to accurately estimate the transmission map and makes the transmission map more accurate. The image after defogging uses an adaptive gamma correction function for color compensation to obtain a better defogging effect. Experimental results indicate that the algorithm can effectively restore the blurred image and maintain image edges and details.

2   Red Dark Channel Prior Algorithms

2.1   Atmospheric Scattering Model

In computer image processing, the foggy image formation model is defined as:

$$I(x) = J(x)t(x) + A(1 - t(x)) \tag{1}$$

In the formula, $J(x)$ is the fogless image, $I(x)$ is a foggy image, A is a value that is atmospheric light, $t(x)$ is the transmittance.

According to the formula (1), the fog image restoration formula can be obtained, that is:

$$J(x) = \frac{I(x) - A}{t(x)} + A \tag{2}$$

2.2   Dark Channel Prior Theory

To achieve the purpose of clear defogging effect, He et al. [6] collected and established many outdoor fogless images, and statistically analyzed its pixel characteristics, and proposed a dark channel prior defogging algorithm. In most dehazing images, their pixels in non-sky areas is at least one color channel with minimal value which close to zero.

$$J^{DCP}(x) = min_{c \in \{R,G,B\}} \left[min_{y \in \varphi(x)} J^c(y) \right] \to 0 \tag{3}$$

In the formula, $J^{DCP}(x)$ is the dark channel gray value of the fogless image, $\varphi(x)$ is the local region centered on x, and $J^c(y)$ is the pixel value in one of the color channels of R, G, and B. According to the formula (2), in foggy images, the dark channel value of the image can roughly indicate the relative concentration of the fog.

2.3   Red Dark Channel Prior Theory

In view of the characteristics of light absorption and scattering in foggy images, we find that the RDCP theory [9] which is applicable to underwater images is also applicable to foggy images.

$$J^{RDCP}(x, c) = min_{c \in \{R,G,B\}} \left[min_{y \in \varphi(x)} (1 - J(y, R)), J(y, G), J(y, B) \right] \tag{4}$$

In the formula, R, G, B represent the three color channels of the image, $J^{RDCP}(x)$ represents the gray value of the red dark channel, $J(y, R)$, $J(y, G)$, $J(x, B)$ represent the gray value of the three color channels respectively.

2.4   Transmittance

According to the derivation of He et al. [6], the transmittance of each channel can be calculated by the following formula (5).

$$t(x) = 1 - min_{c \in \{R,G,B\}} \left[min_{y \in \varphi(x)} \frac{J^c(y)}{A^c} \right] \tag{5}$$

In the fog imaging process, not only the presence of light scattering, but also need to consider the aerosol particles on selective absorption of light waves and attenuation. Because aerosol particles are selective for absorbing different wavelengths of atmospheric light during atmospheric imaging. Its attenuation coefficient is proportional to the wavelength. The propagation distance is inversely proportional to the wavelength of the light wave. In foggy weather, the red light of foggy images is most attenuated and absorbed by aerosol particles relative to green and blue light. The dark channel values of some colors of the blurred image calculated directly according to formula (5) may be different from the actual channel values. In turn, the transmission map of each color channel is larger.

According to the MIE scattering theory, the attenuation coefficient of each channel in the image is defined by the wavelength of the corresponding visible light. Therefore, it is necessary to calculate the transmission map of each channel separately, i.e.

$$t(x, R) = 1 - min(\frac{min_{y \in \varphi(x))}[1 - I(x, R)]}{1 - A_{R,\infty}}, \frac{min_{y \in \varphi(x)}I(x, G)}{A_{G,\infty}}, \frac{min_{y \in \varphi(x)}I(x, B)}{A_{B,\infty}}) \tag{6}$$

$$t(x, G) = \{exp[-c(R)d(x)]\}^{\frac{c(G)}{c(R)}} = t(x, R)^{\frac{c(G)}{c(R)}} \tag{7}$$

$$t(x, B) = \{exp[-c(R)d(x)]\}^{\frac{c(B)}{c(R)}} = t(x, R)^{\frac{c(B)}{c(R)}} \tag{8}$$

In the formula, $t(x, R)$, $t(x, G)$, $t(x, B)$ represent transmission maps of R, G and B channels, $c(R)$, $c(G)$, $c(B)$ is R, G and B channels of which the attenuation coefficient, and $d(x)$ denotes the depth of field.

In haze weather, the attenuation of light of different wavelengths in aerosol particles is different, and the longer the wavelength, the greater the degree of absorption attenuation. In visible light, the longest wavelength is red light, so the degree of attenuation of red light is the largest, followed by green light, and finally blue light. In view of red dark channel prior theory, the transmission map of red channel can be calculated by formula (6). Formulas (7) and (8) can be used to combine the attenuation coefficients of the other two channels according to the transmittance of the red channel, and then the atmospheric transmittance maps of the blue and green channels can be obtained. Zhao et al. [10] give the numerical relationship between atmospheric light and scattering coefficient and total attenuation coefficient during imaging, namely:

$$A_\infty(x) \infty \frac{b(\lambda)}{c(\lambda)} \tag{9}$$

In the formula, the scattering coefficient is $b(\lambda)$.

It can be seen from Eq. (9) that in the atmospheric imaging process, the pixel value of the background light is inversely proportional to the wavelength attenuation coefficient and the wavelength scattering coefficient. After extensive experiments, it is found by Gould et al. [11] that the scattering coefficient is usually linearly related to the wavelength of the light wave in the haze.

$$b(\lambda) = (-0.00113\lambda + 1.62517)b(555) \tag{10}$$

The wavelengths of the light waves corresponding to the three channels of red, green and blue are 620, 540, 450 respectively [12]. The atmospheric light values calculated by formula (4) and scattering coefficients calculated by formula (10) are substituted into formula (9). Finally, the proportional relationship of attenuation coefficients between three channels is calculated. That is the following formulas.

$$\frac{c(G)}{c(R)} = \frac{b(G)A_{R,\infty}}{b(R)A_{G,\infty}} \tag{11}$$

$$\frac{c(B)}{c(R)} = \frac{b(B)A_{R,\infty}}{b(R)A_{B,\infty}} \tag{12}$$

By substituting formula (11) and formula (12) into formula (7) and formula (8), the transmission maps of different color channels can be obtained.

2.5   Atmospheric Light

In the image, the traditional dark channel defogging algorithm regards the brightest point as the atmospheric light value A. In this way, the selected atmospheric light value will be disturbed by objects that are brighter than atmospheric light, and eventually lead to larger atmospheric light value. In order to make the atmospheric light value more accurate, we use the quad-tree partitioning algorithm [13] and Fig. 1 shows the segmentation structure.

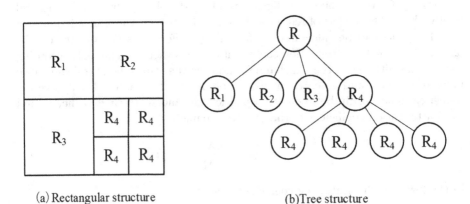

(a) Rectangular structure   (b) Tree structure

Fig. 1. Structures of quad-tree algorithm.

The first step is to split the image into four sub-regions, and define the regional mean scoring result as s(x). The formula is:

$$S_{score}(x) = I(x, R) - max\left[I(x, G), I(x, B)\right] \qquad (13)$$

In the formula, $I(x, R)$, $I(x, G)$, $I(x, B)$ respectively represent the original image gray values of the R, G, and B channels.

Then, sort the values of the four sub-regions from largest to smallest, and the region with the largest value is denoted as M. Assume that the median value of pixels in the M area is equal to V. And x_m is the minimum difference between the original pixel and the median value V in the M area.

$$I(x_m) - V = min\left\{I(x, M) - V\right\} \qquad (14)$$

The atmospheric light value A is the intensity value of point x_m.

$$A = I(x_m) \qquad (15)$$

2.6 Final Fogless Image Restoration

The R, G, B each channel transmittance $t(x, R)$, $t(x, G)$, $t(x, B)$ combined with atmospheric optical value A plug into the atmospheric scattering model respectively, got each channel to defogging figure $J(x, R)$, $J(x, R)$, $J(x, R)$, and according to the type (4) to restore the final image without fog.

3 Post Processing of Defogging Image

3.1 Gamma Correction

After defogging, the overall brightness of the image will be reduced, which will lead to the loss of a lot of detail information, and the distant scene in the image will be distorted. Therefore, we performed color correction and visual enhancement on the defogged image. We use gamma correction to compensate for the information on the defogged image. The expression of Gamma curve in Gamma correction [13] is:

$$y(x) = x^{\gamma} \qquad (16)$$

In the formula, x represents the color image's the pixel value, y(x) is the pixel value after correction, and the γ value is the gamma correction parameter. When the γ takes 1, it is a linear transformation; when the value of the γ is less than 1, the visual effect of reduced contrast will be produced; when the value of the γ is greater than 1, the visual effect of increased contrast will be produced, making the image more vivid.

3.2 Maximum Between-Class Variance Method

OTSU [14] is derived from the ordinary least squares method. It divides the image to be processed into foreground modules and background modules according to the gray level of image pixels, and maximize the difference between the two modules as much as possible, while minimizing the gray level difference of the pixels within each module.

Let all the pixels of the image lie in the interval [0, L−1], where the number of pixels of each gray value i is n_i. If there are a total of N pixels, the probability P_i at any gray level is:

$$P_i = \frac{n_i}{N} \tag{17}$$

Image pixels are divided into two different parts according to the threshold size, C_0 and C_1. These two parts are composed of gray level pixels in the interval [0, T − 1] and [T, L − 1]. Pixels located at C_0 and C_1 probabilities are:

$$P_0(T) = \sum_{i=0}^{T-1} p_i \tag{18}$$

$$P_1(T) = \sum_{i=T}^{L-1} p_i = 1 - P_0 \tag{19}$$

The average gray value of C_0 and C_1:

$$\mu_0 = \frac{1}{P_0(T)} \sum_{i=0}^{T-1} i p_i = \frac{\mu(T)}{P_0(T)} \tag{20}$$

$$\mu_1 = \frac{1}{P_1(T)} \sum_{i=T}^{L-1} i p_i = \frac{\mu - \mu(T)}{1 - P_0(T)} \tag{21}$$

Then the average gray value of the image is μ:

$$\mu = \sum_{i=0}^{L-1} i p_i = P_0(T)\mu_0 + P_1(T)\mu_1 \tag{22}$$

The final interclass variance lambda can be obtained as:

$$\sigma_B^2 = P_0(T)(\mu_0 - \mu)^2 + P_1(T)(\mu_1 - \mu)^2 \tag{23}$$

Let the threshold T be sequentially taken in the range of [0, L − 1], and T which can make σ_B^2 the maximum value is the most suitable threshold.

3.3 Gamma Correction Based on OTSU

In foggy images, due to the influence of aerosol particles in the atmosphere, the incident light that eventually reaches the camera is less than that in natural environment. This will lead to a relatively close distance from the camera scene brightness and contrast are relatively high, and the brightness of the scene far from the camera will be relatively low and blurred, which will lead to the loss of information.

In the post-processing part of the algorithm, the image is divided into three parts: highlight region, transition region and shadow region. In the first segmentation, the image is divided into bright region and dark region; in the second segmentation, the bright region is divided into highlight region and transition region according to pixel level, and the dark region is divided into shadow region and transition region. Because the transition region is almost not affected by the change of light, there is no need for gamma correction. In this paper, we only use different parameters of gamma correction for highlight and shadow areas (Fig. 2).

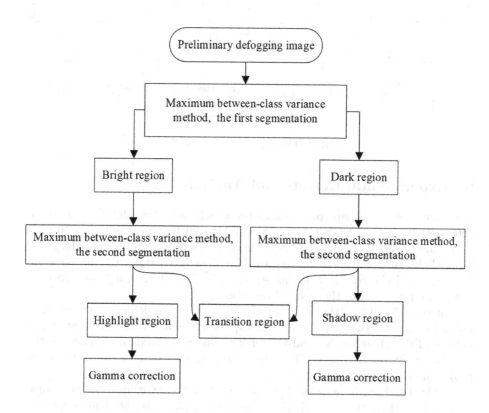

Fig. 2. Gamma correction based on OTSU.

4   Algorithm Flow Chart

In summary, the proposed image dehazing algorithm is mainly divided into four steps:

(1) Estimation of atmospheric light values for foggy images.
(2) The transmission map of each color channel in the image is obtained respectively from the red dark channel prior theory,
(3) The atmospheric light value and transmittance are substituted into the formula (1) to obtain the preliminary restored images.
(4) The restored image is further adaptively corrected to get the last restored image after information enhancement.

Figure 3 shows the algorithm flow of this paper.

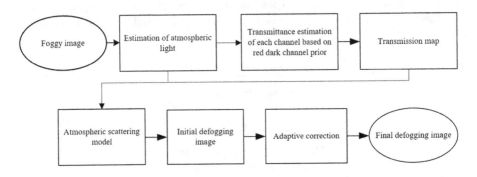

Fig. 3. The algorithm flow chart.

5   Experimental Results and Analysis

The experiment was run on a computer which have Intel(R) Core(TM) i5-6500CPU @3.20 GHz 8 GB RAM in MATLAB R2016a under Windows 10.

In the experiment, the red visible light wavelength was 620 nm, the green visible light wavelength was 540 nm, the blue light was 450 nm, the initialization K = 0.2, and the search step was set to 0.05. The algorithm parameters for comparison were set to the optimal conditions.

For the sake of test the versatility and robustness of dehazing algorithm in our paper, part of the data used in the experiment comes from the foggy image dataset of the Shanghai Normal University campus series photographed by the camera, as shown in Fig. 4. The other parts shown in Fig. 5 comes from the project home page of HE, Fattal, etc.

In Fig. 4 and Fig. 5, (a) is the foggy image, (b) is the defogging image obtained by the dark channel prior dehazing algorithm, and (c) is the defogged result obtained by the color attenuation prior algorithm [15], (d) The defogging result obtained by Dana Berman's dehazing algorithm [16], (e) is the dehazing result obtained by our proposed dehazing algorithm.

5.1   Subjective Evaluation

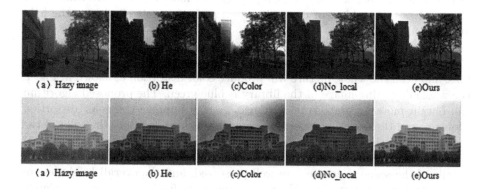

Fig. 4. Dehazing effect of different algorithms based on SHNU campus data.

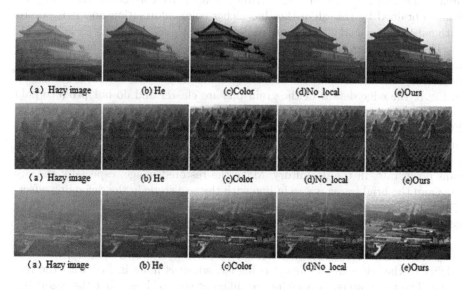

Fig. 5. Dehazing effect of different algorithms based on the data in He's article.

From the image comparison of defogging results, the dark channel defogging algorithm which has a clearer defogging effect can be obtained, but the defogging effect in the sky area is not ideal. There is also a serious loss of information in the dark foggy image itself, as shown in Fig. 5 for pedestrians and roadside trees. In this paper, the image is adaptively corrected after defogging, which effectively enhances the information of lower pixel values of images and solves the problem of information loss in low pixel value regions. The traditional dark channel a priori algorithm defogged image will have color distortion problems in the sky area, and there will be a slight halo at the edge of the sky, as shown in the sky edge above the dormitory building in Fig. 4 and the sky image edge of Tiananmen in Fig. 5. In this paper, the defogging image has more accurate transmittance, which solves the problem of color distortion and effectively eliminates the halo at the edge of the sky.

The color attenuation prior algorithm can remove the fog in the image to a certain extent, but the brighter areas in the image will produce blue-green bias, and even the whole picture will produce color distortion as shown in Fig. 4, the whole defogging image of the library is blue-green. The proposed algorithm can obtain more accurate transmittance, greatly improve the color distortion problem, and the adaptive correction algorithm can compensate the color of the image, making the restored image more in line with the subjective vision.

After removing the fog by using the non-local defogging algorithm, the edge details of the scene in images are well preserved, and the overall brightness of the image is greatly improved. However, some of the fog has not been completely removed, which does not conform to the subjective visual image, and the image will have color deviation, such as the wall of the library in Fig. 4 and the sky area of Tiananmen Gate in Fig. 5. After self-adaptive correction, the defogging image obtained by this algorithm has richer color information and it is accord with subjective visual effects more and more.

This paper uses the red dark channel method to obtain a more accurate image transmittance, so that the image after defogging does not produce color deviation, and the details of the defogged image are well restored. As shown in Fig. 5, the edge details of the grain pile are clearer and do not produce halo edges. The image after fog removal is self-adaptively corrected to enhance image brightness and increase the color saturation. Reduce the loss of image details and color distortion caused by low brightness after fog removal, and make the image more in line with subjective visual effects. As shown in Fig. 4, the garbage cans downstairs in the dormitory. Make the restored image, especially the sky area and the bright area, more in line with the real scene in the defogging effect. The sky area above the library in Fig. 4 and the car below the library, and the scenery in the mountain village in Fig. 5.

In summary, the restored image details obtained by the algorithm have better subjective visual effects of fog removal, and have higher definition, and the color fidelity of the scene in the image is higher, which is more in line with the real scene. The foggy image processing for different scenes shows that the algorithm in this paper has preferable versatility and has ideal defogging effect for foggy images in different scenes, and the defogging effect is better than other defogging algorithms.

5.2   Objective Evaluation Indicators

For objectively evaluate the dehazing effect of each algorithm, the image quality was evaluated using the comprehensive quality evaluation indicators such as image information entropy, average gradient and structural definition.

1) Average gradient

It can clearly reflect the details of images. An image with a larger average gradient value has more detailed information and clearer image. The average gradient can be expressed by Eq. (22):

$$\overline{G} = \frac{1}{(M-1)(N-1)} \sum_{i=1}^{M-1} \sum_{j=1}^{N-1} \sqrt{\frac{(l(i,j) - l(i+1,j))^2 + (l(i,j) - l(i,j+1))^2}{2}}$$

(24)

$\overline{G}$ represents the average gradient of each pixel in the image, M and N are the number of rows and columns of the image respectively.

2) Information entropy

It represents the average information amount. The greater the entropy value, the more detailed information carried in the image. In this paper, the average of three channel information entropy in the image is counted as the result. The formula for information entropy is shown in (23):

$$H(x) = -\sum_{i} P(x_i) log P(x_i)$$

(25)

H(x) represents information entropy, and $P(x_i)$ represents the probability of occurrence of gray level x_i.

3) Structural definition (NRSS)

The Human Visual System (HVS) is well suited to extract the characteristics of structural information of a target. Wang et al. proposed the concept of image structure similarity (SSIM), and thought that as long as the change of target structure information can be calculated, the perceived image distortion value can be obtained. Based on this idea, Yang Chunling et al. [16], introduced the method into the definition evaluation of the full reference image, and thought that the image's definition can be expressed by SSIM between target images and reference images. Xie et al. [1] calculates the SSIM of each x_i and y_i. The definition of no-reference structure clarity of the image is as follows:

$$NRSS = 1 - \frac{1}{N} \sum_{i=1}^{N} SSIM(x_i, y_i)$$

(26)

x_i, y_i represents the image sub-block of the same area of original images and restored images, N represents the number of blocks of image, and SSIM represents the structural similarity of the image.

The larger the NRSS value is, the clearer the image is, the more complete the structure information of the image is retained, and it is more in line with the subjective visual characteristics of the human eye.

5.3   Objective Evaluation

Table 1. Average gradient before and after processing of each algorithm.

Algorithm	Dorm	Library	Tiananmen	Cones	Canon
Hazy image	5.6616	3.4505	3.805	7.5786	2.6633
He	7.2115	4.0621	5.0963	9.4807	4.8532
Zhu	7.4297	3.9821	5.1045	9.4996	4.8286
Nonlocal	3.9367	3.6036	4.0613	8.0185	4.4963
Ours	7.8549	4.722	5.3293	9.6559	5.2049

Table 2. Information entropy before and after processing by each algorithm.

Algorithm	Dorm	Library	Tiaananmen	Cones	Canon
Hazy image	7.4371	7.4371	6.4313	7.2157	6.4315
He	7.2663	7.2663	6.9970	6.9140	6.4200
Zhu	7.5545	7.5545	7.6417	7.1823	7.0501
Nonlocal	7.7054	7.7054	6.6521	7.2218	7.1054
Ours	7.4644	7.4644	7.6605	7.2290	7.1851

Table 3. Structure clarity before and after processing of each algorithm.

Algorithm	Dorm	Library	Tiaananmen	Cones	Canon
Hazy image	0.9929	0.8023	0.9870	1.0040	0.9704
He	0.9983	0.8148	0.9897	0.9930	0.9667
Zhu	0.9897	0.9097	0.9838	0.9580	0.9814
Nonlocal	0.9730	0.8045	1.0033	0.9961	0.9730
Ours	1.0007	0.9430	1.0161	1.0024	0.9849

From Table 1 can be analyzed that the information entropy of fogless images increases in varying degrees according to different scenes after defogging. Compared with all the restored results, the information entropy in this algorithm is higher than others algorithms, indicating that the restored image in this algorithm has greater detail intensity, more information and clearer image.

From the comparison of the average gradient of different scene images in Table 2, we can see that besides the dark channel defogging algorithm, others algorithm are higher than the original fog image. Compared with the average gradient of all images, the average gradient of the restored image in this paper is the highest. This indicates that the image clarity of the image is more obvious, the edge detail is better, the texture level of the image is more abundant, and the fog image processing effect is more excellent.

From Table 3 can be analyzed that foggy images are processed in different scenes, and the structural clarity of all restored images is compared. The reconstructed image obtained by the algorithm has the highest structural definition and the structural information of the image is preserved. More complete, the defogging effect is more in line with subjective visual characteristics.

6 Conclusion

In this paper, the theory and method of red dark channel are used to solve the color distortion of image after defogging and the distortion when defogging in the sky area. Taking the absorption and attenuation of light in different degrees during the imaging process in fog and haze as the breakthrough point, the more accurate image transmittance can be obtained. Then the image after defogging is adaptively corrected to enhance the image information. As is known by the experimental results, the improved algorithm has better defogging effect. It is superior to the existing dark channel defogging algorithm in image details, image quality and subjective vision, making the restored image closer to the natural scene image.

References

1. Zhou, S.L., Zou, H.X., Xing, X.W., Ji, K.F., Leng, X.G.: Hybrid bilateral filtering algorithm based on edge detection. IET Image Process. **10**(11), 809–816 (2016)
2. Qiao, T., Ren, J.C., Wang, Z., Zabalza, J.: Effective denoising and classification of hyperspectral images using curvelet transform and singular spectrum analysis. IEEE Trans. Geosci. Remote Sens. **55**(1), 119–133 (2017)
3. Li, Y., et al.: Fast morphological filtering haze removal method from a single image. J. Comput. Inf. Syst. **11**(16), 5799–5806 (2015)
4. Tian, H.Y., Xue, M., Ming, Z., Meng, H.: An improved multi-scale retinex fog and haze image enhancement method. In: Proceedings of the 2016 International Conference on Information System and Artificial Intelligence, Piscataway, pp. 557–560. IEEE (2017)
5. He, K.M., Sun, J., Yang, X.O.: Single image haze removal using dark channel prior. IEEE Trans. Pattern Anal. Mach. Intell. **33**(12), 2341–2353 (2011)
6. Liu, Y., Zhang, H., Wu, Y., et al.: A fast single image defogging algorithm based on semi-inverse method. J. Graph. **36**(1), 68–76 (2015)
7. Xiao, J., Peng, H., Zhang, Y., et al.: Fast image enhancement based on color space fusion. Color Res. Appl. **41**(1), 22–31 (2014)
8. Garldran, A., Pardo, D., Picon, A., Alvarez-Gila, A.: Automatic red-channel underwater images restoration. J. Vis. Commun. Image Represent. **26**, 132–145 (2015)
9. Zhao, X.W., Jin, T., Qu, S.: Deriving inherent optical properties from background color and underwater image enhancement. Ocean Eng. **94**, 163–172 (2015)
10. Gould, R.W., Arnone, R.A., Martinolich, P.M.: Spectral dependence of the scattering coefficient in case 1 and case 2 waters. Appl. Opt. **38**(12), 2377–2383 (1999)

11. Fergus, K.: Dark flash photography. ACM SIGGRAPH **28**(3) (2009)
12. Huang, S.C., Cheng, F.C., Chiu, Y.S.: Efficient contrast enhancement using adaptive gamma correction with weighting distribution. IEEE Trans. Image Process. Publ. IEEE Signal Process. Soc. **22**(3), 1032–1041 (2013)
13. Wang, S., Rehman, A., Zhou, W., et al.: SSIM-motivated rate-distortion optimization for video coding. IEEE Trans. Circ. Syst. Video Technol. **22**(4), 516–529 (2012)
14. Hao, C., Jian, C., Qingzhou, Y.E., et al.: Autofocus algorithm based on adjacent pixel difference and NRSS. Comput. Eng. **41**(9), 261–265 (2015)
15. Zhu, Q.S., Mai, J.M., Shao, L.: A fast single image haze removal algorithm using color attenuation prior. IEEE Trans. Image Process. **24**(11) (2015). https://doi.org/10.1109/TIP.2015.2446191
16. Berman, D., Treibitz, T., Avidan, S.: Non-local image dehazing (2015)

Human Instance Segmentation

Chengguo Ju and Guodong Wang[✉]

College of Computer Science and Technology, Qingdao University, Qingdao 266071,
Shandong, China
doctorwgd@gmail.com

Abstract. Currently, the more popular instance segmentation frameworks are
based on powerful object detection methods, such as Faster R-CNN, Mask R-
CNN, etc. Although they use different methods and different structures, these
methods are roughly similar: first generating multiple regions proposal in the
image, and then using the non-maximum suppression algorithm (NMS) to delete
the regions proposal that do not meet the requirements in the generated regions
proposal. However, when there are two highly overlapping objects in the image,
the NMS will treat the bounding box of one of them as a duplicate candidate area
and delete it. This means that these algorithms cannot distinguish between two
highly overlapping objects. However, in instance segmentation, people are a special category, and we can use human bones to segment people. Also in the example
is divided, an example of the classification confidence score is used as a mask quality divided frame most instances. However, it is quantified as IoU mask quality
is usually not a good correlation between the scores and classification instance
masks its basic facts. Through this problem, we propose a new module scoring
module (Evaluation), using the scoring module to combine instance features with
corresponding masks, which can improve the quality of instance segmentation.

Keywords: Convolutional neural network · FPN · Evaluation module

1 Introduction

Research on "people" in the field of computer vision has attracted more and more attention, such as: face recognition [1–6], pedestrian detection [7–9] and tracking, abnormal
behavior detection, etc. This article uses a special group of people and uses human bones
to subdivide people. It can segment people better than other instance segmentation networks, and can better solve problems such as overlapping and occlusion of candidate
frames.

Deep learning method for the special category of human detection also has good
results, but the segmentation structure using proposal will have disadvantages, such as:
Two objects may share the same or very similar bounding box, the main reason is that
when two targets of the same category overlap in an image, the NMS algorithm used
by most target detection algorithms will only retain the frame with the highest category
confidence, and delete the rest as repeated useless frames; The number of instances is

G. Zhai et al. (Eds.): IFTC 2020, CCIS 1390, pp. 41–51, 2021.
https://doi.org/10.1007/978-981-16-1194-0_4

usually limited by the number of proposals that the network can process (usually hundreds), moreover, the effect of segmentation is affected by the double error of target detection and recognition and detection frame positioning. People will generally have closely-connected pictures in their lives, so using the method based on the candidate frame mentioned above, there will be a person who will not be segmented, resulting in inaccurate experimental results. In addition, in the current network framework, the detection score (that is, assumed to be determined by the largest element in the classification score) due to background clutter, occlusion and other issues, the classification score may be higher, but the mask quality is low, use the candidate, The score of the instance Mask obtained by using the candidate box is usually related to the box classification confidence. It is unsuited to apply the classification score to evaluation the quality of the mask, because it is only used to distinguish the semantic category of the proposal without knowing the examples of Mask of the real quality and integrity.

Through the study of the above problems, this article finds that using the particularity of human bones can better accurately segment the people in the picture, thereby avoiding the missed detection caused by the candidate frame, so this article uses human bones to segment the human body and segmentation is more accurate, the human bones are connected through the key points of the people, and the people posture [10–13] is used to accurately segment the human; A new module Evaluation module is proposed, the function of this module is to make IoU regress the predicted Mask and its ground truth Mask, therefore, Evaluation module solves situation where the Mask score does not match the Mask quality.

2   Related Work

2.1   Instance Segmentation

Prior to this, many people have proposed algorithms [14, 15] for instance segmentation. These methods were simply divided into two sorts: One is based on traditional segmentation ways, for example, threshold-based segmentation methods, watershed algorithms, etc. The basic idea is to calculate one or more grayscale thresholds based on the grayscale characteristics of the image, and then compare grayscale value of each pixel in an image with threshold, and finally sort the pixels into appropriate categories based on the comparison results. Therefore, the most critical step of this method is to solve the optimal gray threshold according to a certain criterion function. His disadvantage is that it only considers the characteristics of the gray value of the pixel itself, and generally does not consider the spatial characteristics, so it is more sensitive to noise and not robust. Another segmentation algorithm is currently a more popular mainstream method. It is a segmentation method based on deep learning [16–18]. The ResNet [19] network framework is a more commonly used network structure for feature extraction. It solves the phenomenon that the gradient disappears when the deep learning network is stacked to a certain depth, and back propagation cannot feedback the gradient to the previous network layer; The Fast R-CNN [20] network structure extracts the features in the image through the basic network, and then use the RoI Pooling layer to read the feature relative to each RoI on the feature map of the full image and then perform classification and regression through the fully connected layer; Faster R-CNN [21] is an improved version of the former, which replaces the time-consuming selective search algorithm with RPN (Region Proposal Network), and has a breakthrough optimization of the entire network structure; Mask R-CNN [22] is based on the structure of Faster R-CNN and it adds Mask prediction branch, it also improves ROI Pooling and proposes ROI Align; PANet [23] can be seen as an improvement on Mask R-CNN, it makes full use of feature fusion, cites the bottom-up path augmentation structure, and makes full use of network shallow features for segmentation, the introduction of adaptive feature pooling makes the extracted ROI features richer; the introduction of fully-connected fusion to fuse the output of a foreground and background binary classification branch to obtain more accurate segmentation results.

2.2 Multi-person Human Pose Estimation

The single-person pose estimation method has a better effect in single-person recognition, but it is still relatively poor when applied to multi-person pose recognition [11, 24, 25]. The same multi-person pose estimation effect is better, and the effect of single-person pose estimation is not ideal. There are two people pose estimation mainstream research methods, namely top-down, first detected more than one person, then evaluate each person's posture. The detection way may pose estimation by adding single achieved. Bottom-up: first detecting joints, each joint point then determines which person belongs.

3 Method

3.1 Overview

In this part, we will propose a brand-new module by which we can calculate the pixel-level IOU value between the mask obtained by the mask branch and the mask corresponding to the ground truth to measure the accuracy of the segmentation.

First of all, this article selects the ResNet50 network as the feature extraction network. The ResNet network is actually formed by the fusion of multiple shallow networks, avoiding the disappearing gradient problem, because it is formed by the fusion of multiple shallow networks. The shallow network will not have the disappearing gradient problem during training, so it can accelerate the convergence of the network.

The network structure will further adopt FPN network [26] for feature extraction. Advanced features from top to bottom horizontal connecting low-resolution and high semantic information as well as low-level features high resolution and low semantic information, so all levels of features have a wealth of semantic information. FPN network low-level features may be accumulated and processed advanced features have been processed under the premise of reducing the amount of calculation. Because low-level functions may supply more precise location information, while high-level functions may supply more detailed message. Deep-level features can distinguish complex targets; using deeper networks to construct feature pyramids, which can increase robustness. Figure 1 shows its network structure.

Bottom-top: The lower layer reflects the shallower image information features like edges; the higher layer reflects the deeper image features like object contours and even categories;

Top-bottom: The feature output of the upper layer generally has a smaller feature map, but it can represent larger-dimensional image information. This type of high-level information has been experimentally proven to play a key role in subsequent tasks such as target detection and object classification. Therefore, when processing each layer of information, we will refer to the higher-layer information for its input, and enlarge the upper-layer feature map to the same scale and then make a horizontal connection with the feature map of this layer;

The expression correlation between the convolution feature and the output of each level: here we use 1×1 convolution to generate better output features, which can effectively reduce the number of channels in the middle level. These 1×1 convolutions allow us to output feature maps of different dimensions with the same number of channels.

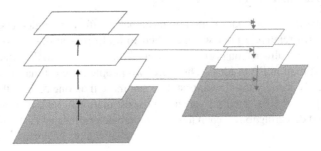

Fig. 1. FPN network structure

In order to solve the undesirable factors such as human body occlusion and overlap, the human skeleton is used to segment the human body. Human bone is more appropriate to distinguish between overlapping area larger of the two people, and they can provide clearer personal information than bounding boxes. In most instance segmentation tasks, most instance segmentation frameworks use the confidence of instance classification as the Mask quality score. However, it is quantized to mask instance IoU between the mask and the basic situation of the quality of the correlation between the classification score is usually not strong, so in this text, I will put forward a brand new module through that we can calculate the pixel-level IOU value between the mask obtained by the mask branch and the mask corresponding to the ground truth, to evaluate the precision of the segmentation. Figure 2 shows the network structure of the entire article. In general, the

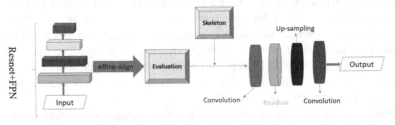

Fig. 2. Overview of our network structure

article proposes a convolutional neural network which uses human bones to segment and score the human body.

3.2 Evaluation

RoIs processed by the alignment module Affine-Align enter the Evaluation module, first enter the mask branch, output the mask of each RoI, and then use the output result and the features processed by the Affine-Align as the input of the Evaluation branch after concat. This paper uses a max pooling layer with a convolution kernel size of 2 and a step size of 2 so that the predicted mask has the same spatial size as the RoI. The input of the Evaluation module consists of two parts, one is the RoI feature map obtained by the feature extraction network through the alignment module, and the other is the Mask output from the Mask branch. After MaxPooling, Mask and the aligned RoI feature map are conacted, and then go through 4-layers of convolution and 3-layers of fully connected layers to output the score, the output score is the ratio of the mask obtained by the Mask branch to the IoU processed by the alignment module. Figure 3 shows the network structure of the Evaluation module.

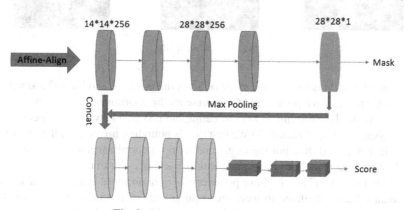

Fig. 3. The structure of "Evaluation"

In short, the proposed convolutional neural network that uses human bones to segment and score the human segmentation has the following advantages:

(1) Through the FPN network adopts a multi-scale fusion method, each level has rich semantic information.
(2) A scoring mechanism is proposed, the Evaluation branch is added, directly learn IoU's network and the pixel-level IOU value between the mask obtained by the mask branch and the mask corresponding to the ground truth is calculated to evaluate the precision of the separation.

4 Experiments

K-means are used to gather human poses into a set $S(S = S1, S2, \ldots\ldots, Sn\})$, and use a formula to define the distance between two poses, as follows:

$$\text{Dist}(P, Pu) = \sum\nolimits_{m=1}^{n} ||Cm - Cum||^2 \tag{1}$$

$$Cm = \begin{cases} (x, y, 2) & \textit{if Cm is visible} \\ (x, y, 1) & \textit{if Cm is not visible} \\ (0.5, 0.5, 1) & \textit{if Cm is not in image} \end{cases} \tag{2}$$

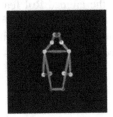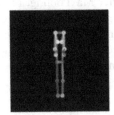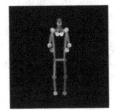

Fig. 4. Pose template

Among them, Pu is the average value of Sn in the pose set, and Pu > 0.5 key points are regarded as effective points, and Ck represents the coordinates of the key points of the human body. Use formula (1) (2) to define the distance between two people. The specific operation is as follows: (1) We first use its bounding box to crop the square RoI of each instance, and then put the target and its pose coordinates to the center of the RoI. (2) We adjust the size of this square RoI to 1 × 1 in order to normalize the posture coordinates to (0, 1). (3) Only those postures that contain more than 8 effective points in the data set are calculated to meet the requirements of posture template. Too little efficient point gesture not provide sufficient information, and as the K-means clustering outlier rejection. The two most common postures are the half-length posture and the full-body posture (full body rear view and front view) (as shown in Fig. 4), which are also in line with daily life. We use the radiation transformation matrix to convert the other postures as much as possible.

4.1 Datasets

The data set has two parts, the COCO data set and the OCHuman data set. The COCO data set is a large and rich object detection, segmentation and captioning data set. But, in this article, the COCO data set uses pictures containing people for training. Since there are few public data sets that have both human pose and human instance segmentation labels, COCO data sets simultaneously satisfies both requirements of the largest data set, so all of our models have been focused on training in COCOPersons training, and with a posture critical point and split masks comment; OCHuman dataset includes 8110 human-body image example 4731, each instance by one or more other instances serious obstruction. MaxIoU is used to evaluate the importance of occluded objects. MaxIoU > 0.5, said the instances severe occlusion, and is chosen to compose the data set. MaxIoU OCHuman average of 0.67 per person, which is the most difficult associated with human examples of data sets. Table 1 indicates the basic information of the data set:

Table 1. The information of data set

	COCOPersons	OCHuman
Images	64115	4731
Persons	273469	8110
Persons (oc0.5)	2619	8110
Persons (oc0.5)	214	2614
Average MaxIoU	0.08	0.67

4.2 Results

The basic process of the experiment first uses the basic network resnet50 + FPN to extract features, and then uses the Affine-Align module to align the ROI into a consistent size according to the human pose (the size of this article is unified as 64 * 64). Then, the aligned ROI is sent to the scoring module for processing. Then use this method in real-time multi-person 2D pose estimation. This method uses the part affinity field to detect the joint points of the body through the part confidence map [27], then uses PAF to connect the joint points, and finally combines them to obtain the skeleton of each instance feature. Finally, it is segmented through the SegMoudule module, and the resulting picture is output.

We tested our proposed Evaluation module on two data sets: (1) OCHuman was the biggest verification data set, which is mainly suitable for people who are heavily occluded. (2) COCOPersons (COCO personnel category) [28], which is included common situations in ordinary living. In experiment, the OCHuman dataset is tested, and the occlusion and overlap of people are tested, while the coco dataset was only trained on the category of people. This method has achieved good results in the OCHuman data set. Compared with the previous algorithm, there is a significant improvement. Adding a scoring module (Evaluation) to pose2seg gives a better result than the original, and the segmentation result is more accurate. The experimental results conducted on OCHuman have been significantly improved, which is 1.9 AP higher than Pose2seg [29], and AP@0.5 and AP@0.75 are also improved to varying degrees. The experimental results are as follows (Tables 2 and 3):

In contrast to the latest work, PersonLab and Mask R-CNN, the module we proposed has made instance segmentation a greater improvement in people, and the experimental

Table 2. Results under the OCHman validation dataset.

	AP	AP@0.5	AP@0.75
Pose2seg	0.544	0.945	0.599
Our	0.563	0.948	0.609

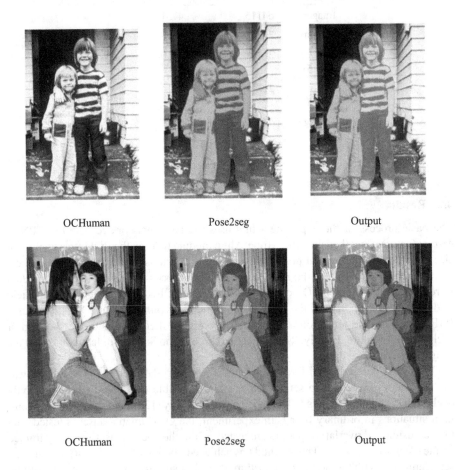

OCHuman   Pose2seg   Output

OCHuman   Pose2seg   Output

results are more accurate. We compare the experimental data with their experimental data. Among them, the category of people in the COCO data set was trained and tested. For the convenience of comparison, we only compare the medium category and the large category. Table 4 shows the comparative results of the experiment.

Table 3. Results under the COCOPerson validation dataset.

	AP	AP@0.5	AP@0.75
Pose2seg	0.579	0.914	0.669
Our	0.582	0.916	0.680

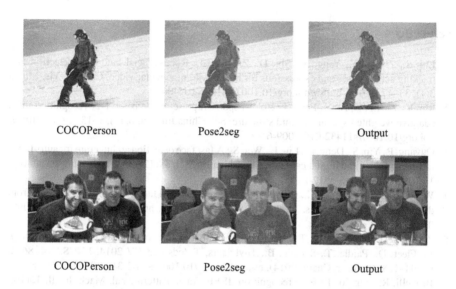

COCOPerson   Pose2seg   Output

COCOPerson   Pose2seg   Output

Table 4. Comparison with other experimental data

Method	Backbone	AP	APm	APl
Mask R-CNN	Resnet50-FPN	0.532	0.433	0.648
PersonLab	Resnet152		0.497	0.621
PersonLab	Resnet101		0.492	0.621
Our	Resnet50-FPN	0.582	0.537	0.685

5 Conclusion

In the field of CV, research on "people" has attracted more and more attention, such as: face recognition, pedestrian detection and tracking, abnormal behavior detection, etc. These have broad application prospects in areas such as intelligent safety and unmanned driving. This article uses human bones and a scoring mechanism (calculating the pixel-level IOU value between the mask obtained by the mask branch and the mask corresponding to the ground truth to measure the accuracy of the segmentation) to segment the human body. The scoring mechanism we proposed can be very good to predict the quality of the mask, the FPN network is able to integrate the semantic information of the multi-layer feature map and the unique bone information of the human body, the human body can be segmented well. In actual application scenarios, human body segmentation still needs to be further improved due to human body occlusion and camera angle, which is also a big challenge.

References

1. Liu, S., Zhang, Y., Yang, X., Shi, D., Zhang, J.J.: Robust facial landmark detection and tracking across poses and expressions for in-the-wild monocular video. Comput. Vis. Media **3**(1), 33–47 (2016). https://doi.org/10.1007/s41095-016-0068-y
2. Ma, X., Zhang, F., Li, Y., Feng, J.: Robust sparse representation based face recognition in an adaptive weighted spatial pyramid structure. Sci. China Inf. Sci. **61**(1), 1–13 (2017). https://doi.org/10.1007/s11432-016-9009-6
3. Ouyang, P., Yin, S., Deng, C., Liu, L., Wei, S.: A fast face detection architecture for auto-focus in smart-phones and digital cameras. Sci. China Inf. Sci. **59**(12), 1–3 (2016). https://doi.org/10.1007/s11432-015-5312-z
4. Wang, J., Zhang, J., Luo, C., Chen, F.: Joint head pose and facial landmark regression from depth images. Comput. Vis. Media **3**(3), 229–241 (2017). https://doi.org/10.1007/s41095-017-0082-8
5. Zhang, Z., Luo, P., Loy, C., Tang, X.: Facial landmark detection by deep multi-task learning. In: Fleet, D., Pajdla, T., Schiele, B., Tuytelaars, T. (eds.) ECCV 2014. LNCS, vol. 8694, pp. 94–108. Springer, Cham (2014). https://doi.org/10.1007/978-3-319-10599-4_7
6. Brunelli, R., Poggio, T.: Face recognition. IEEE Trans. Pattern Anal. Mach. Intell. **15**(10), 1042–1052 (1993)
7. Mao, J., Xiao, T., Jing, Y., et al.: What can help pedestrian detection? In: IEEE Computer Vision and Pattern Recognition, pp. 153–168 (2017)
8. Zhang, L., Lin, L., Liang, X., He, K.: Is faster R-CNN doing well for pedestrian detection? In: Leibe, B., Matas, J., Sebe, N., Welling, M. (eds.) ECCV 2016. LNCS, vol. 9906, pp. 443–457. Springer, Cham (2016). https://doi.org/10.1007/978-3-319-46475-6_28
9. Zhang, S., Yang, J., Schiele, B.: Occluded pedestrian detection through guided attention in CNNs. In: 2018 IEEE/CVF Conference on Computer Vision and Pattern Recognition (CVPR), pp. 6995–7003. IEEE (2018)
10. Chen, Y., Wang, Z., Peng, Y., et al.: Cascaded pyramid network for multi-person pose estimation. In: Conference on Computer Vision and Pattern recognition (CVPR), pp. 733–747 (2017)
11. Fang, H., Xie, S., Tai, Y., et al.: RMPE: regional multi-person pose estimation. Comput. Sci. **34**(2), 256–271 (2016)
12. Lifkooee, M.Z., Liu, C., Liang, Y., Zhu, Y., Li, X.: Real-time avatar pose transfer and motion generation using locally encoded Laplacian offsets. J. Comput. Sci. Technol. **34**(2), 256–271 (2019). https://doi.org/10.1007/s11390-019-1909-9
13. Xia, S., Gao, L., Lai, Y.-K., Yuan, M.-Z., Chai, J.: A survey on human performance capture and animation. J. Comput. Sci. Technol. **32**(3), 536–554 (2017). https://doi.org/10.1007/s11390-017-1742-y

14. Chen, H., Sun, K., Tian, Z., et al.: BlendMask: top-down meets bottom-up for instance segmentation. In: Conference on Computer Vision and Pattern Recognition (CVPR), pp. 112–126. IEEE (2020)

15. Li, Y., Qi, H., Dai, J., et al.: Fully convolutional instance-aware semantic segmentation. In: Computer Vision and Pattern Recognition, pp. 625–650. IEEE (2017)

16. Bolya, D., Zhou, C., Xiao, F., et al.: YOLACT++: better real-time instance segmentation. IEEE Trans. Pattern Anal. Mach. Intell. **99**, 1 (2020)

17. Hariharan, B., Arbeláez, P., Girshick, R., et al.: Hypercolumns for object segmentation and fine-grained localization. In: Computer Vision and Pattern Recognition, pp. 715–724. IEEE (2015)

18. Dai, J., He, K., Li, Y., Ren, S., Sun, J.: Instance-sensitive fully convolutional networks. In: Leibe, B., Matas, J., Sebe, N., Welling, M. (eds.) ECCV 2016. LNCS, vol. 9910, pp. 534–549. Springer, Cham (2016). https://doi.org/10.1007/978-3-319-46466-4_32

19. He, K., Zhang, X., Ren, S., et al.: Deep residual learning for image recognition. In: IEEE Conference on Computer Vision and Pattern Recognition, pp. 229–241. IEEE Computer Society (2016)

20. Girshick, R.: Fast R-CNN. Comput. Sci. (2015)

21. Ren, S., He, K., Girshick, R., et al.: Faster R-CNN: towards real-time object detection with region proposal networks. IEEE Trans. Pattern Anal. Mach. Intell. **39**(6), 1137–1149 (2017)

22. He, K., Georgia, G., Piotr, D., et al.: Mask R-CNN. IEEE Trans. Pattern Anal. Mach. Intell. **36**(2), 1 (2017)

23. Liu, S., Qi, L., Qin, H., et al.: Path aggregation network for instance segmentation. In: 2018 IEEE/CVF Conference on Computer Vision and Pattern Recognition (CVPR), pp. 536–544. IEEE (2018)

24. Chen, Y., Wang, Z., Peng, Y., et al.: Cascaded pyramid network for multi-person pose estimation. In: Computer Science - Computer Vision and Pattern Recognition (2018)

25. Kocabas, M., Karagoz, S., Akbas, E.: MultiPoseNet: fast multi-person pose estimation using pose residual network. In: Ferrari, V., Hebert, M., Sminchisescu, C., Weiss, Y. (eds.) ECCV 2018. LNCS, vol. 11215, pp. 437–453. Springer, Cham (2018). https://doi.org/10.1007/978-3-030-01252-6_26

26. Lin, T., Dollar, P., Girshick, R., et al.: Feature pyramid networks for object detection. In: Conference on Computer Vision and Pattern Recognition (CVPR), pp. 304–311 (2017)

27. Cao, Z., Simon, T., Wei, S.E., et al.: Realtime multi-person 2D pose estimation using part affinity fields. In: 2017 IEEE Conference on Computer Vision and Pattern Recognition (CVPR). IEEE (2017)

28. Lin, T.-Y., Maire, M., Belongie, S., Hays, J., Perona, P., Ramanan, D., Dollár, P., Zitnick, C.: Microsoft COCO: common objects in context. In: Fleet, D., Pajdla, T., Schiele, B., Tuytelaars, T. (eds.) ECCV 2014. LNCS, vol. 8693, pp. 740–755. Springer, Cham (2014). https://doi.org/10.1007/978-3-319-10602-1_48

29. Zhang, S.H., Li, R.L., Dong, X., et al.: Pose2Seg: detection free human instance segmentation. In: Conference on Computer Vision and Pattern Recognition (CVPR), pp. 297–312. IEEE (2019)

UAV Aerial Image Detection Based on Improved FCOS Algorithm

Pengju Zhang[1], Peimin Yan[1], Tao Zhang[2], Wennan Cui[2], and Qiuyu Zhu[1(✉)]

[1] Shanghai University, 99 Shangda Road, Baoshan District, Shanghai, China
zhuqiuyu@staff.shu.edu.cn
[2] Key Laboratory of Intelligent Infrared Perception, Chinese Academy of Sciences, Shanghai, China

Abstract. In order to solve the problem of small target detection in large-scale aerial images, on the basis of FCOS detection framework, the feature fusion layer and the problem of positive and negative sample balance are improved. GIOU is used to improve the loss function, the training scale is modified and multi-scale training strategy is used. At the same time, because the pre-selection box is not used, the training parameter adjustment time is greatly reduced, and the reasoning speed is improved under the condition of maintaining the accuracy. Under the same conditions, compared with the original FCOS, the accuracy of the improved FCOS is improved by about 6% and the speed is improved by 3 FPS.

Keywords: Unmanned aerial vehicles · Small object detection · FCOS · Feature fusion.

1 Introduction

Unmanned aerial vehicle (UAV) can ignore the ground obstacles from high altitude and scan the open places such as landform, traffic and military territory. Its monitoring range is very wide. Therefore, the task of UAV based aerial image detection has great commercial value and application space. Compared with the ground detection task, UAV has air superiority, clear vision and no occlusion. It also can detect a large number of objects and track quickly in multiple regions. However, there are also some problems in UAV aerial images. Due to UAV detection in the air, the detected objects often present small object and overhead viewing angle. Moreover, the aerial images themselves are generally high pixels, which makes the proportion of small object in the whole aerial images smaller. Therefore, small object detection in UAV aerial images is still a challenging and practical task.

For aerial images, the traditional object detection algorithm was used in the early years, and the sliding window mechanism was used to locate the target

This research was funded by the open project fund of the Key Laboratory of intelligent infrared perception, Chinese Academy of Sciences (grant number: CAS-IIRP-2030-03).

in the image grid using features and classifiers. Viola and Jones [1] use HAAR feature and AdaBoost algorithm to build cascader to detect. Felzenszwalb [2] et al. Developed an effective target detection algorithm based on multi-scale hybrid deformation, which extracted HoG features and trained latent support vector machine (MI-SVM) to obtain robustness. However, the overall effect of traditional target detection algorithms is not good in challenging scenarios.

With the development of deep learning technology, more aerial detection models based on deep learning algorithm appear. The models based on deep learning can be divided into two categories: high-precision two-stage algorithm and high-speed single-stage algorithm. To inherit the merits of both two-stage and one-stage methods, [3] propose a single-shot detector formed by two interconnected modules, i.e., the anchor refinement module and the object detection module. Moreover, [4] propose a multi-stage object detection architecture. That is, a sequence of detectors is trained with increasing IOU thresholds to be sequentially more selective against close false positives. [5] propose the channel-aware deconvolutional network to detect small objects, especially for drone-based scenes. To keep the favourable performance independent to the network architecture, [6] train detectors from scratch using BatchNorm with larger learning rate. Recently, with the emergence of anchor-free network (FCOS [7], Center-Net [8], CornerNet [9]), the object detection algorithm based on pixel level has also been developed, and its effect on small object detection has been further improved. Moreover, it does not need the calculation of IOU and the setting of anchor parameters, so the training process becomes very fast and simple.

The VISDRONE [10,18] data set is composed of aerial images of different types of UAVs from different angles and distances for different scenes, and its data volume is very large. Because most of the objects in aerial images are small objects with similar sizes. It is difficult to adjust anchor frame parameters. Moreover, there are many objects in aerial images, so it takes a lot of time to calculate IOU. Therefore, based on FCOS network, aiming at the problem of poor small target detection in VISDRONE aerial image, the network structure and training method are improved by us.

Our main contributions are as follows:

1) In order to better explore the information of small objects, the original FPN [11] structure of FCOS [7] is modified to HR-FPN [12] structure.
2) Most of the VISDRONE datasets are small objects, and the objects are relatively dense. Therefore, in the detection process, high layer's information is not helpful to small objects, even harmful. In this paper, the P6 and P7 layers in HR-FPN structure are removed, which can not only achieve the acceleration effect, but also avoid the influence of useless information on small object detection.
3) Because the object of aerial image is small and dense, it is easy to cause the imbalance of positive and negative samples by using the original method. In this paper, the center sampling method is used to sample the positive and negative samples only in the central area of the ground-truth box, which can effectively balance the number of positive and negative samples.

2   FCOS Algorithm

FCOS [7] algorithm is a kind of full convolution single-stage algorithm, which solves the problem of object detection in a pixel by pixel manner and similar to semantic segmentation. It does not need to use the pre-set anchor box, and directly carries out regression prediction for each pixel of the target, also known as anchor-free algorithm. Compared with SSD [13], Faster RCNN [14] and other anchor-based models, it can avoid the complex calculation related to anchor box in the training process, such as the calculation of IOU during training process. It also can improve the training speed and reduce the training memory. Besides, there is no need to adjust and set the super parameters of the anchor box which has a great impact on the training results. Therefore, the training results of FCOS [7] are more stable and less affected by the super parameters, which greatly improves the training efficiency.

The network structure of FCOS [7] use RESNET [15] as the backbone network, and uses FPN structure to fuse the features of C3, C4 and C5 in the backbone network to get P3, P4 and P5. It down sample the P5 feature layer to get P6 and P7, which can adapt to the target of various scales. Then, the five feature layers are classified and regressed. Therefore, the class output for each feature layer is $H \times W \times C$, where C represents the number of categories (13 categories in VISDRONE [10]), and the position output is $H \times W \times 4$. that is, each pixel corresponds to class and position. The coordinates (x, y) of each point in the feature layer are mapped to the original image. If the mapped points fall within the area of the ground-truth box, they are marked as positive samples, otherwise they are negative samples. The regression target is (L, t, R, b), which is the distance from the left, upper, right and lower boundary of the border to the central point. In order to make the feature space larger and the recognition more powerful, the $exp()$ function is used to stretch the training target, and better training results can be obtained.

$$l = x - x_0^{(i)}, t = y - y_0^{(i)} \tag{1}$$

$$r = x_1^{(i)} - x, b = y_1^{(i)} - y \tag{2}$$

where (x, y) is the coordinate of the center point associated with the border, and $(x_0, y_0), (x_1, y_1)$ are the coordinates of the upper left corner and the lower right corner of the border respectively.

Because FCOS expands the center point area to the whole target area, many low-quality prediction boxes will appear. Most of the low-quality prediction boxes deviate from the center of the actual target. In order to solve this problem, the center ness branch is added to suppress the emergence of low-quality boxes. This strategy is very simple and convenient, and does not introduce super parameters, which is equivalent to introducing a loss to constrain the training process. The specific measure is to add a branch parallel to the classification, and use the following formula as the loss to ensure that the prediction boundary box is as close as possible to the center of the ground-truth box.

$$centerness^* = \sqrt{\frac{min(l^*, r^*)}{max(l^*, r^*)} \times \frac{min(t^*, b^*)}{max(t^*, b^*)}} \qquad (3)$$

where (L^*, T^*, R^*, B^*) is the regression object value of the prediction box. Due to gradient descent algorithm. $1 - centrerness^*$ is used to optimize to make the loss close to zero.

3 Improved FCOS for Aerial Images

In aerial images, the target often presents the characteristics of small objects, and the pixel area is small and densely distributed. When anchor-based network is used, it is very difficult to set anchor frame parameters, and the training and testing speed is very slow. However, the accuracy of FCOS [7] network in the original paper is not good enough in small object detection, which is related to its input size and network structure of the training. The improved FCOS [7] network algorithm can better adapt to small object detection by modifying the network structure, input size, sample selection strategy and feature fusion layer.

3.1 Improved Fusion Layer

Since FCOS [7] is a pixel by pixel method for object detection and the object's pixels in aerial images are relatively small, we need to obtain high-resolution representation to avoid information loss after down sampling. So how to maintain high resolution information? In the semantic segmentation task, many models enhance the information expression ability of the high-resolution feature layer by upsampling the low-resolution feature layer and fusing the high-resolution feature layer with it. Because FCOS is similar to semantic segmentation to calculate the whole feature map, it can also be used to enhance the feature expression of high-resolution feature layer. This method can improve the accuracy of small object detection.

The backbone network Resnet uses $C3$, $C4$ and $C5$ as the input of feature fusion layer. After 1×1 convolution, $P3$, $P4$ and $P5$ are obtained. $P6$ and $P7$ which are down sampled by $P5$ are used for large object detection. The detection scales are $(256, 256)$ and $(512, 512)$. However, there are almost no such large-scale objects in the VISDRONE [10] dataset. So, the $P6$ and $P7$ layer will not only reduce the detection speed, but also produce redundant information, which will reduce the recall rate and accuracy of small object detection. In our paper, $P6$ and $P7$ layers are removed, $C3$ and $C4$ are upsampled to $C5$'s size and concat with $C5$ as $P5$, Then, $P5$ and $P4$ are upsampled to $P3$'s size, and then spliced to enhance the feature expression ability of high-resolution feature map. Finally, the down sampling operation is carried out, as shown in the Fig. 1.

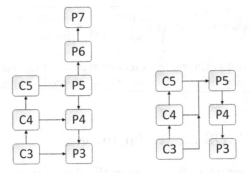

Fig. 1. Feature fusion layers (a) original structure; (b) modified structure

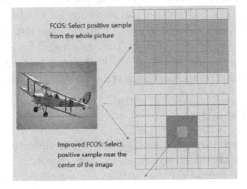

Fig. 2. Comparison of using center sampling strategy

3.2 Center-Sampling Strategy

In order to increase the number of positive samples, FCOS [7] regards all the points in the ground-truth box as positive samples. Although it can effectively relieve the pressure of unbalanced positive and negative samples, the features produced by the points far away from the center of the ground-truth box are not very good. It will lead to optimization difficulties, and a large number of low-quality prediction boxes will be produced in the prediction. In order to solve this problem, this paper uses a central sampling strategy in Fig. 2 to obtain positive samples. The center of the ground-truth is taken as the origin, and the region around it is regarded as a positive sample, which makes it easier to get the optimal optimization results. The positive sample region is selected to extend from the center point to four directions, and the specific extension length on each feature layer is the step size multiplied by radius. Radius is the super parameter, which is set to 1.5 in this paper.

3.3 Improved Loss Function

FCOS algorithm uses focal loss for object classification and IOU loss for position regression. Focal loss can effectively balance positive and negative samples, which makes the optimizer's optimization direction biased to difficult samples and IOU loss can optimize (L, T, R, B) four variables at the same time. However, IOU loss has a problem, which does not consider the optimization scheme without overlapping samples. The IOU of non-overlapping samples is 0, which will lead to zero gradient and cannot be optimized normally. In this paper, GIOU [16] is used instead of IOU, and the GIOU [16] of without overlapping samples is -1. The calculation formula is as follows:

$$GIOU = IOU - \frac{|C\backslash\backslash(A \cup B)|}{|C|} \tag{4}$$

where C is the smallest box that can contain A and B, and $C\backslash\backslash(A\cup B)$ represents the area of C minus the union of A and B. Therefore, the loss function of the improved FCOS [7] is obtained as follows:

$$L(p,t) = L_{focal}(p,c) + L_{giou}(t,t^*) \tag{5}$$

where p and c are the prediction probability and the real class label respectively, t and t^* represent the four position variables which is the distance from the left, upper, right and lower boundary of the border to the central point of the prediction box and the groundtruth box.

3.4 Multi-scale Training Strategy

In the view of UAV, the distance to the target or the shooting angle will cause the scale change of the target. In order to solve this problem, this paper adopts the multi-scale comprehensive training method to optimize the sensitivity of the model to the scale change. And through the analysis of the image size of VIS-DRONE [10] dataset, it is found that there are three kinds of image resolution $(1920, 1080), (1360, 765), (960, 540)$. Generally, deep learning models can only use a single scale in model design, and the images will be scaled while inputting. Therefore, using multi-scale comprehensive training can reduce the sensitivity of the model to scale changes. The specific method is as follows: using multiple scales, each batch will change the input scale randomly when training input. Since FCOS [7] is also a full convolution network, this scheme can be implemented. And through the analysis of the data set, it is found that the image aspect ratio is 1.78. In order to avoid image deformation during image scaling, the original scale $(1333, 800)$ used by FCOS [7] does not meet this aspect ratio, which will reduce the detection effect. Therefore, we must correct the aspect ratio of the scale, but at the same time, we should not make the scale too large to avoid insufficient memory and training, so as to correct $(1333, 800)$ to $(1425, 800)$. When the scale increases, it will make the small target detection more accurate. Therefore, by expanding the scale of $(1425, 800)$, we can get

$(1510, 850)$, $(1600, 900)$, $(1690, 950)$, $(1780, 1000)$, etc. Through the comparison of experiments, it is found that the best training effect is obtained by using the two scales ($1600, 900$ and $1510, 850$).

4 Experiment and Result Analysis

4.1 Data Set Preparation and Model Training

The data set used in this paper is the UAV aerial image data set VISDRONE 2019 [10], which is collected by the AISKYEYE team of the machine learning and data mining Laboratory of Tianjin University of China. Aerial photos of ground targets are carried out by UAVs and marked. The dataset consists of 288 video clips composed of 261908 frames and 10209 still images, covering factors such as location (14 different regions of China), environment (urban and rural areas), density (congestion and sparsity). At the same time, different video clips are collected from different types of UAVs and lighting conditions. There are 13 categories of labeled classes. Some images of the dataset are shown in Fig. 3.

The training is carried out in the environment of CPU Intel Core i7-7550u, main frequency 2.8 GHz, eight cores, memory 16g, Ubuntu 18.04 and video card 2080ti. Due to the multi-scale training strategy, the input image is randomly scaled to $(1600, 900)$ or $(1510, 850)$. Then random horizontal flipping, random saturation, chroma, brightness adjustment and other data enhancement methods are carried out. Specifically, the input 8 images are taken as a batch, and four 2080ti GPUs are used to train 50 epochs, with a total of 40450 iterations. The learning rate is 0.005 and the weight attenuation is 0.0001. The SGD algorithm is used to optimize the parameters, and the warmup strategy is used to linearly increase the learning rate from zero to 0.005 before 300 iterations. In order to find the optimal solution, the learning rate is reduced to 0.1 times in 35 and 45 cycles.

4.2 Experimental Results and Theoretical Analysis

In order to prove the effectiveness of this method, the evaluation indexes of coco dataset are used to evaluate and compare the two models before and after the improvement under the same experimental conditions. In COCO [17] competition, the evaluation results are generally compared with the mean average precision (MAP) and average recall rate (MAR) under the condition of target frame intersection ratio and area size. In this paper, all indicators are compared under the standard of IOU threshold of 0.5.

The calculation formula of MAP and MAR is as follows:

$$precision = \frac{TP}{TP + FP} \tag{6}$$

$$recall = \frac{TP}{TP + FN} \tag{7}$$

Fig. 3. VISDRONE dataset

Table 1. Test result of different models

Model	mAP	mAR	FPS
Faster RCNN	0.275	0.248	5.32
RefineDet	0.288	0.154	12.12
Retinanet	0.213	0.115	13.24
YOLOV3	0.214	0.183	25.41
FCOS	0.263	0.232	14.28
Improved FCOS	0.321	0.270	17.36

where TP is the number of frames with $IOU > 0.5$, FP is the number of frames with $IOU < 0.5$, FN is the number of frames without detection. AP is the area under the precision recall curve, which is defined as follows:

$$AP = \int_0^1 P_r dr \tag{8}$$

Since the data sets in this paper have multiple classes, we need to get the *AP* value of each class, and then the MAP after averaging. The model optimization degree can be judged by limiting the size of the target scale and viewing its recall rate. Since most aerial images are small targets, we mainly focus on the recall rate of small targets.

Under the condition of GPU 2080ti, the performance test results of FCOS [7] before and after improvement are shown in Table 1.

In order to better analyze the effect of the measures adopted in this paper on the detection accuracy, comparative experiments are carried out from the following three aspects.

1) Whether to use center-sample and GIOU
2) Whether to change feature fusion layer and remove *P*6, *P*7 high-level features
3) Whether to use multi-scale training strategy

Table 2. The comparative experimental results of different improving strategy

Experiment	Model 1	Model 2	Model 3	Model 4
Method 1		✓	✓	✓
Method 2			✓	✓
Method 3				✓
mAP(%)	26.3	27.8	30.6	32.1

Model 1, 2, 3 and 4 are models obtained in turn without using or using the above three methods respectively. The comparative experimental results are as Table 2.

Through the above comparative experiments, it is found that changing the fusion layer and removing P6 and P7 high-level features can significantly improve the accuracy of the model. Then, by comparing the recall rate of small targets before and after strategy 2, we can see that the improvement of detection accuracy is mainly due to the increase of recall rate of small objects, which can detect more small targets, thus improving AP. It can be seen that for large objects, the recall rate is reduced from 0.449 to 0.403, which is due to the removal of high-level features. However, the number of large objects in this data set is relatively small, so it does not affect the total precision, while the recall rate of small objects can greatly improve the overall accuracy. It is worth mentioning that since most of the data sets in this paper are small objects, the existence of P6 and P7 layers does not change the overall accuracy. In order to improve the reasoning speed, we choose to remove them.

Comparison of recall rate of the model before and after strategy 2 are shown in Table 3.

Using the improved FCOS, the image detection results of different angles and different scenes are shown in the Fig. 4.

Table 3. Comparison of recall rate of the model before strategy

Scale/Recall	Before	After
Small	0.171	0.182
Middle	0.405	0.416
Large	0.449	0.403

Fig. 4. The test result of datasets

5 Conclusion

In this paper, the FCOS detection model is improved to make it more suitable for aerial images by analyzing the characteristics of small and medium-sized targets in VISDRONE data set. Center sample sampling is used to balance the positive and negative samples. $GIOU$ is a better optimization model instead of IOU. At the same time, the feature fusion layer to enhance the expression of high-level resolution information and the strategy of multi-scale sum training are used to make the model more suitable for aerial images. The recall rate of small target is greatly improved, and the overall accuracy is also greatly improved. At the same time, the feature fusion layers are used to enhance the high-level resolution information expression, and the strategy of multi-scale sum training improve greatly the overall accuracy. Besides, due to the removal of $P6$ and $P7$, the monitoring speed is greatly improved.

References

1. Viola, P.A., Jones, M.J.: Rapid object detection using a boosted cascade of simple features. In: CVPR, pp. 511–518 (2001)

2. Felzenszwalb, P.F., Girshick, R.B., McAllester, D.A., Ramanan, D.: Object detection with discriminatively trained part-based models. TPAMI **32**(9), 1627–1645 (2010)
3. Zhang, S., Wen, L., Bian, X., Lei, Z., Li, S.Z.: Single-shot refinement neural network for object detection. In: CVPR, pp. 4203–4212 (2018)
4. Cai, Z., Vasconcelos, N.: Cascade R-CNN: delving into high quality object detection. In: CVPR, pp. 6154–6162 (2018)
5. Duan, K., Du, D., Qi, H., Huang, Q.: Detecting small objects using a channel-aware deconvolutional network. IEEE Trans. Circuits Syst. Video Technol. **30**, 1639–1652 (2019)
6. Zhu, R., et al.: ScratchDet: exploring to train single-shot object detectors from scratch. In: CVPR (2019)
7. Tian, Z., Shen, C., Chen, H., He, T.: FCOS: fully convolutional one-stage object detection. CoRR, abs/1904.01355 (2019)
8. Zhou, X., Wang, D., Krähenbühl, P.: Objects as points. CoRR, abs/1904.07850 (2019)
9. Law, H., Deng, J.: CornerNet: detecting objects as paired keypoints. In: Ferrari, V., Hebert, M., Sminchisescu, C., Weiss, Y. (eds.) Computer Vision – ECCV 2018. LNCS, vol. 11218, pp. 765–781. Springer, Cham (2018). https://doi.org/10.1007/978-3-030-01264-9_45
10. Zhu, P., et al.: VisDrone-DET2018: the vision meets drone object detection in image challenge results. In: Leal-Taixé, L., Roth, S. (eds.) ECCV 2018. LNCS, vol. 11133, pp. 437–468. Springer, Cham (2019). https://doi.org/10.1007/978-3-030-11021-5_27
11. Lin, T., Dollár, P., Girshick, R.B., He, K., Hariharan, B., Belongie, S.J.: Feature pyramid networks for object detection. In: CVPR, pp. 936–944 (2017)
12. Sun, K., Xiao, B. Liu, D., Wang, J.: Deep high-resolution representation learning for human pose estimation. In: CVPR (2019)
13. Liu, W., Anguelov, D., Erhan, D., Szegedy, C., Reed, S., Fu, C.-Y., Berg, A.C.: SSD: single shot multibox detector. In: Leibe, B., Matas, J., Sebe, N., Welling, M. (eds.) ECCV 2016. LNCS, vol. 9905, pp. 21–37. Springer, Cham (2016). https://doi.org/10.1007/978-3-319-46448-0_2
14. Ren, S., He, K., Girshick, R.B., Sun, J.: Faster R-CNN: towards real-time object detection with region proposal networks. In: NeurIPS, pp. 91–99 (2015)
15. He, K., Zhang, X., Ren, S., Sun, J.: Deep residual learning for image recognition. In: CVPR, pp. 770–778 (2016)
16. Rezatofighi, H., Tsoi, N., Gwak, J.Y., et al.: Generalized intersection over union: a metric and a loss for bounding box regression. In: 2019 IEEE/CVF Conference on Computer Vision and Pattern Recognition (CVPR). IEEE (2020)
17. Lin, T.-Y., et al.: Microsoft COCO: common objects in context. In: Fleet, D., Pajdla, T., Schiele, B., Tuytelaars, T. (eds.) ECCV 2014. LNCS, vol. 8693, pp. 740–755. Springer, Cham (2014). https://doi.org/10.1007/978-3-319-10602-1_48
18. Zhu, P., Wen, L., Du, D., et al.: Vision meets drones: past, present and future. arXiv: Computer Vision and Pattern Recognition (2020)

FaceCode: An Artistic Face Image with Invisible Hyperlink

Yi Deng, Jun Jia, Dandan Zhu, Hua Yang, and Guangtao Zhai[⊠]

Institute of Image Communication and Network Engineering,
Shanghai Jiao Tong University, Shanghai, China
{deng_yi,jiajun0302,ddz,hyang,zhaiguangtao}@sjtu.edu.cn

Abstract. With the widespread use of mobile social software, QR code plays an important role in acquiring messages from offline to online. However, the plain black and white blocks of QR code cannot attract users in social software, thus some popular software like Wechat beautify the QR code to improve its visual appeal. Inspired by the mentioned fact, this paper proposes a novel 2D image code named FaceCode. FaceCode is a Convolution Neural Network (CNN) based framework to embed information into a picture and beautify it simultaneously. For an input picture, FaceCode firstly uses a style transfer neural network to make the picture artistic, and then an embedding network cascading to the style transfer network embeds the personal information of users into the picture. The information is invisible but can be recognized by a phone camera. With the help of FaceCode, the users can hide their personal information in their profile pictures in social software. Experiments show that FaceCode can generate personalized profile pictures while maintaining the accuracy of recognizing the hidden information.

Keywords: Style transfer · Digital watermarking · 2D barcode

1 Introduction

In our daily life, people often need to hide some information into their profiles. QR Code [6] is an effective way to hide information. However, it has two main deficiencies: it not only takes space but also looks ugly. It also lacks attraction to social media users. To address these problems, we propose a novel 2D image network to hide information into personal profiles and generate artistic profiles at the same time. Through our network, we can generate artistic profiles appealing to social media users and also hide information to make it invisible to users. The network architecture is shown in Fig. 1.

In image style transfer, Gatys *et al.* was the first to use Convolution Neural Network [5,7] to synthesize textures in style image transfer. He used VGG-19 [4] as a feature extraction to extract style features in style images and semantic content information in content images and output images that transfer the style of style images to the content images in our view. During his transfer process,

© Springer Nature Singapore Pte Ltd. 2021
G. Zhai et al. (Eds.): IFTC 2020, CCIS 1390, pp. 63–72, 2021.
https://doi.org/10.1007/978-981-16-1194-0_6

he proposed a method that can quantitatively measure the content and style features. His method can synthesize high-quality output images but takes a lot of time because of a large number of computational costs.

Johnson *et al.* named the loss in VGG-19 as perceptual loss and used a feed-forward network to train the network that output images in a given style. It can achieve a real-time image style transfer. His network's results are similar to Gatys' both quantitatively and as measured by objective function value but are three orders of magnitude faster to generate. However, the network has its deficiencies. Once the network has been trained using a specific style image, the network is fixed and can only output images that have the same style as the given style image.

As for embedding information into images, Tancik *et al.* invented StegaStamp based on a neural network, which can hide hyperlinks into natural images and make hyperlinks detectable for cameras. StegaStamp contains an encoder to embed hyperlinks and a decoder to recover the information hidden in the image. To simulate the actual physical world, between the encoder and the decoder they use a distortion network to attack the output image of the encoder and send the distorted image to the decoder. It performs well in recovering the information from physical photographs.

However, StegaStamp simplifies the camera imaging process into a series of imaging process methods, which may not work in many physical situations with various lightings and shadows. Besides, it does not consider the characteristics of the Human Vision System (HVS) when training the decoder [9]. Thus, the hidden information in images can be easily noticed by human eyes although it's invisible to the cameras. To solve this problem, Jia *et al.* proposed a method simulating the actual physical distortion to achieve a better visual effect. They exploit 3D rendering to simulate the camera imaging process in the real world: lighting, perspective warp, noise, blur, and photo compression of cameras. Their approach outperforms StegaStamp in many physical scenes.

In this paper, we propose a new architecture to hide information into artistic profiles. We combine a style transfer network with an information embedding network. First, we input personal profiles into the style transfer network to generate artistic profiles. Then we input personal information into the cascading embedding network to embed personal information of users into the artistic profiles. Experimental results show that the network can generate artistic images of good visual experience while hiding information perfectly well. And we can achieve a high decoding accuracy in various physical environments.

The main contributions of this paper are summarized below:

- We first employ the image style transfer network to generate personalized profiles in given styles to make it more attractive. Moreover, the artistic profiles can hide some actual face information to avoid being misused by other people.
- We first combine the style transfer network and image hidden network to embed personal information into artistic profiles. We can generate images of good visual experience containing invisible hyperlinks that are detectable by

cameras under various unconstrained environments and achieve high accuracy in decoding the information.

- We can use the network to generate personalized profiles in social media with some hidden hyperlinks containing some personal information such as identity or home page. Users who are interested in the profile can get the information they need by taking photos.

2 Methodology

The framework of FaceCode consists of two cascading networks: (1) a style transfer neural network, (2) an information embedding neural network. Considering the typical application scenario in social software, we assume that the input of FaceCode is a facial picture used as the profile picture of the user. When an input image is fed into the framework, the style transfer network firstly beautifies the image into a specific artistic style, and then the embedding network embeds specific information into the artistic facial picture. When training the embedding network, we train an extracting network simultaneously to recognize the embedded information. Figure 1 presents the framework of FaceCode.

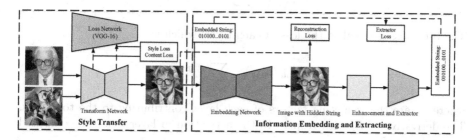

Fig. 1. The framework of the proposed FaceCode. Our framework consists of two cascading CNNs based neural networks: (1) a style transfer network to beautify the input picture (left), (2) an information hiding architecture to embed personal information and extract the hidden information. To make the hidden information extractable to the camera, we insert an enhancement module between the embedding network and the extractor. The enhancement uses a perspective transformation to simulate different camera views and uses differentiable 3D rendering to model the light condition.

2.1 Style Transfer

We select the method proposed by Johnson *et al.* [11] as our style transfer network.

Style Representation. A convolution layer with N_l filters can generate N_l feature maps each of size M_l, where M_l is the product of the height and width of each feature map. The output in layer l is the feature of the image in certain dimension, and can be described as a matrix $F_l \in R^{N_l \times M_l}$, where $F_{i,j}^l$ is the activation of the ith filter at position j in layer l.

The style of an image can be represented through feature correlations by the Gram Matrix $G^l \in R^{N_l \times N_l}$ [8], where $G_{i,j}^l$ is the inner product between the vectorized feature maps i and j in layer l:

$$G_{ij}^l = \sum_k F_{ik}^l F_{jk}^l. \tag{1}$$

By summing the feature correlations of different layers, we can obtain a stationary and multi-scale representation of the input image, which can describe its texture information very well, but will lose its global arrangement information. From the input of low-level layers, we can easily find the texture of the original image. Let a and x separately be the original image and the image that is generated, and matrix A^l and G^l be their style representation in layer l.

The loss of layer l contributing to the total loss can be described as:

$$E_l = \frac{1}{4N_l^2 M_l^2} \sum_{i,j} (G_{ij}^l - A_{ij}^l)^2. \tag{2}$$

The total loss is equal to the loss of each layer, which is

$$L_{style}(a, x) = \sum_{l=0}^{L} w_l E_l, \tag{3}$$

where w_l are the weighting factors of each layer contributing to the total loss. The derivative of E_l with respect to the activation in layer l can be computed as:

$$\frac{\partial E_l}{F_{ij}^l} = \begin{cases} \frac{1}{N_l^2 M_l^2}((F^l)^T (G^l - A^l))_{ji} & if F_{ij} > 0 \\ 0 & if F_{ij} < 0. \end{cases} \tag{4}$$

The gradient of E_l with respect to the pixel values x can be computed using standard error back-propagation algorithm [1].

Content Representation. In practical objection recognition tasks, higher layers in the neural network can capture high-level contents in terms of object recognition. Based on this, we refer to the feature responses in higher layers of the network as the content representation.

Let p and x be the original image and the image which is generated, and P^l and F^l be their respective feature matrix in layer l. We can define the squared-error loss between two feature representations as follows:

$$L_{content}(p, x, l) = \frac{1}{2} \sum_{i,j} (F_{ij}^l - P_{ij}^l)^2. \tag{5}$$

The derivative of this loss with respect to the activations in layer l is

$$\frac{\partial L_{content}}{\partial F_{ij}^l} = \begin{cases} (F^l - P^l)_{ij} & if F_{ij} > 0 \\ 0 & if F_{ij} < 0. \end{cases} \qquad (6)$$

From the gradient with respect to input x, we can see that it can be readily computed using the standard error back-propagation algorithm. Therefore, we can change the initial random image x until it can generate the same response in layer l of VGG-19 as the original image p.

2.2 Information Hiding

The information hiding architecture accepts an image and hidden information as inputs. In this paper, the input image is an artistic facial picture with a specific style and the input information is a binary string. The information hiding architecture is shown in the right of Fig. 1. As analyzed in the first section, the embedded information can be extracted after the picture is taken by a camera. Thus, we insert an enhancement module between the embedding network and the extractor. The enhancement can simulate different camera views and light conditions of the camera. The output image of the embedding network is enhanced by this module and then fed into the extractor. After the enhancement, the image can be simulated as a physical photo.

Embedding Network. The embedding network embeds the hidden information into the input picture (stylized image). Inspired by [10], we reshape the input information (a binary string in this paper) and concatenate it to the input picture. We select U-Net [12] as the backbone of our embedding network. The goal of the embedding network is to generate an image that contains the hidden string and is visually close to the input image. To maintain the similarity to the input image, we use L_2 and $LPIPS$ [2] as the loss functions to supervise the training of the embedding network:

$$L_{embedding}(x, x') = ||x - x^2||^2 + LPIPS(x, x'), \qquad (7)$$

where x is the input image and x' is the output image.

Enhancement Network and Extracting Network. The extracting network accepts the output of the embedding network and extracts the hidden information. The output is a binary string that has the same length as the input string of the embedding network. To supervise the extracting network, we use cross-entropy as the loss function. If we directly train the embedding network and extracting network, the loss functions can converge easily. However, there is a trade-off between the visual quality of the embedding result and the accuracy of the extracting result. Considering the application example mentioned in the first section, the embedded information is invisible but can be recognized after the picture is taken by a camera, which requires enough high accuracy under the camera imaging process. Inspired by [13] and [14], we add an enhancement module between the embedding network and the extracting network.

When we take photos with a camera, two major distortions may be introduced to the original image. The first distortion is the perspective deformation caused by different camera views. We generate random perspective transformation matrices and apply them to the output of the embedding network during training. After that, the hidden information can become robust against the perspective deformation. The second distortion is the color change caused by different light conditions. To simulate different light conditions, we use two light models to process the output of the embedding network. After these two enhancements, the output of the embedding network can be simulated as a physical photo. Different from the embedding and extracting networks, the enhancement module does not contain any parameters so that it can be omitted in inference. However, this module is inserted in the end-to-end training framework, thus the mentioned enhancements need to be differentiable.

3   Experimental Results and Analysis

3.1   Implementation Details

The resolution of a style transfer output is 224×224. The backbone of the embedding network is UNet [12] which contains a series of residual connections. We define the resolution of the input of our embedding network is 400×400. The hidden information of this paper is a binary string of 100 bits. The string is generated randomly during training and encoded with error-correcting code BCH in inference.

The dataset used in our experiments is a subset of the IMDB-WIKI dataset [15]. We select 20k images from this dataset as the training set of our style transfer network. We select 5 kinds of training style: Udnie, Starry Night, the Scream, Composition vii, and Wave. Then, we select 5k images that are not included by the 20k images mentioned above as the test set of the style transfer network and generate 25k stylized images. These 25k stylized images are then resized to 400×400 and used to train the information hiding framework. After training, we select the other 100 images from the IMDB-WIKI dataset as the final test set.

3.2   Results of Visual Quality

In this subsection, we present the results of visual quality. To measure the visual quality of the stylized image with hidden information, we use SSIM [3] and PSNR to measure the quality of the FaceCode compared to the stylized image. The quantitative result is presented in Table 1.

In addition to the quantitative result, we also present some qualitative results in Fig. 2. Figure 2 presents two samples for each style. We can find that the hidden information has almost no effect on the visual appealing of the stylized images.

Table 1. SSIM and PSNR values.

Metric	Value
SSIM	0.89
PSNR	27.53

3.3   Results of Information Extracting

To measure the robustness of information extracting, we take 250 photos from different camera angles and different light conditions. The pictures are displayed on a Dell monitor and the distance from the camera to the screen is 60 cm. Figure 3 presents some samples in our experiments. Different camera angles can introduce different moire patterns, which can change the brightness, hue, and contrast of the image. In experiments, we use BCH(96,56) to encode the hidden string, which has 56 bits to encode the message and 40 bits to correct errors. When the error number is less than 5 bits, the hidden string can be decoded accurately. We present the decoding accuracy of each kind of style under different camera angles and the bit accuracy in Table 2. From Table 2, we can find that the decoding accuracy and bit accuracy of the Starry Night style is the lowest among these five kinds of style. Although the bit accuracy of these false samples is range from 0.91 to 0.94, they cannot be decoded. Through analysis, we find that the cause of this problem may be the narrow color gamut of this kind of style. Thus, it is difficult to hide too much information for this style.

Table 2. Decoding accuracy under different camera angles and average bit accuracy.

Style	Left 45	Left 30	0	Right 30	Right 45	Average bit accuracy
Udnie	90%	100%	100%	100%	100%	0.99
Starry Night	50%	70%	80%	80%	50%	0.92
The Scream	100%	100%	100%	90%	90%	0.98
Composition vii	90%	100%	100%	90%	80%	0.96
Wave	80%	90%	90%	90%	70%	0.95

Fig. 2. The qualitative results of the proposed FaceCode. In experiments, we select five kinds of style images. The first column of each group is the original facial image, the second column is the stylized image, and the third column is the stylized image containing hidden string. The resolution of the second column is 224×224 and the resolution of the third column is 400×400.

(a)   (b)   (c)   (d)

(e)   (f)   (g)   (h)

(i)   (j)   (k)   (l)

(m)   (n)   (o)   (p)

Fig. 3. Some samples in real environments.

4   Conclusion

This paper proposes FaceCode, named An Artistic Face Image with Invisible Hyperlink. With the help of our work, the users of social software can generate personalized profile pictures and embed their personalized information into this picture. The hidden information is invisible to human eyes but can be recognized by the cameras of the cell phone. The experiment results show that our approach has both visually appealing and decoding robustness.

Acknowledgement. This work is supported by Science and Technology Commission of Shanghai Municipality (STCSM, GrantNos. 19DZ1209303, 18DZ1200102).

References

1. Rumelhart, D.E., Hinton, G.E., Williams, R.J.: Learning representations by back-propagating errors. Nature **323**(6088), 533–536 (1986)
2. Zhang, R., Isola, P., Efros, A.A., Shechtman, E., Wang, O.: The unreasonable effectiveness of deep features as a perceptual metric. In: IEEE Conference on Computer Vision and Pattern Recognition (CVPR) (2018)
3. Wang, Z., Bovik, A.C., Sheikh, H.R., Simoncelli, E.P.: Image quality assessment: from error visibility to structural similarity. IEEE Trans. Image Process. **13**(4), 600–612 (2004)
4. Simonyan, K., Zisserman, A.: Very deep convolutional networks for large-scale image recognition. arXiv preprint arXiv:1409.1556 (2014)
5. Gatys, L.A., Ecker, A.S., Bethge, M.: Image style transfer using convolutional neural networks. In: IEEE Conference on Computer Vision and Pattern Recognition (CVPR) (2016)
6. Gao, Z., Zhai, G., Hu, C.: The invisible QR code. In: Proceedings of the 23rd ACM International Conference on Multimedia, pp. 1047–1050 (2015)
7. Gatys, L.A., Ecker, A.S., Bethge, M.: Texture synthesis using convolutional neural networks. In: IEEE Conference on Neural Information Processing Systems (NIPS) (2015)
8. Portilla, J., Simoncelli, E.P.: A parametric texture model based on joint statistics of complex wavelet coefficients. Int. J. Comput. Vis. **40**(1), 49–70 (2000)
9. Jaderberg, M., Simonyan, K., Zisserman, A., Kavukcuoglu, K.: Spatial transformer networks. In: Advances in Neural Information Processing Systems, pp. 2017–2025 (2015)
10. Zhu, J., Kaplan, R., Johnson, J., Fei-Fei, L.: HiDDeN: hiding data with deep networks. In: Ferrari, V., Hebert, M., Sminchisescu, C., Weiss, Y. (eds.) ECCV 2018. LNCS, vol. 11219, pp. 682–697. Springer, Cham (2018). https://doi.org/10.1007/978-3-030-01267-0_40
11. Johnson, J., Alahi, A., Fei-Fei, L.: Perceptual losses for real-time style transfer and super-resolution. In: Leibe, B., Matas, J., Sebe, N., Welling, M. (eds.) ECCV 2016. LNCS, vol. 9906, pp. 694–711. Springer, Cham (2016). https://doi.org/10.1007/978-3-319-46475-6_43
12. Ronneberger, O., Fischer, P., Brox, T.: U-Net: convolutional networks for biomedical image segmentation. In: Navab, N., Hornegger, J., Wells, W.M., Frangi, A.F. (eds.) MICCAI 2015. LNCS, vol. 9351, pp. 234–241. Springer, Cham (2015). https://doi.org/10.1007/978-3-319-24574-4_28
13. Tancik, M., Mildenhall, B., Ng, R.: StegaStamp: invisible hyperlinks in physical photographs. In: Proceedings of the IEEE/CVF Conference on Computer Vision and Pattern Recognition, pp. 2117–2126 (2020)
14. Jia, J., et al.: Robust invisible hyperlinks in physical photographs based on 3D rendering attacks. arXiv preprint arXiv:1912.01224 (2019)
15. Rothe, R., Timofte, R., Van Gool, L.: DEX: Deep EXpectation of apparent age from a single image. In: IEEE International Conference on Computer Vision Workshops (ICCVW) (2015)

Single Image Deraining via Multi-scale Gated Feature Enhancement Network

Hao Luo, Hanxiao Luo, Qingbo Wu$^{(\boxtimes)}$, King Ngi Ngan, Hongliang Li,
Fanman Meng, and Linfeng Xu

University of Electronic Science and Technology of China, Chengdu 611731, China
{haoluo,lhx}@std.uestc.edu.cn,
{qbwu,knngan,hlli,fmmeng,lfxu}@uestc.edu.cn

Abstract. With the widespread popularity of computer vision applications, single image deraining problem has attracted more and more attentions. Though various deep-learning based algorithms are designed for single image rain steak removal, deraining performance is still limited due to the insufficient utilization of multi-scale features, which either fails to remove rain steaks completely or damages the original image content. In our paper, a novel deraining network called Multi-scale Gated Feature Enhancement Network (MGFE-Net) is proposed to deal with different types of rain streaks meanwhile achieve a satisfied restoration effect. In MGFE-Net, a multi-scale gated module (MGM) is first utilized between the encoder and decoder to extract multi-scale features according to image content and keep the consistence between high-level semantics and low-level detail features. Furthermore, to cope with diverse rain streaks with different representative characteristics, we integrate the receptive field block (RFB) into encoder and decoder branches to enhance extracted rain features. Multi-level outputs of decoder are fused to obtain a final refined result. Extensive deraining results on synthetic and realistic rain-streak datasets present that our MGFE-Net performs better than recent deraining methods.

Keywords: Single image deraining · Gated feature enhancement · Multi-scale features

1 Introduction

Due to the occlusion of rain steaks with various shapes and sizes, the images captured under different rainy conditions usually tend to seriously damage the texture details and loss image contents, which hampers the further applications [3,13,19]. In this way, designing an efficient single-image deraining algorithm is highly necessary, which can remove diverse rain streaks while preserve more image details, especially in the complicated outdoor scenes. In the past few years, deraining researches have drawn considerable attentions, which mainly revolve around rain removal in video and single image [10,23,25]. Compared with video rain removal which exploits the temporary correlations between successive

© Springer Nature Singapore Pte Ltd. 2021
G. Zhai et al. (Eds.): IFTC 2020, CCIS 1390, pp. 73–84, 2021.
https://doi.org/10.1007/978-981-16-1194-0_7

frames to restore clean background video, single image deraining [6,9,12] is more challenging due to the shortage of temporary information.

The widespread popularity of deep learning-based methods in other visual tasks [13,19,20], has promoted convolutional neural networks (CNN) applied into single image deraining. In [5], Fu et al. propose that it is tough to separate background from rainy image by directly using convolution network, thus they adopt CNN to cope with high frequency feature map rather than the original rainy image. Besides, joint detection [26], density estimation [29], and residual learning [11] are also introduced for rain steak detection and removal. Zhang et al. [29] propose a two-stage algorithm, which first predicts rain steak distribution and then removes them from background. Wang et al. [21] utilize an attention network to guide deraining process and generate clear background. Yang et al. [27] focus on hierarchy of local features which influences deraining effect a lot. Although these methods have achieved considerable performance improvements, existing deep learning-based deraining algorithms are still restricted in the details restoration of deraining photos. From the perspective of human visual perception, the restoration effects of some methods are not very satisfactory, which either fail to remove rain steaks completely or have an over-deraining effect resulting in distortion of original image content. For example, some methods tend to blur the background or remove some image details while removing rain steaks, because of the different levels of overlaps between background texture details and rain streaks. Besides, most deep-learning based methods are trained on synthetic data sets that results in limited generalization capability to cope with real-life rainy images well.

To cope with the restrictions of prior frameworks, we propose a novel Multi-scale Gated Feature Enhancement Network (MGFE-Net), which is based on a typical framework of encoder and decoder. More specifically, the receptive field block (RFB) [13] is embedded into encoder and decoder to cope with diverse rain steaks removal and clean background restoration. Furthermore, we design the multi-scale gated module (MGM) to control propagation of multi-scale features, which can not only selectively combine multi-scale features acquired from different layers of encoder and decoder, but also keep the consistence between high-level semantics and low-level detail features. At last, several coarse deraining results are obtained by subtracting the feature maps generated by decoder from the original rainy image, and the final refined restored image is obtained by a fusion of these coarse deraining results. The proposed MGFE-Net can remove diverse rain steaks while well preserve the background content details. The comparison results validate that our MGFE-Net achieves best performance among recent designed deraining methods.

In general, the following three contributions are included in our paper:

1. We propose a novel network named Multi-scale Gated Feature Enhancement Network (MGFE-Net) based on a typical framework of encoder and decoder to deal with various rain streaks accumulated from different directions with different shapes and sizes while ensure the background content details well-preserved.

2. In MGFE-Net, we introduce receptive field block (RFB) into the encoder and decoder respectively to enhance multi-scale feature extraction. Besides, we design the multi-scale gated module (MGM) to selectively combine multi-scale features and keep the consistence between high-level semantics and low-level detail features for satisfied rain-free image restoration.
3. The comparison results on several benchmark synthetic and realistic datasets indicate that our MGFE-Net can present an excellent deraining performance and generalize well to real-life photos, which significantly improves the deraining effect and human visual perception quality of restored images.

2 The Proposed Method

2.1 Network Architecture

In our paper, the Multi-scale Gated Feature Enhancement Network (MGFE-Net) based on a typical encoder and decoder framework [26] is designed to deal with single image deraining task. Figure 1 presents the overall architecture. First, we embed the receptive field block (RFB) into diverse layers to strengthen the receptive field of filtering kernels in encoder and enhance the extracted deep features of decoder. Then, different from normal skip-connection in U-net framework, we design a gated module to selectively concatenate the shallow features and deep features, which can benefit to keep the consistence between shallow detail content and deep semantics. At last, in order to generate a refined restored rain-free image, a fusion strategy is adopted to integrate coarse deraining results obtained from different outputs of decoder layers.

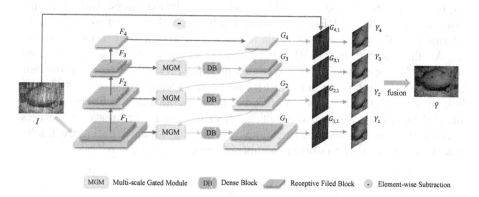

Fig. 1. Illustration of the MGFE-Net. The designed receptive filed block (RFB) and multi-scale gated module (MGM) are embedded in encoder and decoder. The final deraining result is acquired by fusing several coarse outputs of decoder.

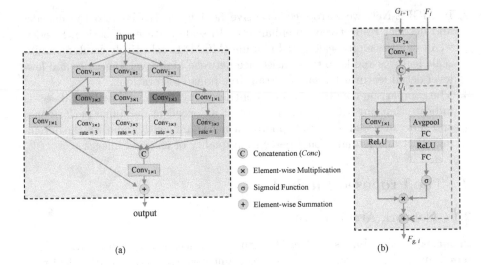

Fig. 2. The schematic illustration of designed modules in our MGFE-Net. (a) The integrated receptive filed block (RFB) for enhancing feature extraction. (b) Our proposed multi-scale gated module (MGM) with well consistence between high-level semantics and low-level details.

2.2 Enhanced Feature Extraction with Receptive Filed Block

The shapes, sizes and extension directions of rain steaks in real life are randomly varied, which makes the single image deraining a challenging problem. The performance of typical single image methods is always restricted, due to the limited receptive filed of simple cascaded convolution filters. To handle this issue, we integrate the RFB to promote model capability of extracting enough information by leveraging multi-scale features between adjacent convolution layers. As illustrated in Fig. 1, RFB is embedded after each layers of encoder and decoder. More specifically, RFB contains multiple forward paths with different kernel sizes, as can be seen in Fig. 2(a). For the input feature map $F_I \in \mathbb{R}^{H \times W \times C}$ from previous layers in encoder or decoder, RFB adopts different filtering kernels followed by diverse dilation rates [3] to effectively extract rain streak features in complex scenes. These feature maps in multiple forward paths are finally concatenated together to obtain the output feature map $f_O \in R^{H \times W \times C}$.

2.3 Multi-scale Gated Module

Except the inability to completely remove rain steaks, another common shortage of most rain removal methods is over-deraining, which leads to damage original image content and seriously affect the visual perception quality of restored images. Thus we design a gated module to control the propagation of multi-scale features, which can not only selectively combine multi-scale features acquired from different layers of encoder and decoder but also keep the consistence between image semantics in high level and texture details in low level. By adding the gated module between different layers of encoder and decoder, the model can achieve a good deraining effect meanwhile keep background content details well-preserved.

As described in Fig. 2(b), F_i and G_{i+1} denote the corresponding shallow and deep features in encoder and decoder, respectively. We first employ an upsampling layer $UP_{2\times}$ and a 1×1 convolution layer to make the spatial size of F_i same as G_{i+1}. Then the output feature maps are stacked with F_i using a concatenation operator $Conc$ along the channel dimension. The cascaded feature maps can be denoted as:

$$U_i = \text{Conc}\left(F_i, \text{Conv}_{1 \times 1}\left(UP_{2\times}\left(G_{i+1}\right)\right)\right), i = H - 1, \ldots, 1 \qquad (1)$$

where $U_i \in \mathbb{R}^{H \times W \times C}$ indicates the concatenation result of F_i and G_{i+1}, H indicates the number of convolution layers in total.

As shown in Fig. 2(b), the right branch includes average pooling layer and two fully connected layers, and a weight map for gated feature is generated by selecting sigmoid function after the fully connected network layer. For the left branch, a 1×1 conv-layer and relu activation function [1] are adopted to change channel number of U_i. Then the gated feature is generated by multiply outputs from two branches, which contains consistent low-level detail information and abstract semantic features. The whole process can be denoted as follow:

$$F_{g,i} = \left(f_{Right}\left(U_i\right) \otimes f_{Left}\left(U_i\right)\right) \oplus U_i, i = H - 1, \ldots, 1 \qquad (2)$$

where $F_{g,i}$ denotes the gated features in the ith layer, $\otimes$ and $\oplus$ are element-wise product and sum operation, respectively. Before being sent into deeper layer of decoder, the gated feature $F_{g,i}$ is refined by as a dense block:

$$G_{i,1} = f_{\text{Dense}}\left(F_{g,i}\right), i = H - 1, \ldots, 1 \qquad (3)$$

where $G_{i,1}$ denotes the final output feature in i^{th} layer of decoder and f_{Dense} denotes a dense block (DB) [7], which consists of three consecutive convolution layers with dense connections. The predicted derained image Y_i in the ith layer is obtained by subtracting the decoder output feature maps from the original rain maps,

$$Y_i = I - G_{i,1}, i = H, \ldots, 1 \qquad (4)$$

In the end, we further fuse the coarse deraining results (i.e., $Y_H, \ldots, Y_1$) to obtain final refined deraining image $\hat{Y}$, which can be denoted as follow:

$$\hat{Y} = \text{Conv}_{1 \times 1}\left(\text{Conc}\left(Y_H, \ldots, Y_1\right)\right) \qquad (5)$$

2.4 Loss Function

In order to guarantee the satisfied deraining effect and visual perception of restored image, the proposed MGFE-Net is optimized by combining content loss, SSIM loss and gradient loss. Specifically, we first conduct content loss to effectively measure the differences between restored images and corresponding rain-free images by leveraging a L_1 loss, which is formulated as follow:

$$L_1 = \sum_{i=1}^{H} \|Y_i - Y\|_1 + \|\hat{Y} - Y\|_1 \tag{6}$$

where H represents the amount of coarse deraining outputs of decoder, Y is the groundtruth image, Y_i and $\hat{Y}$ denote the restored image obtained from the ith layer of decoder and the final predicted deraining image, respectively.

Besides, the SSIM loss is utilized to evaluate structural similarity between restored images and rain-free images, which can ensure the preservation of content textures and is formulated as follow:

$$L_{ssim} = \sum_{i=1}^{H} (1 - \text{SSIM}(Y_i - Y)) + (1 - \text{SSIM}(\hat{Y} - Y)) \tag{7}$$

Furthermore, inspired by the advantages of sobel operator in edge prediction during image reconstruction [2,24], we compare the derained images with its rain-free images in gradient domain to keep the same gradient distribution. Thus the gradient loss is defined as:

$$L_{grad} = \left\|\nabla_x(\hat{Y}) - \nabla_x(Y)\right\|_1 + \left\|\nabla_y(\hat{Y}) - \nabla_y(Y)\right\|_1 \tag{8}$$

Finally, the total loss function for MGFE-Net is defined as follows:

$$L_{\text{total}} = L_1 + \lambda_g L_{grad} + \lambda_s L_{ssim} \tag{9}$$

where λ_g and λ_s are coefficients to balance different loss items.

3   Experiment

3.1   Experiment Setup

Implementation Details. The MGFE-Net is applied on the deep learning-based PyTorch [17] framework. The training image samples are cropped into patches with size of 256×256 and we further horizontally flip these patches in a probability of 0.5. The Adam optimizer is utilized with a batch size of 10 while the learning rate is 2×10^{-4} at the beginning stage and then decreased to 1×10^{-5} after 50,000 training iterations. During testing, these input rainy images keep original sizes without any data augmentations.

Datasets. In our paper, we compare MGFE-Net with other recent deraining algorithms on three synthetic benchmark datasets and a real world rainy image set. For specific, Rain1200 [29] contains a total of $24,000$ pairs of rainy/rain-free images, of which $12,000$ pairs are in training/testing image set, respectively. Besides the pairs in Rain1200 are conducted with three levels of rainy density.

Rain1400 [5] collects 1,000 clean images and each of them is transformed into 14 different rainy images. There are 12,600/1400 sample pairs for training/testing set. Rain1000 [21], covering a wide range of realistic scenes, is the largest single image deraining dataset including 28,500/1,000 pairs for training/testing set respectively. In addition, we collect 146 realistic rainy photos from [21,26], in which rain steaks vary in content, intensity, and orientation.

Evaluation Metrics. We adopt two typical measures, PSNR [8] and SSIM [22], to compare the performance of our MGFE-Net with recent methods. For real-world set which lacks corresponding ground truth, we use another two quantitative indicators, NIQE [15] and BRISQUE [14], to evaluate the visual quality of deraining photos. Smaller values of NIQE and BRISQUE mean better restoration effect and better visual perceptual quality. The recent deraining models we compared with are Clear [4], JORDER [26], DID-MDN [29], DualCNN [16], RESCAN [11], SPANet [21], UMRL [28] with cycle spinning, and PReNet [18].

3.2 Comparison with the State-of-the-Art Methods

Comparison Results on Synthetic Datasets. Table 1 summarizes the quantitative comparison results of different single image deraining methods where our MGFE-Net outperforms previous methods on all the benchmark datasets. Note that the performance of PReNet is very close to our MGFE-Net, the possible main reason we consider is that PReNet [18] adopts frequent image cropping to expands dataset by several times. Specifically, on Rain1200, Rain1400, and Rain1000 datasets, our method promotes the PSNR values by an average of 0.28 db, 0.68 db, 2.78 db compared with the second best results of each dataset. It is a remarkable fact that our method has an excellent performance on Rain1000, which collects images in kinds of natural scenes and contains lots of real rain steaks.

We then qualitatively compare our MGFE-Net with other methods by demonstrating details of the restored deraining images. As shown in Fig. 3, our MGFE-Net is the only model to successfully handle with different rainy situations. For the first two rows in Fig. 3 where the rain steaks are very densely distributed or different significantly in shapes, we can observe that the recent three methods cannot removal rain steaks completely while our method generates a clean deraining result. For the last two rows, other methods either leave obvious artifacts in restored images or blur the original background, while our method obtain a better visual effect and keep the content details well preserved.

Comparison Results on Real-World Dataset. Considering most deraining models are trained with synthetic rainy images, it is necessary to evaluate the generalization ability of deraining methods on realistic rainy photos. As shown in Table 2, it is obvious that our MGFE-Net performs better than previous methods according to NIQE and BRISQUE for reference-free evaluation. We also present

Table 1. Comparison results in PSNR and SSIM between our MGFE-Net and other recent methods for single image deraining on three synthetic datasets.

Methods	Rain1200		Rain1400		Rain1000	
	PSNR	SSIM	PSNR	SSIM	PSNR	SSIM
Clear [4]	22.02	0.7889	24.73	0.8448	31.14	0.9248
JORDER [26]	30.29	0.8782	29.03	0.8881	37.45	0.9680
DID-MDN [29]	27.98	0.8626	26.96	0.8642	26.44	0.9052
DualCNN [16]	27.79	0.8210	26.10	0.8403	32.57	0.9272
RESCAN [11]	32.12	0.8998	30.92	0.9095	36.37	0.9578
SPANet [21]	26.97	0.8091	28.46	0.8801	38.51	0.9750
PReNet [18]	32.30	0.9136	30.73	0.9172	38.97	0.9782
UMRL [28]	30.49	0.8917	27.82	0.8924	28.10	0.9169
MGFE-Net(Ours)	**32.58**	**0.9140**	**31.60**	**0.9230**	**41.75**	**0.9837**

(a) Input   (b) SPANet   (c) UMRL   (d) PReNet   (e) MGFE-Net (Ours)   (f) Ground Truth

Fig. 3. Qualitative comparison of SPANet [21], UMRL [28], PReNet [18] and our proposed MGFE-Net on three synthetic datasets.

several restored images for qualitative comparison in real-world rainy situation in Fig. 4. Whether it is in the case of heavy rain with dense rain steaks or spare rain steak distribution with complicated shapes, our MGFE-Net has a better generalization ability to remove rain steaks in the realistic scenes than other methods.

3.3   Ablation Study

To verify the effectiveness of designed modules in MGFE-Net, we conduct four different experimental settings and evaluate their performances on Rain1200 [29]. As shown in Table 3, the four experimental settings are used to present the

Table 2. Comparison results in NIQE and BRISQUE on the real-world photos.

Method	DualCNN [16]	SPANet [21]	UMRL [28]	PReNet [18]	MGEF-Net
NIQE	5.425	5.105	5.047	5.641	**4.477**
BRISQUE	34.74	30.92	27.58	33.42	**26.44**

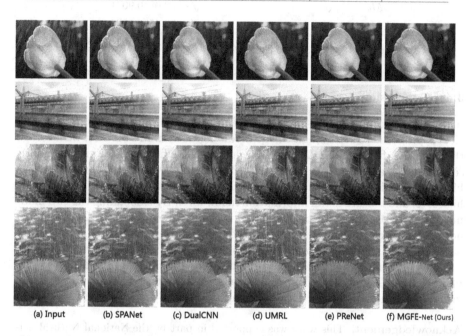

(a) Input   (b) SPANet   (c) DualCNN   (d) UMRL   (e) PReNet   (f) MGFE-Net (Ours)

Fig. 4. Comparison results in real-world rainy situations of SPANet [21], DualCNN [16], UMRL [28], PReNet [18] and our proposed MGFE-Net. Intuitively, our MGFE-Net performs better than recent deraining methods.

effectiveness of receptive filed block (RFB), multi-scale gated module (MGM) and gradient loss (GL), respectively. Note that, the Backbone means the simple encoder and decoder framework under the only optimization of L_1 loss and L_{ssim} loss. It can be seen obviously that supervising rain-free image generation by adding gradient loss does have a great effect on performance improvements. By integrating RFB and MGM into the experimental setting M_b sequentially, the fourth setting M_d (i.e., our proposed MGFE-Net) enhances the extracted deep features in larger receptive fields and effectively utilizes the multi-scale features, which could further promote the model capability and generate rain-free images with best visual effects.

Table 3. Ablation study on four experimental settings of MGFE-Net. Performances are evaluated on Rain1200 [29] dataset.

Settings	Backbone	RFB	MGM	GL	PSNR/SSIM
M_a	$\checkmark$				31.61/0.8963
M_b	$\checkmark$			$\checkmark$	32.08/0.9071
M_c	$\checkmark$	$\checkmark$		$\checkmark$	32.45/0.9127
M_d	$\checkmark$	$\checkmark$	$\checkmark$	$\checkmark$	**32.53/0.9151**

3.4 Conclusion

In our paper, a novel multi-scale gated feature enhancement network (MGFE-Net) is proposed to solve single image deraining task. In MGFE-Net, we leverage the receptive field block (RFB) to strengthen the efficient extraction of multi-scale features and use the multi-scale gated module (MGM) to selectively combine multi-scale features and keep the consistence between image semantics in high level and texture detail information in low level. By embedding the two modules into typical framework of encoder and decoder, the proposed MGFE-Net can not only generate a clean deraining image but also keep the background content well preserved. Sufficient comparison results demonstrate that our MGFE-Net not only presents an excellent performance but also generalize well to real-life photos, which significantly improves the deraining effect and enhance human visual perception quality of derained images.

Acknowledgement. This work was supported in part by the National Natural Science Foundation of China under Grant 61971095, Grant 61871078, Grant 61831005, and Grant 61871087.

References

1. Agarap, A.F.: Deep learning using rectified linear units (ReLU). arXiv preprint arXiv:1803.08375 (2018)
2. Barbosa, W.V., Amaral, H.G., Rocha, T.L., Nascimento, E.R.: Visual-quality-driven learning for underwater vision enhancement. In: ICIP, pp. 3933–3937. IEEE (2018)
3. Chen, L.C., Papandreou, G., Kokkinos, I., Murphy, K., Yuille, A.L.: Deeplab: semantic image segmentation with deep convolutional nets, atrous convolution, and fully connected CRFs. IEEE TPAMI **40**(4), 834–848 (2017)
4. Fu, X., Huang, J., Ding, X., Liao, Y., Paisley, J.: Clearing the skies: a deep network architecture for single-image rain removal. IEEE TIP **26**(6), 2944–2956 (2017)
5. Fu, X., Huang, J., Zeng, D., Huang, Y., Ding, X., Paisley, J.: Removing rain from single images via a deep detail network. In: CVPR, pp. 3855–3863 (2017)
6. Huang, D.A., Kang, L.W., Wang, Y.C.F., Lin, C.W.: Self-learning based image decomposition with applications to single image denoising. IEEE TMM **16**(1), 83–93 (2013)

7. Huang, G., Liu, Z., Van Der Maaten, L., Weinberger, K.Q.: Densely connected convolutional networks. In: CVPR, pp. 4700–4708 (2017)
8. Huynh-Thu, Q., Ghanbari, M.: Scope of validity of PSNR in image/video quality assessment. Electron. Lett. **44**(13), 800–801 (2008)
9. Kang, L.W., Lin, C.W., Fu, Y.H.: Automatic single-image-based rain streaks removal via image decomposition. IEEE TIP **21**(4), 1742–1755 (2011)
10. Kim, J.H., Sim, J.Y., Kim, C.S.: Video deraining and desnowing using temporal correlation and low-rank matrix completion. IEEE TIP **24**(9), 2658–2670 (2015)
11. Li, X., Wu, J., Lin, Z., Liu, H., Zha, H.: Recurrent squeeze-and-excitation context aggregation net for single image deraining. In: Ferrari, V., Hebert, M., Sminchisescu, C., Weiss, Y. (eds.) ECCV 2018. LNCS, vol. 11211, pp. 262–277. Springer, Cham (2018). https://doi.org/10.1007/978-3-030-01234-2_16
12. Li, Y., Tan, R.T., Guo, X., Lu, J., Brown, M.S.: Rain streak removal using layer priors. In: CVPR, pp. 2736–2744 (2016)
13. Liu, S., Huang, D., Wang, Y.: Receptive field block net for accurate and fast object detection. In: Ferrari, V., Hebert, M., Sminchisescu, C., Weiss, Y. (eds.) ECCV 2018. LNCS, vol. 11215, pp. 404–419. Springer, Cham (2018). https://doi.org/10.1007/978-3-030-01252-6_24
14. Mittal, A., Moorthy, A.K., Bovik, A.C.: No-reference image quality assessment in the spatial domain. IEEE TIP **21**(12), 4695–4708 (2012)
15. Mittal, A., Soundararajan, R., Bovik, A.C.: Making a "completely blind" image quality analyzer. IEEE SPL **20**(3), 209–212 (2012)
16. Pan, J., et al.: Learning dual convolutional neural networks for low-level vision. In: CVPR, pp. 3070–3079 (2018)
17. Paszke, A., et al.: PyTorch: an imperative style, high-performance deep learning library. In: NeurIPS, pp. 8026–8037 (2019)
18. Ren, D., Zuo, W., Hu, Q., Zhu, P., Meng, D.: Progressive image deraining networks: a better and simpler baseline. In: CVPR, pp. 3937–3946 (2019)
19. Saleh, F.S., Aliakbarian, M.S., Salzmann, M., Petersson, L., Alvarez, J.M.: Effective use of synthetic data for urban scene semantic segmentation. In: Ferrari, V., Hebert, M., Sminchisescu, C., Weiss, Y. (eds.) ECCV 2018. LNCS, vol. 11206, pp. 86–103. Springer, Cham (2018). https://doi.org/10.1007/978-3-030-01216-8_6
20. Song, T., Cai, J., Zhang, T., Gao, C., Meng, F., Wu, Q.: Semi-supervised manifold-embedded hashing with joint feature representation and classifier learning. Pattern Recogn. **68**, 99–110 (2017)
21. Wang, T., Yang, X., Xu, K., Chen, S., Zhang, Q., Lau, R.W.: Spatial attentive single-image deraining with a high quality real rain dataset. In: CVPR, pp. 12270–12279 (2019)
22. Wang, Z., Bovik, A.C., Sheikh, H.R., Simoncelli, E.P.: Image quality assessment: from error visibility to structural similarity. IEEE TIP **13**(4), 600–612 (2004)
23. Wei, W., Yi, L., Xie, Q., Zhao, Q., Meng, D., Xu, Z.: Should we encode rain streaks in video as deterministic or stochastic? In: ICCV, pp. 2516–2525 (2017)
24. Wen, Q., Tan, Y., Qin, J., Liu, W., Han, G., He, S.: Single image reflection removal beyond linearity. In: CVPR, pp. 3771–3779 (2019)
25. Yang, W., Liu, J., Feng, J.: Frame-consistent recurrent video deraining with dual-level flow. In: CVPR, pp. 1661–1670 (2019)
26. Yang, W., Tan, R.T., Feng, J., Liu, J., Guo, Z., Yan, S.: Deep joint rain detection and removal from a single image. In: CVPR, pp. 1357–1366 (2017)
27. Yang, Y., Lu, H.: Single image deraining via recurrent hierarchy enhancement network. In: ACM MM, pp. 1814–1822 (2019)

28. Yasarla, R., Patel, V.M.: Uncertainty guided multi-scale residual learning-using a cycle spinning CNN for single image de-raining. In: CVPR, pp. 8405–8414 (2019)

29. Zhang, H., Patel, V.M.: Density-aware single image de-raining using a multi-stream dense network. In: CVPR, pp. 695–704 (2018)

Cancelable Face Recognition with Mask

Chengcheng Liu[1], Jing Li[2], Hui Ji[1], Wenbo Wan[1], and Jiande Sun[1]($\boxtimes$)

[1] School of Information Science and Engineering, Shandong Normal University,
Jinan 250358, China
sdnu_liuchengcheng@hotmail.com, {hui.ji,wanwenbo}@sdnu.edu.cn,
jiandesun@hotmail.com
[2] School of Journalism and Communication, Shandong Normal University,
Jinan 250358, China
lijingjdsun@hotmail.com

Abstract. Cancelable biometrics are the effective methods to solve the problem that biometrics cannot be reissued after leakage. As far as we know, the existing methods of cancelable biometrics are implemented by irreversible transformation or encryption of biometrics. In this paper, we propose a method that we add a mask to face image to realize cancelable biometrics. We use relative entropy to study the statistical relationship between the face images with mask and original face images. Then we change the positions of same mask to achieve the same effective cancelable biometrics while keeping the statistical relationship invariant as far as possible. In addition, we divide the whole mask into blocks, which can be used as cancelable biometrics template as same as the whole one. Similarly, we also maintain the statistical relationship between the original face images and the face images with the blocks as close as possible to the statistical relationship between the face images with the whole one and the original face images. Our experiments on CanBiHaT and LFW dataset show that our method achieve cancelable face recognition.

Keywords: Cancelable biometrics · Face recognition · Relative entropy

1 Introduction

Biometrics play an increasingly important role in daily life and are used in various security authentication fields, which brings great convenience to users [5,6]. However, biometrics authentication also has some disadvantages [9]. For example, those biometrics are always exposed to public, which brings great threat to users' privacy security. At the same time, biological characteristics are unique to individuals and cannot be cancelled or reissued. Once the biometrics are stolen by the attacker, they will be compromised forever. In addition, same biometric may be used in multiple identity recognition systems. If the database of one of those systems is leaked, it will also bring threat to other systems. In order to solve these problems, cancelable biometrics [8,9,15] have been proposed as one of the research hotspots.

© Springer Nature Singapore Pte Ltd. 2021
G. Zhai et al. (Eds.): IFTC 2020, CCIS 1390, pp. 85–95, 2021.
https://doi.org/10.1007/978-981-16-1194-0_8

Cancelable biometrics means that different templates can be generated for the same biometrics. Through a series of transformation of the original biological characteristics, such as irreversible transformation, biometrics salting, hashing-based methods and so on, templates are generated. Templates can only represent the users' biological characteristics, and can be cancelled or reissued. If the used template is leaked, a new biometric template can be generated by another methods or parameters. The old template will also been removed and no longer work. As far as we know, all the methods of cancelable biometrics are implemented by irreversible transformation or encryption of biometrics. In this paper, we propose a method for cancelable biometrics that we realize cancelable face recognition with face images with mask. Specifically, we implement the cancelable biometrics by changing the position of mask or dividing the mask into blocks. We study the statistical relationship between the face images with mask and the original face images. Then we study the same mask that pasted in different positions in order to create effective cancelable biometrics. And then, we divide whole mask into blocks to form cancelable biometrics, which can achieve the same effect as the whole one. The change of mask's position and blocks of mask provide more options for generating cancelable biometrics.

2   Related Work

Biometrics, such as fingerprint, iris, face and so on, are often used in variety of recognition applications [5,6]. However, these biological characteristics are unique to individuals, they cannot be cancelled or reissued and they are exposed to the public. As a result, they are at risk of being easily leaked, which brings a lot of security concerns. Cancelable biometrics [9] are the most commonly used methods to solve the problem that biological characteristics cannot be cancelled and reissued.

The popular cancelable biometrics methods include irreversible transformation [2,9,13], biological filtering [14,16,17], random mapping [7,10–12] and biometrics salting [20]. Irreversible transformation transform the original biometrics to another subspace. Among them, Ratha et al. [13] proposed cartesian transformation, polar transformation and function transformation to generate cancelable fingerprint templates. Savvides et al. [16] proposed random convolution method to convolve the original face image, and then encrypted the convolved images to synthesize the single minimum average energy biofilters for recognition. In addition, hashing-based [18] methods are increasingly used to generate cancelable biometrics. J.K.Pillai et al. [10] proposed sectored random projections (SRPs) method to generate cancelable iris templates by extracting the user's iris and calculates Gabor features and performing different random mappings on the feature sectors. Zuo et al. [20] mixed the original binary biological image with random noise to get cancelable biometrics. Although the existing methods can generate effective cancellable biometrics, all the methods are implemented by irreversible transformation or encryption of biometrics. In this paper, we propose a method for cancelable biometrics that we realize cancelable face recognition with mask.

3   Our Method

We believe that the two distributions can be easily distinguished when the difference between them reaches a certain degree. Relative entropy is a method measuring the difference between two probability distributions. In our method, we use the relative entropy to study the difference between the original face images and the face images with mask. At the same time, we also measure the difference between the face images with whole mask and the images with mask blocks. Our goal is to construct more convenient and universal cancelable biometrics templates.

3.1   Relative Entropy

Relative entropy, also known as KL divergence or information divergence, is an asymmetric measure of the difference between two probability distributions. In the information theory, relative entropy is equivalent to the difference of information entropy of two distributions. For two discrete probability distributions $P(x)$ and $Q(x)$ which defined on random variable X, the relative entropy of P relative to Q is calculated as follows.

$$KL(P\|Q) = \sum_{x\in X} P(x)\log\frac{P(x)}{Q(x)} \tag{1}$$

Where $P(x)$ is same to $Q(x)$, $KL(P\|Q) = 0$. Similarly, the greater the difference between $P(x)$ and $Q(x)$, the value of $KL(P\|Q)$ becomes greater.

3.2   Change Positions of the Same Mask

We believe that the personalized masks pasted on different positions of the face could be used as effective cancelable biometrics, under the premise that the relative entropy between the images with mask on different positions and original images can be very similar. At the same time, we also consider the relative entropy of the personalized masks and the covered parts of the face. The overall idea is shown in Fig. 1, and we will introduce it in detail below.

We first calculate the relative entropy $KL(I_{s_s}\|O)$ (we abbreviate it as KL_{I_sO}) between the face images with mask on the selected position and original images. The selected position is the area that used to generate personalized mask. We use this relative entropy as an anchor.

$$KL(I_{s_s}\|O) = \sum_{x=0}^{255} I_{s_s}(x)\log\frac{I_{s_s}(x)}{O(x)} \tag{2}$$

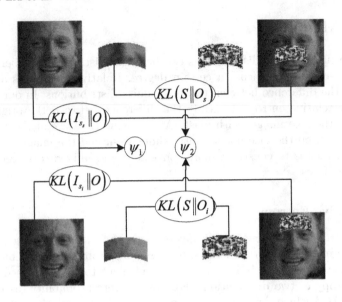

Fig. 1. The overall idea of changing positions of the same mask.

Then we calculate the relative entropy $KL\left(I_{s_i}\|O\right)$ (we abbreviate it as KL_{I_iO}) between the face images with mask on different positions and original images. These positions are obtained by using a mask to traverse the mask on the face. The number of positions is determined by the size $M \times N \times C$ of original face images, the step ε and the size $m \times n$ of the mask.

$$KL\left(I_{s_i}\|O\right) = \sum_{x=0}^{255} I_{s_i}\left(x\right)\log\frac{I_{s_i}\left(x\right)}{O\left(x\right)} \tag{3}$$

All the relative entropy must subtract the anchor respectively, and then the absolute value operation is performed to measure the distance between them.

$$\psi_1 = \left|KL\left(I_{s_i}\|O\right) - KL\left(I_{s_s}\|O\right)\right|, \tag{4}$$
$$i \in \left[1, \left(\frac{M-m}{\varepsilon}+1\right) \times \left(\frac{N-n}{\varepsilon}+1\right)\right]$$

where, x represents the pixel value, O represents the original face images, I_{s_s} represents the images with mask on the selected position and I_{s_i} represents the images with mask on other positions.

Then, we calculate the relative entropy $KL\left(S\|O_s\right)$ (we abbreviate it as KL_{SO_s}) between the mask S and the selected region on the face O_s, this entropy is also used as an anchor.

$$KL\left(S\|O_s\right) = \sum_{x=0}^{255} S\left(x\right)\log\frac{S\left(x\right)}{O_s\left(x\right)} \tag{5}$$

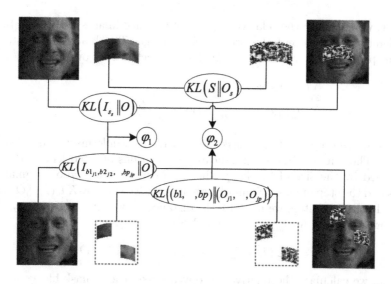

Fig. 2. The overall idea of dividing the whole mask into blocks.

Then we calculate the relative entropy $KL(S \| O_i)$ (we abbreviate it as KL_{SO_i}) between the mask S and the covered face regions O_i when the mask traverses the face.

$$KL(S \| O_i) = \sum_{x=0}^{255} S(x) \log \frac{S(x)}{O_i(x)} \tag{6}$$

Similarly, we calculate the absolute distance between these relative entropies and anchor.

$$\psi_2 = |KL(S \| O_i) - KL(S \| O_s)|, \tag{7}$$

$$i \in \left[1, \left(\frac{M-m}{\varepsilon}+1\right) \times \left(\frac{N-n}{\varepsilon}+1\right)\right]$$

Finally, we define the objective function as follows. $\lambda > 0$ balances the contribution of the two absolute distances ψ_1 and ψ_2. By optimizing the equation, we can find another region on the face to replace the previously selected mask position.

$$\min_{i,i \neq s} (\lambda \times \psi_1 + (1-\lambda) \times \psi_2) \tag{8}$$

3.3 Divide Whole Mask into Blocks

The whole mask is directly pasted on the face, which is really eye-catching. Therefore, we consider to separate the mask into blocks and paste them on the face to reduce attention. The overall idea is shown in Fig. 2, and we will introduce it in detail below.

First, we calculate the relative entropy of the face images with mask blocks on different positions and the original face image. The blocks are pasted on different positions by traversing masks. Every block has its own mask.

$$KL\left(I_{b1_{j1},b2_{j2},\cdots,bp_{jp}}\|O\right) = \sum_{x=0}^{255} I_{b1_{j1},b2_{j2},\cdots,bp_{jp}}(x)\log\frac{I_{b1_{j1},b2_{j2},\cdots,bp_{jp}}(x)}{O(x)} \tag{9}$$

where $b1,\cdots,bp$ represent the mask blocks and the whole mask is divided into p blocks. Those index $j1,\cdots,jp$ indicate the positions of p blocks and they are determined by the size of blocks, p, the size of mask, the size of original face images and the step of mask. Similarly, we use relative entropy $KL\left(I_{s_s}\|O\right)$ as an anchor. In the next step, we measure the distance between $KL\left(I_{b1_{j1},\cdots,bp_{jp}}\|O\right)$ (we abbreviate it as $KL_{I_{b1j1},\cdots,bp_{jp}O}$) and $KL\left(I_{s_s}\|O\right)$.

$$\varphi_1 = \left|KL\left(I_{b1_{j1},b2_{j2},\cdots,bp_{jp}}\|O\right) - KL\left(I_{s_s}\|O\right)\right| \tag{10}$$

Then, we calculate the relative entropy between those mask blocks and the face areas covered by them.

$$KL\left((b1,\cdots,bp)\|(O_{j1},\cdots,O_{jp})\right) = \sum_{x=0}^{255}(b1(x),\cdots,bp(x))\log\frac{(b1(x),\cdots,bp(x))}{(O_{j1}(x),\cdots,O_{jp}(x))} \tag{11}$$

Similarly, we use the relative entropy between the whole mask and the selected region on the face $KL\left(S\|O_s\right)$ as an anchor. We calculate the distance between the anchor and $KL\left((b1,\cdots,bp)\|(O_{j1},\cdots,O_{jp})\right)$ (we abbreviate is as $KL_{(b1,\cdots,bp)O_{j1',\cdots,jp'}}$).

$$\varphi_2 = \left|KL\left((b1,\cdots,bp)\|(O_{j1},\cdots,O_{jp})\right) - KL\left(S\|O_s\right)\right| \tag{12}$$

Finally, we define our objective function as follows.

$$\min_{\substack{j1,j2,\cdots,jp \\ j1\neq j2\neq\cdots\neq jp}} \left(\gamma \times \varphi_1 + (1-\gamma) \times \varphi_2\right) \tag{13}$$

where $\gamma > 0$ balances the contribution of the two absolute distances φ_1 and φ_2. By optimizing this function, we can find some regions on the face pasting blocks to get effective cancelable biometrics.

4   Experiments

In this section, we evaluate our proposed method in face recognition task. We choose masks pasted on nose to test. By optimizing the objective function, we can find the replacement position of the whole mask and the positions of the mask blocks. At last, we paste the personalized whole mask or mask blocks on those areas to prove that these face images can be used as effective cancelable biometrics.

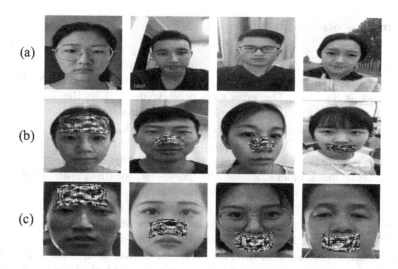

Fig. 3. Face examples of CanBiHaT dataset. (a) shows the original faces; (b) shows users wear their own masks and (c) shows the face images are pasted masks in digital domain.

4.1 Datasets and Models

In our experiments, we mainly use the currently popular CASIA-WebFace dataset [19], LFW-Clean dataset [1,4], LFW-Clean-Nose dataset [1] and the CanBiHaT dataset [1]. We use the ArcFace [3], a face recognition model with good performance in recent two years, to verify the effectiveness of the cancelable biometrics with mask.

CASIA-WebFace Dataset. This dataset contains 494414 images of 10575 people. We use images of 1000 people to pre-train the face recognition model. This dataset has a large amount of data and many races of people, which can make our pre-trained model more robust.

LFW-Clean and LFW-Clean-Nose Dataset. In our previous work [1], we cleaned the LFW dataset. The cleaned LFW (LFW-Clean) dataset includes 6,778 images of 3,445 people. LFW-Clean-Nose dataset contains all images in LFW-Clean dataset with personalized masks on nose. We test our method on LFW-Clean-Nose dataset.

CanBiHaT Dataset. We collected and generated CanBiHaT dataset in [1]. This dataset contains 9138 images of 30 people. It consists of original face images, face images with personalized masks in the physical world and face images with personalized masks in the digital domain, as shown in Fig. 3. We mainly use the face imaged with masks on nose in digital domain to test our method.

4.2   Implementation Details

In our experiments, we first use MTCNN model to process all images to $128 \times 128 \times 3$. For changing position of mask, we get the rectangle of the outermost edge of the mask on the face images, and process it to get the mask. The size of the mask is 34×62. The area with pixel value of 1 in the mask is used to pasted mask. The step size $\varepsilon = 1$. We first calculate the relative entropy $KL\left(I_{s_s} \| O\right)$ and $KL\left(S \| O_s\right)$. As we traverse the mask, we calculate the relative entropy $KL\left(I_{s_i} \| O\right)$ and $KL\left(S \| O_i\right)$ of the mask at different positions. We set the balance parameter $\lambda = 0.5$ to optimize our objective function.

For pasting mask blocks on different positions, we divide one whole mask into two mask blocks. We also use mask to traverse the mask blocks. The size of each mask is 34×31 and the step size of mask is 1. When the mask blocks traverse the face image, we first fix the position of one block and traverse the other. Then, we move the position of the first block and traverse the other. We repeat the whole process until the two mask blocks have both traversed the face image. Throughout the process, we keep the two mask blocks from overlapping. In the process of traversing the mask blocks, we calculate the relative entropy $KL\left(I_{b1_{j1},\cdots,bp_{jp}} \| O\right)$ and $KL\left((b1,\cdots,bp) \| (O_{j1},\cdots,O_{jp})\right)$. We set the balance parameter $\gamma = 0.5$ to optimize the objective function.

4.3   Experiment Results

We calculate the relative entropy of the face images with mask on nose of 10 users and their original face images, the relative entropy between the mask and the nose area covered by the mask. Then we calculate the two kinds of entropy in the process of masks moving and two mask blocks. We find the optimal solution of

Table 1. The relative entropy results. i', $j1'$ and $j2'$ represent the face region that satisfies our objective function.

users \ KL	$KL_{I_s O}$	KL_{SO_s}	$KL_{I'_i O}$	$KL_{SO'_i}$	$KL_{I_{b1j1',b2j2'} O}$	$KL_{(b1,b2)O_{j1',j2'}}$
user1	1.85843	42.19054	1.62511	42.18581	1.59378	42.19246
user2	2.34524	38.68674	2.05619	38.67342	2.01666	38.70417
user3	2.17719	39.17494	1.94334	39.17633	1.91987	39.17481
user4	2.95010	50.80214	2.54322	50.30637	2.52083	48.36947
user5	2.51844	36.28748	2.04520	36.29317	1.95708	36.29543
user6	1.78244	52.35710	1.25810	51.45221	1.16163	48.73423
user7	2.71471	48.12767	2.23449	48.11992	2.18438	48.12503
user8	1.21780	31.04045	0.97505	31.03642	0.97138	31.04065
user9	0.51818	38.09812	0.40750	38.10044	0.40486	38.09930
user10	2.61041	42.74774	2.23952	42.75877	2.24566	42.73581

the objective function to get the positions of the whole mask and mask blocks. Their corresponding relative entropy results are shown in Table 1. The Fig. 4 shows some examples that the changed positions of the whole mask and the positions of blocks we calculated.

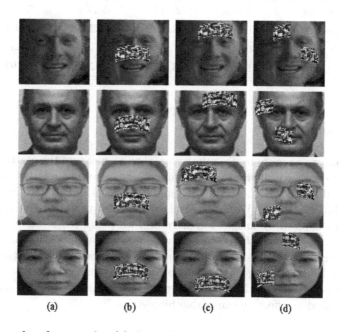

Fig. 4. Examples of our results. (a) shows the original face images. (b) shows the faces wear the whole masks on nose. (c) shows the changed positions of wholes masks. (d) shows the face images with mask blocks on the positions we calculated.

Then, we input the original face images (Or-img), the face images with the whole mask on the nose (Sn-img), the face images with mask on the changed position (Si'-img), and the face image with the mask blocks (Bl-img) into the arcface model respectively. We calculate the accuracy when users register with one of the four types of images and test them with these four types of images. The results are shown in Table 2. From the table, we can see that when the position of the mask changes, the face recognition accuracy is 98.12%, while that of the face with whole mask on nose drops to 47.24%. When the mask is divided into two blocks, the recognition accuracy is 98.79%, while that of face with whole mask on nose drops to 38.03%. From the data in the table, we can see no matter where the mask is worn or whether it is divided into blocks, as long as the relative entropy between the face image with mask and the original face is as close as possible to the relative entropy between the face image with mask on the nose and the original face, these images with masks can realize cancelable face recognition.

Table 2. The recognition accuracy corresponding to four types images.

Tested / Entered	Or-imgs	Sn-img	Si'-img	Bl-img
Or-img	95.74%	2.11%	5.17%	7.92%
Sn-img	0.19%	98.07%	10.23%	3.01%
Si'-img	36.81%	47.24%	98.12%	33.33%
Bl-img	15.33%	38.03%	20.23%	98.79%

5   Conclusion

In this paper, we propose to use relative entropy to measure the statistical relationship between two different classes images. Then we use relative entropy to measure the difference between the original face images and the face images with masks on different areas. We also calculate the relative entropy of masks and the face area covered by masks. Furthermore, we study the relative entropy of original face images and the face images with mask blocks. We find an area that can replace the selected position when generating masks and some areas to paste mask blocks by optimizing our objective function. Our experiments show that the mask is pasted on another position or the whole mask is divided into blocks can also be used as effective cancelable biometrics.

References

1. Canbihat: cancelable biometrics with hard-template. submitted to IEEE T-IFS
2. Bolle, R.M., Connell, J.H., Ratha, N.K.: Biometric perils and patches. Pattern Recogn. **35**(12), 2727–2738 (2002)
3. Deng, J., Guo, J., Xue, N., Zafeiriou, S.: Arcface: Additive angular margin loss for deep face recognition. arXiv: Computer Vision and Pattern Recognition (2018)
4. Huang, G.B., Ramesh, M., Berg, T., Learned-Miller, E.: Labeled faces in the wild: a database for studying face recognition in unconstrained environments. Technical report 07–49, University of Massachusetts, Amherst, October 2007
5. Huang, T.S., Xiong, Z., Zhang, Z.: Face recognition applications. In: Li, S.Z., Jain, A.K. (eds.) Handbook of Face Recognition, 2nd edn., pp. 617–638. Springer (2011). https://doi.org/10.1007/978-0-85729-932-1_24
6. Li, L., Mu, X., Li, S., Peng, H.: A review of face recognition technology. IEEE Access **8**, 139110–139120 (2020). https://doi.org/10.1109/ACCESS.2020.3011028
7. Lingli, Z., Jianghuang, L.: Security algorithm of face recognition based on local binary pattern and random projection. In: 9th IEEE International Conference on Cognitive Informatics (ICCI 2010), pp. 733–738 (2010)
8. Manisha, K.N.: Cancelable biometrics: a comprehensive survey. Artif. Intell. Rev. **53**(5), 3403–3446 (2020). https://doi.org/10.1007/s10462-019-09767-8
9. Patel, V.M., Ratha, N.K., Chellappa, R.: Cancelable biometrics: a review. IEEE Signal Process. Mag. **32**(5), 54–65 (2015)

10. Pillai, J.K., Patel, V.M., Chellappa, R., Ratha, N.K.: Sectored random projections for cancelable iris biometrics. In: 2010 IEEE International Conference on Acoustics, Speech and Signal Processing, pp. 1838–1841 (2010)
11. Pillai, J.K., Patel, V.M., Chellappa, R., Ratha, N.K.: Secure and robust iris recognition using random projections and sparse representations. IEEE Trans. Pattern Anal. Mach. Intell. **33**(9), 1877–1893 (2011)
12. Punithavathi, P., Geetha, S.: Dynamic sectored random projection for cancelable iris template. In: 2016 International Conference on Advances in Computing, Communications and Informatics (ICACCI), pp. 711–715 (2016)
13. Ratha, N.K., Chikkerur, S., Connell, J.H., Bolle, R.M.: Generating cancelable fingerprint templates. IEEE Trans. Pattern Anal. Mach. Intell. **29**(4), 561–572 (2007)
14. Rathgeb, C., Wagner, J., Tams, B., Busch, C.: Preventing the cross-matching attack in bloom filter-based cancelable biometrics. In: 3rd International Workshop on Biometrics and Forensics (IWBF 2015), pp. 1–6 (2015)
15. Rathgeb, C., Uhl, A.: A survey on biometric cryptosystems and cancelablebiometrics. EURASIP J. Inf. Secur. **2011**, 3 (2011).https://doi.org/10.1186/1687-417X-2011-3
16. Savvides, M., Kumar, B.V.K.V., Khosla, P.K.: Cancelable biometric filters for face recognition. In: 17th International Conference on Pattern Recognition, ICPR 2004, Cambridge, UK, 23–26 August 2004, pp. 922–925. IEEE Computer Society (2004). https://doi.org/10.1109/ICPR.2004.1334679
17. Takahashi, K., Hirata, S.: Cancelable biometrics with provable security and its application to fingerprint verification. IEICE Trans. Fundam. Electron. Commun. Comput. Sci. **94**-A(1), 233–244 (2011)
18. Teoh, A.B.J., Kuan, Y.W., Lee, S.: Cancellable biometrics and annotations on biohash. Pattern Recogn. **41**(6), 2034–2044 (2008)
19. Yi, D., Lei, Z., Liao, S., Li, S.Z.: Learning face representation from scratch. arXiv: Computer Vision and Pattern Recognition (2014)
20. Zuo, J., Ratha, N.K., Connell, J.H.: Cancelable iris biometric. In: International Conference on Pattern Recognition, pp. 1–4 (2008)

Adaptive Noise Injection for Quality Improvement of Blurry Images

Yiming Yang[1], Guangtao Zhai[1(✉)], Menghan Hu[2], and Wei Jiang[3]

[1] Department of Electronic Engineering, Shanghai Jiao Tong University,
Shanghai 200240, China
{yangyiming_97,zhaiguangtao}@sjtu.edu.cn
[2] Shanghai Key Laboratory of Multidimensional Information Processing,
East China Normal University, Shanghai 200240, China
mhhu@ce.ecnu.edu.cn
[3] Shanghai University of Electric Power, Shanghai 200090, China
shiepjw@shiep.edu.cn

Abstract. In image processing, noise are often regarded as non-ideal pixel changes. However, these changes may have a positive effect on the blurred images. By adding suitable amount of noise to the right positions, the image quality can be improved. This study makes an investigation of this phenomenon and conducts experiments on the corresponding datasets. Though noise may have a negative impact on the images with good quality, as to the images deteriorated by Gaussian blurriness distortion, noise can improve their subjective image quality.

Keywords: Noise injection · Image quality improvement · Blurriness

1 Introduction

This world is full of noise. Noise in photos is always assumed to be annoying, so most noise reduction methods try to reduce the noise on images as much as possible.

However, the photographers tend to add a small amount of noise for a better visual quality, which indicates that the image with best perceptual quality may not necessarily be free of noise. It is because the final receptors of the image are the human eyes which have the specific perception methods and perceptual limitations.

Fairchild *et al.* [1] evaluated the impact of spatial resolution, uniformly distributed noise and contrast on human perceptual sharpness increment, which is highly related to the quality of the image. According to their subjective sharpness perception experiment, it is shown that "additive uniform noise also increases sharpness up to a certain level of noise, and then decreases sharpness to a certain extent". Therefore, we infer that increasing noise under a specific constraint can increase the perception of sharpness, but has a negative impact when exceeding a certain constraint.

© Springer Nature Singapore Pte Ltd. 2021
G. Zhai et al. (Eds.): IFTC 2020, CCIS 1390, pp. 96–106, 2021.
https://doi.org/10.1007/978-981-16-1194-0_9

Kashibuchi and Kobayashi *et al.* [2] examined whether noise addition could improve the quality of digital photographic prints. Fairchild *et al.* [3] proposed the concept of noise adapting–when people is influenced by a certain amount of noise, the image perception quality can be improved. However, this conclusion can only be drawn when keeping participants observing the image with noise for a period of time so that they can get adapted to the noise, and making them compare two image stimuli simultaneously. But people usually look at one image for a short time, so they may not have the chance to get adapted to the noise. Besides, in most cases there is only one stimulus showing up every time, so people do not have another image to compare.

Kurihara *et al.* [4] analysed the noise injection behavior of the photographers and found the relationship between the pixel values and the distributions of noise added to the image. For the positions of pixels with intensity near 0 and 1 (for the rest of this paper, the image pixel value is assumed to be within 0 and 1), the author said that it is recommended to add chi-square distributed noise. However, adding noise to these pixels will mostly lead to undesirable effects in our experiments. Later, Kurihara *et al.* [5] found that "image noise might reduce sharpness at edges, but be able to improve sharpness of lower frequency component or texture in image". This is a very impressing discovery, but the experiment is not so sufficient. Because the authors only use the bark image as the experiment object, which is similar to the noise pattern. In addition, they manually selected the injection positions without providing the underlaying reason.

Kayargadde and Martens [6] found "adding noise to sharp image makes them appear blurred, whereas adding noise to very blurred image makes them slightly less blurred". It is a significant point shown in our paper. Wan *et al.* [7] added noise to color images, which extended their previous work only to experiment with black and white images. However, with only four types of biscuit images being selected as the experimental objects, their experiments are not really extensive enough.

Kobayashi *et al.* [8,9], getting the intuition from the "memory color" [10], proposed that memory texture is the mechanism for adding image noise to improve image preference. They found that the texture of the memory is related to the preference of the image and further discussed the individual differences. However, the study did not discuss about how to calculate the optimal amount of added noise.

The remainder of this paper is organized as follow. Section 2 introduces this phenomenon. In Sect. 3, we provide the experiment details. Section 4 discusses the model and the validation result. Section 5 is the conclusion part.

2   Noise Injection

2.1   Blur and Noise

Blurriness's negative impacts on the image are mainly concentrated on the high-frequency spectrum positions, as shown in Fig. 1 (a). According to the previous description, adding noise can compensate for the high frequency loss of the blurry image, thereby improving the image quality. Most of previous work chose to add white or $\frac{1}{f}$ noise, however, the low-frequency parts of the original images are actually less affected. So adding the noise which contains low-frequency information is redundant. In this paper, we intend to modify the spectrum of noise to specifically restore the badly damaged high-frequency parts.

The natural scenes have fixed patterns and have shaped our perceptual systems through evolution [11]. Image distortion affects the natural scenes statistics (NSS) in a characteristic way [12] and many researchers recommend using the generalized Gaussian distribution (GGD) to model the radial spectrum of natural scene. The GGD is:

$$f_X\left(x; \mu, \sigma^2, \gamma\right) = ae^{-[b|x-\mu|]^\gamma} \quad x \in \Re \tag{1}$$

where, μ, σ^2, γ are the mean, variance and shape-parameter of the distribution and $a = \frac{b\gamma}{2\Gamma(1/\gamma)}$, $b = \frac{1}{\sigma}\sqrt{\frac{\Gamma(3/\gamma)}{\Gamma(1/\gamma)}}$, where $\Gamma(\cdot)$ is the gamma function: $\Gamma(x) = \int_0^\infty t^{x-1}e^{-t}dt, \quad x > 0$.

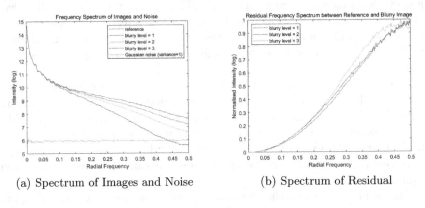

(a) Spectrum of Images and Noise   (b) Spectrum of Residual

Fig. 1. Comparison of Spectrum

The parameters of the GGD can be estimated using the approach proposed in [13]. From Fig. 1 (b), we can easily conclude that the residual between the original image and the blurry image is also GGD. According to different blurry levels, we use different GGD functions to approximate the radial frequency spectrum distributions of the residual between the reference and the corresponding blurry images. Then we use it to generate the colored noise for injection. See more details in Sect. 3.1.

2.2   Position for Noise Injection

Previous work added noise to the whole image, but this is not the best method to realize the full potential of noise. Our experimental results show that adding noise to all positions cannot produce good results in most cases. The most unpleasant positions, shown in Fig. 2, are listed as follows:

- Flat block. The flat area is significantly deteriorated by noise because of the huge discrepancy between the spectrum of the flat block and the noise. When the noise pattern dominates the image appearance, its perceptual image quality drops considerably.
- Structural edge block. The joint part of objects which sharpness chiefly depend on, is an important indicator of the image quality and is consequently vulnerable to the negative impact of noise.
- Extreme luminance block. For areas whose pixel value near 0 or 1, the injection of noise can be easily perceived by human eyes. The empirical conclusion is that human attention on an image is not uniformly distributed. People are easily attracted by the greatly dark or bright parts on image, so they are highly likely to perceive the noise patterns on them.
- Contrast block. According to Weber contrast theory, the luminance perception of human is in a relative, rather than an absolute way. Resembling the extreme luminance block, more focus on these parts will help people distinguish the extra noise and the 'reference' image.
- Deep depth of field block. This block has a very high level of blurriness, which is not suitable for noise injection. It will be demonstrated by the following content.

Therefore, we firstly conduct a pre-experiment on where to inject the noise. Subjects can freely add noise to any part of an image to test whether the noise can improve the image quality. Then, the injection mask of every test image is used to build the corresponding noise injection image datasets for further analysis. In Fig. 3, we can see that the lost high frequency details are made up by the injected noise, which means that injecting noise to the right positions can improve the subjective image quality (the standard deviation σ is used to control the intensity of noise and will be declared in Sect. 3.)

3   Subjective Experiment

3.1   Datasets

In this paper, we utilize CSIQ and TID2013 datasets, containing 30 and 25 scenes respectively, as the experimental objects. These two datasets are combined together as the reference set named $\mathbf{S}$. For every image in $\mathbf{S}$, we use 5 levels of Gaussian filter to get its corresponding blurry distortion images. So $\mathbf{S}$ is expanded to another dataset, named as $\mathbf{S}_1$, totally containing 330 (55+5*55) images.

For every image in $\mathbf{S}_1$, we inject the modified colored noise with 100 different intensities to get the images set $\mathbf{S}_2$. The step of injection intensity is set to 0.001.

The injection process is: 1) the normal Gaussian distribution is used as the base of noise, 2) the standard deviation σ is used to control the intensity of noise,

(a) Flat block

(b) Structural edge block

(c) Extreme luminance block

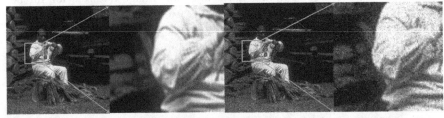

(d) Contrast block

(e) Deep depth of field block

Fig. 2. Unpleasing noise examples

3) the final modified noise is generated by using the radial spectrum intensity filter mentioned in Sect. 2.1 to process the Gaussian noise base. Notably, we use the GGD-like noise with fixed parameters. The parameters are chosen by averaging the statistics of all the images in S_1. For instance, to inject noise into the image with blurry level of 1, we average the radial frequency spectrum of all reference images and images with blurry level of 1, then we get the frequency spectrum intensity filter with default parameters.

Finally, we use the injection mask acquired in the pre-experiment to constrain the injection position and repeat the procedure to get the S_3 .

3.2   Subjective Assessment Experiment

Subjects participating in this experiment are all with normal vision or corrected-to-normal vision, including 30 males and 20 females.

We prepare a tutorial experiment for the subjects one day before the experiment, which includes 1) learning basic knowledge about image features, 2) observing some scoring data from experienced people, and 3) scoring some test samples and receiving feedback from us.

To determine the optimal injection amount for each scene with a certain blurry level, the subject can quickly switch from these 100 images and select the one he/she thinks with the best quality. After averaging the subjective injection opinions, we get S_2' and S_3' from S_2 and S_3 respectively. Then we conducted the scoring experiment. All experimental settings are under the guidelines in the recommendations of the ITU-R BT.500-13 [14] and the viewing distances are set strictly according to [15]. To assess the overall image quality, participants are required to rate their perceived quality in the continuous range at the scale of 0 – 100. In our experiments, each stimulus is randomly selected and presented for about 15 s and the followed resting time was 5 s using the mid-gray image.

Table 1. Most preferred amount of injection noise

$\sigma(10^{-3})$ Injection \ Blurry Level	Original	1	2	3	4	5
Wholly	4	8	10	12	6	5
Selectively	10	34	45	47	8	6

3.3   Experimental Setup

The results of most preferred amount of noise are shown in Table 1. For wholly injected noise, there is no absolute dependence on the relationship of blurry levels. Subjects' tolerance toward the wholly injected noise is low because the injected noise will apparently exert bad influence on the inappropriate positions, as we discuss in Sect. 2. For selectively injected noise, people's tolerance toward

(a) Cactus (CSIQ, blurry level = 2, $\sigma = 0.052$)

(b) 1660 (CSIQ, blurry level = 2, $\sigma = 0.046$)

(c) I14 (TID2013, blurry level = 2, $\sigma = 0.050$)

(d) I20 (CSIQ, blurry level = 2, $\sigma = 0.040$)

Fig. 3. Appropriate injection

Table 2. Overall subject score of $\mathbf{S}_1$, $\mathbf{S}_2^{'}$ and $\mathbf{S}_3^{'}$

MOS Blurry Level Injection	Original	1	2	3	4	5
Without	**87.5**	**84.6**	80.2	73.8	**58.0**	**24.3**
Wholly	85.4	82.9	78.6	72.3	56.4	22.8
Selectively	86.2	84.3	**84.6**	**79.2**	56.7	23.6

them is high, demonstrating their positive impact on the increment of image perceptual quality.

For the original image, a small amount of noise is accepted because of its supplementary effect of high-frequency information. For images with the blurry level from 1 to 3, the amount of preferred noise increases with the blurry level, indicating that people prefer the offset effect of noise on blurry image. However, for images with blurry level 4 and 5, human's tolerance toward noise decreases dramatically, because the high level blurriness has made the image similar to a flatten block. The noise injected on them can be easily perceived and can not help improve the image quality.

Table 2 shows the subjective mean opinion score (MOS) of S_1, S_2' and S_3'. For images with blurry level of 1, 2 and 3, the MOS shows that the quality of the image is obviously improved, which means an appropriate injection of noise can improve the image quality. For images with blurry level of 4 and 5, injection does not make any difference.

4 Adaptive Noise Injection Model

4.1 Model Parameter

From the experimental results and the feedback of participants, it is found that the increase in noise is closely related to certain image features, namely entropy, edge density, edge gradient, colorfulness, skewness, and most importantly the blurriness.

- Entropy. It can indicate the flatness and the texture enrichment of image in some degree. From experiment, people prefer images with a certain level of complexity [20]. Representing the complexity of image, the entropy can be a good feature to control the injection amount.
- Edge density. The density of edges represents the structural complexity of image. After applying the Canny edge algorithm [16], we can get a binary mask from the candidate image. The sum of all the elements in the mask matrix can be the indicator of edge density.
- Gradient. Two images with the same Canny mask may have distinctively different gradient levels at the same edge position, so we introduce gradient to be the complement of the edge density. In our research, we use Sobel gradient kernels to perform image convolution operations, and statistically obtain gradient level information from gradient feature maps.
- Blurriness. We have proven the great link between noise and blurry level, as shown in Table 2. Within limits, the amount of injected noise is positively related to the degree of blurriness. We use the method proposed in [17] to estimate the blurriness map from a single image.
- Colorfulness. From the experiment, we find subjects tend to add noise to the positions with a certain degree of color complexity. This dependence can be used to predict the optimal injection amount. We use the method proposed in [18] to calculate the colorfulness of an image.

– Skewness. Skewness is the third-order statistical data, and often reflects the comprehensive nature of brightness and contrast: glossiness [20]. From experiment, the brightness and contrast of image also relate with the proper position to noise injection. Besides, [19] find that skewness in natural scene images is very close to a constant, which means the skewness can be the barometer of blurriness distortion.

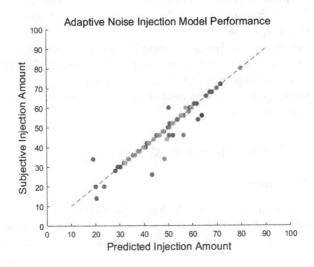

Fig. 4. Comparison of subjective and predicted noise amount

Table 3. Evaluation of proposed model

	Pearson	Spearman	MSE	MAE
Score	0.9577	0.9578	0.0015	1.3620e-05

Those features stated above can be written as $\mathbf{f} = \{f_{en}, f_e, f_g, f_b, f_c, f_s\}$. Applying the features calculation to the entire image, we get the global feature $\mathbf{f}_1$. However, the global statistics contain some redundant feature information. Generally, human's attention will not be uniformly distributed on the whole image. When people evaluate an image, they do not take all the details of one image into consideration. In [5], the author pointed out that the perceptual sharpness of image will be determined by the most sharp part of the image. Therefore, it is reasonable to say that the human's main perception of one image is dominated by its prominent characteristics. For this reason we partition the image into 64 blocks and recapture the features blockwisely, then we pick the top

24 of these 64 values as f_2. Additionally, to capture the feature mostly relative to injection, we repeat the above process with the injection mask to get f_3 and f_4.

We use the Neural Fitting API of NFTOOL in MATLAB to fit the input training features and output recommended injection amount.

4.2   Evaluation Results

Figure 4 shows the scatter plots between subjective and predicted injection amount scores.

To further evaluate the performance of the proposed adaptive noise injection model, we employ commonly used performance measures, which are Pearson linear correlation coefficient (PLCC), Spearman rank order correlation coefficient (SROCC), mean square error (MSE), and mean absolute error (MAE). The results are listed in Table 3.

The predicted noise amount and the preferred noise amount are highly correlated under the measurement of PLCC and SROCC, though there are inevitably some outliers. On the one hand, it is because the existence of the particularity of natural scenes. One the other hand, the hand crafted features we select in Sect. 4.1 is not sufficient to completely describe interaction between blurriness and noise. However, the result shows that the adaptive noise injection model does make a good example for capturing the intrinsic relationship between the image statistics and the optimal injection amount.

5   Conclusion

In this work, we verify the feasibility of quality improvement of blurry images by noise injection. In the pre-experiment, we find noise does not work well in some areas, for instance the flatten area, due to their specific structure. In subjective experiments, we find injecting a certain amount of noise with the injection mask helps counteract the negative effect of blurriness. Based on these experiments, we propose an adaptive noise injection model for the prediction of injection amount, using the selected statistical features of an image. The evaluation score shows that our model, which achieves a high performance in accuracy, can capture the intrinsic relationship between blurriness and noise.

Acknowledge. This work is supported by Science and Technology Commission of Shanghai Municipality (STCSM, GrantNos.19DZ1209303, 18DZ1200102).

References

1. Johnson, G.M., Fairchild, M.D.: Sharpness rules. In: Color Imaging Conference, vol. 3, pp. 24–30 (2000)
2. Kashibuchi, Y., Aoki, N., Inui, M., Kobayashi, H.: Improvement of description in digital print by adding noise. J. Soc. Photo. Sci. Tech. Japan **66**(5), 471–480 (2003) (in Japanese)

3. Fairchild, M.D., Johnson, G.M.: On the salience of novel stimuli: adaptation and image noise. In: Color Imaging Conference, pp. 333–338 (2005)
4. Kurihara, T., et al.: Digital image improvement by adding noise: an example by a professional photographer. J. Imaging Sci. Technol. **55**, 030503 (2011)
5. Kurihara, T., et al.: Analysis of sharpness increase by image noise. J. Imaging Sci. Technol. **55**, 030504 (2011)
6. Kayargadde, V., Martens, J.B.: Perceptual characterization of images degraded by blur and noise: experiments. J. Opt. Soc. Am. A Opt. Image Sci. Vis. **13**(6), 1166–1177 (1996)
7. Wan, X., Aoki, N., Kobayashi, H.: Improving the perception of image sharpness using noise addition (2014)
8. Zhao, Y., Aoki, N., Kobayashi, H.: Memory texture as a mechanism of improvement in preference by adding noise. In: 2014 Electronic Imaging, pp. 9014–9013 (2014)
9. Wan, X., Kobayashi, H., Aoki, N.: Improvement in perception of image sharpness through the addition of noise and its relationship with memory texture. In: Proceedings of SPIE, vol. 9394, pp. 93941B–93941B-11 (2015)
10. Bartleson, C.J.: Memory colors of familiar objects. J. Opt. Soc. Am. **50**, 73–77 (1960)
11. Zhai, G., Min, X.: Perceptual image quality assessment: a survey. Sci. China Inf. Sci. **63**(11), 1–52 (2020). https://doi.org/10.1007/s11432-019-2757-1
12. Tang, C., Yang, X., Zhai, G.: Noise estimation of natural images via statistical analysis and noise injection. IEEE Trans. Circ. Syst. Video Technol. **25**, 1283–1294 (2015)
13. Sharifi, K., Leon-Garcia, A.: Estimation of shape parameter for generalized Gaussian distributions in subband decompositions of video. IEEE Trans. Circ. Syst. Video Technol. **5**, 52–56 (1995)
14. Methodologies for the subjective assessment of the quality of television images, document ITU-R BT.500-14 (2019)
15. Gu, K., Liu, M., Zhai, G., Yang, X., Zhang, W.: Quality assessment considering viewing distance and image resolution. IEEE Trans. Broadcast. **61**, 520–531 (2015)
16. Canny, J.F.: A computational approach to edge detection. IEEE Trans. Pattern Anal. Mach. Intell. PAMI **8**, 679–698 (1986)
17. Karaali, A., Jung, C.R.: Edge-based defocus blur estimation with adaptive scale selection. IEEE Trans. Image Process. **27**(3), 1126–1137 (2018)
18. Hasler, D., Susstrunk, S.: Measuring colourfulness in natural images. In: Proceedings of IST/SPIE Electronic Imaging 2003: Human Vision and Electronic Imaging VIII, vol. 5007, no. LCAV-CONF-2003-019, 2003, pp. 87–95 (2003)
19. Zhai, G., Wu, X.: Noise estimation using statistics of natural images. In: 2011 18th IEEE International Conference on Image Processing, pp. 1857–1860 (2011)
20. Motoyoshi, I., Nishida, S., Sharan, L., Adelson, E.H.: Image statistics and the perception of surface qualities. Nature **447**, 206–209 (2007)

Adaptive Enhancement Technology for Screen Content Photos

Yazhen Zhou[1,2,3,4,5]($\boxtimes$), Dakurah Collins Kyefondeme[1], Huayi Zhou[1],
Min Zhao[1,2,3,4,5], Nan Guo[1], and Li Wu[1]

[1] Faculty of Information Technology, Beijing University of Technology, Beijing, China
zyz@emails.bjut.edu.cn
[2] Key Laboratory of Artificial Intelligence, Ministry of Education, Shanghai, China
[3] Engineering Research Center of Intelligent Perception and Autonomous Control,
Ministry of Education, Beijing, China
[4] Beijing Key Laboratory of Computational Intelligence and Intelligent System,
Beijing, China
[5] Beijing Artificial Intelligence Institute, Beijing, China

Abstract. Recent years have witnessed the widespread applications of
mobiles and other portable electronic devices, involving a variety of
screen content photos. Different from natural scene photos, screen content photos are composed of more lines, fewer colors and unique text messages. Thus, it is difficult to realize the satisfactory enhancement effect of
screen content photos using traditional image enhancement technology
since they are designed for the natural scene. In this paper, we develop a
novel enhancement model for screen content photos by considering text
and picture separately. To be specific, we first use a fully convolutional
network to divide a screen content photo into three independent parts:
picture region, foreground text region, and background. Second, an optimal modification of histogram is used to automatically enhance the picture region's contrast, and the guided image filter is used to enhance the
foreground text region. Third, the enhanced picture region, the enhanced
foreground text region, and background are fused to obtain the final
enhanced image. Experimental results show that our model has produced
less noise and derived outstanding enhancement effect than the popular
enhancement techniques.

Keywords: Screen content photos · Adaptive enhancement · Image
Segmentation

1 Introduction

With the development of smart phones and portable electronic devices with
visualization function, screen content photos are playing an increasingly important role in almost all applications [1–4]. In various remote operations or frame

Supported by the National Natural Science Foundation of China under Grant 61703009,
and National Science and Technology Major Project of the Ministry of Science and
Technology of China under Grant 2018ZX07111005.

G. Zhai et al. (Eds.): IFTC 2020, CCIS 1390, pp. 107–118, 2021.
https://doi.org/10.1007/978-981-16-1194-0_10

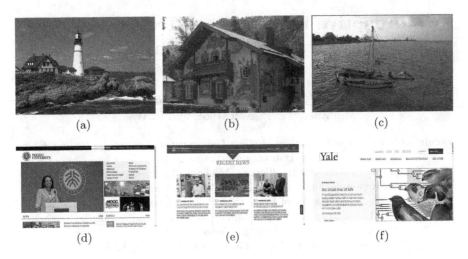

(a)   (b)   (c)

(d)   (e)   (f)

Fig. 1. Examples with different scenes: (a)–(c) Natural scene photos; (b)–(f) Screen content photos.

transmission scenarios, the refreshed screen content will compress and transmit to the local client when the user interacts with the computer [5]. The visual device presents these frames together with the computer-generated text content [6]. However, it inevitably leads to image distortion or low image quality during such process, which reduces users' experiences. Therefore, image quality enhancement technology is one of the research tasks that application developers focus on [7–9].

Image enhancement has been an important research topic in the field of image processing and computer vision and has a long history, which covers many aspects of image, such as image sharpness, denoising, saturation, contrast, resolution, etc. [10–16]. Image enhancement technology can effectively improve the recognition accuracy of related tasks in industrial scene photos [17–21]. In recent years, some image enhancement techniques which can automatically find the optimal parameters based on image quality assessment (IQA) have emerged, which can realize adaptive enhancement according to the information of the image itself [22,23]. Unfortunately, different from natural scene photos captured by cameras, screen content photos consist of fewer colors, more thin lines, and simpler shapes [24–28]. Figure 1 shows the difference between natural scene photos and screen content photos. For most enhancement techniques, it is a common phenomenon that any single technique may not be fully adapted well to all images due to the various characteristics in distinct regions of an image, while this is more common for screen content photos [29].

To solve the above problems, and inspired by recent semantic segmentation techniques based on deep learning, we propose a screen content photo enhancement method based on image segmentation. Specifically, we first divide a screen photo into three different regions by using a fully convolutional neural

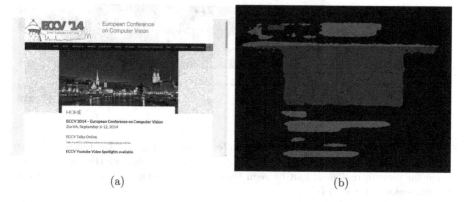

(a)   (b)

Fig. 2. Illustration of semantic segmentation results of a screen content photo using FCNN: (a) Original screen content photo; (b) FCNN segmentation result after median filter.

network (FCNN): picture region, foreground text region, and background. In FCNN, VGG-16 is used as the high-level semantic information extractor of the screen content photo [30]. Then, for the picture region, a histogram modification method is used to improve the picture's contrast, which combines three different types of histograms to implement adaptive enhancement. Second, in order to enhance the display effect of the foreground text region, the guided image filter is used to modify the foreground text region. Third, we fuse the enhanced picture, enhanced foreground text region, and background region to obtain the final enhanced screen content photo.

The rest of this paper is organized as follows. The second section describes the entire model architecture of this paper in detail, including image segmentation, contrast enhancement based on histogram modification, and guided image filter. In the third section, the validity of the proposed model in this paper is proved by experiments. The fourth section summarizes this paper and discusses future work.

2   Methodology

Unlike common natural scene photos captured by the digital camera, the screen content photos are mostly composed of pictures, foreground texts, and some background areas in many applications such as online shopping, electronic photo album, and webpage [31]. Popular image enhancement techniques are difficult to implement appropriate enhancement for all the content in the screen due to their quite different characteristic in distinct regions [32,33]. In this section, our proposed model will be described in detail, including semantic segmentation of screen content, image contrast enhancement, and guided image filter.

(a) (b) (c)

Fig. 3. Histogram equalization results of different image regions: (a) Original screen content photo; (b) Histogram equalization of the whole photo; (c) Histogram equalization for picture region. It can be seen that there is a serious distortion in (b) and excessive enhancement in (c).

2.1   Semantic Segmentation of Screen Content

In most cases, a screen content photo consists of three parts: the picture region, the foreground text region, and the background. How to achieve accurate semantic segmentation of screen content is one of the most important issues for enhancing the whole screen content photo.

In our work, we first use FCNN to segment the semantics of screen content photos [34]. FCNN is a kind of convolutional neural network (CNN). In CNN, the shallow convolutional layers in the front adopts a smaller perception field to learn some local features of the image (such as texture features), while the deep convolutional layers possess a greater perception field to learn more high-level features, such as object size, position, and direction information, etc. FCNN uses convolution operation instead of the full-connection layers of traditional CNN to obtain the high-level information of the target object. Meanwhile, the deconvolution layer is introduced to realize the fine segmentation of images at the pixel level.

For organizing FCNN, we replaced the last three full connection layers of VGG-16 with convolutional layers to reduce parameters, thus forming a total of sixteen convolutional layers as high-level semantic feature extraction modules. For each convolutional layers with filter size 3×3, the side of each photo is zero-padding by one pixel to keep the size of the feature map consistent with the input. Max-pooling is used after two convolutional layers at the first four layers and three convolutional layers at the middle nine layers, respectively. At the end of the network, the upsampling layers is used to reconstruct the feature map to the same size as the original input.

It is noted that there are some noises around the different semantics after FCNN segmentation since the deconvolution layers are not a strict inverse operation in mathematics. To solve this problem, we used 9×9 median filters for segmented images to achieve smoother semantic information where is shown in Fig. 2(b).

2.2 Image Contrast Enhancement

For the picture region of the screen content photo, our work mainly focuses on improving the image contrast. In general, contrast-enhanced screen photos could produce a more perceptually satisfying image. Histogram equalization is one of the most classic contrast enhancement methods, which could reallocate the pixel value of an image and thus makes the contrast of the image more balanced [35]. However, histogram equalization is often prone to excessive enhancement, leading to a sharp decrease in image comfort. Moreover, if histogram equalization is used to enhance the whole screen content photo, it will be a visual disaster, as shown in Fig. 3.

Fortunately, some IQA methods could provide guidance for image enhancement technology since they can simulate the human visual system to objectively estimate the image quality. In our work, an automatic robust image contrast enhancement (RICE) model is used to improve the contrast of pictures [36]. Specifically, given an input picture $\mathbf{I}$, we denote $\mathbf{h_i}$ as the histogram of $\mathbf{I}$, and $\mathbf{h_u}$ as a uniformly distributed histogram. Appropriate contrast enhancement techniques are intended to obtain more visual information while minimizing perceptual degradation, thus the desired target histogram translates into an optimization problem as follows:

$$\hat{\mathbf{h}} = \min_{\mathbf{h}} \|\mathbf{h} - \mathbf{h_i}\| + \alpha \|\mathbf{h} - \mathbf{h_e}\| \tag{1}$$

where $\mathbf{h_e}$ is the histogram equalization result of $\mathbf{I}$ and α is a constraint parameter. Note that the Eq. (1) tries to find the optimal solution between the two parts of the histogram and will converge to $\mathbf{I}$ when α is close to zero. Another feature $\mathbf{h_s}$ is obtained by calculating the histogram of $\mathbf{I}$ through a nonlinear mapping to $\mathbf{I_s}$, which can be represented as follows:

$$\mathbf{I_s} = \frac{\beta_1 - \beta_2}{1 + \exp\left(-\frac{\mathbf{I_i} - \beta_3}{\beta_4}\right)} + \beta_2 \tag{2}$$

where $\beta = \{\beta_1, \beta_2, \beta_3, \beta_4\}$ are free parameters that need to be solved.

Then, we combine the histogram $\mathbf{h_s}$ into Eq. (1), thus obtaining the final objective optimization function:

$$\hat{\mathbf{h}} = \min_{\mathbf{h}} \|\mathbf{h} - \mathbf{h_i}\| + \alpha \|\mathbf{h} - \mathbf{h_e}\| + \gamma \|\mathbf{h} - \mathbf{h_s}\| \tag{3}$$

where γ is another constraint parameter similar to α. In our research, a quality assessment metric of contrast is used to automatically find the optimal solution according to the picture content, which is defined as:

$$\mathcal{Q}(\mathbf{I}, \mathbf{I_e}) = \|sign(DCT(\mathbf{I})), sign(DCT(\mathbf{I_e}))\|_0 + \theta(E(\mathbf{I}) - E(\mathbf{I_e})) \tag{4}$$

where $\mathbf{I_e}$ is the a contrast enhanced version of $\mathbf{I}$; $DCT(\cdot)$ is discrete cosine transform; $sign(\cdot) = \{-1, 1\}$ is the sign of a variable; θ is a fixed parameter to adjust the weight between two parts; $E(\cdot)$ shows the information entropy of

Fig. 4. Illustration of the foreground text region of the screen content photo after enhancing with the guide image filter (GIF): (a) Original part of foreground text region; (b) Enhanced result after GIF, $r = 4, \epsilon = 0.1^2$; (c) Enhanced result after GIF, $r = 1, \epsilon = 0.05^2$; (d) Enhanced result after GIF, $r = 2, \epsilon = 0.05^2$.

an image, which is an important concept in statistics. Generally speaking, a high-contrast image tends to have greater entropy.

Based on this assessment metric, the optimal solution $\{\alpha, \gamma\}$ in Eq. (3) can be solved by optimizing the following problem:

$$\alpha, \gamma = \min_{\alpha, \gamma} \mathcal{Q}\left(\mathbf{I}, T_{hm}\left(\mathbf{I}, \frac{\mathbf{h_i} + \alpha\mathbf{h_e} + \gamma\mathbf{h_s}}{1 + \alpha + \gamma}\right)\right) \tag{5}$$

where $T_{hm}(\cdot)$ is a histogram matching function given in [37]. In this way, for the picture region of the screen content photo, the algorithm could adaptively find the optimal histogram to better improve the image contrast.

2.3   Guided Image Filter

For the foreground text part of the screen content photo, we adopt the guided image filter (GIF) as an unsharpness mask for denoise and smoothing text edge. The GIF is a linear transform filter based on the local-linear model and is one of the fastest edge-preserving filters, which has been successfully applied to many tasks, such as image smoothing, image fusion, image enhancement, etc. Different other filters, for an image $\mathbf{I}$ to be filtered, the input of GIF requires a guidance image $\mathbf{g}$, which can be the image $\mathbf{I}$ itself or an image related to $\mathbf{I}$.

Fig. 5. Segmentation results by FCNN. We highlight the picture region and foreground text region with blue and red rectangles, respectively.

Despite the great filtering power achieved by GIF in image processing, it can still be over-enhanced and may have artifacts when the core of the filter kernel size is large like Fig. 4(b). Conversely, it will amplify the noise when kernel is small as shown in Fig. 4(c). Based on this, The improved GIF is shown as follows:

$$\alpha_j = \frac{\frac{1}{|r|}\sum_{i \in r_j} \mathbf{I_i}h_i - \mu_j\hat{\mathbf{g}}_j}{\sigma_j^2 + \epsilon}, \quad r = 2, \epsilon = 0.05^2 \tag{6}$$

$$\beta_j = \hat{\mathbf{g}}_j - \alpha_j\mu_j, \qquad o_i = \hat{\alpha}_i\mathbf{I_i} + \hat{\beta}_i$$

where $\mathbf{I}$ is the original screen content photo; $\mathbf{g} = \mathbf{I}$ is the guidance image; μ_j and σ_j^2 are the mean and variance of image $\mathbf{I}$ in a path where kernel radius is $|r|$; ϵ is a regularization parameter and o_i is the output pixel value after smoothing. Based on the above optimization, we can achieve satisfactory enhancement effect on the foreground text, as shown in Fig. 4(d).

3   Experimental Results

Based on the analysis in the above sections, we will demonstrate the effectiveness of our proposed model in terms of subjective assessment. In this section, we adopted eight photos from the prevalent Webpage Dataset as the test dataset, which includes 149 screen content photos [38]. Finally, we conducted subjective experiments with several popular image enhancement methods to quantify the model enhancement results.

For training the FCNN, the pre-training VGG-16 model is fine-tuned in the dataset with 10 epoches to complete the semantic feature segmentation of the screen content photos. We train the FCNN with ADAM optimizer by setting the default hyper-parameters and the learning rate is initialized as 10^{-4}. To complete the semantic segmentation at pixel level, L2 loss is used to measure the

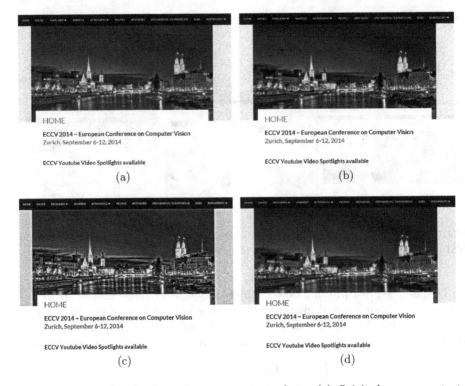

Fig. 6. An example of enhanced screen content photo: (a) Original screen content photo; (b) Enhanced result only using RICE; (c) Enhanced result by GIF; (d) Our result.

segmentation accuracy. We implemented the FCNN with torch1.6 and trained with an Intel(R) Core i7-7820X CPU at 3.6GHz and an NVIDIA GeForce GTX 1080. Figure 5 shows that some examples of screen photo segmentation results.

Figure 6 shows the enhancement result of a screen content photo. It can be seen that when the image is enhanced only by RICE, the visual perception of the text region is not improved subjectively [Fig. 6(b)], while the picture region will appear large distortion when the image is filtered to improve the quality of the text region [Fig. 6(c)]. Our proposed method has achieved a significantly superior enhancement effect and less noise in the text region edge than only using a single enhancement technique [Fig. 6(d)].

In addition, we also enhanced some other screen content photos, as shown in Fig. 7–Fig. 8 [(a)–(f)]. In these results, histogram equalization all leads to the visual disaster of screen content photos [Fig. 7, 8(b)]. In Fig. 7, 8(e), GIF has a good visual effect in the foreground text region, while leads to serious distortion in the picture region. In Fig. 7, 8(d), there is a significant over-enhancement relative to Fig. 7, 8(e), which is due to the large radius of the filtering kernel. Note that, our filtering kernel radius is still much smaller than it given in [16].

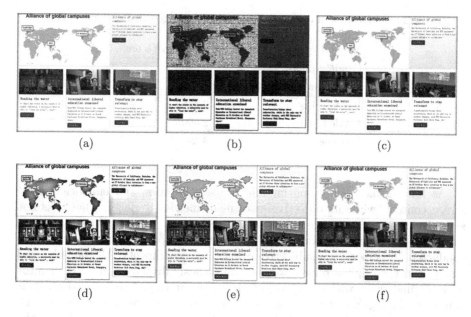

Fig. 7. Enhanced screen content photo. (a) Original screen content photo; (b) Output of Histogram Equalization [11]; (c) Output of RICE [36]; (d) Output of GIF [16], $r = 4, \epsilon = 0.1^2$; (e) Output of GIF [16], $r = 2, \epsilon = 0.05^2$; (f) Output of our model.

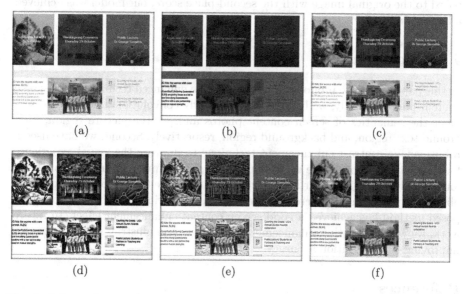

Fig. 8. Enhanced screen content photo. (a) Original screen content photo; (b) Output of Histogram Equalization [11]; (c) Output of RICE [36]; (d) Output of GIF [16], $r = 4, \epsilon = 0.1^2$; (e) Output of GIF [16], $r = 2, \epsilon = 0.05^2$; f) Output of our model.

Table 1. Comparison of our model and popular image enhancement models.

Method	Subjective score
Original photo	3.6905
Histogram equalization [11]	1.4048
RICE [36]	3.4762
Guided image filter [16]	2.6905
Propose	**4.2857**

As far we know, only one method for segmentation and enhancement of screen content, while its objective assessment metrics is global. Thus it is not suitable for assessing image enhancement techniques based on image segmentation [39]. To further quantify the effectiveness of our proposed method, we conducted 30 person-time subjective evaluation experiments. All the enhanced results and the original photos were simultaneously displayed on a 2K monitor with original scale, with each subject given a score from 1 to 5 based on their subjective feelings about the image. All the photo scores are averaged to get the final score, which is shown in Table 1. It can be seen that our model achieves the best subjective evaluation result, as highlight in the table. The rest of the image enhancement model all have varying degrees of excessive enhancement. Compared to the original image with the second-place score, our model was achieved a large gain of 11.9%.

4   Conclusion

In this paper, we have proposed a novel adaptive enhanced technology for screen content photos. Firstly, we have developed a fully convolutional network to segment the semantics of screen content photos and get the picture region, foreground text region, and background region, respectively. Second, we have used a robust image contrast enhancement technique to improve the visual experience for the picture region, while we have used the guided image filter to enhance the foreground text region. Third, we have fused the above three separate regions to obtain the final enhanced screen content photo. Experiments show that our proposed method has achieved a good screen content enhancement effect. In future work, we will extend this enhancement technology to industrial scene photos for improving its recognition accuracy.

References

1. Gu, K., Zhou, J., Qiao, J., Zhai, G., Lin, W., Bovik, A.C.: No-reference quality assessment of screen content pictures. IEEE Trans. Image Process. **26**(8), 4005–4018 (2017)
2. Wang, S., Gu, K., Zhang, X., Lin, W., Ma, S., Gao, W.: Reduced-reference quality assessment of screen content images. IEEE Trans. Circ. Syst. Video Technol. **28**(1), 1–14 (2016)

3. Gu, K., Jakhetiya, V., Qiao, J.F., Li, X., Lin, W., Thalmann, D.: Model-based referenceless quality metric of 3D synthesized images using local image description. IEEE Trans. Image Process. **27**(1), 394–405 (2018)

4. Min, X., Ma, K., Gu, K., Zhai, G., Wang, Z., Lin, W.: Unified blind quality assessment of compressed natural, graphic, and screen content images. IEEE Trans. Image Process. **26**(11), 5462–5474 (2017)

5. Lu, Y., Li, S., Shen, H.: Virtualized screen: a third element for cloud-mobile convergence. IEEE Multimed. **18**(2), 4–11 (2011)

6. Sun, W., Min, X., Zhai, G., Gu, K., Ma, S., Yang, X.: Dynamic backlight scaling considering ambient luminance for mobile videos on LCD displays. IEEE Trans. Mob. Comput. (2020)

7. Gu, K., Zhai, G., Lin, W., Yang, X., Zhang, W.: Learning a blind quality evaluation engine of screen content images. Neurocomputing **196**, 140–149 (2016)

8. Zhan, K., Shi, J., Teng, J., Li, Q., Wang, M., Lu, F.: Linking synaptic computation for image enhancement. Neurocomputing **238**, 1–12 (2017)

9. Li, C., et al.: An underwater image enhancement benchmark dataset and beyond. IEEE Trans. Image Process. **29**, 4376–4389 (2019)

10. Arici, T., Dikbas, S., Altunbasak, Y.: A histogram modification framework and its application for image contrast enhancement. IEEE Trans. Image Process. **18**(9), 1921–1935 (2009)

11. Gonzalez, R.C., Woods, R.E.: Digital Image Processing. Addison-Wesley, Reading (1992)

12. Kim, Y.T.: Contrast enhancement using brightness preserving bi-histogram equalization. IEEE Trans. Cons. Electron. **43**(1), 1–8 (1997)

13. Xu, H., Zhai, G., Wu, X., Yang, X.: Generalized equalization model for image enhancement. IEEE Trans. Multimed. **16**(1), 68–82 (2013)

14. HaCohen, Y., Shechtman, E., Goldman, D.B., Lischinski, D.: Non-rigid dense correspondence with applications for image enhancement. ACM Trans. Graph. **30**(4), 1–10 (2011)

15. Li, M., Liu, J., Yang, W., Sun, X., Guo, Z.: Structure-revealing low-light image enhancement via robust retinex model. IEEE Trans. Image Process. **27**(6), 2828–2841 (2018)

16. He, K., Sun, J., Tang, X.: Guided image filtering. IEEE Trans. Pattern Anal. Mach. Intell. **35**(6), 1397–1409 (2012)

17. Gu, K., Zhang, Y., Qiao, J.: Vision-based monitoring of flare soot. IEEE Trans. Instrument. Meas. **69**, 7136–7145 (2020)

18. Gu, K., Xia, Z., Qiao, J., Lin, W.: Deep dual-channel neural network for image-based smoke detection. IEEE Trans. Multimed. **22**(2), 311–323 (2019)

19. Ren, W., et al.: Low-light image enhancement via a deep hybrid network. IEEE Trans. Image Process. **28**(9), 4364–4375 (2019)

20. Gu, K., Qiao, J., Li, X.: Highly efficient picture-based prediction of PM2.5 concentration. IEEE Trans. Ind. Electron. **66**(4), 3176–3184 (2019)

21. Gu, K., Zhang, Y., Qiao, J.: Ensemble meta learning for few-shot soot density recognition. IEEE Trans. Ind. Inf. **17**, 2261–2270 (2020)

22. Gu, K., Lin, W., Zhai, G., Yang, X., Zhang, W., Chen, C.W.: No-reference quality metric of contrast-distorted images based on information maximization. IEEE Trans. Cybernet. **47**(12), 4559–4565 (2016)

23. Wang, S., Gu, K., Ma, S., Lin, W., Liu, X., Gao, W.: Guided image contrast enhancement based on retrieved images in cloud. IEEE Trans. Multimed. **18**(2), 219–232 (2015)

24. Gu, K., Xu, X., Qiao, J., Lin, W., Thalmann, D.: Learning a unified blind image quality metric via on-line and off-line big training instances. IEEE Trans. Big Data **6**(4), 780–791 (2020)
25. Xia, Z., Gu, K., Wang, S., Liu, H., Kwong, S.: Toward accurate quality estimation of screen content pictures with very sparse reference information. IEEE Trans. Ind. Electron. **67**(3), 2251–2261 (2019)
26. Jakhetiya, V., Gu, K., Lin, W., Li, Q., Jaiswal, S.P.: A prediction backed model for quality assessment of screen content and 3-D synthesized images. IEEE Trans. Ind. Inf. **14**(2), 652–660 (2017)
27. Wang, S., et al.: Subjective and objective quality assessment of compressed screen content images. IEEE J. Emerg. Sel. Top. Circ. Syst. **6**(4), 532–543 (2016)
28. Wang, S., Gu, K., Zeng, K., Wang, Z., Lin, W.: Objective quality assessment and perceptual compression of screen content images. IEEE Comput. Graph. Appl. **38**(1), 47–58 (2016)
29. Minaee, S., Wang, Y.: Screen content picture segmentation using robust regression and sparse decomposition. IEEE J. Emerg. Sel. Top. Circ. Syst. **6**(4), 573–584 (2016)
30. Simonyan, K., Zisserman, A.: Very deep convolutional networks for large-scale image recognition. In: International Conference on Learning Representations (2015)
31. Zhang, Y., Chandler, D.M., Mou, X.: Quality assessment of screen content images via convolutional-neural-network-based synthetic/natural segmentation. IEEE Trans. Image Process. **27**(10), 5113–5128 (2018)
32. Min, X., Gu, K., Zhai, G., Hu, M., Yang, X.: Saliency-induced reduced-reference quality index for natural scene and screen content images. Signal Process. **145**, 127–136 (2018)
33. Wang, S., Ma, L., Fang, Y., Lin, W., Ma, S., Gao, W.: Just noticeable difference estimation for screen content images. IEEE Trans. Image Process. **25**(8), 3838–3851 (2016)
34. Long, J., Shelhamer, E., Darrell, T.: Fully convolutional networks for semantic segmentation. In: Proceedings of the IEEE Conference on Computer Vision and Pattern Recognition, pp. 3431–3440 (2015)
35. Wang, Y., Chen, Q., Zhang, B.: Image enhancement based on equal area dualistic sub-image histogram equalization method. IEEE Trans. Cons. Electron. **45**(1), 68–75 (1999)
36. Gu, K., Zhai, G., Yang, X., Zhang, W., Chen, C.W.: Automatic contrast enhancement technology with saliency preservation. IEEE Trans. Circ. Syst. Video Technol. **25**(9), 1480–1494 (2014)
37. Arici, T., Dikbas, S., Altunbasak, Y.: A histogram modification framework and its application for image contrast enhancement. IEEE Trans. Image Process. **18**(9), 1921–1935 (2009)
38. Shen, C., Zhao, Q.: Webpage saliency. In: Fleet, D., Pajdla, T., Schiele, B., Tuytelaars, T. (eds.) ECCV 2014. LNCS, vol. 8695, pp. 33–46. Springer, Cham (2014). https://doi.org/10.1007/978-3-319-10584-0_3
39. Che, Z., et al.: Adaptive screen content image enhancement strategy using layer-based segmentation. In: 2018 IEEE International Symposium on Circuits and Systems (ISCAS), pp. 1–5. IEEE (2018)

Machine Learning

Accelerated Object Detection for Autonomous Driving in CVIS Based on Pruned CNN Architecture

Changyi Wang[1]([✉]), Liang Qian[1,2], Lianghui Ding[1], Feng Yang[1], Cheng Zhi[1], and Youshan Xu[3]

[1] Department of Electronic Engineering, Shanghai Jiao Tong University, Shanghai, China
wchangyi@sjtu.edu.cn
[2] Shenzhen Institute of Guangdong Ocean University, Shenzhen, China
[3] Wuhan Maritime Communication Research Institute, Wuhan, China

Abstract. While processing delay has become the primary consideration for future Cooperation Vehicle Infrastructure Systems (CVIS), different enhanced methodologies based on pruned network has widely studied. More efficient pruned architecture can be accomplished by considering prior information like motion feature prediction (optical flow, etc.) to achieve optimized feature computing. With consideration of continuous features backward propagation methods, an accelerated neural network pruning method is proposed in this paper, to achieve real-time pruning based on prior information in CNN inference time. Furthermore, proposed method can fully utilize the information from CVIS to maximize pruning ratio in feature space from the CVIS monitoring stream, with significant improvement for recall index, a more suitable performance evaluation index for object detection in autonomous driving. With comparison to general detection framework, like YOLOv3 based on darknet-52, more than 20% processing speed gain can be significantly achieved in our proposed method, with minimum loss of recall index. At the same time, the basic recall rate has also been increased by 13.7%.

Keywords: Autonomous driving · CNN accelerating · Video-based object detection

1 Introduction

Cooperation Vehicle Infrastructure Systems (CVIS) is an important part of Intelligent Transport Systems (ITS). CVIS realizes the intelligent coordination between vehicles and infrastructure through information sharing between vehicles and roads and between vehicles. CVIS needs the support of wireless communication and sensor technology, which has been studied a lot and are constantly improving. Obtaining road condition from the video captured by camera on the vehicles or roadside base station is one of the most important tasks in CVIS. And the object detection method based on computer vision is popular and effective.

© Springer Nature Singapore Pte Ltd. 2021
G. Zhai et al. (Eds.): IFTC 2020, CCIS 1390, pp. 121–134, 2021.
https://doi.org/10.1007/978-981-16-1194-0_11

In recent researches, object detection algorithms are widely used to process a single image, like RCNN [1], faster RCNN [2], YOLO [3,4], SSD [5], etc. But video-based applications, such as providing real time traffic information in CVIS, have high requirements for processing speed. The genera treatment is to split the video into continuous single-frame images for processing, and use model compression algorithms to compact and accelerate the models. But continuous frames of video have motion correlation. There are a lot of redundant information between several adjacent frames, especially under the CVIS environment perspective. CVIS environment perspective means the enhanced monitoring stream obtained from a fixed monitoring perspective. The repeated information should be fully utilized.

The traffic information obtained by base stations on the roadside and vehicles on the road needs to be processed collaboratively in CVIS, which provides a natural multi-node cooperative structure, and the MEC (Mobile Edge Computing) architecture can be easily applied. The rapid development and application of 5G make this structure more reliable. We designed a distributed computing framework which is suitable for multi-node information fusion structure. We use hash rules to split the convolution computation of CNN to edge computing devices, and use different calculation distribution strategies at different CNN depths to avoid frequent information exchange. The distributed framework will also undertake some auxiliary computing tasks. The computing devices loaded on each base station and each vehicle are available distributed computing units, and they can provide different computing capabilities. Each computing unit connected to the CVIS network can be awakened when needed, and computing tasks will be allocated according to different computing capabilities, the number of idle nodes and certain computing distribution rules and restrictions, which will be discussed in Sect. 3.3.

Inspired by network pruning and feature propagation of continuous video frames, combined with the distributed computing auxiliary framework, we propose a new method of channel pruning to accelerate CNN for video-based object detection tasks. Different from the traditional pre-training, pruning and fine-tuning pipeline, we collect prior information in the CNN inference time and apply it to the dynamic pruning process in real time. In our algorithm, we select a key frame as the baseline and the subsequent frames do not fluctuate much relative to it. Some of the features in the subsequent frames can be replaced by the corresponding features in the key frame, that is, the calculation needed to generate these features is omitted, and the feature extraction process has been accelerated. The feature lost by the omitted calculations can be compensated by the features passed from the key frame. Of course, we switch key frames according to certain rules. The overall pipeline and detailed explanation are shown in Fig. 1. The frame k is the key frame we selected for the first time. When the program runs to frame k', it judges that the image has large fluctuations, then switches the key frame to frame k'. Our framework will take effect in CNN inference time under the CVIS environment perspective.

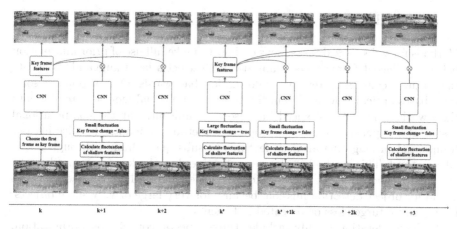

Fig. 1. The overall pipeline. The blue line at the bottom indicate consecutive video frames over time. In this example, the first frame k is the key frame selected at the beginning. Each frame will produce features and use these features to generate prediction results. Before feature extraction, some frames will be sampled for key frame verification to determine whether there are fluctuations that cannot be ignored, like the bottom blue rectangle in frame $k + 1$, k', $k' + 1$ and $k' + 3$. If the fluctuation does not occur, the pruned network, shown as a narrower CNN module rectangle, is used for feature extraction and receive the redundant features propagating from key frame. If the fluctuation occurs, as shown at frame k', program will use the complete network to extract the features and set it as a new key frame. In practice, after detecting a fluctuation, it is necessary to continuously detect some subsequent frames to ensure the fluctuation is not caused by the noise introduced by accident. (Color figure online)

CVIS environment perspective is more appropriate in object detection task than vehicle perspective for autonomous driving. The vehicle perspective needs to adapt to different sizes and the blur of the targets caused by viewing distance. At the same time, all angles of the target should be considered. The most serious problem is occlusion. This is why even in a particular usage scenarios, many models cannot obtain very high accuracy in autonomous driving object detection. From CVIS environment perspective, these problems can be alleviated. The problem is that the information cannot be processed locally in the vehicle, so we need to consider the delays caused by information transmission. It can be solved easily rely on 5G and MEC architecture, which matches our distributed framework very well.

We conducted an object detection experiments on YOLOv3 [4] based on DarkNet, and applied it to an automatic driving scene under CVIS environment perspective. Without the aid of distributed computing, we obtain a 20% speed increase in feature extraction, and the recall loss was less than 1.5%.

2   Related Work

Methods for video-based tasks focus on how to make full use of prior information between adjacent frames. The main idea is to select a key frame and propagate the features containing repeated information backwards. One of popular solutions bases optical flow [6–8], which introduce traditional motion detection into their work. The effect of speed increase is significant, but the computational cost is also expensive. Paper [9] proposes a method of adaptively selecting key frames and propagating all deep features to subsequent frames through a specific method. This method is also very effective, but the key frame needs to be switched frequently if the FPS of video is not enough. Inherit all deep features is bad for object detection mission, because for very large or very small objects, it may cause target loss or repeated judgments.

CNN acceleration mainly includes three aspects: convolution optimization, quantification and structured simplification. Convolution optimization and quantification make the calculation more efficient. Convolution optimization accelerates the calculation by using specific methods and changing the process of convolution, like FFT [10]. Quantification [11] reduces the complexity of floating-point calculations.

The training-based pruning methods are easy to implement and widely used in structural simplification. Method based on sparse connection eliminates redundant connections between neurons and is very effective in simplifying structure and storing weight. This method works mainly based on weights, including calculating the importance of weights [12,13] or using random pruning methods and turning pruning the problem into a combinatorial optimization problem [14]. These fine-grained pruning method make most of the weights in the network become zero and require special sparse matrix calculation library or hardware to accelerate. Channel-wise pruning is a coarse-grained pruning method [15] used to remove redundant channels in the feature map. It can also use LASSO regression [16] or geometric media [17] to select and delete redundant channels in CNN inference time then retrain the model. Although the flexibility is not as good as sparse connection methods, channel pruning is easier to implement and usually produce obvious results as long as the network is deep enough.

But training-based methods mentioned above need a lot of computation, and need retrain to make up for the pruned accuracy, known as fine-tune. Every specific network needs specific computation and pruning. And these methods dependent too much on the large redundancy in the structure and training data of the network to be pruned.

3   Model and Approach

In this section, we analyze the advantages of the CVIS environment perspective in autonomous driving, propose a channel pruning algorithm based on the redundant information between adjacent frames and then introduce the distributed architecture for computing auxiliary.

3.1 CVIS Environment Perspective

We use CVIS environment perspective for theoretical analysis and experiment. This is not only to simulate the high viewing angle of roadside base station, but also because CVIS environment perspective has many advantages compared to traditional vehicle perspective in this scenario.

CVIS environment perspective brings implicit feature simplification. From the perspective of vehicle, the features extracted for each category are very complex. The classifier needs to consider that the target of each category will have different angles, including the front, back, sides and several other different rotation angles. At the same time, it is necessary to fully consider different occlusion problems, such as vehicle occlusion and crossroads. Therefore, the features extracted from each category are not smooth enough. Actually, this non-smoothness makes the model more robust to adapt to various scenarios, but it has a greater impact on the final recognition accuracy of the model. Under the CVIS environment perspective, the features extracted from category are stable, and the size of each category is relatively fixed. There is no need to consider the problem of different scales of the same category caused by the distance, and the problem of occlusion between targets can also be alleviated. These characteristics are conducive to the work of category integration.

Category fusion is an important part of our work. In the field of autonomous driving, we are not considered about the specific category of the detected target, but pay more attention to whether it has an impact on the driving of the vehicle. Therefore, we can merge similar categories in the labeling stage, which is very difficult in the traditional vehicle perspective. For example, we hope to merge pedestrians riding two-wheeled vehicles of different sizes together. From the perspective of the vehicle, different angles will bring some differences, which is not conducive to the convergence of the classifier. But under the CVIS environment perspective, they are very similar. The fusion of categories can bring higher accuracy, although it will also make the model more over fitting. We deploy an over fitting model based on the CVIS environment perspective for each base station, and they show very stable performance. Through experiments, based on the fusion category and CVIS environment perspective, the same object detection model can increase the recall by more than 10%, which is more important for autonomous driving.

3.2 Pruning Method

The pruning process in a single convolution layer has showed in Fig. 2. This method focuses on feature extraction process of CNN, cares about those features that have not changed significantly, rather than those are relatively unimportant to the final feature extraction results. We aim to reduce unnecessary calculations. After selecting the key frame, we calculate and obtain the repetition factor, which represents the degree of repetition between feature maps in current frame and key frame. We choose those features with a smaller repetition factor and replace them with corresponding parts of key frame under a certain pruning ratio.

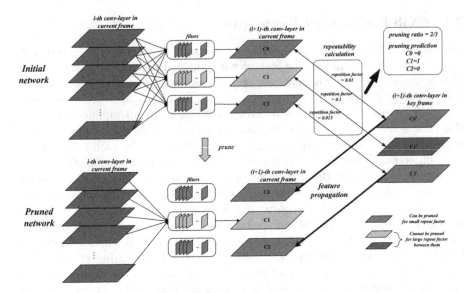

Fig. 2. Pruning in a single convolution layer. The green parts indicate that they can be replaced by the key frame under the guidance of pruning ratio, while the yellow parts cannot. This is because the yellow part is not repetitive enough compared to the same channel marked as red in the key frame. (Color figure online)

The key problem is how to determine which features can be replaced, we need to confirm which features have not changed or changed little compared to key frame. We use repeatability to measure it. Assuming that F_k is the currently selected key frame and F_c is the current frame. The feature maps in ith layer and jth channel of them are f_k^{ij} and f_c^{ij}. We use $Frobenius norm$ to calculate the repeatability between F_c and F_k, named as repetition factor, so that we can obtain more statistical results. The formula to obtain the repetition factor of F_c is:

$$R_c^{ij} = \left\| (f_k^{ij} - f_c^{ij}) \right\|_F^r \cdot \qquad (1)$$

R_c^{ij} is the repetition factor of the feather map in ith layer and jth channel in F_c. $().^r$ represents a power function acts on each element of the matrix with an even power r(the default is 2). This power function helps to enlarge obvious difference and makes numerical analysis more convenient. $\|.\|_F$ is the $Frobenius\ norm$. A small repetition factor means that feature is highly repetitive.

In practice, since the shallow features of CNN contain a lot of more obvious and important information and require much less calculation than deep features, we tend to set a higher pruning ratio for the deeper layers of CNN. It also makes the accuracy change smoother.

The calculations mentioned in this section are carried out along with the object detection, all the computing resources will be supplied by the auxiliary calculation module in distributed.

3.3 Distributed Framework

The entire framework depends on distributed environment for computing allocation and data communication. As shown in Fig. 3, the detection device will run the complete initial CNN and output the results first. At the same time, prediction device and sub-devices will take the task of feature storage in parallel.

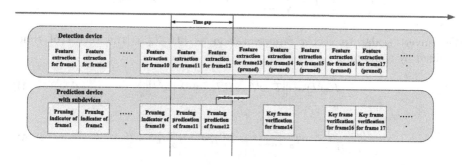

Fig. 3. Distributed framework pipeline. The blue line at the top is the time axis. The upper blue boxes represent the operation performed by the detection device, and the lower red boxes represent the operation performed by the prediction device. In this example, in the first 10 frames, the detection device uses the complete CNN network to extract features, and the prediction device calculates the repetition factors of these then frames. The 11th and 12th frames are the time difference, the prediction device synchronizes the time series of the repetition factors to the current time through forecasting. After the 13th frame, the detection device uses the time series to generate pruning indicator variable and extract features by the pruned CNN network. On the 14th,16th and 17th frames, the prediction device performs key frame verification. (Color figure online)

After a few frames $F_1, \ldots, F_N$, detection device continues the detection task using the initial network, while the prediction device and sub-devices calculate the repetition factor $R_c(c = 2, \ldots, N)$ of $F_2, \ldots, F_N$ relative to F_1, which is the current key frame. These repetition factors are summarized to the prediction device to select the features needed to be pruned under the conduct of pruning ratio in each layer. If a feature in ith layer and jth channel in frame c can be pruned, we mark it as 0, otherwise mark it as 1. We set an indicator variable p_c^{ij} to represent it, note that $p_c^{ij} = \{0, 1\}$.

The R_c^{ij} in these several frames will form a frame-related time series, and the prediction device will predict the $R_c^{ij}(c > N)$ according to the state of frame read in detection device by regression methods, which means that the prediction sequence is supplemented to the current frame. We use linear regression to predict the repetition factor in latter frames, the cost function is:

$$J(\omega^{ij}) = \frac{1}{N}\sum_{c=1}^{N}(\omega^T t_c - R_c^{ij})^2 \tag{2}$$

The number of repetition factors in each frame is greater than the total number of sample frames, so the input data is not full rank. At the same time, repetition factors are not zero at most of the time. So, we introduce L_2 norm to make this regression become a ridge regression problem. The cost function and the problem become:

$$\min_{\omega^{ij}} J(\omega^{ij}) = \frac{1}{N}\sum_{c=1}^{N}\left(\omega^{ij^T} t_c - R_c^{ij}\right)^2 + \lambda\left\|\omega^{ij}\right\|_2^2 \tag{3}$$

We convert scalar to vector representation as (4), T_a is the vector of time obtained by combining t_c:

$$J(\omega^{ij}) = \left\|T_a\omega^{ij} - R^{ij}\right\|_2^2 + \lambda\left\|\omega^{ij}\right\|_2^2 \tag{4}$$

so,

$$\frac{\partial J(\omega^{ij})}{\partial \omega^{ij}} = 2T_a^T T_a\omega^{ij} - T_a^T R^{ij} - T_a^T R^{ij} + 2\omega^{ij} \tag{5}$$

then let $\frac{\partial J(\omega^{ij})}{\partial \omega^{ij}} = 0$, we can get the regression parameters of ith layer and jth channel by (6):

$$\omega^{ij} = (T_a^T T_a + \lambda E)^{-1} T_a^T R^{ij} \tag{6}$$

This supplement will create a time delay, the number of sub-devices can reduce the delay. Detection device uses this sequence to predict the pruning indicator in subsequent frames and prune the network.

Then detection device can use the pruning prediction to extract features faster, and the prediction device will run the key frame verification task. The features extracted by the shallow CNN are the surface features of the picture. As the basis for subsequent feature extraction, they can represent the similarities and differences between different images. Similar to the hash code representing the picture identification information in the picture storage, these shallow features can also be used as the identification features of the image. Take shallow features (10%) in current frame and compare it with the key frame, if the difference is greater than a threshold presupposed, it can be reasonably considered that the frame has a large fluctuation. If this happens, then in subsequent continuous frames, we use current frame as a new key frame.

Note that our method is different from the traditional pruning methods in principle and application stage, and there is no conflict between them. In this way, the model simplified by traditional compression methods can also be accelerated by our framework. And retrain is not needed in our method, the initial model itself will not change.

4   Experiment

We collect several one hour video data with high traffic flow in different time, different weather and light conditions both in CVIS environment and vehicle perspective. All the devices are based on the Intel CPU i7 7700 and Nvidia GPU GTX 1060 6G.

YOLOv3 is an object detection algorithm based on darnet52, which has 52 convolution layers, including 23 residual blocks. As shown in Table 1, we divide these convolution layers into 6 parts according to the down-sampling layers, and set different pruning ratio for each part. The visual results are shown in Fig. 4, our method can achieve significant results.

Table 1. Slicing parts of darknet52

Block names	Number of layers	Slicing part
Convolutional Layer 0	1×1	1
Downsample Layer 0	1×1	
Residual Layer 0	2×1	2
Downsample Layer 1	1×1	
Residual Layer 1	2×2	3
Downsample Layer 2	1×1	
Residual Layer 2	2×8	4
Downsample Layer 3	1×1	
Residual Layer 3	2×8	5
Downsample Layer 4	1×1	
Residual Layer 4	2×4	6

We tend to use recall to characterize the performance of models or methods in experiments. Recall represents the proportion of samples that are correctly predicted in ground truth. This indicator can be more important for autonomous driving, because we hope to more accurately identify the original road conditions, so the risk of missed detection is very high.

4.1   Experiment in Different Perspective

The YOLOv3 models are trained by the same amount of data both in CVIS environment perspective and vehicle perspective. For each frame, if the IOU between predicted box and labeled box is greater than 0.5 and the category prediction is correct, the prediction is correct. The recall of each frame is the proportion of correct predictions among all objects. The average recall is shown in Table 2.

We select 250 continuous frames at the same time and place but at different perspective for experiment. There are more than 5 objects in each frame. In the

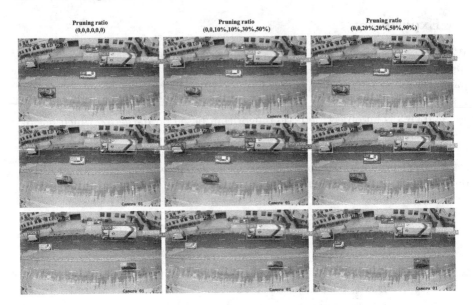

Fig. 4. The performance of the algorithm on our dataset under different pruning ratio. The six numbers of pruning ratio each column represent the pruning rate of six parts shown in Table 1. The first column is the result of no pruning. Each column contains three different frames and each row shows the detection result of the same frame. The results obtained by the model accelerated by our algorithm have no visual deviation.

Table 2. Recall in two perspective

Perspective mode	Average recall
CVIS environment perspective	**99.52%**
Vehicle perspective	87.50%

experiment, we found that if the key frame switching threshold set for vehicle perspective is the same as the CVIS environment perspective, the key frames will be changed very frequently. In order to confirm that the same feature extraction speed can be obtained, key frames will not be changed adaptively, but they will be changed every 50 frames. The recall drop in each frame is shown in Fig. 5, the CVIS environment perspective has better performance in recall maintenance.

4.2   Experiment of Precision and Speed-Up

We only change the pruning ratio of a certain part of the network and fix the others at 0 to show the recall and running time change curve. The results are shown in Fig. 6. It can be clearly seen from Fig. 6 that which pruning ratio is acceptable according to the reduction in recall. Some curves tend to be gentle at last because of the unmoved objects. Deep features are more suitable for pruning because of better precision maintenance and speed improvement. We

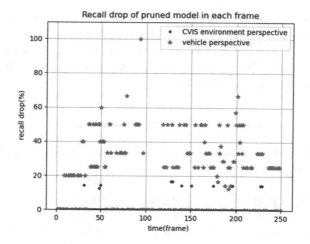

Fig. 5. The recall drop in each frame in CVIS environment perspective and vehicle perspective. The axis y is the decrease in recall relative the model without pruning. The large the value, the more the recall drops. The pruning ratio in each part is (0, 0, 20%, 20%, 50%, 50%)

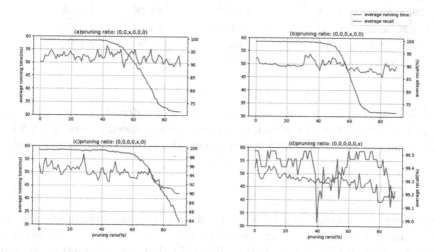

Fig. 6. Recall change and speed increase under different trimming ratios. The y-axis on the left of each figure is the average running time of feature extraction, and the y-axis on the right is the average recall. (a) and (b) show that pruning the shallow layer cannot produce obvious acceleration effect, and the recall maintenance performance is poor. The recall in (c) decreases slower than (a) and (b). And (c) has obvious acceleration effect. The average recall in (d) fluctuates above 99.0%, and (d) has the same acceleration effect as (c). As shown in (c) and (d), the effect of pruning deeper networks is more obvious.

always set the pruning ratio of the first two shallow parts to 0, because they are the surface features of the image and have a great impact on the subsequent feature extraction, and the calculation involved in them are much smaller than the subsequent ones. This is also one of the important reasons why we choose these parts for key frame verification.

Table 3. Results of different pruning ratio

Pruning ratio in part 3 to 6 (%)	Average running time (ms)	*Accelerate rate*	Average recall	*Recall decrease*
(0,0,0,0)	46.88	0	99.52%	0
(10,10,30,50)	**41.80**	**10.83%**	**99.22%**	**0.30%**
(10,10,50,50)	39.93	14.83%	98.92%	0.60%
(10,10,60,50)	40.30	14.03%	97.37%	2.12%
(10,10,30,90)	**38.88**	**17.06%**	**98.81%**	**0.71%**
(10,10,40,90)	**38.10**	**18.72%**	**98.69%**	**0.83%**
(10,10,50,90)	37.86	19.23%	97.79%	1.73%
(20,20,30,50)	40.61	13.37%	98.81%	0.71%
(20,20,50,50)	39.37	16.01%	98.38%	1.14%
(20,20,30,90)	**38.20**	**18.52%**	**98.32%**	**1.20%**
(20,20,40,90)	**37.51**	**19.96%**	**98.15%**	**1.37%**
(20,20,50,90)	37.18	20.68%	97.07%	2.45%
(30,30,50,50)	38.93	16.95%	96.42%	3.10%

The average running time and average recall of different pruning ratio are showed in Table 3. Our framework could have 10.83% speed improvement with 0.3% recall loss and almost 20% improvement with a recall loss less than 1.5%.

5   Conclusion

To conclude, the current deep CNN has excellent performance in detection accuracy with expensive computing cost. However, the existing object detection methods based on CNN cannot make full use of redundant information between frames in videos and cannot easily meet the high requirements of processing speed and latency in autonomous driving and other real time scenarios. This paper proposes a channel pruning method based on a distributed framework to accelerate CNNs for video-based object detection tasks. We have explained that the fixed CVIS environment perspective is more suitable for autonomous driving in CVIS and our framework than vehicle perspective through experiment. In the case of autonomous driving under CVIS environment perspective, it can obtain a significant speed improvement and guarantee competitive accuracy with a reasonable pruning ratio. Our framework could have 10.83% speed improvement by only 0.3% recall loss and almost 20% improvement with a recall loss less than

1.5%. Deep features are more suitable for pruning because of better accuracy maintenance and speed improvement. The distributed computing framework we proposed can allocate CNN calculations to edge devices, and use the concepts of MEC and 5G to speed up the calculation process. It is also important that our framework works during CNN inference time and does not change the initial model itself. Our method can be easily combined with other model compression method.

In the future, we plan to pay more attention to the distributed framework mentioned in this paper. We will discuss how to handle the access and distribution of edge nodes more efficiently, and design information exchange logic and exception handling under different communication conditions.

Acknowledgment. This paper is supported in part by NSFC China (61771309, 61671301), Shanghai Commission of Science and Technology Funding (SCST 15DZ2270400), Shanghai Key Laboratory Funding (STCSM 18DZ1200102), Medical Engineering Cross Research Foundation of Shanghai Jiao Tong University (YG2017QN47), and Big Data Modeling based on Optical Coherence Tomography Asymmetric Scanning Technology for Early Diagnosis of Glaucoma (YG2019QNA61).

References

1. Girshick, R., Donahue, J., Darrell, T., Malik, J.: Rich feature hierarchies for accurate object detection and semantic segmentation. In: 2014 IEEE Conference on Computer Vision and Pattern Recognition, Columbus, OH, pp. 580–587 (2014)
2. Ren, S., He, K., Girshick, R., Sun, J.: Faster R-CNN: towards real-time object detection with region proposal networks. IEEE Trans. Pattern Anal. Mach. Intell. **39**(6), 1137–1149 (2017)
3. Redmon, J., Divvala, S., Girshick, R., Farhadi, A.: You only look once: unified, real-time object detection. In: 2016 IEEE Conference on Computer Vision and Pattern Recognition (CVPR), Las Vegas, NV, pp. 779–788 (2016)
4. Redmon, J., Farhadi, A.: YOLOv3: An Incremental Improvement. CoRR, abs/1804.02767 (2018)
5. Liu, W., Anguelov, D., Erhan, D., Szegedy, C., Reed, S.: SSD: single shot multibox detector. arXiv:1512.02325 (2015)
6. Gadde, R., Jampani, V., Gehler, P.V.: Semantic video CNNs through representation warping. In: 2017 IEEE International Conference on Computer Vision (ICCV), Venice, pp. 4463–4472 (2017)
7. Zhu, X., Xiong, Y., Dai, J., Yuan, L., Wei, Y.: Deep feature flow for video recognition. In: 2017 IEEE Conference on Computer Vision and Pattern Recognition (CVPR), Honolulu, HI, pp. 4141–4150 (2017)
8. Xu, Y., Fu, T., Yang, H., Lee, C., Yang, H.K.: Dynamic video segmentation network. In: Proceedings of the IEEE Conference on Computer Vision and Pattern Recognition (CVPR), pp. 6556–6565 (2018)
9. Li, Y., Shi, J., Lin, D.: Low-latency video semantic segmentation. In: 2018 IEEE/CVF Conference on Computer Vision and Pattern Recognition, Salt Lake City, UT, pp. 5997–6005 (2018)
10. Vasilache, N., Johnson, J., Mathieu, M., Chintala, S., Piantino, S., LeCun, Y.: Fast convolutional nets with fbfft: a GPU performance evaluation. arXiv preprint arXiv:1412.7580 (2014)

11. Wu, J., Leng, C., Wang, Y., Hu, Q., Cheng, J.: Quantized convolutional neural networks for mobile devices. In: 2016 IEEE Conference on Computer Vision and Pattern Recognition (CVPR), Las Vegas, NV, pp. 4820–4828 (2016)
12. Li, H., Kadav, A., Durdanovic, I., Samet, H., Graf, H.P.: Pruning filters for efficient convnets. CoRR, abs/1608.08710 (2016)
13. Yang, T., Chen, Y., Sze, V.: Designing energy-efficient convolutional neural networks using energy-aware pruning. In: 2017 IEEE Conference on Computer Vision and Pattern Recognition (CVPR), Honolulu, HI, pp. 6071–6079 (2017)
14. Anwar, S., Sung, W.Y.: Coarse pruning of convolutional neural networks with random masks. In: Proceedings of the International Conference on Learning and Representation (ICLR), pp. 134–145. IEEE (2017)
15. Liu, Z., Li, J., Shen, Z., Huang, G., Yan, S., Zhang, C.: Learning efficient convolutional networks through network slimming. In: 2017 IEEE International Conference on Computer Vision (ICCV), pp. 2755–2763 (2017)
16. He, Y., Zhang, X., Sun, J.: Channel pruning for accelerating very deep neural networks. In: 2017 IEEE International Conference on Computer Vision (ICCV), Venice, pp. 1398–1406 (2017)
17. He, Y., Liu, P., Wang, Z., Hu, Z., Yang, Y.: Filter pruning via geometric median for deep convolutional neural networks acceleration. In: 2019 IEEE/CVF Conference on Computer Vision and Pattern Recognition (CVPR), Long Beach, CA, USA, pp. 4340–4349 (2019)

Bi-LSTM Based on Attention Mechanism
for Emotion Analysis

Hanyang Song, Dan-Ting Duan, and Long Ye[✉]

Key Laboratory of Media Audio and Video (Communication University of China),
Ministry of Education, Beijing 100024, China
songsong_shy@163.com, {dantingduan,yelong}@cuc.edu.cn

Abstract. In the process of intelligent human-machine interaction, speech emotion recognition (SER) is paramount. In this project, we presented a structure to promote the accuracy of SER. In the task of SER, the extracted features are inputted into the network, and then we added an attention mechanism to the structure to focus on the salient sections of emotion. In order to reduce the impact of over fitting, we also add a global pooling branch to the structure. Eventually, we used a softmax classifier to classify the emotion information. To manifest the benefit of the proposed architecture, we evaluate it on the TSCBE dataset constructed by our group. Our results can be indicative of that the model proposed in this work can achieve higher accuracy compared with baseline.

Keywords: Speech emotion recognition · Attention mechanism · Bi-LSTM

1 Introduction

Emotional information is very paramount in the daily interaction. In verbal communication, emotional information in voice can help the listener understand the speaker's intention effectively. This is also true in the process of human-machine interaction.

Since the mid-1980s, growing researchers enjoy devoting themselves to the study of speech recognition, and have made quiet a few remarkable achievements, but at the same time, researchers are facing a host of challenging problems [1–4]. The task of SER is to extract the acoustic features which express emotion from the collected voice signals, and deal with the mapping relationship between these features and emotions of human. Quintessential SER system is mainly composed of signal of speech acquisition, emotion feature excavation and emotion classification recognition, as present in Fig. 1.

SER is a quintessential problem of pattern identification. Up to now, most of the pattern identification and classification methods have been applied to SER in speech. These methods include ANN, HMM [5], GMM, SVM and maximum likelihood Bayesian classification.

This work is supported by the National Natural Science Foundation of China under Grant Nos. 61971383, 61631016, the Fundamental Research Funds for the Central Universities under Grant No. YLSZ180226, and the CETC funding.

© Springer Nature Singapore Pte Ltd. 2021
G. Zhai et al. (Eds.): IFTC 2020, CCIS 1390, pp. 135–142, 2021.
https://doi.org/10.1007/978-981-16-1194-0_12

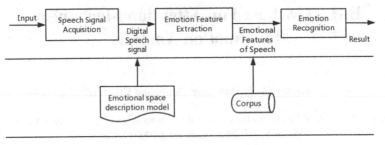

Fig. 1. A quintessential SER system.

In recent years, deep learning to automatically learn features from emotional audio data captures researchers' attention increasingly. In [6], the author applied a DNN on the basis of the quintessential statistical features of speech level, which improves the recognition accuracy compared with the quintessential support vector machine (SVM) and other classifiers. References [7] and [8] learned short-term acoustic features by using depth feedforward and recurrent neural network which called RNN at frame level, and then used extreme learning machine (ELM) to map the quintessential representation to the sentence level. [9] used convolution layer and recursion layer to learn the mapping of continuous values from time-domain speech signal to emotion around the model space. [10] recently proposed a weighted pool RNN algorithm based on weights to extract auditory representation. The results manifest that the performance of weighted pool RNN is better than the quintessential average, maximum or minimum pool methods. In addition, it demonstrates that the RNN can focus on the things of interest. In recent years, multi-task learning has manifested the superiority in emotion recognition tasks [11, 12].

In this paper, we focused on the research of SER based on the Bi-LSTM. The organizes as follows. Section 2 explains the details of the suggested method. Section 3 presents the experiments and experimental data. Finally, Sect. 4 provides a summary and the conclusion.

2 Approach

The proposed network has two network branches, presented in Fig. 2. The first branch uses a simple attention mechanism combined with Bi-LSTM to make the network pour attention into the emotional part of discourse. In the other branch, the global average pooling (GAP) layer is added to to avert over-fitting. After that, we concatenate the prediction results of the two network branches and then input them into a softmax layer to get the result of the entire network.

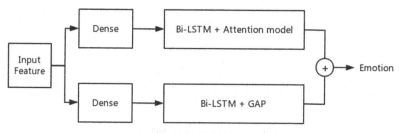

Fig. 2. Architecture of the proposed system.

2.1 Bi-LSTM and Attention Branch

LSTM Neural Network. In the current research on artificial intelligence, deep learning (DL) is a very popular research field. Deep learning suggests a DL network model, which effectively solves many problems [13–16]. At present, there are two typical deep learning network: CNN and RNN. Unlike with CNN, RNN is adept in processing sequence data with context information, which manifests promising performance in the kind of problem. By modeling the time series information, we can obtain the change of local feature and periodic information from the feature sequence, and then extract the features of discourse level, classify the emotional audios. Therefore, for problems like machine translation and speech recognition, RNN can manifest outstanding performance.

Nevertheless, there are also quiet a few cases of RNN that cannot be handled. Some problems in the training of neural network model with many layers, including gradient vanishing and gradient explosion. With the increasing of network layers, these problems will become more and more obvious.

RNNs have a characteristic, which gives rise to its unfavorable performance in most tasks due to its struggle with short-term memory. Long-Short Term Memory (LSTM) [17, 18] have active memory. In fact, LSTM is a kind of RNN. Different from typical RNN, LSTM has gating mechanism. A great contribution of this character is to solve the problem that RNN can only memorize short-term information. The emergence of LSTM is mainly to establish a long-term dependence model to determine the optimal time delay for time series problems. In the hidden layer of RNN, LSTM adds quiet a few special computing nodes. With the participation of these nodes, the mode of gradient transmission is changed in the process of back propagation, and the problems of gradient disappearance and gradient explosion can be reduced effectively. The long-range time dependencies of sequence classification can also be obtained effectively [19].

The architecture of LSTM is manifested in Fig. 3.

As present in the Fig. 3, h_{t-1} refers to the output of the front cell, X_t refers to the input of the present cell, and σ is interpreted as sigmoid function. Unlike RNN, LSTM has a "processor", which called unit, to determine the validity of information. Each unit has a input gate, a forget gate and a output gate. LSTM obtain a sequence information by input gate, and then the information will be judged whether it is useful. Useful information will be delivered to the network layer behind, while useless information will be forgotten through the forgetting gate [17].

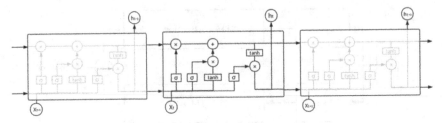

Fig. 3. LSTM model structure.

Weighted-Pooling with Local Attention. Not every frame of voice data contains emotional information. The emotion type of a voice data is usually affected by the strong emotional part, not every frame. In this network branch, which inspiration comes from [10], we use an attention mechanism to make the network focus on the emotional part of a voice data. We replace the typical average pooling by calculating the weighted sum, where the weight is determined by a set of additional parameters of the attention model. The diagram is presented as follows.

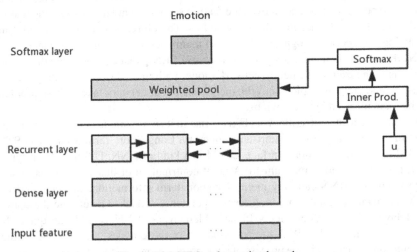

Fig. 4. Bi-LSTM and attention branch.

The network structure are represented in Fig. 4, We calculate the multiplication between the attention parameters vectors and the LSTM output y_t, which is required for each frame t. The calculated result is used to represent the contribution score of the frame to the final result. Finally, we add a softmax layer.

$$\alpha_t = \frac{\exp(u^T y_t)}{\sum_{\tau=1}^{T} \exp(u^T y_\tau)}. \tag{1}$$

We need to use the weight obtained in time for the weighted average:

$$z = \sum_{t=1}^{T} \alpha_t y_t. \tag{2}$$

The final output is transmitted to the softmax layer at the end of the network to obtain the posterior probability of each emotion. As for the internal parameters of the attention models, all these parameters will be trained with RNN parameters by the way of backpropagation.

2.2 Bi-LSTM and GAP Branch

Global Average Pooling Layer. [18] pointed out that the global average pool (GAP) can solve the problem of too many parameters effectively in the fully connected network model. Gap is mainly used to calculate the average value of all elements of the input feature map. In [19], a GAP is added after the convolution layer at the end of the network structure. The experimental results also confirm that GAP can replace the traditional full connection layer.

The network framework of this branch is presented in Fig. 5. The speech features are fed into dense layer, and then input into Bi-LSTM. Different from the first branch, we take the output of Bi-LSTM as the input of GAP.

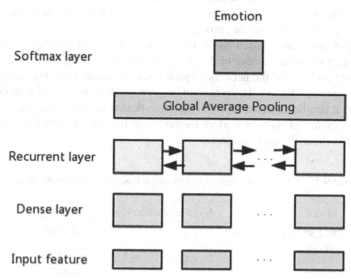

Fig. 5. Bi-LSTM and GAP branch.

3   Experiments

3.1   Corpus Description

In order to make the experimental results more accuracy and convincing, we cooperated with the broadcasting and hosting major of Communication University of China to provide professional and representative audio data for the research of this subject. In the present study, 13 speakers (7 males and 6 females) were placed in induced situations arousing the three basic emotions of positive, neutral, and negative in order to create the Text-Speech Chinese Bimodal Emotion (TSCBE) proprietary database. The database contains 657 audio data, the average duration of each audio is 7.3 s. The sampling rate was setted as 48 kHz and the voice datas were recorded through using high quality microphones.

Audio recording is completed in a professional recording studio, which requires the speakers to evoke their emotions by recalling their real experiences before giving the performance of a specific emotional segment, so as to enhance the emotional authenticity. The high quality of audio datas ensure the smooth progress of the experiment.

3.2   Implementation Details

For the input data of this network, we extracted a set of 36D acoustic features as mention in [20]. In the process of feature extraction, we use a 25 ms window and set the moving step to 10 ms. Finally, the extracted acoustic feature are z-normalized.

We use a modified ReLu dense layer with 512 nodes for feature learning process, a Bi-LSTM recursive layer with 128 memory cells for feature learning process. Drop out rate is setted as 50% in the training process.

The experiments was carried out in three groups. In the first group, we balanced the results with different number of dense layers before Bi-LSTM and make the best one to be the baseline. All the network structure were based on attention model. These data are presented in Table 1. In the second one, we combine Bi-LSTM with GAP and apply different number of dense layers in the network structure to compare their results, presented in Table 2. Finally, we adopt the proposed framework, which combines the best two networks in the first two parts.

Table 1. Accuracy of emotion classification based on different models.

Model	Number of dense layers	Accuracy
Bi-LSTM + Attention model	1	69.47%
	2	71.21%
	3	69.82%

The baseline method combines Bi-LSTM with attention model to make the model to focus on emotionally salient parts of the test audio data. For baseline, two layers of dense can achieve the best effect. GAP is usually used to replace the fully connection layer

Table 2. Accuracy of emotion classification based on different models.

Model	Number of dense layers	Accuracy
Bi-LSTM + GAP	1	71.72%
	2	70.70%
	3	69.93%

Table 3. Accuracy of emotion classification based on different models.

Model	Accuracy
Bi-LSTM + Attention model	71.21%
Bi-LSTM + GAP	71.72%
Ours	72.22%

in the classifier. The second network structure with multiple dense layers can not get outstanding results. Result in [10] manifests that the performance of the attention model achieve the best results than the other models. Our method combines the advantages of the two methods, so that the network can ignore the influence of silent frames, and avert over-fitting by using GAP branch. Table 3 presents that the proposed method achieves 72.22% accuracy, higher than the other methods.

4 Conclusion

In this work, we combine Bi-LSTM based on an attention mechanism with GAP to proposed a new network for SER. Through the attention pattern, our network can ignore both the silent frame and the other frames of the discourse that without emotional content. And the Bi-LSTM-GAP branch can help to avert over-fitting. To manifest the benefit of the proposed structure, we evaluate it through the TSCBE dataset constructed by our group. Our results can be indicative of that the model proposed in this work can get higher accuracy compared with baseline.

References

1. Wang, K., et al.: Speech emotion recognition using fourier parameters. IEEE Trans. Affect. Comput. **6**, 69–75 (2015)
2. Ramakrishnan, S., Emary, I.M.M.E.: speech emotion recognition approaches in human computer interaction. TS **52**(3), 1467–1478 (2011)
3. Zhang, S., et al.: Speech emotion recognition using deep convolutional neural network and discriminant temporal pyramid matching. Inst. Electr. Electron. Eng. **20**, 1576–1590 (2017)
4. Peng, Z., et al.: Speech emotion recognition using 3D convolutions and attention-based sliding recurrent networks with auditory front-ends. Inst. Electr. Electron. Eng. Access **8**, 16560–16572 (2020)

5. Rabiner, L.R.: A tutorialon hidden Markov models and selected applications in speech recognition. Inst. Electr. Electron. Eng. **77**, 257–286 (1989)
6. Stuhlsatz, A., Meyer, C., Eyben, F., Zielke, T., Meier, G., Schuller, B.: Deep neural networks for acoustic emotion recognition: raising the benchmarks. In: ICASSP. IEEE (2011)
7. Han, K., et al: Speech emotion recognition using deep neural network and extreme learning machine. In: Interspeech (2014)
8. Lee, J., et al.: High-level feature representation using recurrent neural network for speech emotion recognition. In: Interspeech (2015)
9. Trigeorgis, G., et al.: Adieu features? End-to-end speech emotion recognition using a deep convolutional recurrent network. In: ICASSP. IEEE (2016)
10. Mirsamadi, S., et al.: Automatic speech emotion recognition using recurrent neural networks with local attention. In: 2017 ICASSP, New Orleans, U.S.A. IEEE, March 2017
11. Parthasarathy, S., et al.: Jointly predicting arousal, valence and dominance with multi-task learning. In: Interspeech (2017)
12. Busso, C., et al.: IEMOCAP: interactive emotional dyadic motion capture database. JLRE **43**, 335–359 (2008)
13. Yu, X., et al.: Development of deep learning method for predicting firmness and soluble solid content of postharvest Korla fragrant pear using Vis/NIR hyperspectral reflectance imaging. Postharvest Biol. Technol. **141**, 39–49 (2018)
14. Cui, K., et al.: Virtual reality research of the dynamic characteristics of soft soil under metro vibration loads based on BP neural networks. Neural Comput. Appl. **29**(5), 1233–1242 (2017). https://doi.org/10.1007/s00521-017-2853-7
15. Sun, Y., et al.: Adaptive neural-fuzzy robust position control scheme for maglev train systems with experimental verification. IEEE Trans. Ind. Electron. **66**, 8589–8599 (2019)
16. Hussain, S., et al.: Implications of deep learning for the automation of design patterns organization (2018)
17. Gers, F.A., et al.: LSTM recurrent networks learn simple context-free and context-sensitive languages. IEEE Trans. Neural Netw. **12**, 1333–1340 (2001)
18. Gers, F.A., et al.: Applying LSTM to time series predictable through time-window approaches. In: Tagliaferri, R., Marinaro, M. (eds.) Neural Nets WIRN Vietri-01, pp 193–200. Springer, London (2002). https://doi.org/10.1007/978-1-4471-0219-9_20
19. Ma, X., et al.: Long short-term memory neural network for traffic speed prediction using remote microwave sensor data. TRCET **54**, 187–197 (2015)
20. Tao, F., et al.: Advanced LSTM: a study about better time dependency modeling in emotion recognition. In: ICASSP. IEEE (2018)

Visual and Audio Synchronization of Pedestrian Footstep Based on Human Pose Estimation

Qiutang Qi[1] , Xin Ma[1] , Chuanzhen Li[1], and Long Ye[2(✉)]

[1] School of Information and Communication Engineering,
Communication University of China, Beijing, China
[2] Key Laboratory of Media Audio and Video, Ministry of Education,
Communication University of China, Beijing, China
yelong@cuc.edu.cn

Abstract. In the film, the sounds related to characters' actions, such as clothing friction and footsteps, are difficult to be directly collected through recording and add manual sound effects requires a lot of time and energy. Aiming at the sound of footstep, which is highly related to human motion, this paper proposes a method to generate the sound of footsteps. First, the method of pedestrian gait detection is used to extract the landing frames, and then the relative parameters of footfall are obtained by the alignment of sampling rate. Finally, through these parameters, the sound effect of footsteps synchronized with the pedestrian gait picture is synthesized to obtain reasonable audio and video. In addition, we tested on UCF-ARG and HMDB datasets, and solved the problems of different directions, different speeds, and half length in pedestrian video by feature selection and fusion, show the effectiveness of our proposed method.

Keywords: Human pose estimation · Gait cycle detection · Audio - video synchronization

1 Introduction

Having the appropriate audio in a video can greatly enrich our visual experience. However, the sounds associated with human motion in video recording, such as clothing friction and footsteps, are difficult to collect directly and are mostly synthesized through post-production of sound effects. Adding sound effects by hand undoubtedly takes a lot of time and effort. For pedestrians walking, if the correlation between movement and sound is found, the method of automatic sound generation is conducive to the improvement of efficiency and the saving of manpower and time by referring to the law of human movements.

This work is supported by the National Natural Science Foundation of China under Grant Nos. 61971383, 61631016, the Fundamental Research Funds for the Central Universities under Grant No. YLSZ180226, and the CETC funding.

© Springer Nature Singapore Pte Ltd. 2021
G. Zhai et al. (Eds.): IFTC 2020, CCIS 1390, pp. 143–157, 2021.
https://doi.org/10.1007/978-981-16-1194-0_13

We focus on the video of pedestrian walking, hoping to analyze the landing frames of footstep, from the pedestrian walking pattern, then add footstep sounds appropriatly to realize audio and video synchronization. The detection of footstep landing frames is the main problem we have to deal with. In the video, the uncertainty of pedestrian walking direction and speed and the blocking of body also affect the detection to some extent.

At present, most of the research on pedestrian walking focuses on the field of gait recognition, that is, to distinguish different people from the walking posture, while there are few research on pedestrian walking and footstep landing sound. The traditional gait cycle detection method uses background subtraction to obtain the binary image of the human in the background, and detects the characteristics of the person's width and height and contour in the binary image for the detection of gait cycle. Part of the joint position is obtained by simple stick model, and the joint position is not accurate enough.

To tackle these problems, the characteristics and information of each joint of the pedestrian in the video were firstly obtained by using human pose estimation. Secondly, the detected joint features are screened and processed to determine the walking gait cycle and then determine the landing frames. Finally, according to the detected landing frames information, add and adjust the audio, synthesize the sound effect of footsteps synchronizing with the pedestrian gait picture. We fuse different features to deal with several known difficult detection conditions, which ensures that the algorithm can achieve good detection effect for the three special cases in the video.

Aiming at the sound of footstep, which is highly related to human motion, this paper proposes a method to generate the sound of footsteps. This paper trained and tested on UCF-ARG and HMDB respectively, and good experimental results are obtained from both datasets.

The innovations introduced by our paper are: 1) We propose a method to detect the sound time of pedestrian landing and prove that this method has high accuracy. 2) Aiming at the three types of problems: different directions, different speeds and half length, we ensured that the algorithm could achieve good detection effect for the three special cases in the video through feature selection and fusion. 3) On the basis of detecting the accurate landing frame and matching the corresponding footstep audio, the sound effect of footstep landing in audio and video synchronization is realized.

2   Related Work

Our work is closely related to the study of pedestrian gait cycle detection and human pose estimation.

2.1   Gait Cycle Detection for Pestrians

The detection of pedestrian landing frame is equivalent to the detection of gait cycle to some extent. Gait cycle detection is realized by detecting key frames in gait cycle.

In an early work, Johansson studied gait with the MLD (Moving Lighting Displays) experiment. Light sources are installed at key points of human beings, and the movement track of the light source is recorded as the characteristics in the process of gait recognition. From the movement of these light sources, the cyclical characteristics of gait can be seen [1,2]. Although this is only a research on visual motion perception, it is proved that the motion characteristics of joints can reflect the gait cycle, which lays a foundation for further research [3,4]. Subsequently, Kale [8], Zeng [5], Lee [9] and others analyzed the periodicity of gait by using various characteristics [5,6] such as the aspect ratio of human body [7], the norm of human body width vector [8], and the normalized body contour [9]. Gait cycle detection has also entered a flourishing period.

The algorithm of pedestrian periodic detection has made remarkable progress, but most of them are the overall features of binarization images, such as the feature of human body width and height and contour, etc., seldom uses the detailed features such as human joints. We use the human pose estimation to obtain the detailed features of human joints to supplement the pedestrian gait detection features.

2.2 Human Pose Estimation

The reason for the lack of detailed features such as joints in pedestrian periodic detection is that early joint detection is based on specific structural models, which are complex in model construction and lack of flexibility and accuracy.

With the development and improvement of related theories of deep learning, human pose estimation based on deep convolutional neural network has become the mainstream. DeepPose [10] first applied the deep convolutional neural network method for feature extraction, which greatly improved the accuracy, and then most of the methods were carried out on this basis. Later, CPM [11] and Stacked Hourglass [12] respectively proposed algorithms for multi-scale processing features and hourglass structure combined with deconvolution, which fully utilized multi-scale features and captured the spatial location information of each joint in the human body, once again greatly improving the accuracy. These algorithms are representative of early single-person pose estimation.

However, in most video scenes, characters appear in groups rather than individually. In general, multi-person posture estimation networks are divided into two categories: top-down and bottom-up. RMPE [13] and CPN [14] are typical top-down algorithms, in which RMPE proposes a symmetric space transformation network, and the detection accuracy is also higher. PAF [15] is a typical bottom-up algorithm, which can achieve real-time effect, but its accuracy is slightly lower than that of top-down algorithm.

We hope to get the accurate landing frame by accurately detecting the joint positions. Therefore, our first choice is the RMPE algorithm to implement the part of our joint detection.

3   Methodology

3.1   A Framework of Visual and Audio Synchronization of Pedestrian Footstep

Given the original video sequence, our goal is to add footstep sounds consistenting with the pedestrian's walking frequency. We divided the task into three parts. First, we used the human pose estimation network to process the video and get the characteristics and information of each joint of the pedestrian. Secondly, the detected joint features are screened and processed to determine the walking gait cycle and then determine the landing frame. Finally, according to the detected landing frame information, add and adjust the audio, synthesize the sound effect of footsteps synchronizing with the pedestrian gait picture, and get the reasonable audio and video (Fig. 1).

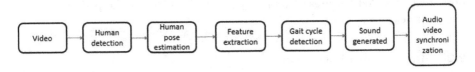

Fig. 1. A high level overview of our approach for generating synchronized audio and video of pedestrian footsteps.

3.2   Detection of Human Joint Characteristics

2D coordinate detection of human bone joints is the basis to describe human walking motion. In order to obtain high accuracy human joints, we introduce human pose estimation network. RMPE algorithm is selected because of its high precision of joint detection.

The video sequence was sent to RMPE network. First, the video was decomposed into a single frame image according to the video frame rate, and the image was detected by SSD to obtain the Human proposal. The resulting proposal was input into two parallel branches, the upper branch being the structure of STN+SPPE+SDTN, STN received the human proposal, while SDTN generated the pose proposal. The following parallel branches act as additional regularized orthotics. Finally, pose NMS (non-maximum suppression) is performed on the pose proposal to eliminate the redundant pose proposal, so as to obtain more accurate 2D human body joint coordinates. We only keep a set of optimal detection results for each frame, and we stored the human joint coordinates as the feature of subsequent landing frame detection.

3.3   Video Frame Detection of Foot Landing

How to find the gait cycle though the detected body joints will be the focus of the following discussion.

Generally, the characteristics of gait cycle detection include contour features and the aspect ratio of human body. We used the joint coordinates after pose estimation to extract: the distance feature, trajectory feature, angle feature of each joint, and calculate the width to height ratio of the human body. By using the above features, we detected the gait cycle and obtained the landing frame. Figure 2 shows the process of the detection of foot landing.

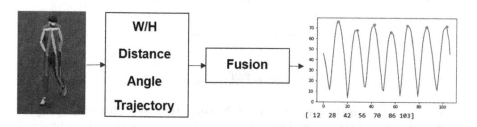

Fig. 2. Ground frame detection process.

Feature Extraction. Since the walking behavior is more closely related to the lower part of the human body, we take the ankle joint as an example to briefly introduce the characteristic calculation process.

Ankle Distance Feature. A full gait cycle is represented by the interval between the legs opening to the maximum width when walking and the interval between the legs opening to the maximum width the next time. Therefore, we can determine the gait cycle by measuring the width of the stride of the legs. The ankle joint is located at the end of the lower leg and can be accurately detected. We use the distance between the ankles as the feature of the interval between the legs. The ankle joint distance is defined as follows:

$$D_x = |x_{Lfoot} - x_{Rfoot}|. \tag{1}$$

$$D_y = |y_{Lfoot} - y_{Rfoot}|. \tag{2}$$

$$D_{xy} = \sqrt{(x_{Lfoot} - x_{Rfoot})^2 + (y_{Lfoot} - y_{Rfoot})^2}. \tag{3}$$

Where, D_x, D_y, D_{xy} are the x-direction, y-direction, and the distance between two points of the left and right feet, and the coordinate positions of the left and right feet are (x_{Lfoot}, y_{Lfoot}) and (x_{Rfoot}, y_{Rfoot}).

Ankle Track Feature. The most intuitive feature to judge the landing frame of a pedestrian is the running track feature of the foot. However, in the process of motion, the movement of the foot is not strictly in accordance with the smooth parabola, and the accuracy of the position of the foot detected through the video is not 100%, so the actual track of the foot is not smooth. Taking the change of displacement along the X-axis as an example, we drew a waveform with the number of video frames as the X-axis and the x-coordinate of the joint as the Y-axis, and the trajectory showed a step-like increase or decrease. For the subsequent experiments, we need to adjust the waveform direction to the horizontal direction. Based on the stability characteristics of the hip joint, we can calculate the modified coordinate point through Eq. 4 and Eq. 5:

$$x_{footr}[i] = \frac{x_{hip}[0]}{x_{hip}[i]} x_{foot}[i]. \tag{4}$$

$$y_{footr}[i] = \frac{y_{hip}[0]}{y_{hip}[i]} y_{foot}[i]. \tag{5}$$

Where $x_{footr}[i]$ is the x-coordinate of the corrected foot at frame i, $x_{foot}[i]$ is the x-coordinate of the original foot, $x_{hip}[0]$ and $x_{hip}[i]$, are the x-coordinate of the hip joint at frame 0 and frame i, respectively. Equation 5 is the calculation in y-coordinate.

Angle Between Legs. Use a straight line to connect the left foot and the midpoint of the hip, left and right feet, and the right foot to the midpoint of the hip. The distance is D_{L_Hip}, D_{L_R}, D_{Hip_R}. According to Eq. 6, the angle between the two legs can be obtained.

$$Angle_{leg} = \arccos \frac{D_{L\_Hip}^2 + D_{Hip\_R}^2 - D_{L\_R}^2}{2D_{L\_Hip}D_{Hip\_R}}. \tag{6}$$

Width to Height Ratio of Human Body. The width to height ratio of human body is also a common feature in gait periodic detection. We choose the maximum and minimum values of X and Y axes in all joints to replace the actual height and width of human body, calculate the ratio, and get the features of the width to height ratio of human body.

Common Landing Frame Detection

3.4   Detection of Human Joint Characteristics

The detection of landing frame in ordinary circumstances refers to the video frame of landing of footsteps in the process of walking under the condition of human body side (90°). Four features were used for detection respectively, and the peak value of the characteristic waveform was detected after smooth processing. Different feature peaks represented different meanings. Take the ankle joint distance feature as an example, and the peak value represents the moment when the legs open up the most and that is the moment when the foot hits the ground. Record the video frames corresponding to all peaks to obtain all required landing frames under this video.

In addition, we take the foot landing frame (ankle) with the best detection effect as the ground truth. Other joint features of the body are selected and fused, and the foot landing frame is detected with the fused features. We hope to replace the single feature with the fusion of multiple features to make the detection result more stable.

Special Landing Frame Detection. In addition to the detection of ordinary landing frames, experiments were carried out for the special situations in three kinds of pedestrian videos, including different directions, different speeds and half-lengths.

Different Directions. A person can move in an arbitrary direction under real circumstances. For pedestrians walking from different directions, different features have different tolerances to the scope of vision. It is not realistic to use a single feature to detect gait cycle at all directions. However, through experiments, we can find that some features have better detection effect on specific directions. For example, in the side case, the distance feature of the ankle joint can detect the landing frame of the foot very well, but in the front case, the detection effect is poor. The detection results of shoulder track characteristics were accurate in the front condition, but the detection results were worse in the lateral condition. Therefore, we fuse these features and adjust the parameters to ensure that accurate detection results of landing frames can be obtained in all directions.

Half-Lengths. Pedestrians may also appear to have only the upper body during the detection. When the lower part of the body is occluded, especially when the foot position is occluded, we will not be able to continue to use the characteristics of the ankle joint for detection. Therefore, in order to be able to detect the landing frame in the half body, we need to look for other features, especially the upper body features instead of the ankle features. Through experiments, it can be found that the distance of ankle joint, the distance of knee joint and the track of shoulder joint are correlated (with the same period). Therefore, we can use shoulder joint and knee joint instead of ankle joint to achieve the effect of half-body detection.

3.5   Video Synchronized with Sound

Synchronous at Same Speed. In order to synchronize the added audio with the footstep action in the video, we select the position where the footstep landing frame is detected to add audio. First, the time of this frame in the video is calculated according to the position of the landing frame obtained by gait cycle detection. Assuming that the detected landing frame is the Nth frame and the image frame rate is F (frame/second), then the time of the Nth frame in the video is T ms.

$$T = \frac{N}{F}1000. \tag{7}$$

Similarly, after calculating the time of all the landing frames, calculate the time difference for every two landing frames, and then cut the audio with this time difference as the condition.

It should be emphasized that the audio we chose is the standard footfall audio, and we need to ensure that the audio clipped by the time difference between two landing frames is exactly the sound of footfall landing, otherwise the sound will not be matched with the video.

After that, we spliced the clipped audio and ensured that the audio duration obtained after splicing was equal to that of the video. Finally, we combined the audio and video to get the final result.

Synchronous at Different Speeds. When pedestrians walk at different speeds, the gait law remains unchanged, only the density of the waveform changes, which has no influence on the detection of landing frames. However, in audio clipping, due to the fixed duration of sampled audio, the problem of missing and repeating of landing sound is very likely to occur. Therefore, we adopt different degrees of double speed processing for the original audio. However, when the audio is processed at a slow speed, the audio tone will change. To solve this problem, we introduce SOLA Time-scaling algorithm [16], which can ensure that the audio pitch remains the same when we shift gears. Through these operations, we guarantee the synchronization effect of video and sound at different walking speeds.

4   Experiments

To evaluate the effectiveness of our approach, we conduct a lot of experiments.

4.1   Dataset

The dataset consists of UCF-ARG Dataset and HMDB (Large Human Motion Database) and part of the video data shot by ourselves.

UCF-ARG Dataset consists of 12 volunteers' multi-angle human motion recognition data. The human movements are filmed in 10 categories. We only selected the walking movement data, each of whom had 4 angles: 90° for the close distance, 135° for the side, 90° for the long distance, and 15° for the back (we set 0° for the front and 180° for the back). The video length varies from 3 s to 9 s, and the video frame rate is 29.97 (frames per second).

HMDB Dataset is one of the most important data sets in the field of action recognition. Most of the videos in this data set are from movies. As the video quality is different, and the video perspective is relatively unfixed, which makes action recognition more difficult, but it is closer to the real effect. We only select the walking action data, whose video length ranged from 2 s to 5 s, and the frame rate is 30(frames per second).And we will manually filter out videos that do not make sense.

The data captured by ourselves mainly include pedestrian walking videos at different speeds, between 9 s to 20 s for each video, which is mainly used to verify the effectiveness of our landing detection at different speeds.

4.2 Experimental Results of Pose Estimation

We feed the video sequence from the data set into the RMPE network to get the pose estimation AP (Average Precision). In the table we present only the results of the foot and the body. Quantitative results on the UCF-ARG are given in Table 1. We can find that the AP of the foot is slightly lower than that of the body, and the AP reaches its maximum when the angle is close to 90°. Comparing the results in HMDB data set given in Table 2, it can be found that the detection results of UCF-ARG dataset is better than HMDB dataset, because the video background of UCF-ARG is relatively clean and the walking posture is relatively standardized. However, the video in the HMDB dataset is a movie clip with a complex background and is subject to light and occlusion. The accuracy of attitude estimation results will have a certain influence on the follow-up experiments.

Table 1. Human pose estimation results on the UCF-ARG Dataset (AP).

UCF-ARG	90° (Close)	135°	90° (far)	15°
Foot (AP)	82.1	73.5	65.3	63.5
Body(AP)	91.3	81.2	72.1	70.1

Table 2. Human pose estimation results on the HMDB Dataset (AP).

HMDB	0°–90°	90°	90°–180°
Foot (AP)	67.2	78.1	65.7
Body(AP)	75.3	84.2	74.3

4.3 Experimental Results of Landing Frame Detection

Feature Selection. Of gait cycle are commonly used to detect features include: distance, trajectory characteristics, Angle and the ratio of high to width of the human body, and so on, through the heat map to find the correlation between the data set different characteristics. It can be seen from Fig. 3 that the features most relevant to the ankle joint distance feature are the angle between legs and the ratio of body width to height. However, none of these features is effective in the half body. Besides, the features with high correlation are the shoulder, knee and hand, etc., which are selected for fusion instead of the feature of ankle spacing.

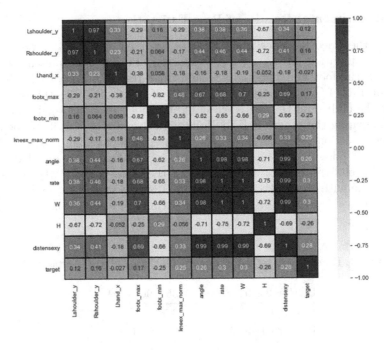

Fig. 3. Heat map of characteristic correlation

Left and Right Trajectory Fusion. We fused the tracks of the left and right joints of the body, as shown in Fig. 4. Firstly, the ankle joint is horizonted according to the stability of the hip joint, and then the maximum value of the left and right ankle joints is fused, so that the information of the left and right feet can be greatly utilized.

Weighted Fusion of Features. Features are weighted and fused, and feature weights are learned from the voting mechanism. First, four SVM classifiers are trained under training dataset, each classifier is about a single feature, for example, the classifier is about a single feature shoulder joint. Secondly, the classification effect of the four classifiers was tested under the test set, and the number of correct classification was counted to represent the number of correct classification under the four characteristics. Finally, the weight of the feature

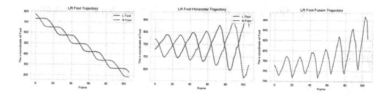

Fig. 4. Heat map of characteristic correlation

can be obtained by normalizing the second step. The results of feature-weighted fusion are shown in Fig. 5.

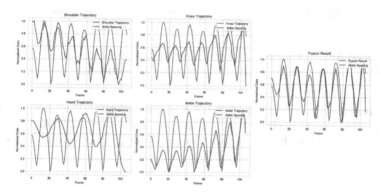

Fig. 5. Weighted fusion diagram. Green is the waveform of ankle joint distance, and red is the track waveform of shoulder, knee, hand, ankle and final fusion result respectively. (Color figure online)

Different Directions. Features were tested from different directions. The front side was set as 0° and the back side as 180°. Take the ankle distance, angle, track and aspect ratio features as an example, and the feature waveforms in the directions of 90° and 135° were drawn as shown in Fig. 6. It can be seen from the figure that landing frames can be well detected in all features on the side. When the angle changes, the waveform changes to varying degrees, and even some waveform detection results become inaccurate, such as the width to height ratio. The experimental results show that the ankle distance feature has good detection results under most directions except front and back. The track of shoulder showed better detection results at the directions close to front and back. Therefore, we fuse the two features, choosing ankle distance feature as the main feature when walking direction is the side, and shoulder joint feature as the main feature when walking direction is the front and the back, so as to ensure that accurate landing frame detection results can be obtained at all directions.

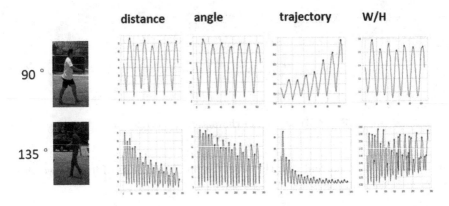

Fig. 6. Characteristic waveform from different directions.

The fusion results are shown in Fig. 7. For test videos, we classify the videos manually in advance, and then test the results of the videos.

Half-Lengths. The waveform in Fig. 8 is a comparison of the knee-ankle and shoulder-ankle respectively. The red line is the waveform of ankle, and the green line is the waveform of knee and shoulder respectively. It can be seen from the

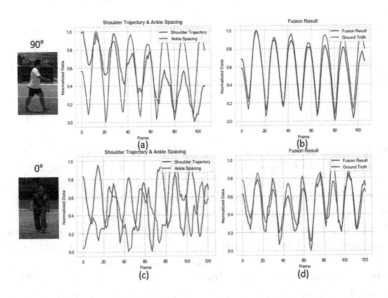

Fig. 7. Fusion results from different directions. The first line is the feature fusion result of side direction, and the second line is the feature fusion result of front direction. In (a) and (c), red and green are the characteristic waveforms of shoulder track and ankle distance, respectively. In (b) and (d), red is the fusion result, and green is ground truth. (Color figure online)

figure that the knee has a high degree of similarity. Although the waveform of shoulder and ankle does not have a high degree of coincidence, they have periodic consistency, which can ensure the identity of our landing frames. Therefore, when there are only the half-lengths, we can choose the upper body features instead of the lower body features for detection.

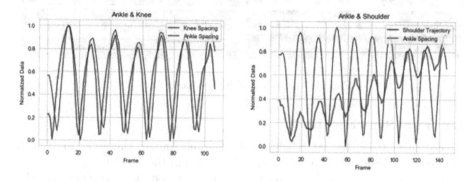

Fig. 8. Waveform contrast diagram.

Different Speeds. When the walking speed is different, the corresponding audio interval will also change greatly. In order to ensure the synchronization of audio and video, the audio speed is processed and clipped to obtain the results as shown in Fig. 9.

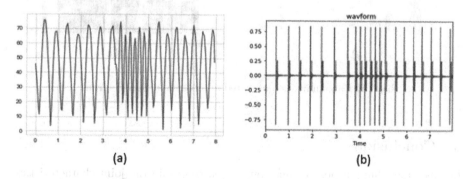

Fig. 9. The results of landing frame detection and the generated audio when the walking speed is different.

Fig. 10. Audio and video synthesis result.

4.4 Final Synthesis Result

According to the detection results of the landing frames, the audio and video can be synthesized to obtain the results as shown in the Fig. 10.

Moreover, we found the video with sound for testing, and compared the generated audio with the original audio, as shown in Fig. 11, we could find that the occurrence frame of its footsteps was basically the same.

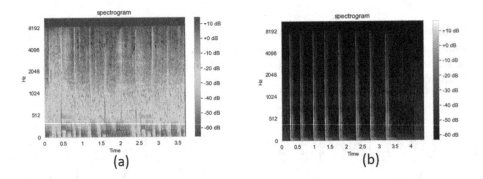

Fig. 11. Raw audio vs. generated audio comparison diagram.

5 Conclusion

In this paper, human pose estimation is used to obtain the joint characteristics of the pedestrian in the video, which solves the problem of inaccurate joint position in the traditional gait cycle detection. By analyzing the joint features, the footstep landing frame of the pedestrian is determined, and the footstep signal processed by editing is added at the corresponding time point, so as to add synchronous audio for the video with missing footstep. Verification experiments on UCF-ARG and HMDB show that the synchronization between video and audio is good.

References

1. Johansson, G.: Visual perception of biological motion and a model for its analysis. Percept. Psychophys. **14**(2), 201–211 (1973)
2. Johansson, G.: Visual motion perception. Sci. Am. **232**(6), 76–89 (1975)
3. Makihara, Y., Sagawa, R., Mukaigawa, Y., Echigo, T., Yagi, Y.: Gait recognition using a view transformation model in the frequency domain. In: Leonardis, A., Bischof, H., Pinz, A. (eds.) ECCV 2006. LNCS, vol. 3953, pp. 151–163. Springer, Heidelberg (2006). https://doi.org/10.1007/11744078_12
4. Huang, C.C., Hsu, C.C., Liao, H.Y.: Frontal gait recognition based on spatio-temporal interest points. J. Chin. Inst. Eng. **39**(8), 997–1002 (2016)
5. Zeng, Y.: Research on gait Recognition Method based on Angle and contour Features. Central South University (2008)
6. Ben, X., Meng, W., Yan, R.: Dual-ellipse fitting approach for robust gait periodicity detection. Neurocomputing **79**(3), 173–178 (2012)
7. Wang, L., Tan, T., Ning, H.: Silhouette analysis-based gait recognition for human identification. IEEE Trans. Pattern Anal. Mach. Intell. **25**(12), 1505–1518 (2003)
8. Kale, A., Sundaresan, A., Rajagopalan, A.N.: Identification of humans using gait. IEEE Trans. Image Process. **13**(9), 1163–1173 (2004)
9. Lee, C.P., Tan, A.W.C., Tan, S.C.: Gait Recognition with Transient Binary Patterns. Academic Press (2015)
10. Toshev, A., Szegedy, C.: DeepPose: human pose estimation via deep neural networks. In: Computer Vision and Pattern Recognition (CVPR) (2014)
11. Wei, S.E., Ramakrishna, V., Kanade, T.: Convolutional pose machines. In: Proceedings of the IEEE Conference on Computer Vision and Pattern Recognition, pp. 4724–4732 (2016)
12. Newell, A., Yang, K., Deng, J.: Stacked hourglass networks for human pose estimation (2016)
13. Fang, H.S., Xie, S., Tai, Y.W.: RMPE: regional multi-person pose estimation. In: Proceedings of the IEEE International Conference on Computer Vision, pp. 2334–2343 (1975)
14. Chen, Y., Wang, Z., Peng, Y.: Cascaded pyramid network for multi-person pose estimation. In: Proceedings of the IEEE Conference on Computer Vision and Pattern Recognition (2018)
15. Cao, Z., Simon, T., Wei, S.E.: Realtime multi-person 2D pose estimation using part affinity fields. In: Proceedings of the IEEE Conference on Computer Vision and Pattern Recognition, pp. 7291–7299 (2017)
16. Zölzer, U.: DAFX: Digital Audio Effects, 2nd edn. Wiley, Hoboken (2011)

Research on Face Aging Synthesis Based on Hybrid Domain Attention Mechanism GAN Network

Liuyin Dong, Xiangfen Zhang$^{(\boxtimes)}$, Feiniu Yuan$^{(\boxtimes)}$, Chuanjiang Li, and Dawei Hao

The College of Information, Mechanical and Electrical Engineering, Shanghai Normal University, Shanghai 200234, China
{xiangfen,yfn}@shnu.edu.cn

Abstract. Facial aging synthesis refers to the rendering of young people's facial images from an aesthetic point of view by adding wrinkles, eye bags, stains, or changing hair color, so that they can finally show the effect of natural facial aging. Facial aging synthesis needs to consider both the authenticity of the aging effect and the consistency of identity information. The authenticity of the aging effect is based on the accurate expression of aging characteristics and the clarity of aging details. The consistency of identity information means that during the aging process, the aging face needs to maintain a certain similarity with the original young face in terms of feature information. Based on the above two issues and the instability of GAN training, this paper proposes a face aging method based on the hybrid domain attention mechanism to generate an anti-network. A large number of experiments show that this method can synthesize aging human face while ensuring the aging effect and the requirements of identity information.

Keywords: Hybrid domain attention mechanism · Generative Adversarial Networks · Face aging synthesis

1 Introduction

Facial aging aims to render a given facial image with natural aging effects under a certain age or age group. In recent years, due to its strong practical value in digital entertainment (cross-age recognition and age editing), criminal investigation (looking for missing children), etc., the research on facial aging has attracted widespread attention.

In terms of face aging research, predecessors have proposed many methods, which can be roughly divided into two types: traditional face aging methods and

Supported by: National Natural Science Foundation of China (61862029) and Shanghai Normal University (Research on Automatic Focus Algorithm (209-AC9103-20-368005221)).

© Springer Nature Singapore Pte Ltd. 2021
G. Zhai et al. (Eds.): IFTC 2020, CCIS 1390, pp. 158–168, 2021.
https://doi.org/10.1007/978-981-16-1194-0_14

face aging methods based on deep learning. Recently, face aging methods based on deep learning, especially Generative Adversarial Networks (English full name, GAN), have shown excellent capabilities in face aging. Compared with the traditional face aging method, the face aging method based on deep learning has improved the image quality, identity consistency and the authenticity of the aging effect to a certain extent, but the overall effect is not ideal. For example, Zhang et al. proposed a conditional adversarial autoencoder (CAAE), which can perform age progression and regression (getting old and getting younger) in both directions, but it cannot well maintain the identity information of aging faces [1]. In order to achieve a balance between identity information consistency and authenticity of aging effects, we propose a framework based on the attention mechanism conditional GAN network to achieve face aging. The main contributions of our work can be summarized as follows:

(1) Using the hybrid domain attention mechanism, in the process of feature learning, the important features are strengthened by filtering the features in the channel dimension and the space dimension, so that the aging characteristics are well presented, and the synthesized aging face has a realistic aging effect.

(2) Introduce a structure to maintain identity information in the model, and calculate the perceptual loss through pre-training VGG16, so that the generated aging face can maintain the original facial feature information, and at the same time, it also avoids artifacts and ghosting in the composite image.

(3) This method is based on the GAN (ACGAN) structure with auxiliary classifiers, and does not need to add a separate pre-trained age classifier. It can supervise the age information and guide the input face image to better synthesize the aging image of the specified target age, The WGAN loss function is used as a counter loss to stabilize the training of GAN, and the final objective function is a combination of multiple loss functions.

2   Network Framework

This method is mainly based on the network structure of ACGAN.The network framework we proposed is shown in Fig. 1. The network mainly includes two modules:

2.1   Generator Module

The face image and age conditions are input to the generator together, and the hybrid domain attention module is introduced into the generator, and the aging face composite image is generated by training the generator.

2.2   Discriminator Module

The composite image of the aging face and the real face image (original young and aging face image) are used as the input of the discriminator. The discriminator performs true and false judgment and category judgment, and finally makes the generated face look realistic and accurately located in the target age group.

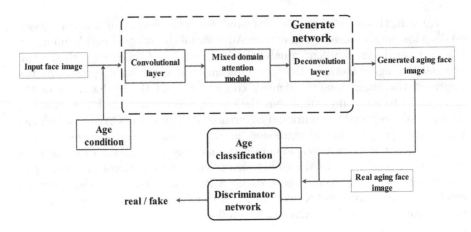

Fig. 1. Overall network framework.

3   Generate Network Structure Based on Hybrid Domain Attention Mechanism

Figure 2 is our generate network structure. The size of the convolution kernel is (5, 5), and the step size is 2. The input face is subjected to 3-layer convolution to extract the features of the high-dimensional face, and the output feature map enters the hybrid domain attention module, and then enters the next level network, and the image is restored through the 3-layer deconvolution structure.

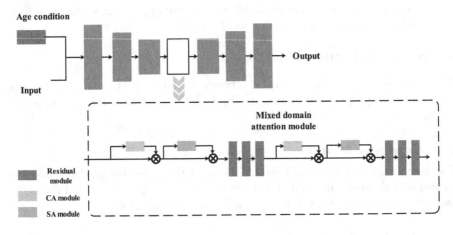

Fig. 2. Generate network structure.

We divide faces of different ages into 5 age groups, corresponding to ages 11–20, 21–30, 31–40, 41–50, and over 50. Given a face image x_s, we use $y_t \in R^{H*W*5}$

to represent the age group to which x belongs, where H and W represent the height and width of the picture, and 5 represents the age group number. Like one-hot encoding, only one feature map is filled with 1, and the other feature maps are all 0. Regarding the position of conditional joining, we refer to previous work [2]. Since the age condition has been introduced into the generation network at the beginning, the age condition can be better reflected. A key element to achieve the aging effect is to make the generator pay attention to the area related to the aging feature in the image, so the hybrid domain attention module is introduced [3].

4   Loss Function Design

This paper defines the loss function of 3 parts. The WGAN loss function is used as a counter loss to make the training of GAN more stable; the pre-trained VGG16 is used to calculate the perceptual loss, and the extraction of low-level features can keep the identity information consistent and have a better performance in the overall visual experience; the age classification loss makes The generated aging face image is more accurate in age classification.

4.1   Fight Against Loss

The original GAN formula is based on the JS divergence loss function, which aims to maximize the possibility of the generator trying to deceive the discriminator to correctly classify fake images. For the parameters of the generator, this loss may not be continuous and may be locally saturated, thus As a result, the discriminator gradient disappears and the generator is guided in the wrong direction. In order to stabilize the training of GAN, this paper uses Wasserstein distance as the training loss function.

$$L_G = -E_{x \sim p(x_s)} \left[D_I \left(G \left(x_s, y_t \right) \right) \right] \tag{1}$$

$$L_D = E_{x \sim p(x_s)} \left[D_I \left(G \left(x_s, y_t \right) \right) \right] - E_{x \sim p(x_s)} \left[D_I \left(x_s \right) \right] \tag{2}$$

$$L_{adv} = E_{x \sim p(x_s)} \left[D_I \left(x_s \right) \right] - E_{x \sim p(x_s)} \left[D_I \left(G \left(x_s, y_t \right) \right) \right] \tag{3}$$

4.2   Perceptual Loss of Keeping Identity Information

Existing GAN-based networks usually use the pixel-by-pixel gap between the synthesized image and the input image as a loss function to maintain the invariance of identity information. Using the pixel gap as a loss function will reduce the perceptual quality, and eventually blur the generated face or even appear artifacts, making people have a bad visual experience. The generated aging face and the input face image have obvious differences in wrinkles, beards, etc., but the facial features and facial contours are basically unchanged. In this case, the use can compare the high-level perception and semantic differences between the images The perceptual loss function is more appropriate [4].

In this paper, Conv1_1-Conv3_3 of VGG16 is used as the network structure of the identity retention module. The features obtained from the real picture via VGG16 and the features obtained from the generated picture via VGG16 are compared, so that the content information of the generated picture is close to that of the real picture, which plays a role in monitoring the retention of identity information. The perceived loss is:

$$L_{identity} = E_{x_s \sim p_{data(x_s)}} \left[\left\| h\left(G\left(x_s, y_t\right)\right) - h\left(x_s\right) \right\|^2 \right] \tag{4}$$

Where h(.) is the feature extracted from a specific feature layer in a pre-trained neural network. In this article, we use the pre-trained lower feature layer of VGG16 [5] as h(.). $G\left(x_s, y_t\right)$ represents the face image synthesized by the generator. The reason for not using the mean square error (MSE) between x_s in the pixel space and the specified age aging face $G\left(x_s, y_t\right)$ synthesized by the generator is: Compared with the input face x_s, $G\left(x_s, y_t\right)$ has significant changes in hair color, beard, facial wrinkles, etc. The MSE loss will make $G\left(x_s, y_t\right)$ and x_s too consistent.

4.3   Age Classification Loss

The loss of age classification causes the parameters of the generator to be changed to generate faces of a specified age. While reducing the loss of image confrontation, the generator must also reduce the age error through the age classifier Dy. The age classification loss is defined by two parts: the age estimation loss of the generated face image used to optimize G, and the age estimation loss of the real image used to learn the age classifier Dy. y_s is the age label of the input image x_s, and l(.) corresponds to the softmax loss. The age classification loss is:

$$L_{age} = E_{x_s \sim p_{data}(x_s)} \left[l\left(D_y\left(G\left(x_s, y_t\right), y_t\right) + l\left(D_{y(x_s)}\right), y_s\right) \right] \tag{5}$$

5   Experiment

5.1   Face Data Set Selection

UTK face consists of more than 23708 face images with age and gender tags that have been cropped at the same time. The age span is between 1–116 years old. We only keep the age label, filter out a total of 17,029 face images of 10–70 years old, and divide the 16,200 images in the training set into 5 age ranges 11–20, 21–30, 31–40, 41–50 and 51+.

CACD includes about 160,000 pictures of celebrities between the ages of 16 and 62. The public face age data set lacks face images in old age. The face images supplemented by this part are crawled on the Internet and the face images without age labels are age-labeled through age estimation. Removal of the interference of complex backgrounds and better retention of the aging feature area can allow the network to learn better, so we used mtcnn for face detection and alignment during cropping [6]. The filtered data set is divided into two parts, 90% for training and 10% for testing.

The FG-NET data set contains a total of 1002 real images of 82 people at different ages.

5.2 Experimental Details

We compare our method with the latest work, namely the Conditional Adversarial Autoencoder Network (CAAE) [1] and the Conditional Generative Adversarial Network Based on Identity Preservation (IPCGAN) [7]. We choose the Adam optimization algorithm and set the learning rate and batch size to 0.002 and 64 to optimize G and D. The experiment shares the same hyperparameter settings, and trains G and D alternately for 100 iterations on a GTX 1080Ti GPU. For CAAE, to be fair, we deleted gender information and used 5 age groups. On the premise of not changing the hyperparameter settings, for CAAE and IPCGAN, we use the released code to retrain the model.

5.3 Experimental Qualitative Comparative Analysis

Qualitative Comparison with CAAE, IPCGAN and OldBooth. In order to compare the performance with the previous aging synthesis method, we first perform a qualitative evaluation of the aging synthesis face of different methods on the UTK FACE dataset. Figure 3 shows the aging synthetic face of different methods on UTK FACE. The first line of each group is the IPCGAN method, the second line is the CAAE method, and the third line is the method of this paper. We can see that the results of CAAE have poor performance in terms of aging effect, identity information and picture quality. IPCGAN has a good performance in maintaining identity information, but the facial texture of the synthesized aging face is not significant. Compared with CAAE and IPCGAN, The aging face generated by this method not only performs well in maintaining identity information, but also has more prominent facial wrinkles and stains. At the same time, lighter eyebrows and hair can be observed.

In order to obtain more accurate evaluation results, we conducted experiments on the CACD dataset with more pictures. Figure 4 shows the aging synthetic face on CACD by different methods. Due to the poor results of CAAE, we replaced it with OldBooth [8], which is popular now. The first line of each group is the IPCGAN method, and the second line is the OldBooth method. Compared with OldBooth, our method has a significant improvement in image quality. Compared with IPCGAN, the face image generated by our method has more detailed texture, so the authenticity of the aging effect is stronger.

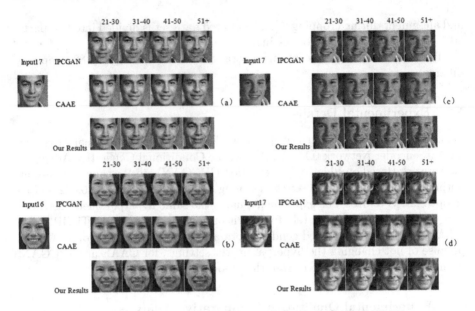

Fig. 3. Different methods of aging synthetic face on UTK FACE.

Qualitative Comparison with Other Aging Methods. In order to get a more accurate evaluation, we further compare with the previous method and use the form of voting for subjective investigation. Each option group has three

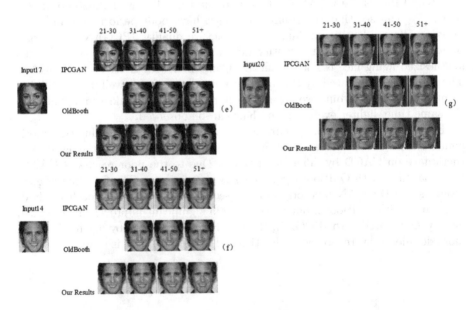

Fig. 4. Different methods of aging synthetic face on CACD.

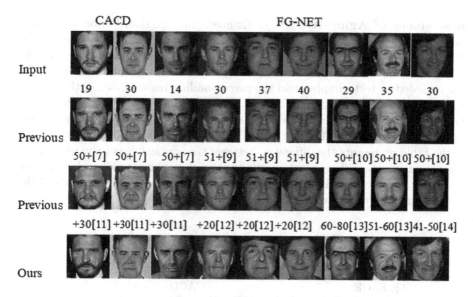

Fig. 5. Some options for subjective investigation.

images, which are the input face, the previous method and the method in this chapter. From the perspective of the authenticity of the aging effect and the consistency of the identity information, the voters are provided with three options, respectively, the face synthesized by the previous method is more realistic And it is closer to the input face; the method in this chapter is more realistic and closer to the input face; the previous method is similar to the method in this chapter and cannot be selected. The statistical result is that 50.4% of voters think the method in this chapter is better, 38.2% of voters think the previous method is better, and 11.4% of voters cannot choose. Figure 5 shows some of the options in the subjective investigation.

The second line is the aging face image obtained by the previous method, which are [7] face image of age 50+, [9] face image of age 51+ and [10] face image of age 50+. The third line is the aging face image obtained by using the popular aging app and the previous method, which are the face image with the age increase of 30 years by the method [11] and the face image with the age increase by 20 years by the method [12]. Images and [13] face images aged 60–80, [13] face images aged 51–60, and [14] face images aged 41–50.

5.4 Experimental Quantitative Evaluation

We made a quantitative assessment of the results. There are two key evaluation indicators for age development, namely the accuracy of aging and the consistency of identity. This section will introduce the evaluation results of the accuracy of aging and the retention of identity information on the Face++ API [15]. We compare the performance of this method with CAAE method and IPCGAN method.

Assessment of Aging Accuracy. Estimate the age distribution of the real image and the generated aging face image in each age group. The smaller the difference between the average age, the more accurate the simulation of the aging effect. On UTK FACE and CACD, the face images of 11–20 years old are regarded as test samples, and the corresponding test samples in the other 4 age groups (21–30, 31–40, 41–50, 51+) are synthesized Aging synthetic human face. Table 1 is the experimental data of age aging accuracy, showing the age estimation results of UTK FACE and CACD. The difference in the lower layer of the table represents the difference between the average age of the real image. By comparing the difference, it is found that our method is always better than the other two methods in all age groups, which proves the effectiveness of the method in the accuracy of aging effect simulation.

Table 1. Ageing accuracy test results.

Age distributions								
UTK FACE					CACD			
Age group	21–30	31–40	41–50	51+	21–30	31–40	41–50	51+
Generic	26.31	36.51	45.12	53.86	30.67	38.68	46.14	54.39
Syntheic	26.19	35.81	42.33	50.14	30.13	38.09	45.26	53.18
Deviation from the mean age of generic images (in absolute value)								
CAAE	2.19	6.99	9.33	16.09	2.55	5.31	11.21	17.47
IPCGAN	0.6	2.93	6.47	8.84	1.72	3.47	5.18	7.17
ACGAN	0.12	0.7	2.79	3.72	0.36	0.59	0.88	1.21

Table 2. Identity information consistency experiment results.

Verification confidence								
UTK FACE					CACD			
Age group	21–30	31–40	41–50	51+	21–30	31–40	41–50	51+
11–20	95.72	93.12	91.25	90.88	94.25	93.46	93.14	92.89
21–30	–	94.82	92.57	91.76	–	94.19	93.76	93.11
31–40	–	–	93.04	92.45	–	–	–	93.52
41–50	–	–	–	92.64	–	–	–	93.88
Verication Rate (%) between Young and Aged Faces (threshold = 76.5, FAR = 1e−5)								
CAAE	40.12	38.15	37.62	37.33	60.81	57.23	56.11	53.96
IPCGAN	100	99.28	99.36	98.57	100	99.28	98.97	98.52
ACGAN	100	100	98.92	97.26	100	99.84	99.12	98.74

Identity Information Maintenance Evaluation. A facial verification experiment was conducted to investigate whether the identity information was retained during the facial aging process. We used Face++ API to continue to verify the identity of the identity information and compared the aging synthetic faces of the same sample with different age groups. The results of the face verification experiment are shown in Table 2. The verification confidence level above represents the mapping between the two age groups, and the verification rate below represents the verification rate of all methods. The higher the verification rate, the stronger the method's ability to retain identity.

It can be seen that compared with the other two methods, CAAE has a poor ability to retain identity information. On CACD, our method achieves the highest verification rate in the first three groups of age translations, indicating that the proposed method achieves permanent retention of identity information during facial aging.

6   Conclusion

In this article, we propose a new method of face aging based on hybrid domain attention mechanism to generate anti-network. A large number of experiments show that this method can synthesize aging faces while ensuring the aging effect and the requirements of identity information.

References

1. Zhang, Z.F., Song, Y., Qi, H.R.: Progression/regression by conditional adversarial autoencoder. In: IEEE Conference on Computer Vision and Pattern Recognition (2017). https://doi.org/10.1109/CVPR.2017.463
2. Perarnau, G., van de Weijer, J., Álvarez, J.M., Raducanu, B.: Invertible conditional GANs for image editing. In: IEEE Conference and Workshop on Neural Information Processing Systems (2016)
3. Woo, S.H., Park, J.C., Lee, J.-Y., Kweon, I.S.: CBAM: convolutional block attention module. In: Ferrari, V., Hebert, M., Sminchisescu, C., Weiss, Y. (eds.) ECCV 2018. LNCS, vol. 11211, pp. 3–19. Springer, Cham (2018). https://doi.org/10.1007/978-3-030-01234-2_1
4. Johnson, J., Alahi, A., Fei-Fei, L.: Perceptual losses for real-time style transfer and super-resolution. In: Leibe, B., Matas, J., Sebe, N., Welling, M. (eds.) ECCV 2016. LNCS, vol. 9906, pp. 694–711. Springer, Cham (2016). https://doi.org/10.1007/978-3-319-46475-6_43
5. Qassim, H., Verma, A., Feinzimer, D.: Compressed residual-VGG16 CNN model for big data places image recognition. In: 2018 IEEE 8th Annual Computing and Communication Workshop and Conference (CCWC), pp. 169–175. IEEE (2018)
6. Chen, Y.W.: Face detection and facial key point location based on improved MTCNN model. Donghua University (2019)
7. Wang, Z.X., Tang, W.L., Gao, S.: Face aging with identity-preserved conditional generative adversarial networks. In: IEEE Conference on Computer Vision and Pattern Recognition (2018)
8. OldBooth. https://apps.apple.com/cn/app/id357467791
9. Li, Q., Liu, Y.F., Sun, Z.N.: Age Progression and Regression with Spatial Attention Modules (2019). https://arxiv.org/pdf/1903.02133.pdf

10. Yang, H., Huang, D., Wang, Y., Jain, A.K.: Learning face age progression: a pyramid architecture of GANs. In: IEEE Conference on Computer Vision and Pattern Recognition, pp. 31–39 (2018)
11. AgingBooth. https://apps.apple.com/cn/app/id1056567576
12. oldify. https://apps.apple.com/cn/app/bian-lao-2-oldify-2-face-your/id621561671
13. Wang, W., et al.: Recurrent face aging. In: IEEE Conference on Computer Vision and Pattern Recognition, pp. 2378–2386 (2016)
14. Shu, X., Tang, J., Lai, H., Liu, L., Yan, S.: Personalized age progression with aging dictionary. In: IEEE International Conference on Computer Vision, pp. 3970–3978 (2015)
15. Face++ research toolkit. www.faceplusplus.com/

NCLRNet: A Shallow Network and Non-convex Low-Rank Based Fabric Defect Detection

Ban Jiang[1], Chunlei Li[1(✉)], Zhoufeng Liu[1], Yaru Zhao[1], and Shuili Tang[2]

[1] School of Electrical and Information Engineering,
Zhongyuan University of Technology, Zhengzhou 450007, China
lichunlei1979@sina.com
[2] Hengtian Heavy Industry Co., Ltd., Zhengzhou 450001, China

Abstract. Fabric images have complex and regular texture features, and defects destroy this regularity, which can be considered as sparse parts in background. Low rank representation technique has been proven applicable in fabric defect detection, which decomposes fabric image into sparse parts and redundant background. Traditional low-rank representation model is resolved by convex surrogate, which results in an inaccurate solution. In addition, the performance of low-rank representation model relies on the characterization capabilities of feature descriptor. But the hand-crafted features cannot effectively describe the complex fabric texture. To solve these issues, we propose a fabric defect detection algorithm based on a shallow network and Non-convex Low rank representation (NCLRNet). In this process, we design a shallow convolutional neural network to improve the efficiency of feature extraction, and the non-convex method is introduced into the low rank representation model to get the accurate solution. Moreover, the detection results of different feature layers are fused together by the double low rank matrix representation algorithm to achieve a better detection performance. Experimental results on fabric images demonstrate the effectiveness and robustness of our proposed method.

Keywords: Fabric defect detection · Low rank representation · Non-convex · Neural networks

1 Introduction

With the industrial revolution, traditional hand-knitting industry has been replaced by modern machinery manufacturing equipments. Despite evolution

This work was supported by NSFC (No. U1804157), Henan science and technology innovation team (CXTD2017091), IRTSTHN (18IRTSTHN013), Scientific research projects of colleges and universities in Henan Province (19A510027, 16A540003), Program for Interdisciplinary Direction Team in Zhongyuan University of Technology.

G. Zhai et al. (Eds.): IFTC 2020, CCIS 1390, pp. 169–180, 2021.
https://doi.org/10.1007/978-981-16-1194-0_15

in manufacturing processes, the occurrence of defects in fabrics during the production process is still inevitable, which largely affects the value and sales of textiles. At present, most domestic production lines are manually inspected by skilled workers, thus their accuracy and speed are subjectively affected by the workers [1]. Therefore, it is urgent to seek efficient, high-precision, stable and adaptable detection models to replace traditional manual detection methods.

Defect detection technique based on machine vision has stable and objective detection results, and has been a research hotspot over the past few years. The complexity texture and various kinds of defects in the fabric images, making it difficult to detect defects of fabric images. The existing fabric defect detection algorithms based on machine vision are mainly divided into four categories: statistical-based [2], spectral-based [3], dictionary learning based [4] and model-based methods [5]. Statistical-based methods first divide the fabric image into several blocks, then calculate the statistical characteristics of each image block, and finally, identifie the image blocks with different statistical characteristics as defects. However, such methods are only applicable to certain kinds of defects and lack adaptability. Spectral-based methods transform the image into frequency domain and then adopt energy criterion for defect detection. The detection performance of these methods depend on the selected filter bank and their computational complexity are too high. Dictionary learning based methods reconstruct the defect-free image by dictionary, and then compare with the original image to realize defect detection, but its detection results are affected by dictionary selection. In the model-based method, fabric texture is modeled as a random process, defect detection is regarded as a hypothesis test problem of statistical information derived from the model. However, the results of this method for small size defects are not satisfactory.

Low-rank representation (LRR) model has been proved effective to recover low-rank and noise matrices from a given observation matrix contaminated by noise [6], and has been applied in many computer vision fields, including object detection [7] and image classification [8], etc. For fabric detect detection, the background is usually macroscopically uniform and has high redundancy, which can be considered as a low rank part. Defect regions deviate from this subspace can be considered as a sparse part. Therefore, LRR is suitable for fabric defect detection. Li et al. [9] proposed a low rank representation algorithm based on biological vision model. Li et al. [7] proposed a defect detection algorithm based on low rank by using eigenvalue decomposition instead of singular value decomposition. These methods adopt convex optimization in solving stage, which leads to poor accuracy.

Meanwhile, effective feature descriptors can enlarge the gap between background and defect, so as to improve the performance of low rank model. Therefore, it is crucial to design an efficient feature descriptor for LRR-based models. Recently, due to the powerful feature representation ability of convolutional neural network (CNN) in various machine vision filed, which perform extraordinary superiority than traditional hand-crafted features [10]. Therefore, we take advantages of deep features in representing images. However, the existing convolution neural networks, such as VGG16 [11], often have many convolution layers which are not suitable for characterizing fabric defects. Compared with other detection objects such as human face and pedestrian, the fabric image is relatively simple, and it is redundancy to adopt too many layers to represent fabric image. Therefore, we decided to design a shallow convolution neural network with only several convolution layers, which is specially used to extract the shallow features of fabric images.

In previous work, we noticed that the detection results generated by a single feature layer are often not ideal. Considering that the detection results generated by each layer always have a higher significance at the defect location, while the defect-free area has a lower significance. Therefore, the DLRMR [12] is adopted to fuse the detection structure of a single layer to generate the final detection result.

In this paper, a fabric defect detection algorithm based on shallow convolutional neural network (S-NET) and non-convex low rank representation (NLRR) is proposed. The contributions are as follows

1) Designed a shallow convolutional network to extract fabric features, which improves the characterization ability of fabric features.
2) Integrating non-convex regularization to improve the accuracy of solution.

2   Proposed Method

Firstly, we established a shallow convolutional neural network (S-NET) with three convolutional layers to represent the fabric image. Then a non-convex NLRR model is constructed, which can detect fabric defect with a more accurate detection result. In addition, the DLRMR is used to fuse the saliency maps obtained from different convolutional layers to obtain a more comprehensive detection result. Finally, the defect region is located by threshold segmentation algorithm. The flowchart is shown in Fig. 1.

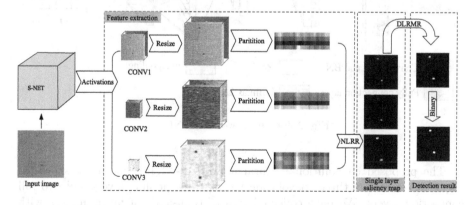

Fig. 1. The flowchart of the proposed method.

2.1 Feature Extraction

An effective representation of features is very important for the method based on low rank. Recent years, convolution neural network has made great progress in image processing. In fact, CNN can be regarded as a transferable feature extractor, which can automatically represent representative features through a continuous propagation channel from layer to layer, and most importantly, we do not need to design complex hand-crafted feature descriptors. It is recognized that Deep features extracted by CNN are more universal and portable than traditional hand-crafted features [10]. Inspired by this, the CNN-based deep features are adopted to characterize fabric images in this paper.

VGG16 [11], as a classic deep convolution neural network, is widely used in the machine vision. The features extracted from its shallow layer tend to represent edge information, and with the increase of the number of layers, the extracted features will be more abstract. However, with respect to complex natural scene images, it is detrimental to represent fabric image using CNN with excessive convolution layers. Texture information, which plays an important role in fabric image detection, is mainly reflected in the edge information. Therefore, we decided to design a customized convolutional neural network with fewer convolutional layers, which is dedicated to extracting the shallow features of fabric image.

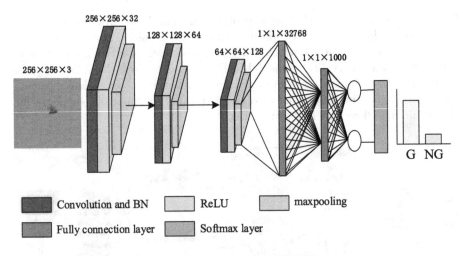

Fig. 2. The framework of S-NET.

The proposed convolutional neural network S-NET structure is shown in Fig. 2. It consists of three convolution layers, three pooling layers and two full connection layers. We have collected tens of thousands of fabric images with linear array camera, and trained the network with defect free images as positive samples and defect images as negative samples. Considering the inconsistency of feature maps generated by convolution and pooling operations, these deep feature maps are adjusted to the same size before the next section.

2.2   Model Construction

Normal fabric images are formed by regular interlacing of warp and weft, but the appearance of defects destroy the regularity. Therefore, the background can usually be regarded as a low rank part. With respect to background, the defect usually occupies a smaller size and can be considered as sparse part. The LRR has been shown to recover low-rank and noise matrices from a given observation matrix contaminated by noise [6]. Therefore, the LRR can be used to deal with fabric defect detection. This can be achieved by minimizing the following problems:

$$\min_{L,E} \text{rank}(L) + \lambda(\|E\|_{2,0}) \quad s.t. \ D = AL + E \tag{1}$$

Where D is the deep feature matrix, L and E are low-rank matrix and sparse matrix respectively. A is a dictionary. $\lambda > 0$ is a balance factor.

Since $rank(L)$ and $\|E\|_{2,0}$ are a non-convex combination optimization function [13]. It is an NP-hard problem, so we often relax it to the following convex optimization problems:

$$\min_{L,E} \|L\|_* + \lambda(\|E\|_{2,1}) \quad s.t. \ D = AL + E \tag{2}$$

Where $\| \cdot \|_*$ is matrix nuclear norm, $\| \cdot \|_{2,1} = \sum_{i=1}^{n} \|[\cdot]_{:,i}\|_2$.

In Eq. (2), we can choose the observation matrix D as the dictionary matrix and get the following problems [6]:

$$\min_{L,E} \|L\|_* + \lambda(\|E\|_{2,1}) \quad s.t. \ D = DL + E \tag{3}$$

However, convex relaxation method will produce imprecise results and affect the final performance. Non-convex optimization is proved to be able to get more accurate estimates. Therefore, non-convex regularization is integrated into the LRR model:

$$\min_{L,E} \|L\|_{w,S_p}^p + \lambda\|E\|_{2,1} \quad s.t. \ D = DL + E \tag{4}$$

Where $\| \cdot \|_{w,S_p} = \left(\sum_{i=1}^{\min(m,n)} w_i \sigma_i^p \right)^{1/p}$ is the non-convex relaxation of $rank(\cdot)$ based on weighted nuclear norm [14] and Schatten p norm [15].

For the convenience of solving, we introduce the intermediate variable $J = E$:

$$\min_{L,E} \|J\|_{w,S_p}^p + \lambda\|E\|_{2,1} \quad s.t. \ D = DL + E, \ J = L \tag{5}$$

Algorithm 1. Solving NLRR

Input: D; $\lambda > 0$;

Initialize: $L^0 = 0$, $E^0 = 0$, $J^0 = 0$, $Y_1^0 = 0$, $Y_2^0 = 0$, $\mu^0 = 1e-4$, $\mu^{\max} = 10^5$, $k = 0$, $\rho = 1.1$, $tol = 1e-8$

while not converged **do**

1. Update J^{k+1}:

$$\arg\min_J \xi(J^k, E^k, D, Y_1^k, Y_2^k, \mu^k)$$
$$= \arg\min_J \frac{1}{\mu}\|J^k\|_{w,S_p}^p + \frac{1}{2}\|J^k - (L^k + \frac{Y_2^k}{\mu^k})\|_F^2$$

2. Update L^{k+1}:

$$L = (I + D^T D)^{-1}(D^T D - D^T E + J^{k+1} + \frac{D^T Y_1^k - Y_2^k}{\mu^k})$$

3. Update E^{k+1}:

$$\arg\min_E \xi(J^{k+1}, E^k, D, Y_1^k, Y_2^k, \mu^k)$$
$$= \arg\min_E \frac{\lambda}{\mu}\|E^k\|_{2,1} + \frac{1}{2}\|E^k - (D - DL^k + \frac{Y_1^k}{\mu^k})\|_F^2$$

4. Update Y_1^{k+1}, Y_2^{k+1} and μ^{k+1}:

$$Y_1^{k+1} = Y_1^k + \mu^k(D - DL^{k+1} - E^{k+1})$$
$$Y_2^{k+1} = Y_2^k + \mu^k(L^{k+1} - J^{k+1})$$
$$\mu^{k+1} = \min(\mu_{\max}, \rho\mu^k)$$

5. Check the convergence condition:

$$\|D - DL^{k+1} - E^{k+1}\|_\infty < tol \quad and \quad \|L^{k+1} - J^{k+1}\|_\infty < tol$$

6. $k = k + 1$

end while

Output: E^{k+1}

Then, the Langrange function of formula (5) is obtained:

$$
L(J, E, D, Y_1, Y_2, \mu) \\
= \|J\|_{w,S_p}^p + \lambda\|E\|_{2,1} + \langle Y_1, D - DL - E\rangle + \langle Y_2, L - J\rangle \qquad (6) \\
+ \frac{\mu}{2}\left(\|D - DL - E\|_F^2 + \|L - J\|_F^2\right)
$$

Where Y_1 and Y_2 are the Lagrange multipliers, $\langle\cdot\rangle$ indicate the inner product, $\|\cdot\|_F$ is Frobenius norm, μ is a penalty parameter. The ADMM model [16] is adopted to solve the optimization problem, and the specific steps are shown in Algorithm 1:

Step 1 can be solved by generalized soft threshold (GST) [17], while step 3 can be solved by Lemma 1.

Lemma 1 [18]: *For a given matrix Q, if W^* is the optimal solution of the following optimization problem:*

$$\min_{W} \alpha \|W\|_{2,1} + \frac{1}{2}\|W - Q\|_F^2 \tag{7}$$

then we can obtain W^* by the following formula

$$W_{:,i}^* = \begin{cases} \frac{\|Q_{:,i}\|_2 - \alpha}{\|Q_{:,i}\|_2} Q_{:,i}, & if \ \|Q_{:,i}\|_2 > \alpha \\ 0, & \text{otherwise.} \end{cases} \tag{8}$$

After the decomposition by NLRR, each convolution layer can get a sparse matrix, and then combine it into a new matrix. Next, the DLRMR is used to fuse it [12]. Finally, the position of defect region is obtained by threshold segmentation algorithm.

3   Experiment Result

In this section, we used defective fabric imagesobtained on the cloth inspection machine through the line array camera as the experimental dataset. The performance is conducted by comparing the difference between the detection results and the manually calibrated GT image. The parameters in each experiment are fixed, and the resolution of the input fabric images are set to 256 pixels 256 pixels.

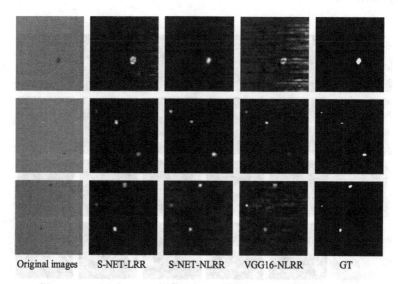

Original images   S-NET-LRR   S-NET-NLRR   VGG16-NLRR   GT

Fig. 3. Comparison of detection results based on different CNN and LRR-based methods. The first and last columns are the original image and GT image, respectively. The second column is the detection result based on the S-NET and LRR method. The third column is based on the detection results of the S-NET and NLRR method, and the fourth column is based on the detection results of the VGG16 and NLRR method.

3.1 Performance Evaluation of Different Deep Features

We compare detection results based on CNN and LRR-based methods. We set the following three methods as test Benchmarkes: methods based on S-NET and LRR, methods based on S-NET and NLRR, and methods based on VGG16 and NLRR. It should be noted that here we only use a single convolution layer to extract features, where the convolution layer used in S-NET is conv1, and the convolution layer used in VGG16 is conv1_2. The detection results are shown in Fig. 3. The first and last columns are the original image and GT image, respectively. The second column is the detection result based on the S-NET and LRR method. The third column is based on the detection results of the S-NET and NLRR method, and the fourth column is based on the detection results of the VGG16 and NLRR method. From the detection results of the third and fourth column, we can see that the detection results based on VGG16 are significantly worse than those based on S-NET. There is serious noise in the detection results based on VGG16, which proves the effectiveness of S-NET. From the second and third column, Although the method based on S-NET and LRR can also locate the position of the defect area, its positioning accuracy is inferior, especially the detection result of the first image is much larger than the actual defect area. We integrate the non-convex method into LRR to improve the accuracy of the solution and achieve the expected results. For example, in the second image, only the method proposed in this paper can detect all the defect locations, while the original LRR model and the method using vgg16 have the phenomenon of missing detection.

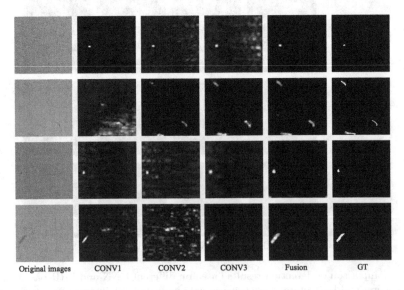

Fig. 4. Compare the detection results of deep features from different convolution layers in S-NET. The first and last columns are the original image and GT image, respectively. From the second to the fourth column, the detection results of Conv1, Conv2 and Conv3 are listed. The fifth column is the fusion result of three-layer detection results.

In addition, the detection results of deep features from different convolution layers in S-NET are compared in Fig. 4, and the detection results after double low rank matrix representation fusion is also shown. It can be seen that there are a lot of noises in the saliency maps generated by single convolution layer features, and most of them are suppressed after DLRMR fusion. Combined with Fig. 3 and Fig. 4, we find that the final saliency image not only has a high detection accuracy, but also suppresses most of the noise.

3.2   Comparison with State-of-the-Art

Qualitative Evaluations: The proposed method is compared with other methods, such as histogram of oriented gradient (HOG) [19], least squares regression (LSR) [20], and the Gabor filter and low-rank decomposition (GABOR) [21]. The experimental results are shown in Fig. 5. The first and last columns are the original image and GT image, respectively. From the second column to the fifth column, the detection results of HOG, LSR, Gabor and our method are listed respectively. The sixth column is a binary segmentation image of NLRR detection results.

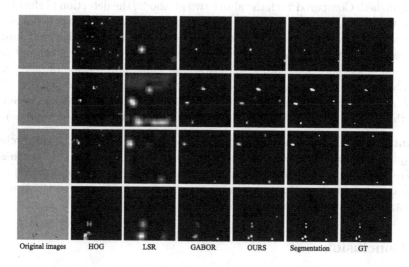

Original images   HOG   LSR   GABOR   OURS   Segmentation   GT

Fig. 5. Comparison the results using different detection methods. The first and last columns are the original image and GT image, respectively. From the second to the fifth column, the detection results of HOG, LSR, GABOR and OURS are listed. The sixth column is the binary segmentation image of the NLRR detection result.

As can be seen from Fig. 5, the saliency image generated by hog method can locate the location of some defects, but it contains more serious noise, and the detected defect areas are relatively scattered. LSR method can detect all defects, but the defect area detected by LSR method is much larger than the actual defect

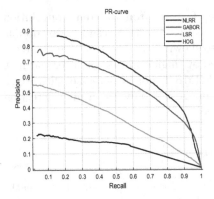
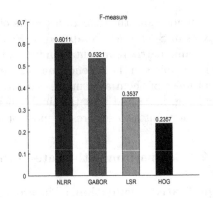

Fig. 6. Quantitative comparison of four methods: PR curve on the left and F-measure on the right.

area, resulting in poor detection accuracy. In particular, the detection result of the fourth image is much larger than that of the GT image. And the defects with smaller distance are connected together in saliency image and cannot be distinguished. Compared with the above two methods, the detection performance of the GABOR method has been greatly improved, but it still has deficiencies. For example, it is sensitive to detect small defects, especially is defect that similar to background texture. The saliency map generated by our method can not only detect all defect locations, but also outline the shape information of defects. In the second and fourth images, only our method can detect all the defects, while other methods either fail to detect or have serious errors. In conclusion, it can be seen that our method has the highest detection accuracy and the lowest noise.

Quantitative Evaluations: Two criteria are used to evaluate the comprehensive quality of different methods, including the precision recall (PR) curve and F-measure. From Fig. 6, the area of PR curve under the curve of our proposed method is larger than that of other methods and the F-measure is also the largest, which revels the superiority of our proposed method.

4   Conclusion

In this paper, we proposed a fabric defect detection algorithm based on S-NET and NLRR. To solve the problem that hand-crafted descriptors cannot comprehensive represent the texture of fabric, we establish a shallow neural network with three convolution layers to better represent the characteristics of fabric image. Then, LRR is used to separate the defective part from the fabric image. In addition, the non-convex optimization is used in the solution process of the LRR model, which improves the solution accuracy. Finally, the detection results of each convolution layer are fused to obtain the optimal saliency map by using the DLRMR. Experiments on fabric images show that this method is better than the existing methods. Besides, the method can also be applied to remote sensing technology and other surface anomaly detection, and has broad development prospects.

References

1. Wang, M., Li, Y., Du, S.: Research progress of defect detection method based on machine vision. Adv. Text. Technol. **27**(05), 57–61 (2019)
2. Shi, M., Fu, R., Guo, Y., et al.: Fabric defect detection using local contrast deviations. Multimed. Tools Appl. **52**(1), 147–157 (2011)
3. Tolba, A.S.: Fast defect detection in homogeneous flat surface products. Expert Syst. Appl. **38**, 12339–12347 (2011)
4. Zhoufeng, L., Lei, Y., Chunlei, L.I., et al.: Fabric defect detection algorithm based on sparse optimization. J. Text. Res. **37**, 56–63 (2016)
5. Li, M., Cui, S., Xie, Z.: Application of Gaussian mixture model on defect detection of print fabric. J. Text. Res. **36**(8), 94–98 (2015)
6. Liu, G., Lin, Z., Yan, S., et al.: Robust recovery of subspace structures by low-rank representation. IEEE Trans. Pattern Anal. Mach. Intell. **35**(1), 171–184 (2013)
7. Li, P., Liang, J., Shen, X., et al.: Textile fabric defect detection based on low-rank representation. Multimed. Tools Appl. **78**(3), 1–26 (2017)
8. Zhang, T., Ghanem, B., Liu, S., et al.: Low-rank sparse coding for image classification. In: International Conference on Computer Vision. IEEE Computer Society (2013)
9. Li, C., Gao, G., Liu, Z., et al.: Fabric defect detection based on biological vision modeling. IEEE Access 1 (2018)
10. Mei, S., Jiang, R., Ji, J., et al.: Invariant feature extraction for image classification via multichannel convolutional neural network. In: 2017 International Symposium on Intelligent Signal Processing and Communication Systems (ISPACS), pp. 491–495. IEEE (2017)
11. Simonyan, K., Zisserman, A.: Very deep convolutional networks for large-scale image recognition. Comput. Sci. (2014)
12. Li, J., Luo, L., Zhang, F., et al.: Double low rank matrix recovery for saliency fusion. IEEE Trans. Image Process. **25**(9), 1 (2016)
13. Liu, G., Lin, Z., Yu, Y.: Robust subspace segmentation by low-rank representation. In: International Conference on Machine Learning. DBLP (2010)
14. Gu, S., Xie, Q., Meng, D., et al.: Weighted nuclear norm minimization and its applications to low level vision. Int. J. Comput. Vis. **121**(2), 183–208 (2017). International Conference on Machine Learning, Haifa, Israel, pp. 663–670
15. Nie, F., Huang, H., Ding, C.: Low-rank matrix recovery via efficient schatten p-norm minimization. In: Twenty-Sixth AAAI Conference on Artificial Intelligence (2012)
16. Lin, Z., Liu, R., Su, Z.: Linearized alternating direction method with adaptive penalty for low-rank representation. In: Advances in Neural Information Processing Systems, pp. 612–620 (2011)
17. Zuo, W., Meng, D., Zhang, L., et al.: A generalized iterated shrinkage algorithm for non-convex sparse coding. In: Proceedings of the IEEE International Conference on Computer Vision, pp. 217–224 (2013)
18. Yang, J., Yin, W., Zhang, Y., et al.: A fast algorithm for edge-preserving variational multichannel image restoration. SIAM J. Imaging Sci. **2**(2), 569–592 (2009)

19. Li, C., Gao, G., Liu, Z., et al.: Fabric defect detection algorithm based on histogram of oriented gradient and low-rank decomposition. J. Text. Res. **38**(3), 153–158 (2017)
20. Cao, J., Zhang, J., Wen, Z., et al.: Fabric defect inspection using prior knowledge guided least squares regression. Multimed. Tools Appl. **76**(3), 4141–4157 (2017)
21. Zhang, D., Gao, G., Li, C.: Fabric defect detection algorithm based on Gabor filter and low-rank decomposition. In: Eighth International Conference on Digital Image Processing. International Society for Optics and Photonics (2016)

Saliency Model Based on Discriminative Feature and Bi-directional Message Interaction for Fabric Defect Detection

Zhoufeng Liu[✉], Menghan Wang, Chunlei Li, Zhenduo Guo, and Jinjin Wang

Zhongyuan University of Technology, ZhengZhou 450007, China
lzhoufeng@hotmail.com

Abstract. Due to the complexity of the texture background and the diversity of the defect types of the fabric image, the traditional method of fabric defect detection shows poor detection performance. Recent advances on salient object detection benefit from Fully Convolutional Neural Network (FCN) and achieve the good performance. Meanwhile, the deficiencies in a fabric image are salient compared to the texture background, so the saliency model is very feasible for fabric defect detection. In this paper, we propose a novel saliency model based on discriminative feature and bi-directional message interaction for fabric defect detection. Firstly, we design a multi-scale attention-guided feature extraction module in which the multi-scale context-aware feature extraction block and channel attention block are respectively used to capture multi-scale contextual information and assign greater weight to more discriminative features corresponding to the right fabric defect scale. Then a bi-directional message interaction module is designed to promote the effectiveness of feature with specific resolution by interacting message along both directions, which further improves the availability of the feature extraction. After the bi-directional message interaction module, we use a cross-level contrast feature extraction module, which elevates features with locally strong contrast along each resolution axis, to predict saliency maps. Finally, the predicted saliency maps are efficiently merged to produce the final prediction result. We conduct extensive experiments to evaluate our net and experiment results demonstrate that the proposed method outperforms the state-of-the-art approaches.

Keywords: Fabric defect detection · Saliency model · Discriminative feature · FCN

This work was supported by NSFC (No. 61772576, 61379113, U1804157), Science and technology innovation talent project of Education Department of Henan Province (17HASTIT019), The Henan Science Fund for Distinguished Young Scholars (184100510002), Henan science and technology innovation team (CXTD2017091), IRTSTHN (18IRTSTHN013), Scientific research projects of colleges and universities in Henan Province (19A510027, 16A540003), Program for Interdisciplinary Direction Team in Zhongyuan University of Technology.

G. Zhai et al. (Eds.): IFTC 2020, CCIS 1390, pp. 181–193, 2021.
https://doi.org/10.1007/978-981-16-1194-0_16

1 Introduction

Fabric defect detection in the textile industry is a basic and challenging problem, whose goal is to identify and locate deficiencies rapidly and accurately in a given fabric image. Traditional methods mostly rely on human eyes to capture defects for quality control and assurance of textiles, but the manual method has onerous inspection cost and impairs the health of the inspectors. Meanwhile, the success rate of manual inspection was only 60%–75% [1]. Luckily, benefiting from the mushroom growth of computer vision, the realization of automatic fabric defect detection becomes an effective path to guarantee the quality of fabrics.

Benefiting from the enlightenment of human visual system, salient object detection aims to imitate this system which automatically discerns and locates predominant objects of a visual scene. The deficiencies in a fabric image correspond to the foreground objects, so saliency model is very feasible for fabric defect detection. In recent years, several attempts have been performed and many valued models have been proposed in saliency prediction. Although these models [2,3,5–7,9,10] have shown promising results, some problems remain when they are applied to fabric images. Firstly, most existing saliency detection models [7,11] based on FCN stack single scale convolutional layers and max pooling layers successively to generate deep-level features. Due to fabric defect appear in various sizes, the correct size of defect object cannot be captured using only single scale convolution operation, and the limited receptive fields makes the network unable to learn the features containing rich context information, thus failing to accurately detect various types of fabric defects. Secondly, many previous papers directly use the deep-level features to perform the prediction task [8,13,14] or try to incorporate multi-level features in a unidirectional manner for saliency map prediction [4,12,15,16]. For instance, Lou et al. [16] propose non-local deep feature (NLDF) model, which adopt the local contrast features through subtracting the features obtained by average pooling layer and simply deconvolution layer to integrate features from different levels. Another work by Hou et al. [15] build several short connections from deep layers to shallow layers to fuse features of different layers. Nevertheless, these unidirectional frameworks are merely performed from deep side output layers to shallow side output layers, neglecting the knowledge transmission in the reverse direction. Therefore, the high-level outputs inevitably lack spatial detail information embraced in shallow layers. Correspondingly, insufficient contextual information would lead to inaccurate predictions or even wrong prediction results. To identify defective parts of a fabric image, we would require both local detailed information and global semantic knowledge. Hence, the effective combination of multi-level features is a key step in the detection model. In view of above discussion, the valid extraction of multi-scale feature maps and the Reasonable integration of multi-layer side outputs can boost the performance of fabric defect detection.

In this paper, we propose a novel saliency model based on discriminative feature and bi-directional message interaction for fabric defect detection. For the first problem, we use a multi-scale attention-guided feature extraction module in which the multi-scale context-aware feature extraction block (MCFEB) and channel attention block (CAB) are used to capture multi-scale contextual information and reweight multi-scale features respectively. Concretely, the MCFEB obtain multiple feature maps for each side output via stacking multiple convolutional layers with different receptive fields, and the CAB assign different weights to multi-scale features by reweighting operation. For the second problem, we propose a bi-directional message interaction module as a modified version of the gated bi-directional message passing module (GBMPM) in the [18]. The more global high-level semantic knowledge from deeper layers are transmitted to shallower layers, while low-level detailed information contained in shallower layers are transmitted in the reverse direction, to form bi-directional message interaction module. Serially, we introduce the cross-level contrast features extraction module to promote features with locally strong contrast along cross-level of each resolution axis. Finally, multi-level feature maps are integrated to generate final saliency map.

To summarize, this paper makes three following contributions:

1. With a multi-scale attention-guided feature extraction module, our model is able to generate features that covers a very large-scale range and assign more attention to more discriminative features corresponding to the right fabric defect scale.
2. A bi-directional message interaction module is designed as a modified version of the GBMPM to integrate multi-level feature maps more suitable for fabric defect detection.
3. A cross-level contrast feature extraction module is introduced to promote features with strong local contrast along each resolution axis and integrate multi-level features effectively for prediction task.

2   Proposed Method

In this section, we will describe the proposed framework for fabric defect detection and some implementation details. We describe the multi-scale attention-guided feature extraction module (MAFEM) of our proposed network in Sect. 2.2, and then provides the implementation of the bi-directional message interaction module (BMIM) in Sect. 2.3. Section 2.4. furnishes the detailed depiction of the cross-level contrast feature extraction module (CCFEM). Before that, let us first take a look at the overall framework of our proposed method in Sect. 2.1.

2.1   Overview of Network Architecture

In this paper, we propose a novel saliency model based on discriminative feature and bi-directional message interaction to address fabric defect detection problem. Our network consists of three components: multi-scale attention-guided feature extraction module, bi-directional message interaction module and cross-level contrast feature extraction module. The overall framework is shown in Fig. 1. We tackle the fabric defect detection problem based on FCN. Our proposed model is based on the VGG16 [17] network. Specifically, for purpose of

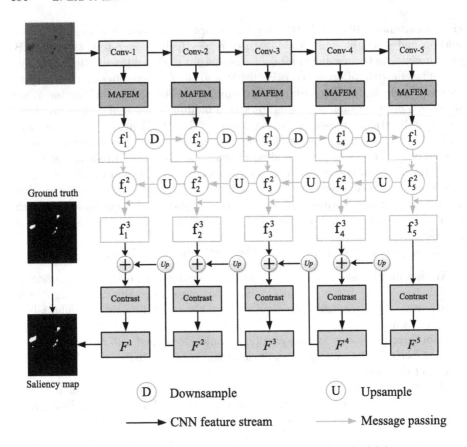

Fig. 1. The overall framework of our proposed model. Each colorful box represents an operating block. We take an RGB image $256 \times 256 \times 3$ as input, and utilize the VGG16 network to extract multi-level features. The multi-scale attention-guided feature extraction module (gray boxes) is designed to generate discriminative features that covers a very large-scale range. Then, the bi-directional message interaction module (orange boxes) is used to integrate multi-level features that generated from different level layers. Finally, the cross-level contrast feature extraction module (green boxes) is introduced, which promote features with strong local contrast along each resolution axis, to predict saliency maps. The predicted multi-level saliency maps are integrated to generate final saliency map. (Color figure online)

adapting the network model to the task of fabric defect detection, we carry out relevant modification operations on VGG16 in advance. We remove all the original fully connected layers and the last max pooling layer. Firstly, we feed the fabric image into the modified VGG16 net to produce multi-level feature maps at five levels. Then, after each level output of the modified VGG16 net, we design to add a multi-scale attention-guided feature extraction module that used to extract multi-scale context-aware features and reweight multi-scale features. As followed, we utilize the bi-directional message interaction module that was

Table 1. Details of MCFEB. The filter with (k*k, c) signify the channel and kernel size are c and k.

Layer	Filter	Kernel size (k)	Output
Conv1-2	k*k, 32	1/3/5/7	256*256*128
Conv2-2	k*k, 64	1/3/5/7	128*128*256
Conv3-3	k*k, 64	1/3/5/7	64*64*256
Conv4-3	k*k, 128	1/3/5/7	32*32*512
Conv5-3	k*k, 128	1/3/5/7	16*16*512

used to incorporate the fine spatial details and semantic knowledge at each level. Finally, we utilize cross-level contrast feature extraction module to promote features with locally strong contrast along cross-level of each resolution axis. And multi-level feature maps are integrated for final saliency prediction.

2.2 Multi-scale Attention-Guided Feature Extraction Module

Visual context information is quite vital to aid fabric defect detection, so a multi-scale attention-guided feature extraction module is designed to capture discriminative multi-scale contextual information. Multi-scale attention-guided feature extraction module can be divided into two sub-block structures: MCFEB and CAB. To reduce the computation, the existing model [18] capture multi-scale contextual information via using dilated convolutional layers with different fields of view and fuse multi-scale features by simple concatenate operation that treat all features equally. Nevertheless, using dilated convolutional layers inevitably drop some significant contextual information as many of fabric defects belongs to minor objects. At the same time, because treating all features equally may introduce unnecessary information misleading the network, only using concatenate operation lacks self-adaptability. Hence, we waive dilated convolution layers and we show the details of the MCFEB in Table 1. MCFEB learn features of defect objects and image context by parallel multiple convolutions. Then, the feature maps are integrated via cross-channel concatenation operation, which can capture the useful knowledge of image context at multiple scales. Finally, channel attention block is used to assign more attention to more discriminative features corresponding to the right fabric defect scale by reweight multi-scale feature maps, and the implementation of the CAB is displayed in Fig. 2.

The input image I with size $W \times H$ is first fed into the VGG16 network to extract multi-level feature maps, which are expressed as $X = \{x_i, i = 1, \ldots, 5\}$ with spatial resolution $\tau = \left[\frac{W}{2^{i-1}}, \frac{H}{2^{i-1}}\right]$. For feature map x_i, we then use four convolutional layers with different receptive fields, which could obtain the useful image context knowledge at different scales. The four parallel convolutional layers have the different convolutional kernel size, which are set to 1, 3, 5 and 7. We combine the multi-scale contextual features via cross-channel concatena-

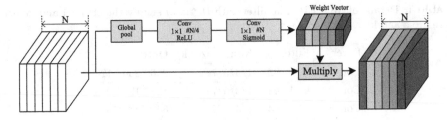

Fig. 2. The operational details of the channel attention block.

tion operation. The we apply CAB to multi-level features, and get multi-scale discriminative features $X^m = \{x_i^m, i = 1, \ldots, 5\}$.

2.3 Bi-directional Message Interaction Module

Sensibly, the knowledge between each layer is isolated. In FCN, the bottom layer extracts the spatial details and the upper layers extract the semantic knowldge. Considering that the information of each layer can be stored and used separately, the unique direction is avoided in a FCN model that straight passes from deep layer to shallow layer or the opposite direction. Therefore, bi-directional message interaction module is added to coalesce information at each level. Compare with the GBMPM, the gate functions are abandoned as repeated convolution operation seriously loses context information from the shallow layer. Through this structure, the spatial details at the bottom layers can receive more guidance from the upper location information, while the shallower layers transfer more fine spatial details to the deeper ones. Therefore, multi-level features can cooperate with each other to produce more accurate results.

It takes feature maps $X^m = \{x_i^m, i = 1, \ldots, 5\}$ with different spatial resolutions as input and outputs features $F^3 = \{f_i^3, i = 1, \ldots, 5\}$. The connections among multi-level side outputs is along two directions in our bi-directional message interaction module. One connection begin with the feature from the bottom layer (*i.e.*, x_1^m) with the maximum resolution $[W, H]$ and ends up with the feature from the top layer (*i.e.*, x_5^m) with the minimum resolution ($[\frac{W}{2^4}, \frac{H}{2^4}]$). The other direction is the opposite. For example, the process of transferring messages from shallower side output layers to deeper side output layers is performed by:

$$f_i^1 = \begin{Bmatrix} \phi\left(x_i^m + Down\left(f_{i-1}^1\right)\right) & , i > 1 \\ f_i^0 & , i = 1 \end{Bmatrix} \tag{1}$$

where $f_i^0 = x_i^m$ with resolution $\tau = [\frac{W}{2^{i-1}}, \frac{H}{2^{i-1}}]$. $\phi()$ is a ReLu activation function. $Down()$ is a average pooling operation with the stride of 2. And f_i^1 represents the updated features after receiving lower-level fine spatial details from f_{i-1}^1. The rightabout of transferring messages from deeper layers to shallower layers is:

$$f_i^2 = \begin{Bmatrix} \phi\left(x_i^m + Up\left(f_{i+1}^2\right)\right) & , i < 5 \\ f_i^0 & , i = 5 \end{Bmatrix} \tag{2}$$

where $Up()$ is a up sampling operation to match the size of lower-level feature maps. And f_i^2 is the updated features after receiving global sematic information from higher-level feature f_{i+1}^2. For generating the better representation of $i-th$ level features, the features are incorporated from both directions as follows:

$$f_i^3 = \text{Conv}\left(\text{Cat}\left(f_i^1, f_i^2\right); \theta_i^3\right) \tag{3}$$

where f_i^3 contains both low-level spatial details and high-level semantic information. $Conv(*; \theta)$ denotes the convolution operation with parameter $\theta = \{W, b\}$. $Cat()$ represents the channel concatenation operation. Through the bi-directional message interaction module, multi-level features f_i^3 can adaptively encode local and global saliency cues for accurate saliency prediction. In this module, MCFEB and CAB work cooperatively to accurately detect fabric defects.

2.4   Cross-Level Contrast Feature Extraction Module

The defects in the fabric image are unique and stand out from the surrounding texture background. Salient features must thus be consistent within the foreground defect object and inside the texture background but be diverse between foreground objects and background region. In order to capture this kind of contrast information, we add a cross-level contrast feature extraction module (CCFEM) to extract and fuse cross-level contrast feature associated to each local feature. In each level, the CCFEM performs an initial conversion to accommodate to the following contrast extraction operation: we perform convolution operation and ReLu function on local features as the original input feature for contrast extraction operations. Then the contrast extraction operation is implemented by subtracting its local average from original input feature. After, a fusion operation is used to fuse the features of double branch from the contrast extraction operation and its original input. Integrating the CCFEMs into the decoder enables the model to adaptively process the spatial neighborhood contrast of different regions during the training phase. The entire process is written as:

$$F^3 = \text{Conv}(\text{Cat}\left(f_i^o, f_i^c\right)) \tag{4}$$

Where F^i represents the output of the $CCFEM^i$. $Conv()$ is a 1×1 convolution layer having the same number of channels with f_i^o to adapt to the following cross-level contrast feature extraction. f_i^o and f_i^c are the $i-th$ level original input feature and its contrast feature, which are respectively computed as follow:

$$f_i^c = f_i^o - \text{Avg}\left(f_i^o\right) \tag{5}$$

$$f_i^o = \begin{cases} \phi\left(\text{con}\,v\left(f_i^3 + Up\left(F^{i+1}\right)\right)\right), i < 5 \\ \phi\left(\text{Conv}\left(f_i^3\right)\right), i = 5 \end{cases} \tag{6}$$

We show the details of the CCFEM in Fig. 3. The cross-level contrast features extraction module is introduced to promote features with strong local contrast

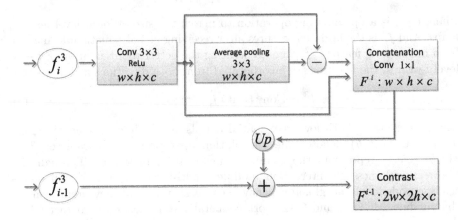

Fig. 3. The operational details of the cross-level contrast feature extraction module.

along each resolution axis, which further integrate multi-level feature maps effectively for final saliency prediction. Furthermore, our fusion loss function in which the consistency-enhanced loss (CEL) is introduced as an aid to the binary cross-entropy loss, guides our model to output saliency maps with higher certainty and less fuzzy salient objects, which have better performance than using only binary cross-entropy loss. The loss function is defined as:

$$L = L_{CEL} + L_{BCE} \tag{7}$$

where consistency-enhanced loss L_{CEL} is computed as:

$$L_{CEL}(\hat{Y}, Y) = \frac{|FP + FN|}{|FP + 2TP + FN|} \tag{8}$$

where Y is the ground-truth, $\hat{Y}$ is the binary prediction, TP, FN and FP represent true-positive, false-negative and false-positive respectively, the calculation is as follows:

$$TP(Y, Y) = \sum_i \hat{y}_i \cdot y_i \tag{9}$$

$$FP(Y, Y) = \sum_i \hat{y}_i \cdot (1 - y_i) \tag{10}$$

$$FN(Y, Y) = \sum_i (1 - \hat{y}_i) \cdot y_i \tag{11}$$

where i is the spatial location of the input image. The binary cross-entropy loss L_{BCE} is computed as:

$$L_{BCE}(\hat{Y}, Y) = -\sum_i^{|Y|} (y_i \log y_i + (1 - y_i) \log (1 - \hat{y}_i)) \tag{12}$$

Where $|Y|$ is the number of pixels in the input image.

3 Experiment

3.1 Experiment Setup

For our model, we use our fabric image dataset which contains 1600 images with scratches, stains and many other types of defects. We divide the dataset into 2 parts: 1100 images for training and the remaining 500 images for testing. Besides, the training set is expanded via flipping fabric images horizontally to alleviate the over-fitting problem. The input fabric images were resized to 256 × 256 for training. Our model is implemented in PyTorch. The weights in the backbone network are initialized with the pretrained weights of VGG16 [17]. All the weights of newly added convolution layers are initialized by the default setting of PyTorch. The momentum SGD optimizer is used to train our network with an initial learning rate of $1e-3$, a weight decay of $5e-4$, and a momentum of 0.9. Moreover, we adopt a poly strategy [19] with the factor of 0.9. Our model is trained to complete the entire training procedure for 50 epochs with a mini-batch of 4.

We use three metrics to evaluate the performance of the proposed model as well as other state-of-the-art salient object detection methods on our testing set. Evaluation metrics include F-measure (F_β), mean-F (F_{avg}) and mean absolute error (MAE). The F-measure is an overall performance indicator, it is computed as:

$$F_\beta = \frac{(1+\beta^2) \cdot \text{Precision} \cdot \text{Recall}}{\beta^2 \cdot \text{Precision} + \text{Recall}} \tag{13}$$

Where $\beta^2 = 0.3$. Furthermore, the mean-F can image the spatial consistency of the prediction results. Hence, we calculate F_{avg} by an adaptive threshold that is twice the mean value of the prediction. And we also calculated the MAE to measure the average difference between predicted saliency map S and ground truth G, which is expressed as:

$$MAE = \frac{1}{W \times H} \sum_{x=1}^{W} \sum_{y=1}^{H} |S(x,y) - G(x,y)| \tag{14}$$

Where W and H is the width and height of a fabric image. In addition, we also trained the advanced saliency models NLDF [16], BMPM [18] and BASNet [20] and compare them with ours. The visual comparisons results and quantitative evaluation results are shown in Fig. 4 and Table 2. Figure 4 shows some representative saliency maps generated by the proposed model as well as other state-of-the-state algorithms. The fabric images are selected from testing dataset. As we can see, our method can accurately detect defect objects. F-measure scores, mean-F scores and MAE scores are given in Table 2. It can be seen that our approach produces the best score across our dataset, which means that our method has a good perception of salient region and can generate accurate saliency prediction maps close to the ground truth masks.

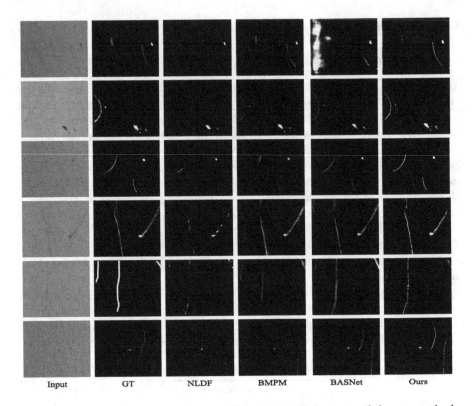

| Input | GT | NLDF | BMPM | BASNet | Ours |

Fig. 4. Visual comparison of the proposed method and the state-of-the-art methods. It is clear that our method generates more accurate saliency maps than others.

3.2   Ablation Analysis

In this section, we build a ablation analyse to illustrate the effectiveness of the MAFEM. Figure 5 and Table 3 show the improvements of the proposed MAFEM from the visual and quantitative perspectives, respectively. To prove its contribution to the model, we remove MAFEM for experiments. It can be easily observed from Fig. 5 that the performance of the network is greatly improved by the proposed module. And their F-measure scores, mean-F scores and MAE scores are shown in Table 3. Therefore, the comparison between BMIM+CCFEM and MAFEM+BMIM+CCFEM verifies that MAFEM contribute to the final result.

Table 2. The maximum F-measure (larger is better), mean-F (larger is better) and MAE (smaller is better) of different detection approaches on the testing dataset.

Method	Max (F_β)	F_{avg}	MAE
NLDF [16]	0.5632	0.4661	0.0041
BMPM [18]	0.5980	0.2332	0.0048
BASNet [20]	0.6058	0.4195	0.0107
Ours	0.6367	0.5352	0.0039

Table 3. The maximum F-measure (larger is better) and MAE (smaller is better) of different detection methods on the testing dataset.

Model setting	Max (F_β)	F_{avg}	MAE
BMIM+CCFEM	0.5922	0.1496	0.0136
MAFEM+BMIM+CCFEM	0.6367	0.5352	0.0039

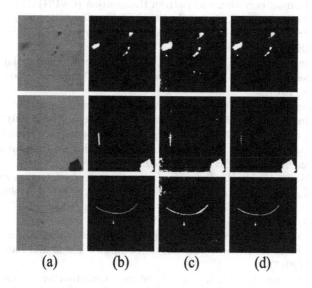

(a)   (b)   (c)   (d)

Fig. 5. Illustrations for the effectiveness of MAFEM. (a) Original images; (b) Ground truth; (c) BMIM+CCFEM; (d) MAFEM+BMIM+CCFEM.

4   Conclusion

In this paper, we investigate the scale variation issue of fabric defects and feature integration issue to design a novel saliency model, for fabric defect detection. Our network consists of multi-scale attention-guided feature extraction module, bi-directional message interaction module and cross-level contrast feature extraction module. Firstly, we use the multi-scale attention-guided feature extraction module to extract multi-scale discriminative contextual information. As followed, we utilize bi-directional message interaction module to incorporate the fine spatial details and semantic knowledge at each level. Finally, cross-level contrast feature extraction module is introduced to promote features with locally strong contrast along cross-level of each resolution axis and integrate multi-level features effectively for final saliency prediction. Experimental results demonstrate that our proposed approach outperforms other state-of-the-art methods under different evaluation metric.

References

1. Srinivasan, K., Dastoor, P.H., Radhakrishnaiah, P., et al.: FDAS: a knowledge-based framework for analysis of defects in woven textile structures. J. Text. Inst. Proc. Abstracts **83**(3), 431–448 (1990)
2. Li, G., Yu, Y.: Visual saliency based on multiscale deep features. In: 2015 IEEE Conference on Computer Vision and Pattern Recognition (CVPR). IEEE (2015)
3. Li, G., Yu, Y.: Deep contrast learning for salient object detection. In: IEEE Conference on Computer Vision and Pattern Recognition (CVPR). IEEE (2016)
4. Tian, Z., Shen, C., Chen, H., et al.: FCOS: fully convolutional one-stage object detection. In: 2019 IEEE/CVF International Conference on Computer Vision (ICCV). IEEE (2020)
5. Liu, N., Han, J., Zhang, D., Wen, S., Liu, T.: Predicting eye fixations using convolutional neural networks. In: IEEE Conference on Computer Vision and Pattern Recognition (2015)
6. Liu, N., Han, J.: DHSNet: deep hierarchical saliency network for salient object detection. In: Computer Vision and Pattern Recognition. IEEE (2016)
7. Wang, L., Lu, H., Ruan, X., et al.: Deep networks for saliency detection via local estimation and global search. In: 2015 IEEE Conference on Computer Vision and Pattern Recognition (CVPR). IEEE (2015)
8. Wang, L., Wang, L., Lu, H., Zhang, P., Ruan, X.: Saliency detection with recurrent fully convolutional networks. In: Leibe, B., Matas, J., Sebe, N., Welling, M. (eds.) ECCV 2016. LNCS, vol. 9908, pp. 825–841. Springer, Cham (2016). https://doi.org/10.1007/978-3-319-46493-0_50
9. Wang, L., Lu, H., Wang, Y., et al.: Learning to detect salient objects with image-level supervision. In: IEEE Conference on Computer Vision and Pattern Recognition. IEEE (2017)
10. Zhao, R., Ouyang, W., Li, H., et al.: Saliency detection by multi-context deep learning, pp. 1265–1274 (2015)
11. Zhang, P., Wang, D., Lu, H., et al.: Learning uncertain convolutional features for accurate saliency detection (2017)
12. Zhang, P., Wang, D., Lu, H., et al.: Amulet: aggregating multi-level convolutional features for salient object detection. In: IEEE International Conference on Computer Vision. IEEE (2017)
13. Li, G., Yu, Y.: Visual saliency based on multiscale deep features. In: IEEE Conference on Computer Vision and Pattern Recognition (CVPR). IEEE (2015)
14. Lee, G., Tai, Y.W., Kim, J.: Deep saliency with encoded low level distance map and high level features (2016)
15. Hou, Q., Cheng, M., Hu, X., Borji, A., Tu, Z., Torr, P.H.S.: Deeply supervised salient object detection with short connections. IEEE Trans. Pattern Anal. Mach. Intell. **41**(4), 815–828 (2019). https://doi.org/10.1109/TPAMI.2018.2815688

16. Luo, Z., Mishra, A., Achkar, A., et al.: Non-local deep features for salient object detection. In: IEEE Conference on Computer Vision and Pattern Recognition (CVPR). IEEE (2017)

17. Simonyan, K., Zisserman, A.: Very deep convolutional networks for large-scale image recognition. Comput. Sci. (2014)

18. Zhang, L., Dai, J., Lu, H., et al.: A bi-directional message passing model for salient object detection. In: 2018 IEEE/CVF Conference on Computer Vision and Pattern Recognition (CVPR). IEEE (2018)

19. Liu, W., Rabinovich, A., Berg, A.C.: ParseNet: looking wider to see better. Comput. Sci. (2015)

20. Qin, X., Zhang, Z., Huang, C., et al.: BASNet: boundary-aware salient object detection. In: IEEE/CVF Conference on Computer Vision and Pattern Recognition (CVPR). IEEE (2019)

An Empirical Study of Text Factors and Their Effects on Chinese Writer Identification

Yu-Jie Xiong[1,2](✉)(iD), Yue Lu[2](iD), and Yan-Chun Cao[3](iD)

[1] School of Electronic and Electrical Engineering,
Shanghai University of Engineering Science, Shanghai 201620, China
xiong@sues.edu.cn
[2] Shanghai Key Laboratory of Multidimensional Information Processing,
East China Normal University, Shanghai 200241, China
[3] School of Public Administration, Faculty of Economics and Management,
East China Normal University, Shanghai 200062, China

Abstract. In this paper, we analyze the relationship between the performance of the text-independent feature and text factors of the handwriting on Chinese writer identification. Text factors contain two types of information: the number of characters in both query and reference and the number of the same characters in both query and reference. We conclude that the performance increases when the query and reference contain more characters, and the minimum number of needed characters is 50. The number of the same characters in both query and reference has little influence on the identification when the number of characters is more than 50. The conclusions are verified by repeated writer identification tests with different amount of characters on the handwriting document pages.

Keywords: Chinese writer identification · Empirical study · Text factors · Text-independent

1 Introduction

Biometrics are becoming a key aspect of information security [1]. Conventional authentication techniques use a special product (i.e., key, ID card, etc.) or a unique information (i.e., password, etc.) to perform personal recognition. However, biometrics refers to individual recognition based on a person's physical or behavioral traits. Physiological and behavioral biometrics are two main branches of biometrics, and writer identification is a kind of behavioral biometrics using handwriting as the individual feature for personal authentication. Handwriting with a natural writing attitude is an effective way to represent the uniqueness of individual, and plays an essential role in the biometric traits [2].

Writer identification can be divided into text-dependent and text-independent approaches [3]. According to the common sense, the more characters are appeared in both query and reference, the better the performance is

© Springer Nature Singapore Pte Ltd. 2021
G. Zhai et al. (Eds.): IFTC 2020, CCIS 1390, pp. 194–205, 2021.
https://doi.org/10.1007/978-981-16-1194-0_17

achieved. When there are only few characters (e.g. phrase, name), the text content of the handwriting documents should be the same to ensure the credibility of writer identification. On the other hand, if there are lots of characters (e.g. text-lines, paragraphs, or pages), the text content of handwriting documents could be the different. Compared to text-dependent approaches, it is well known that text-independent approaches have no limitations on character amount on the handwriting documents. Text-independent approaches require sufficient characters created by different people for features representation. If training samples are not enough, the approaches are not text-independent any more. Thus, the definition of text-independent is rather qualitative than quantitative. Actually the factors of text content are of crucial importance for the text-independent approachs, and influence the performance of an identification system to some extent.

Generally the researchers attempted to propose a novel feature which is distinctive and at the same time robust to changes under different conditions. Zhu et al. [4] extracted texture features with the two-dimensional Gabor filtering technique. In order to with reduce the calculational cost, Shen et al. [5] used the wavelet technique to improve the Gabor filters. Zhang et al. [6] proposed a hybrid method combining Gabor model with mesh fractal dimension. Li and Ding [7] focuses on different locations of linked pixel pairs, and presented the grid microstructure feature (GMF). Inspired by the idea of GMF, Xiong et al. [8] proposed a contour-directional feature.

In this paper, we try to investigate the text-independent approaches from another perspective. An empirical study of text factors and its effects on Chinese writer identification is presented. This study has two. The first one is to find the experimental minimum number of characters for reliable writer identification. Though the performance of identification not only depends on the number of characters, but also depends on the capacity of datasets and the quality of feature and handwriting, the minimum character amount is still quite useful and meaningful when we try to design a new dataset or test the performance of a new text-independent feature. The second goal is to make clear the relationship between the identification performance and text factors.

2   Experiments

Usually, researchers believe that the number of characters is the main factor which carry the greatest responsibility for good performance. This implies that with more characters in both query and reference, the performance will be better. Brink et al. [9] reported that the minimum character amount of needed text for text-independent writer identification is 100 characters (Dutch and English). In our opinion, text factors consist of two types of information: the number of characters in both query and reference (ACQR) and the number of the same characters in both query and reference (ASCQR). They can reflect the integrated relationship of text content between the query and reference. We design two specific experiments to measure the impact of each factor on the performance and analyze the interactions between them.

2.1   Dataset

The HIT-MW dataset [10] is a famous Chinese dataset for writer identification. It includes 853 documents and 186,444 characters. Our experiments attempt to explore the impacts of text factors under different conditions, therefore the number of characters and text content in both query and reference should to be controlled accurately. The HIT-MW dataset cannot satisfy for this demand. In order to meet this requirement, the documents for our experiments are dynamic generated. We choose CASIA-OLHWDB1.0 [11] as the initial isolated character database to generate new document images which have alterable text content and characters. CASIA-HWDB1.0 contains isolated handwritten Chinese characters samples, and the samples were contributed by 420 persons, and each writer was asked to write 3,866 Chinese characters. 3,740 characters are in the GB2312-80 level-1 set which includes 3755 most frequently used Chinese characters. There are two obvious advantages for this dataset. Firstly, we have more than 1,680,000 characters from 420 writers to generate various documents. Only based on sufficient data, we can evaluate the impacts of each factor on writer identification correctly. Secondly, the character samples are isolated and each writer has the same 3,866 characters, thus we can have perfect control of text content in every documents to simulate the documents under different conditions.

2.2   Document Image Generation

A simple but effective method is employed to generate document images for our experiments. The generated document is line based handwriting document. In order to create a document of writer α with n characters $\{C_i|i = x_1, x_2, \cdots, x_n\}$, the isolated character samples $\{C_i^\alpha|i = x_1, x_2, \cdots, x_n\}$ are selected to create the text-lines. Each text-line $\{L_i|i = 1, 2, \cdots, \lceil n/10 \rceil\}$ is formed by a sequence of close connected characters. The generated document I is arranged by text-lines from top to bottom, and the space between adjacent text-lines are five pixels. Some generated images are shown in Fig. 1, and they are similar to the handwriting with a natural writing attitude.

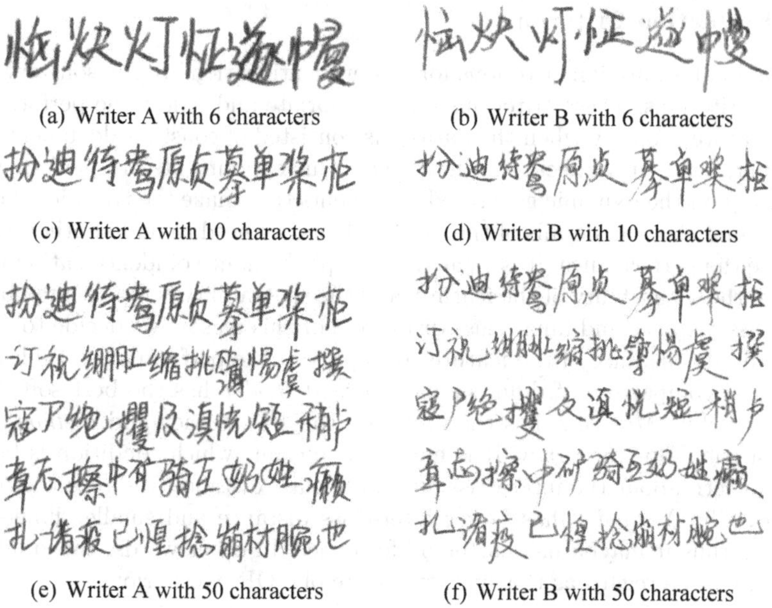

(a) Writer A with 6 characters

(b) Writer B with 6 characters

(c) Writer A with 10 characters

(d) Writer B with 10 characters

(e) Writer A with 50 characters

(f) Writer B with 50 characters

Fig. 1. Generated images of two writers with different characters

2.3 Contour-Directional Feature

In our previous work, we proposed a histogram based feature called as contour-directional feature (CDF) [8] for text-independent Latin writer identification. Our proposed CDF utilizes directional information to describe the distribution of pixel pairs, and represents the the writing style for different writers. We compare the CDF with other common text-independent features. There are the contour-hinge feature (CHF) [12], the multi-scale contour-hinge (MCHF) [13], the GMF [7] and the SIFT based features (SDS+SOH) [14]. As done in [7], we conduct the test using the handwritings of 240 writers in the HIT-MW dataset. Table 1 shows the writer identification performance of different features.

Table 1. The performance of different features on the HIT-MW dataset

#	CHF	MCHF	GMF	SDS+SOH	CDF
Soft-Top-1	84.6%	92.5%	95.0%	95.4%	**95.8%**
Soft-Top-5	95.4%	97.1%	98.3%	98.8%	**99.2%**
Soft-Top-10	96.7%	97.5%	98.8%	**99.2%**	**99.2%**

2.4   Evaluation Criterion

Conventional evaluation criterions for writer identification are the soft and hard TOP-N criterions. These criterions are appropriate and reflect the performance of the feature properly when the dataset is consisted of constant documents and the experiments only executed a few times. Our experiments are performed by repeatedly on the dynamic generated documents that make the traditional criterions cannot show all details of the results. Thus, we need to find another way to evaluate the performance. It is clear that the performance of identification is relevant to the separability of the feature, and the separability is represented by the inter-class distance and inner-class distance. For this reason, we decide to utilize the similarity distance of the features to represent the performance. Table 2 is a simulation comparison of different methods. *Method 1* has the best soft Top-5 accuracy, while *Method 2* has the best soft Top-10 accuracy and *method 3* has the best soft Top-1 accuracy. It is hard to determine which condition is better. If we concern about the inter-class and inner-class distance, the result is pretty obvious. The *Method 2* has larger inter-class distance and smaller inner-class distance, thus it maybe has batter performance. In other words, the similarity distance can be regard as the synthetic score of TOP-N criterions.

Table 2. A simulation comparison of different methods

#	Method 1	Method 2	Method 3
Soft-Top-1	68.2%	69.9%	**70.2%**
Soft-Top-5	**83.5%**	81.8%	82.4%
Soft-Top-10	86.8%	**89.4%**	88.6%
Inter-class distance	4.2E−06	5.5E−06	4.5E−06
Inner-class distance	2.4E−06	1.8E−06	2.2E−06

2.5   Experimental Setup

Text factors consist of two types of information: the number of characters in both query and reference (ACQR) and the number of the same characters in both query and reference (ASCQR). We design two experiments to analyze the relationship among the performance and ACQR and ASCQR. Experiment 1 is to calculate the similarity distance (SD) of the features extracted from the dynamic generated images with the same number of characters. There are three conditions between the query and reference: 1. They are from the same person and have totally different characters (SPDC); 2. They are from different persons and have the same characters (DPSC); 3. They are from the different persons and have totally different characters (DPDC). The SDs of SPDC, DPSC, and DPDC are computed by 126,000 (420 * 300) times repeated trials. It is noted that the characters in each trial are randomly assigned, and the writer of the query in each trial of DPSC and DPDC is also randomly assigned.

When the number of characters in the reference is constant, the number of the same characters in both query and reference (ASCQR) also has an effect on the performance. Experiment 2 is to calculate the SD of the features extracted from the dynamic generated images with different number of the same characters. There are two additional conditions between the query and reference: 1. The numbers of the characters in the query (ACQ) is equal to the number of characters of the characters in the reference (ACR); 2. ACQ is not equal to ACR. The SDs of SPDC, DPSC, and DPDC in two conditions are also computed by 126,000 (420*300) times repeated trials. Through the statistical analysis of the result, we can find the relationship between the performance and ASCQR.

2.6   Experimental Results

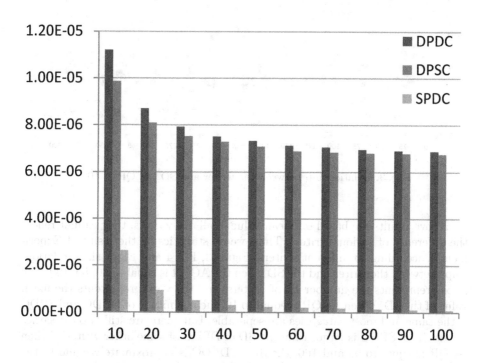

Fig. 2. Relationship between ACQR and SD

Figure 2 shows the statistical result of the Experiment 1 according to ACQR. The x-axis represents ACQR and the y-axis represents the mean value of the SD. As shown in figure, the SDs of all conditions become smaller when ACQR is increased. However, the decline rate of SPDC is much greater than the decline rates of DPSC and DPDC. This implies the separability of the feature becomes better with increasing characters. On the other hand, the SD of DPDC is always larger than the SD of DPSC. It shows that the same characters in both query and reference can influence the similarity of the features. The difference of the SDs of DPDC and DPSC is smaller when ACQR is increased, and the SD of DPDC is approximately equal to the SD of DPSC when ACQR is larger than 50. It demonstrates the feature is really text-independent when ACQR is larger than 50.

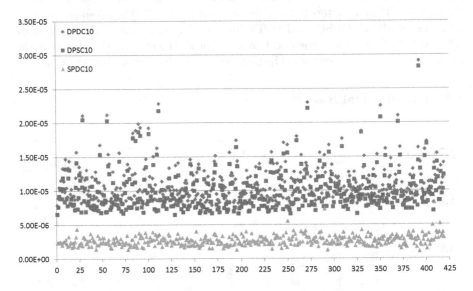

Fig. 3. Relationship between the writer and SD (ACQR = 10)

Above results are based on mean value of all 420 writers, they cannot reflect the difference of various writers. Thus, we do statistics on the result of Experiment 1 according to different writers. Figure 3, Fig. 4 and Fig. 5 show relationships between the writer and the SD when the ACQR is equal to 10, 50, 100. The x-axis represents the number ID of writers, and the y-axis represents the mean value of the SD. When ACQR is equal to 10, the magnitude of DPDC and SPDC is the same and most categories are separable. But there are still two categories whose SD of SPDC is larger than the SD of DPDC of some other writers. When ACQR is equal to 50 and 100, the SD of DPDC is approximately equal to the SD of DPSC, and the magnitude of DPDC is larger ten times than the magnitude of SPDC. It supports that separability the feature is text-independent when ACQR is larger than 50.

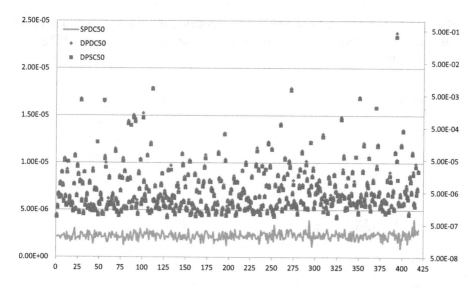

Fig. 4. Relationship between the writer and SD (ACQR = 50)

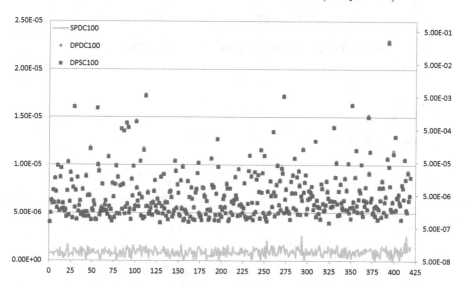

Fig. 5. Relationship between the writer and SD (ACQR = 100)

We also obtain the probability distributions of SD with different characters in both query and reference. Figure 6, Fig. 7 and Fig. 8 are the probability distributions of SD when the ACQR is equal to 10, 50, 100. The x-axis represents the value of the SD and the y-axis represents the probability of the occurrence. Figure 6 shows that the probability distribution of SPDC and DPDC are overlapped. However, there is no overlap between the probability distributions of

SPDC and DPSC in Fig. 7 and Fig. 8. It implies that if a fixed threshold is used to identify different writers, the classification accuracy is 100% when ACQR is larger than 50.

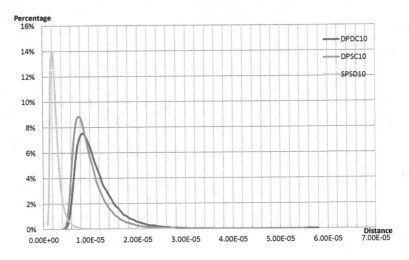

Fig. 6. The probability distribution of SD (ACQR = 10)

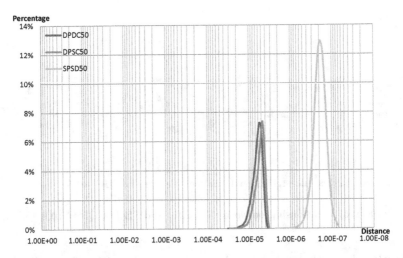

Fig. 7. The probability distribution of SD (ACQR = 50)

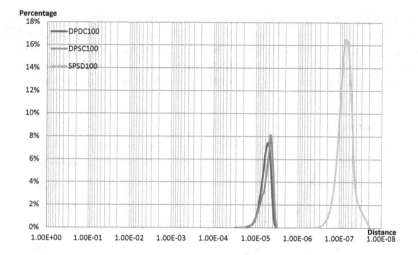

Fig. 8. The probability distribution of SD (ACQR = 100)

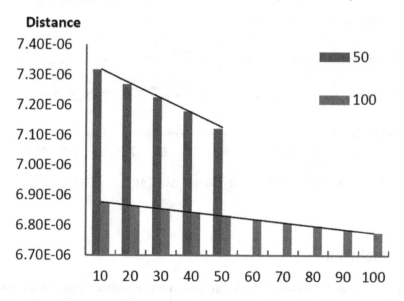

Fig. 9. The SD with different ASCQR(ACQ = ACR)

Figure 9 shows that the SD of the query and reference from different persons with different ASCQR when ACQ is equal to ACR, and the ACQR is 50 and 100. The x-axis represents the value of ASCQR and the y-axis represents the mean value of the SD. It is clear that the SD of different persons is reduced when ASCQR is increased. The relationship between the SD and ASCQR is linear, and the decline rate decreases with the increasing ACQR. Figure 10 shows that the SD of the query and reference from different persons with different ACR when ASCQR is from 10 to 50. The x-axis represents the value of ACR and the y-axis represents the mean value of the SD. The figure indicates that the SD of different persons is reduced when ACR is increased and ASCQR is fixed. The decline rate of the SD decreases with the increasing ACR, and the decline rate of the SDs with different ASCQR and the same ACR seems to the same.

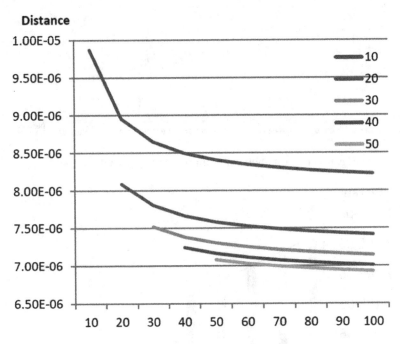

Fig. 10. The SD with different ACR(ACQ ≠ ACR)

3   Conclusion

As a rule of thumb, 50 characters is the minimum character amount for Chinese writer identification when using a strong text-independent feature such as CDF. In general, the more difficult the identification task, the more text are needed. More characters in handwriting documents are always better in every cases, even the amount of characters is only increased in the reference handwriting documents.

Acknowledgements. This work is jointly sponsored by National Natural Science Foundation of China (Grant No. 62006150), Shanghai Young Science and Technology Talents Sailing Program (Grant No. 19YF1418400), Shanghai Key Laboratory of Multidimensional Information Processing (Grant No. 2020MIP001), and the Fundamental Research Funds for the Central Universities.

References

1. Jain, A.K., Ross, A., Pankanti, S.: Biometrics: a tool for information security. IEEE Trans. Inf. Forensics Secur. **1**(2), 125–143 (2006)
2. Bulacu, M.L.: Statistical pattern recognition for automatic writer identification and verification. Ph.D. thesis, University of Groningen (2007)
3. Plamondon, R., Lorette, G.: Automatic signature verification and writer identification - the state of the art. Pattern Recogn. **22**(2), 107–131 (1989)
4. Zhu, Y., Tan, T.N., Wang, Y.H.: Biometric personal identification based on handwriting. In: Proceedings of the International Conference on Pattern Recognition, pp. 797–800 (2000)
5. Shen, C., Ruan, X.G., Mao, T.L.: Writer identification using Gabor wavelet. In: Proceedings of the World Congress on Intelligent Control and Automation, pp. 2061–2064 (2002)
6. Zhang, J., He, Z., Cheung, Y., You, X.: Writer identification using a hybrid method combining gabor wavelet and mesh fractal dimension. In: Corchado, E., Yin, H. (eds.) IDEAL 2009. LNCS, vol. 5788, pp. 535–542. Springer, Heidelberg (2009). https://doi.org/10.1007/978-3-642-04394-9_65
7. Li, X., Ding, X.: Writer identification of Chinese handwriting using grid microstructure feature. In: Tistarelli, M., Nixon, M.S. (eds.) ICB 2009. LNCS, vol. 5558, pp. 1230–1239. Springer, Heidelberg (2009). https://doi.org/10.1007/978-3-642-01793-3_124
8. Xiong, Y.-J., Wen, Y., Wang, P.S., Lu, Y.: Text-independent writer identification using sift descriptor and contour-directional feature. In: Proceedings of the International Conference on Document Analysis and Recognition, pp. 91–95 (2015)
9. Brink, A., Bulacu, M.L., Schomaker, L.: How much handwritten text is needed for text-independent writer verification and identification. In: Proceedings of the International Conference on Pattern Recognition, pp. 1–4 (2008)
10. Su, T.H., Zhang, T.W., Guan, D.J.: Corpus-based HIT-MW database for offline recognition of general purpose Chinese handwritten text. Int. J. Doc. Anal. Recogn. **10**(1), 27–38 (2007)
11. Liu, C.-L., Yin, F., Wang, D.-H., Wang, Q.-F.: Online and offline handwritten Chinese character recognition: benchmarking on new databases. Pattern Recogn. **46**(1), 155–162 (2013)
12. Bulacu, M.L., Schomaker, L., Vuurpijl, L.: Writer identification using edge-based directional features. In: Proceedings of the International Conference on Document Analysis and Recognition, pp. 937–941 (2003)
13. Van Der Maaten, L., Postma, E.: Improving automatic writer identification. In: Proceedings of the Belgium-Netherlands Conference on Artificial Intelligence, pp. 260–266 (2005)
14. Wu, X.Q., Tang, Y.B., Bu, W.: Offline text-independent writer identification based on scale invariant feature transform. IEEE Trans. Inf. Forensics Secur. **9**(3), 526–536 (2014)

Events-to-Frame: Bringing Visual Tracking Algorithm to Event Cameras

Sixian Chan[1], Qianqian Liu[1], XiaoLong Zhou[1,2], Cong Bai[1], and Nan Chen[3(✉)]

[1] College of Computer Science and Technology, Zhejiang University of Technology,
Hangzhou 310023, China
[2] College of Electrical and Information Engineering, Quzhou University,
Quzhou 324000, China
[3] College of Continuing Education, Qilu Normal University, Jinan 250013, China
20153410@qlnu.edu.cn

Abstract. Event based cameras mean a significant shift to standard cameras by mimicking the work of the biological retina. Unlike the traditional cameras which output the image directly, they provide the relevant information asynchronously through the light intensity changes. This can produce a series of events that include the time, position, and polarity. Visual tracking based on event camera is a new research topic. In this paper, by accumulating a fixed number of events, the output of events stream by the event camera is transformed into the image representation. And it is applied to the tracking algorithm of the ordinary camera. In addition, the data sets of the ground-truth is relabeled and with the visual attributes such as noise events, occlusion, deformation and so on so that it can facilitate the evaluation of the tracker. The data sets are tested in the existing tracking algorithms. Extensive experiments have proved that the data sets created is reasonable and effective. And it can achieve fast and efficient target tracking through the SOTA tracking algorithm test.

Keywords: Dynamic vision sensor · Visual tracking · Correlation filters · Deep learning

1 Introduction

Event-based cameras are driven by the events which occur in a scene like their biological counterparts. They are different from conventional vision sensors, on the contrary, they are driven by the timing and control signals by man-made, and that have nothing to do with the source of visual information [18]. Dynamic Vision Sensor (DVS) [27] (Fig. 1a) is a kind of the event based, it provide a series of asynchronous events [9] (Fig. 1b). And these bio-inspired sensors overcome some of the limitations of traditional cameras: high temporal resolution, high dynamic range, low power consumption and so on. Hence, event cameras can take an advantage for high-speed and high dynamic range visual applications

© Springer Nature Singapore Pte Ltd. 2021
G. Zhai et al. (Eds.): IFTC 2020, CCIS 1390, pp. 206–216, 2021.
https://doi.org/10.1007/978-981-16-1194-0_18

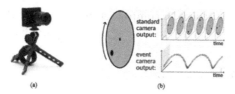

(a)   (b)

Fig. 1. (a) The Dynamic Vision Sensor (DVS). (b) The difference between event camera with traditional camera when a blackspot move on the platform.

in challenging scenarios with large brightness contrast. Since these advantages, vision algorithms based on event cameras have been applied in the areas of like event-based tracking, Simultaneous Localization and Mapping (SLAM), and object recognition [26,31,32,35], etc.

Visual tracking is a hot topics and it is widely used in video surveillance, unmanned driving, human-computer interaction and so on. While tracking algorithms are well established and have achieved successful applications in many aspects. Their visual image acquisition methods are based on traditional fixed-frequency acquisition frames which suffer from high redundancy, high latency and high data volume. Event-based sensors provide a continuous steam of asynchronous events. The position, time and polarity of the each event is encoded by address event representation (AER) [19]. The AER is triggered by the event. The pixels work asynchronously and only outputs the address and information of the pixel whose light intensity changes. Instead of passively reading out each pixel information in the frame, they can eliminate redundant information from the source. Real-time dynamic response with scene change, image super-sparse representation, and the events of output asynchronously can be widely used in high-speed object tracking and robot vision.

The current visual tracking algorithm works on nature images. Since each pixel of the frame needs a uniform time for exposure, it will cause image blur and information loss when the object moves quickly. And the tracking algorithms are susceptible to lighting, fast movement of targets, etc. Event-based tracking maybe solve this problem. Event-based cameras cannot directly output the frames. Therefore, it cannot be directly applied to the computer vision algorithm of ordinary cameras.

In our work, we convert the event stream generated by the event camera into image representations. The converted image is formed by integrating a certain a mount of events with a sliding event window. We select seven event data records from the DVS benchmark data sets [14]. By accumulating the DVS data into the frames, we have remarked the ground-truth to further accurately determine the locations of tracking object for the current tracking algorithms evaluation. All of the frames are annotated with axis-aligned bounding boxes, the sequences are relabeled with the visual attributes such as noise events, occlusion, deformation and so on. The experiments test and verify the reasonable validity of the labeled data and show that the tracking algorithms can track the specific targets with high accuracy and robustness in complex scenes based on the output frames of the event camera.

2   Related Work

Many methods for the event-based tracking have been presented up to now. Because of the low data processing and latency of the event based cameras, early researchers track targets which moving in a static scene as the clusters of events, and they achieve good performances in applications such as traffic monitoring, high-speed robot tracking and so on [7]. At the same time, the event-by-event adaptive tracking algorithm has been proved in some high contrast user-defined shapes. Ni et al. [25] proposed the nearest neighbor strategy, which linked the incoming event with the target form and updated its conversion parameters. Glover et al. [10] proposed an improved particle filter which can automatically adjust the time window of the target observation for tracking a single target in event-space. All of the above methods need a experience premise or user-defined to define the target to be tracked. When the motion range of the object is gradually enlarged, other methods determine to distinct the natural features to track by analyzing the event [8]. Zhu et al. [36] proposed a soft data association modeled with probabilities, which relying on grouping events into a model. Features were generated by the motion compensated events, which generated to pointsets based on registered templates of new events. Lagorce et al. [18] proposed an event-based multi kernel algorithm, which tracked the characteristics of incoming events by integrating various kernels like Gaussian and user-defined kernels and so on. The appearance features of the event stream objects were obtained from a multi-scale space independent of the data foundation, and the original features could not be retained. Kogler et al. [17] presented an event-to frame converter and tested on two conventional stereo vision algorithms. Schraml et al. [30] proposed to integrate DVS events in a period of 5–50 ms and used them to track moving objects in stereo vision. However, one difference between an event camera and a normal camera is that the stationary object is not imaged, which result in the sparse data on the space and time. When integrating events at a fixed time, the time information is destroyed and the spatial data is sparse in different frames. Li et al. [20] proposed a tracking algorithm based on the CF mechanism by encoding the event-stream object by the rate coding. But it produces a lot of noise events.

3   Event-Image Representation Based on Event Time-Stamp

Event based cameras have independent pixels and response to changes in logarithm of light intensity $e_m = (X_m, t_m, p_m)$. In the ideal case of no noise, the event is triggered by the address-event representation combines the position, time, and polarity of the event (a signal with a change in brightness, an ON

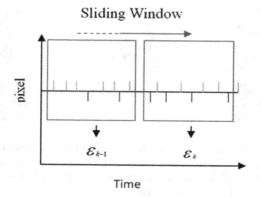

Fig. 2. The sliding event window diagram. The incoming event stream is depicted as red (positive events)/green (negative events) in the timeline). Events are divided into N events windows (blue box) by sliding windows. Each window is formed into each frame. In this example, N = 8. (Color figure online)

event is a positive event indicating an increase in brightness, and an OFF event is a negative event indicating a decrease in brightness). The event as:

$$e_m = (X_m, t_m, p_m) \tag{1}$$

Where: $X_m = (x_m, y_m)^T$ indicates the pixel address; t_m indicates the time when the event occurs; $p_m \in \{+1, -1\}$ indicates the polarity of event, $p_m = +1$ indicates the brightening event, otherwise it becomes dark. The triggered event means that the brightness increase from the last event reaches a preset threshold $\pm C$, namely:

$$\Delta L(X_m, t_m) = p_m C \tag{2}$$

where:

$$\Delta L(X_m, t_m) = L(X_m, t_m) - L(X_m, t_m - \Delta t_m) \tag{3}$$

Δt_m indicates the time elapsed since the last trigger event of pixel's X_m.

As mentioned above, the event camera outputs the captured image as an asynchronous event stream. Since a single data stream contains a lot of data, it should be processed in batches firstly. In this paper, a sliding event window [28, 29] with a fixed number of N events is used to slide on the data stream, thereby completing the transition from an event stream which containing huge amounts of data to a small batch of data with a fixed number of events. The sliding window divides the event stream into multiple small windows, and controls the flow of one small window every time. This method can overcome the large of traffic data. The sliding window works as shown in Fig. 2.

The valid information of the event stream rely on the number of events are processed at the same time. There are generally two methods for event processing: One is based on event-driven that work on event by event, and the other method that work on a set of events. The former process the every of

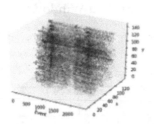

Fig. 3. An example of a girl scene that accumulates a certain number of events. The (a) shows a girl captured by a normal camera. The (b) shows the visualization of the space-time information within the stream of events of the girl. The (c) shows the girl image of corresponding Integral reconstruction.

incoming single event. However, an independent event does not provide enough information frequently and may generate a large number of noise events. The later method integrate all of the information contained in the events. we choose the fixed events information to integrate the event stream, which can achieve better results. We define E(t) as the sum of events during a little time interval of the sliding window:

$$E(t) = \sum_{t \in eventwindow} (event_x \pm 1, event_y \pm 1, t) \tag{4}$$

We accumulate 7500 events into the frames in this paper. By the process of accumulating framing, the position where the event occurs is converted to the pixel position and formed the image frame. The position of the event in the world coordinates is mapped to the image coordinates by the mapping relationship by the Eq. 5:

$$\begin{bmatrix} u \\ v \\ 1 \end{bmatrix} = 1/z_c \begin{bmatrix} f_x & 0 & c_x & 0 \\ 0 & f_y & c_y & 0 \\ 0 & 0 & 1 & 0 \end{bmatrix} \begin{bmatrix} R & t \\ 0 & 1 \end{bmatrix} \begin{bmatrix} X_w \\ Y_w \\ Z_w \\ 1 \end{bmatrix} \tag{5}$$

Fixed events can make the deviation range between two adjacent frames not too big.

To reduce the effect of the image surface's noise, we add an event counter synchronously during accumulating the events. At the same time, we record the every pixel's coordinate position (x, y) and times in the event. The more events accumulate, the higher weight of events, and the higher of the activity in the process of data accumulating and framing. It is easier to get strongly vitality in the event selection and it is not easy to eliminate. On the contrary, the fewer the number of event accumulations, the easier to obtain a higher elimination rate in the event selection, and it is easy to die. Compared to the time surface [23, 34], the ability to handle the local patch is flat (weaker), but the speed of processing is faster and the resource of consumption is less.

The accumulated events are represented by image binarization, and the pixel's gray value is set to 0 or 255. Hence, the entire image exhibit a distinct between black and white effect. Since the size of the data sets provided by DVS benchmark data sets is different, we divide them into 200*200 pixels, and adjust the object to the middle of the lens to obtain effective information. The way of processing can improve the robustness of the input data. The Fig. 3 shows a scene by accumulating a fixed number of events.

Table 1. The distribution of the video sequence attributes and the length of the video recording table, 1 means the attribute, 0 means no.

Sequence	Long(s)	Noise events	Complicated background	Occlusion	Deformation	Scale variation
singer	13	1	1	1	1	1
figure_skating	34	1	1	1	1	1
girl	36	1	0	1	1	1
Sylvester	21	1	0	0	1	1
Vid_J_person_floor	21	1	1	1	1	1
Vid_E_person_part_occluded	8	1	1	1	0	0
Vid_D_person	22	1	1	0	0	0

4 Experiment and Evaluation

4.1 The DVS Data Sets

We choose seven event data records from the DVS benchmark which recorded by the DVS output of a DAVIS camera [14]. The tracking targets including the person, head, doll. These seven sequences are "figure_skating" , "singer", "girl", "sylvester", "Vid_D_person", "Vid_E_person_part_occluded", "Vid_J_person_floor", which are accumulated into 696, 263, 731, 437, 443, 160 and 422 frames, respectively.

The ground-truth provided by the tracking data sets is slightly offset from the actual position and size. Therefore, we relabel the locations of tracking object in the seven sequences. Each frame is annotated with an axis aligned bounding box. The description of boxes is (x, y, w, h), where (x, y) is the left-top corner vertex position, and w, h represent the width and height. Moreover, all of the sequences are labeled with five visual attributes, including the noise events, occlusion, complicated background, scale variation and deformation. The distribution of these attributes and the long of recordings are presented in Table 1.

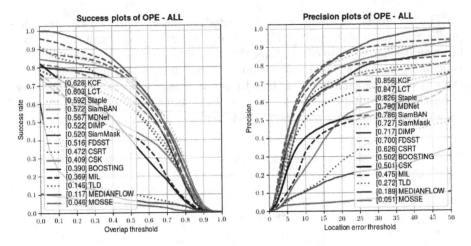

Fig. 4. The performance comparison of the tracking algorithms. The success and accuracy rate are shown in the left and right figures respectively.

4.2 Evaluation

The evaluation methodology: The success rate and accuracy are used to the tracking algorithms for evaluating. The former is measured by average overlap rate (AOR), that is, the percentage of sequence frames whose overlap exceeds the set threshold. And the latter is measured by the center location error (CLE), that is, the distance between the target and actual location is less than the percentage of the sequence frame with the set threshold.

The evaluation tracking algorithms: According to the learning mechanism of algorithms, we divide them into the tracking algorithms based on deep learning (SiamBAN [5], MDNet [24], DIMP [3], SiamMask [33]), the Correlation filtering tracking algorithms with hand-crafted features (CSK [12], KCF [13], FDSST [6], LCT [22], Staple [2], CSRT [21]), and other tracking algorithms like (CT [15], BOOSTING [11], MIL [1], TLD [16], MOSSE [4]).

Quantitative Analysis. It is found through the experiments that the visual tracking algorithms can effectively track our event stream sequences and achieve good performance. Among them, the KCF tracking algorithm performs best. The comparsion results of accuracy and success rate plot are showed in Fig. 4. From the Fig. 4 we can see that the SOTA deep learning algorithms perform not well. The improved feature extraction algorithm (such as KCF with hog feature) can track accurately and effectively. The pre-20 and suc-50 are 0.856 and 0.628, respectively. It performs better than the CSK algorithm that use a cyclic matrix based on gray features, which is beyond doubt. But its accuracy is better than that the staple tracking algorithm that combine the Hog and color histogram Fortunately, this may be related to our video sequence with the binary grayscale images. In addition, the effect of tracking drift is easily caused

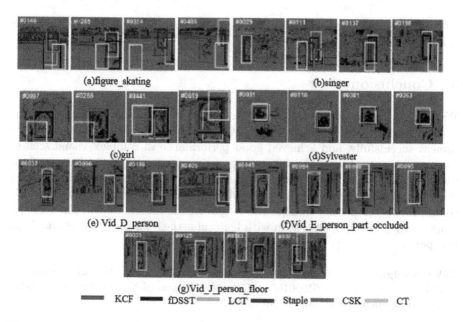

(a)figure_skating   (b)singer

(c)girl   (d)Sylvester

(e) Vid_D_person   (f)Vid_E_person_part_occluded

(g)Vid_J_person_floor

▬▬ KCF ▬▬ fDSST ▬▬ LCT ▬▬ Staple ▬▬ CSK ▬▬ CT

Fig. 5. Examples of the results of some tracking algorithms in seven event stream sequences.

by scale change, the FDSST algorithm introduce to the scale estimation, and the LCT algorithm add a confidence filter to the scale is slightly better than its performance, but they are worse than the KCF tracking algorithm. In summary, the data transformed by event camera is valid and reasonable.

Quantitative Analysis. The tracking results of some trackers in the seven event stream sequences are shown in Fig. 5. The scale of the skater change repeatedly for the figure_skating sequence. At the beginning, all of the six tracking algorithms are able to track the object, but when it continue to change, the tracker will drift gradually. At the 485th frame, the other five tracking algorithms completely lose the target, and the KCF can still keep tracking. In the singer sequence, under the disturbance of the background, the singer is blurred. Due to the sudden change of the stage (the 111th frame and the 131th frame), the target is lost for the CT and CSK tracking algorithm. Similarly, in the Vid_D_person and Vid_E_person_part_occluded sequence, the CSK and CT also drift. However, for the Sylvester sequence, even if the target is deformed, all the trackers can still track robustly. In the girl sequence, The face target is constantly deformed and changed, and the tracker gradually drift. At the 619th frame, only Staple and FDSST can keep effective tracking. In the Vid_J_person_floor sequence, When the target is interfered by another person, the CT and CSK will track the wrong target, which makes the tracking fail. But the rest of the tracking algorithm can still achieve stable tracking when the two are separated (via. the 125th frame and 183th frame).

5   Conclusion

We accumulated the events stream into frames by integrating a certain number of asynchronous events. It applied to the SOTA tracking algorithm of the ordinary camera successfully, and achieved good performance in complex visual scenes. The experiments showed the rationality of converting the event stream into a frame image. At the same time, the processing of the method not only avoided the effects of lighting, but also reduced the effects of the background, which could protect the privacy outside the target. In the future, we will put forward a novel target tracking algorithm with high robustness for the data sets made in this paper.

Acknowledgment. This work is supported by National Natural Science Foundation of China under Grant No. 61906168 and Zhejiang Provincial Natural Science Foundation of China under Grant No. LY18F020032.

References

1. Babenko, B., Yang, M.H., Belongie, S.: Robust object tracking with online multiple instance learning. IEEE Trans. Pattern Anal. Mach. Intell. **33**(8), 1619–1632 (2010)
2. Bertinetto, L., Valmadre, J., Golodetz, S., Miksik, O., Torr, P.H.: Staple: complementary learners for real-time tracking. In: Proceedings of the IEEE Conference on Computer Vision and Pattern Recognition, pp. 1401–1409 (2016)
3. Bhat, G., Danelljan, M., Gool, L.V., Timofte, R.: Learning discriminative model prediction for tracking. In: Proceedings of the IEEE International Conference on Computer Vision, pp. 6182–6191 (2019)
4. Bolme, D.S., Beveridge, J.R., Draper, B.A., Lui, Y.M.: Visual object tracking using adaptive correlation filters. In: 2010 IEEE Computer Society Conference on Computer Vision and Pattern Recognition, pp. 2544–2550. IEEE (2010)
5. Chen, Z., Zhong, B., Li, G., Zhang, S., Ji, R.: Siamese box adaptive network for visual tracking. In: Proceedings of the IEEE/CVF Conference on Computer Vision and Pattern Recognition, pp. 6668–6677 (2020)
6. Danelljan, M., Häger, G., Khan, F.S., Felsberg, M.: Discriminative scale space tracking. IEEE Trans. Pattern Anal. Mach. Intell. **39**(8), 1561–1575 (2016)
7. Drazen, D., Lichtsteiner, P., Häfliger, P., Delbrück, T., Jensen, A.: Toward real-time particle tracking using an event-based dynamic vision sensor. Exp. Fluids **51**(5), 1465 (2011). https://doi.org/10.1007/s00348-011-1207-y
8. Gallego, G., et al.: Event-based vision: a survey. arXiv preprint arXiv:1904.08405 (2019)
9. Gehrig, D., Rebecq, H., Gallego, G., Scaramuzza, D.: Asynchronous, photometric feature tracking using events and frames. In: Ferrari, V., Hebert, M., Sminchisescu, C., Weiss, Y. (eds.) ECCV 2018. LNCS, vol. 11216, pp. 766–781. Springer, Cham (2018). https://doi.org/10.1007/978-3-030-01258-8_46

10. Glover, A., Bartolozzi, C.: Robust visual tracking with a freely-moving event camera. In: 2017 IEEE/RSJ International Conference on Intelligent Robots and Systems (IROS), pp. 3769–3776. IEEE (2017)

11. Grabner, H., Leistner, C., Bischof, H.: Semi-supervised on-line boosting for robust tracking. In: Forsyth, D., Torr, P., Zisserman, A. (eds.) ECCV 2008. LNCS, vol. 5302, pp. 234–247. Springer, Heidelberg (2008). https://doi.org/10.1007/978-3-540-88682-2_19

12. Henriques, J.F., Caseiro, R., Martins, P., Batista, J.: Exploiting the circulant structure of tracking-by-detection with kernels. In: Fitzgibbon, A., Lazebnik, S., Perona, P., Sato, Y., Schmid, C. (eds.) ECCV 2012. LNCS, vol. 7575, pp. 702–715. Springer, Heidelberg (2012). https://doi.org/10.1007/978-3-642-33765-9_50

13. Henriques, J.F., Caseiro, R., Martins, P., Batista, J.: High-speed tracking with kernelized correlation filters. IEEE Trans. Pattern Anal. Mach. Intell. **37**(3), 583–596 (2014)

14. Hu, Y., Liu, H., Pfeiffer, M., Delbruck, T.: DVS benchmark datasets for object tracking, action recognition, and object recognition. Front. Neurosci. **10**, 405 (2016)

15. Zhang, K., Zhang, L., Yang, M.-H.: Real-time compressive tracking. In: Fitzgibbon, A., Lazebnik, S., Perona, P., Sato, Y., Schmid, C. (eds.) ECCV 2012. LNCS, vol. 7574, pp. 864–877. Springer, Heidelberg (2012). https://doi.org/10.1007/978-3-642-33712-3_62

16. Kalal, Z., Mikolajczyk, K., Matas, J.: Tracking-learning-detection. IEEE Trans. Pattern Anal. Mach. Intell. **34**(7), 1409–1422 (2011)

17. Kogler, J., Sulzbachner, C., Kubinger, W.: Bio-inspired stereo vision system with silicon retina imagers. In: Fritz, M., Schiele, B., Piater, J.H. (eds.) ICVS 2009. LNCS, vol. 5815, pp. 174–183. Springer, Heidelberg (2009). https://doi.org/10.1007/978-3-642-04667-4_18

18. Lagorce, X., Meyer, C., Ieng, S.H., Filliat, D., Benosman, R.: Asynchronous event-based multikernel algorithm for high-speed visual features tracking. IEEE Trans. Neural Netw. Learn. Syst. **26**(8), 1710–1720 (2014)

19. Lazzaro, J., Wawrzynek, J.: A multi-sender asynchronous extension to the AER protocol. In: Proceedings Sixteenth Conference on Advanced Research in VLSI, pp. 158–169. IEEE (1995)

20. Li, H., Shi, L.: Robust event-based object tracking combining correlation filter and CNN representation. Front. Neurorobot. **13**, 82 (2019)

21. LuNežič, A., Vojíř, T., Čehovin Zajc, L., Matas, J., Kristan, M.: Discriminative correlation filter tracner with channel and spatial reliability. Int. J. Comput. Vision **126**(7), 671–688 (2018)

22. Ma, C., Yang, X., Zhang, C., Yang, M.H.: Long-term correlation tracking. In: Proceedings of the IEEE Conference on Computer Vision and Pattern Recognition, pp. 5388–5396 (2015)

23. Manderscheid, J., Sironi, A., Bourdis, N., Migliore, D., Lepetit, V.: Speed invariant time surface for learning to detect corner points with event-based cameras. In: Proceedings of the IEEE Conference on Computer Vision and Pattern Recognition, pp. 10245–10254 (2019)

24. Nam, H., Han, B.: Learning multi-domain convolutional neural networks for visual tracking. In: Proceedings of the IEEE Conference on Computer Vision and Pattern Recognition, pp. 4293–4302 (2016)

25. Ni, Z., Pacoret, C., Benosman, R., Ieng, S., RÉGNIER*, S.: Asynchronous event-based high speed vision for microparticle tracking. J. Microsc. **245**(3), 236–244 (2012)

26. Paredes-Vallés, F., Scheper, K.Y.W., De Croon, G.C.H.E.: Unsupervised learning of a hierarchical spiking neural network for optical flow estimation: from events to global motion perception. IEEE Trans. Pattern Anal. Mach. Intell. **42**, 2051–2061 (2019)

27. Patrick, L., Posch, C., Delbruck, T.: A 128x 128 120 db 15μ s latency asynchronous temporal contrast vision sensor. IEEE J. Solid-State Circuits **43**, 566–576 (2008)

28. Ramesh, B., Zhang, S., Lee, Z.W., Gao, Z., Orchard, G., Xiang, C.: Long-term object tracking with a moving event camera. In: BMVC, p. 241 (2018)

29. Rebecq, H., Ranftl, R., Koltun, V., Scaramuzza, D.: Events-to-video: bringing modern computer vision to event cameras. In: Proceedings of the IEEE Conference on Computer Vision and Pattern Recognition, pp. 3857–3866 (2019)

30. Schraml, S., Belbachir, A.N., Milosevic, N., Schön, P.: Dynamic stereo vision system for real-time tracking. In: Proceedings of 2010 IEEE International Symposium on Circuits and Systems, pp. 1409–1412. IEEE (2010)

31. Seok, H., Lim, J.: Robust feature tracking in DVS event stream using Bézier mapping. In: The IEEE Winter Conference on Applications of Computer Vision, pp. 1658–1667 (2020)

32. Vidal, A.R., Rebecq, H., Horstschaefer, T., Scaramuzza, D.: Ultimate SLAM? Combining events, images, and IMU for robust visual SLAM in HDR and high-speed scenarios. IEEE Robot. Autom. Lett. **3**(2), 994–1001 (2018)

33. Wang, Q., Zhang, L., Bertinetto, L., Hu, W., Torr, P.H.: Fast online object tracking and segmentation: a unifying approach. In: Proceedings of the IEEE Conference on Computer Vision and Pattern Recognition, pp. 1328–1338 (2019)

34. Wang, Q., Zhang, Y., Yuan, J., Lu, Y.: Space-time event clouds for gesture recognition: from RGB cameras to event cameras. In: 2019 IEEE Winter Conference on Applications of Computer Vision (WACV), pp. 1826–1835. IEEE (2019)

35. Xu, J., Jiang, M., Yu, L., Yang, W., Wang, W.: Robust motion compensation for event cameras with smooth constraint. IEEE Trans. Comput. Imaging **6**, 604–614 (2020)

36. Zhu, A.Z., Atanasov, N., Daniilidis, K.: Event-based feature tracking with probabilistic data association. In: 2017 IEEE International Conference on Robotics and Automation (ICRA), pp. 4465–4470. IEEE (2017)

Extending Chest X-Ray with Multi Label Disease Sequence

Anqi Zheng[1], Cong Bai[1,2], and Ning Liu[3]($\boxtimes$)

[1] College of Computer Science, Zhejiang University of Technology, Hangzhou 310023, China
[2] Key Laboratory of Visual Media Intelligent Processing Technology of Zhejiang Province, Hangzhou 310023, China
[3] School of Electronic, Information and Electrical Engineering, Shanghai Jiao Tong University, Shanghai 200000, China
ningliu@sjtu.edu.cn

Abstract. Doctors need to spend a lot of time and energy on reading the patient's medical images to write the corresponding diagnosis report. Therefore, it is interesting to use the artificial intelligence technology on the research of automatic generation of medical imaging reports. In order to improve the accuracy of the report generation, we extend the Chest X-Ray dataset with multi label of disease combining the medical characteristics of imaging reports. In this paper, we give the concrete steps of expanding the dataset. The original dataset contains 8121 chest X-ray images from different perspectives and 3996 diagnostic reports. Based on the original dataset, we pick out the complete data pair and use a multi label classification network named CheXNet to expand the dataset with the multi label disease sequence. The multi disease label sequence includes the judgment results of 14 common thoracic diseases. After manual correction, we get a dataset which contains 3119 multimodal data pairs. Each data pair is composed of two chest X-ray images and corresponding diagnostic reports, as well as a binary multi label sequence. The extended dataset is more useful for the task of medical diagnostic reports generation.

Keywords: Report generation · Medical imaging · Multi label · Chest X-ray

1 Introduction

In recent years, with the continuous development of deep learning technology and the diversification of methods, its application scenarios gradually expand to the medical field. As an important evidence of disease diagnosis, medical imaging has become one of the most potential branches of artificial intelligence. Medical imaging is the key basis for early screening of diseases, diagnosis of symptoms and targeted treatment in clinical medicine. Medical imaging diagnosis has developed from simple morphological examination to tissue, organ metabolism and function diagnosis, from simple auxiliary diagnostic examination means to clinical discipline integrating examination, diagnosis and treatment now. In clinical practice, it is the radiologist's duty to read medical images

© Springer Nature Singapore Pte Ltd. 2021
G. Zhai et al. (Eds.): IFTC 2020, CCIS 1390, pp. 217–226, 2021.
https://doi.org/10.1007/978-981-16-1194-0_19

and write diagnostic reports so as to give the right conclusion to the doctor. Diagnosis report is used by doctors to describe their findings and conclusions for a specific medical image, and it is also an important medical certificate for patients.

However, for most radiologists, writing a report is time-consuming, tedious and error prone. In addition, the growth rate of the number of doctors is far behind the number of medical images. The exponential growth of medical image data has brought huge diagnostic pressure and report writing load to doctors, and also led to the emergence of an urgent situation of "supply exceeding demand".

Because of the emergence of contradiction, automatic generation of medical imaging diagnosis report has attracted more and more attentions. There are several related literatures published, most of which use Chest X-Ray [1] dataset. These methods generally use Encoder-Decoder structure. Although the structure used is similar, there are great differences in the specific implementation. With the deepening of people's cognition of neural network, the algorithm model used has become more and more complex, and the performance improves continuously.

As early as 2016, Shin H C et al. [2] proposed a method to mine the joint context from the collection of chest X-ray images and diagnostic reports. Through the trained CNN-RNN model, this method inferred the context vector of the labeled content such as the location and severity of the abnormality for the input medical image. Strictly speaking, the final output of this research was not a complete diagnosis report, but it was a big step towards this goal by outputting various annotations related to the diagnosis report. Then Jing B et al. [3] proposed a multi task model based on text generation and multi label classification, which realized the generation of complete diagnostic reports. The algorithm used the pre-trained CNN-LSTM model to obtain the image features and text labels of the input chest X-ray image, and generated the diagnosis report statement by controlling the variables. In 2018, Li CY et al. [4] also used the CNN-RNN model to generate the diagnosis report by using a hybrid method of retrieval and reinforcement learning. Through the pre-trained Encoder-Decoder, several topics were obtained, and each topic was enhanced to generate a single sentence diagnosis report. In 2019, Li CY et al. [5] proposed a new knowledge-driven encode, retrieve, paraphrase method which used knowledge graph. This method combined traditional knowledge-based and retrieval methods with modern learning based methods to achieve accurate and robust medical report generation. In 2019, Harzig P et al. [6] tried to solve the problem of data bias in Chest X-Ray dataset. On the basis of the common CNN-RNN model, the abnormal sentence prediction module was used to distinguish the normal description and abnormal description of the sentence to be generated, and the double-word LSTM was used to generate the normal and abnormal sentences respectively.

As one of the most common radiological examinations, Chest X-Ray is used to screen and diagnose many thoracic diseases. This dataset contains medical image pairs with different perspectives and diagnosis reports corresponding to image. However, it is difficult for the well trained model to find the tiny lesions in images only by depending on image features, and it is impossible to describe the lesions accurately after combining with the text features. For imaging diagnosis, finding abnormalities in the image to get the conclusion of pathological changes is the most important task that people should pay attention to. For the diagnosis report, the keyword in the sentence is the name of disease, but different from the common image caption, the emergence of keyword does not necessarily represent a specific semantic understanding. Therefore, the corresponding multi label disease sequence for common disease keywords is very necessary in the process of report generation training.

In this paper, we propose a multimodal medical dataset, which expands Chest X-Ray dataset with multi label disease sequence. It can not only guide the generation of diagnostic reports, but also improve the accuracy of abnormal lesions description in the generated reports to a certain extent.

The contribution of this paper can be summarized as follows:

Firstly, we select the multimodal pairs, each pair includes an image pair and corresponding diagnosis report in the Chest X-Ray, so as to facilitate the research of generating diagnostic reports by inputting images from different perspectives at the same time, and increase the availability of the dataset.

Secondly, we establish a multimodal medical dataset, and establish a preliminary multi label disease sequence with the help of multi label classification network CheXNet [7] to annotate common thoracic diseases in images.

Thirdly, to improve the accuracy of multi label disease sequence, we correct the multi label disease sequence corresponding to the image according to the content of the dataset diagnosis report.

The rest of this paper is organized as follows. The second section introduces the original structure of Chest X-Ray, and analyzes the motivation of expanding the dataset in detail. The third section describes the way we expand. In the fourth section, we introduce the multi label classification network CheXNet, show the analysis of the experimental results. Finally, conclusion and perspectives are shown in the fifth part.

2 Dataset

2.1 Original Chest X-Ray

In recent years, automatic generation of medical imaging reports is one of the hot topics in research, Chest X-Ray is the most commonly used open medical imaging dataset for this research. This dataset contains 7470 chest X-rays and 3955 diagnostic reports from two large hospital systems in the Indiana patient care network database. Each report is associated with a pair of front and side view images. The report contains the comparison, instruction, discovery and impression sections. So far, this is the only open chest X-ray medical imaging dataset that contains diagnostic reports (Figs. 1 and 2).

2.2 Motivation for Expansion

The basic content of automatic generation of medical imaging reports is to shape long narrative from visual content. Although its essential is image caption, there is a big gap between it and the common image caption task. In report generation, the most important thing that people pay attention to is to find the abnormal lesions in image and get the conclusion of pathology. In other words, the keyword of the sentence is the name of the disease mentioned, but in most cases, even if there is no disease, it will be mentioned in the description, which greatly increases the difficulty of image caption (Fig. 3).

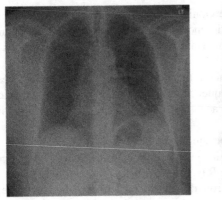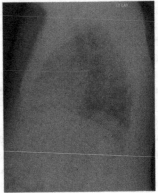

Impression: No acute cardiopulmonary abnormality.

Findings: Stable cardiomediastinal silhouette. No focal pulmonary opacity pleural effusion or pneumothorax. No acute bony abnormality. There are stable degenerative changes of the spine.

Fig. 1. A typical healthy chest X-ray film and its report sample. In the impression section, the diagnosis results of the patient are provided. The findings section lists the observations of the chest X-ray image.

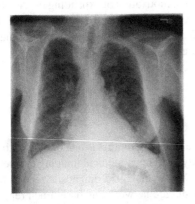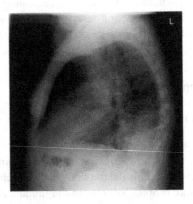

Impression: Question of left lower lobe pneumonia andor pleural effusion.

Findings: Borderline heart size with mild central vascular congestive changes. There is opacity at posterior aspect of lower chest seen on lateral view which probably represents left lower lobe consolidation. There may also be small bilateral pleural effusion. Upper limits of normal heart size. Mild central vascular prominence. Old fracture deformities of multiple right ribs.

Fig. 2. An unhealthy chest X-ray and its report sample. In the impression section, the diagnosis results of the patient are provided. The findings section lists the observations of the chest X-ray images, including a description of the disease.

At the same time, this dataset has some defects when it is used for report generation research. For example, the proportion of describing normal representation is much

Images	Ground Truth	Generated report

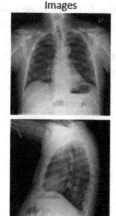

Impression: No acute process.

Findings: Stable appearance of the chest. There are xxxx sternotomy xxxx identified. The heart is within normal limits in size. **The aorta is calcified and tortuous.** There are scattered calcified granulomas throughout both lungs. **No focal infiltrate pleural effusion or pneumothorax. Mild degenerative changes of the thoracic spine.**

Impression: No acute cardiopulmonary abnormality

Findings: The heart size is normal.The lungs are clear.There is no focal airspace consolidation.There is no pneumothorax or pleural effusion.There is no acute bony abnormality.

Fig. 3. Comparison of the ground observation and the output by model. The image on the left is a pair of chest X-ray images of a patient. In the middle is the diagnosis report corresponding to the image pair. On the right is the output of the report generation model. Therefore, it is difficult for the generated model to distinguish the anomaly in the image (bold part in ground truth).

higher than that of describing abnormal disease, resulting in the generation model which dependents on data probability distribution unable to focus on abnormal lesions in the image in this dataset.

However, for this subject, it is the key point to find and accurately describe the lesions in the image. The data bias problem exists in the Chest X-Ray, namely, the number of images is small, the proportion of abnormal reports is small, and the lesion points are difficult to detect, which makes the machine learning model produce deviation, and most of the sentences in the generated report are used to describe the normal situation. Simultaneously, it is not conducive to the evaluation of model performance and goes against the essential of the subject.

Therefore, it is better to be able to generate high accuracy multi label disease sequences about common chest diseases through a pre-trained multi label classification network based on diagnostic reports, which can be used as the multimodal input of report generation task to assist report generation, improve the performance of model in finding abnormal lesions, and improve the proportion and accuracy of abnormal description in the generated report.

3 Method

We extend the Chest X-Ray dataset by model prediction and manual adjustment. We manually compare and adjust the results of these images in the multi label classification network, and finally obtain the multi label disease sequence of these images.

Firstly, the CheXNet is trained with the pretreated Chest X-Ray14 [8] dataset. The multi label disease sequence in the dataset is used as ground truth to improve the performance of the model, and a trained multi label of disease classification network is obtained.

Then, we screen out 3119 groups of image pairs with both front view and side view as well as the corresponding diagnostic reports in the Chest X-Ray dataset. After preprocessing, the chest X-ray images with a frontal view are taken as the test set of multi label classification network CheXNet, and 3119 sets of binary multi label disease sequences about 14 common chest diseases are obtained. These 14 kinds of chest diseases include Atelectasis, Cardiomegaly, Effusion, Infiltration, Mass, Nodule, Pneumonia, Pneumothorax, Consolidation, Edema, Emphysema, Fibrosis, Pleural Thickening, Hernia (Fig. 4).

Images   Part of The Report

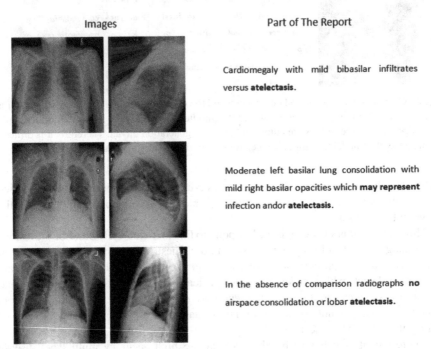

Cardiomegaly with mild bibasilar infiltrates versus **atelectasis**.

Moderate left basilar lung consolidation with mild right basilar opacities which **may represent** infection andor **atelectasis**.

In the absence of comparison radiographs **no** airspace consolidation or lobar **atelectasis**.

Fig. 4. About atelectasis. The bold sections in the figure show three different situations about atelectasis mentioned in the report.

After getting the initial multi label disease sequence, the model generated sequence is adjusted manually by comparing with the content of corresponding diagnostic report.

In the diagnosis report, there are many types of descriptions in the sentence which mentions a certain disease, and each description represents a different result meaning. For example, we can see "atelectasis" in several reports but they have different meanings, it representatives that it is confirmed sometimes, sometimes it representatives that it is not confirmed, and sometimes it representatives that it might have atelectasis. Because medical imaging diagnosis focuses on finding the disease that the patient has or may have, so as to facilitate further diagnosis and treatment, we label the "uncertainty" as "1", which represents that in this image, we can detect this disease.

In addition, due to the fact that there are multiple report writers who writes the original reports, the reports have different writing styles, and the description of a specific disease in the reports is quite different. For example, the "obstructive pulmonary disease" mentioned in some reports may not be included in the 14 target diseases at the time of preliminary judgment. However, obstructive pulmonary disease is a chronic bronchitis and emphysema characterized by airflow obstruction, which indicates that those patients may have "emphysema". "Emphysema" can also be described as "large lung volumes" and "lung hyperinflation" or something like that in the diagnosis report (Fig. 5).

Images   Part of The Report

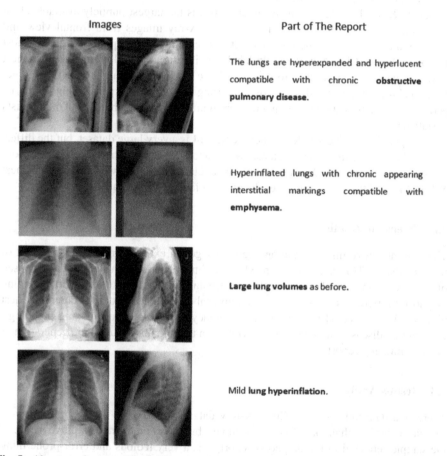

The lungs are hyperexpanded and hyperlucent compatible with chronic **obstructive pulmonary disease.**

Hyperinflated lungs with chronic appearing interstitial markings compatible with **emphysema.**

Large lung volumes as before.

Mild **lung hyperinflation.**

Fig. 5. About emphysema. The bold sections in the figure show the four different descriptions of emphysema mentioned in the report.

Therefore, in order to ensure the accuracy of the multi label disease sequence, we determine some manual correction rules by consulting a source or authority. After several adjustments, we finally complete the work of multi label of disease expansion for Chest X-Ray dataset.

4   Implementation

4.1 Multi Label Classification Network

CheXNet is a 121-layer Dense Convolutional Net-work (DenseNet) [9], which is trained on the open dataset Chest X-Ray14. It is used to generate detection results for 14 common chest diseases with high accuracy.

Chest X-ray 14, released by Wang et al. [8], is the largest publicly available chest X-ray image dataset. It contains 112120 chest X-ray images from frontal view and uses automatic extraction method to annotate each image with up to 14 different chest pathology labels. CheXNet, the multi label classification network trained on the Chest X-Ray14 dataset, can be used to detect a single disease, and can also be used to get the probability of multiple diseases by modifying the output to expansion algorithm. Its performance on the test set is very good, even significantly higher than that of radiologists in statistics.

Compared with Chest X-Ray, Chest X-Ray 14 is a very large dataset, but the difference of the chest X-ray images in these two databases is small.. Therefore, we can adopt transfer learning and CheXNet, the multi label classification network trained on Chest X-Ray 14, to obtain preliminary results of multi label disease sequence.

4.2 Extension Results

Through the above implementation, we finally get an extended multimodal dataset of medical images. This dataset contains 3119 multimodal pairs. Each data pair is composed of chest X-ray images of the patient's from frontal and lateral views and corresponding diagnostic reports, as well as a binary multi label sequence about 14 common chest diseases. It is expected to improve the accuracy of the detection of lung pathological changes, disease diagnosis and description in the task about automatic generation of medical imaging reports.

4.3 Results Analysis

There is a data unbalance in Chest X-Ray dataset, that is, the number of abnormal samples is far less than that of normal samples, but based on the non-intuitive nature of the sample reflected in the diagnosis report, it is a very tedious and error-prone thing to count the proportion of specific abnormal samples. The multi label of disease has a certain intuitive, so it's statistics will be very convenient. Therefore, according to the types of diseases, we make statistics on the diseases in the multimodal group (Table 1).

Table 1. Normal samples and abnormal samples in dataset.

Type of sample	Quantity	Proportion
Normal samples	2180	69.89%
Abnormal samples	939	30.11%

The statistical results show that there are 2180 normal samples and 939 abnormal samples. These abnormal samples only account for 30.11% of the dataset. Among the abnormal samples, pneumothorax account for the least, only 1.81% while the atelectasis account for the most, but it is still far less than 50% (Table 2).

Table 2. Statistics of the frequency of diseases in 939 abnormal samples.

Type of disease	Quantity	Proportion
Atelectasis	292	31.10%
Cardiomegaly	228	24.28%
Effusion	147	15.65%
Infiltration	74	7.88%
Mass	29	3.09%
Nodule	140	14.91%
Pneumonia	70	7.45%
Pneumothorax	17	1.81%
Consolidation	27	2.88%
Edema	56	5.96%
Emphysema	152	16.19%
Fibrosis	24	2.56%
Pleural Thickening	39	4.15%
Hernia	39	4.15%

For the trained model which needs a large amount of data and depends on probability, the number of these abnormal images is far from enough to detect the lesions accurately. From the side, it is necessary to distinguish whether the input sample is normal or abnormal in the task of automatic generation of medical imaging diagnosis report. In order to enhance the ability of the model to detect and descript these diseases, it is necessary to expand this type of the sample. There is still a long way to go for the data collection of multimodal medical images.

5 Conclusion

This paper introduces a multimodal dataset of medical images, which contains 3119 pairs of chest X-ray images from frontal and lateral views, corresponding diagnostic reports and multi label disease sequences. With the help of transfer learning and manual proofreading, we extend the medical image dataset Chest X-ray with multi disease label sequence. The expanded dataset can help the task of generating diagnostic reports to find abnormal lesions in images, partly improve the accuracy of abnormal symptoms description in the generated reports, and alleviate the difficulty of small proportion of abnormal descriptions in existing research reports. We will use this dataset as an input to the report generation research in the future and evaluate its role in reducing the data bias. In the future, we will try to expand the medical details of this dataset in more multimodal forms that can be used to provide a more detailed description of the patient's specific disease and make appropriate treatment suggestions.

Acknowledgement. This work is partially supported by Natural Science Foundation of China under Grant No. U1908210, 61976192.

References

1. Dina, D.F., et al.: Preparing a collection of radiology examinations for distribution and retrieval. J. Am. Med. Inform. Assoc. **23**(2), 304–310 (2015)
2. Shin, H. C., Roberts, K., Lu, L., Demner-Fushman, D., Yao, J., Summers, R.M.: Learning to read chest x-rays: recurrent neural cascade model for automated image annotation. In: Proceedings of the IEEE Conference on Computer Vision and Pattern Recognition, pp. 2497–2506 (2016)
3. Jing, B., Xie, P., Xing, E.: On the automatic generation of medical imaging reports. In: Proceedings of the 56th Annual Meeting of the Association for Computational Linguistics, pp. 2577–2586. Association for Computational Linguistics (2017)
4. Li, C.Y., Liang, X., Hu, Z., Xing, E.P.: Hybrid retrieval-generation reinforced agent for medical image report generation. arXiv preprint arXiv:1805.08298 (2018)
5. Li, C.Y., Liang, X., Hu, Z., Xing, E.P.: Knowledge-driven encode, retrieve, paraphrase for medical image report generation. In: AAAI Conference on Artificial Intelligence (2019)
6. Harzig, P., Chen, Y.Y., Chen, F., Lienhart, R.: Addressing data bias problems for chest x-ray image report generation (2019)
7. Rajpurkar, P., et al.: CheXNet: radiologist-level pneumonia detection on chest x-rays with deep learning (2019)
8. Wang, X., Peng, Y., Lu, L., Lu, Z., Bagheri, M., Summers, R.M.: Chestx-ray8: hospital-scale chest x-ray database and benchmarks on weakly-supervised classification and localization of common thorax diseases. arXiv preprint arXiv:1705.02315 (2017)
9. Huang, G., Liu, Z., Laurens, V.D.M., Weinberger, K.Q.: Densely connected convolutional networks. arXiv preprint arXiv:1608.06993 (2016)

Synchronous Prediction of Continuous Affective Video Content Based on Multi-task Learning

Mingda Zhang[1], Wei Zhong[1(✉)], Long Ye[2], Li Fang[1], and Qin Zhang[2]

[1] Key Laboratory of Media Audio and Video (Communication University of China), Ministry of Education, Beijing 100024, China
{mingdazhang,wzhong,lifang8902}@cuc.edu.cn

[2] State Key Laboratory of Media Convergence and Communication, Communication University of China, Beijing 100024, China
{yelong,zhangqin}@cuc.edu.cn

Abstract. In this paper, we develop an approach for the continuous prediction of affective video contents by employing multi-modal features and multi-task learning in valence and arousal dimensions. In the proposed framework, three deep features SoundNet, VGGish and YAMNet are selected for the audio modality. And we also extract the global visual features and moving information through adapting two VGG19 models, whose inputs are separately the key frames of sample videos as well as their optical-flow images. Further by fusing the audio features together with the visual ones, the multi-task learning strategies in valence and arousal dimensions are also given to improve the regression performance. The performance of the audio and visual features selected is evaluated on the Emotional Impact of Movies Task 2018 (EIMT18) in the experiments. Compared to the competitive teams of EIMT18, our approach can obtain better MSE result in the arousal dimension and much better PCC performance in the valence dimension, along with the comparable PCC metric in the dimension of arousal and slightly lower MSE metric in the dimension of valence, indicating that the joint prediction of valence and arousal dimensions can help to improve the regression performance in both of the valence and arousal dimensions, especially on the metric of PCC.

Keywords: Affective video content analysis · Multi-modal features · Multi-task learning · LIRIS-ACCEDE · LSTM

1 Introduction

In light of the rapid advance of multimedia technologies, the emotional video content analysis is becoming an extremely important part of video understanding, with the purpose of predicting the videos' emotional influence on audiences. In the recent years, growing attentions have been paid to evaluate the videos' quality and model their affective video content framework.

This work is supported by the National Natural Science Foundation of China under Grant No. 61801440, the Fundamental Research Funds for the Central Universities under Grant No. 2018XNG1824 and the CETC funding.

G. Zhai et al. (Eds.): IFTC 2020, CCIS 1390, pp. 227–238, 2021.
https://doi.org/10.1007/978-981-16-1194-0_20

The related works of emotional video content prediction can be broadly classified into two types: the global and the continuous [1–3]. For the type of global affective video content analysis, a multi-modal local-global attention network [2] was proposed based on attention-mechanism. Yi et al. [3] constructed a network to address the adaptive weights of modalities and the temporal inputs were also brought into loss functions for model training. This paper pays attention to the continuous emotional video analysis which predicts each video's expected emotional scores in the dimensions of valence and arousal continuously. In the research of the continuous affective video content analysis, the Emotional Impact of Movies Task in 2018 (EIMT18) [4] competition organized by the MediaEval aims at predicting the expected values of valence and arousal for each second of the movie. The dataset used in the EIMT18 competition includes a total of 54 movies (total duration of 96,540 s) as the development set and additional 12 movies (total duration of 32,106 s) as the test set with continuous valence and arousal annotations, which are all selected from the set of 160 movies provided in the LIRIS-ACCEDE dataset [5].

There are seven teams participated in the regression task of EIMT18, and six of them [6–11] submitted results in the valence and arousal dimensions. Among them, GLA [6] achieved the best performance in the arousal dimension and the best result with Mean Square Error (MSE) in the valence dimension. This method used the Inception-Image and VGGish features in the long short-term memory (LSTM) models, regularization with dropout and batch normalization were also used in order to prevent overfitting. THUHCSI [7] obtained the best performance on the metric of Pearson's Correlation Coefficient (PCC) in the valence dimension. Besides the baseline features including Emobase 2010 feature set, EIMT17's visual features being one big feature except the CNN and VGG-16 fc6 feature, this method also selected the eGeMAPS and the final layer of Inception network as extended deep visual features in the LSTM models. Yi and Wang et al. [8] utilized the two-stream ConvNet to capture the action feature, the SENet for the object feature and ResNet-50 for the scene feature, in addition to the VGGish for the audio feature. The CERTH-ITI team [9] extracted the pre-trained VGG-16 features and Emobase 2010 feature set to predict the valence and arousal scores by adopting a linear regression model. Quan et al. [10] only adopted the 2048-dimensional ResNet-50 features and a two-layer fully connected neural network was used for regression. Ko et al. [11] utilized a two-stage learning framework, which first conducts the subspace learning using emotion preserving embedding to uncover the informative subspace from the baseline feature space according to the emotional labels, and then the SVR with RBF kernel was used for the regression.

It is worth noting that, although some of the above methods can perform well, they all consider the affective regression task separately in the valence and arousal dimensions and maybe different models are used respectively for the valence and arousal predictions. Since the affective state is a joint representation of the valence and arousal dimensions, it is necessary to introduce the multi-task learning to predict the valence and arousal dimensions synchronously.

A novel framework is developed for the continuous emotional video prediction in this paper based on the multi-modal features and multi-task learning in the dimensions of valence and arousal. For the audio modality, three deep features SoundNet, VGGish and YAMNet are selected. In the visual modality, we extract the global visual features and moving information through adapting two VGG19 models, whose inputs are the sample videos' key frames and their optical-flow images, separately. Fusing the audio and visual features together, the multi-task learning strategies are given to predict the valence and arousal dimensions synchronously, further improving the regression performance. We evaluate the selected audio and visual features in the experiments on the dataset of EIMT18. The comparison results between the competitive teams participated in EIMT18 [6–11] and the proposed method illustrate that, the latter can reach better MSE performance in the dimension of arousal and much better PCC performance in the dimension of valence, along with the comparable PCC metric in the dimension of arousal and slightly lower MSE metric in the dimension of valence, indicating that the joint prediction of valence and arousal scores could contribute to improve the regression performance in both of the valence and arousal dimensions, especially on the metric of PCC.

In the following parts, the proposed framework including the selected audio and visual features and multi-task learning strategy is briefly introduced in Sect. 2. Section 3 demonstrates the experimental results and analysis. Finally, this paper concludes in Sect. 4.

2 Proposed Method

The proposed approach of the continuous emotional video prediction is illustrated in Fig. 1, which consists of three major steps as described below. Firstly, the pre-trained convolutional neural network models are selected to design and finetune new feature extraction networks, obtaining the audio and visual features. Specifically, three deep features SoundNet, VGGish and YAMNet are selected for the audio modality. In the analysis of visual modality, the global visual features and moving information are extracted through adapting two VGG19 models, whose inputs are the sample videos' key frames and the optical-flow images of them respectively. Subsequently, the LSTM model [12] is employed for training the unimodal feature sets and the feature-level fusion is adopted to explore the complementarity of the multi-modal features. Finally, the multi-task learning

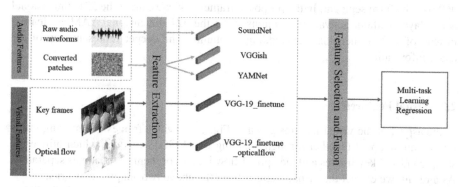

Fig. 1. The continuous emotional video prediction approach.

strategies are introduced in the valence and arousal dimensions to improve the results for model learning and prediction.

2.1 Audio Features

In the aspect of the audio features given in Fig. 1, three convolutional networks are utilized to obtain the audio features. In their midst, SoundNet could directly deal with the variable length audio waves, while VGGish and YAMNet are both the variants of image processing networks.

SoundNet: The one-dimensional convolutional network SoundNet [13] consists of the fully convolutional layers and pooling layers, it could directly process the audio waves with variable length. It learns the original audio waveform directly through employing a large number of unlabeled videos, which is trained by diverting visual information of well-trained visual model to the audio model. In the proposed framework, considering the good generalization ability of convolutional networks, the sampling rate of the raw waveform is set as 44,100 and the outputs of the conv5 layer are directly extracted as the 256-dimensional SoundNet features for each second audio segment.

VGGish and YAMNet: In order to deal with audio event detection, Google's sound understanding team released a dataset named AudioSet [14, 15], which provides a common large-scale evaluation task in March 2017. Further, the neural networks VGGish and YAMNet are both pre-trained on the AudioSet. These two networks have the same inputs, those audios are resampled into 16kHz mono and then converted to the 96×64 patches through preprocessing. VGGish is a variation of VGG model with eleven layers, and the last set of convolution and maxpooling layers are removed. Meanwhile the 128-wide dense layer is finally applied instead of the 1000-wide one, forming a compact embedded layer. The 128-dimensional VGGish feature is extracted from the 128-dimensional embeddings for each second audio segment. YAMNet is a variant of the Mobilenet_v1 model. Those 96×64 patches are fed into the Mobilenet_v1 model to yield an 3×2 array of activations for the 1024 kernels at the top of the convolution. These activations are averaged to give a 1024-dimensional embedding, and then put through a single logistic layer to get the 521 per-class output scores corresponding to the 960ms waveform segment. In the proposed framework, we extract the 521-dimensional dense layer without activation functions to be the 521-dimensional YAMNet feature instead of 1024-dimensional embeddings, obtaining the deeper representation of the audio information.

2.2 Visual Features

In the aspect of the visual features given in Fig. 1, the video frames and moving information are adopted together through adapting two VGG19 models, which utilize the sample videos' key frames and the optical-flow images of them as the inputs separately. As a result, we extract the visual features from the above two adapted networks.

VGG19 [16], which was developed by the Visual Geometry Group of Oxford University, is one of the most widely used networks in image classification and positioning.

It studies the influence of the depth of the convolutional network on the accuracy rate in large-scale image recognition tasks. Through the use of a convolutional layer with convolution kernel, the effect is greatly improved and the network depth reaches to 16–19 layers. Due to its good generalization characteristic, VGG19 is selected as the backbone to obtain the visual features of the video frames and moving information.

As shown in Fig. 2, the fully convolutional part of original VGG19 network is maintained as the backbone in the adapted VGG19 model. In order to get the information from each channel, the GAP layer is concatenated after the fully convolutional part. The deep visual features are extracted from the "dense_1" layer with 512 filters. In order to train the adapted VGG19 network on the EIMT18's dataset, we add the "dense_2" layer with two filters and set the MSE between these two filters and provided labels as the loss function.

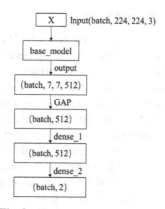

Fig. 2. The adapted VGG19 model.

The adapted VGG19 model described above is trained by two kinds of inputs. The first type of inputs is the sample videos' key frames, and the second is the optical-flow images' key frames calculated from the sample videos. For the inputs being sample videos' key frames, we choose the last frame of each second in video as its key frame. As for the inputs being the key frames of optical-flow images, we utilize the PWC-Net [17] to compute the optical-flow images of sample video frames, which includes the moving information of the videos. Although the PWC-Net is a compact CNN model, it is effective for calculating optical-flow. The current optical-flow prediction is utilized to warp the CNN features of the second image and then the warped features and features of the first image are employed to build a cost volume, which is dealt with a CNN to estimate the optical-flow. Subsequently the key frames of sample videos in each second and optical-flow images as illustrated in Fig. 3 are fed into the adapted VGG19 models to obtain the 512-dimensional visual features, respectively.

Fig. 3. The key frames of sample videos in each second and the optical-flow images.

2.3 Multi-task Learning Framework

For the continuous affective video regression task of EIMT18, the affective state is a joint representation of the valence-arousal space for each second of the video, and thus it is necessary to introduce the multi-task learning to make a joint prediction in the valence and arousal dimensions. The advantage of multi-task learning strategy is capable of boosting the generalization performance of a model through learning the main task and related ones synchronously which share the same feature representation. Here choosing the appropriate related tasks is very important. Learning the relationships between the dimensions of valence and arousal is helpful in improving the prediction of the correlations between the multi-modal features and affective dimensions.

In the proposed framework, the LSTM network is adopted to perform the multi-task learning, which can capture the complicated and long-term dependency information of the video sequences. The training process of the LSTM regression network also takes into accounts the intrinsic correlations between valence and arousal dimensions inherently. The main part of the LSTM takes notes the inputs' history before the present time step, which is represented as the memory cell c_t. The functions of past output state and present input are represented as h_{t-1} and x_t respectively. As for how many new messages of the present input x_t can be taken into account, it is controlled by the input gate i_t. Whether the network should forget its past information c_{t-1} is decided by the state of the forget gate f_t, and the output gate o_t is used to control the amount of information from memory cell c_t to output state h_t. The followings are the formulas of the LSTM at time step t:

$$\text{input gate:} \qquad i_t = \sigma(W_{ix}x_t + W_{ih}h_{t-1} + b_i), \qquad (1)$$

$$\text{forget gate:} \qquad f_t = \sigma\left(W_{fx}x_t + W_{fh}h_{t-1} + W_{fc}c_{t-1} + b_f\right), \qquad (2)$$

$$\text{output gate:} \qquad o_t = \sigma(W_{ox}x_t + W_{oh}h_{t-1} + W_{oc}c_{t-1} + b_o), \qquad (3)$$

$$\text{cell input:} \qquad g_t = f\left(W_{gx}x_t + W_{gh}h_{t-1} + b_g\right), \qquad (4)$$

$$\text{cell state:} \qquad c_t = i_t \odot g_t + f_t \odot c_{t-1}, \qquad (5)$$

cell output:$$h_t = o_t \odot \phi(c_t),$$ (6)

where σ and ϕ denote the sigmoid function and tanh function respectively, the notation "$\odot$" is the dot production of the matrices, $\{W_{**}, b_*\}$ are the parameters in the LSTM.

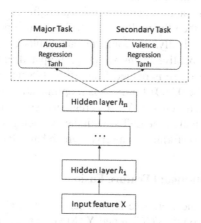

Fig. 4. The proposed multi-task learning strategy in the valence and arousal dimensions.

For the multi-task learning framework, considering the fact that the affective state is a joint representation of the valence-arousal space for each second of the video and these two dimensions are highly correlated with each other, we propose to learn the regression model both in the valence and arousal dimensions simultaneously as shown in Fig. 4. Here the MSE metric between the predictions $\hat{y}_t^{(*)}$ and actual labels $y_t^{(*)}$ is used as the loss function, which minimizes

$$L = \frac{1}{2T} \sum_{t=1}^{T} \left(\alpha \left(\hat{y}_t^{(a)} - y_t^{(a)} \right)^2 + \beta \left(\hat{y}_t^{(v)} - y_t^{(v)} \right)^2 \right),$$ (7)

$$\hat{y}_t^{(a)} = W_y^{(a)} h_t + b_y^{(a)},$$ (8)

$$\hat{y}_t^{(v)} = W_y^{(v)} h_t + b_y^{(v)},$$ (9)

where $W_y^{(a)}$ and $b_y^{(a)}$ as well as $W_y^{(v)}$ and $b_y^{(v)}$ are parameters being trained in LSTM, which are utilized to forecast the arousal and valence groundtruth $y_t^{(a)}$ and $y_t^{(v)}$ respectively, T is the data's entire time steps, hyper-parameters α and β are used to balance the two dimensions.

3 Experiments and Analysis

The developed emotional video regression strategy is tested and verified on the EIMT18 task, which predicts the expected scores of valence and arousal for each second of the movie. The dataset used in the EIMT18 task includes a total of 54 movies as the development with total duration of 96,540 s set and additional 12 movies as the test set with total duration of 32,106 s, which are all selected from the set of 160 professionally made and amateur movies provided in the LIRIS-ACCEDE dataset [5]. Both of the development and test sets are provided with continuous annotations of valence and arousal for each second of the movies.

First of all, the performance evaluation of the feature fusion is given in the modalities of audio and visual, and then the multi-task learning is also performed in the valence and arousal dimensions. Finally, we compare our results on the multi-task learning framework with the competitive teams which participated in the EIMT18. Here the temporal LSTM model we use is ranged from 16 to 128 units and 1 to 3 layers, and the learning rate is set to be 0.0001 for the Adam optimization algorithm [18]. The time step of our framework is chosen as 8. We also regularize our models by using the batch normalization and dropout after the LSTM with the rate being 0.5 to prevent overfitting. And the experiments are performed on a server which has 8 RTX 2080Ti.

3.1 Evaluation of Multi-modal Feature Fusion

As described in Sect. 2, there are five feature sets selected in all. Among them, three feature sets (SoundNet_conv5, VGGish and YAMNet) are for the audio modality, and two feature sets (VGG19 finetuned with sample videos' key frames, VGG19 finetuned with the optical-flow images) are for the visual modality. In this subsection, considering the fact that the features in the audio and visual modalities are complementary for the emotional video regression task, we concatenate these multi-modal features together and then evaluate their fusion performance on the LSTM regression model. The experimental results of representative feature combinations are given in Table 1. More concretely, the upper part of Table 1 shows the experimental results of feature fusion in the audio modality, and the lower part gives the experimental results of representative feature

Table 1. Evaluation of multi-modal feature fusion on the LSTM regression model.

Feature fusion	Arousal		Valence	
	MSE	PCC	MSE	PCC
A: Soundnet_Conv5 + VGGish	0.129	0.251	**0.116**	0.420
B: Soundnet_Conv5 + YAMNet	**0.128**	**0.254**	0.117	**0.437**
C: VGGish + YAMNet	**0.128**	0.250	0.125	0.410
D: Soundnet_Conv5 + VGGish + YAMNet	**0.128**	0.251	0.126	0.414
E: A + VGG19_finetune + VGG19_finetune_opticalflow	0.124	0.319	**0.120**	**0.408**
F: B + VGG19_finetune + VGG19_finetune_opticalflow	0.125	0.308	0.128	0.403
G: D + VGG19_finetune + VGG19_finetune_opticalflow	**0.123**	**0.325**	0.121	**0.408**

Note: "VGG19_finetune" denotes the VGG19 finetuned with the sample videos' key frames. "VGG19_finetune_opticalflow" denotes the VGG19 finetuned with optical-flow images combinations in the audio and visual modalities. The best results for both parts are shown in bold respectively.

As illustrated in Table 1 that, for the selection of audio features, the combination B obtains the best regression performance in the dimension of arousal and best PCC in the dimension of valence. And then considering the feature fusion of both audio and visual modalities, the combination G obtains the best regression performance in the dimensions of valence and arousal. More concretely for the combination G, its MSE metric is 0.123 and PCC performance is 0.325 in the arousal dimension, while its MSE metric is 0.121 and PCC performance is 0.408 in the valence dimension, showing the complementarity of audio and visual modalities.

3.2 Evaluation on Multi-task Learning Framework

For the continuous affective video regression task of EIMT18, the affective state is a joint representation of the valence-arousal space for each second of the video, and thus it is necessary to perform the multi-task learning to make a joint prediction in the valence and arousal dimensions. In this subsection, in order to get the complicated and long-term dependency information of the sequences, we adopt the LSTM network to perform the multi-task learning for the dimensions of valence and arousal.

From the experimental results of Subsect. 3.1, we can see that the audio-visual feature combination G obtains the best regression results in both of the valence and arousal dimensions. Therefore, in this subsection, we choose the audio-visual feature combination G to perform the multi-task learning for the dimensions of valence and arousal. Considering the fact that the regression performance in the arousal dimension is always inferior to those in the valence dimension, the regression task in the arousal dimension is regarded as the major task in the proposed multi-task learning framework. Table 2 gives the results of multi-task learning on the combination G, where the best results are shown in bold respectively for the valence and arousal dimensions.

Table 2. The results of multi-dimension learning on the combination G.

α: β (Arousal: Valence)	Arousal		Valence	
	MSE	PCC	MSE	PCC
(0.85: 0.15)	**0.124**	**0.349**	0.119	0.383
(0.80: 0.20)	0.125	0.341	0.118	0.384
(0.75: 0.25)	0.126	0.325	0.118	0.411
(0.70: 0.30)	0.125	0.313	**0.113**	0.400
(0.60: 0.40)	0.127	0.306	0.122	0.413
(0.50: 0.50)	0.128	0.284	0.119	**0.418**

It can be seen from Table 2 that, for the arousal dimension, the higher the weight is assigned, the better the obtained results can be. Due to the rationality of multi-modal feature selection, the valence dimension also has the similar trends and better robustness. Furthermore as shown in Table 2, the experimental results also verify that the multi-task learning for the valence and arousal dimensions is helpful to improve the regression performance in the dimensions of arousal and valence, especially on the metric of PCC.

3.3 Comparisons with the Competitive Teams of EIMT18

In this subsection, we compare our approach with the competitive teams participated in EIMT18 [6–11] as shown in Table 3, validating the effectiveness of the proposed framework. The best results are shown in bold respectively for the valence and arousal dimensions.

It can be seen from Table 3 that, compared with the competitive teams participated in EIMT18 [6–11], the proposed method can obtain better MSE metric in the dimension of arousal and much better PCC performance in the dimension of valence, along with the comparable PCC metric in the dimension of arousal and slightly lower MSE in the dimension of valence. The above comparison results show that the chosen features in the modalities of audio and visual can improve the prediction capability, indicating their complementarity to each other. In addition, the proposed multi-task learning strategy for the valence and arousal dimensions can also help to improve the regression performance in the dimension of arousal and valence, especially on the metric of PCC.

Table 3. Comparisons to the competitive teams in EIMT18.

Methods	Arousal		Valence	
	MSE	PCC	MSE	PCC
GLA [6]	0.133	**0.351**	**0.084**	0.278
THUHCSI [7]	0.140	0.087	0.092	0.305
Yi and Wang et al. [8]	0.136	0.175	0.090	0.301
CERTH-ITI [9]	0.138	0.054	0.117	0.098
Quan et al. [10]	0.171	0.091	0.115	0.146
Ko et al. [11]	0.149	0.083	0.102	0.114
Ours	**0.124**	0.349	0.113	**0.418**

4 Conclusions

A new approach is developed in this paper for the continuous emotional video analysis based on multi-modal features and multi-task learning. In the proposed framework, we choose three deep features including SoundNet, VGGish and YAMNet for the modality of audio. As for the modality of visual, we adopt the video frames and moving information together through adapting two VGG19 models, whose inputs are the sample videos' key frames and the optical-flow images separately. With the features in the audio and visual modalities fused together, the multi-task learning strategies in valence and arousal dimensions are also given to improve the regression performance. The performance of the audio and visual features selected is evaluated on the Emotional Impact of Movies Task 2018 (EIMT18) in the experiments. With the comparisons to the competitive teams participated in EIMT18 [6–11], our approach can obtain better MSE result in the arousal dimension and much better PCC performance in the valence dimension, along with the comparable PCC metric in the dimension of arousal and slightly lower MSE metric in the dimension of valence, indicating that the joint prediction of valence and arousal dimensions can help to improve the regression performance in the dimensions of valence and arousal, especially on the metric of PCC.

References

1. Baveye, Y., Chamaret, C., Dellandréa, E., Chen, L.M.: Affective video content analysis: a multidisciplinary insight. IEEE Trans. Affect. Comput. **9**(4), 396–409 (2017)
2. Ou, Y., Chen, Z., Wu, F.: Multimodal local-global attention network for affective video content analysis. IEEE Trans. Circuits Syst. Video Technol. **PP(99)**, 1 (2020)
3. Yi, Y., Wang, H., Li, Q.: Affective video content analysis with adaptive fusion recurrent network. IEEE Trans. Multimed. **22**(9), 2454–2466 (2020)
4. Dellandréa, E., Huigsloot, M., Chen, L., Baveye, Y., Xiao, Z., Sjöberg, M.: The mediaeval 2018 emotional impact of movies task. In: Emotional Impact of Movies task, MediaEval (2018)
5. Baveye, Y., Dellandrea, E., Chamaret, C., Chen, L.: Liris-accede: A video database for affective video content analysis. IEEE Trans. Affect. Comput. **6**(1), 43–55 (2015)
6. Sun, J., Liu, T., Prasad, G.: GLA in mediaeval 2018 emotional impact of movies task. In: Emotional Impact of Movies task, MediaEval (2018)
7. Ma, Y., Liang, X., Xu, M.: THUHCSI in mediaeval 2018 emotional impact of movies task. In: Emotional Impact of Movies task, MediaEval (2018)
8. Yi, Y., Wang, H., Li, Q.: CNN features for emotional impact of movies task. In: Emotional Impact of Movies task, MediaEval (2018)
9. Batziou, E., Michail, E., Avgerinakis, K., Vrochidis, S., Patras, I., Kompatsiaris, I.: Visual and audio analysis of movies video for emotion detection. In: Emotional Impact of Movies Task, MediaEval (2018)
10. Quan, K., Nguyen, V., Tran, M.: Frame-based evaluation with deep features to predict emotional impact of movies. In: Emotional Impact of Movies task, MediaEval (2018)
11. Ko, T., Gu, Z., He, T., Liu, Y.: Towards learning emotional subspace. In: Emotional Impact of Movies task, MediaEval (2018)
12. Hochreiter, S., Schmidhuber, J.: Long short-term memory. Neural Comput. **9**(8), 1735–1780 (1997)
13. Aytar, Y., Vondrick, C., Torralba, A.: SoundNet: learning sound representations from unlabeled video. In: Daniel. D., Ulrike, L., Roman, G., Masashi, S., Isabelle, G. (eds.) Advances in Neural Information Processing Systems 2016, pp. 892–900, Curran Associates Inc., New York (2016)
14. Gemmeke, J., Ellis, D., Freedman, D., et al.: Audio set: an ontology and human-labeled dataset for audio events. In: The 42nd International Conference on Acoustics, Speech and Signal Processing 2017, New Orleans, USA, pp. 776–780. IEEE (2017)
15. Hershey, S., Chaudhuri, S., Ellis, D., et al.: CNN architectures for large-scale audio classification. In: The 42nd International Conference on Acoustics, Speech and Signal Processing 2017, New Orleans, USA, pp. 131–135. IEEE (2017)

16. Simonyan, K., Zisserman, A.: Very deep convolutional networks for large-scale image recognition. arXiv preprint arXiv:1409.1556 (2014)
17. Sun, D., Yang, X., Liu, M., Kautz, J.: PWC-Net: CNNs for optical-flow using pyramid, warping, and cost volume. In: IEEE Conference on Computer Vision and Pattern Recognition 2018, Utah, USA, pp. 8934–8943. IEEE (2018)
18. Kingma, D., Ba, J.: Adam: a method for stochastic optimization. arXiv preprint arXiv:1412. 6980 (2014)

Insights of Feature Fusion for Video Memorability Prediction

Fumei Yue[1] , Jing Li[2], and Jiande Sun[1(✉)]

[1] School of Information Science and Engineering, Shandong Normal University,
Jinan 250358, Shandong, China
fumei.yue@hotmail.com, jiandesun@hotmail.com
[2] School of Journalism and Communication, Shandong Normal University,
Jinan 250358, Shandong, China
lijingjdsun@hotmail.com

Abstract. Researches on video memorability focus on predicting the probability of the content being remembered, which does make sense in both academic types of research and practical commercial. Therefore, we explore various feature fusion strategies on different regression models and give valuable suggestions for improving the prediction performance. To conclude persuasively, we test and analyze abundant performances derived from classical Random Forest (RF) and Support Vector Regression (SVR) algorithms with 7 state-of-the-art features and their combinations. Specifically, we first test the performances of the RF and SVR with the perspective of a single feature. And then we test the performance of each feature on RF and SVR by fusing semantic features, respectively. According to the single feature training results, the top-3 best features are selected to further evaluate the performance of their combinations. Then, we test the performance of the multi-feature fusion features on RF and SVR by adding semantic features. Finally, the comprehensive results indicate that the C3D feature fusing semantic features yield the best performance with the RF model for the long-term video memorability scores, and the LBP feature fusing semantic features yield the best performance with the SVR model for the short-term video memorability scores.

Keywords: Video memorability · Regression algorithms · Feature fusion

1 Introduction

Memory is a very important element in our study and life, and media memorability is also indispensable to us. However, different images and videos are remembered in different degrees in human minds, either impressing us or passing us by. Researches on the memorability of media information such as images and videos have gradually emerged. Isola et al. [9] find that memorability is

© Springer Nature Singapore Pte Ltd. 2021
G. Zhai et al. (Eds.): IFTC 2020, CCIS 1390, pp. 239–248, 2021.
https://doi.org/10.1007/978-981-16-1194-0_21

an intrinsic character of an image and prove that memorability is highly consistent across different observers. In experiments, Isola et al. prove that object and scene semantics are related to image memorability, and some features of the image can predict image memorability. After that, most of the researches focus on feature extraction and feature fusion, trying to predict image memorability by improving features. Khosla et al. [11] first propose the use of Convolutional Neural Network (CNN) to extract image features and put forward a new model MemNet. Subsequently, people try to use CNN to extract depth features and adjust algorithm performance to improve image memorability scores [29].

As the research on image memorability continues to deepen, experts and scholars have shifted their focus to video. With the researches of images, memorability are developing at an exponential rate, and moving towards the direction of video memorability is an important field of computer vision science. Due to the global development of the Internet, billions of videos are posted on popular websites each day, such as Twitter, YouTube, Instagram, and Flickr, and there are millions of people watching these videos every hour [22]. The data processed by media platforms such as media advertising, social networks, information retrieval, and recommendation systems are increasing exponentially day by day. Improving the relevance of multimedia in our daily lives requires new ways to organize or retrieve digital content. Just like other standards(such as interestingness) required for vertical videos, memorability can be considered feasible to choose from among competing videos. This is more true when considering specific use cases for creating advertising or educational content. Since different multimedia content (images or videos) have different effects on human memory, predicting the memorability level of a given content is very important for advertising experts [7]. In addition to advertising, other fields, such as academic research, film production, education, content retrieval, etc., may also be affected by the proposed task. With the MediaEval [14] conference, researches of predicting media memorability have gradually attracted everyone's attention. More and more experts and scholars have researched video descriptions and regression methods.

Based on this, more and more experts and scholars devote themselves to the study of video memorability. Similar to image memorability, the current research on video memorability is to extract features and fuse features, on the other hand, to improve the image memorability prediction algorithm. Akanksha Kar et al. [10] use CNN to propose a VM prediction model based on algorithm extraction of features, considering two types of features, i.e., semantic features and visual features. To be sure, this provides new ideas for the study of video memorability. Sumit Shekhar et al. [10] develop a predictive model for video memorability focusing on feature fusion, including saliency, C3D, video semantic features, spatiotemporal features, color features, etc. Most of the current researches are based on the extraction or fusion of video features, semantic features, color features, etc., and improve the video memory score through enhancement algorithms. Few papers take out semantic features, keyframe features, and video features separately for research and analysis of the results of each feature on different regression algorithms.

In this paper, we use 7 state-of-the-art features to train on different regression algorithms. These features include video features (C3D [24]), traditional image features (RGB [8], HOG [18], HSV [23], LBP [16]), and deep features (VGG [21], AlexNetFC7 [13]). We test and analyze abundant performances derived from classical Random Forest (RF) and Support Vector Regression (SVR) algorithms with the 7 state-of-the-art features and the influence of fusion of semantic features on video memorability performance. According to the results of the single feature training, the three best features are selected to further evaluate the performance of their combinations [27]. Then, we test the effect of the multi-feature fusion features on RF and SVR by adding semantic features. The purpose of this paper is to analyze the performance of feature fusion for video memorability prediction based on experimental results and propose our suggestions for predicting video memorability scores. It is worth noting that experiments are conducted on the TRECVid 2019 Video to Text Dataset [2]. Compared with previous experiments, the semantic features changed from one video corresponding to one semantic description to one video corresponding to multiple semantic descriptions.

The main contributions of this paper are summarized as follows:

- We test and analyze abundant performances derived from classical Random Forest (RF) and Support Vector Regression (SVR) algorithms with 7 state-of-the-art features. According to the training results of a single feature on RF and SVR model, the best three features are selected for feature fusion, and the feature performance after fusion is tested and analyzed on RF and SVR.
- We test and analyze the performance of each feature and their combinations on the RF and SVR by fusing semantic features. The performance of fusing semantic features are tested separately.
- For the long-term memorability score, C3D feature fusing semantic features yield the best performance with RF model. For the short-term memorability score, LBP feature fusing semantic features yield the best performance with the SVR model.

2   Related Work

We introduce the previous related work on media memorability. As far as memorability is concerned, it is mainly divided into image memorability and video memorability. We briefly introduce image memorability and mainly discuss the related work of video memorability. Recent works had explored the memorability of images. Papers using image features to predict image memorability were studied in [3,9,11,28], in which the features involved mainly include pixel histogram, saliency, HOG, SIFT, SSIM, deep features, depth, and motion, etc. Soodabeh Zarezadeh et al. [28] used deep features to predict image memorability on the SUN memorablity dataset. Basavaraju et al. [3] proposed that depth and motion can also affect image memorability. [5,15,26] studied objects in images, which

[15] studied objects in natural scenes. Isola et al. [9] proved that memorability was an inherent property of images, while Erdem Akagunduz et al. [1] came up with the concept of Visual Memory Schema (VMS). For the study of image memorability, some researchers focused on feature extraction, and others focused on algorithm improvement.

Researches on the memorability of videos had emerged in recent years [4,7,10,19], whose purposes were to improve videos memorability by extracting features and fusing features. Romain et al. [4] proposed the idea of predicting short-term and long-term separately. For the processing of video memorability, some features extraction directly extracted features from the video, some extracted keyframes from the video. At this level, image memorability and video memorability were described. For extracting features directly from the video, Du Tran et al. [24] proposed a simple and effective method for Spatio-temporal features. For video, C3D descriptors were versatile, compact, simple, and efficient, it also better described the characteristics of time and space. Compared with extracting features directly in the video, extracting video keyframes using image features on keyframes was much easier. For keyframes, there were many features, such as color features (RGB). The deep features extracted by the VGG [21] network and the AlexNet [13] network proposed. The deep feature extracted by the VGG [21] was an operator used to describe the local texture features of an image. AlexNetFC7 was also a new research point in recent years.

3   Understanding Video Memorability

In this section, we will introduce what video is memorability, video memorability games, and the video dataset used in this paper.

3.1   Video Memorability Game

Video memorability games [10,19] are usually divided into two stages, the short-term memorability video stage and the long-term memorability video stage. The short-term memorability stage refers to a series of videos of a given participant, including a target video and a filler video. During the observation of the participant, there will be repeated target videos. If the participant thinks that he/she has seen this video, click the space bar. After 1–2 days, perform the long-term memorability video stage for the participants who passed the first stage. Given a series of videos of the participant, there are still target videos and filler videos. If the participant thinks that he/she has seen the video, he/she can just hit the space bar. Video memorability refers to the probability that all participants correctly recognize the target video.

3.2   TRECVid 2019 Video to Text Dataset

As the MediaEval 2020 conference is held, the TRECVid 2019 Video to Text Dataset [2] is provided. The dataset provides ground truth of short-term memorability scores and long-term memorability scores, as well as the text description of each video. The difference is that a video has multiple text descriptions. We perform regression algorithm training on features based on the provided features.

Data is composed of 6,000 short videos retrieved from TRECVid 2019 Video to Text Dataset [2]. In a sense, each video consists of a coherent unit and is associated with two memorability scores, which are the probabilities of being remembered after two different periods of memorability. Similar to previous editions of the task [14], memorability has been measured using recognition tests. Now, a subset of the dataset is practicable including 590 videos as part of the training set. All of our model training have been done on this subset.

4   Predicting Video Memorability

4.1   Model and Data Preprocessing

4.1.1   Data Preprocessing

(1) Captions preprocessing: For data processing on the text description provided in the TRECVid 2019 Video to Text dataset, the difference from the previous text description is that the data we use different multiple text descriptions for a video. For the text description, we use the bag of word model to vectorize it, and then group and splice the vectorized data into a vector according to the video, to resolve the situation that the number of videos and text does not correspond in the future. Normalize the spliced vector so that the pre-processed data is restricted to a certain range $(-1,1)$, thereby removing the negative impacts caused by the singular sample data. Since the dimensionality of the spliced vector is too large, we use PCA for dimensionality reduction processing. The processed text is called a semantic feature. (2) Other features preprocessing: Normalize the spliced vector so that the preprocessed data is limited to a certain range $(-1,1)$, thereby eliminating the negative impacts caused by singular sample data. C3D is a 4096-dimensional feature. PCA is used to reduce its dimensionality. Other features also use the same method for normalization and PCA dimensionality reduction.

4.1.2   Support Vector Regression Algorithm

For general regression problems, given a training data $P = (a_1, b_1), (a_2, b_2), \dots, (a_n, b_n), b_i \epsilon R$, we aim to study a $f(a)$ such that it is as approach to b as possible, which ω and v are the parameters to be determined. In the traditional model, only when $f(a)$ and v are the same, the loss is zero. Support vector regression [25] supposes that we can accept a deviation of ε between $f(a)$ and b at most. The loss is calculated if and only if $f(a)$ when the absolute value of the difference between a and b is bigger than ε [6]. Consequently, we think that it is equal to taking $f(a)$ as the center and building an interval band with a width of 2ε. It is considered as predicted correctly if the training data drops into this interval band [6].

Thus, the SVR problem can be formalized as

$$\min_{w,v} \frac{1}{2} \parallel w \parallel^2 + C \sum_{i=1}^{m} \ell_\varepsilon(f(a_i) - b_i) \tag{1}$$

where C is the regularization constant, ℓ_ε is ε insensitive loss function

$$\ell_\varepsilon(z) = \begin{cases} 0, & if \mid z \mid \le \varepsilon; \\ \mid z \mid -\varepsilon, & otherwise. \end{cases} \tag{2}$$

4.1.3   Random Forest Algorithm

Random Forest [17] is an algorithm that integrates multiple trees through the idea of ensemble learning. There are two keywords in the name of a random forest, one is "random" and the other is "forest". "Forest" is well understood. This analogy is still very appropriate. This is also the main idea of the random forest-the embodiment of integrated thinking. Accurately, the traditional decision tree chooses a series of best attributes of the current node in the option of partition attributes, while in Random Forest, for each merit of the decision tree, a subset of k attributes is randomly chosen from the attribute set of the node, and then a best attribute is selected from this subset for the division [20].

4.2   Spearman Correlation Coefficient

The Pearson correlation coefficient between rank variables is called the Spearman correlation coefficient. The correlation coefficient ρ is formulated as [12]:

$$\rho = \frac{\sum_i (a_i - \bar{a})(b_i - \bar{b})}{\sqrt{\sum_i (a_i - \bar{a})^2 \sum_i (b_i - \bar{b})^2}} \tag{3}$$

Spearman's coefficient is used for the predicted video memorability score and ground truth. When $\rho > 0$, it means that the video memorability score is positively correlated with ground truth, and the closer to 1, the better the result.

4.3   Feature Prediction

4.3.1   Single Feature Prediction

We take C3D, HOG, AlexNetFC7, HOG, LBP, VGG, HSV, RGB as input, and use RF and SVR algorithms for training. It can be seen from Table 1 that for long-term video memorability, the Spearman correlation coefficient obtained by using the random forest algorithm to train the input HOG feature is better than the results obtained by other features. For short-term memorability videos, the results obtained by using the random forest algorithm with input HSV features are better than those obtained by other features.

Table 1. Single feature prediction

Features	RF		SVR	
	Short-term	Long-term	Short-term	Long-term
C3D	−0.158	0.022	0.091	−0.143
AlexNetFC7	0.015	−0.087	−0.239	0.022
HOG	−0.006	0.066	−0.062	−0.017
LBP	0.006	−0.033	0.002	−0.018
VGG	−0.153	−0.11	−0.087	−0.071
HSV	0.124	−0.045	−0.191	−0.089
RGB	−0.016	−0.165	0.023	−0.001

Table 2. Single feature fusion semantic feature prediction

Features	RF		SVR	
	Short-term	Long-term	Short-term	Long-term
Captions+C3D	−0.033	**0.284**	0.091	−0.131
Captions+AlexNetFC7	0.092	0.034	0.047	0.037
Captions+HOG	−0.031	0.016	−0.025	−0.011
Captions+LBP	0.043	−0.032	**0.173**	0.083
Captions+VGG	0.051	−0.048	0.143	0.065
Captions+HSV	−0.043	−0.095	−0.182	−0.079
Captions+RGB	0.135	−0.168	0.031	−0.013

4.3.2   Single Feature Fusion Semantic Feature Prediction

Semantic features and other features are separately fused, and the fused features are used as input for training using random forest and supporting vector regression. The obtained results are shown in Table 2. For long-term video memorability, the results using random forest algorithm training which after fusion of semantic features and C3D video features are significantly better than the results of single feature training and the results of other feature fusion semantics.

4.3.3   Multi-feature Prediction

According to the results of single-feature training, we selected several features with relatively good training results for multi-feature fusion and analyzed whether the multi-feature fusion has a better effect on predicting video memorability. The results are shown in Table 3.

Table 3. Multi-feature Prediction

Features	RF		SVR	
	Short-term	Long-term	Short-term	Long-term
HSV+C3D+RGB	0.076	0.076	−0.054	−0.033
AlexNetFC7+C3D+HOG	0.138	0.059	0.062	0.054
LBP+VGG+RGB	0.141	−0.142	0.008	0.016
C3D+LBP+VGG	−0.086	0.135	0.098	0.001

4.3.4 Multi-feature Fusion Semantic Feature Prediction

Multi-feature fusion is performed on the features that have been trained with semantic features and the training results are described in Table 4.

Table 4. Multi-feature fusion semantic feature prediction

Features	RF		SVR	
	Short-term	Long-term	Short-term	Long-term
Captions+HSV+C3D+RGB	0.076	0.076	−0.054	−0.024
Captions+AlexNetFC7+C3D+HOG	0.067	−0.024	−0.123	−0.095
Captions+LBP+VGG+RGB	−0.131	0.113	0.104	0.104
Cptions+C3D+LBP+VGG	−0.014	0.107	−0.129	−0.071

4.4 Results Analysis

Through the comparison of the four-level training results of a single feature, single feature fusion semantic feature, multi-feature, and multi-feature fusion semantic features, it is found that in general, the results obtained after training the data by fusion of semantics and single features are the best. For long-term video memorability, the feature obtained by fusing semantic features and C3D video features using a random forest algorithm is the best, which is 0.284. For short-term video memorability, the feature obtained by fusing the semantic feature and the LBP feature using the support vector regression algorithm is the best, which is 0.173. Compared with single features, the fusion of semantic features can promote the improvement of video memorability prediction results to a certain extent, and semantic features play an inseparable role in the study of video memorability. After a multi-feature fusion of semantic features, the prediction results decreased. We analyzed that the feature dimension became larger after multi-feature fusion semantics. After the PCA method was used to reduce the dimensionality, the number of samples was only 590, and the extraction of principal components was insufficient, resulting in data loss.

Based on the above results, we suggest that the C3D feature fusing semantic features yield the best performance with the RF model for the long-term memorability scores and the LBP feature fusing semantic features yield the best performance with the SVR model for the short-term memorability scores.

5 Conclusion

The main work what we do in this paper is to analyze the effects of four levels of features on the random forest algorithm and support vector regression algorithm for predicting video memorability. By using features as input to train the model, both in feature extraction and model selection, it provides constructive suggestions for the next step in predicting video memorability.

Acknowlegement. This work was supported in part by Natural Science Foundation of China (U1736122), and in part by Natural Science Foundation for Distinguished Young Scholars of Shandong Province (JQ201718).

References

1. Akagunduz, E., Bors, A.G., Evans, K.K.: Defining image memorability using the visual memory schema. IEEE Trans. Pattern Anal. Mach. Intell. **42**(9), 2165–2178 (2020)
2. Awad, G., et al.: Trecvid 2019: an evaluation campaign to benchmark video activity detection, video captioning and matching, and video search & retrieval. arXiv preprint arXiv:2009.09984 (2019)
3. Basavaraju, S., Sur, A.: Image memorability prediction using depth and motion cues. IEEE Trans. Comput. Soc. Syst. **7**(3), 600–609 (2020)
4. Cohendet, R., Demarty, C., Duong, N., Engilberge, M.: Videomem: constructing, analyzing, predicting short-term and long-term video memorability. In: 2019 IEEE/CVF International Conference on Computer Vision (ICCV), pp. 2531–2540 (2019)
5. Dubey, R., Peterson, J., Khosla, A., Yang, M., Ghanem, B.: What makes an object memorable? In: 2015 IEEE International Conference on Computer Vision (ICCV), pp. 1089–1097 (2015)
6. Gong, H., Qian, C., Wang, Y., Yang, J., Yi, S., Xu, Z.: Opioid abuse prediction based on multi-output support vector regression. In: Proceedings of the 2019 4th International Conference on Machine Learning Technologies, pp. 36–41 (2019)
7. Goswami, G., Bhardwaj, R., Singh, R., Vatsa, M.: MDLFace: memorability augmented deep learning for video face recognition. In: IEEE International Joint Conference on Biometrics, pp. 1–7 (2014)
8. Hunt, R.W.G.: The reproduction of colour in photography, printing and television. J. Photogr. Sci. **36**(1), 30 (1988)
9. Isola, P., Xiao, J., Torralba, A., Oliva, A.: What makes an image memorable? In: CVPR 2011, pp. 145–152 (2011)
10. Kar, A., Mavin, P., Ghaturle, Y., Vani, M.: What makes a video memorable? In: 2017 IEEE International Conference on Data Science and Advanced Analytics (DSAA), pp. 373–381 (2017)
11. Khosla, A., Raju, A.S., Torralba, A., Oliva, A.: Understanding and predicting image memorability at a large scale. In: 2015 IEEE International Conference on Computer Vision (ICCV), pp. 2390–2398 (2015)

12. Kong, X., Shi, Y., Wang, W., Ma, K., Wan, L., Xia, F.: The evolution of turing award collaboration network: bibliometric-level and network-level metrics. IEEE Trans. Comput. Soc. Syst. **6**(6), 1318–1328 (2019)

13. Krizhevsky, A., Sutskever, I., Hinton, G.: ImageNet classification with deep convolutional neural networks. In: Advances in Neural Information Processing Systems, vol. 25, no. 2 (2012)

14. Larson, M., Soleymani, M., Gravier, G., Ionescu, B., Jones, G.J.F.: The benchmarking initiative for multimedia evaluation: mediaeval 2016. IEEE Multimed. **24**(1), 93–96 (2017)

15. Lu, J., Xu, M., Yang, R., Wang, Z.: Understanding and predicting the memorability of outdoor natural scenes. IEEE Trans. Image Process. **29**, 4927–4941 (2020)

16. Ojala, T., Pietikainen, M., Maenpaa, T.: Multiresolution gray-scale and rotation invariant texture classification with local binary patterns. IEEE Trans. Pattern Anal. Mach. Intell. **24**(7), 971–987 (2002)

17. Robert, C.: Machine learning, a probabilistic perspective. Chance **27**(2), 62–63 (2014)

18. Schüller, C., Brewster, J.L., Alexander, M.R., Gustin, M.C., Ruis, H.: The hog pathway controls osmotic regulation of transcription via the stress response element (STRE) of the saccharomyces cerevisiae CTT1 gene. EMBO J. **13**(18), 4382–4389 (1994)

19. Shekhar, S., Singal, D., Singh, H., Kedia, M., Shetty, A.: Show and recall: learning what makes videos memorable. In: 2017 IEEE International Conference on Computer Vision Workshops (ICCVW), pp. 2730–2739 (2017)

20. Shi, H., Liu, S., Chen, J., Li, X., Ma, Q., Yu, B.: Predicting drug-target interactions using lasso with random forest based on evolutionary information and chemical structure. Genomics **111**(6), 1839–1852 (2019)

21. Simonyan, K., Zisserman, A.: Very deep convolutional networks for large-scale image recognition. arXiv preprint arXiv:1409.1556 (2014)

22. Struck, J., et al.: Pd23-12 utilization of facebook, twitter, youtube and instagram in the prostate cancer community. J. Urol. **199**(4), e484–e485 (2018)

23. Tobian, A.A.R., et al.: Male circumcision for the prevention of HSV-2 and HPV infections and syphilis. N. Engl. J. Med. **329**(13), 1298–1309 (2004)

24. Tran, D., Bourdev, L., Fergus, R., Torresani, L., Paluri, M.: Learning spatiotemporal features with 3d convolutional networks. In: IEEE International Conference on Computer Vision, vol. 45, pp. 1692–1703 (2015)

25. Wang, H., Shi, Y., Xuan, Z., Zhou, Q., Bouguettaya, A.: Web service classification using support vector machine. In: IEEE International Conference on Tools with Artificial Intelligence (2010)

26. Yoon, S., Kim, J.: Object-centric scene understanding for image memorability prediction, pp. 305–308 (2018)

27. Yu, E., Sun, J., Li, J., Chang, X., Han, X.H., Hauptmann, A.G.: Adaptive semisupervised feature selection for cross-modal retrieval. IEEE Trans. Multimed. **21**(5), 1276–1288 (2019)

28. Zarezadeh, S., Rezaeian, M., Sadeghi, M.T.: Image memorability prediction using deep features, pp. 2176–2181 (2017)

29. Zhang, H.Y., Liu, J., Wang, D.D.: Review of the application of deep learning in image memorability prediction. In: 2020 International Workshop on Electronic Communication and Artificial Intelligence (IWECAI), pp. 142–146. IEEE (2020)

GaLNet: Weakly-Supervised Learning for Evidence-Based Tumor Grading and Localization in MR Imaging

Tianqing Ding[1,4], Zhenyu Zhang[2], Jing Yan[3], Qiuchang Sun[1], Yuanshen Zhao[1], and Zhi-Cheng Li[1,4(✉)]

[1] Shenzhen Institutes of Advanced Technology, Chinese Academy of Sciences, Shenzhen, China
zc.li@siat.ac.cn
[2] Department of Neurosurgery,
The First Affiliated Hospital of Zhengzhou University, Zhengzhou, China
[3] Department of MRI, The First Affiliated Hospital of Zhengzhou University, Zhengzhou, China
[4] University of Chinese Academy of Sciences, Beijing, China

Abstract. Learning grading models directly from magnetic resonance imaging (MRI) without segmentation is more challenging. Existing deep convolutional neural network-based tumor grading algorithms rely on pixel-level annotation and lack of interpretability for clinical applications. This paper proposes a tumor Grading and Localization Network, or GaLNet, for providing evidence-based tumor grading from original magnetic resonance images (MRI) without tumor segmentation using a weakly-supervised approach. By employing malignancy attention blocks, GaLNet learns multi-scale malignancy-aware features with both strong semantics and fine spatial information. By adapting GaLNet trained with image-level tumor grading labels, the network jointly localizes malignant regions to provide supporting evidence of why and what GaLNet predicts. GaLNet achieves an AUC of 0.86 and an accuracy of 87% on testing dataset, which outperforms the tradition ResNet (0.83, 80%) and SENet (0.84, 86%) trained with images of segmented tumor.

Keywords: Weakly-supervised learning · Localization · Grading

1 Introduction

Gliomas are primary brain tumors deriving from neuroglias stem or progenitor cells [1]. Gliomas account for ∼80% of all primary brain tumors [2]. Gliomas are assigned into four WHO grades from I to IV, indicating different degree of malignancy. In clinical setting, tumor grading is a critical factor affecting treatment strategy [1]. The lower-grade gliomas (LGGs, WHO grade II and

Supported by the National Natural Science Foundation of China (61571432), Shenzhen Basic Research Program (JCYJ20170413162354654).

III) are the most common gliomas in young adults, characterized by diffuse infiltration of the brain parenchyma and an inherent tendency to recurrence and progression [3]. LGGs possess a favorable prognosis, where possible management includes watch-and-wait, biopsy assessment or immediate resection. The high-grade gliomas (HGGs, WHO grade IV), or glioblastomas (GBMs), are the most frequent and most malignant gliomas that predominantly occur in patients more than 50 years of age. The standard of care of HGG is complete macroscopic resection followed by combination chemoradiotherapy [4].

Previous studies have demonstrated that features learned from magnetic resonance imaging (MRI) are predictive of glioma WHO grading, survival, and genomic characteristics [5–8]. Recently, deep convolutional neural networks (CNNs) trained on MRI have shown superior performance in glioma diagnosis and prognosis compared with handcrafted features [9–11]. However, most image-based learning methods rely on accurate tumor segmentation. Supervised automated tumor segmentation requires pixel-level annotations, which is time-consuming and costly. On the other hand, most methods lack of interpretable evidence supporting for the grading decision made. These motivate us to develop evidence-based grading algorithm without preacquired tumor annotations. A learning method predicting WHO grades directly from MRI data without tumor segmentation has undoubtedly clinical benefits.

Learning grading models directly from MRI without segmentation is more challenging than from tumoral area, because most regions in brain MRI are healthy parts without grading-associated information. Therefore, we consider learning to focus on the tumor area. This problem can be reconsidered in a weakly-supervised learning way [12]: learning to localize the tumor by a CNN trained with image-level grading labels only. We hypothesize that learning malignancy aware features for tumor grading could identify the malignant regions, while extracting features from the localized malignant regions could enhance the tumor grading. In such a case, learning to localize the discriminative evidence in MRI can offer visually interpretable information for clinicians. It is a challenging and interesting task, aiming to learn "malignant" features showing where and how malignant the tumor is.

In this paper, we for the first time present an evidence-based joint Grading and Localization Network, or GaLNet, which (1) is end-to-end trainable for evidence-based glioma grading using MRI slices without pre-delineated tumor annotations, and (2) can jointly localize the discriminative evidence in a weakly-supervised way trained with binary grading labels (HGG or LGG) only. The main contributions of this study include:

(1) *Malignancy attention*:
   To learn malignant features for grade prediction, malignancy attention blocks (MABs) are incorporated into the GaLNet. A multi-scale attention mechanism based on a mini-pyramidal structure is used to focus on malignant regions in multiple MRI sequences.

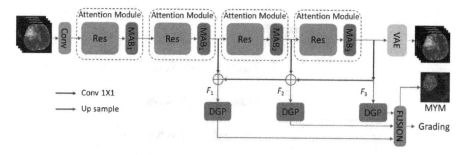

Fig. 1. Architecture of the proposed GaLNet for glioma grading and localization from multiple MRI sequences.

(2) *Malignancy map*:

To localize malignant regions, malignancy map (MYM) is generated inspired by the class activation map (CAM) technique [13]. MYM highlights malignant regions with high resolution. It enables nearly pixel-level localization of malignancy for providing visually interpreted evidence of the predicted tumor grade.

2   The Proposed GaLNet

We aim to predict binary grade (HGG or LGG) for glioma patients using multiple MRI sequences. We first introduce the architecture of the proposed GaLNet. Then we elaborate how GaLNet provides visually interpretable evidence by jointly handling grade prediction and malignancy localization.

2.1   Data Preprocessing

The MRI data used include T1-weighted, T1-weighted Gadolinium contrast-enhanced, T2-weighted, and T2-weighted FLAIR images (short for T1w, T1C, T2w, and FLAIR). The MRI images (T1w, T1C, T2w, and FLAIR) are preprocessed to normalize the intensity and geometry. First, N4 is employed for bias field correction. After skull stripping, all voxels are resampled into $1 \times 1 \times 1$ mm^3 with a linear interpolater. Rigid registration is performed using T1C image as a template with the mutual information similarity metric. Histogram matching is performed for intensity normalization.

2.2   GaLNet Framework

As observed, lower stages of CNN have poor semantic consistency while encode finer spatial information; higher stages extract semantically strong but spatially coarse features. Therefore, we fuse multi-scale information to combine the advantages of accurate semantic prediction and finer spatial localization. On the other hand, we employ attention mechanism to focus on the malignant regions, which

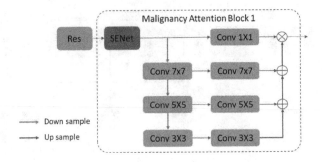

Fig. 2. The proposed malignancy attention block (MAB₁).

could significantly improve the prediction performance of the multi-scale network especially when original MR images rather than ROIs are used as input.

The framework of the proposed GaLNet is illustrated in Fig. 1. GaLNet is built based on a multi-scale fusion architecture, comprising a malignant feature extraction path containing four MABs, a variational auto-encoder (VAE) branch, and a multi-scale feature fusion structure. The binary tumor grade, g_i, is used as the training label. The output $\hat{g}_\theta$ is the estimated grade, where θ is the network parameters (weights). Meanwhile, at the last convolutional layer we obtain the MYMs, from which the malignancy can be localized as discriminative evidence.

The feature extractor starts with a convolution layer followed by four attention modules, where ResNet is used as the basic recognition unit [14]. The feature extractor can be divided into four stages according to the size of the feature maps. At each bottleneck between two adjacent ResNet stages, a MAB is employed to learn malignancy-aware features. Note that considering the feature map size, at different bottlenecks we integrate three types of MABs, as described in Sect. 2.3.

Along the top-down path the features maps are gradually upsampled by a factor 2 using nearest neighbor interpolation. Lateral connections are built to merge the upsampled semantically-stronger feature maps with the corresponding spatially-finer maps by pixel-wise addition, generating three merged maps at different scales. The three feature maps at different scales before the fusion stage are $\{F_1, F_2, F_3\}$, as shown in Fig. 1. Before each lateral connection a 1×1 convolution is applied to adjust the channel dimensions. The merged features are then fused to enhance both the classification and localization.

Instead of the global averaging pooling (GAP) employed in original CAM technique [13], dual global pooling (DGP) is performed on $\{F_1, F_2, F_3\}$ respectively. DGP comprises a GAP operator for searching for the best discriminative features and a global max pooling (GMP) operator for identifying all discriminative parts over the image. After DPG on each feature map, two vectors are generated and concatenated into one. The concatenated vectors are followed by a fully convolutional layer (kernel size 1×1) and a final sigmoid node, generating the final estimated grade. Note that GaLNet is fully convolutional and therefore is efficient at inference phase. To show the discriminative evidence, MYMs indicating malignancy localizations are calculated at different scales.

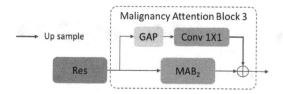

Fig. 3. The proposed malignancy attention block (MAB$_3$).

2.3 Malignancy Attention Block

To focus on representing the malignant evidence while ignore the healthy background, attention mechanism is employed. To capture both large and subtle malignant contents, a multi-scale attention block, or MAB, is proposed as shown in Fig. 2. Three types of attention block are used, i.e. MAB$_1$, MAB$_2$, and MAB$_3$. MAB$_1$ is integrated at the first and second ResNet bottlenecks. For MAB$_1$, first, channel attention is used to select channel-wise malignancy-aware features using SENet [15]. Then, a triple-scale attention branch is employed to emphasize malignant regions using a mini-pyramidal U-shape structure. To better approximate the importance of different locations at different scales, 7×7, 5×5 and 3×3 convolutions are used in MAB$_1$. Then, multi-scale features are fused by the mimi-pyramid scale-by-scale, which can make good use of context features at adjacent scales. The final output of MAB$_1$ is an pixel-wise multiplication of the multi-scale attention features and the original features from the SENet after a 1×1 convolution.

MAB$_2$ is integrated in the third ResNet bottleneck, while MAB$_3$ is added on top of the feature extraction path. In MAB$_2$, considering the reduced feature size after two ResNet stages, a two-scale attention structure is used instead of the triple-scale one, employing only 5×5 and 3×3 convolutions. In MAB$_3$, a GAP followed by a 1×1 convolution is used as shown in Fig. 3, which incorporates the strongest global information into the fused feature by adding with the output features of an MAB$_2$ block.

2.4 Malignancy Map

The CAM technique previously proposed in [13] can localize class-specific objects with image-level classification labels only. However, CAM is obtained from the last convolutional layer and therefore is spatially coarse.

We propose a malignancy map, or MYM technique by taking the weighted sum of features maps from different scales using multiple DGPs. Note that MYM follows the approach of Grad-CAM [17] rather than the original CAM [13] as GaLNet is fully convolutional. MYM localizes the malignant regions on the input image, showing the importance of regions to the predicted tumor grade. Therefore, it provides clinicians a visualized evidence of why and what the GaLNet predicts.

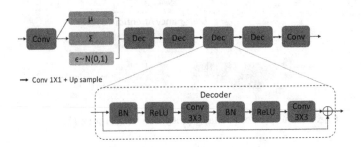

Fig. 4. The VAE decoder branch.

Given the target feature map at scale s as $F_s \in \{F_1, F_2, F_3\}$, the MYM at scale s, M_s, can be computed as a weighted sum of F_s with the weights $\{w_s^n\}$, where w_s^n indicates the importance of the n-th feature map F_s^n in F_s. The weight w_s^n is calculated by spatially averaging the gradients of the tumor grade g_θ with respect to F_s^n as

$$w_s^n = Avg_{(i,j)}(\frac{\partial g_\theta}{\partial F_s^n(i,j)}), \tag{1}$$

where the gradients $\frac{\partial g_\theta}{\partial F_s^n(i,j)}$ can be obtained in back propagation. M_s can then be calculated

$$M_s = \mathrm{ReLU}(\sum_n w_s^n F_s^n), \tag{2}$$

where ReLU is used to discard negative features.

The final MYM is a weighted sum of M_s at all three scales and can be calculated as

$$MYM = a \cdot M_1 + b \cdot \mathrm{UP}(M_2) + c \cdot \mathrm{UP}(M_3), \tag{3}$$

where UP upsamples M_2, M_3 to the size of M_1 using bilinear interpolation and $a + b + c = 1$.

2.5   VAE Decoder Branch

Considering the limited size of training dataset, an additional VAE decoder-like branch [16] is appended at the endpoint of the feature extractor (after MAB$_3$) to reconstruct the original input images.

The VAE branch is illustrated in Fig. 4. This branch is used to regularize and guide the feature extractor. First, the channels of the feature maps from MAB$_3$ are adjusted to 256 where 128 represents mean and 128 represents standard deviation (std). Given the mean and std, a sample is randomly generated from a Gaussian distribution and is decoded to reconstruct the input images.

2.6   Loss Function

The loss function consists of three parts as

$$\mathbf{L} = \mathbf{L}_{\mathrm{ce}} + \alpha \cdot \mathbf{L}_{\mathrm{rec}} + \beta \cdot \mathbf{L}_{\mathrm{KL}}, \tag{4}$$

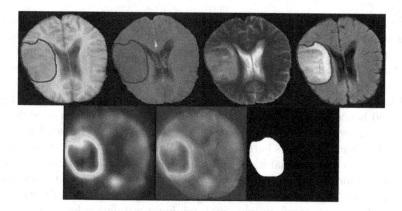

Fig. 5. First row: From left to right: T1w, T1c, T2w and FLAIR image overlapped with pixel-level tumor segmentation delineated manually by clinicians; Second row: From left to right: MYM, MYM overlapped with FLAIR, malignancy localization from MYM using fixed thresholding.

where α, β are both 0.05 determined empirically. $\mathbf{L}_{ce}$ is a cross-entropy loss between the predicted grade and the ground truth. $\mathbf{L}_{rec}$ is an ℓ_2 loss measuring the error between the original and VAE reconstructed images as $\mathbf{L}_{rec} = \|I_{in} - I_{VAEout}\|_2^2$. $\mathbf{L}_{KL}$ is a KL divergence used as the penalty term in standard VAE [16].

3   Results

3.1   Data and Setup

In total 681 glioma patients are collected from The First Affiliated Hospital of Zhengzhou University and Sun Yat-sen University Cancer Center. The inclusion criteria were that patients with (1) newly diagnosed histologically-confirmed WHO grade II, III, or IV gliomas and (2) pretreatment MRI including axial T1-weighted, axial T1-weighted Gadolinium contrast-enhanced, axial T2-weighted, and T2-weighted fluid attenuation inversion recovery images (short for T1w, T1c, T2w, and FLAIR). Exclusion criteria were that (1) patients without confirmed grading data and (2) MRI with motion artifact.

All local MR images were acquired with 1.5 and 3.0-T MRI systems (Magnetom Verio or Trio TIM, Siemens Healthcare, Erlangen, Germany and Discovery MR 750, GE Healthcare, Milwaukee, Wisconsin). The scanning sequences and parameters were: (1) T1w sequences at repetition time msec, 210–720; echo time msec, 4–20; section thickness, 2.0–5.0mm; (2) T1c images at repetition time msec, 260–950; echo time msec, 4–20; section thickness, 2.0–5.0mm; (3) T2w images at repetition time msec, 2137–10000; echo time msec, 80–140; section thickness, 3.0–5.0mm; (4) T2w FLAIR images at repetition time msec, 6000–11000; echo time msec, 85–155; section thickness, 2.5–6.0mm.

The tumor grade is pathologically confirmed. The cohort is randomly divided into a training set of 545 patients (225 HGGs and 320 LGGs) and a testing set of 136 patients (59 HGGs and 77 LGGs) at a ratio of 4:1. All computing is done using Tensorflow on NVidia Tesla V100 32G GPU. For each patient, 4 transverse slices with the largest tumor area are selected from T1w, T1c, T2w and FLAIR respectively. The are resized into 256×256 and are used as input. ResNet-50 is used as the basic unit. The network is trained from scratch using Adam optimizer with a initial learning rate of 10^{-4} and a batch size of 16 for 150 epochs. The learning rate is halved at 75 and 125 epochs. ℓ_2-norm regularization is used on the convolutional kernel parameters with a weight of 10^{-5}. Random rotation, random shear and random zoom are used for data augmentation. In the training set, 436 are used for training while 109 are used for validation with a ratio of 4:1. The network weights with minimum validation loss is used in the final model for testing.

Table 1. Performance comparison on both training and testing datasets. Acc, tr and te are short for accuracy, training and testing. ResNet ROI and SE-ResNet ROI are trained using ROI. GaLNet$^-$ removes all MABs from GaLNet.

Model	AUC_{tr}	Acc_{tr}	AUC_{te}	Acc_{te}
ResNet	0.83	80%	0.76	74%
SE-ResNet	0.83	83%	0.78	75%
ResNet ROI	0.91	90%	0.83	80%
SE-ResNet ROI	0.93	90%	0.84	86%
GaLNet	**0.93**	**92%**	**0.86**	**87%**
GaLNet$^-$	0.85	86%	0.79	80%

3.2   Tumor Grade Classification Results

We compare the proposed GaLNet with ResNet-50 [14] and SE-ResNet-50 [15]. For further comparison, the ROI of segmented tumor is used as input instead of the original MRI. The tumor is segmented from the input MRI using a 3D U-Net based automated algorithm proposed in [18]. The ROI is resized into 224×224 and fed into a CNN trained with cross-entropy loss. To assess the importance of the proposed attention mechanism, ablation experiments are also performed by removing all MABs.

The results are shown in Table 1. On the testing dataset, GaLNet achieves the highest AUC of 0.86 and the highest accuracy of 87%. Note that GaLNet outperforms the ResNet and SENet trained with ROI on testing dataset. One reasonable explanation is that GaLNet has seen not only the intratumoral structures but also peritumoral and "healthy-looking" tissues, which may contain malignant information and therefore could contribute in tumor grading.

3.3   Malignancy Evidence Localization Results

Given the accurate tumor grading from MR images, the proposed GaLNet can localize the supporting evidence. An example is shown in Fig. 5. For precise localization, a nearly pixel-level segmentation can be generated from MYM using a simple fixed thresholding, as shown in the seventh column in Fig. 5. The MYM and the localized malignant regions provide a visualized evidence of what and why GaLNet predicts.

4   Conclusion

In clinical practice, it is important to reduce image annotation burden and to improve interpretability of CNN. Our study shows the potential of weakly-supervised learning with GaLNet in evidence-based tumor grading from MRI in glioma patients. GaLNet does not require tumor segmentation. More importantly, GaLNet can provide discriminative evidence with accurate malignancy localization, which can serve as visual assistance supporting for the grading decision.

References

1. Weller, M., et al.: Glioma. Nat. Rev. Dis. Primers **1**, 15017 (2015)
2. Ostrom, Q.T., et al.: CBTRUS statistical report: primary brain and other central nervous system tumors diagnosed in the United States in 2013–2017. Neuro-Oncology, **22**, iv1–iv96 (2020)
3. Brat, D.J., et al.: Cancer genome atlas research network. Comprehensive, integrative genomic analysis of diffuse lowergrade gliomas. N. Engl. J. Med. **372**, 2481–2498 (2015)
4. Wen, P.Y., et al.: Glioblastoma in adults: a society for neuro-oncology (SNO) and European society of neuro-oncology (EANO) consensus review on current management and future directions. Neuro Oncol. **22**, 1073–1113 (2020)
5. Mohan, G., Subashini, M.M.: MRI based medical image analysis: survey on brain tumor grade classification. Biomed. Signal Process. Control **39**, 139–161 (2018)
6. Li, Q., et al.: A fully-automatic multiparametric radiomics model: towards reproducible and prognostic imaging signature for prediction of overall survival in glioblastoma multiforme. Sci. Rep. **7**, 14331 (2017)
7. Li, Z.-C., et al.: Multiregional radiomics profiling from multiparametric MRI: identifying an imaging predictor of IDH1 mutation status in glioblastoma. Cancer Med. **7**, 5999–6009 (2018)
8. Li, Z.-C., et al.: Multiregional radiomics features from multiparametric MRI for prediction of MGMT methylation status in glioblastoma multiforme: a multicentre study. Eur. Radiol. **28**, 3640–3650 (2018). https://doi.org/10.1007/s00330-017-5302-1
9. Decuyper, M., Bonte, S., Van Holen, R.: Binary glioma grading: radiomics versus pre-trained CNN features. In: Frangi, A.F., Schnabel, J.A., Davatzikos, C., Alberola-López, C., Fichtinger, G. (eds.) MICCAI 2018. LNCS, vol. 11072, pp. 498–505. Springer, Cham (2018). https://doi.org/10.1007/978-3-030-00931-1_57

10. Lao, J., et al.: A deep learning-based radiomics model for prediction of survival in glioblastoma multiforme. Sci. Rep. **7**, 10353 (2017)
11. Choi, K.S., et al.: Prediction of IDH genotype in gliomas with dynamic susceptibility contrast perfusion MR imaging using an explainable recurrent neural network. Neuro Oncol. **21**, 1197–1209 (2019)
12. Diba, A., et al.: Weakly supervised cascaded convolutional networks. In: CVPR, pp. 5131–5139 (2017)
13. Zhou, B., et al.: Learning deep features for discriminative localization. In: CVPR, pp. 2921–2929 (2016)
14. He, K., et al.: Deep residual learning for image recognition. In: CVPR, pp. 770–778 (2016)
15. Hu, J., Shen, L., Sun, G.: Squeeze-and-excitation networks. In: CVPR, pp. 7132–7141 (2018)
16. Doersch, C.: Tutorial on variational autoencoders. arXiv:1606.05908 (2016)
17. Selvaraju, R.R., et al.: Grad-CAM: visual explanations from deep networks via gradient-based localization. In: ICCV, pp. 618–629 (2017)
18. Isensee, F., Kickingereder, P., Wick, W., Bendszus, M., Maier-Hein, K.H.: No new-net. In: Crimi, A., Bakas, S., Kuijf, H., Keyvan, F., Reyes, M., van Walsum, T. (eds.) BrainLes 2018. LNCS, vol. 11384, pp. 234–244. Springer, Cham (2019). https://doi.org/10.1007/978-3-030-11726-9_21

Image Retrieval Under Fine-Grained and Long-Tailed Distribution

Shuai Chen, Fanman Meng$^{(\boxtimes)}$, Qingbo Wu, Yuxuan Liu, and Yaofeng Yang

University of Electronic Science and Technology of China,
Chengdu 611731, China
{s-chen,liuyuxuan1,202022011513}@std.uestc.edu.cn,
{fmmeng,qbwu}@uestc.edu.cn

Abstract. Image retrieval is a promising task that aims to retrieve relevant images from a large-scale database based on user's requests. This paper is a solution to the Huawei 2020 digital device image retrieval competition. The core idea of the proposed solution is to employ metric-learning to perform fine-grained image retrieval. To be specific, to address the long-tailed distribution caused by the imbalance of samples in the dataset, an image retrieval tailored causal graph is first constructed, and a causal intervention is performed for counterfactual reasoning, which proves to be effective to alleviate the influence of long-tailed distribution. To solve the challenging fine-grained image retrieval issues, this paper proposes a novel global and local attention image retrieval framework, which simultaneously mines global and local features to obtain the most discriminative feature. In addition, an object detector is further developed to capture the object of interest, thereby an accurate representation of the foreground area can be acquired. Furthermore, some additional testing and model ensemble skills, such as re-ranking, fine-tuning on larger images, and multi-scale testing, are implemented to further boost the performance. Extensive experiments on the benchmark demonstrate the effectiveness of the proposed method.

Keywords: Fine-grained image retrieval · Long-tailed distribution · Attention mechanism · Causal intervention

1 Introduction

Image retrieval technology aims at retrieving user-interested images from a large-scale database according to the user's specific needs. Image retrieval is a fundamental task in the modern computer vision community and has a large number of application scenarios, such as e-commerce [8], fashion landmark detection [10,23], and so on. In the past few years, due to the rapid growth of multimedia technology and the continuous increase of social information, image retrieval has aroused growing attention and many effective image retrieval methods have been developed [3,7,19]. Although considerable progress has been made in image

© Springer Nature Singapore Pte Ltd. 2021
G. Zhai et al. (Eds.): IFTC 2020, CCIS 1390, pp. 259–270, 2021.
https://doi.org/10.1007/978-981-16-1194-0_23

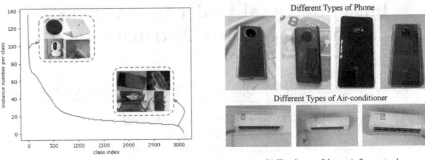

(a) The distribution of the dataset is long-tail distribution.   (b) The classes of dataset is fine-grained.

Fig. 1. Illustration of the long-tailed (a) and fine-grained (b) essence of the given dataset. In (a), some classes have hundreds of instances, while there are many classes whose instances are less than twenty. In (b), different brands of phones and air-conditioners belong to different classes, although they are very similar to each other.

retrieval, most existing image retrieval methods still face some challenges, such as long-tailed distribution and fine-grained classification problems, which will affect the practicability of image retrieval algorithms.

The long-tailed essence of the given dataset is shown in Fig. 1(a), some classes (termed as tail classes) only contain rarely few images, while their counterparts (termed as head classes) contain hundreds of images. This unbalanced distribution can inevitably lead to an inferior training process predominated by the head class, while deterioration of tail class is gained. The previous methods mainly adapt the re-sampling [11] or re-weighting [4] strategy to alleviate such an issue, however, these two strategies need future data distribution before training, thus cannot be applied to a variety of dynamic data streams. Motivated by [15,21], we establish a Structural Causal Model (SCM) [15], which considers the SGD momentum term as a confounder in long-tailed image retrieval, playing two roles simultaneously: benefiting the head class and misleading the tail class to the representation of the head class. The details of the utilized causal graph can be found in [21]. After establishing the causal graph, we perform backdoor adjustment [13] to obtain the real representation of tail class by wiping out the influence of the SGD momentum term. We refer readers to [15,21] for more details about SCM and it's applications in long-tailed image classification.

Fine-grained image retrieval is a challenging problem and needs further research. This issue mainly locates on the following two technical points. First, the category-level of fine-grained retrieval is much lower than traditional image retrieval. Take category 'cellphone' as an example, the traditional image retrieval only needs to identify 'cellphone' from other categories (such as 'air-conditioner' and 'watch'), but the fine-grained retrieval need to distinguish the specific kinds (such as 'Huawei' and 'iPhone') of 'cellphone' additionally, and even the 'Huawei cellphone' is also split into some tiny classes according to its specific type. Figure 1(b) illustrates some samples of 'cellphone' and 'air-conditioner'. Second, the fine-grained categories belonging to tail classes have a big difference in posture, texture, color, and background, which brings great difficulty to fine-grained classification. Previous methods [1,2,5,12,16,18] propose a global structure in a single-forward pass to solve this task but the performance is limited. In our opinion, fine-grained image retrieval has a high demand for local details but such a global strategy cannot capture detailed and local information, thus it has poor performance. [2] proposes a local self-attention module combining with global structure and achieves great improvement. This module uses 1×1 convolution layers to convert middle feature maps into a coefficient matrix, and then the matrix is used to re-weight feature maps to filter information. Motivated by group convolution, we propose our structure: Global and Local Attention Network (GLANet) to solve such an issue. The key innovation is the multi-head attention module, and a fusion module is proposed to fuse the local features and global features, forming the final descriptor. In this way, each output has highlighted local channel-specific information, which can promote the network to get better recognition capability on fine-grained retrieval task.

Noted that the fusion module plays two roles in our method, fusing the global and local features in the GLANet, and simultaneously acting as a sampling method to perform the backdoor adjustment in the utilized causal graph. Moreover, a foreground detector and some additional strategies are implemented to further enhance performance. To summarize, the main contribution of the proposed method are four-fold:

1. Different from the existing methods, the proposed method utilizes an image retrieval tailored causal graph and a causal intervention strategy to perform counterfactual reasoning, capable of boosting performance under a long-tailed distribution setting.
2. To cope with the challenge of fine-grained retrieval, this paper proposes a global and local attention image retrieval framework, which jointly uses the global and local descriptors to fully exploit the most discriminative features.
3. Observing that the interesting object is usually located in the center of each picture, this paper develops an object detector for foreground detection, so that the model can focus on the object region and a precise representation of the interesting object can be obtained.
4. A series of additional strategies, namely re-ranking, fine-tuning on larger images, and model ensemble, are implemented to further improve the performance of the proposed model. Extensive experiments on the benchmark demonstrate the effectiveness of the proposed method.

2   Method

In this section, we will elaborate the strategies adopted to deal with long-tailed distribution, namely the causal graph and casual intervention firstly. Then we describe the detailed architecture of the proposed GLANet, addressing the fine-grained image retrieval task. Finally, we present the core idea of the foreground detector.

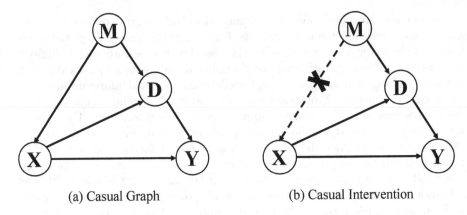

(a) Casual Graph   (b) Casual Intervention

Fig. 2. Illustration of the causal graph and the causal intervention process. M, D, X, Y denote momentum term, projection on head class, image feature, image label respectively. By cutting off the $M \longrightarrow X$ edge, the true $X \longrightarrow Y$ is obtained.

2.1   Causal Graph for Long-Tailed Distribution

Causal Graph Establishment. To deal with the long-tailed distribution of the given dataset, a causal graph is established, shown in Fig. 2, containing four data variables: the SGD momentum M, the image feature X, projection on the head direction D, and the image label Y. The directed edges among these variables indicate how each variable influences each other, where the root is the cause and the goal is the effect. The edges are explained as follows:

$M \longrightarrow X$. This edge denotes the image feature X form a specific image, with the influence of optimizer momentum M.

$M \longrightarrow D \longleftarrow X$. These two edges illustrate that the momentum M makes X deviating from its real direction.

$X \longrightarrow Y \longleftarrow D$. The final model prediction Y is determined by two variables, where $X \longrightarrow Y$ is the real effect, and also what we want, while $Y \longleftarrow D$ can be taken as a median that X influence Y indirectly.

Causal Intervention. To obtain the direct representation of head class and tail class, known as the Total Direct Effect (TDE) [14,22]. A de-confound training step is needed, in other words, the classifier of the image retrieval model should be normalized:

$$Y_i = \frac{\tau}{M} \sum_{m=1}^{M} \frac{(w_i^m)^T x^m}{(\|w_i^m\| + \gamma) \|x^m\|} \tag{1}$$

where τ, γ is two hyper-parameters controlling the classifiers, M is the multi-head number, Y_i is the logits of ith class, and w_i^m is the weight of mth classifier without bias.

To accomplish such a de-confound training, a moving average feature $\bar{x}_i$ should be maintained across training iterations, and the direction of such a moving average feature is considered as the inclination direction $\hat{d}$ of training dynamics on the head class.

$$\overline{x}_i = \alpha\overline{x}_{i-1} + (1-\alpha)x_i \tag{2}$$

$$\hat{d} = \overline{x}/\|\overline{x}\| \tag{3}$$

where α is the momentum term, and x_i is the image feature under current model.

During the validation and test step, a counterfactual TDE inference step is performed, that is, part of the class logits, having the excessive tendency towards the head class, should be taken out:

$$TDE\left(Y_i\right) = \frac{\tau}{M}\sum_{m=1}^{M}\left(\frac{\left(w_i^m\right)^T x^m}{\left(\|w_i^m\| + \gamma\right)\|x^m\|} - \alpha\cdot\frac{\cos\left(x^m, \hat{d}^m\right)\cdot\left(w_i^m\right)^T \hat{d}^m}{\|w_i^m\| + \gamma}\right) \tag{4}$$

After obtaining the TDE logits of a specific image, the image retrieval process can be built on this representation.

2.2   Global and Local Attention Network

To extract the efficient representation of images, we propose the GLANet, which is shown in Fig. 3. GLANet mainly contains three components: a local feature extraction module, a global feature extraction module, and a feature fusion module. Furthermore, when extracting local features, we introduce an attention mechanism to obtain local features at diverse spatial locations.

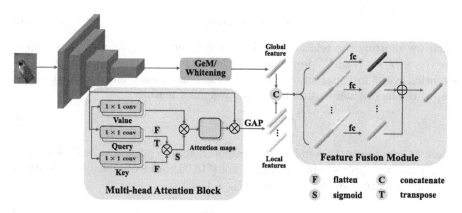

Fig. 3. Overview of our method. It contains three components: local feature extraction module, global feature extraction module and feature fusion module.

Global Feature Extraction Module. For the extraction of global features, we implement it based on the deep features to obtain global and high-level semantic information of images. Specifically, the deep features of size $C_D \times H_D \times W_D$ is obtained from the output of the last layer firstly. Then, we apply Generalized Mean Pooling (GeM) [16] to aggregate deep features into a global feature. Afterward, whitening is applied to remove redundant information, which utilizes a fully connected layer F with learning bias b to get the final global features v_G.

$$v_G = F \times \left(\frac{1}{H_D W_D} \sum_{h,w} d_{h,w}^p \right)^{1/p} + b, \tag{5}$$

where p denotes the generalized mean power parameter, $d_{h,w}$ is the feature vector of size C_D at location h, w.

Local Feature Extraction Module. As for local features with low-level information, we apply our proposed local feature extraction module to obtain them from the features of the penultimate layer. In addition, to obtain richer local features from diverse locations, a Multi-Head Attention Block is constructed during the process of local features generation.

Given an input feature of size $C_M \times H_M \times W_M$. Firstly, we apply three 1×1 convolutions to the features to get query, value, and key. Then tensor $q \in N_M \times C_M$ is obtained through flattening and transposing the query, and tensor $k \in C_M \times N_M$ is obtained through flattening the key, where $N_M = H_M \times W_M$. Then We multiply q and k together and use softmax to get a relationship matrix S of size $N_M \times N_M$

$$S = softmax(q^\top k). \tag{6}$$

Then we multiply the relation matrix S and value to get the attention map of size $C_M \times H_M \times W_M$. We implement the attention operation M times to get M attention maps focusing on different locations and then multiply the attention map with the original feature to get the weighted feature

$$F_{Li} = S \cdot F_i, i \in [1, M] \tag{7}$$

where M represents the number of attention maps, F_{Li} denotes the ith local feature. Then, we apply Global Average Pool (GAP) to the obtained local features to obtain a feature vector v_{Li} of size $C_M \times 1$.

$$v_{Li} = f_{GAP}(F_{Li}) \tag{8}$$

Feature Fusion Module. New feature vectors $f_C = \{f_{C1}, \ldots, f_{CM}\}$ are obtained by concatenating the global feature vector and each local feature vector. We reduce the dimension of the newly obtained feature vectors through the fully connected layer and then perform the average operation on the obtained results. In this way, we get the feature vector v_{out} that we finally output.

$$v_{\text{out}} = \frac{1}{M} \sum_{i=1}^{M} f_{FC}(f_{Ci}) \tag{9}$$

Subsequently, we adapt the Sphere loss [9] for global and local features learning. Specifically, the Sphere loss can be described as follows:

$$L_{\text{ang}} = \frac{1}{N} \sum_{i} - \log \left(\frac{e^{\|v_{out}\|\psi(\theta_{y_i,i})}}{e^{\|v_{out}\|\psi(\theta_{y_i,i})} + \sum_{j \neq y_i} e^{\|v_{out}\| \cos(\theta_{j,i})}} \right) \tag{10}$$

where $\psi(\theta_{y_i,i})$ denotes angular margin, which can be formulated as follows:

$$\psi(\theta_{y_i,i}) = (-1)^k \cos(m\theta_{y_i,i}) - 2k \tag{11}$$

where $\theta_{y_i,i} \in \left[\frac{k\pi}{m}, \frac{(k+1)\pi}{m} \right]$, and m is used to control the size of angular margin.

2.3 Foreground Detector

Observing that the images of the given dataset have the following characteristics: each image in the dataset has only one object. Moreover, small objects occupy a certain proportion of the dataset. Based on the above observations, the proposed method adopts an object detector [17] to firstly extract the object of interest from the image, and subsequently extract features based on the detection result. By adopting the above measures, the interference of some useless information, such as the background area, can be eliminated to some extent, thus an accurate representation of the foreground area can be acquired.

3 Experiment

In this section, the dataset and experiment setup, comparison with previous methods, and the tricks and model ensemble strategy will be introduced.

3.1 Dataset and Experiment Setup

Dataset. The track B of the 2020 Digix Global AI Challenge is a digital device image retrieval competition, and the given dataset contains three parts: the training part, the test-A part, and test-B part. The training part contains 3094 classes of common digital devices and 68811 images in total. As shown in Fig. 1, the training data is long-tailed and fine-grained, making the competition especially challenging. The test-A part contains a query set of 9600 images and a gallery set of 49804 images. The organization of test-B part is the same as test-A part, but with different images inside. Note that only the class label of the training part is available, no other information except the images is available in test-A and test-B part. To validate the trained models, the original training part is split into a new training part and validation part.

Basic Configuration. The model framework is shown in Fig. 3, the ImageNet pre-trained ResNet-101 [6] is used as the backbone in our baseline method, while some larger models are also used, such as EfficientNet [20] and ResNext [24]. And the dim of GLANet is set to 512 because larger dim leads to over-fitting, the multi-head number is set to 10 for the balance of total parameters and efficiency. The sphere-loss and a common cross-entropy loss without weighting are used. For image augmentation, several strategies are adapted, such as horizontally flip, brightness, saturation, and contrast change, center-crop. The baseline model takes the 512×512 training images as input. The SGD optimizer is selected for training, where learning rate, momentum, weight decay are set to 5e−5, 0.9, 1e−5, a cosine annealing adjustment is performed. The batch-size is set to 16. The total epoch is set to 200. For the validation set and test set, the baseline model also takes the 512×512 training images as input. All the experiments are based on the PyTorch framework with 4 Nvidia Titan XP GPUs.

Evaluation Metric. The top-1 accuracy and the mean average precision of top-10 (mAP@10) are used, the final average score is formed as:

$$Score = 0.5Acc + 0.5mAP@10 \tag{12}$$

3.2   Comparison with Previous Methods

To accomplish the comparison, we select some current image retrieval method, such as R-MAC [5], GeM [16], GeM-AP [18], GEM-SOLAR [12], GEM-SmoothAP [1]. As shown in Table 1, we compare the proposed method with some existing methods on the given image retrieval dataset. As can be seen, compared with these methods, our method can achieve the best retrieval performance in both the validation set and the test-A set, with a 70.52 top-1 accuracy, 67.12 mAP@10, and an average score of 68.82 in the validation set, and an average score of 65.50 in test-A set.

To demonstrate the effectiveness of the proposed solution, some images from the query set and their corresponding retrieved images from the gallery set are illustrated in Fig. 4.

Table 1. Comparison with other image retrieval method

Methods	Val set			Test-A
	Top-1 acc	mAP@10	Avg	Avg
R-MAC [5]	67.16	63.12	65.14	62.10
GeM [16]	68.55	64.19	66.37	63.12
GeM-AP [18]	69.94	65.74	67.84	64.14
GEM-SOLAR [12]	69.62	66.42	68.02	64.73
GEM-SmoothAP [1]	70.30	66.84	68.57	65.28
Ours	70.52	67.12	68.82	65.50

Query
Rank1
Rank2
Rank3
Rank4
Rank5
Rank6
Rank7
Rank8
Rank9
Rank10

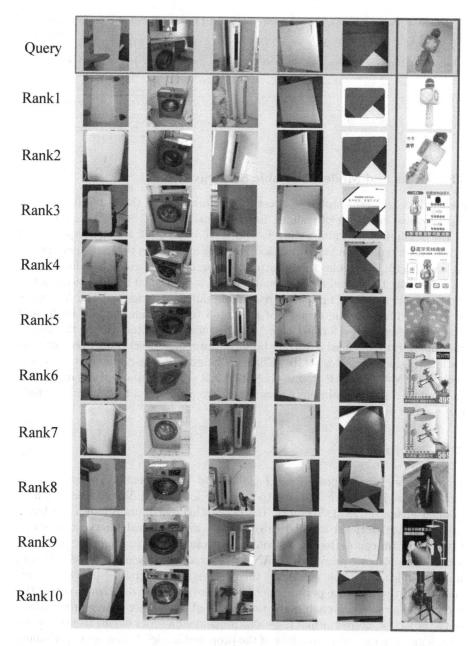

Fig. 4. The visualization results of our method. For each query image, the top 10 retrieval results are shown ranked up-down. The first 5 columns indicate some good cases, while the last column shows the failure case.

Table 2. Some additional tricks are adapted to further boost the performance.

Tricks				Val set			Test-A
Larger-Size	Multi-Scale	Re-ranking	Ensemble	Top-1 acc	mAP@10	Avg	Avg
				70.52	67.12	68.82	65.50
√				71.3	68.14	69.72	66.34
√	√			72.81	71.55	72.18	69.36
√	√	√		74.6	72.68	73.64	71.3
√	√	√	√	76.8	74.16	75.48	73.32

3.3   Tricks and Model Ensemble Strategy

Some tricks are also adapted to boost the performance on the test-A part. First, a progressive enlarging of training images is utilized. 512×512 image is used at the beginning, and alternating to 786×768 and 1024×1024 sequentially, when converged to the last input size. Second, multi-scale testing is performed. At each testing, we collect the outputs under different scales, varying among $[512, 768, 840, 1024]$, and a concatenation step is performed before searching the most similar samples. Third, some re-ranking skills are performed, the descriptor of a query image is the average of the top-3 retrieved images and itself, and a second search is performed based on this new descriptor. Forth, the model ensemble strategy is used to further boost performance, descriptors from different backbones, including ResNet101, Efficient-7, and Efficient-8, different methods, such as GEM-SmoothAP [1] and GEM-SOLAR [12]. The above tricks make that the proposed solution obtains an average score of 73.32 on test-A data. Details can be seen in Table 2.

4   Conclusion

In this paper, we propose a novel global and local attention image retrieval network based on metric learning to solve the long-tailed distribution and fine-grained image retrieval. To tackle the long-tailed distribution issues, we leverage an image retrieval tailored causal graph and a causal intervention strategy to perform counterfactual reasoning. By jointly constructing the global and local descriptors, we propose a GLANet to extract the efficient representation of images, which is capable of solving the challenging fine-grained image retrieval task. To further improve performance, we utilize an object detector to detect the foreground area, which enables the network to obtain an accurate representation of the object of interest. Finally, we also implement a series of effective strategies to enhance the retrieval capability of the proposed model. Extensive experiments on the benchmark demonstrate the effectiveness of the proposed method.

References

1. Brown, A., Xie, W., Kalogeiton, V., Zisserman, A.: Smooth-AP: smoothing the path towards large-scale image retrieval. arXiv preprint arXiv:2007.12163 (2020)

2. Cao, B., Araujo, A., Sim, J.: Unifying deep local and global features for image search. arXiv (2020)
3. Chen, B., Deng, W.: Hybrid-attention based decoupled metric learning for zero-shot image retrieval. In: Proceedings of the IEEE Conference on Computer Vision and Pattern Recognition, pp. 2750–2759 (2019)
4. Cui, Y., Jia, M., Lin, T.Y., Song, Y., Belongie, S.: Class-balanced loss based on effective number of samples. In: Proceedings of the IEEE Conference on Computer Vision and Pattern Recognition, pp. 9268–9277 (2019)
5. Gordo, A., Almazán, J., Revaud, J., Larlus, D.: Deep image retrieval: learning global representations for image search. In: Leibe, B., Matas, J., Sebe, N., Welling, M. (eds.) ECCV 2016. LNCS, vol. 9910, pp. 241–257. Springer, Cham (2016). https://doi.org/10.1007/978-3-319-46466-4_15
6. He, K., Zhang, X., Ren, S., Sun, J.: Deep residual learning for image recognition. In: Proceedings of the IEEE Conference on Computer Vision and Pattern Recognition, pp. 770–778 (2016)
7. Jang, Y.K., Cho, N.I.: Generalized product quantization network for semi-supervised image retrieval. In: Proceedings of the IEEE/CVF Conference on Computer Vision and Pattern Recognition, pp. 3420–3429 (2020)
8. Lang, Y., He, Y., Yang, F., Dong, J., Xue, H.: Which is plagiarism: fashion image retrieval based on regional representation for design protection. In: Proceedings of the IEEE/CVF Conference on Computer Vision and Pattern Recognition, pp. 2595–2604 (2020)
9. Liu, W., Wen, Y., Yu, Z., Li, M., Raj, B., Song, L.: SphereFace: deep hypersphere embedding for face recognition. In: Proceedings of the IEEE Conference on Computer Vision and Pattern Recognition, pp. 212–220 (2017)
10. Liu, Z., Luo, P., Qiu, S., Wang, X., Tang, X.: DeepFashion: powering robust clothes recognition and retrieval with rich annotations. In: Proceedings of the IEEE Conference on Computer Vision and Pattern Recognition, pp. 1096–1104 (2016)
11. Mahajan, D., et al.: Exploring the limits of weakly supervised pretraining. In: Ferrari, V., Hebert, M., Sminchisescu, C., Weiss, Y. (eds.) ECCV 2018. LNCS, vol. 11206, pp. 185–201. Springer, Cham (2018). https://doi.org/10.1007/978-3-030-01216-8_12
12. Ng, T., Balntas, V., Tian, Y., Mikolajczyk, K.: Solar: second-order loss and attention for image retrieval. arXiv preprint arXiv:2001.08972 (2020)
13. Pearl, J.: Causal diagrams for empirical research. Biometrika **82**(4), 669–688 (1995)
14. Pearl, J.: Direct and indirect effects. arXiv preprint arXiv:1301.2300 (2013)
15. Pearl, J., Glymour, M., Jewell, N.P.: Causal Inference in Statistics: A Primer. Wiley, Hoboken (2016)
16. Radenović, F., Tolias, G., Chum, O.: Fine-tuning CNN image retrieval with no human annotation. IEEE Trans. Pattern Anal. Mach. Intell. **41**(7), 1655–1668 (2018)
17. Ren, S., He, K., Girshick, R., Sun, J.: Faster R-CNN: towards real-time object detection with region proposal networks. In: Advances in Neural Information Processing Systems, pp. 91–99 (2015)
18. Revaud, J., Almazán, J., Rezende, R.S., de Souza, C.R.: Learning with average precision: training image retrieval with a listwise loss. In: Proceedings of the IEEE International Conference on Computer Vision, pp. 5107–5116 (2019)
19. Song, Y., Soleymani, M.: Polysemous visual-semantic embedding for cross-modal retrieval. In: Proceedings of the IEEE Conference on Computer Vision and Pattern Recognition, pp. 1979–1988 (2019)

20. Tan, M., Le, Q.V.: EfficientNet: rethinking model scaling for convolutional neural networks. arXiv preprint arXiv:1905.11946 (2019)
21. Tang, K., Huang, J., Zhang, H.: Long-tailed classification by keeping the good and removing the bad momentum causal effect. In: NeurIPS (2020)
22. VanderWeele, T.J.: A three-way decomposition of a total effect into direct, indirect, and interactive effects. Epidemiology (Cambridge, Mass.) **24**(2), 224 (2013)
23. Wang, W., Xu, Y., Shen, J., Zhu, S.C.: Attentive fashion grammar network for fashion landmark detection and clothing category classification. In: Proceedings of the IEEE Conference on Computer Vision and Pattern Recognition, pp. 4271–4280 (2018)
24. Xie, S., Girshick, R., Dollár, P., Tu, Z., He, K.: Aggregated residual transformations for deep neural networks. In: Proceedings of the IEEE Conference on Computer Vision and Pattern Recognition, pp. 1492–1500 (2017)

Multispectral Image Denoising by Multi-scale Spatial-spectral Residual Network

Xiujuan Lang[1], Tao Lu[1(✉)], Jiaming Wang[2], Junjun Jiang[3], Huabin Zhou[1], Zhongyuan Wang[4], and Yanduo Zhang[1]

[1] Hubei Key Laboratory of Intelligent Robot, School of Computer Science and Engineering, Wuhan Institute of Technology, Wuhan 430073, China
lutxyl@gmail.com
[2] The State Key Laboratory for Information Engineering in Surveying, Mapping and Remote Sensing, Wuhan University, Wuhan 430079, China
[3] The Peng Cheng Laboratory, School of Computer Science and Technology, Harbin Institute of Technology, Harbin 150001, China
[4] NERCNS, School of Computer Science, Wuhan University, Wuhan 430072, China

Abstract. Image denoising algorithm has made impressive progress in the last decades. However, most of them can not be directly applied to noisy multispectral images (MSI) because of complex spectral noise patterns which always result in spectral distortion. For the purpose of solving this issue, we propose a multiscale spatial-spectral residual network (MSSRN) for MSI denoising task. Firstly, a multi-scale feature discovery strategy is used for extracting rich spectral structure information. Secondly, we design a spatial-spectral decomposing block, which performs convolution from the spatial and spectral dimensions to maximize the use of both spatial and spectral information. Finally, the obtained multiscale spatial-spectral information leverages the denoising performance stably and efficiently. Whether subjective or objective image qualities, experimental results over the CAVE dataset outperform outstanding MSI denoising algorithms.

Keywords: MSI denoising · Multi-scale module · Spatial-spectral decomposing block

1 Introduction

Multispectral images (MSI) are the images captured across a number of different wavelengths with the amount of bands from tens to hundreds in the same scene.

Compared with single band image, MSI provide abundant information from multiple specific frequencies across the electromagnetic spectrum, which facilitates the fine representation of a real-world scene. The nature of MSI's multiple bands, is always believe

This work has been supported by the National Natural Science Foundation of China (62072350, U1903214, 62071339), Hubei Technology Innovation Project (2019AAA045), the Central Government Guides Local Science and Technology Development Special Projects (2018ZYYD059), the High value Intellectual Property Cultivation Project of Hubei Province, the Enterprise Technology Innovation Project of Wuhan(202001602011971).

G. Zhai et al. (Eds.): IFTC 2020, CCIS 1390, pp. 271–281, 2021.
https://doi.org/10.1007/978-981-16-1194-0_24

as a help to exceedingly promote the performance of numerous computer vision tasks, for instance classification [11], super-resolution [6], image fusion [3]. However, due to the unstable sensor, photon effect, and calibration errors, the acquired multispectral images are inevitably interfered with multiple noise. The complex spectral noise patterns brings great challenges to MSI quality and other high-level tasks such as understandings and object recognition. Thus, MSI denoising is widely used in various applications.

Generally, existing MSI denoising algorithms can often be looked up as the extensions of grayscale image denoising methods. They disregarded the rich spectral information contained in each MSI pixel. This kind of nature attribute has been proved useful for the task of analysis of spectral information. For example, the famous filtering-based approaches (BM3D) [2] and weighted nuclear norm minimization (WNNM) [4] or one of the learning-based algorithms expected patch log likelihood (EPLL) [15], have been applied to MSI by considerable datas in a band by band manners, which did not utilize a link between the spatial and spectral information in each bands, leading to larger spectral distortions. These methods, including the up-to-date the 3D-cube-based algorithm BM4D [7] performs better in MSI denoising, while only take the non-local self-similarity across space(NSS) of the MSI into account. However, they neglect the global correlation along the spectrum (GCS) of MSI which may lead to distortions and artifacts in the spectral domain, then, it can't obtain good performance in real applications.

In the last couple of years, deep learning, especially convolutional neural networks (CNNs), has been successfully used in the automatic processing of image data and performed well in some computer tasks such as object detection and classification. Some methods which are based on residual CNN also emerge more and more, such as image noise reduction algorithm DnCNN [14]. In these methods, CNN learns the mapping function between the target image (ground-truth) and the degraded image by an end-to-end framework. Due to its powerful ability to learn non-linear mapping functions from training data, the expressive power of residual CNN-based methods exceeds that of traditional algorithms. Yuan et al. [13] proposed a hyperspectral image denoising method based on residual CNN (HSID-CNN). This method considers both spatial and spectral information and does not need to manually adjust the hyperparameters of each HSI. As a matter of fact, among the existing denoising methods, this method achieves the best HSI denoising effect. However, it needs to train different models for each level of noise existing in the data, which does not furnish an across-the-board solution to the denoising problem. And the 3D-DnCNN only extracted one scale feature maps without using the multi-scale information. It is meaningful to recover a noisy MSI. Moreover, extending 2D CNN directly to 3D CNN will extremely augment the amount of parameters and thus make the calculation more complicated. The spatial-spectral decomposing block can greatly decrease the amount of network parameters and keep low computing complexity.

In this paper, the noise existing in MSI data is able to be represented by a deep learning model between clean and noise data, and a multi-scale spatial spectral residual network is proposed to restore the noisy MSI. The proposed MSSRN model takes a 3D MSI scene as input containing spatial and spectral information concurrently. Instead of using one scale filter in the first layer for the network to learn fixed scale features, we extract multi-scale features by designing a multi-scale module, which is expected to obtain more structures information to help denoising. Correspondingly, to avoid the increasing number of parameters from 2D CNN to 3D CNN, we proposed a spatial-spectral decomposing block to speed time without losing performance. The contributions of this article include the following.

1) We present a multi-scale neural residual network for MSI denoising task, which can extract multi-scale features for spatial-spectral correlation. The proposed MSSRN can obtain simultaneously different receptive field sizes for MSI denoising task.
2) To my knowledge, we first design a spatial-spectral decomposing block for multi-scale information with low computational complexity for denoising task.

In the rest of this section: Sect. 2 introduces the MSSRN approach for MSI denoising. Extensive experimental results on the CAVE database are showed in Sect. 3. The last conclusions are drawn in Sect. 4.

2 Multi-scale Spatial-spectral Residual Network

We know that a MSI is a 3D tensor data, $Y \in R^{W \times H \times C}$ where W and H represent the spatial dimension including height and width, C represents the spectral dimension, the MSI degradation model can be formulated as:

$$Y = X + v \tag{1}$$

where $X \in R^{W \times H \times C}$ represents the clean MSI, $v \in R^{W \times H \times C}$ denotes the additive noise which obeys the Gaussian distribution.

To remove the Gaussian noise in MSI, we presented a multi-scale spatial-spectral residual network to learn the relationship function between the clean MSI and the noisy one. The proposed method learns the mapping relationship in an end-to-end manner. The details about the network are as followed:

2.1 Network Architecture

The whole framework of the MSSRN framework is displayed in Fig. 1. Through the residual CNN, MSSRN can learn a non-linear mapping between the noisy data and original data in a end-to-end manner. We know that a MSI has rich spectral information across all bands. Regarding them as the extensions of the grayscale image will lead to spectral distortion. In order to retain it, we take a full 3D MSI patch as input. The input noisy MSI of size m × m × c first goes through the multi-scale module to generate multi-scale features. This part composed of 4 convolutional layers with the filters size are $1 \times 1 \times 1$, $3 \times 3 \times 3$, $5 \times 5 \times 5$ and $7 \times 7 \times 7$, respectively. Each size filter has the same quantity which is 32. After, those features were added up to be fed the spatial-spectral decomposing block. And then, we adopt two kinds of residual blocks. The first has 15 layers which are stacked by Convolution (Conv), Batch Normalization (BN), and Rectified Linear Unit (Relu). However, after the 8th layers, a concatenation operation was used to concatenate the output with the input of the network. This is to enhance the details of the recovery. The second residual block also consists of the before components, but the order has some differences. It is Conv+BN+Relu+Conv+BN except for the last layer. Those residual blocks have $1 \times 1 \times 1$ size of filters, there is no need to be equipped with spatial-spectral decomposing block.

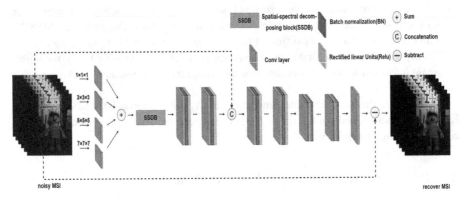

Fig. 1. This is the whole architecture of the MSSRN framework.

2.2   Multi-scale Extracting Module

We know that a MSI has redundant spectral information across all bands, which is useful for improving the precision of restoration. Whether in the surface properties or textural features, the completely spatial-spectral 3D cube has a high similarity and correlation. Therefore, we never split any bands of the MSI in the whole network, this operation can promise the spectral information is completely in the denoising process. In the data pre-preprocessing stage, the spatial-spectral information is preserved as much as possible.

What's more, because the ground objects ordinarily have multiplicative sizes in different non-local areas, the feature representation might depend on contextual information in different scales in remote sensing imagery. Therefore, a multi-scale feature discovery strategy is presented for our network architecture, which significantly enhances the performance of the network. The effectiveness of a multi-scale module has been proven in many computer vision works. In this paper, the multi-scale extracting module consists of four convolutional layers, which extract multi-scale features for the same context information simultaneously, and get diverse receptive field sizes for denoising processing. Different receptive fields are very useful in recovering spectral structural information. To obtain both the multi-scale spatial features and spectral features, this module adopts different convolutional kernel sizes, as showed in Fig. 1 which gives a clear indication of kernel size in the green blocks. From top to bottom, the sizes of convolution kernel are respective $1 \times 1 \times 1, 3 \times 3 \times 3, 5 \times 5 \times 5$ and $7 \times 7 \times 7$. The four outputs of the feature maps are then added to a single 32-channels feature map. Following, we have extracted the feature information with different scales, then the subsequent processing can jointly utilize both the spatial information and spectral information. The add up representation is defined as follow:

$$f_c = f_1 + f_2 + f_3 + f_4 \tag{2}$$

where f_1, f_2, f_3, f_4 stand for the different level feature representations. The add layer f_c is the follow-up input of the network, which has feature maps of different scales.

2.3 Spatial-spectral Decomposing Block

For the given MSI patch with a size of $m \times m \times c$, it can be used to take advantage of the spatial-spectral correlation by the 3D convolution filter with the size of r × r × s. It is useful to deal with MSI data. However, as a matter of fact, directly performing 3D convolution will lead to lots of parameters, which leads to high computation complexity. Inspired by previous work [8], we propose a spatial-spectral decomposing block, which decomposes a 3D convolution filter (e.g. 3 × 3 × 3) into a 1D spectral filter with a size of 1 × 1 × 3 and a 2D spatial filter with a size of 3 × 3 × 1. And the spatial and spectral striding of 3D convolution is correspondingly decomposed into its spatial and spectral dimensions. The Fig. 2 shows the spatial-spectral filter. Use 2D spatial filter and 1D spectral filter to continuously filter the input MSI data. The number of parameters can be significantly decreased by the separable 3D convolution.

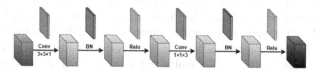

Fig. 2. Spatial-spectral decomposing block.

Furthermore, compared with full 3D convolution, our spatial-spectral decomposition convolution offers two advantages. First, reduce the number of parameters, for example, a filter with a size of 3 × 3 × 3, we assume that has 27 parameters. While a spatial-spectral filter with a size of 3 × 3 × 1 and 1 × 1 × 3 has 12 parameters. The second merit is that the number of non-linear layers in the network is increased, that is, an additional Relu layer is added between 2D convolution and 1D convolution. The advantage of this is that as the number of non-linear layers increases, the non-linear expression ability of the network will increase, as noted in the VGG network, which applying several smaller filters and additional nonlinearity between the two will approximate the effect of a large filter.

2.4 Loss Function

In our MSSRN, the residual learning strategy was adopted to learn the residual relationship, it can be formulated as $R(y)$ v, then recover data can obtain by $x = y R(y).R(y)$ is the mapping function, x represents the clean MSI, and y represents the noisy one. Furthermore, we use the averaged mean squared error between the desired residual datas and estimated ones from input existing noise. The loss function is as follows:

$$l(\theta) = \frac{1}{2N} \sum_{i=1}^{N} \left\| R(y_i; \theta) - (y_i - x_i) \right\|_2^2 \tag{3}$$

where θ is the function that needs to learn the network parameters in MSSRN, y_i and x_i are tensor patches which are $\in R^{W \times H \times C}$. Corresponding, N noisy and clean training data patch pairs is denoted $\{(y_i, x_i)\}_{i=1}^{N}$. We show the loss curve in Fig. 3, MSSRN (only with multi-scale module) and MSSRN+ (with multi-scale module and spatial-spectral decomposing block) are close to each other, but the difference is also obvious. We can observe that the MSSRN+ converges more quickly than MSSRN.

3   Experiments

In this part, we compared the simulation data with the comparison algorithms, and analyzed the objective and subjective aspects to validate the effectiveness of the proposed MSSRN for MSI denoising.

3.1   CAVE Datasets

In our simulated experiment, we employ the CAVE MSI dataset [12][1] as the simulated dataset. It contains 32 objects of daily life. Its spatial resolution is 512×512, the spectral resolution is 31, and the range of spectral dimension reflectance is from 400 nm to 700 nm in 10 nm steps. For convenience, each of these MSI is scaled into the interval [0, 1] in our experiments. We randomly select 25 multispectral images from the database to regard as the training data, the rest part was the test data to validate the effectiveness of the proposed method.

In the simulated MSI noise reduction process, Gaussian noise exists in each band of MSI. Different from the Gaussian noise at a certain level, in our experiments, the noise intensity was different in the different spectra bands, but conformed to a random probability distribution [10].

3.2   Parameter Setting and Network Training

In order to give full play to the non-linear expression ability of the network and obtain adequate spatial and spectral information for MSI denoising, we set the network depth to 18 in the designed MSSRN framework. We adopt the method in [5] to initialize the weight. The stochastic gradient descent(SGD) method is used as the optimization algorithm of the network, and set the decay to 0.001, a momentum to 0.9, last, regard 16 as the batch size. In our MSSRN models, we cost 50 epoch to training and the initial value of the learning rate is 0.1 and decreases 10 times every 10 epoches.

In the training processing, we employ the Keras framework to train MSSRN models. Our experiment can run on a PC with NVIDIA 1080Ti GPU.

---

[1] https://www.cs.columbia.edu/CAVE/databases/multispectral/.

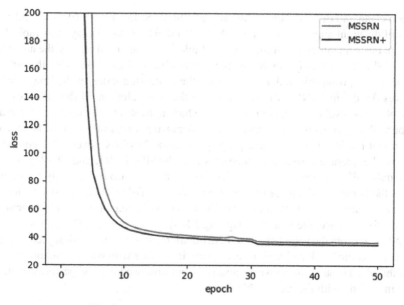

Fig. 3. Training loss in MSSRN and MSSRN+.

3.3 Comparison Methods

We compare the proposed MSSRN method with several classic denoising methods. They are non-local similarity based methods (BM4D) [7], intrinsic tensor sparsity regularization (ITSReg) [9], Hyper-Laplacian Regularized Unidirectional Low-rank Tensor Recovery (LLRT) [1], deep learning method (DnCNN) [14] and a spatial-spectral deep residual CNN (HSID-CNN) [13]. We download implementation codes from the authors' website and use default parameter settings in our experiments.

3.4 Evaluation Measures

We select five commonly metrics to estimate the performance of the proposed approach MSSRN on the simulated data, including peak signal-to-noise-ratio (PSNR), structural similarity index (SSIM), feature similarity (FSIM), the spectral angle mapper (SAM), relative dimensionless global error in synthesis (ERGAS). The larger the first three metrics, the closer the output is to the reference value. The last two are opposite.

3.5 Performance on CAVE Dataset

Objective Performance Comparison. In this part, we show objective performance that is the five evaluation measures's values of the proposed methods (MSSRN and MSSRN+) against 5 existing competing methods. That MSSRN denotes the method with the multi-scale extracting module which that no spatial-spectral decomposing block. Another MSSRN+ denotes the method with the multi-scale extracting module and spatial-spectral decomposing block. We calculated the PSNR, SSIM and FSIM values all bands in MSI between clean and denoised one. The average PSNR, SSIM, FSIM, ERGAS and SAM results of different approaches on the CAVE MSI database are displayed in Table 1.

From these quantitative comparisons in Table 1 and the visual results, the advantage of the MSSRN can be obviously obtained. It is observed from the table that spatial-spectral decomposing block does not reduce the evaluation index of the image, which improves 0.5 dB in PSNR. Although it is not the best value on all the indicators, the whole objective evaluation value is the best, which indicates that convoluted for spatial and spectral, respectively, is effective for MSI denoising. From values of the table, it can be seen that the PSNR gains of the proposed method MSSRN+ over other competing methods, the average PSNR enhancements over BM4D, LLRT, and ITSReg base on traditional methods are as large as 0.85 dB, 1.62 dB and 3.93 dB respectively. Comparing with methods base on deep learning HSID-CNN and 3D-DnCNN, improvements over them are as large as 2.35 dB and 5.41 dB. It should be stated that some benchmark methods, for instance, the goal of designing BM4D is for general 3D video frames but not MSI data. From the results of those benchmark methods, most are designed based on noise at a specific level, and their effectiveness in dealing with noise at unknown levels drops sharply. Through the above comparison, our proposed method performs well and robust in dealing with the changeable noise.

Table 1. Quantitative results of competing methods on CAVE dataset (We use bold-face to highlight the best results in each row).

Index	Noisy	BM4D	LLRT	ITSReg	HSID-CNN	3D-DnCNN	MSSRN	MSSRN+
PSNR	21.42	33.82	33.05	30.74	32.32	29.26	34.17	**34.67**
SSIM	0.1954	0.6857	0.7964	0.5976	0.7325	0.4937	0.7709	**0.7983**
FSIM	0.6810	0.8798	0.8993	0.8245	0.8616	0.8486	**0.9322**	0.9139
ERGAS	849.38	249.14	284.32	472.74	217.19	252.02	140.11	**133.33**
SAM	0.8755	0.8749	0.7797	1.0705	0.8348	0.7414	**0.5376**	0.5628

Subjective Performance Comparison. In order to evaluate the subjective quality of denoised images, we compare ours (MSSRN and MSSRN+) with five other contrast algorithms. In all testing cases, it can be seen that MSSRN+ (with spatial-spectral decomposing block) can restore spatial information close to MSSRN (no spatial-spectral decomposing block). Figure 4 contains the visual comparison of denoised images for all methods, as we will elaborate next.

To further explain the performance of our denoising method, we show in Fig. 4 two bands in the chart and stuffed toy, which that center at 410 nm (the darker and noisy intensity is weaker one) and 680 nm(the brighter and stronger one), respectively. It can be seen from the resulting figures that the noise level in the 410 nm band is low, and the traditional algorithm can restore the image quality better than the deep learning method. Among them, the restoration effect of ITSReg is the best, and the result of LLRT is similar to the result of ITSReg. BM4D has already experienced the loss of detailed information. In fact, the 410 nm band of the deep learning algorithm has noise and loss of details. However, in the 680 nm band where the noise level is high, traditional algorithms have varying degrees of noise and retain fewer details; For HSID-CNN, the results have been deformed, which may be affected by the pre-trained model. The noise of 3D-DnCNN is serious. In contrast, the proposed MSSRN+ is clearer in particulars conservation, and the algorithm that adds spatial-spectral decomposing block has higher image quality overall. In summary, the traditional algorithm performs well in the case of the low noise intensity, while the proposed method has a stronger ability to adapt to changes in noise and is more robust.

Runtime Analysis. For a fair comparison, we selected 2 traditional algorithms BM4D and LLRT, 2 deep learning algorithms HSID-CNN and 3D-DnCNN, compared the test time with our proposed method. From Table 2, we can see that the test time of MSSRN+

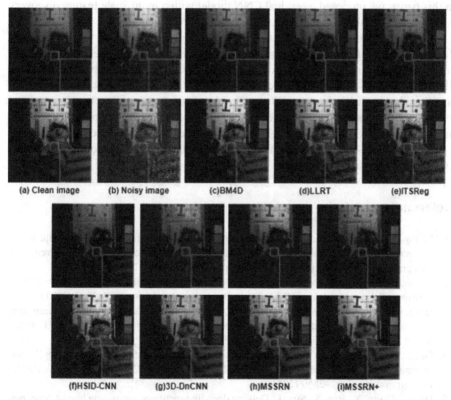

Fig. 4. (a) The clean image at two bands (410 nm above and 680 nm below) of the chart and staffed toy; (b) For the Gaussian noisy image correspondingly, where the 410 nm band's noisy intensity is weak while the other is strong; (c)–(g) are all recovered results by the 5 employed MSI denoising method; (h) is the results of our method with a multi-scale module but no spatial-spectral decomposing block; (i) is the results with multi-scale module and spatial-spectral decomposing block. It should note that for easy observation of details, the marked area in each image is enlarged by 4x.

Table 2. Run time for all algorithms.

Index	BM4D	LLRT	HSID-CNN	3D-DnCNN	MSSRN	MSSRN+
Time(s)	315.8	1287.8	23.8	7.8	7.7	6.9

is the shortest, far beyond the traditional algorithms. It is similar between 3D-DnCNN and MSSRN. In summary, the spatial and spectral decomposing block save time.

4   Conclusion

In this paper, we proposed a residual CNN model with a multi-scale feature discovery strategy and spatial-spectral decomposing block for MSI denoising.

Among the multi-scale extracting module is adopted to acquire feature maps on different scales. The spatial-spectral decomposing block reduces the parameters and keeps the image quality higher. We did not train specific models for certain noise levels, like traditional discriminative models, our MSSRN has the capacity of handling the situation that each band exists different levels of noise. According to the simulated experiments, we can observe that the proposed approach have a good performance than many of the SOTA methods in both evaluation indexes and visual effects. However, for a darker situation, our method can not handle well, there will be improvements for this problem in the future.

References

1. Chang, Y., Yan, L., Zhong, S.: Hyper-Laplacian regularized unidirectional low-rank tensor recovery for multispectral image denoising. In: Proceedings of the IEEE Conference on Computer Vision and Pattern Recognition, pp. 4260–4268 (2017)
2. Dabov, K., Foi, A., Katkovnik, V., Egiazarian, K.: Image denoising by sparse 3-D transform-domain collaborative filtering. IEEE Trans. Image Process. 16(8), 2080–2095 (2007)
3. Deng, L.J., Vivone, G., Guo, W., Dalla Mura, M., Chanussot, J.: A variational pansharpening approach based on reproducible kernel Hilbert space and heaviside function. IEEE Trans. Image Process. 27(9), 4330–4344 (2018)
4. Gu, S., Zhang, L., Zuo, W., Feng, X.: Weighted nuclear norm minimization with application to image denoising. In: Proceedings of the IEEE Conference on Computer Vision and Pattern Recognition, pp. 2862–2869 (2014)
5. He, K., Zhang, X., Ren, S., Sun, J.: Delving deep into rectifiers: surpassing human-level performance on ImageNet classification. In: Proceedings of the IEEE International Conference on Computer Vision, pp. 1026–1034 (2015)
6. Jiang, J., Sun, H., Liu, X., Ma, J.: Learning spatial-spectral prior for super-resolution of hyperspectral imagery. IEEE Trans. Comput. Imaging 6, 1082–1096 (2020)
7. Maggioni, M., Foi, A.: Nonlocal transform-domain denoising of volumetric data with group-wise adaptive variance estimation. In: Computational Imaging X, vol. 8296, p. 829600. International Society for Optics and Photonics (2012)

8. Tran, D., Wang, H., Torresani, L., Ray, J., LeCun, Y., Paluri, M.: A closer look at spatiotemporal convolutions for action recognition. In: Proceedings of the IEEE Conference on Computer Vision and Pattern Recognition, pp. 6450–6459 (2018)

9. Xie, Q., et al.: Multispectral images denoising by intrinsic tensor sparsity regularization. In: Proceedings of the IEEE Conference on Computer Vision and Pattern Recognition, pp. 1692–1700 (2016)

10. Xie, W., Li, Y.: Hyperspectral imagery denoising by deep learning with trainable nonlinearity function. IEEE Geosci. Remote Sens. Lett. **14**(11), 1963–1967 (2017)

11. Xu, Y., Zhang, L., Du, B., Zhang, F.: Spectral–spatial unified networks for hyperspectral image classification. IEEE Trans. Geosci. Remote Sens. **56**(10), 5893–5909 (2018)

12. Yasuma, F., Mitsunaga, T., Iso, D., Nayar, S.K.: Generalized assorted pixel camera: postcapture control of resolution, dynamic range, and spectrum. IEEE Trans. Image Process. **19**(9), 2241–2253 (2010)

13. Yuan, Q., Zhang, Q., Li, J., Shen, H., Zhang, L.: Hyperspectral image denoising employing a spatial–spectral deep residual convolutional neural network. IEEE Trans. Geosci. Remote Sens. **57**(2), 1205–1218 (2018)

14. Zhang, K., Zuo, W., Chen, Y., Meng, D., Zhang, L.: Beyond a Gaussian denoiser: residual learning of deep CNN for image denoising. IEEE Trans. Image Process. **26**(7), 3142–3155 (2017)

15. Zoran, D., Weiss, Y.: From learning models of natural image patches to whole image restoration. In: 2011 International Conference on Computer Vision, pp. 479–486. IEEE (2011)

CZ-Base: A Database for Hand Gesture Recognition in Chinese Zither Intelligence Education

Wenting Zhao, Shigang Wang[✉], Xuejun Wang[✉], Yan Zhao, Tianshu Li, Jiehua Lin, and Jian Wei

College of Communication Engineering, Jilin University,
Nanhu Road No. 5372, Changchun 130012, China
wangshigang@vip.sina.com, xjwang@jlu.edu.cn

Abstract. Training proper hand shapes is the key to learning a musical instrument, and a timely feedback plays an important role in improving the efficiency for trainees. In this paper, we establish a comprehensive database of Chinese zither performance gestures (CZ-Base) with a collection of hand shape subsets based on multi-view image acquisition. In addition, combined zither pedagogy with image analysis technology a classification standard is put forward. In our experiment, deep neural networks (VGG19, ResNet50 and InceptionV3) are used to realize the classification and recognition of zither playing gestures. The feasibility and practicability of the CZ-Base is thus verified. The tentative exploration of this paper is expected to inspire more interdisciplinary researches on science and fine arts.

Keywords: Hand gesture database · Chinese zither · Multi-view acquisition · Standard of classification · Neural network · Gesture recognition

1 Introduction

Chinese zither is a traditional string plucking instrument of China with a history of more than 2,500 years. It is a heritage of Chinese culture and tradition with an unparalleled popularity both in ancient and contemporary China. Nowadays, a zest of learning to play the ancient musical instrument can be noticed all around the country, and a higher requirements have been put forward for a quality teaching, which also poses a challenge for constant innovation of teaching methodology and self-learning modes. With the development of artificial intelligence, there are a large number of remarkable achievements applying advanced science and technology to various fields, such as industry, military, medical treatment, etc. While

Supported by National Key Research and Development Program of China (NO. 2017YFB0404800), National Natural Science Foundation of China (No. 61631009) and "the Fundamental Research Funds for the Central Universities" under the grant (No. 2017TD-19).

G. Zhai et al. (Eds.): IFTC 2020, CCIS 1390, pp. 282–292, 2021.
https://doi.org/10.1007/978-981-16-1194-0_25

its extension is still gradually expanding. We have made some attempts to build a bridge between science and fine arts by exploring the intersections and seeking for integration and innovation.

As for instrumental learning, beginners are usually in the face of the following challenge: in the absence of guidance, they cannot identify the problem without a timely feedback after class, thus leading to low efficiency in practice. Meanwhile, machine vision technology is able to analyze and discriminate the image content taken by the acquisition equipment. So trainees can take photos of their hands conveniently to make a judgment. To that end, it is required to build a corresponding database for Chinese zither hand shapes and set a evaluation criterion combining teaching experience and image technology.

Recently, the exploration of applying engineering technology to musical instrument is mainly from the following aspects: augmented reality, human-computer interaction [1–4] and audio transcription and visualization [5,6]. Moreover, due to the perfect western music theory, most of researchers take western instruments as objectives. In this paper, we make use of image analysis and recognition technology to research on the traditional instrument, aiming at hand shapes classification in Chinese zither practice from the perspective of music education. In terms of science and technology, the main process of image recognition is preprocessing, extracting image features, detecting objects, classifying and recognizing. Different from the traditional method of artificial image feature modeling, deep learning can autonomously learn the high-dimension and low-dimension information of images through training a large number of data sets, and extract more abundant image features for classification. There are some landmark researches on image recognition based on deep learning, i.e. LeNet [7], AlexNet [8], VGG [9], GoogLeNet [10,11] and ResNet [12]. In this paper, three deep neural networks are selected to verify the feasibility and practicability of the CZ-Base, which can be treated as baselines.

This paper is organized as follows: Sect. 2 builds the CZ-Base by collecting multi-view images. Section 3 introduces classification and recognition method based on deep learning. Section 4 proposes a classification standard for Chinese zither hand shapes combined teaching experience and image analysis. Section 5 presents experimental baselines for hand gesture recognition using neural networks. Section 6 concludes the paper.

2 The Establishment of the CZ-Base Based on Multi-view Acquisition

In this paper, We establish a comprehensive database of Chinese zither performance gestures (CZ-Base) with a collection of hand shape datasets based on multi-view image acquisition. In this section, we first introduce the Hand shape of Chinese zither performance, and then show the process of image acquisition based on multiple viewpoints.

2.1 Hand Shape of Chinese Zither Performance

Training proper hand shapes is the primary task for Chinese zither playing. It lays the foundation for further study such as zither skills, performance and musical expression. In addition, a rational and accurate performance gesture not only show the beauty from the visual perspective, but also can affect the timbre directly in the aspect of the auditory. As for the Chinese zither, the generation of sound relies on the vibration of strings through the use of physiological functions. Thus, a rational and accurate hand shape should be payed more attention to, involving mechanics, acoustics, medicine and other multidisciplinary fields. The standard hand shape of Chinese zither performance is shown in Fig. 1. Hand shall be naturally positioned and relaxed, wrist poised paralleled with instrument. A hollow shall be shaped in the hand and finger knuckles bent outward with strength.

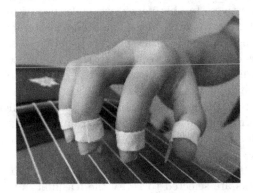

Fig. 1. Hand shape of Chinese zither performance

Proper hand shapes for zither playing are featured by the fingers that are naturally bent and parted at average distance with thumb and index finger forming a circle and the pinkie finger relaxed. Through many years of zither teaching experience we conclude frequent wrong hand shapes, including tightened fingers, dented joints, loosely formed thumb-index finger circle, and kinky pinkie. A stringed instrument vibrates and produces sound by the fingertips forcing on the string. However, common errors above may lead to the dispersion of the force due to local tension, thus affecting the performance of Chinese zither. The state of the hand shape can be fully presented by the multi-view image acquisition method.

2.2 Image Acquisition Based on Multiple Viewpoints

In consideration of the practicality and convenience, the portable camera is selected as the acquisition equipment, which can give access to the expansion of practical application in the future. In order to present the hand gesture as comprehensively as possible, we adopt the image acquisition method based on multiple viewpoints. For one hand gesture, the mobile camera is used to take photos from the front, left and right, respectively. The schematic diagram is shown in Fig. 2. From the performer's perspective, set the front shooting angle as viewpoint A, the left shooting angle as viewpoint B, and the right shooting angle as viewpoint C.

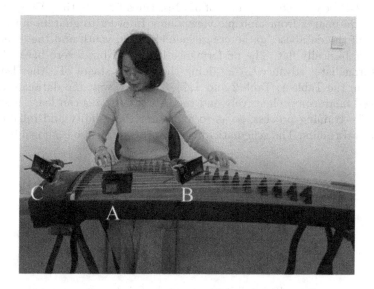

Fig. 2. Gesture image acquisition based on multi-view point

The results of gesture image acquisition based on multi-view point are shown in Fig. 3. (a) is the hand gesture image taken from the viewpoint A, (b) is the hand gesture image taken from the viewpoint B, and (c) is the hand gesture image taken from the viewpoint C.

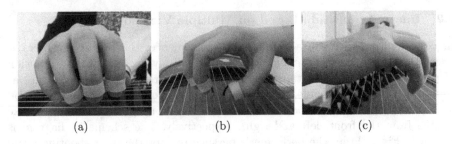

(a)   (b)   (c)

Fig. 3. Results of gesture image acquisition based on multi-view point

The CZ-Base consists of a total of 3272 pictures by collecting 256 gatherers' hand gesture images from multiple viewpoints. In order to guarantee the completeness of the database, gatherers include children, youth and the elder. The sex ratio is basically flat. The performance level distributes zero-base, elementary, intermediate, advanced, containing the various stages of zither learners, as shown in the Table 1, Table 2 and Table 3. In this way, the database can be established more comprehensively and the neural networks can learn more features in the training process, so as to guarantee the validity and reliability of experimental results. The schematic diagram of the CZ-Base is shown in Fig. 4.

Table 1. Age distribution of the CZ-Base

Age	Children (4, 17]	Youth [18, 45]	Elder [46, +)
Number	87	124	45

Table 2. Sex ratio of the CZ-Base

Gender	Male	Female
Ratio	54%	46%

Table 3. Distribution of performance level

Level	Zero Basis	Primary	Intermediate	Advanced
Number	118	54	36	48

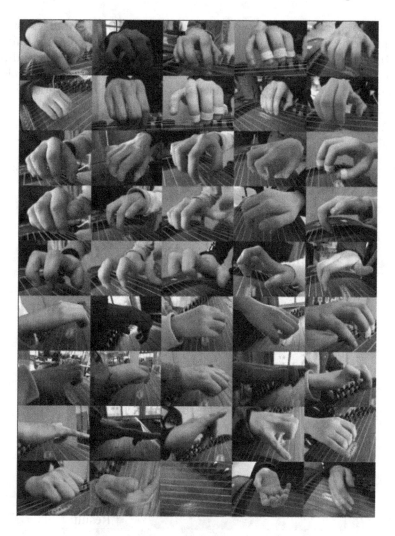

Fig. 4. Schematic diagram of the CZ-Base

3 Image Classification and Recognition Method Based on Deep Learning

Based on the self-built CZ-Base, this paper utilizes the image recognition technology to realize the classification and discrimination of Chinese zither playing gestures. The main process of image recognition is to preprocess input images, extract features, classify and recognize, and output results, as shown in Fig. 5. Compared with traditional machine learning methods by modeling image feature manually, deep learning can self-learn image features through training sets and desired targets. And then, test sets can output actual results through the trained neural network. The process is shown in Fig. 6. Deep learning solves two major problems: image approximation of high-dimensional complex functions and extraction of hierarchical structure features. Convolutional layer and pooling layer in the network mainly realize the image feature extraction, while the full connection layer completes the image classification and recognition.

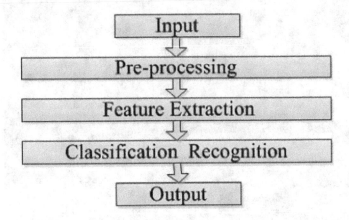

Fig. 5. Flow diagram of image recognition

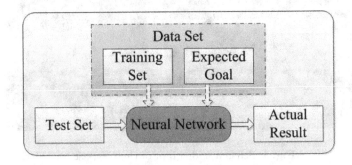

Fig. 6. Flow diagram of deep learning

In this paper, three deep neural networks, VGG19, ResNet50, InceptionV3, are used for gesture recognition based on the CZ-base.

4   Classification Standard for Hand Shapes Combined Chinese Zither Pedagogy with Image Analysis Technology

In this paper, we propose a classification standard for Chinese zither hand shapes, which is combined years of teaching and tutoring experience with machine vision technology, as shown in Table 4. This classification criteria mainly include 9 categories: three correct categories, five error categories and one other category. The subset of correct hand shapes from viewpoint A is labeled A1, the one from viewpoint B is labeled B1 and the other one from viewpoint C is labeled C1. With years of teaching experience, five common error categories are summarized in order to establish corresponding image subsets labeled A2, B2, B3, C2 and C3 respectively. In addition, category D is other than the 8 categories above, such as unusual errors, non-performance state, images without hands, etc. The detailed description of each category is shown in Table 5, including 9 categories, discriminant results, detailed description and corresponding suggestions for improvement.

Table 4. Classification criteria of Chinese zither hand shapes

	Viewpoint A	Viewpoint B	Viewpoint C
Correct	A1	B1	C1
Error	A2	B2	C2
		B3	C3
Other	D		

Table 5. Detailed description of gesture categories

Category	Result	Detailed description	Suggestions
A1	Viewpoint A Correct	Correct	—
A2	Viewpoint A Error	Tightened fingers	Relax, Open fingers widely and naturally
B1	Viewpoint B Correct	Correct	—
B2	Viewpoint B Error	Loosely formed thumb-index finger circle	Fingers pointing approximately to strings for plucking, a circle formed with thumb and index finger
B3	Viewpoint B Error	Dented joints	Make a hollow fist with all knuckles bulged
C1	Viewpoint C Correct	Correct	—
C2	Viewpoint C Error	Kinky pinkie	Little finger relaxed, naturally dropped
C3	Viewpoint C Error	Cocked pinkie	Little finger relaxed, naturally bent
D	Other	Unusual mistakes, nonperforming status, images without hand shapes	Readjust and shoot again

In this paper, we establish a comprehensive database (CZ-base) and put forward a classification standard so that it could enable the image recognition technology to distinguish hand shapes of Chinese zither performance effectively. The number of each category annotated in the CZ-base is shown in Table 6.

Table 6. Number of each category

Category	Number
A1	526
A2	395
B1	380
B2	500
B3	293
C1	327
C2	337
C3	358
D	156
Total	3272

5   Image Classification and Recognition Experiment Based on the CZ-Base

The data of each category in CZ-Base is distributed in a ratio of 9:1. The number of training set and test set is obtained as shown in the Table 7. The training set is used to guide the neural network to gain the ability of classification and recognition for hand gestures, and the test set is used to evaluate the generalization ability of the deep neural network.

Experimental environment: GPU is used as the experimental platform. The server is configured as the processor Intel Core I9-9900K, the main frequency is 3.6 GHz, and the display card is GeForce RTX 2080Ti*4 blocks. Based on the Python programming language, the Keras framework is used to build a neural network in order to complete the experiment in this paper.

First, the initial weight of the network is obtained by pre-training on the ImageNet database. Adjust the input image to the resolution of 224*224, and then normalize the data distribution to the interval of [0,1]. The cross entropy is used as the loss function during the training, the batch size in each training round is set to 32, and the gradient descent is adopted as Adadelta. The initial learning rate is set as 0.1. When the value of loss function does not continue to decline, the learning rate is reduced to one tenth of the original, and the lowest learning rate is 0.00001. Set the epoch to 50 times.

Table 7. The number of training and test sets allocated

Subset	Training set	Test set
Number	2949	323

The test set in CZ-Base has been trained and learned through the deep neural network model. The classification and recognition accuracy of each subset is shown in Table 8, and the comprehensive accuracy of CZ-Base is shown in Table 9.

Table 8. Recognition accuracy of each subset (%)

Accuracy	VGG19	ResNet50	InceptionV3
A1	92.30	92.30	96.15
A2	89.74	87.18	89.74
B1	100.00	100.00	100.00
B2	98.00	100.00	100.00
B3	89.65	93.10	93.10
C1	87.50	96.87	96.87
C2	90.90	93.93	90.90
C3	100.00	100.00	100.00
D	66.66	73.33	86.66

Table 9. Comprehensive recognition accuracy

Neural network	VGG19	ResNet50	InceptionV3
Accuracy	92.56%	94.42%	95.66%

As for the CZ-Base we established, the experimental results show that the accuracy of the image classification recognition network VGG19, ResNet50 and InceptionV3 is 92.56%, 94.42% and 95.66% respectively.

6 Conclusion

In this paper, we propose a classification standard for hand shapes recognition in Chinese zither practice which is combined zither pedagogy with image analysis technology. According to the standard we put forward, the CZ-Base is constructed by collecting nine subsets of hand gesture images based on multi-view acquisition. In our experiment, three neural networks (VGG19, ResNet50, and InceptionV3) are used to verify the feasibility and practicability of the CZ-Base, and ideal results of recognition accuracy are obtained. The tentative exploration in this paper is intended for an interdisciplinary application between science and fine arts. More related researches on music education via science and techniques are hopefully to be inspired.

References

1. Zhang, Y., Liu, S., Tao, L., Yu, C., Shi, Y., Xu, Y.: ChinAR: facilitating Chinese Guqin learning through interactive projected augmentation. In: ACM International Conference Proceeding Series, pp. 23–31 (2015)
2. Chow, J., Feng, H., Amor, R., Wünsche, B.C.: Music education using augmented reality with a head mounted display. In: Conferences in Research and Practice in Information Technology Series, vol. 139, pp. 73–80 (2013)
3. Huang, F.: Piano AR: a markerless augumented reality based piano teaching system. In: Proceedings of the International Conference on Intelligent Human-Machin Systems and Cybernetics (IHMSC) (2011)
4. Löchtefeld, M., Krüger, A., Gehring, S., Jung, R.: GuitAR - supporting guitar learning through mobile projection. In: Conference on Human Factors in Computing Systems - Proceedings, pp. 1447–1452 (2011)
5. Yin, J., Wang, Y., Hsu, D.: Digital violin tutor: an integrated system for beginning violin learners. In: Proceedings of the 13th ACM International Conference on Multimedia, pp. 976–985 (2005)
6. Rogers, K., et al.: PIANO: faster piano learning with interactive projection. In: ITS 2014 - Proceedings of the 2014 ACM International Conference on Interactive Tabletops and Surfaces, pp. 149–158 (2014)
7. Lecun, Y., Bottou, L., Bengio, Y., Haffner, P.: Gradient-based learning applied to document recognition. Proc. IEEE **86**(11), 2278–2324 (1998). https://doi.org/10.1109/5.726791
8. Krizhevsky, A., Sutskever, I., Hinton, G.E.: ImageNet classification with deep convolutional neural networks. Commun. ACM **60**(6), 84–90 (2017)
9. Simonyan, K., Zisserman, A.: Very deep convolutional networks for large-scale image recognition. In: 3rd International Conference on Learning Representations, ICLR 2015 - Conference Track Proceedings, pp. 1–14 (2015)
10. Szegedy, C., et al.: Going deeper with convolutions. In: Proceedings of the IEEE Computer Society Conference on Computer Vision and Pattern Recognition, pp. 1–9. https://doi.org/10.1109/CVPR.2015.7298594
11. Szegedy, C., Vanhoucke, V., Ioffe, S., Shlens, J., Wojna, Z.: Rethinking the inception architecture for computer vision. In: Proceedings of the IEEE Computer Society Conference on Computer Vision and Pattern Recognition, pp. 2818–2826 (2016)
12. He, K., Zhang, X., Ren, S., Sun, J.: Deep residual learning for image recognition. In: Proceedings of the IEEE Computer Society Conference on Computer Vision and Pattern Recognition, pp. 770–778 (2016)

A Novel Hand Gesture Recognition System

Ying Zhao$^{(\boxtimes)}$ and Ming Li

School of Electronic Engineering, Shanghai Dianji University, Shanghai, China
zhaoy@sdju.edu.cn

Abstract. Aims to recognize static hand gestures and track fingertips in real time, a single camera based gesture recognition method is proposed in this paper. First of all, difference of the two neighbor frames is computed to remove the influence of background. Key points brightness and geometry constrain is considered to get the locations of the possible fingertip candidates in ROI. In second step, the classify decision is made by a random tree classifier. And the processing of locating and racking the fingertips is by mean shift method. In the experiment, six different hand gestures and their meanings are defined which are swipe left(page up), swipe right(page down), thumb up(volume up), thumb down(volume down), open palm(open) and making fist(close) to control the device. Recognize all the possible pattern and then track the shape of trajectory and make the instruction in time. The results demonstrate that the proposed method can solve the problem in time and avoid the influence of the complex background.

Keywords: Dynamic hand gesture recognition · Skin color detection · EM cluster · Mean shift · Random tree classifier

1 Introduction

In the last few years, gesture recognition became one of the most natural way of human machine interaction in the field of computer vision. It complete the process of human-computer interaction in a friendly and flexibility way, which has been widely used in human-computer interaction, virtual reality, sign language aided recognition, multimedia entertainment and Artificial intelligence.

In generally, there are two kinds of features are used to hand gesture recognition, which are global features and local features. Global such as Fourier transform descriptors, Moments and spatial distribution. These are the classical methods but required exactly image segmentation. In the other hand, SIFT, SURF, HOG are belongs to local features. SIFT and SURF image features are immune to various transformations like rotation, scaling, translation [1].

In this paper, a new hand gesture recognition method is proposed. First, remove a part of the complex background environment. IR filter is used to cut off the visible light and only the lights which wavelength is similar with the one emitted by the IR LED could go into the camera sensor. And detect ROI to obtain the area of the human hand in real time. Second, the classify decision is made by a random tree multi-class classifier.

© Springer Nature Singapore Pte Ltd. 2021
G. Zhai et al. (Eds.): IFTC 2020, CCIS 1390, pp. 293–301, 2021.
https://doi.org/10.1007/978-981-16-1194-0_26

The structure of this paper is organized as follows. Section 2 demonstrate the framework and details of our method. Discussion and analysis of experimental results in Sect. 3. Finally, Sect. 4 is the conclusion.

2   Gesture Recognition System

Our system framework includes: hand detection, hand pose estimation, finger tracking, and gesture classification (see Fig. 1).

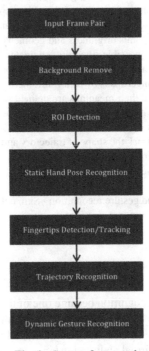

Fig. 1. System framework

2.1   Background Removing

In order to split the gesture from the background, IR filter is used to cut off visible light and only the lights which has the similar wavelength with the one emitted by the IR LED could go into the camera sensor. The processor will sync the camera and IR LED to make the IR LED switch on and off in every two camera frames. So the input frame sequence will be pair of frames with and without LED light. Then the absolute difference of two consequential frames will just keep the intensity of IR LED light, so the background will be removed such as Fig. 2.

IR Led On   IR Led Off   Foreground

Fig. 2. Remove background with IR Led Assistant

2.2 ROI Detection

Due to the clustering character of skin color, gesture recognition methods based on skin color have become popular in recent years [2]. A novel algorithm for real-time evaluation of the position and orientation of the human head using depth image was propose in reference [3]. Topological Data Analysis for object detection is proposed in reference [4]. The lack of large datasets is one of the main difficulties to develop a reliable automatic classification system. In paper [5], a deep learning framework for skin cancer detection is presented. Reference [6] proposed a color space containing error signals for real-time skin color detection. The HSV space has good clustering performance and it's suitable to detect the skin area.

2.2.1 Look-Up Table

1027 sample images are collected from internet and the skin color region of each picture are manually labeled. In HSV space, V component is removed first, and then a look-up table is trained from the Bayesian theory. Figure 3(b) shows the results of skin color in simple background. Figure 3(b) is the situation in complex background. It is shown that when the background is changed to the color like wood, the classification effect is poor, and the skin color part in the video cannot be detected.

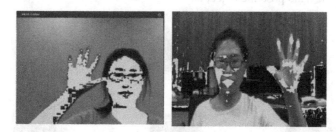

Fig. 3. Skin detection by Look-up table (Color figure online)

2.2.2 EM Cluster

As can be seen from Figure 3(b), when the background is changed to the wood background, the classification effect is poor, and the skin color part in the video cannot be detected. Therefore, Look-up table is only used as the rough detection, and then the skin color is detected by EM clustering algorithm.

Due to the different lighting conditions and different contents of videos, a general skin color classifier is difficult to meet the requirements of each video. In our method, the first 50 frames of each video are considered as the sample database to learn the online skin color classifier to meet the accuracy requirements.

Incremental EM clustering is adopted for higher accuracy. Firstly, the skin color of the first frame is detected by the look-up table method to get the initial skin color sample. Then the initial Gaussian distribution model is established by EM clustering of this sample. The skin color of the second video frame is classified by the initial Gaussian model, and the new skin color sample is clustered to update the initial Gaussian distribution model until the 50th frame. Figure 4 is the results of skin detection by incremental EM clustering.

Fig. 4. Skin detection by Incremental EM clustering

2.3 Static Hand Pose Recognition

The ROI detection will get a rough object area. And the area may involve some background thing like face, arms and etc. We use a classifier with a tree structure as shown in Fig. 5. In the classification tree, every node is a multi-class classifier. The root node just does rough classification. The leaf node will make the final decision to make sure what kind of the hand pose the object is.

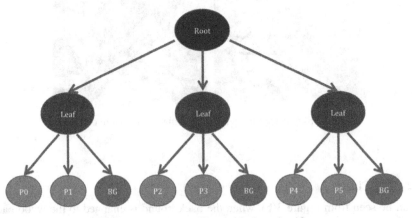

Fig. 5. Tree structure like multi-class classifier

2.4   Fingertips Detection/Tracking

2.4.1   Fingertips Candidates Generation

Generally, there are two views of fingertips as shown in Fig. 6. For the left case, The image will be threshold to get a binary mask. The binary mask could be regarded as a 2D graph. Then the mask center will be used as the initial extreme point. All other extreme points will be calculated by 2D geodesic distance. As in Fig. 7, the red points are the extreme points, the center red point is the initial extreme point.For the right case, the top ten brightest areas centers will be regarded as candidates as in Fig. 8.We combined the two methods together to get all possible candidate fingertips and then use random forests classifier to make the final decision.

Fig. 6. Two views of fingertips

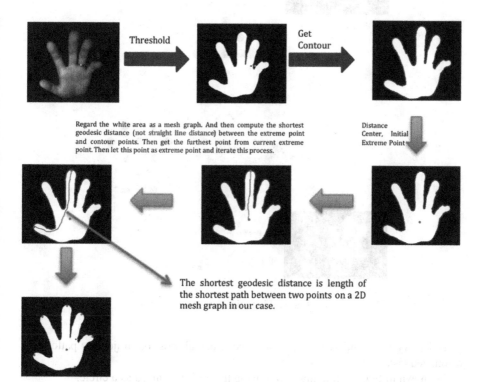

Fig. 7. Candidate method one (Color figure online)

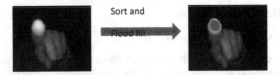

Fig. 8. Candidate method two

2.4.2 Fingertips Detection

Fingertips detection is very important for static gesture recognition. How to identify the fingertips' positions accurately in hand images is vital for a human-computer interaction system.

There are two steps in our method. Key points brightness and geometry constrain is considered to get the locations of the possible fingertip candidates in ROI. And then the classify decision is made by a random tree classifier. And the processing of locating and racking the fingertips is by mean shift method. The steps are shown in Fig. 9.

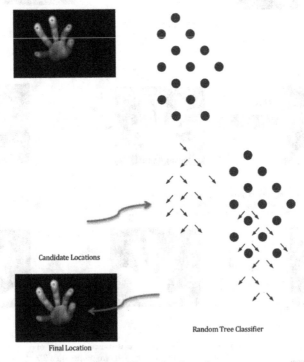

Fig. 9. Fingertips detection

Trajectory Recognition module could recognize all possible trajectory pattern for customized task.

As shown in Fig. 10, the fingertip moving trace is recognized as a circle.

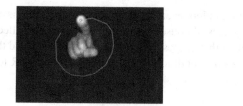

Fig. 10. Fingertip trajectory recognition

2.5 Dynamic Hand Gesture Recognition

Dynamic gesture refers to the gesture whose shape and position change with time. We used image processing to detect a swipe motion. The swipe action is detected as Fig. 11.

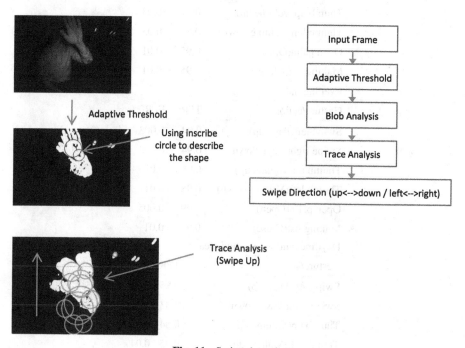

Fig. 11. Swipe detection

3 Experiment

6 actions are defined: page up, page down, volume up, volume down, open and close to control the device.

With active IR lighting and sequential frame difference, the gesture system could work in wide lighting conditions like in door day time, evening and our door. According to possible application scenarios, we designed 3 experiments. The first is indoor daytime with good natural light. The second if indoor evening without light. The Third is outdoor with good natural light and under eaves of house. For every condition, we collect 4000 pictures of those gestures and each of these types of gesture pictures is 600, and the total background class is 400. And for every condition, we give out TPR and FPR to prove the efficiency (Table 1).

Table. 1 Statistical results of our experiment

Daytime indoor		
Gesture/action	TPR	FPR
Swipe left(Page up)	0.92	0.03
Swipe right(Page down)	0.90	0.01
Thumb up(Volume up)	0.91	0.03
Thumb left(Volume down)	0.92	0.03
Open palm(Open)	0.95	0.01
Making fist(Close)	0.95	0.01
Evening indoor		
Gesture/action	TPR	FPR
Swipe left(Page up)	0.94	0.003
Swipe right(Page down)	0.94	0.003
Thumb up(Volume up)	0.98	0.01
Thumb left(Volume down)	0.98	0.01
Open palm(Open)	0.99	0.005
Making fist(Close)	0.97	0.01
Daytime outdoor and under eave		
Gesture/action	TPR	FPR
Swipe left(Page up)	0.85	0.03
Swipe right(Page down)	0.83	0.01
Thumb up(Volume up)	0.84	0.05
Thumb left(Volume down)	0.95	0.04
Open palm(Open)	0.94	0.01
Making fist(Close)	0.94	0.01

4   Conclusion

In this paper, the construction of online classifier and the realization of gesture dynamic recognition system are discussed in detail. At present, most gesture recognition systems are offline learning systems. Our method is a meaningful attempt. The experimental results show that the proposed method is robust to complex background. With IR light and sequential frame difference the system could work stably under different lighting condition like indoor outdoor daytime and evening. In the next work, it will be focus on the real time performance and use it in many possible application scenarios.

References

1. Tiantian, L., Jinyuan, S., Runjie, L., Yingying, G.: Hand gesture recognition based on improved histograms of oriented gradients. In: The 27th Chinese Control and Decision Conference, pp. 4211–4215 (2015)
2. Vladimir, V., Vassili, S., Alla, A.: A survey on pixel-based skin color detection techniques. In: International Conference Graphicon, pp. 85–93 (20030
3. Ying, Y., Wang, H.: Dynamic random regression forests for real-time head pose estimation. Mach. Vis. Appl. **24**(8), 1705–1719 (2013). https://doi.org/10.1007/s00138-013-0524-y
4. Vandaele, R., Nervo, G.A., Gevaert, O.: Topological image modification for object detection and topological image processing of skin lesions. Sci. Rep. **10**(1), 1–15 (2020)
5. Thurnhofer-Hemsi, K., Domínguez, E.: A convolutional neural network framework for accurate skin cancer detection. Neural Process. Lett. (1) (2020). https://doi.org/10.1007/s11063-020-10364-y
6. Zhang, Y., Dong, Z., Zhang, K., et al.: Illumination variation-resistant video-based heart rate monitoring using LAB color space. Opt. Lasers Eng. (12) (2020)

Media Transfer

A Hybrid Bitrate Control Approach
for Smooth Video Streaming in DASH

Tong Liu[1], Yawen Sun[2], Lianghui Ding[1($\boxtimes$)], Cheng Zhi[1], Feng Yang[1],
Liang Qian[1], and Youshan Xu[3]

[1] Institute of Image Communication and Network Engineering, Shanghai, China
{liutong96,lhding,zhicheng,yangfeng,lqian}@sjtu.edu.cn
[2] Department of Radiology, Ren Ji Hospital, School of Medicine,
Shanghai Jiao Tong University, Shanghai, China
cjs1119@hotmail.com
[3] Wuhan Maritime Communication Research Institute, Wuhan, China
gogoxys@163.com

Abstract. Adaptive bitrate (ABR) has been widely used in video streaming to adjust the bitrate of video chunks and optimize user's quality of experience (QoE). In this paper, we propose a novel client-side ABR algorithm, called *Dynamic Buffer Control* (DBC), by taking both bitrate smoothness and rebuffering into consideration. We formulate the QoE optimization problem by taking the perceived bitrate as the utility while taking bitrate smoothness and rebuffering as penalty functions. To solve this problem, we propose virtual queues to translate penalty functions' constraints into queueing problems and use Lyapunov Drift Optimization to achieve maximum bitrate and stable queues. We evaluate the performance of DBC and compare it with both model-based and learning-based ABR algorithms under multiple QoE metrics and trace datasets. Evaluation results show that DBC outperforms model-based algorithms, i.e., MPC, BOLA and FESTIVE with 13%, 20% and 27% gain respectively. DBC outperforms learning-based ABR schemes, i.e., Comyco and Pensieve, with 4% and 11% gain respectively.

Keywords: Video streaming · ABR · DASH · Lyapunov Drift Penalty Optimization

1 Introduction

Video traffic has dramatically risen in recent years, especially HTTP based video streaming [1]. Offering good *quality of experience* (QoE) for all clients under varying network conditions is the main objective of all service providers. In

This paper is supported in part by NSFC China (61771309, 61671301), Shanghai Commission of Science and Technology Funding (SCST 15DZ2270400), Shanghai Key Laboratory Funding (STCSM 18DZ1200102), and Medical Engineering Cross Research Foundation of Shanghai Jiao Tong University (YG2017QN47).

© Springer Nature Singapore Pte Ltd. 2021
G. Zhai et al. (Eds.): IFTC 2020, CCIS 1390, pp. 305–317, 2021.
https://doi.org/10.1007/978-981-16-1194-0_27

video streaming structure based on HTTP, such as MPEG-DASH [2], video is segmented into small chunks (e.g., 4-second block) with different bitrates. Different clients can fetch the stored video chunks in different video bitrates according to the network conditions.

QoE perceived by users is mainly impacted by three factors, namely, perceived bitrate, rebuffering and bitrate smoothness [3]. However, the requirements are conflicting. For instance, a higher bitrate leads to better video quality, while it may result in rebuffering. Fast rate adjusting for higher perceived bitrate may result in bad bitrate smoothness. Therefore, *adaptive bitrate* (ABR) algorithms are proposed to adjust bitrates of chunks to balance all these factors to maximize QoE of each client in the network conditions.

Existing ABR solutions can be divided into two categories, i.e., the model-based and the learning-based methods.

Model-based methods set up a model between the selected bitrate and the network conditions reflecting by the estimated end-to-end throughput [4,5], the buffer occupancy at the client [6,7], or both [8], etc.

Throughput estimation approach tries to predict future throughput between the video server and the client and determines the future bitrate matching the throughput. FESTIVE [4] estimates the future throughput from that in past chunks via harmonic mean. PANDA [5] uses the probe packet continuously to test the throughput. However, the end-to-end throughput is hard to be estimated accurately considering the complicated and varying network conditions.

Buffer occupancy tries to stabilize downloaded video chunks in buffer to avoid video stalling. A higher buffer level that is more stored video chunks in buffer can tolerate the worse network condition when downloading the successive chunks. BBA [6] proposes a positive linear function for bitrate selection in terms of buffer level. BOLA [9] uses Lyapunov Optimization theory to control the buffer and develop the algorithm that is making video bitrate choice as a step function of buffer level. Since the buffer control algorithms require only local information. They have been widely used in state-of-the-art HTTP video services, e.g., BOLA has been included in MPEG-DASH reference player *dash.js*. However, they are set up with presumptions which suffer from bitrate oscillation under unexpected network conditions especially at dense buffer thresholds. A variant of BOLA, called BOLA-O, mitigates bitrate oscillation by using last chunk's average throughput as an indicator. When it identifies that network throughput is between two neighboring selection thresholds such that bitrate may oscillate between them to make buffer stable, algorithm will pause bitrate selection until network throughput and buffer level are under appropriate value. However, it will waste throughput resources [9].

Joint consideration of throughput estimation and buffer control uses both estimated throughput and the buffer occupancy to choose the most suitable bitrate. MPC [8] solves an optimization problem based on current throughput estimation and buffer occupancy by relaxing overall bitrate control into finite steps using model predictable control theory. At each selection, it simulates finite n steps video playing ahead to get final QoE scores by considering network throughput is unchanged. It relies heavily on throughput estimation and incurs higher calculating consumption in simulating video playing. This motivates us to develop an algorithm to fit changing network conditions in low computation complexity.

Learning-based methods [10–12] are trying to learn the optimal bitrate strategies from large-scale network traces by Reinforcement Learning (RL) framework. CS2P [12] uses Hidden Markov Model (HMM) to model state evolution patterns of network throughput with collected data. Pensieve [10] uses A3C network in Deep Reinforcement Learning (DRL) to find the suitable bitrate for future chunks. Comyco [11] uses Imitation Learning model which uses expert data generated from MPC to train DRL model to achieve better performance in terms of training epochs. However, the generalization ability of Comyco is worse than Pensieve, which means Comyco needs to be trained under a specific video dataset and bitrate ladder. In practical deployment, low-granularity quantization of the neural networks [13] performs worse than original networks, and neural models on servers require an update after a cluster of weeks [14]. Thus, video content providers need a client-side ABR algorithm to adapt to various circumstances.

In this paper, we propose a novel QoE-aware bitrate adaption algorithm, DBC, based on buffer status and throughput estimation using Lyapunov Drift Optimization of queueing. Following aforementioned motivations, we develop a model-based method in client's side without trainings and updates. And our solution leverages Lyapunov Drift Optimization to solve ABR control problem which includes three main QoE factors as considered by MPC but in low complexity. Firstly, we formulate perceived bitrate as bitrate utility. Secondly, we formulate the video chunks arranged in buffer as a queueing problem. And we combine bitrate smoothness and rebuffering into control policy by introducing the related Lyapunov drift penalty functions and *virtual queues*. We use throughput estimation result only as a reference for rebuffering penalty, which is not relying on high accuracy. Finally, we combine bitrate utility maximization and queueing stability problems as ABR control problem. We compare DBC with state-of-the-art solutions under a broad set of video datasets, network traces and QoE metrics. Results show that DBC outperforms model-based algorithms, i.e., MPC, BOLA and FESTIVE with 13%, 20% and 27% improvement. DBC outperforms learning-based ABR schemes, i.e., Comyco and Pensieve, with 4% and 11% improvement respectively.

The rest of the paper is arranged as follows. We introduce the background of HAS and DASH in Sect. 2, and formulate the problem in Sect. 3. Then we propose the solution using DBC approach in Sect. 4 and give the details of DBC in Sect. 5. After that, the performance of DBC is evaluated and compared with state-of-the-art solutions in Sect. 6. Finally, the whole paper is concluded in Sect. 7.

2   Background of HAS

HTTP-based adaptive streaming (HAS) is the dominant form of video delivery today. Relying on existing CDN infrastructure, servers can offer high-quality

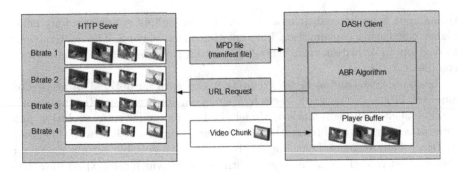

Fig. 1. Basic work flow of DASH

video sources for clients in different places [15]. The widely-used HAS technologies include Microsoft Smooth Streaming, Apple's HLS, and Adobe's HDS. These protocols have been standardized under Dynamic Adaptive Streaming over HTTP (DASH) [2]. The video is segmented into chunks with different bitrates and the same length. Chunks in different bitrates are aligned so that video player can switch bitrate between chunks without video freezing.

As illustrated in Fig. 1, DASH client gets a manifest file of required video from HTTP server after being authorized. Following the information in the file, video player chooses an appropriate bitrate of chunks and downloads the chunk file by URLs from CDNs. The video player can dynamically adjust bitrate by ABR algorithm to adapt to the varying network conditions. This design has several advantages over other streaming protocols such as Real-Time Message Protocol, RTMP [16]. DASH can provide seamlessly bypass middleboxes, using existing commodity of CDN and implement better services by using multiple servers [16,17].

3   Problem Formulation

3.1   Video Model

A video is modeled as a set of chunks with the same length Δt and index $\Gamma \triangleq \{1, 2, 3, ..., K\}$. Define time slot $k, k \in \Gamma$, starts from t_k, and $t_1 = 0$. There are M bitrates for each chunk denoted as $\mathcal{R} \triangleq \{R_1, R_2, R_3, ..., R_M\}$ and the related chunk size set at t_k is $\mathcal{A}_{t_k} \triangleq \{a_1^{t_k}, a_2^{t_k}, a_3^{t_k}, ..., a_M^{t_k}\}$. At the beginning of each slot, video player makes the decision $\pi_k \triangleq (r(t_k), \alpha(t_k))$ on the successive chunk and sends the request to server, where $r(t_k) \in \mathcal{R}$ and $\alpha(t_k) \in \mathcal{A}_{t_k}$. Clients can get $\mathcal{R}$ and $\mathcal{A}_{t_k}$ from manifest file.

3.2   Network Model

The network is modeled as a random process $\omega(t)$ (byte/sec). In the ABR algorithm, the bitrate decision is made discretely. Thus we define the available average throughput at slot t_k defined as C_{t_k}.

$$C_{t_k} \triangleq \frac{\int_{t_k}^{t_{k+1}} \omega(t)dt}{\Delta t}. \tag{1}$$

3.3 Buffer Queue Model

At the client's side, the video playback data is stored in a finite buffer. As the chunks arrive at buffer discretely, we model it as a queue $B(t)$. Let B_{max} denote the maximum buffer length (byte), and $B(t) \in [0, B_{max}]$. The discrete queuing dynamics at t_k are

$$B(t_{k+1}) \triangleq \max[B(t_k) - b(t_k), 0] + \alpha(t_k) \tag{2}$$

where $b(t_k)$ is the size of video that has been played between t_k to t_{k+1}.

3.4 Problem Formulation of ABR Control

The perceived bitrate, rebuffering and bitrate smoothness are the three main factors influencing QoE. To include all these factors into the optimization problem, we formulate perceived bitrate as the utility, while formulate bitrate smoothness and rebuffering as constraints.

Since the user's QoE is not strictly linear with perceived video bitrates, we define a transition function for mapping the bitrate into QoE. We denote $\Phi(t_k)$ reflects the bitrate utility.

$$\Phi(t_k) \triangleq q(r(t_k)), \tag{3}$$

where $q(\cdot)$ can be QoE_{log} or QoE_{vmaf} [18] in different QoE metrics. More details will be given in Sect. 6.2.

To consider smoothness as a constraint, we define the difference between rates of two successive chunks as the smoothness penalty.

$$p_1(t_k) \triangleq r(t_{k-1}) - r(t_k). \tag{4}$$

To consider rebuffering as a constraint, we define the difference between the estimated downloaded video size in the next slot and the queue size $B(t_k)$ as the rebuffering penalty.

$$p_2(t_k) \triangleq \frac{\widehat{C_{t_k}} \cdot \Delta t}{\alpha(t_k)} - B(t_k), \tag{5}$$

where $\widehat{C_{t_k}}$ is the estimated available bandwidth for next chunk. Note that the throughput estimation in (5) impacts the constraint indirectly, thus its accuracy has low impact on the final bitrate decision and QoE. More details will be given in Sect. 5.1.

Considering the overall ABR control, we use the time average penalties in $K \to \infty$, instead of instantaneous values to guarantee the long-term QoE performance. Therefore, we formulate the time average constraints of smoothness and rebuffering factor as:

$$\overline{p_i(t_k)} \leq 0, i = 1, 2, \tag{6}$$

where $\overline{p_i(t_k)}, i = 1, 2$ denotes the time average of the penalty functions, that is $\lim_{k \to \infty} \frac{1}{k} \sum_{j=1}^{k-1} p_i(t_j)$. Thus $\overline{p_1(t_k)} \leq 0$ means the long-term average bitrate is not decreasing. The $\overline{p_2(t_k)} \leq 0$ means that the next chunk will be smaller than the downloaded chunks in buffer, which means the video can avoid stalling.

Note that queueing *stable* [19, Definition 2.3] in format (2) is $\lim_{t \to \infty} \frac{\mathbb{E}\{|B(t)|\}}{t} = 0$. We formulate ABR control problem at t_k by maximizing bitrate utility.

$$\max_{\pi_k} \quad \Phi(t_k)$$
$$\text{s.t.} \quad \overline{p_i(t_k)} \leq 0, i = 1, 2, \qquad (7)$$
$$B(t_k) \text{ is stable.}$$

4   Lyapunov Optimization of ABR Control

4.1   Virtual Queues

We introduce *virtual queues* related to smoothness and rebuffering functions to convert time average constraints (6) into queueing problems to solve the control problem (7).

Define virtual queues as

$$Z_i(t_{k+1}) = \max[Z_i(t_k) + p_i(t_k), 0], i = 1, 2. \qquad (8)$$

$Z_i(t)$ is used to enforce $\overline{p_i(t)} \leq 0$ based on the relation [19, pp. 57],

$$\limsup_{t \to \infty} \frac{\mathbb{E}(Z_i(t))}{t} \geq \limsup_{t \to \infty} \overline{p_i(t)}. \qquad (9)$$

Thus, if $Z_i(t), i = 1, 2$ is stable then

$$\limsup_{t \to \infty} \overline{p_i(t)} \leq 0, \qquad (10)$$

which makes long-term constraint for $p_i(t), i = 1, 2$ satisfied.

4.2   Lyapunov Optimization of Queue Stability

We leverage Lyapunov optimization to solve buffer and virtual queues stability problem. Define $\Theta(t_k) = [B(t_k), Z_1(t_k), Z_2(t_k)]$, where $\Theta(t_k)$ is the combined vector of buffer queueing $B(t_k)$ and virtual queueings $Z_i(t_k), i = 1, 2$. In order to take a scalar measure of the size of the vector, define a quadratic Lyapunov function $L(\Theta(t))$ as follows

$$L(\Theta(t_k)) \triangleq \frac{1}{2}(\beta_1 Z_1^2(t_k) + \beta_2 Z_2^2(t_k) + \beta_3 B^2(t_k)) \qquad (11)$$

where $\beta_i, i = 1, 2, 3$ are the positive weights of each queue. For a queueing problem, Lyapunov drift can be used to describe the stability of queue. Thus the drift is the optimization variable for queues. Define the Lyapunov drift as follows

$$\Delta(\Theta(t_k)) \triangleq \mathbb{E}\{L(\Theta(t_{k+1})) - L(\Theta(t_k))|\Theta(t_k)\}. \tag{12}$$

This drift is the expected change in Lyapunov function (11) over one slot when given the current state in t_k, $\Theta(t_k)$.

To maximize $\Phi(t_k)$ and make queues stable, we formulate the initial optimization target at t_k as $\Delta(\Theta(t_k)) - V\mathbb{E}\{\Phi(t_k)|\Theta(t_k)\}$, where V is the factor of bitrate maximization.

Note that video chunk size $\alpha(t_k)$ in the same bitrate is different. Thus final optimization target $\rho(t_k, R(t_k), \alpha(t_k))$ is normalized by $\alpha(t_k)$ as follows

$$\rho(t_k, r(t_k), \alpha(t_k)) = \frac{\Delta(\Theta(t_k)) - V\mathbb{E}\{\Phi(t_k)|\Theta(t_k)\}}{\alpha(t_k)}. \tag{13}$$

We reformulate the problem at t_k is as follows

$$\min_{\pi_k} \quad \rho(t_k, r(t_k), \alpha(t_k)) \tag{14}$$

$$\text{s.t.} \quad B(t_k), Z_i(t_k) \text{ are stable}, i = 1, 2.$$

We can derive that $[B(t_{k+1})]^2 \leq [B(t_k) - b(t_k) + a(t_k)]^2$ from (2). It also has similar result with $Z_i(t)$, that is $[Z_i(t_{k+1})]^2 \leq [Z_i(t_k) + p_i(t_k)]^2$ from (8). Then we have the inequality of drift

$$\begin{aligned}\Delta(\Theta(t_k)) \leq &D + \beta_1 p_1(t_k)\mathbb{E}\{Z_1(t_{k+1})\} \\ &+ \beta_2 p_2(t_k)\mathbb{E}\{Z_2(t_{k+1})\} - \beta_3 b(t_k)\mathbb{E}\{B(t_k)\}\end{aligned} \tag{15}$$

where D has the finite positive upper bound

$$\begin{aligned}D \leq &\frac{1}{2}\beta_1 p_1^2(t_k) + \frac{1}{2}\beta_2 p_2^2(t_k) + \frac{1}{2}\beta_3 b^2(t_k) + \\ &\frac{1}{2}\beta_3(\alpha_M^{t_k})^2 + \beta_3 B_{max}\alpha_M^{t_k}.\end{aligned} \tag{16}$$

According to definition, we have $\beta_i p_i(t_k) < 0, i = 1, 2, -\beta_3 b(t_k) < 0$ and $D \geq 0$. And our case is based on actual scenarios so we have $\mathbb{E}\{L(\Theta(0)\} < \infty$. Based on [19, Theorem 4.2], all the queues can achieve stable by minimizing Lyaunov drift.

Then we can relax the initial problem as follows

$$\begin{aligned}\min_{\pi_k} \quad &(\beta_1 p_1(t_k)Z_1(t_k) + \beta_2 p_2(t_k)Z_2(t_k) \\ &- \beta_3 B(t_k) - V\Phi(t_k))/(\alpha(t_k))\end{aligned} \tag{17}$$

where β_1 and β_2 represent the weights of two penalty functions. Recall that $b(t_k)$ represents played video in time slot t_k. In order to simplify the control policy, we relax $b(t_k)$ as a fixed value considered in β_3.

At last, because the action space of the algorithm is finite, the DBC algorithm greedily chooses the action π_k which can get the minimum target value at t_k based on the observation at t_{k-1}.

5   Algorithm Design

5.1   Throughput Estimation

In our algorithm, throughput is one part of control policy to prevent rebuffering rather than choosing bitrate based on bandwidth directly, which is not depending on high accuracy. Thus, we suggest using the efficient bandwidth estimation method in FESTIVE [4] using the harmonic mean. We denote the estimation result $\widehat{C_{t_k}}$ with former L chunks in $Mbps$ is

$$\widehat{C_{t_k}} = \frac{L}{\sum_{l=1}^{L} \frac{1}{\widehat{C_{t_{k-l}}}}}. \tag{18}$$

5.2   DBC: Dynamic Buffer Control

In the implementation, our algorithm is shown in Algorithm 1. For each bitrate selection, DBC uses former L chunks recorded throughput to estimate average throughput of successive chunk using (18). Then, it greedily chooses the best bitrate based on (17) in M bitrates. Finally, DBC updates $Z_1(t)$ and $Z_2(t)$ for next selection.

6   Evaluation

In this section, we evaluate the proposed DBC algorithm which is compared with other ABR schemes. Under multiple real network traces and QoE metrics, our algorithm shows a great improvement.

6.1   Setup

Virtual Player. We design a player to simulate video streaming following the basic work-flow of DASH [2]. The parameters in DBC is set as $\beta_1 = 12, \beta_2 = 15, \beta_3 = 1, V = 17$ and we record last $L = 4$ chunks' average throughput to estimate future bandwidth.

Video Dataset. We use the video *EnvivoDash3* [20] which is widely used in [10,11]. The video is encoded by the H.264/MPEG-4 codec at bitrates in Kbps of {300, 750, 1200, 1850, 2850, 4300}.

Network Traces. To fully evaluate the performance of DBC, we collect over hundreds of traces from public datasets for testing. These traces included HSDPA[21]: widely-used logs from TCP streaming sessions which are collected on multiple means of transportation from Telenor's 3G mobile wireless network in Norway; FCC dataset [22]: a broadband dataset provided by the FCC. All the traces above are cooked into no more than one-second granularity to simulate actual scenarios better.

Algorithm 1: Design of DBC at t_k

Input: Former L chunks' recorded throughput: C_{t_k-l}; Virtual queues' value: $Z_i(t_k), i = 1, 2$; Buffer queue: $B(t_k)$;
        Former birtrate selection: $r(t_k)$;
        Chunks' size in slot t_k: $\mathcal{A}_{t_k} = \{a_1^{t_k}, ..., a_M^{t_k}\}$;
        Chunks' bitrate: $\mathcal{R} = \{R_1, R_2, ..., R_M\}$;
Output: Bitrate and size selection: $\pi_k = (\alpha(t_k), r(t_k))$.

1 Initialize $\rho = 0, p_1 = 0, p_2 = 0$;
2 Computing future throughput: $\widehat{C_{t_k}} = \frac{L}{\sum_{l=1}^{L} \frac{1}{C_{t_k-l}}}$

3 **for** $i = 1$ *to* M **do**
4 | $\widehat{B} \leftarrow max[B(t_k) - b(t_k), 0] + a_i^{t_k}$
5 | $\widehat{p_1} \leftarrow r(t_{k-1}) - R_i$
6 | $\widehat{Z_1} \leftarrow max[Z_1(t_k) + \widehat{p_1}, 0]$
7 | $\widehat{p_2} \leftarrow \frac{\widehat{C_{t_k}} \cdot \Delta t}{a_i^{t_k}} - B(t_k)$
8 | $\widehat{Z_2} \leftarrow max[Z_2(t_k) + \widehat{p_2}, 0]$
9 | $\widehat{\Phi} \leftarrow q(R_i)$
10 | $\rho' = (\beta_1\widehat{p_1}\widehat{Z_1} + \beta_2\widehat{p_2}\widehat{Z_2} - \beta_3\widehat{B} - V\widehat{\Phi})/a_i^{t_k}$
11 | **if** $\rho' \leq \rho$ **then**
12 | $\alpha(t_k) = a_i^{t_k}$
13 | $r(t_k) = R_i$
14 | $\rho = \rho'$
15 | $p_1 = \widehat{p_1}$
16 | $p_2 = \widehat{p_2}$
17 | **end**
18 **end**
19 $Z_1(t_{k+1}) \leftarrow max[Z_1(t_k) + p_1, 0]$
20 $Z_2(t_{k+1}) \leftarrow max[Z_2(t_k) + p_2, 0]$
21 **return** $\pi_k = (\alpha(t_k), r(t_k))$

6.2 QoE Metrics

Motivated by the linear-based QoE metric which widely used in evaluation of ABR schemes [8,10,11,23], we conclude the metric as follow

$$QoE = \alpha \sum_{k=1}^{K} q(r(t_k)) + \gamma \sum_{k=1}^{K} [q(r(t_{k+1})) - q(r(t_k)]_+$$
$$- \delta \sum_{k=1}^{K} [q(r(t_{k+1})) - q(r(t_k)]_- - \mu \sum_{k=1}^{K} T_k. \tag{19}$$

where $q(\cdot)$ maps video bitrate to video quality to users, defined as bitrate utility. We use two kinds of $q(\cdot)$, $QoE_{log} : q(R_m) = log(R_m/R_{min})$ used by Pensieve [10] and $QoE_{vmaf} : q(R_m) = \text{VMAF}(R_m)$ [18] used in Comyco [11]. T_k represents the rebuffering time of chunk k. The last two components reflect the quality

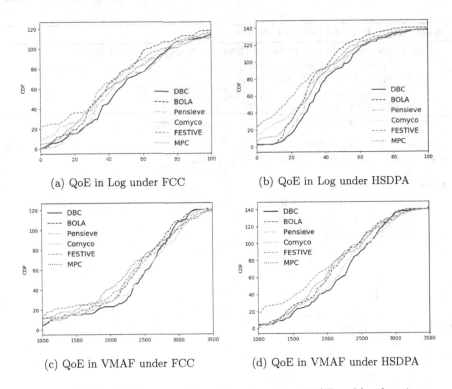

(a) QoE in Log under FCC   (b) QoE in Log under HSDPA

(c) QoE in VMAF under FCC   (d) QoE in VMAF under HSDPA

Fig. 2. CDFS of QoE scores of two datasets under VMAF and log functions

smoothness, including bitrate increasing and decreasing. We set the parameters in QoE metrics as suggested in [10,11] shown in Table 1.

Table 1. Parameters in QoE Metrics

	α	μ	γ	θ
QoE_{log}	1	4.3	2.3	2.3
QoE_{vmaf}	0.8469	28.7959	0.2979	1.0610

6.3 Comparison with Other ABR Schemes

In this part, we compare performances of DBC with other ABR schemes under real network traces and different QoE metrics above. Figure 2 shows the CDFs of total QoE scores under QoE_{log} and QoE_{vmaf} for each trace in HSDPA and FCC.

By analyzing CDFs in Fig. 2, we can have high-level conclusions. First of all, we find that DBC performs best in model-based ABR methods and exceeds

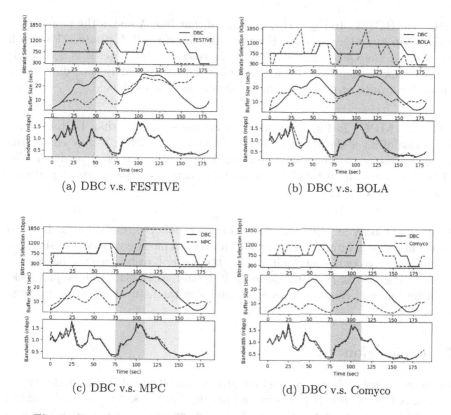

Fig. 3. Comparisons with DBC and other ABR schemes under one trace

learning-based schemes, Pensieve and Comyco, in plenty of traces. In the model-based methods, DBC performs the best and MPC is the second. What's more, FESTIVE performs worst in most of the cases, that is because it relies on throughput estimation only.

Then we use one same trace to get the detailed performance of DBC and other ABR baselines. In the Fig. 3, we compare FESTIVE, BOLA, MPC and Comyco with DBC. We record the bitrates, buffer status and actual bandwidth in the trace for each comparison. Note that the actual network bandwidth is cooked into no more than 1s granularity and ABR decision time is sampled from the same cooked trace data, showed in the third sub-figure, which may be a little different for each scheme.

DBC vs. FESTIVE. In Fig. 3 (a), FESTIVE choose the bitrate according to the previous bandwidth. But it does not take player's buffer into consideration. Thus it will stall when the bandwidth decreases suddenly, e.g., from 0–50 s to 50–75 s of this trace.

DBC vs. BOLA. In Fig. 3 (b), we can see that BOLA makes the buffer more stable than any other scheme. However, the bitrate will fluctuate a lot which will damage the QoE, e.g. 75–150 s in this trace. In that case, it is acceptable that the downloaded video chunks in buffer can change partly according to the future bandwidth or previous chunks' bitrate, as DBC is showed.

DBC vs. MPC. In Fig. 3 (c), MPC shows more stability than BOLA, which is because of its n ahead optimization. Comparing to DBC, it may choose the higher bitrate when the short-time bandwidth is increasing, such as during 75–110 s. But when the network situation takes a turn to the worse, it performs worse than DBC in 110–150 s.

DBC vs. Comyco. In Fig. 3 (d), Comyco's policy is similar with DBC as shown in figure of bitrate variation. But it makes a more aggressive decision. For example, Comyco will continually choose the higher bitrate when the bandwidth is increasing such as 75–110 s. However, it doesn't accumulate enough playbacks in buffer and will choose the lower bitrate after the network situation becomes worse.

7   Conclusion

In this work, we presented a novel adaptive video bitrate algorithm DBC, which optimizes QoE with buffer control and penalty functions. To accurately control the bitrate, we formulated the problem as a queueing problem and leveraged Lyapunov Optimization to solve it. Over a large bandwidth dataset, QoE metrics and video dataset, evaluation results showed that DBC performs better than most popular ABR schemes.

References

1. Cisco Visual Networking Index: Forecast and Methodology, 2016–2021, White Paper, June 2017
2. Sodagar, I.: The MPEG-dash standard for multimedia streaming over the internet. IEEE Multimed. **18**(4), 62–67 (2011)
3. Dobrian, F., et al.: Understanding the impact of video quality on user engagement. ACM SIGCOMM Comput. Commun. Rev. **41**(4), 362–373 (2011)
4. Jiang, J., Sekar, V., Zhang, H.: Improving fairness, efficiency, and stability in HTTP-based adaptive video streaming with festive. In: Proceedings of the 8th International Conference on Emerging Networking Experiments and Technologies, pp. 97–108 (2012)
5. Li, Z., et al.: Probe and adapt: rate adaptation for HTTP video streaming at scale. IEEE J. Sel. Areas Commun. **32**(4), 719–733 (2014)
6. Huang, T.-Y., Johari, R., McKeown, N., Trunnell, M., Watson, M.: A buffer-based approach to rate adaptation: evidence from a large video streaming service. In: Proceedings of the 2014 ACM conference on SIGCOMM, pp. 187–198 (2014)

7. Spiteri, K., Urgaonkar, R., Sitaraman, R.K.: BOLA: near-optimal bitrate adaptation for online videos. In: IEEE INFOCOM 2016-The 35th Annual IEEE International Conference on Computer Communications, pp. 1–9. IEEE (2016)
8. Yin, X., Jindal, A., Sekar, V., Sinopoli, B.: A control-theoretic approach for dynamic adaptive video streaming over HTTP. In: Proceedings of the 2015 ACM Conference on Special Interest Group on Data Communication, pp. 325–338 (2015)
9. Spiteri, K., Urgaonkar, R., Sitaraman, R.K.: BOLA: near-optimal bitrate adaptation for online videos. IEEE/ACM Trans. Netw. **28**(4), 1698–1711 (2020)
10. Mao, H., Netravali, R., Alizadeh, M.: Neural adaptive video streaming with pensieve. In: Proceedings of the Conference of the ACM Special Interest Group on Data Communication, pp. 197–210 (2017)
11. Huang, T., Zhou, C., Yao, X., Zhang, R.-X., Wu, C., Sun, L.: Quality-aware neural adaptive video streaming with lifelong imitation learning. IEEE J. Sel. Areas Commun. **38**, 2324–2342 (2020)
12. Sun, Y., et al.: CS2P: improving video bitrate selection and adaptation with data-driven throughput prediction. In: Proceedings of the 2016 ACM SIGCOMM Conference, pp. 272–285 (2016)
13. Mao, H., et al.: Real-world video adaptation with reinforcement learning (2019)
14. Yan, F.Y., et al.: Learning in situ: a randomized experiment in video streaming. In: 17th {USENIX} Symposium on Networked Systems Design and Implementation, NSDI 2020, pp. 495–511 (2020)
15. Bentaleb, A., Begen, A.C., Zimmermann, R.: SDNDASH: improving QoE of HTTP adaptive streaming using software defined networking. In: Proceedings of the 24th ACM International Conference on Multimedia, pp. 1296–1305 (2016)
16. Bentaleb, A., Taani, B., Begen, A.C., Timmerer, C., Zimmermann, R.: A survey on bitrate adaptation schemes for streaming media over HTTP. IEEE Commun. Surv. Tutor. **21**(1), 562–585 (2018)
17. Da Silva, S., Bruneau-Queyreix, J., Lacaud, M., Negru, D., Réveillère, L.: Muslin: A QoE-aware CDN resources provisioning and advertising system for cost-efficient multisource live streaming. Int. J. Netw. Manag. **30**(3), e2081 (2020)
18. Rassool, R.: VMAF reproducibility: validating a perceptual practical video quality metric. In: IEEE International Symposium on Broadband Multimedia Systems and Broadcasting (BMSB), pp. 1–2. IEEE (2017)
19. Neely, M.J.: Stochastic network optimization with application to communication and queueing systems. Synth. Lect. Commun. Netw. **3**(1), 1–211 (2010)
20. Lederer, S., Müller, C., Timmerer, C.: Dynamic adaptive streaming over HTTP dataset. In: Proceedings of the 3rd Multimedia Systems Conference, pp. 89–94 (2012)
21. Riiser, H., Vigmostad, P., Griwodz, C., Halvorsen, P.: Commute path bandwidth traces from 3G networks: analysis and applications. In: Proceedings of the 4th ACM Multimedia Systems Conference, pp. 114–118 (2013)
22. FM Broadband America: Fixed Broadband Report. Technical Report and Appendix, Technical report (2016)
23. Akhtar, Z., et al.: Oboe: auto-tuning video ABR algorithms to network conditions. In: Proceedings of the 2018 Conference of the ACM Special Interest Group on Data Communication, pp. 44–58 (2018)

Quality Assessment

Learning a No Reference Quality Assessment Metric for Encoded 4K-UHD Video

Jingwen Xu[1](✉), Yu Dong[1], Li Song[1](✉), Rong Xie[1], Sixin Lin[2], and Yaqing Li[2]

[1] Cooperative Medianet Innovation Center, Shanghai Jiao Tong University,
Shanghai, China
{ariel1996,thesmallfish,song_li,xierong}@sjtu.edu.cn
[2] Tencent Technology (Shenzhen) Company Limited, Shenzhen, China
{andersomlin,fredli}@tencent.com

Abstract. 4K-UHD videos have become popular since they significantly improve user's visual experience. As video coding, transmission and enhancement technology developing fast, existing quality assessing metrics are not suitable for 4K-UHD scenario because of the expanded resolution and lack of training data. In this paper, we present a no-reference video quality assessment model achieving high performance and suitability for 4K-UHD scenario by simulating full-reference metric VMAF. Our approach extract deep spatial features and optical flow based temporal features from cropped frame patches. Overall score for video clip is obtained from weighted average of patch results to fully reflect the content of high-resolution video frames. The model is trained on automatically generated HEVC encoded 4K-UHD dataset which is labeled by VMAF. The strategy of constructing dataset can be easily extended to other scenarios such as HD resolution and other distortion types by modifying dataset and adjusting network. With the absence of reference video, our proposed model achieves considerable accuracy on VMAF labels and high correlation with human rating, as well as relatively fast processing speed.

Keywords: No reference (NR) · Video quality assessment (VQA) · 4K- UHD · HEVC codec

1 Introduction

With the rapid development of broadcasting and internet technology, demand for high quality video is increasing. On the premise of satisfying the demand for contents, viewers tend to pursue better viewing experience, which leads to increasing popularity of ultra high definition videos with 4K (4K-UHD) resolution and rapid development in all aspects of video processing technologies. Due to large amount of raw data acquired by professional UHD cameras, video compression plays an important role among processing procedures. In order to monitor performance

© Springer Nature Singapore Pte Ltd. 2021
G. Zhai et al. (Eds.): IFTC 2020, CCIS 1390, pp. 321–330, 2021.
https://doi.org/10.1007/978-981-16-1194-0_28

of algorithms and system, it is crucial to accurately evaluate video quality perceived by human eyes during the process. Such tasks are called video quality assessment (VQA) and can be performed subjectively or objectively depending on the existence of human rating during assessment. Although subjective VQA provides a more accurate judgement, the high consumption of time and human resource make it not suitable for real-world applications. Therefore, researchers consider using objective methods to simulate human visual system and reflect perceptual quality. Objective VQA can be devided into 3 categories according to the information of pristine video needed: full-reference (FR), reduced-reference (RR) and no-reference (NR). While FR and RR metrics require certain amount of information from pristine video, NR metrics have extensive application prospect because of their independency of reference and suitability in most scenarios.

Existing NR-VQA algorithms can be devided into two categories: methods utilizing handcrafted natural scene statistical (NSS) features and methods based on deep learning (DL). For the first category, handcrafted quality-related NSS features are first extracted. The performance of these methods is largely influenced by the accuracy of manually extracted features for measuring video distortions and hard to adjust according to different tasks. BRISQUE [14] first proposed that the distribution of subtracted mean correlation (MSCN) coefficients varies with the type and degree of distortion. By fitting MSCN coefficients into asymmetric generalized gaussian distribution and extracting parameters from the fitted distribution, loss of image 'naturalness' can be quantified, which has been considered as a most basic NSS feature. VIIDEO [15] analyses local statistics of videos by computing low pass filtered frame difference coefficients. Higher resolution of 4K-UHD videos causes more spatial complexity which leads to different texture details and NSS features compared with low-resolution videos, limiting the accuracy of these methods.

The second category uses jointly optimized deep neural networks (DNNs) for high-dimensional feature extraction and quality score generation. DNNs enjoy more flexibility when extracting features targeting different problems and some DNN based methods achieve good performance in practical application. However, due to the high cost of human annotation and limitation of dataset size in field of quality assessment, such methods usually need to adopt data enhancement technology or fine tune from pre-trained models targeting other scenarios such as distortion level ranking [1] and distortion type classification [2]. For 4K-UHD scenario, because of the limitation of receptive field size of neural network and high resolution of video frames, appropriate spatial and temporal pooling strategies should be applied for better reflection of the overall content and video quality. Bosse S [3] put forward a NR IQA metric which trained a DNN to extract features from image patches, showing the potential to get overall score of image from patch aggregation.

Considering above problems, we propose a DNN based NR-VQA metric for HEVC [11] encoded 4K-UHD videos in this work. By using Video Multi-Method Assessment Fusion (VMAF) label to generate scalable dataset, lack of training data is relived and high correlation with human rating is achieved, which could be a good solution to relief the limitation of dataset size in other scenarios. And by a patch aggregation strategy, overall quality for high resolution videos are reflected while maintaining a low computational complexity, which is also effective for videos with lower resolution and other quality evaluation tasks.

The structure of remainders of this paper is described as follows. Detailed information and overall architecture of proposed method are illustrated in Sect. 2. Several experiments on proposed model are conducted in Sect. 3. Section 4 finally summarizes presented model as well as provides a brief outlook for future work.

2 Proposed Method

The framework of our method is described as follows. HEVC encoded 4K-UHD dataset which is labeled by FR metric VMAF without human annotation is first built. After cropping consecutive video frames into patches, patch wise weights and quality scores are obtained from deep spatial features extracted by DNN and temporal features extracted from optical flow. Overall quality score is defined as weighted average of patch wise scores and weights. Model architecture is shown in Fig. 1. There are three main aspects of proposed method: building VMAF labeled dataset, quality feature extraction and weighted aggregation of patch scores.

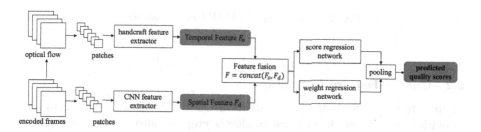

Fig. 1. Architecture of our proposed model

2.1 VMAF Labeled Dataset

In order to comprehensively utilize the ability of FR metrics to extract quality-related features and eliminate the dependence of reference video, we consider using the strong learning ability of DNNs to train a NR model to approximate the performance of a FR one. At the same time, using FR score as label can reflect the spatial and temporal fluctuations of quality accurately, making the production and setting of datasets more flexible and targeted. FR metric VMAF [5] is chosen as the ground truth label of generated dataset. As a fusion of multiple FR quality metrics and inter-frame temporal information estimation, VMAF achieves high correlation with human ratings and has been deployed as an indicator for quality in other research fields such as video coding. Meanwhile, the accuracy of VMAF in new application scenarios is being constantly verified, ensuring consistency of our label with human perception. However, VMAF is nondifferentiable, making it unusable as a perceptual control indicator in algorithm optimization processes, and its demand for reference limits the application scenarios.

Specific codecs are designed for and applied to 4K-UHD videos. Among them High efficiency video coding (HEVC) particularly target 4K UHD applications and is widely applied. Therefore, we add different degrees of HEVC compression distortion to pristine videos and train our model on the dataset to simulate performance of VMAF. This procedure significantly enlarge the scale of the data set and can be easily extended to other scenarios such as other distortions with no need of human annotation. Figure 2 illustrates the method to generate VMAF labels.

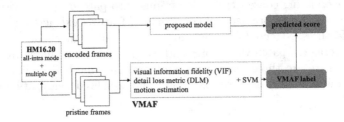

Fig. 2. Generation of VMAF labeled dataset

2.2 Quality Feature Extraction

In order to fully reflect the content distribution in video frames with ultra-high resolution, continuous frames are randomly cropped into patches and spatio-temporal features are extracted from each patch, which is a main difference between proposed method and the existing deep learning methods. In the proposed method, DNN is used to extract spatial features from each patch. VGG net [10] is adopted as a basis of our model which has shown good performance in the field of quality assessment to extract quality-related features. In order to fit for size of cropped patches and appropriate number of deep features, the VGG net is adjusted and a sequence of $conv3 - 32, conv3 - 32, maxpool, conv3 - 64, conv3 - 64, maxpool, conv3 - 128, conv3 - 128, maxpool, conv3 - 256, conv3 - 256, maxpool, conv3 - 512, conv3 - 512, maxpool, maxpool$ layers is adopted and patch normalization is used to speed up the convergence. For each patch, a 512-dimensional spatial feature is extracted.

Temporal features are extracted from optical flow which contains pixel-level temporal information such as motion intensity and motion direction with rich details and variations. Humans are more sensitive to areas with intense motion, making the introduction of motion-related optical features beneficial for reflecting video saliency. As VMAF taking temporal information of adjacent frames as one feature in SVM model, our choice of using optical flow corresponds to it well. Instead of using an end-to-end network, handcrafted low-dimension features are extracted from each optical flow patch to reduce parameters in regression part of network and lower network complexity. Most importantly, spatial information redundancy is reduced.

Once dense optical flow [13] of one patch is obtained, within kth 8×8 mini-patch, let H_k and V_k denote the horizon and vertical component matrix. Mean value $\mu_{|\cdot|}$ and standard deviation $\sigma_{|\cdot|}$ of magnitude $\sqrt{H_k^2 + V_k^2}$ are calculated to depict motion intensity. Minimum eigenvalue $\lambda_{|\cdot|}$ of covariance matrix of H_k and V_k is obtained to represent local motion randomness. Thus for each cropped patch of frame containing $K \times L$ mini-patches, extracted temporal features can be defined as follows.

$$f_0 = [\mu_0, \mu_1, ..., \mu_{K \times L}] \tag{1}$$

$$f_1 = [\sigma_0, \sigma_1, ..., \sigma_{K \times L}] \tag{2}$$

$$f_2 = [\lambda_0, \lambda_1, ..., \lambda_{K \times L}] \tag{3}$$

Mean value for each feature of mini-patches μ_f is taken as a component of patch-wise temporal feature. While the inconsistency and dispersion of natural statistic features can characterize perceivable distortion, standard deviation of feature vectors σ_f is calculated as well. Thus for each patch, temporal feature F_o can be expressed as

$$F_o = [\mu_{f_0}, \mu_{f_1}, \mu_{f_2}, \sigma_{f_0}, \sigma_{f_1}, \sigma_{f_2}] \tag{4}$$

With deep spatial features F_d and handcrafted temporal features F_o extracted, the overall feature for each patch is obtained by

$$F = concat(F_d, F_o) \tag{5}$$

2.3   Weighted Average of Patch Scores

As mentioned above, when patches of a high-resolution video clip are cropped, it is vital to select the appropriate spatial and temporal pooling method. It's inaccurate to ignore differences between frames and high resolution and use the rating of whole video as the label of a single patch for training. So we adopt a patch aggregation strategy to get predicted score for whole video clip from multiple patches.

To be specific, for each patch, the 518-dimensional vector of fused spatial-temporal feature is regressed to patch-wise score s_i and weight w_i by 2 branches of regression networks. The two branches of network are respectively made up of a series of fully connected layers of $FC518, FC512$ with different weights and biases. Dropout regularization is applied to prevent overfitting. Thus among $m \times n$ patches of n frames, weighted average score for jth frame can be obtained from patch score s_i and weight w_i

$$\widehat{S}_j = \frac{\sum_{i=j \times m}^{(j+1) \times m} s_i \times w_i}{\sum_{i=j \times m}^{(j+1) \times m} w_i} \tag{6}$$

While scores for a single frame is defined, there are two strategies for inter frame temporal pooling. The simplest way is to average score of each frame

$$\widehat{S} = \frac{1}{n} \sum_{j=0}^{n-1} \left(\frac{\sum_{i=j \times m}^{(j+1) \times m} s_i \times w_i}{\sum_{i=j \times m}^{(j+1) \times m} w_i} \right) = \frac{1}{n} \sum_{j=0}^{n-1} \widehat{S}_j \tag{7}$$

In order to put more emphasis on quality fluctuation between frames, a strategy of weight average patch aggregation is introduced which attach a weight W_j to the frame score $\widehat{S}_j$

$$\widehat{S} = \sum_{j=0}^{n-1} \left(\widehat{S}_j \frac{\sum_{i=j \times m}^{(j+1) \times m} w_i}{\sum_{i=0}^{n \times m} w_i} \right) = \sum_{j=0}^{n-1} \left(\widehat{S}_j \times W_j \right) \tag{8}$$

As the predicted score $\widehat{S}$ of video clip is defined and obtained from video patches, with ground truth label S, loss function is defined as

$$Loss = |S - \widehat{S}| \tag{9}$$

$|\cdot|$ denotes $l1$ loss which is less outlier-sensitive. By minimizing the loss function, whole network of deep feature extraction and two branches of regression network is jointly optimized.

3   Experiments

Due to the limitation in size of public 4K-UHD datasets, we first build our own VMAF labeled 4K encoded dataset. The joint dataset contains 162 distorted video sequences from 27 different high quality pristine video sequences of 4K-UHD resolution from 3 sources: SJTU 4K video dataset [16], reference videos of MCML 4K-UHD video quality database [12] and test sequences from UltraVideoGroup [6]. Video clips of each dataset contain a variety of contents with extensive spatial and temporal perceptual complexity. HM16.20 reference software is used for HEVC encoding and 6 QP values (22, 27, 32, 37, 40, 46) are selected for each video with all-intra encoding mode basing on prior experience. Compressed sequences with various bitrates are obtained, leading to distinguishable differences for both human eyes and VMAF score. The joint HEVC encoded dataset eliminates overfitting of training on individual small MOS labeled dataset, and is further augmented by extracting consecutive 8 frames with a stride of 100, which enlarges the dataset and reflects the temporal quality fluctuation. With the reference of undistorted video, VMAF score of each video clip is calculated as ground-truth for further training and validation. We use a 60% training and 40% validation approach to ensure that our model gets completely new frames for validation. Prior experiments are performed and we determined a 64 × 64 patch size for 4K-UHD videos. For each frame, a number of 6 × 8 patches are extracted. Models are individually trained using two temporal pooling strategy mentioned in last section, denoted as Ours-avg and

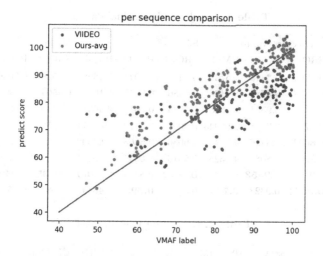

Fig. 3. Predict score of VIIDEO and ours-avg

Ours-fw. Models are trained for 800 epochs. The initial learning rate is 10^{-4} and is multiplied by a factor 0.1 every 200 epochs.

As a second step, we calculate correlation indexes between the trained model and other state-of-the-art IQA, VQA metrics with VMAF. Open sourced FR metrics PSNR, SSIM [4], MS-SSIM [8] and NR metric NIQE [9] are adopted. Besides we compare the performance of features extracted by NSS-based metric: BRISQUE and VIIDEO by training a SVM respectively on the same training dataset as our proposed method. Figure 3 shows the scatter plot of predicted score of proposed method with average pooling (Ours-avg) and VIIDEO. The X-axis represents the VMAF label score, and it can be seen from the scatter diagram that our method achieves a higher correlation with VMAF.

For benchmarking performance, we calculate SROCC, PLCC to reflect the correlation and RMSE to reflect prediction error. Before calculating PLCC and RMSE, five-parameter regression is used to eliminate nonlinearity between predicted score and human rating.

$$f(s) = \tau_1 \left(0.5 - \frac{1}{1 + exp[\tau_2(s - \tau_3)]}\right) + \tau_4 q + \tau_5 \qquad (10)$$

Results listed in Table 1 and Table 2 show that both proposed methods outperforms other state-of-the-art NR models and most FR models, achieving a correlation of 0.89 on the whole dataset. While the results have a fluctuation on different subsets, it shows strong applicability on joint dataset. Because the video clips are made up of consecutive frames which shares a slight difference, performance of two temporal pooling strategies of purposed method are quite similar.

Though the models are trained on VMAF labels, a test on video sets with human rating is required. SJTU 4K-HEVC Video Subjective Quality Database

Table 1. Results on individual datasets

	UltraVideoGroup			SJTU			MCML		
	SROCC	PLCC	RMSE	SROCC	PLCC	RMSE	SROCC	PLCC	RMSE
PSNR	0.8064	0.8343	7.5731	0.8426	0.8047	5.4898	0.7528	0.7036	5.8516
SSIM	0.7373	0.7780	8.8439	0.8486	0.8647	5.1051	0.8504	0.8254	7.3707
MS-SSIM	0.9773	0.9591	3.9848	0.9773	0.9618	2.4631	0.9530	0.9394	4.6324
NIQE	0.3756	0.3448	12.8943	0.6026	0.5872	10.4311	0.0259	0.1368	12.9582
VIIDEO	0.8093	0.8486	4.3041	0.6036	0.5863	10.4392	0.7452	0.7594	8.5098
BRISQUE	0.8251	0.8081	4.3528	0.6616	0.6335	11.6611	0.7790	0.7790	5.4551
Ours-avg	0.9453	**0.9453**	3.8390	**0.8922**	0.8734	**6.2750**	**0.9335**	**0.9427**	4.3643
Ours-fw	**0.9534**	0.9323	**3.7336**	0.8710	**0.8902**	6.4344	0.9083	0.8591	5.1122

Table 2. Results on joint dataset

	PSNR	SSIM	MS-SSIM	NIQE	VIIDEO	BRISQUE	Ours-avg	Ours-fw
SROCC	0.7355	0.6319	0.9431	0.2757	0.7034	0.7114	0.8847	**0.8979**
PLCC	0.7255	0.6319	0.9431	0.3106	0.7069	0.6571	**0.9133**	0.8880
RMSE	9.2187	10.5099	5.2257	12.7334	9.4753	7.3302	5.4558	**5.0685**

[17] labeled by MOS and HEVC encoded 4K-UHD sequences from MCML database [12] labeled by DMOS are selected for further test. Two datasets are carefully devided to ensure that no test sequences appeared during training procedure. In real-world application, random access mode of HEVC codec adopting inter-prediction between I,P,B frames will cause fluctuation in calculated quality, which barely damage perceptual quality because of the visual hysteresis of human eyes. Thus our test is conducted on I-frames selected from encoded videos. Results are listed in Table 3. Among all tested FR-metrics, VMAF shows a good performance, justifying our approach of using VMAF as ground truth label. While accuracy of VMAF on SJTU dataset declined, the joint dataset guaranteed the universality for trained model. Because the extracted frames are not continuous, the frame wise weighted pooling strategy can better reflect the quality fluctuation over whole video and achieve relative high performance. Thus by imitating the full reference method VMAF, our method achieves high correlation with human ratings in case of extreme limited data set.

In 4K-UHD scenarios, computational complexity is an important aspect to consider. Therefore, we compare average processing time on a single frame of selected methods and results are listed in Table 4. Our method is implemented using Pytorch [7] on PC with Intel Core i7-8700K CPU and a TITAN XP GPU. VIIDEO and BRISQUE features are first extracted and then regressed using pre-trained SVM on the same computer. It is worth to note that speed of the proposed metric is significantly faster than the other two conventional metrics, validating efficiency of our patch selection and aggregation strategy.

Table 3. Results on human ratings

	MCML			SJTU		
	SROCC	PLCC	RMSE	SROCC	PLCC	RMSE
PSNR	0.8535	0.8030	1.4825	0.7254	0.7418	0.3568
SSIM	0.8174	0.7662	1.5987	0.7359	0.7435	0.3558
MS-SSIM	0.9237	0.9082	1.0411	**0.8460**	**0.8736**	**0.2589**
VMAF	**0.9460**	**0.9521**	**0.7602**	0.8022	0.8529	0.2777
NIQE	0.3248	0.3033	2.3726	0.4054	0.3892	0.5059
VIIDEO	0.7905	0.8398	1.3505	0.6612	0.6907	0.3749
BRISQUE	0.7535	0.7425	1.6665	0.5382	0.6116	0.4101
Ours-avg	0.8646	0.8222	1.3910	0.7035	0.6551	0.4632
Ours-fw	**0.8853**	**0.8973**	**1.1446**	**0.9009**	**0.8948**	**0.2731**

Table 4. Average time to process a single frame

Model	VIIDEO	BRISQUE	Ours-avg
Processing speed(second/frame)	11.91	6.84	**3.79**

4 Conclusion

In this paper, we present a NR video quality assessment model which extracts deep spatial features and optical flow based temporal features from cropped patches. By patch aggregation, overall quality of high resolution frames is obtained and by building a VMAF labeled joint dataset, the problem of lack in human annotated dataset is mitigated. Evaluation experiments on HEVC encoded 4K-UHD videos show that our model possess strong quality predicting ability learnt from VMAF and achieve high correlation with human rating score, exceeding various state-of-art quality assessment models. It's worth mentioning that our solutions are not limited to HEVC encoded 4K-UHD videos and can be extended to other scenarios such as HD resolution and other distortion types by simply modifying dataset or fine-tuning network. Test results of our model on open sourced human rating datasets are presented, which could be a benchmark for further studies.

Acknowledgements. This work was partly supported by the Shanghai Key Laboratory of Digital Media Processing and Transmissions and the 111 Project (B07022 and Sheitc No. 150633).

References

1. Liu, X., Van De Weijer, J., Bagdanov, A.D.: RankIQA: learning from rankings for no-reference image quality assessment. In: 2017 IEEE International Conference on Computer Vision (ICCV), Venice, pp. 1040–1049 (2017). https://doi.org/10.1109/ICCV.2017.118
2. Zhang, W., Ma, K., Yan, J., Deng, D., Wang, Z.: Blind image quality assessment using a deep bilinear convolutional neural network. IEEE Trans. Circuits Syst. Video Technol. **30**(1), 36–47 (2020). https://doi.org/10.1109/TCSVT.2018.2886771
3. Bosse, S., Maniry, D., Müller, K., Wiegand, T., Samek, W.: Deep neural networks for no-reference and full-reference image quality assessment. IEEE Trans. Image Process. **27**(1), 206–219 (2018). https://doi.org/10.1109/TIP.2017.2760518
4. Wang, Z., Bovik, A.C., Sheikh, H.R., Simoncelli, E.P.: Image quality assessment: from error visibility to structural similarity. IEEE Trans. Image Process. **13**(4), 600–612 (2004)
5. VMAF. https://github.com/Netflix/vmaf. Accessed 30 Aug 2020
6. Ultra Video Group. http://ultravideo.cs.tut.fi/. Accessed 30 Aug 2020
7. Pytorch. https://pytorch.org/. Accessed 30 Aug 2020
8. Wang, Z., Simoncelli, E.P., Bovik, A.C.: Multiscale structural similarity for image quality assessment. In: 2003 The Thirty-Seventh Asilomar Conference on Signals, Systems & Computers, Pacific Grove, CA, USA, vol. 2, pp. 1398–1402 (2003). https://doi.org/10.1109/ACSSC.2003.1292216
9. Mittal, A., Soundararajan, R., Bovik, A.C.: Making a "completely blind" image quality analyzer. IEEE Signal Process. Lett. **20**(3), 209–212 (2013). https://doi.org/10.1109/LSP.2012.2227726
10. Simonyan, K., Zisserman, A.: Very deep convolutional networks for large-scale image recognition. Computer Science (2014)
11. Sullivan, G.J., Ohm, J., Han, W., Wiegand, T.: Overview of the High Efficiency Video Coding (HEVC) standard. IEEE Trans. Circuits Syst. Video Technol. **22**(12), 1649–1668 (2012). https://doi.org/10.1109/TCSVT.2012.2221191
12. Cheon, M., Lee, J.: Subjective and Objective Quality Assessment of Compressed 4K UHD Videos for Immersive Experience. IEEE Trans. Circuits Syst. Video Technol. **28**(7), 1467–1480 (2018). https://doi.org/10.1109/TCSVT.2017.2683504
13. Farnebäck, G.: Two-frame motion estimation based on polynomial expansion. In: Bigun, J., Gustavsson, T. (eds.) SCIA 2003. LNCS, vol. 2749, pp. 363–370. Springer, Heidelberg (2003). https://doi.org/10.1007/3-540-45103-X_50
14. Mittal, A., Moorthy, A.K., Bovik, A.C.: No-reference image quality assessment in the spatial domain. IEEE Trans. Image Process. **21**(12), 4695–4708 (2012). https://doi.org/10.1109/TIP.2012.2214050
15. Mittal, A., Saad, M.A., Bovik, A.C.: A completely blind video integrity Oracle. IEEE Trans. Image Process. **25**(1), 289–300 (2016). https://doi.org/10.1109/TIP.2015.2502725
16. Song, L., Tang, X., Zhang, W., Yang, X., Xia, P.: The SJTU 4K video sequence dataset. In: 2013 Fifth International Workshop on Quality of Multimedia Experience (QoMEX), Klagenfurt am Wörthersee, pp. 34–35 (2013). https://doi.org/10.1109/QoMEX.2013.6603201
17. Zhu, Y., Song, L., Xie, R., Zhang, W.: SJTU 4K video subjective quality dataset for content adaptive bit rate estimation without encoding. In: 2016 IEEE International Symposium on Broadband Multimedia Systems and Broadcasting (BMSB), Nara, pp. 1–4 (2016). https://doi.org/10.1109/BMSB.2016.7521936

Optimization-Based Tone Mapping Evaluation

Huiqing Zhang[1,2,3], Donghao Li[1,3(✉)], Yonghui Zhang[1], Weiling Chen[4], Nan Guo[1], and Hongyan Liu[1]

[1] Faculty of Information Technology, Beijing University of Technology, Beijing, China
lidonghao97@163.com
[2] Key Laboratory of Artificial Intelligence, Ministry of Education, Beijing, China
[3] Engineering Research Center of Digital Community, Ministry of Education, Beijing, China
[4] College of Physics and Information Engineering, Fuzhou University, Fuzhou, China

Abstract. In recent years, increasing attention has been paid to devising tone mapping operators, which convert specialized high dynamic range (HDR) images to standard low dynamic range (LDR) ones for visualization on daily monitors. However, there lacks a reliable evaluation criterion for comparing distinct tone mapping operators, which is of great significance to the design and optimization of tone mapping methods. In this paper we propose an effective tone mapping evaluation system (TMES) based on a two-stage framework. In the first stage, features are extracted in view of the observations that luminance information, color saturation, statistical naturalness, structural fidelity and visual saliency have different and determinate influences on the perceptual quality of tone-mapped LDR images. In the second stage, the extracted features are integrated with a data-driven optimization strategy, which iteratively learns the parameters by applying thousands of collected tone-mapped LDR and natural images. Our TMES evaluation system can be implemented with or without reference HDR images, serving for the optimization and monitoring of tone mapping methods. Experiments conducted on three databases prove the superiority of our quality evaluation system.

1 Introduction

One chief and challenging problem of the rendering of a high dynamic range (HDR) natural scene on a conventional and widely applied low dynamic range (LDR) display has received broad attentions [1–7]. Regarding this issue, current solutions were developed based on global- and/or local-based mapping strategies. Reinhard *et al.* came up with a simple global tone-mapping operator by preserving naturalness of the input HDR image based on a monotonic curve for compression [1]. Fattal *et al.* proposed to preserve fine local details by manipulating the gradient field of luminance information [2]. Pattanaik *et al.* developed a local gain control approach towards adaptively preserving detail information

© Springer Nature Singapore Pte Ltd. 2021
G. Zhai et al. (Eds.): IFTC 2020, CCIS 1390, pp. 331–347, 2021.
https://doi.org/10.1007/978-981-16-1194-0_29

[3]. Recently, it has come to an agreement that considering both global and local features for tone mapping can achieve better performance [4–7]. The majority of techniques in this type decompose an HDR image into a base layer and a detail layer, which are independently processed for simultaneously preserving sharp edges and fine details. The decomposition methods of an HDR image can be referred to as edge-preserving filters [6,7]. In spite of the successful applications of existing tone-mapping operators, few of them can handle all types of HDR images with various contents, dynamic ranges, resolutions, etc. So, a universal algorithm or framework for tone mapping is still a tough problem, and thus a reliable evaluation criterion is urgently required for the design, optimization and monitoring of tone mapping algorithms.

Image quality assessment (IQA) is one of practical tools for addressing this problem, since it has the judgement and optimization potentials to choose the optimal LDR images [9,10]. Despite the significance, very limited efforts have been made so far. Recently, Yeganeh *et al.* found that two factors, structural fidelity and statistical naturalness, have great influence on the quality of tone-mapped LDR images. Inspired by this, they came up with the tone-mapped quality index (TMQI) [9], which has achieved promising performance as compared with present full-reference (FR) IQA approaches. Afterwards, Liu *et al.* considered saliency, which has prevailed in many areas such as quality evaluation [12,13], image compression [14], and contrast enhancement [15,16], to improve the TMQI [17]. The above-described two methods belong to FR metrics requiring the whole original HDR image as reference. In use, FR IQA metrics can help to convert specialized HDR images to standard LDR versions [18].

However, during the transmission or at the terminal where the HDR image is not available, FR-IQA methods may not be applicable. No-reference (NR) IQA models adapting to these situations are preferred for quality monitoring. More recently, in [10], Gu *et al.* proposed to blindly evaluate the quality of tone-mapped LDR images, named the blind tone-mapped quality index (BTMQI), which extracts 11 features from the perspectives of information entropy, statistical naturalness and structural preservation, followed by inferring the single quality score via a machine learning tool [19]. Results revealed that these features are effective on quality evaluation of tone-mapped LDR images. Nonetheless, learning the features on the small-size TMID [9] and TMID2015 [10] databases may very likely cause the over-fitting problem.

In this paper, we address the problem by introducing a new tone mapping evaluation system (TMES). The proposed evaluation system can be implemented under the condition with or without reference HDR images, such that FR or NR evaluation in proper application scenarios can be achieved. Furthermore, the parameters utilized in the proposed TMES system are reliably optimized via a new strategy based on abundant collected image samples. In particular, our proposed TMES evaluation system is developed based on a two-step model. Firstly, we extract four types of features, each of which can be explored from a particular perspective to provide complementary functionalities. The first type consists of five features for measuring the luminance information (including basic and detail information), which are inspired from the assumption that a desired tone-mapped image maintains much information regardless of holding/darkening/brightening its original luminance intensity. Saliency- and block-based strategies are further used to enhance the adopted features. The impact of color saturation on the visual quality of tone-mapped LDR images is included in the development of the second type of feature. The third and fourth types of modified structural fidelity and statistical naturalness features stem from the recent work [9], for estimating the visual degradation separately with respect to a large body of natural images and the reference HDR image.

In the second step, we focus on how to fuse features into a single quality score via a reliable optimization scheme. On one hand, the high-performance FR metrics can be used to train the regression module of NR models [20], and on the other hand, FR metrics can be improved by including part or all of features (e.g. natural scene statistics (NSS)-based features) used in NR models [9]. Inspired by these motivations, we introduce a novel optimization strategy using a large sample set, which consists of about 3,000 tone-mapped LDR images and 14,000 natural images, as training data. Our target is to generate FR TMES (F-TMES) and NR TMES (N-TMES) methods simultaneously. More concretely, in this work, we construct an optimization function and solve it with an iterative-based nonlinear programming approach on a great number of training data to derive the optimal model parameters. It is also worth noting that the F-TMES method combines all the 8 features above while the N-TMES method just uses 7 in them, which are extracted from the converted LDR images only.

In this paper, there are four major contributions. First of all, we provide 8 features which are highly relevant to the quality assessment of tone-mapped LDR images. The 8 new features come from four aspects of considerations, by modifying existing works with saliency, patch-based pooling, etc. Second, a data-driven optimization scheme is introduced to reliably combine the features based on a large sample set, in which images are exactly different from those in evaluation databases. Third, the proposed TMES system can be well implemented with or without the reference HDR image for tone mapping methods comparison, optimization and quality monitoring. Lastly, our FR and NR models obtain the state-of-the-art performance in their individual classes.

The rest of this paper is arranged as follows. Section 2 presents the proposed TMES evaluation system and details the four types of features, including luminance information, color saturation, statistical naturalness and structural fidelity, followed by converting features into a single quality score based on a new data-driven optimization strategy. In Sect. 3, a validation of our FR and NR models as compared with FR TMQI and state-of-the-art blind IQA metrics is conducted on three recent databases, including TMID [9], TMID2015 [10], and HDRD [11]. We finally draw the concluding remarks in Sect. 4.

2   Tone-Mapped IQA Framework

In this section, we first describe how to extract luminance information, color saturation, statistical naturalness and structural fidelity based features, and then

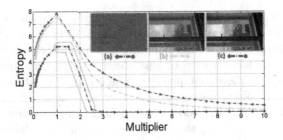

Fig. 1. Correlation of the entropy with varying multiplier. (a), (b) and (c) indicate three LDR images generated from the HDR image. Each of three curves is constituted by 37 entropy values of luminance-changing images, which are respectively generated from the above three tone-mapped LDR images (i.e., (a), (b) and (c)) with distinct multipliers. The rank of these three images in terms of subjective quality is: (a) < (b) < (c).

introduce the method to form these features via an optimization scheme to establish our TMES system.

2.1 Feature Extraction

It is reasonable to suppose that a satisfied tone-mapped LDR image delivers abundant information, especially in the areas that attract visual attention. Along this vein, we further hypothesize that, regardless of protecting/reducing/raising the original luminance intensity, a high-quality tone-mapped LDR image can preserve more features. According to this, we produce some images by changing brightness in the luminance channel:

$$\{I_1, I_2, ..., I_i\} = \{m_1, m_2, ..., m_i\}I_t \tag{1}$$

where I_t represents an input tone-mapped image and m_i is the i-th multiplier. The subsequent step is the normalization, in which the produced images are first rounded to the nearest integer:

$$I_{i,j} = \begin{cases} I_{i,j} - mod(I_{i,j}, 1) + 1 & \text{if } mod(I_{i,j}, 1) \geq \frac{1}{2} \\ I_{i,j} - mod(I_{i,j}, 1) & \text{otherwise} \end{cases} \tag{2}$$

and then clipped into the visible dynamic range:

$$I_{i,j} = \min(I_{i,j}, 2^l - 1) \tag{3}$$

where j indicates the pixel index in I_i. Here, mod is used to find the remainders and $2^l - 1$ is the maximum dynamic range. As for 8-bit LDR images, we assign $l = 8$ and $2^8 - 1 = 255$. Note that all the values of pixels must be non-negative, such that there is no need to restrain them greater than or equal to zero. Subsequently, we measure the luminance information of each created image via the commonly used entropy [21]:

$$E_i = -\sum_{x=0}^{255} p_i(x) \log p_i(x) \tag{4}$$

where $p_i(x)$ is the probability density of grayscale x in I_i. E_i refers to basic information when $m_i = 1$, and it refers to detail information for other cases of m_i [22].

The validity of E_i for quality evaluation of tone-mapped images has been presented in previous conference paper [22]. As displayed in Fig. 1 (a)–(c), there are three tone-mapped images converted from the same HDR image. The three curves reflect the variations of entropy with the multiplier in each of three images respectively. We assign $M = \{1, a, \frac{1}{a} | a \in [1.5, 10]\}$. One can see that, compared with (b) and (c), the curve of (a) quickly fades to a very low level with a small amount of changes in luminance (for example, as the multiplier changed from 1.5 to 2.5, highlighted with a green loop), which is consistent with the fact that (a) contains less information and has a worse visual quality than (b) and (c).

It is obvious that the under-exposure problem exists in (a). What about two normal tone-mapped images (b) and (c) Apparently, these two images do not include over-exposed or under-exposed regions. As can be seen from Fig. 1, the blue curve of (c) is always above the yellow curve of (b) although these two curves are close to each other. Human judgements of quality show the fact that (c) is slightly better than (b). This also demonstrates the effectiveness of the feature E_i when assessing the quality of tone-mapped images. Generally speaking, humans incline to make a judgment via a simpler manner, and thus it is better to deploy sparse features unless the performance is largely reduced. From the experiments, it was found that using 5 representative entropy values can validly save the implementation time, and at the same time preserve a high-level performance. We accordingly assign $M = \{\frac{1}{8.5}, \frac{1}{2}, 1, 2, 8.5\}$.

Despite the substantial contribution of applying global entropy to discriminate the luminance information and the visual quality of tone-mapped images, human visual system (HVS) is overlooked. Therefore, two additional factors are considered to modify the global entropy defined in Eq. (4). One manner is to consider the visual saliency, because human eyes pay more attention to salient areas. A modern visual saliency detection model, image signature model [23], is used for the sake of its efficiency and efficacy. The image signature model makes use of the sign of each DCT component to generate the saliency map. As such, this model just requires a single bit per component, making it efficient with very low cost of computational complexity. The image signature is defined as

$$\text{ImgSign}(I_i) = \text{sign}(\text{DCT2}(I_i)) \tag{5}$$

where $\text{sign}(\cdot)$ is the entrywise sign operator to obtain the sign of the input value. The reconstructed image is computed by

$$\bar{I}_i = \text{IDCT2}(\text{ImgSign}(I_i)) \tag{6}$$

where DCT2 and IDCT2 represent discrete cosine transform and inverse discrete cosine transform for the two dimensional image signal, respectively. The saliency map can be acquired by smoothing the squared reconstructed image:

$$\text{Smap} = g * (\bar{I}_i \circ \bar{I}_i) \tag{7}$$

where g is a Gaussian kernel and 'o' and '*' are the entrywise and convolution product operators respectively. Accordingly, we define the saliency-based entropy to be the entropy of the 30% most salient pixels, denoted as $E_{s,i}$.

Due to the fact that "patch" usually serves as the unit in the image recognition, decomposition and restoration, etc., the other manner makes use of the mean of patch-based entropy computed by

$$E_{p,i} = \frac{1}{J} \sum_{j=1}^{J} E_i(P_{i,j}) \tag{8}$$

where $E_i(P_{i,j})$ indicates entropy of the j-th patch $P_{i,j}$ in the image I_i, and J is the number of all the patches. Finally, we fuse the global entropy and its two HVS-based modified versions to yield the first type of features:

$$E_{t,i} = \frac{E_i + \gamma E_{s,i}^{\phi} + \gamma E_{p,i}^{\phi}}{1 + 2\gamma} \tag{9}$$

where γ and ϕ alter the relative strength of responses of three terms. These two parameters are set to be the same values in [10]. It is clear that a larger value of $E_{t,i}$ corresponds to an image of better quality.

Apart from the luminance information, color saturation also plays a critical role in visual perception [24–26], especially in IQA algorithm design [31]. According to the illustration in [27], colorfulness quantifies the degree of distinguishment between color and gray. After changing form the tone-mapped RGB image into HSV color space via the MATLAB function "rgb2hsv", the color saturation is defined to be the global average of saturation channel. It is natural to consider the HVS-based ways for modification. Note that the mean of patch-based saturation values is itself the global mean. By trials, we find that the saliency-based manner based on the image signature algorithm [23] contributes a certain performance gain. Therefore, the saliency-based mean of color saturation values, denoted as C, constitutes the second type of feature. Intuitively, the larger the saturation value is, the higher quality the image has.

An important index adopted in IQA tasks is the statistical naturalness, which is based on a reliable assumption that an image of high perceived quality looks natural [28–32]. This may be also applied to tone-mapped IQA problem. But it has been found that naturalness closely correlates with luminance and contrast for tone-mapped LDR images [33]. Guided by this observation, a statistical naturalness model is established using 3,000 natural images, in light of patch-based means of luminance and contrast values [9]. These images consist of various natural scenes, e.g. building, mountain, sea, plant, animal, artifact, etc., available at [34,35]. For each natural image, we first remove its chromatic information and keep the luminance channel. Subsequently, each image is separated into a train of patches. Eventually, we compute the global mean of patch-based local mean (c) and that of patch-based local standard deviation (d). It was found that the two histograms of means and standard deviations of 3,000 natural images can be well fitted by a Gaussian function and a Beta probability density function:

$$P_c(c) = \frac{1}{\sqrt{2\pi}\sigma_c} \exp\left[-\frac{c - \mu_c}{2\sigma_c^2}\right] \tag{10}$$

and

$$P_d(d) = \frac{(1-d)^{\kappa_d-1}d^{\iota_d-1}}{\beta(\iota_d, \kappa_d)} \tag{11}$$

where P_c and P_d are the likelihood measures of naturalness given an image; $\beta(\cdot)$ is the Beta function; the optimized model parameters μ_c, σ_c, ι_d and κ_d are set with the values in [10]. By introducing a normalization factor $K = \max\{P_c, P_d\}$, we finally use the third type of statistical naturalness feature as $N = \frac{1}{K}P_cP_d$.

The design philosophy behind the fourth adopted feature, which is designed by modifying the structural fidelity feature in [9], lies in that the HVS is good at extracting structural information from a scene [36,37]. Specifically, the two main targets of seeing a picture are to understand the semantic information included therein and aesthetics. Structures convey important visual information and are beneficial to these two aspects, mainly depending on the analysis of main structures (e.g., contour) and fine structures (e.g., edge) [38–40], so it is crucial to preserve structures of HDR images in tone-mapped LDR images. The structural fidelity performs locally based on two components:

$$S_l = \frac{2\hat{\sigma}_x\hat{\sigma}_y}{\hat{\sigma}_x^2 + \hat{\sigma}_y^2 + c} \cdot \frac{\sigma_{xy}}{\sigma_x\sigma_y + c} \tag{12}$$

where x and y represent HDR and LDR images' local patches respectively. σ_x and σ_y indicate local standard deviations, and σ_{xy} is the cross correlation between two associated local blocks in above two kinds of images. $\hat{\sigma}_x$ and $\hat{\sigma}_y$ are obtained by passing σ_x and σ_y through a fixed nonlinear mapping, and c is a positive stabilizing constant to avoid division-by-zero.

In Eq. (12), the first component conducts the structural comparison while the second component compares the signal strength. Note that the second component only works when one of two kinds of images is important and the other one is unimportant. As such, a nonlinear mapping is utilized to compute $\hat{\sigma}_x$ and $\hat{\sigma}_y$ from σ_x and σ_y, for the purpose of determining the significance of signal strength. The nonlinear mapping should characterize the visual sensitivity via a smooth transition in-between [41]. As such, the term $\hat{\sigma}_x$ is computed by

$$\hat{\sigma}_x = \frac{1}{\sqrt{2\pi}\theta_\sigma} \int_{-\infty}^{\sigma} \exp\left[-\frac{(x-\tau_s)^2}{2\theta_\sigma^2}\right] dx. \tag{13}$$

In Eq. (13), $\theta_\sigma = \frac{\tau_s}{k}$ with $k = 3$ indicates the standard deviation of the normal distribution that controls the slope of detection probability variation. The modulation threshold $\tau_s = \frac{\mu}{\lambda A(f)}$ with μ denotes the average intensity value, λ is a constant to fit psychological data and f represents the spatial frequency.

Then, a sliding window traverses the image to produce local structural fidelity of the overall color blocks, which is combined to predict a single score of the image. The global-based mean ignores the characters of HVS, and we also employ the IS technique [23] on the LDR image to search for salient parts, in order to highlight the visual importance of a local region. Thus, the modified structural fidelity is evaluated by

$$\tilde{S}_l = \frac{\sum_i S_l(i) \cdot V_f(i)}{\sum_i V_f(i)} \tag{14}$$

where i is the index of patches; $V_f(i)$ indicates the saliency map. Several mechanisms have been reported in psychophysical masking studies [42] and neuropsychological recordings [43] that selectively narrow ranges of spatial frequency and orientation. To simulate this function which may happen in visual cortex, multi-scale image decomposition is often used in the construction of visual models, e.g. in recent IQA studies [9,44–48]. Therefore, we use a multi-scale model in our work, in which the input HDR and LDR images are iteratively low-pass filtered and down-sampled to generate the image pyramid structure. Combining scores in each scale level, the overall prediction of the fourth type of the modified structural fidelity feature is defined as $S = \prod_{l=1}^{L} \tilde{S}_l^{\rho_l}$, where the number of scales $L = 5$ and the coefficients $\rho_l = \{0.0448, 0.2856, 0.3001, 0.2363, 0.1333\}$ are acquired via psychophysical experiments [44].

2.2   Parameter Optimization

We have extracted the four types of 8 features applied in our TMES evaluation system. Undoubtedly, they can be used as a vector valued measure, individually or in combination. But a single quality score of an image is more preferable in real application scenarios. Thus, how to reliably combine these 8 features also plays a critical role in the final measure, which will be explicitly described in this subsection.

In [9], Yeganeh and Wang defined a three-parameter function to calibrate the joint measurement of two features U and V:

$$Q = \gamma U^\phi + (1 - \gamma)V^\theta \tag{15}$$

where γ, ϕ and θ are parameters to be determined. Considering the fact that there are 8 features extracted in our study, 15 parameters are required when using such strategy. This is a non-trivial problem to reasonably determine the values of 15 parameters. Instead, machine learning technologies, such as support vector regressor [19] and extreme learning machine [49], can be applied as the pooling stage to combine the features mentioned above following the line of popular IQA researches [28,29]. Based on the estimation of the median performance by repeatedly conducting a procedure of random 80% train-20% test 1,000 times, the effectiveness of a quality metric tested can be reflected. Yet these supervised learning-based pooling schemes may easily lead to over-fitting, such that the learned model is extremely effective on the training set whereas fails on the other testing images.

In order to circumvent this deficiency, it has been provided in [20] that a large quantity of training samples, which are not overlapped with the images in the evaluation database, and high-performance FR metrics that serve to label training samples can be used to combine the features robustly. On the other hand, as mentioned earlier, FR metrics can be improved by including some or all of features (e.g. NSS-based features) used in NR algorithms [9]. Based on these inspirations, a novel optimization strategy using a large dataset as training samples is introduced to generate the FR F-TMES and NR N-TMES methods via an iterative-based strategy.

In particular, we group the 8 features into two classes based on the similarity of definition and function of parameters. One class includes the first type of five features measuring the luminance information, while the other class includes the rest three features. For pooling, we exploit a two-stage method. The principal component analysis (PCA) is used in the first stage [50], because it is a standard dimensionality reduction technique for features of similar attributes and has been applied to an extensive class of image processing and automatic engineering.

In essence, PCA finds linear fusions of variables reflecting major trends in a dataset with the linear assumption of the datasets. For a tone-mapped LDR image, we denote the first type of 5 luminance information features as the vector a. Given a group of n tone-mapped LDR images, we can generate n vectors and combine them into a matrix $A = (a_1, a_2, ..., a_n)$ of dimension $5 \times n$. The objective of PCA is to find a new basis for the dataset by linearly transforming the matrix A into an another matrix E of dimension $p \times n$, $E = PA$, where $p < 5$. The new basis has minimal unwanted clutter and reveals relationships between the data points. The rows of P are the eigenvectors of the covariance matrix $S_A = \frac{1}{n-1} AA^T$ of A, where the superscript "T" means transpose. This requires A to be zero mean across each variable and thus P can be constructed by extracting the eigenvectors of S_A. In the diagonal of the covariance matrix $S_E = \frac{1}{n-1} EE^T$ of E, the elements are the eigenvalues aligned in descending order. The eigenvalues offer an indication of the variation of each variable contributing to the overall variation. We assign $p = 1$ and acquire the transforming matrix P such that the associated modified luminance information feature $E = PA$.

Towards acquiring the reliable transforming matrix P, we construct a new training set, in which about 300 HDR images were collected from websites [51–53]. There are none overlapping between our collected HDR images and the images in TMID, TMID2015 and HDRD evaluation databases. We then generated about 3,000 tone-mapped LDR images from the collected HDR images using ten popular tone-mapping operators [1,2,4,54–60], constituting the new training set. It is worth noting that, different from the supervised learning method, the PCA is an unsupervised learning tool without training labels. Therefore, based on the 3,000 tone-mapped LDR images above, we can finally obtain the transforming matrix P and yield the modified luminance information feature $E = P[E_{t,1}, ..., E_{t,5}]^T$.

In this manner, we can convert 8 features to 4 variables and will focus on how to reliably combine those 4 variables to derive the F-TMES and N-TMES evaluation methods in the second stage. We first define the N-TMES and F-TMES models with simple linear combinations:

$$\text{N-TMES} = E + w_1C + w_2N \tag{16}$$

$$\text{F-TMES} = \text{N-TMES} + w_3S = E + w_1C + w_2N + w_3S \tag{17}$$

where w_1, w_2 and w_3 are fixed positive numbers to control the sensitivities and relative contributions of each term to the final quality score, since each of them is positively correlated to the visual quality of tone-mapped images.

Then, we concentrate on assigning the values of w_1, w_2 and w_3. Subjective experiments are the most reliable strategy to derive the truth labels because the tone-mapped images are displayed to the humans. Increasing the dimension and diversity inevitably enhances the generality of a method. In this paper, we thus carry out the single-stimulus method to label the 3,000 tone-mapped images generated by ourselves, according to the instructions provided by ITU-R BT.500-13 [61]. However, such large amount of testing samples require substantial efforts, which may not be practical. As such, we introduce a novel method to achieve a good trade-off between the cost of subjective test and the reliability of quality ratings. The difference between the current and early works lies in that in the previous works all the images were scored 20~25 times by the subjects and averaged to be a MOS value after outlier elimination, while in our test, the whole images tested were scored only once, so the scores are undoubtedly not exactly reliable[1]. Note that the overall subjective quality scores of tone-mapped images are regarded as labels for parameter tuning, such that it is not required to ensure that all the scores are faithful as we just need to make sure that the majority of them, e.g. 80%, are reliable (more illustrations regarding this will be given later). In essence, many subjective experiments have shown that only a small few quality ratings were outliers and have to be removed [9,10,16,37], which indicates that our test meets the demand stated above. Also, this work introduces another NSS-based constraint that the quality scores of natural images estimated by our IQA algorithm should be close to each other. The subjective test was conducted similarly to [16]. The difference between them is that each image was scored only once, and this can intensively decrease the cost of subjective experiment because rating all the 3,000 images more than 20 times is extremely expensive, labor-intensive and time-consuming.

After obtaining the training labels via the above subjective test, we build the following optimization equation to find the optimal values of w_1, w_2 and w_3:

$$\min_{w_1,w_2,w_3} f(x) = \Theta(w_1,w_2) + \alpha\Theta'(w_1,w_2,w_3) + \beta\Phi(w_1,w_2)$$

$$\text{s.t.} \quad w_1 \geq 0, \ w_2 \geq 0, \ w_3 \geq 0 \tag{18}$$

where α and β are used to balance the relative importance among the three components. In Eq. (18), the first component is defined as $\Theta(w_1,w_2) =$

---

[1] The method belongs to weak supervision. Compared with recent weak supervision works [62,63] by using a FR quality model to label a great quantity of image samples, this method has a wider applications for parameter tuning of FR and NR models.

$R(\mathbf{q}(w_1, w_2), \mathbf{q}^\dagger)$, where $\mathbf{q}(w_1, w_2)$ is the vector of objective quality predictions of tone-mapped images derived by the N-TMES model; $\mathbf{q}^\dagger$ is the vector of quality labels of tone-mapped images; $R(\mathbf{x}, \mathbf{y})$ computes the root mean square error (RMSE) between $\mathbf{x}$ and $\mathbf{y}$ and defined as $R(\mathbf{x}, \mathbf{y}) = \sqrt{\frac{1}{U} \sum_{u=1}^{U} (x_u - y_u)^2}$, where u and U separately represent the index and the length of the vector $\mathbf{x}$. This component aims to find the optimal w_1 and w_2 values through minimizing the distance between the objective quality scores estimated by deploying the N-TMES model and the labels acquired via our subjective experiment. In Eq. (18), the second component $\Theta'(w_1, w_2, w_3) = R(\mathbf{q}'(w_1, w_2, w_3), \mathbf{q}^\dagger)$ is akin to the first component except that $\mathbf{q}'(w_1, w_2, w_3)$ is the vector of objective quality estimations of tone-mapped images derived by using the F-TMES method. In Eq. (18), the third component is defined to be $\Phi(w_1, w_2) = \mathcal{E}(\mathbf{q}^*(w_1, w_2)^2) - \mathcal{E}(\mathbf{q}^*(w_1, w_2))^2$, where $\mathcal{E}$ computes the expectation of a given vector and $\mathbf{q}^*(w_1, w_2)$ is the vector of objective quality measures of a large body of nature images computed by using the N-TMES model. This component is to confine that our N-TMES method conforms to a certain statistical regularity that its quality predictions of a great number of natural images are close to each other, or in other words, have a small variance. Equation (18) is a nonlinear programming problem and we use the 'fmincon' MATLAB function to solve it.

In implementation, the nonlinear programming problem is solved with an iterative-based manner. To specify, firstly, we initialize w_1, w_2 and w_3 as w_1^0, w_2^0 and w_3^0, and compute the N-TMES and F-TMES scores of randomly chosen U tone-mapped images, namely $\mathbf{q}(w_1, w_2)$ and $\mathbf{q}'(w_1, w_2, w_3)$, and extract the associated quality labels, namely $\mathbf{q}^\dagger$. In this work we assign $U = 2400$, i.e., 80% tone-mapped images included in our test, which is able to reduce the ratio of outliers and alleviate their influences on parameter tuning. Secondly, we measure the consistency of our N-TMES model by utilizing lots of natural images. We downloaded the overall 16,873 images in the SUN2012 database [64]. Apparently, there always exist the minority of particular natural images heavily deviated from the others. So in practice, we randomly select 14,000 images (about 80%) from the SUN2012 database followed by computing their N-TMES scores, i.e. $\mathbf{q}^*(w_1, w_2)$, and the associated variance. The above procedure is repeated 1,000 times and the smallest variance serves as $\Phi(w_1, w_2)$. Thirdly, w_1^0, w_2^0 and w_3^0 are updated to be w_1^1, w_2^1 and w_3^1. Finally, we repeatedly perform the second and third steps until the convergence. Via these four steps, we can acquire a group of optimal solutions w_1^*, w_2^* and w_3^*. Next, in order to eliminate the influences of outliers, we repeat the aforesaid procedure 1,000 times and achieve 1,000 groups of optimal solutions. The 3σ-rule is applied to remove the outlier (less than 4%) and eventually maintain 966 groups of optimal solutions. The final w_1^*, w_2^* and w_3^* are assigned to be the mean of the 966 groups of solutions remained.

In real application, the input of the "HDR image" in our TMES system can be vacant. To specify, when only the LDR image is available (i.e., the HDR image cannot be used), we derive the same result from the outputs of the "F-TMES score" and the "N-TMES score". In such situation, we use this result as the quality score of the input LDR image. When the LDR and HDR images are both accessible (i.e., the HDR image can be utilized), the outputs of "F-TMES score" and "N-TMES score" are different. In this case, we use the result from the output of "F-TMES score" as the quality measure of the input LDR image, leading to a more reliable score than without using the reference HDR image.

3   Validation of Evaluation System

In terms of the human ratings obtained through subjective assessment, the validation process is implemented to measure and compare the proposed IQA techniques with 10 most advanced relevant competitors. The human ratings used in our research are associated to three subjective image databases, TMID [9], TMID2015 [10] and HDRD [11]. As far as we know, only these three databases are closely related to tone-mapped IQA problems. The first TMID database was completed at the University of Waterloo in 2013. This database is composed of 15 HDR images and corresponding 120 tone-mapped LDR images generated with 8 tone mapping operators. The second TMID2015 database was completed at Shanghai Jiao Tong University in 2015. In contrast to the TMID database, this database uses 16 tone mapping operators and is composed of 3 commonly occurring HDR images and associated 48 tone-mapped LDR images. The third HDRD database is a large-scale database established at the University of Texas at Austin in 2016. This database includes 821 tone-mapped images, whose opinion scores were derived using a crowdsourcing platform, which can collect 300,000 opinion scores on 1,811 images from more than 5,000 unique observers. Ten recently developed IQA models are included for comparison. Besides the proposed F-TMES and N-TMES methods, other 10 models are respectively FR TMQI [9], NR BRISQUE [28], NFERM [29], NIQE [30], IL-NIQE [31], BMQS [65], BTMQI [10], SSEQ [66], SISBLIM [67], and GMLF [68]. Note that, in building our blind N-TMES metric, a great number of auxiliary image samples are introduced to improve its generality, whereas BRISQUE, NFERM, BTMQI, SSEQ and GMLF methods are demonstrated only using the testing databases. We record the median performance value of 1,000 times 20% testing - 80% training on the TMID database and carry out the cross-validation on TMID2015 and HDRD databases using the regression module trained based on the whole TMID database.

Three typical indices are used for performance evaluation and comparison. According to the recommendations of the video quality experts group, after the regression procedure is used to reduce the nonlinearity of the predicted scores, three indices are calculated. Firstly, the vectors of the original IQA scores, the IQA scores after nonlinear regression, and the subjective scores are respectively expressed as y_o, y_p, and y_s. Then this regression procedure is performed via a logistic regression function as used in [67]. From the perspective of prediction power, the first index is the Pearson linear correlation coefficient (PLCC) between y_p and y_s to measure the prediction accuracy. The other two indices are the Spearman rank order correlation coefficient (SRCC) and the Kendall's rank order correlation coefficient (KRCC) between y_o and y_s, to evaluate the prediction monotonicity. In the three indices stated above, a value close to 1 means superior correlation performance in accordance with human judgement of quality.

Table 1. Comparison on TMID, TMID2015 and HDRD databases. We bold the top models.

TMID Database [9]											
Metric	TMQI	F-TMES	BRISQUE	NFERM	NIQE	IL-NIQE	BQMS	BTMQI	SSEQ	SISBLIM	GMLF	N-TMES
Type	FR [9]	FR (Pro.)	NR [28]	NR [29]	NR [30]	NR [31]	NR [67]	NR [10]	NR [68]	NR [69]	NR [70]	NR (Pro.)
PLCC	0.7715	**0.7934**	0.5481	0.3249	0.5655	0.3352	0.2269	**0.8541**	0.4783	0.2301	0.5146	**0.7659**
SRCC	0.7406	**0.7522**	0.4810	0.2427	0.4967	0.3456	0.2413	**0.8282**	0.3266	0.1464	0.4809	**0.7309**
KRCC	0.5585	**0.5613**	0.3351	0.1693	0.3492	0.2349	0.1643	**0.6545**	0.2116	0.0979	0.3250	**0.5408**

TMID2015 Database [10]											
Metric	TMQI	F-TMES	BRISQUE	NFERM	NIQE	IL-NIQE	BQMS	BTMQI	SSEQ	SISBLIM	GMLF	N-TMES
Type	FR [9]	FR (Pro.)	NR [28]	NR [29]	NR [30]	NR [31]	NR [67]	NR [10]	NR [68]	NR [69]	NR [70]	NR (Pro.)
PLCC	0.6730	**0.8252**	0.0143	0.1757	0.4251	0.5687	0.3186	**0.6824**	0.4834	0.5469	0.1377	**0.7879**
SRCC	0.5551	**0.8310**	0.1247	0.1580	0.4223	0.5745	0.2472	**0.7061**	0.3571	0.4793	0.1580	**0.7927**
KRCC	0.3943	**0.6507**	0.0703	0.1349	0.2857	0.4050	0.1664	**0.5154**	0.2386	0.3498	0.1095	**0.5866**

HDRD Database [11]											
Metric	TMQI	F-TMES	BRISQUE	NFERM	NIQE	IL-NIQE	BQMS	BTMQI	SSEQ	SISBLIM	GMLF	N-TMES
Type	FR [9]	FR (Pro.)	NR [28]	NR [29]	NR [30]	NR [31]	NR [67]	NR [10]	NR [68]	NR [69]	NR [70]	NR (Pro.)
PLCC	--	--	0.1291	0.2032	0.1238	0.2659	0.2393	**0.5721**	0.1470	0.4007	0.1179	**0.7104**
SRCC	--	--	0.1071	0.1447	0.0845	0.2443	0.1257	**0.5162**	0.0900	0.4062	0.1086	**0.6021**
KRCC	--	--	0.0713	0.0961	0.0561	0.1634	0.0835	**0.3520**	0.0610	0.2728	0.0721	**0.4265**

As shown in Table 1, we provide the performance evaluation results of 10 competing IQA methods across three related image databases. The metric with the best performance in each type of FR- and NR-IQA metrics is highlighted with boldface for straightforward comparison. On the TMID database, one can observe that the proposed F-TMES method outperforms the recently designed FR TMQI model. Furthermore, it is transparent that our blind N-TMES metric has achieved very promising result, significantly better than other testing NR-IQA models, and even comparable to the FR TMQI algorithm. On the second TMID2015 database, it can be found that, on one hand, our F-TMES is of overwhelming superiority as compared with other IQA approaches considered, and on the other hand, our N-TMES is also of the optimal performance among other competitors, regardless of the FR TMQI and state-of-the-art blind IQA methods. On the third large-scale HDRD database, in which the HDR images are not included and only NR metrics can be compared, our proposed blind N-TMES model has achieved the optimal result, PLCC over 0.7 and SRCC over 0.6, far beyond other competitors.

4   Conclusion

In this paper, we have addressed the problem of comparing the performance of tone-mapping operators. A new evaluation system has been established based on four types of features to deal with both FR and NR application scenarios. From four aspects of considerations, eight extracted features relevant to luminance information, color saturation, statistical naturalness and structural fidelity play complementary roles in the design of evaluation system. With a two-stage optimization strategy, PCA and linear fusion are applied to reliably combine the features. Experiments show that our FR and NR models are proved to achieve superior performance and comparatively low computational cost.

References

1. Reinhard, E., et al.: High Dynamic Range Imaging: Acquisition, Display and Image-Based Lighting. Morgan Kaufmann, San Mateo (2005)
2. Fattal, R., Lischinski, D., Werman, M.: Gradient domain high dynamic range compression. ACM Trans. Graph. **27**(3), 1–10 (2002)
3. Pattanaik, S., Yee, H.: Adaptive gain control for high dynamic range image display. In: Proceedings of the ACM Conference Computer Graphics, pp. 83–87 (2002)
4. Durand, F., Dorsey, J.: Fast bilateral filtering for the display of high-dynamic-range images. ACM Trans. Graph. **21**(3), 257–266 (2002)
5. Čadík, M.: Perception motivated hybrid approach to tone mapping. In: ICCGVCV, pp. 129–136, January 2007
6. He, K., Sun, J., Tang, X.: Guided image filtering. IEEE Trans. Pattern Anal. Mach. Intell. **35**(6), 1397–1409 (2013)
7. Li, Z., Zheng, J.: Visual-salience-based tone mapping for high dynamic range images. IEEE Trans. Ind. Electron. **61**(12), 7076–7082 (2014)
8. Čadík, M., et al.: Evaluation of Tone Mapping Operators (2010). http://cadik.posvete.cz/tmo/
9. Yeganeh, H., Wang, Z.: Objective quality assessment of tone-mapped images. IEEE Trans. Image Process. **22**(2), 657–667 (2013)
10. Gu, K., et al.: Blind quality assessment of tone-mapped images via analysis of information, naturalness and structure. IEEE Trans. Multimedia **18**(3), 432–443 (2016)
11. Kundu, D., Ghadiyaram, D., Bovik, A.C., Evans, B.L.: Large-scale crowdsourced study for high dynamic range images. IEEE Trans. Image Process. (2017, under review)
12. Gu, K., Wang, S., Yang, H., Lin, W., Zhai, G., Yang, X., Zhang, W.: Saliency-guided quality assessment of screen content images. IEEE Trans. Multimedia **18**(6), 1098–1110 (2016)
13. Gu, K., Jakhetiya, V., Qiao, J., Li, X., Lin, W., Thalmann, D.: Model-based referenceless quality metric of 3D synthesized images using local image description. IEEE Trans. Image Process. **27**(1), 394–405 (2018)
14. Li, S., et al.: Closed-form optimization on saliency-guided image compression for HEVC-MSP. IEEE Trans. Multimedia **20**(1), 155–170 (2018)
15. Gu, K., Zhai, G., Yang, X., Zhang, W., Chen, C.W.: Automatic contrast enhancement technology with saliency preservation. IEEE Trans. Circuits Syst. Video Technol. **25**(9), 1480–1494 (2015)
16. Gu, K., Zhai, G., Lin, W., Liu, M.: The analysis of image contrast: from quality assessment to automatic enhancement. IEEE Trans. Cybern. **46**(1), 284–297 (2016)
17. Liu, X., Zhang, L., Li, H., Lu, J.: Integrating visual saliency information into objective quality assessment of tone-mapped images. In: Huang, D.-S., Bevilacqua, V., Premaratne, P. (eds.) ICIC 2014. LNCS, vol. 8588, pp. 376–386. Springer, Cham (2014). https://doi.org/10.1007/978-3-319-09333-8_41

18. Ma, K., Yeganeh, H., Zeng, K., Wang, Z.: High dynamic range image compression by optimizing tone mapped image quality index. IEEE Trans. Image Process. **24**(10), 3086–3097 (2015)

19. Chang, C.-C., Lin, C.-J.: LIBSVM: a library for support vector machines. ACM TIST **2**(3), 1–27 (2011)

20. Gu, K., Zhou, J., Qiao, J., Zhai, G., Lin, W., Bovik, A.C.: No-reference quality assessment of screen content pictures. IEEE Trans. Image Process. **26**(8), 4005–4018 (2017)

21. Shannon, C.E.: A mathematical theory of communication. Bell Syst. Tech. J. **27**, 379–423 (1948)

22. Gu, K., Zhai, G., Liu, M., Yang, X., Zhang, W.: Details preservation inspired blind quality metric of tone mapping methods. In: ISCAS, pp. 518–521, June 2014

23. Hou, X., Harel, J., Koch, C.: Image signature: highlighting sparse salient regions. IEEE TPAMI **34**(1), 194–201 (2012)

24. Tanaka, J., Weiskopf, D., Williams, P.: The role of color in high-level vision. Trends Cogn. Sci. **5**(5), 211–215 (2001)

25. Solomon, S.G., Lennie, P.: The machinery of colour vision. Nat. Rev. Neurosci. **8**, 276–286 (2007)

26. Gu, K., Qiao, J., Li, X.: Highly efficient picture-based prediction of PM2.5 concentration. IEEE Trans. Ind. Electron. **66**(4), 3176–3184 (2019)

27. Fairchild, M.D.: Color Appearance Models. Wiley, New York (2005)

28. Mittal, A., Moorthy, A.K., Bovik, A.C.: No-reference image quality assessment in the spatial domain. IEEE TIP **21**(12), 4695–4708 (2012)

29. Gu, K., Zhai, G., Yang, X., Zhang, W.: Using free energy principle for blind image quality assessment. IEEE Trans. Multimedia **17**(1), 50–63 (2015)

30. Mittal, A., Soundararajan, R., Bovik, A.C.: Making a 'completely blind' image quality analyzer. IEEE Signal Process. Lett. **22**(3), 209–212 (2013)

31. Zhang, L., Zhang, L., Bovik, A.C.: A feature-enriched completely blind image quality evaluator. IEEE TIP **24**(8), 2579–2591 (2015)

32. Gu, K., Lin, W., Zhai, G., Yang, X., Zhang, W., Chen, C.W.: No-reference quality metric of contrast-distorted images based on information maximization. IEEE Trans. Cybern. **47**(12), 4559–4565 (2017)

33. Čadík, M., Slavík, P.: The naturalness of reproduced high dynamic range images. In: ICIV, pp. 920–925 (2005)

34. UCID - Uncompressed Colour Image Database (2004). http://www-staff.lboro.ac.uk/~cogs/datasets/UCID/ucid.html

35. Computer Vision Test Images (2005). http://www-2.cs.cmu.edu/afs/cs/project/cil/www/v-images.html

36. Wang, Z., Bovik, A., Sheikh, H., Simoncelli, E.: Image quality assessment: from error visibility to structural similarity. IEEE TIP **13**(4), 600–612 (2004)

37. Choi, L.K., Cormack, L.K., Bovik, A.C.: Motion silencing of flicker distortions on naturalistic videos. SPIC **39**, 328–341 (2015)

38. Gu, K., Li, L., Lu, H., Min, X., Lin, W.: A fast reliable image quality predictor by fusing micro- and macro-structures. IEEE Trans. Ind. Electron. **64**(5), 3903–3912 (2017)

39. Hou, X., Zhang, L.: Saliency detection: a spectral residual approach. In: Proceedings of the IEEE Conference on Computer Vision and Pattern Recognition, pp. 1–8, June 2007

40. Singh, A., Singh, M., Singh, B.: Face detection and eyes extraction using sobel edge detection and morphological operations. In: CASP, pp. 295–300, June 2016

41. Barten, P.G.J.: Contrast Sensitivity of the Human Eye and Its Effects on Image Quality. SPIE, Washington, DC (1999)
42. Stromeyer, C.F., Julesz, B.: Spatial-frequency masking in vision: critical bands and spread of masking. J. Opt. Soc. Am. **62**(10), 1221 (1972)
43. De Valois, R., Albrecht, D., Thorell, L.: Spatial frequency selectivity of cells in macaque visual cortex. Vis. Res. **22**(5), 545–559 (1982)
44. Wang, Z., Simoncelli, E.P., Bovik, A.C.: Multi-scale structural similarity for image quality assessment. In: ACSSC, pp. 1398–1402, November 2003
45. Gu, K., Wang, S., Zhai, G., Lin, W., Yang, X., Zhang, W.: Analysis of distortion distribution for pooling in image quality prediction. IEEE Trans. Broadcast. **62**(2), 446–456 (2016)
46. Gu, K., Qiao, J., Lee, S., Liu, H., Lin, W., Le Callet, P.: Multiscale natural scene statistical analysis for no-reference quality evaluation of DIBR-synthesized views. IEEE Trans. Broadcast. **66**(1), 127–139 (2020)
47. Mantiuk, R., et al.: HDR-VDP-2: a calibrated visual metric for visibility and quality predictions in all luminance conditions. TOG **30**(4), 1–14 (2011)
48. Narwaria, M., et al.: HDR-VDP-2.2: a calibrated method for objective quality prediction of high-dynamic range and standard images. JEI **24**(1), 010501 (2015)
49. Huang, G.-B., Zhu, Q.-Y., Siew, C.-K.: Extreme learning machine: theory and applications. Neurocomputing **70**(1–3), 489–501 (2006)
50. Jolliffe, I.T.: Principal Component Analysis. Springer, Heidelberg (1986)
51. High Dynamic Range Image Examples. http://www.anyhere.com/gward/hdrenc/pages/originals.html
52. High Dynamic Range Imaging of Natural Scenes (2002). http://white.stanford.edu/~brian/hdr/hdr.html
53. Krasula, L., et al.: Influence of HDR reference on observers preference in tone-mapped images evaluation. In: QoMEX, pp. 1–6 (2015)
54. Ashikhmin, M.: A tone mapping algorithm for high contrast images. In: Proceedings of the 13th Eurographics Workshop on Rendering, pp. 145–156 (2002)
55. Drago, F., et al.: Adaptive logarithmic mapping for displaying high contrast scenes. In: CGF, vol. 22, no. 3, pp. 419–426 (2003)
56. Krawczyk, G., et al.: Lightness perception in tone reproduction for high dynamic range images. In: CGF, vol. 24, no. 3, pp. 635–645 (2005)
57. Kuang, J., et al.: iCAM06: a refined image appearance model for HDR image rendering. JVCIR **18**(5), 406–414 (2007)
58. Reinhard, E., et al.: Photographic tone reproduction for digital images. ACM Trans. Graph. **21**(3), 267–276 (2002)
59. Reinhard, E., Devlin, K.: Dynamic range reduction inspired by photoreceptor physiology. IEEE TVCG **11**(1), 13–24 (2005)
60. Yee, Y.H., Pattanaik, S.: Segmentation and adaptive assimilation for detail-preserving display of high-dynamic range images. Vis. Comput. **19**(7), 457–466 (2003). https://doi.org/10.1007/s00371-003-0211-5
61. Methodology for the subjective assessment of the quality of television pictures. International Telecommunication Union Recommendation ITU-R BT.500-13 (2012)
62. Gu, K., Tao, D., Qiao, J., Lin, W.: Learning a no-reference quality assessment model of enhanced images with big data. IEEE Trans. Neural Netw. Learn. Syst. **29**, 1301–1313 (2018)
63. Gu, K., Xu, X., Qiao, J., Jiang, Q., Lin, W., Thalmann, D.: Learning a unified blind image quality metric via on-line and off-line big training instances. IEEE Trans. Big Data (2021)

64. Xiao, J., Hays, J., Ehinger, K., Oliva, A., Torralba, A.: SUN database: large-scale scene recognition from abbey to zoo. In: CVPR, pp. 13–18, June 2010
65. Gu, K., Zhai, G., Lin, W., Yang, X., Zhang, W.: Learning a blind quality evaluation engine of screen content images. Neurocomputing **196**, 140–149 (2016)
66. Liu, L., et al.: No-reference image quality assessment based on spatial and spectral entropies. SPIC **29**(8), 856–863 (2014)
67. Gu, K., Zhai, G., Yang, X., Zhang, W.: Hybrid no-reference quality metric for singly and multiply distorted images. IEEE Trans. Broadcast. **60**(3), 555–567 (2014)
68. Xue, W., et al.: Blind image quality assessment using joint statistics of gradient magnitude and Laplacian features. IEEE TIP **23**(11), 4850–4862 (2014)

QoE Assessment and Management of MV/3D Video Services

Yiwen Xu, Jingquan Huang, Wei Liu, Weiling Chen[✉], and Tiesong Zhao

Fujian Key Lab for Intelligent Processing and Wireless Transmission of Media
Information, College of Physics and Information Engineering, Fuzhou University,
Fuzhou, China
weiling.chen@fzu.edu.cn

Abstract. The measurements of Quality of Experience (QoE) are essential to research for better analysis and optimization of Multi-View and 3D (MV/3D) videos. However, there is a lack of systematic description of QoE mechanism in MV/3D videos yet. This paper aims to give a comprehensive account of QoE assessment and management for MV/3D video services. We first conclude distinctive QoE influencing factors (IFs) in MV/3D videos by dividing them into immersion and interaction related IFs. Then the methods of QoE assessment in MV/3D video services (including subjective assessment and objective assessment) are presented. Finally, we summarize QoE management for improving immersion and interaction. We hope our work is capable of providing a useful guideline on the related issues and the future research directions in MV/3D video services.

Keywords: Quality of Experience (QoE) · Multi-View Video (MVV) · 3D video

1 Introduction

With the great booming of video applications on broadband and mobile networks, video display techniques have resulted in a considerable promotion of imaging resolution from High Definition (HD) to 2K, 4K and 8K era. Viewers desire to have a further experience in addition to the improvement of video quality requirements. Thus, whether from media contents or multimedia system perspective, the immersive video services which can produce stronger perceptual stimulation to users have been developing vigorously in recent years. Emerging video services can create a deeper sense of immersion, enable users to interact with video content to a certain extent, and provide a wide range of connections with servers and other users. Compared with traditional 2D videos, Multi-View and 3D (MV/3D) videos enable to provide users with a more immersive experience. Multi-View Video (MVV) allows viewers to watch videos from the angle they want to see. Consequently, it requires multiple cameras to shoot from different angles. While 3D video needs to transmit more data, such as views with texture videos, to satisfy viewers with more realistic experience.

© Springer Nature Singapore Pte Ltd. 2021
G. Zhai et al. (Eds.): IFTC 2020, CCIS 1390, pp. 348–358, 2021.
https://doi.org/10.1007/978-981-16-1194-0_30

The characteristics of MV/3D videos make it produce a large amount of data, so the transmission and storage bring more challenges. According to the Cisco Visual Networking Index (VNI) [1], the growing video traffic would occupy 82% of global traffic by the year 2022. Thereby, it is desirable to explore efficient storage and delivery solutions to satisfy requirements of video contents. Among these methods, the user-centric strategy has become popular toward delivering higher quality videos to serve more users. In this strategy, an essential issue is the Quality of Experience (QoE) of the end-user. QoE is used by users to evaluate their satisfaction with the current quality of service. To introduce the QoE strategy into video delivery, two crucial problems should be addressed: how to assess the QoE Influencing Factors (IFs) and how to evaluate the QoE based on these IFs.

There have been a number of contributions on QoE assessment and management in video delivery and correspondingly so far. Reference [2] divided QoE modeling in HTTP adaptive streaming into parametric models, media-layer models, bitstream models and hybrid models, and provided a comprehensive review of the latest modeling studies. In addition, the video QoE IFs were divided into system IFs, context IFs and human IFs according to the video transmission process in [3]. Moreover, the latest researches on QoE assessment and management following this taxonomy are also summarized. Juluri *et al.* [4] reviewed client factors, network factors, server factors to complete QoE assessment of video on demand services. Reference [5] reviewed QoE management in the video stream, and focused on the application of machine learning in it. Despite of these great efforts, most of their work focuses on traditional 2D video, the QoE issues in MV/3D videos have been less focused. Simultaneously, there is no complete review of the IFs, assessment and management of QoE in MV/3D videos. Compared with traditional 2D videos, MV/3D videos have following characteristics:

1) MV/3D videos can create a deeper sense of immersion;
2) MV/3D videos enable users to interact with video content to a certain extent;
3) MV/3D videos provide a wide range of connections with servers and other users.

Consequently, we first analyse the distinctive QoE IFs for MV/3D videos. Then we summarize the most recent achievements on QoE assessment and management in these applications. The rest of this paper is organized as follows: Sect. 2 presents the distinctive IFs to assess QoE in MV/3D videos. In Sects. 3 and 4, the QoE assessment and management based on these IFs are reviewed, respectively. Section 5 concludes the paper.

2   Distinctive QoE Characteristics in MV/3D Videos

2.1   Description of MV/3D Videos

Existing widely studied QoE researches for 2D videos mainly focus on the quality assessment of video content [6]. However, the assessments of QoE for MV/3D videos are more challenging due to their special IFs.

Fig. 1. MV/3D video service

Figure 1 depicts the key properties of MVV services and 3D video services. MVV is defined as a video includes multiple video sequences captured by several cameras from different locations at the same time. For example, the football game in Fig. 1 is shot from four camera angles. While 3D video is a kind of video that enables users to obtain a stereoscopic effect. On the one hand, MVV is obtained by shooting different viewing angles of the same scene at discrete positions, which can display images of corresponding angles according to the position of the observer. The screen content can also be changed when the user's head moving. This sets up a feeling of looking around. An ordinary plane video is obtained when only one viewpoint of the video is decoded. On the other hand, 3D video has many applications in daily situations such as 3D cinema, exhibition hall and teaching platform. MVV and 3D videos generally use 2D plus depth map coding in encoding for the purpose of improving coding compression efficiency. In this way, the client is required to reconstruct another viewpoint image according to the depth map. In addition, 3D video is obtained when only one video stream of a specific pair of viewpoints is decoded at the MVV decoding end, which is an important reason for introducing MVV and 3D videos together in this paper.

2.2   Immersion-Related IFs

Table 1. Distinctive QoE features of emerging video services

	MVV	3D	VR	AR
Immersion	√	√	√	√
Interaction	√		√	√

Table 1 shows distinctive QoE features of MV/3D videos. We divide these QoE IFs into two categories compared with the unique QoE IFs of traditional video services. They are immersion and interaction related IFs.

The immersion of a video shows how immersive the video is to users. Different devices offer different senses of immersion for users, such as helmets in MVV and glasses in 3D video. The more immersive the video is, the harder users can be disturbed by external environments since they devote themselves wholeheartedly to the video content. Factors related to video immersion include video quality, display format of video content, stereo perception and visual comfort. The qualities of MV/3D videos are affected by more factors owing to their abundant composition. For instance, the positions of different viewpoints and the number of viewpoints are the key IFs for MVV. The reasonable positions and numbers of viewpoint will make users more immersed. Productions of MV/3D videos are different from ordinary video. Firstly, videos need to be captured by a special camera. Then videos stitch or map. Finally, videos are encoded to obtain video streams that can be transmitted in the network. The distinctive video format brings immersion to users. In addition, network congestion can degrade Quality of Service (QoS) thus degrade QoE. Besides, the display mode of these video services and whether there are stereoscopic perceptions will also affect the user's immersion. The impact of these aspects on user immersion is classified and discussed as follows:

1) Arrangement of cameras: MV/3D videos require multiple cameras to arrange video recording in a certain way. The arrangement of the cameras include linear type and circular type. Besides, different density view caused by different density cameras is also considered as QoE IFs in [7].
2) Stereo perception: The stereoscopic sense is the obviously difference between 3D and 2D. The work in [8] investigated disparity, amount of parallax and angular resolution as QoE IFs in MVV. Their results suggested that employing a motion parallax gets better QoE than without any motion parallax and users are sensitive to the angular resolution of MVV systems.
3) Viewing equipment: 3D video technology can be separated into 3D with glasses and naked eye 3D. Reference [9] showed that polarized glasses are better than active shutter glasses and the stereoscopic display gets better QoE than auto stereo display.

2.3   Interaction-Related IFs

In [10], interaction was defined as the extent to which users can participate in modifying the form and content of a mediated environment in real time. In Virtual Reality (VR) and Augmented Reality (AR), users can interact with videos through some auxiliary interactive devices. As for MVV, interactions are completed by switching viewpoints of users. The main IFs of interaction include video content effect on head movement correspondence, the accurate response of the video to the interactive auxiliary device, the freedom of users and the accuracy of combination of virtual and reality. When watching MVV, switching the angle of views frequently easily results in undesirable pause. Reference [6] found that smoothness perception was influenced by the density of the view array and user speed when traveling the views. As we can see from Fig. 1, interaction is a unique feature of MVV relative to 3D video. Furthermore, interactions in MVV are much less than in VR and AR. Thus interaction related IFs are discussed more briefly compared to immersion-related IFs in this paper.

3 QoE Assessments in MV/3D Video Services

QoE assessments are essential for service providers, which can provide a solid indicator for appropriate service level to different users. Key IFs of QoE assessments in MV/3D video services are shown in Fig. 2. According to the distinctive QoE IFs in MV/3D videos, we use both subjective and objective assessment methods.

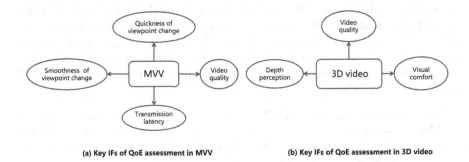

(a) Key IFs of QoE assessment in MVV   (b) Key IFs of QoE assessment in 3D video

Fig. 2. Key IFs of QoE assessment in MV/3D video services

3.1 Subjective Assessment

MV/3D video presentations are distinct from traditional videos. Watching these videos generally requires wearing special devices. Users can also look at these videos to create a stereoscopic view or a panoramic view of a scene. In this case, the user will be intoxicated in the video scene, resulting in a so-called immersion. In this section, we will present the main research directions and trends of subjective assessment for MV/3D videos.

Subjective Assessment on Immersion: The 3D video group of the Video Quality Expert Group (VQEG) has developed a subjective evaluation method for stereoscopic 3D video. They propose the methods assessing and minimizing the visual discomfort and visual fatigue for 3D video. In addition, suggestions on the subjective assessment method of 3D television (3DTV) were also proposed in [11]. Generally, the main factors affecting immersion are depth perception, video quality and visual comfort for 3D video. Users are asked to rate depth perception and video quality in subjective tests while visual comfort can be surveyed in the form of questionnaires. These subjective experiments on immersion for 3D video can be concluded as follows:

1) Depth perception: In the subjective experiment of exploring the effect of 3D stereo perception, Zhang used a Single Stimulus (SS) method with a discrete five-level scale [12]. Subject needed to grade the video quality and depth perception quality separately by five levels. The results confirmed the high correlation between depth quality and video quality.

2) Video quality: Distortion is the main form that affects visual quality. In order to study the effect of asymmetric distortion on the immersion of 3D video, reference [13] set up a subjective experiment. They used a SS procedure using an 11-grade Numerical Categorical Scale (SSNCS) protocol. Then the result is expressed by the mean opinion scores of subjects.

3) Visual comfort: Visual comfort is closely related to simulator disease for 3D video. The Standardized Simulator Disease Questionnaire (SSDQ) [14] was a questionnaire specifically designed to evaluate user simulator diseases in subjective tests. It can be used to evaluate the user's simulator disease in 3D video.

On the other hand, the measurements of immersion for MVV mainly includes video quality and quickness of the viewpoint change and smoothness. In work [15], the author designed subjective experiments for the impact of various Internet Protocol (IP) traffic and delay conditions on MVV QoE. Subject was required to be fluency of the video, video and audio synchronization, quickness of the viewpoint change and comprehensive evaluation rating. Each criterion was evaluated to be one of five levels between 1 (the worst case) and 5 (the best case). In work [7], the authors used an absolute category rating Absolute Category Rating (ACR) method for evaluating test MVV sequences. The test factors included view sweeping speed, smoothness of transition between views and video quality. Two subjective experiments for MVV quality evaluation were proposed in [6]. The first one was the smoothness test of MVV content while the second one was the smoothness of MV static content. The method of rating is also ACR. They found that the IFs of smooth feeling include the density of the view array, the speed of the user when traveling the view and the depth of the object of the scene through their experiments.

Subjective Assessment on Interaction: The interaction of MVV is mainly manifested in that the system can distribute the correct viewpoint video to the user when the user requests to switch the viewpoint. In [17], an interactive task to study the interaction of MVV was designed. In the subjective experiment, one subject was asked to watch the MVV and watch the color or digital information of a dice. Then he told the other subject information he obtained, until the subject who did not watch the video can guess the specific correspondence of the dice, then the task was completed. The subject needed to fill in a questionnaire after the test was completed. The questionnaire included the video quality, whether the viewpoint is switched quickly and the difficulty of the task.

3.2   Objective Assessment

Subjective test requires a lot of manpower and time consumption. Hence, applying subjective test in actual video transmission systems is unrealistic. Consequently, it is necessary to establish objective metric to achieve a broader evaluation of video QoE.

For 3D video, the objective evaluation can be divided into three types: evaluation of depth quality, evaluation of video quality and evaluation of visual comfort. First of all, 3D perception is an important reason for users to feel immersed. Reference [12] proposed a full-reference Depth Quality Assessment (DQA) algorithm based on monocular and binocular 3D content features to measure the degradation of depth quality. In order to evaluate the sense of depth in the video, reference [18] proposed a Layered Random Dot Stereogram (LRDS) for subjective depth perception assessment. Secondly, distortion will reduce user's immersion. In the 3D composite view, the most common distortion comes from depth lossy compression. Zhang *et al.* proposed a 3D quality prediction model to estimate the 3D quality effusion stereopairs based on depth map distortion and neural mechanism [19]. Furthermore, the challenge of Visual Comfort Assessment (VCA) was solved in two stages according to reference [20]. The first stage was extracting Primary Predictive Feature (PPF) and Advanced Predictive Feature (APF). The second stage was mapping features to mass space using random forest regression.

The objective measurements mainly include the evaluation of video quality and transmission latency for MVV. Reference [7] proposed a model based on perceptual disparity to capture the subjective perception of Super Multi-View (SMV), namely Multi-View Perceptual Disparity Model (MVPDM). User perception disparity refers to the difference between adjacent views. MVPDM summarized the contributions of different parameters that affect user perception. Besides, the quality of MVV is sensitive to transmission latency. Reference [16] proposed an adaptive stereoscopic video streaming mechanism. They proved that the quality of received video can be improved by adaptive streaming mechanism after comparing the Peak Signal to Noise Ratio (PSNR) of the decoded video frames received by the proposed algorithm and the traditional algorithms.

4   QoE Managements in MV/3D Video Services

4.1   QoE Managements for Improving Immersion

QoE managements for improving immersion mainly include improving the quality of the video, reducing the stagnation perceived by users and increasing the fluency of visual signals. Methods that can be taken include:

Dynamic Adaptive Streaming over HTTP (DASH)-Based: The DASH data stream should be able to transmit video streams at the most appropriate bit rate and guarantee end-to-end low latency. Transmitting future immersive video via DASH can reduce latency and maximize video quality. Reference

[21] proposed a cloud-assisted and DASH-based Scalable Interactive Multiview Video Streaming (CDS-IMVS) system, which developed a cross-layer optimization scheme to optimize QoE in MVV. A new cache management method was developed in CDS-IMVS. Despite cache cost was increased, total time cost was reduced compared to the traditional methods.

Error Concealment: Error Concealment (EC) can be utilized to improve video quality when an error occurs in the transmission. Reference [22] introduced recent advances in EC for MV/3D videos, including specific methods for depth maps. A packet discarding strategy was given in [23] and its QoE promotion ability was asserted via subjective experiments in MVV.

Choosing the Appropriate Format in 3D Video Services: In [24], QoS parameters were monitored in order to take an appropriate codification decision for Internet Protocol Television (IPTV) service provider. Stereo video coding format and 2D plus depth format were selected in their experiments. Then they drew a conclusion that we should choose 2D plus depth format when quantization scales was relatively low while choose stereo video coding format when quantization scales was relatively high.

4.2   QoE Managements for Improving Interaction

In the interaction of MVV, the system should distribute the correct viewpoint video quickly when it received the user requests to switch the viewpoint. Hence, the methods to improve interaction of MVV that can be taken include:

Increasing the Number of Viewpoints Appropriately: Reference [25] evaluated the visual effect and the number of available viewpoints. The conclusion that numbers of available viewpoints tend to provide higher QoE was made. Reference [26] dealt with three transmission methods on different viewpoints. Finally, the authors found that even with increased latency, all viewpoints of requested server method can increase QoE.

Providing Better Transmission Service: The core of network resource allocation means to prioritize the allocation of bandwidth and bit rate to important views or blocks under limited bandwidth without decreasing the QoE. In MVV, reference [27] studied on the QoE imparity between two bandwidth allocation methods. They observed that the former achieved higher QoE scores when transferring to a narrow-band network. Besides, a QoE-driven Crowdsourced Multiview Live Streaming (CMLS) system was designed in [28]. Then integer programming was used to make the best cloud site while representation choices were used to meet the required QoE as a resource allocation issue. In MPEG-DASH systems, Constant Bit Rate (CBR) coding and efficient rate control strategies are required to increase QoE. Reference [29] used objective QoE measurements of depth maps and structural similarities to find the optimal ratio of interview rate allocation in CBR of MVV streams. They found that unequal rate allocation increase subjective QoE as 0.3–0.5. Reference [30] proposed a new DASH framework to control MVV streams. They use MV navigation rules to prefetch predicted views as a basis for bitrate allocation and finally achieve maximum QoE.

5   Conclusions

This paper first analyzes the distinctive QoE IFs in MV/3D videos, including arrangement of cameras, stereo perception, viewing equipment, video content effect on head movement correspondence and so on. Then QoE assessment in MV/3D video services are concluded. We observe that depth perception, video quality and visual comfort are essential to QoE assessment in 3D video. While MVV pays more attention to transmission quality such as quickness of the viewpoint change and smoothness. Finally, we provide some management methods for improving immersion and interaction in MV/3D videos. We think that the systematic description of QoE mechanism proposed in this paper will contribute to the further research of MV/3D videos. In the future study, we will continue to evaluate and manage QoE of VR, AR and other emerging video services.

References

1. Forecast CV, Cisco visual networking index: Forecast and trends, 2017–2022, White paper, Cisco Public Information (2019)
2. Barman, N., Martini, M.G.: QoE modeling for HTTP adaptive video streaming–a survey and open challenges. IEEE Access **7**, 30831–30859 (2019)
3. Zhao, T., Liu, Q., Chen, C.W.: QoE in video transmission: a user experience-driven strategy. IEEE Commun. Surv. Tutor. **19**(1), 285–302 (2017)
4. Juluri, P., Tamarapalli, V., Medhi, D.: Measurement of quality of experience of video-on-demand services: a survey. IEEE Commun. Surv. Tutor. **18**(1), 401–418 (2016)
5. Torres Vega, M., Perra, C., De Turck, F., Liotta, A.: A review of predictive quality of experience management in video streaming services. IEEE Trans. Broadcast. **64**(2), 432–445 (2018)
6. Cubelos, J., Carballeira, P., Gutiérrez, J., García, N.: QoE analysis of dense multiview video with head-mounted devices. IEEE Trans. Multimedia **22**(1), 69–81 (2020)
7. Carballeira, P., Gutiérrez, J., Morán, F., Cabrera, J., Jaureguizar, F., García, N.: MultiView perceptual disparity model for super multiView video. IEEE J. Sel. Top. Signal Process **11**(1), 113–124 (2017)
8. Ribeiro, F.M.L., et al.: Quality of experience in a stereoscopic multiview environment. IEEE Trans. Multimedia **20**(1), 1–14 (2018)
9. Gutiérrez, J., Jaureguizar, F., García, N.: Subjective comparison of consumer television technologies for 3D visualization. J. Disp. Technol. **11**(11), 967–974 (2015)
10. Steuer, J.: Defining virtual reality: dimensions determining telepresence. J. Commun. **42**(4), 73–93 (1992)

11. Subjective methods for the assessment of stereoscopic 3DTV systems. International Telecommunication Union, Geneva, Switzerland, April 2020

12. Zhang, Y., et al.: Depth perceptual quality assessment for symmetrically and asymmetrically distorted stereoscopic 3d videos. Signal Process.-Image Commun. **78**, 293–305 (2019)

13. Wang, J., Wang, S., Wang, Z.: Asymmetrically compressed stereoscopic 3D videos: quality assessment and rate-distortion performance evaluation. IEEE Trans. Image Process. **26**(3), 1330–1343 (2017)

14. Kennedy, R.S., Lane, N.E., Berbaum, K.S., Lilienthal, M.G.: Simulator sickness questionnaire: an enhanced method for quantifying simulator sickness. Int. J. Aviat. Psychol. **3**(3), 203–220 (1993)

15. Rodriguez, E.J., Nunome, T., Tasaka, S.: Assessment of user behavior and QoE in multi-view video and audio IP transmission. In: Proceedings of the Asia-Pacific Conference on Communication 2009 (APCC 2009), Shanghai, China, October 2009, pp. 790–793 (2009)

16. Hsu, T., Wu, P., Horng, G., Chen, C., Pai, M.: An adaptive stereoscopic video streaming mechanism using MV-HEVC and 3D-HEVC technologies. In: 2019 Twelfth International Conference on Ubi-Media Computing (Ubi-Media), Bali, Indonesia, August 2019, pp. 140–144 (2019)

17. Ichikawa, T., Nunome, T., Tasaka, S.: Multidimensional assessment and principal component analysis of QoE in interactive multi-view video and audio IP communications. In: Proceedings of the International Conference on Information Networking 2012 (ICOIN 2012), Bali, Indonesia, February 2012, pp. 482–487 (2012)

18. Kang, M., Kim, S.: Depth perception assessment for stereoscopic 3D displays using layered random dot stereogram. IEEE Access **5**, 22855–22862 (2017)

19. Zhang, Y., Jin, X., Dai, Q.: A 3D subjective quality prediction model based on depth distortion. In: Proceedings of the IEEE Conference on Visual Communications and Image Processing (VCIP), Chengdu, China, November 2016, pp. 1–4 (2016)

20. Jiang, Q., et al.: Leveraging visual attention and neural activity for stereoscopic 3D visual comfort assessment. Multimed. Tools Appl. **76**(7), 9405–9425 (2017). https://doi.org/10.1007/s11042-016-3548-2

21. Zhao, M., et al.: QoE-driven optimization for cloud-assisted DASH-based scalable interactive multiview video streaming over wireless network. Signal Process.-Image Commun. **57**, 157–172 (2017)

22. de Faria, S.M.M., Marcelino, S., Debono, C.J., Soares, S., Assunção, P.A.: Error Concealment Methods for Multiview Video and Depth. In: Assunção, P., Gotchev, A. (eds.) 3D Visual Content Creation, Coding and Delivery. Signals and Communication Technology, pp. 115–141. Springer, Cham (2019). https://doi.org/10.1007/978-3-319-77842-6_5

23. Furukawa, K., Nunome, T.: QoE assessment of multi-view video and audio transmission with a packet discarding method over bandwidth guaranteed IP networks. 3PGCIC 2016. LNDECT, vol. 1, pp. 579–588. Springer, Cham (2017). https://doi.org/10.1007/978-3-319-49109-7_55

24. Cánovas, A., et al.: A cognitive network management system to improve QoE in stereoscopic IPTV service. Int. J. Commun Syst **32**(12), e3992 (2019)

25. Nunome, T., Miyazaki, R.: The effect of contents and available viewpoints on QoE of multi-view video and audio over WebRTC. In: 2019 IEEE International Conference on Computational Science and Engineering (CSE) and IEEE International Conference on Embedded and Ubiquitous Computing (EUC), New York, USA, August 2019, pp. 80–85 (2019)

26. Nunome, T., Nakagaito, M.: QoE assessment of multi-view video and audio IP transmission methods from multipoint. In: 2019 2nd International Conference on Communication Engineering and Technology (ICCET), Nagoya, Japan, April 2019, pp. 88–92 (2019)
27. Nunome, T., Furukawa, K.: The effect of bandwidth allocation methods on QoE of multi-view video and audio IP transmission. In: 2017 IEEE 22nd International Workshop on Computer Aided Modeling and Design of Communication Links and Networks (CAMAD), Lund, Sweden, June 2017, pp. 1–6 (2017)
28. Bilal, K., Erbad, A., Hefeeda, M.: QoE-aware distributed cloud-based live streaming of multisourced multiview videos. J. Netw. Comput. Appl. **120**, 130–144 (2018)
29. Ozbek, N., Senol, E.: Optimal inter-view rate allocation for multi-view video plus depth over MPEG-DASH using QoE measures and paired comparison. Signal Image Video Process **13**(6), 1215–1223 (2019). https://doi.org/10.1007/s11760-019-01464-x
30. Yao, C., Xiao, J., Zhao, Y., Ming, A.: Video streaming adaptation strategy for multiview navigation over DASH. IEEE Trans. Broadcast. **65**(3), 521–533 (2019)

Scene-Oriented Aesthetic Image Assessment

Rui Liu[1], Haoran Zhang[1], Lv Yan[1], Xin Tian[1(✉)], and Zheng Zhou[2]

[1] Electronic Information School, Wuhan University, Wuhan 430072, China
`xin.tian@whu.edu.cn`
[2] Information and Communication Branch of Hubei, State Grid,
Wuhan 430077, China

Abstract. In recent years, aesthetic image assessment that can be used
to predict image quality automatically, has attracted a lot of interest.
In most previous work, universal aesthetic features are designed for all
types of scenes, neglecting scenes' special characteristics. As a result, such
universal aesthetic features are not very consistent with aesthetic scores
evaluated by humans. In this study, we propose a scene-oriented aesthetic image assessment method in this paper. Firstly, we design special
aesthetic features for different types of scenes. The contributions of different individual aesthetic features to the subjective feelings of humans
are further considered. To accurately map the aesthetic features into
the aesthetic scores evaluated by human, we propose an aesthetic image
quality classification algorithm based on feature-weighted sparse representation. Finally, a framework of automatic aesthetic image generation
from a high resolution and large view photo is suggested. We conduct
extensive experiments on public databases such as AVA, AADB, and
CUKHPQ to verify the efficiency of the proposed algorithm. Another
experiment on automatic aesthetic photo generation demonstrates its
potential application prospects in our daily life.

Keywords: Aesthetic image assessment · Scene-oriented
classification · Feature-weighted sparse representation

1   Introduction

The requirement of capturing good photographs has rapidly increased in the last
few years. On one hand, people are willing to capture the wonderful moments
experienced in their life. On the other hand, social apps such as Facebook, Twitter and others have provided internet platforms for everyone to show themselves
off. However, it is not easy to capture high quality photographs. We need to
master several photography skills for capturing a good photo. In such a case,

---

This work was supported from the National Natural Science Foundation of China
(61971315) and the Basic Research (Free Exploration) Project from Commission on
Innovation and Technology of Shenzhen (JCYJ20170303170611174).

G. Zhai et al. (Eds.): IFTC 2020, CCIS 1390, pp. 359–370, 2021.
https://doi.org/10.1007/978-981-16-1194-0_31

Fig. 1. An example of automatic aesthetic photo generation

is it possible for us to get high quality photos automatically with the support of a computer-aided system? That is the context we want to investigate in this paper (as shown in Fig. 1). To achieve the target, the aesthetic image assessment algorithm is necessary. The assessment of image aesthetic quality is focused on evaluating the aesthetic degree of images from the human senses. This algorithm is formulated as a classification or a regression problem where the aesthetics features of an image are mapped into aesthetic scores. Therefore, its typical procedures include aesthetic feature extraction and feature-based classification.

In 2006, Datta [4] designed many aesthetic features to evaluate whether a picture meets certain aesthetic standards, including the color, texture, image size, the rule of thirds, and so on. In 2006, Yan [7] presented high level aesthetic features such as picture simplicity, clarity, color, contrast, and exposure. Although only seven-dimensional features were designed in this study, the classification accuracy is better than that presented in Dattas study. Unlike the previous methods using features extracted from the entire image, the study conducted by Luo [10] proposed separating the foreground from the background, and extracting a number of high level features of the foreground and the background separately. Wong [21] combined some of the previous methods and optimized the method of foreground extraction according to the saliency of Luo. Marchesotti [11] used low-level local features for aesthetic image classification to achieve good results. Unfortunately, his theoretical basis is not strong. A comprehensive photo aesthetic assessment method, which integrated several kinds of aesthetic features is proposed in [12]. However, not all features are useful during the aesthetic quality evaluation in different types of scenes.

Support vector machine (SVM) is the most popular classifier among all the aforementioned aesthetic image assessment algorithms for mapping the hand-crafted features into aesthetic scores. To improve the classification accuracy, new classifiers, such as sparse representation-based classification algorithm, have been researched. Based on sparse representation [18], John [22] proposed a general classification algorithm for object recognition. In order to scale up to large training sets, dictionary learning approaches [6,20] have been developed for classification algorithms based on sparse representation. Deep-learning-based image aesthetic quality assessment [16] is considered different from all the aforementioned works. This solution has also shown an excellent performance. However, this method needs sufficient training data which involves a lot of manual marking.

The main contributions of this paper include the following. (1) Most of the previous works have been focusing on universal features for all types of scenes. From the standpoint of photography, the aspects of aesthetic focus are not the same across the different types of scenes. For example, composition is considered an important feature for human photographs while saliency is critical for an architecture. Therefore, we specially design aesthetic features pertaining to a particular scene in this study. Compared with universal features, these specially designed aesthetic features can be more consistent with aesthetic scores evaluated by humans. We select three types of scenes ('Human', 'Plant', and 'Architecture') for demonstration. (2) All aesthetic features of an image are always concatenated into a total feature for classification. However, the contribution of different individual features towards a human's aesthetic feelings are not the same. Thus, weighing these contributions can improve the classification accuracy. Therefore, a classification algorithm based on feature-weighted sparse representation (CFSR) is proposed. It can be further incorporated with the dictionary learning-based approaches [14,17], which will be discussed in our future work. (3) To demonstrate its application, a framework of automatic aesthetic image generation is studied. A scene-oriented set of images can be picked up by a scene classification algorithm. Furthermore, high quality images can be evaluated to produce outputs based on the studied aesthetic image quality assessment method for different types of scenes.

The rest of the paper is organized as follows. Section 2 presents the proposed method. Section 3 illustrates the experiments as well as the comparison studies. Finally, the paper is concluded in Sect. 4.

2   Proposed Method

We elaborate on our method in this section.

2.1   Scene-Based Aesthetic Feature Design

In recent years, researchers have proposed a host of aesthetic features. Therefore, we construct our main aesthetic features (as shown in Fig. 2) for different types of scenes based on the previous works [2,7,9,10,12,13].

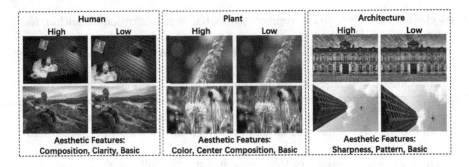

Fig. 2. Scene-based aesthetic features

(i) Human

When capturing human photographs, most professional photographers pay more attention to the position of the person and the clarity within the whole picture. Therefore, aesthetic features such as composition and clarity are considered significant for the human image. Before extracting the composition features, we first need to identify the position of the main object in the image [1]. The composition features include the center composition feature, the landscape composition feature and the trichotomy composition feature [12]. These features match the three composition rules that include the rule of "fill the frame", the rule of thirds and the "landscape" composition. The design of clarity aesthetic features are mostly based on the following principles. (1) Photographers must always blur the background to present the human with increased clarity. Therefore, clarity contrast feature, depth of the field, and background simplicity feature are adopted by calculating the clarity of the subject, clarity of the background and the diversity of background colors, respectively. (2) Compared to the background, additional light must be provided for the human. Therefore, the lighting feature is calculated based on the light difference between the subject and the background [10]. Furthermore, blur, contrast, color and other basic features [7] make the evaluation of human images more accurate.

(ii) Plant

When professional photographers capture the photo of a plant, they often increase the saturation and contrast of these images to make them look more vivid. This indicates that color features are the most important in capturing plant images. Some plant images look messy and inharmonious, because other buildings or messy streets are captured along with the plant. This phenomenon in plant images can be prevented using the center composition feature. Therefore, the color feature and the center composition feature are considered the primary aesthetic features for a plant image. We implement a variety of color related features. Firstly, the color harmony feature of the image is computed based on convolutional neural networks. The average values of H, S, V values are computed for the whole image as well as the central area of the image [9]. Secondly, we build diverse color feeling features including pleasure, arousal, and dominance [13]. Thirdly, we construct the color features based on color dictionary. Some basic features include texture and luminance contrast features [2].

(iii) Architecture

An attractive architectural image always has the characteristic of magnificence or luxury, which correlates to its visual saliency in several ways. Therefore, we compute the detected architecture's sharpness [12] and treat it as a saliency feature. It is calculated based on a no-reference image blur detection algorithm. The repetitiveness of lines and patterns improve the feeling of beauty in architectural images. An example is a symmetrical window on a building, which naturally forms a sense of order and pleases people who view it. Therefore, pattern feature can be identified as a criterion for evaluating the aesthetic quality of architectural images. The whole image is divided into different parts. By matching the feature points such as scale invariant feature transform (SIFT) and speeded up robust feature (SURF) with different parts of the image, the similarities are identified and the pattern feature is built accordingly. We choose some basic features as well, such as the color and different types of contrast features (light/dark contrast, saturation contrast, hue contrast, complementary contrast, warm/cold contrast and comparison of the number of warm/cold zones) [2].

2.2 Aesthetic Image Quality Assessment Based on Feature-Weighted Sparse representation

In [22], a sparse representation-based classification algorithm (SRC) is proposed for human face recognition. Its performance outperforms traditional classification algorithms such as SVM. Similar to SVM, different types of individual aesthetic features are concatenated into a total feature, and then SRC is be used as the classifier directly. As pointed out in the multiple kernel learning [3], individual features for classification are always heterogeneous. Thus, different individual features can have different weights. One simple example is shown in Fig. 3. We suppose that $\mathbf{y} = \left[(\mathbf{y}^1)^T, (\mathbf{y}^2)^T, (\mathbf{y}^3)^T, (\mathbf{y}^4)^T \right]^T$ contains 4 individual features. From Fig. 3, it is obvious that $\mathbf{y}^1$ and $\mathbf{y}^4$ are more important for classification, therefore $\mathbf{y}$ belongs to class 1. However, $\mathbf{y}$ cannot be well classified by SRC from the dictionary $\mathbf{D} = \left[\mathbf{D}_1, \mathbf{D}_2 \right]$ with the sparse coefficient $\mathbf{x}$.

In our algorithm, the training features are represented as $\mathbf{D} = \left[\mathbf{D}_1, \mathbf{D}_2, \ldots, \mathbf{D}_k \right] \in \mathbf{R}^{(m_1+\ldots+m_p)\times(n_1+\ldots+n_k)}$ for k classes. For each $\mathbf{D}_i, i \in [1,k]$, they are concatenated into p individual features denoted as $\mathbf{D}_i^j \in \mathbf{R}^{m_j \times n_i}, j \in [1,p]$. For a test feature $\mathbf{y} = \left[(\mathbf{y}^1)^T, \ldots, (\mathbf{y}^p)^T \right]^T \in \mathbf{R}^{(m_1+\ldots+m_p)\times 1}$, the minimization form is formulated as

$$\begin{cases} \tilde{\mathbf{x}} = \arg\min_{\mathbf{x}} \|\mathbf{y} - \mathbf{D}\mathbf{x}\|_F^2 + \lambda\|\mathbf{x}\|_1 \\ \tilde{\mathbf{x}}^j = \arg\min_{\mathbf{x}} \|\mathbf{y}^j - \mathbf{D}\mathbf{x}\|_F^2 + \lambda\|\mathbf{x}\|_1 \quad j \in [1,p] \end{cases} \quad (1)$$

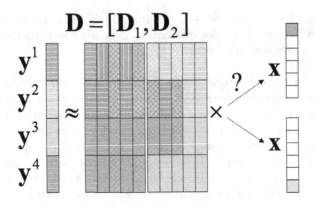

Fig. 3. An example of the importance of CFSR

Then the residual $r_i(\mathbf{y})$ is computed as follows.

$$r_i(\mathbf{y}) = \gamma_{i,0}\|\mathbf{y} - \mathbf{D}\sigma_i(\tilde{\mathbf{x}})\|_F^2 + \sum_{j=1}^{p}\gamma_{i,j}\|\mathbf{y}^j - \mathbf{D}^j\sigma_i(\tilde{\mathbf{x}}^j)\|_F^2 \tag{2}$$

And the class of $\mathbf{y}$ belongs to

$$c = \arg\min_i r_i(\mathbf{y}) \tag{3}$$

$\gamma_{i,j}, i \in [1,k], j \in [0,p]$ are the weights of different individual features ($\gamma_{i,0}$ is the weight of concatenated features). For simplicity, they can be determined through manual tuning. In this work, we also propose an optimization algorithm to automatically determine the suitable weights from the training features. For the tth feature $\mathbf{d}_t \in \mathbf{R}^{(m_1+\cdots+m_n)\times 1}$ in the ith training feature $\mathbf{D}_i$, it can also be well sparse represented by the dictionary $\mathbf{D}_{i,t\notin}$. The subscript $t \notin$ means that $\mathbf{d}_t$ is not included. The objective of picking the right choice of weights is to make the reconstruction error of the same class small and that of the other classes large. In some contents, it means that the reconstruction errors have large variations across all classes. Based on the above idea, the following minimization model is given for each $\mathbf{d}_t$.

$$\begin{cases} \tilde{\mathbf{x}} = \arg\min_{\mathbf{x}} \|\mathbf{d}_t - \mathbf{D}_{t\notin}\mathbf{x}\|_F^2 + \lambda\|\mathbf{x}\|_1 \\ \tilde{\mathbf{x}}^j = \arg\min_{\mathbf{x}} \|\mathbf{d}_t^i - \mathbf{D}_{t\notin}^j\mathbf{x}\|_F^2 + \lambda\|\mathbf{x}\|_1 \end{cases} \tag{4}$$

Then the residual vector $r_i(\mathbf{d}_t)$ is equal to

$$r_i(\mathbf{d}_t) = \gamma_{i,0}\|\mathbf{d}_t - \mathbf{D}_{t\notin}\sigma_i(\tilde{\mathbf{x}})\|_F^2 + \sum_{j=1}^{p}\gamma_{i,j}\|\mathbf{d}_t^i - \mathbf{D}_{t\notin}^j\sigma_i(\tilde{\mathbf{x}}^j)\|_F^2 \tag{5}$$

Thus the weights $\gamma_{i,j}$ can be calculated using the critic method [5] based on the computation of variance from $\|\mathbf{d}_t - \mathbf{D}_{t\notin}\sigma_i(\tilde{\mathbf{x}})\|_F^2$ and $\|\mathbf{d}_t^i - \mathbf{D}_{t\notin}^j\sigma_i(\tilde{\mathbf{x}}^j)\|_F^2, i \in [1,k], j \in [0,p]$.

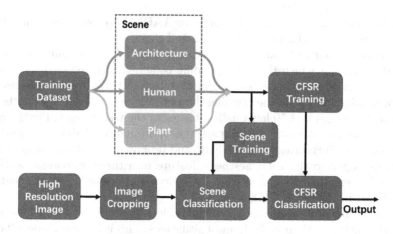

Fig. 4. Framework of scene-oriented aesthetic image generation

2.3 Scene-Oriented Aesthetic Image Generation

The framework of the proposed scene-oriented aesthetic image generation method is shown in Fig. 4. High resolution and large view photos are segmented into small ones with different scales and sizes based on the users' requirements. Then these photos are classified into different types of scenes by a scene classification algorithm. The function of scene classification is to act as a filter and remove some images from ambiguous scenes with low confidence levels in the scene classification algorithm. This ensures that only those images that match our studied scenes very well are selected for further aesthetic image quality assessment. Finally, the aesthetic images from each kind of scene is evaluated based on the proposed aesthetic image quality assessment method.

3 Experimental Results

3.1 Experiments on Scene-Oriented Aesthetic Image Assessment

To evaluate the proposed method, we use the publicly available aesthetic image quality databases including AVA [9], AADB [8] and CUKHPQ [15]. AVA contains over 250,000 images, along with a rich variety of meta-data derived from DPChallenge.com. AADB is a collection of 10,000 images from Flickr.com, which scores the images based on 11 aesthetic elements and then weighs the average to obtain the final score. In AVA and AADB, the highest 20% of the scores are defined for high quality images, and the lowest 20% are for low quality images. The CUHKPQ dataset contains 17,690 photos collected from DPChallenge.com. This dataset consists of seven scenes including "Animal", "Plant", "Still Life", "Architectural", "Landscape", "People" and "Night Scenery". The images are divided into high quality images and low quality images. Three scenes comprising "Architecture," "Plant," and "Human" are built from AVA and CUKHPQ. As adequate plant-like images are not found in AADB, only two scenes, including "Architecture" and "Human" are constructed there.

We compare our method with two other aesthetic image quality assessment methods [9,12], for which the corresponding code has been released. From each scene in the various datasets, we randomly select 150 high quality images and 150 low quality images as the training dataset. We randomly select another 50 high quality images and 50 low quality images as the test dataset. Firstly, SVM is adopted as the classifier to compare the performance of different aesthetic image features. Furthermore, SVM, SRC and proposed CFSR are compared. In CFSR, we separate the total aesthetic feature into three individual aesthetic features. For example, "Composition", "Clarity" and "Basic" aesthetic features are included in the scene "Human".

The experimental results are shown in Table 1. It is observed that Mavridaki [12] performs better than Lo [9] in most situations. This is because, more efficient aesthetic image features are designed in Mavridaki [12]. When compared against Mavridaki [12] and Lo [9], our specially designed aesthetic features based on each scene's requirement are found to be more effective in improving the classification accuracy. With regard to classifiers, SRC outperforms SVM, in general. The proposed CFSR is observed to possess the best performance according to the different weights assigned to individual aesthetic features.

Table 1. Experimental results of classification accuracy

Category	Human			Plant		Architecture		
Dataset	CUHKPQ	AADB	AVA	CUHKPQ	AVA	CUHKPQ	AADB	AVA
Lo [9]	73%	75%	81%	92%	71%	84%	75%	82%
Mavridaki [12]	84%	87%	91%	91%	79%	88%	68%	93%
Prop.+SVM	86%	92%	93%	92%	82%	92%	77%	91%
Prop.+SRC [22]	84%	94%	96%	92%	90%	93%	83%	86%
Prop.+CFSR	88%	98%	98%	95%	93%	93%	85%	88%

A mixed-scene experiment is carried out in order to analyze the influence of misclassification created by the scene classification algorithm. In this experiment, CUHKPQ dataset is used as an example. In the proposed method, the training dataset of each scene is the same as in the above experiment. As the test images are classified into different types of scenes by choosing the confidence level in the scene classification algorithm, its classification accuracy will be under control in some contents. This can be simulated by randomly classifying a certain ratio of images into wrong types of scenes. In this experiment, we randomly choose 300 images from different types of scenes as test images and copy them into different types of scenes of two groups. In group 1 and group 2, the ratio of scene-misclassification are 10% and 15%, respectively. For experimenting other methods, images from different types of scenes in the aforementioned training

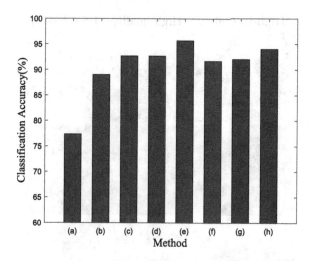

Fig. 5. Performance comparison of different methods in a mixed scene from CUHKPQ dataset. (a) Lo. (b) Mavridaki. (c) Proposed+SVM (group 1). (d) Proposed+SRC (group 1). (e) Proposed+CFSR (group 1). (f) Proposed+SVM (group 2). (g) Proposed+SRC (group 2). (h) Proposed+CFSR (group 2).

dataset are mixed together for training, and the same set of test images are mixed for testing. The experimental results are shown in Fig. 5. When compared to Lo [9] and Mavridaki [12], the classification accuracy of the proposed aesthetic image feature and CFSR has improved by 18.34% and 6.67%, respectively when the accuracy of scene classification is around 90%. If this accuracy is around 85%, the improvement will be reduced to 16.67% and 5%, respectively. Therefore, the efficiency of the proposed method is verified.

3.2   Experiment on Scene-Oriented Aesthetic Image Generation

To demonstrate the application of the proposed method, we carry out the following experiment. In this experiment, images with high resolution and wide view are prepared initially. Then, these images are cropped into smaller ones with different types of scale and size. These small images are classifed into different types of scenes using the histogram of oriented gradients (HOG) feature [19] and SVM with a confidence level more than 90%. The results are treated as the test samples for scene-oriented aesthetic image generation. Some typical high quality and low quality images from the results are chosen for demonstration. The experimental results are shown in Fig. 6. We notice that these results are well consistent with the objective feeling of humans, which ascertain the potential application prospects of automatic aesthetic photo generation in our daily life.

High-resolution   High-quality   Low-quality

Fig. 6. Experimental results of scene-oriented aesthetic image generation

4   Conclusion

We presented a scene-oriented aesthetic image assessment algorithm and demonstrated its application in automatic generation of aesthetic images from high resolution and wide view images. Initially, we designed special aesthetic features for different types of scenes. Furthermore, a classification algorithm based on feature-weighted sparse representation was proposed by considering the significance of different aesthetic features in contributing towards their respective aesthetic scores. In the application of automatic generation of aesthetic images, a candidate image set of different scenes was built from high resolution and wide view images based on a scene classification method. The desired aesthetic images were chosen from this set using the proposed scene-oriented aesthetic image assessment algorithm. Although our work may not constitute a complete solution for this application, it certainly provides a new research direction in this area. Our future work includes creating a more suitable scene classification algorithm and cropping the image into a more appropriate size. We also believe that learning the dictionary from the training features can result in better classification results.

References

1. Alexe, B., Deselaers, T., Ferrari, V.: What is an object? In: 2010 IEEE Computer Society Conference on Computer Vision and Pattern Recognition, pp. 73–80 (2010)
2. Blaha, J.D., Sterba, Z.: Colour contrast in cartographic works using the principles of Johannes Itten. Cartogr. J. **51**(3), 203–213 (2014)
3. Bucak, S.S., Jin, R., Jain, A.K.: Multiple kernel learning for visual object recognition: a review. IEEE Trans. Pattern Anal. Mach. Intell. **36**(7), 1354–1369 (2014)
4. Datta, R., Joshi, D., Li, J., Wang, J.Z.: Studying aesthetics in photographic images using a computational approach. In: Leonardis, A., Bischof, H., Pinz, A. (eds.) ECCV 2006. LNCS, vol. 3953, pp. 288–301. Springer, Heidelberg (2006). https://doi.org/10.1007/11744078_23
5. Diakoulaki, D., Mavrotas, G., Papayannakis, L.: Determining objective weights in multiple criteria problems: the critic method. Comput. Oper. Res. **22**(7), 763–770 (1995)
6. Jiang, Z., Lin, Z., Davis, L.S.: Label consistent K-SVD: learning a discriminative dictionary for recognition. IEEE Trans. Pattern Anal. Mach. Intell. **35**(11), 2651–2664 (2013)
7. Ke, Y., Tang, X., Jing, F.: The design of high-level features for photo quality assessment. In: IEEE Computer Society Conference on Computer Vision and Pattern Recognition, vol. 1, pp. 419–426 (2006)
8. Kong, S., Shen, X., Lin, Z., Mech, R., Fowlkes, C.: Photo aesthetics ranking network with attributes and content adaptation. In: Leibe, B., Matas, J., Sebe, N., Welling, M. (eds.) ECCV 2016. LNCS, vol. 9905, pp. 662–679. Springer, Cham (2016). https://doi.org/10.1007/978-3-319-46448-0_40
9. Lo, K., Liu, K., Chen, C.: Assessment of photo aesthetics with efficiency. In: Proceedings of the 21st International Conference on Pattern Recognition, pp. 2186–2189 (2012)
10. Luo, Y., Tang, X.: Photo and video quality evaluation: focusing on the subject. In: Forsyth, D., Torr, P., Zisserman, A. (eds.) ECCV 2008. LNCS, vol. 5304, pp. 386–399. Springer, Heidelberg (2008). https://doi.org/10.1007/978-3-540-88690-7_29
11. Marchesotti, L., Perronnin, F., Larlus, D., Csurka, G.: Assessing the aesthetic quality of photographs using generic image descriptors. In: 2011 International Conference on Computer Vision, pp. 1784–1791 (2011)
12. Mavridaki, E., Mezaris, V.: A comprehensive aesthetic quality assessment method for natural images using basic rules of photography. In: IEEE International Conference on Image Processing, pp. 887–891 (2015)
13. Mehrabian, A.: Pleasure-arousal-dominance: a general framework for describing and measuring individual differences in temperament. Curr. Psychol. **14**(4), 261–292 (1996). https://doi.org/10.1007/BF02686918
14. Payani, A., Abdi, A., Tian, X., Fekri, F., Mohandes, M.: Advances in seismic data compression via learning from data: compression for seismic data acquisition. IEEE Signal Process. Mag. **35**(2), 51–61 (2018)
15. Tang, X., Luo, W., Wang, X.: Content-based photo quality assessment. IEEE Trans. Multimed. **15**(8), 1930–1943 (2013)

16. Tian, X., Dong, Z., Yang, K., Mei, T.: Query-dependent aesthetic model with deep learning for photo quality assessment. IEEE Trans. Multimed. **17**(11), 2035–2048 (2015)

17. Tian, X.: Multiscale sparse dictionary learning with rate constraint for seismic data compression. IEEE Access **7**, 86651–86663 (2019)

18. Tian, X., Chen, Y., Yang, C., Gao, X., Ma, J.: A variational pansharpening method based on gradient sparse representation. IEEE Signal Process. Lett. **27**, 1180–1184 (2020)

19. Triggs, B., Dalal, N.: Histograms of oriented gradients for human detection. In: 2005 IEEE Computer Society Conference on Computer Vision and Pattern Recognition, vol. 01, pp. 886–893 (2005)

20. Vu, T.H., Monga, V.: Learning a low-rank shared dictionary for object classification. In: 2016 IEEE International Conference on Image Processing, pp. 4428–4432 (2016)

21. Wong, L.K., Low, K.L.: Saliency-enhanced image aesthetics class prediction. In: 2009 16th IEEE International Conference on Image Processing, pp. 997–1000 (2009)

22. Wright, J., Yang, A.Y., Ganesh, A., Sastry, S.S., Ma, Y.: Robust face recognition via sparse representation. IEEE Trans. Pattern Anal. Mach. Intell. **31**(2), 210–227 (2009)

Screening of Autism Spectrum Disorder Using Novel Biological Motion Stimuli

Lei Fan[1,2], Wei Cao[3], Huiyu Duan[1], Yasong Du[4], Jing Chen[4], Siqian Hou[1], Hong Zhu[5], Na Xu[6], Jiantao Zhou[2], and Guangtao Zhai[1(✉)]

[1] Shanghai Jiao Tong University, Shanghai 200240, China
zhaiguangtao@sjtu.edu.cn
[2] University of Macau, Macau 999078, China
[3] Shanghai Mingxiang Information Technology Co., Ltd., Shanghai 200241, China
[4] Shanghai Mental Health Center, Shanghai 200030, China
[5] Pingyang Elementary School, Shanghai 201102, China
[6] Shanghai Zhanyi Children Develop Interlligence Center, Shanghai 200333, China

Abstract. Eye tracking of preferential attention to biological motion is an important approach to Autism Spectrum Disorder (ASD) research and early diagnosis. However, the current method has all time-series information averaged as statistic information, which losing information and features for classification in high-dimensional space. Novel biological motion stimuli with well-designed time-series information could make Insistence on Sameness (IoS) of ASD as an efficient feature for ASD screening. Display area zoning and encoding for eye-tracking data processing improve the spatial resolution of the eye tracking information processing than averaging by side, making it possible to get more information and features for classification from ASD eye-tracking data.

Keywords: ASD · Biological motion · Eye tracking · Insistence on sameness · SVM

1 Introduction

Large-scale census shows that the ASD incidence is about 1–2% [1], with a median of 0.62–0.70% [2]. The incidence of ASD has been rising in the past few decades [3]. In fact, even in developed countries, there are still many adults who have never received a formal ASD diagnosis [4]. 10–33% of ASD patients can't use simple phrases, and their daily lives need a lot of help [5]. In fact, approximately 45% of ASD patients suffer from intellectual disability [2], and 32% suffer from intellectual decline (ie loss of previously acquired skills) [6]. The average diagnosis age of ASD in the U.S in 2016 was 4.7 years, and the average diagnosis age of ASD in China was more than 6.5 years [7]. Two national surveys in the United

---

This work was supported partly by the National Natural Science Foundation of China under Grants 61831015, partly by the Shanghai Municipal Commission of Health and Family Planning under Grant 2018ZHYL0210.

© Springer Nature Singapore Pte Ltd. 2021
G. Zhai et al. (Eds.): IFTC 2020, CCIS 1390, pp. 371–384, 2021.
https://doi.org/10.1007/978-981-16-1194-0_32

States in 2017 [8] found that the diagnosis age of ASD is mostly 36 months later, the diagnosis age of severe ASD is 3.7 to 4.5 years, and that of mild ASD is only diagnosed at school age (5.6–8.6 years), And delays in ASD diagnosis in other underdeveloped countries or regions are more common. Although most parents suspect that children with ASD may have problems around 18–24 months, the median age at diagnosis in the U.S. is still 5.5 years [9]. The impact of ASD on men is 4–5 times higher than that of women [2]. Women are diagnosed at a later age than men [10]. Women need to have more prominent behavioral or cognitive problems than men to get a diagnosis [11], that is, the diagnosis of ASD currently exists Certain male bias [12]. The risk of death in patients with ASD is 2.8 times higher than that of unaffected patients of the same age and sex [13], and it is also related to medical conditions [14]. Studies have shown that 58–78% of adults with ASD have poor or very poor status in terms of independent living ability, education, employment and closed relationships [15]. Even for ASD patients without intellectual disability, their quality of life and professional achievement are often unsatisfactory [15]. At the same time, mainstream media often pay attention to high-functioning ASD patients, and ignore those low-functioning ASD children and adults who need the most attention, reducing the possibility of them being paid attention to, making the social problems of ASD more serious [16]. Therefore, the ASD early diagnosis is a prerequisite for early intervention and training, and it is very necessary.

Eye movement is an important phenotypic feature of mental illness. Eye movement encodes a large amount of information about personal psychological factors, oculomotor nerve control and attention, and eye movement character-istics related to saccades and fixation points have been proven Effectiveness in identifying mental states, cognitive conditions, and neuropathology [17]. Eye tracking technology has been applied to human-computer interaction [18], psy-chology [19] and computer vision [20] and many other fields [21]. As early as the end of the 18th century, there have been related studies trying to record the data of eye movement fixation points [22]. Gaze point estimation algorithms can be roughly divided into two types of estimation algorithms: model-based estimation and appearance-based estimation [21]. The model-based estimation algorithm uses the eye geometric model and can be further sub-divided into two types: shape estimation and corneal reflection. The corneal reflection estimation algorithm [23] relies on an external light source to detect eye features, while the shape estimation formula [24] infers the direction of the eye based on the observed eye shape such as the center of the pupil and the border of the iris. The appearance-based estimation model [25] directly uses eye images as input, and usually requires greatly much of specific user data as training data to achieve the effect of predicting the user's gaze point [26].

Compared with the standard scale-based diagnosis, the automatic collection and quantitative processing of eye movements may make it more objective and easier to analyze and diagnose ASD data. Studies have shown that there are some differences in visual attention between ASD patients and normal people. The dif-ference in attention preference between ASD children and normal-developed children in social situations can be measured by eye tracking. The earliest research of this kind showed that adolescent ASD participants had much less fixation time on the performer, while spent more time on the background scene [27]. A typical experimental setting for studying ASD visual attention is to use social content [28] and use an eye tracker to record the subject's eye movement data [29]. Existing findings include reduced joint attention behavior [30], reduced attention towards social scenes [31], preference for visual stimuli with low-level features [32], and decreased attention towards social stimuli (ie conversations, faces, etc.), but with much more attention towards non-social stimuli, etc. [33]. Studies have shown that the priority of humans and other animals on biological movement (that is, the movement of vertebrates) is an evolutionary ability [34], which is actually a "life detector" [35]. The preference for biological movement can be observed in the first day after the birth of human newborns [17]. A similar phenomenon also occurs in newly hatched chicks [36]. The biological movement of non-human species will also cause priority attention of newborns [17], and this ability is significantly robust [37], and can be retained even after early visual deprivation [38].

2   Motivation

In order to classify the clinical population into a variety of neurodevelopmental disorders (ie Parkinson's disease and attention deficit hyperactivity disorder, other than ASD), Tseng et al. [39] analyzed the effects of watching short video clips Eye movement characteristics of the clinical population. They combined the gaze pattern with the features of the visual attention calculation model, and demonstrated the advantages of incorporating features related to attention into identifying specific diseases. But their model of attention only focuses on early visual saliency, and does not consider the social and high-level semantic information which may affect visual attention much more greatly. In general, the neurobehavioral research we are currently focusing on relies on artificial visual stimuli and structured laboratory tasks for specific hypotheses, which limits the generality of these studies. Wang et al. [40] used linear SVM and three categories of features to quantify the high-functioning ASD adults's visual attention. The feature weights are learned from the recorded eye movement fixation point distribution, and used to quantify the different visual attention preferences between ASD patients and normal controls. This method's main limitation is that it needs to manually set features and manually annotate the area of interest. In addition, they only studied the differences between the two groups of people as a whole, and did not classify the individual subjects. Jiang [41] et al. used deep learning methods to diagnose ASD based on the work of Wang et al. [40]. The ability of deep neural networks to encode high-level semantics and social content is particularly appropriate for describing the behavior of people with ASD. Jiang [41] et al. also used linear support vector machines (SVM) to classify experimental objects after extracting deep features. The problem with this study is that the model of the extracted differential features cannot support the design of the subsequent high-accuracy classification model, and the subject needs to watch all 100 images provided by it and process all the obtained eye movement data. Make a diagnosis. In the actual diagnosis process, it is more difficult to require ASD patients to see all images and provide effective eye movement data for each image. In addition, some related studies have also shown the consistency and robustness of gaze patterns as a phenotypic feature in individuals with ASD [27]. Subsequent research further developed eye tracking and the use of different paradigms to establish reliable objective and quantitative phenotypic markers for ASD. In general, people with ASD tend to show reduced preference for social stimuli [42] and biological movement [43].

The advantage of these studies based on eye tracking is to prove that patients with ASD have different visual preferences, do not require subjects to complete complex tasks, and the test results do not depend on factors such as IQ [44], which means based on eye tracking The type of auxiliary diagnosis of ASD can be used for young children and low-functioning children with ASD. In contrast, eye tracking can be implemented quickly across a wide range of ages and cognitive levels, and it is cheap to directly assess the core social attention deficit of ASD. The above analysis shows that eye movement phenotype analysis is currently the most promising way to achieve early diagnosis of ASD.

Sifre et al. [45] used the difference in percentage of attention between one point-light upright biological motion animation and inverted display to distinguish ASD from the control group. Such a study has achieved a very good early diagnosis of ASD for young infants aged 2–24 months. In the actual experiences of our related research works, since the current median age of children diagnosed with ASD in China is 6.5 years old, this means that, in order to have a sufficient number of ASD samples, it is necessary for us to prepare a sufficiently large sample group according to the proportion of ASD in the population, which labeled by the diagnosis results years later. Considering the sample detachment caused by factors such as population movement, as well as the low degree of adaptability of ASD and the failure rate in actual data collection, the requirements for the total sample group size might be unacceptable for ordinary research teams. It shows how difficult for such research achieved by Sifre's team, and significant value of their work for ASD early diagnosis.

As the data set of Sifre et al. [45] has not open yet, we proposed to repeat their work with our own data set and develop some new methods for ASD screening with biological motion.

Children with autism over 2 years old will form a compensation mechanism. If there are too much temporal- and spatio- information being processed as simplified as average, there will be not so much complex information or features left for classifications in high-dimensional space. Our experiments are proposed to verify whether by redesigning new experimental plots and procedures, and using more complex statistical tools, the compensation mechanism can be bypassed and important differences in behavior between children with autism and the control group can be found as features for classifications. Time-series information-driven testing uses a more complex and higher-level attention mechanism distinction method, which were proposed having a better distinction effect, with great biological and evolutionary significance.

3   Method

3.1   Participants

There were totally 100 children between 3 and 13 years old joining in this test: 21 ASD children with diagnosis information, and 47 children as control group, the rest of the whole group were of cerebral palsy (CP), of developmental delay (DD), or could not finish the test, like operation failure, children turning off monitor, taking away eye-tracker, eating snacks, etc. The gender rate of ASD is male: female = 4.25, and almost 1 for control group, which meets the nature statistic statement in population (Fig. 1).

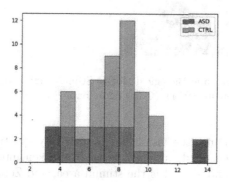

Fig. 1. Test group age profile. ASD Group: 17 boys, 4 girls; CTRL Group: 23 boys, 24 girls.

3.2   Facility and Equipment

Tests were taken in a single close room; Tobii Eye Tracker 4C: View field, horizontal 38°, vertical 29°, max sample rate 90 Hz (set to 50 Hz); Dell U2913WMt displayer: 29" Ultrawide Monitor, 2560 × 1080, 21:9.

3.3   Test and Measurement

The test has 5 experiments, and each experiment has 7 units with upright/inverted person in random side, without any sound accompany. The upright/inverted persons are synchronized with same action, for the same size and shape. And Biological Motion Stimuli applied in the test is below. Raw data updated in 50 Hz: the side of the upright person by 0 or 1, central view angle of the upright person with viewer head distance correction, head tracking with viewer head distance correction, eye tracking with viewer head distance correction (Fig. 2 and Table 1).

Fig. 2. Test facility (left) and Biological Motion Stimuli (right, white light in test, color inverted for better view in paper). (Color figure online)

Visual zone encoding: the vision not recorded by eye tracker is the vision outside the screen, encoded as 0, which used be taken into considerations by researchers; Zone 2 and Zone 4 is the stimuli area, and Zone 3 records the eye tracking shifting between stimuli objects (Figs. 3 and 4).

The visual zoning and encoding simplify the raw data, reducing the processing complexity with state-machine and time-series processing methods. This makes it possible to get more features from higher resolution spatial- information than simple average by side.

Table 1. Biological motion stimuli applied in the test.

Item	Stimuli 1	Stimuli 2	Plot 1	Plot 2	Unit time(s)
Experiment 1	upright	inverted	Mark time	No clap	5.0
Experiment 2	upright	inverted	Approach	No clap	14.0
Experiment 3	upright	upright	Mark time	No clap	5.0
Experiment 4	upright	inverted	Mark time	Clap	6.2
Experiment 5	upright	inverted	Approach	Clap	14.0

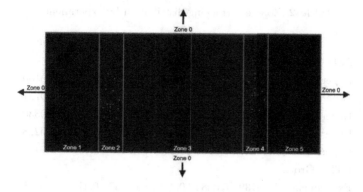

Fig. 3. Display area zoning.

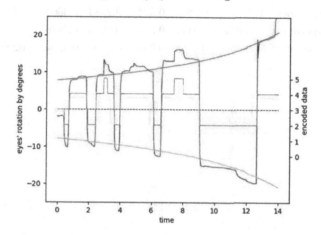

Fig. 4. Display area encoding. Upright person tracking in green, inverted person tracking in yellow, eye tracking in blue, eye tracking zone-encoded from 0 to 5 in red. (Color figure online)

4   Analysis

Data statistics and quality control: All the ASD group were certified by hospitals of Grade III class A in China. All the data with equipment issue were not accepted.

Over all data view: Zone eye tracking distribution by experiment shows that the data in red indicates an event happened in zone 4 at experiment 4, where ASD group intend not to see the upright person clapping (from 26.7% to 17.2%), while control group intend to see the upright person clapping (from 41.4% to 48.5%) (Table 2 and Figs. 5 and 6).

The main difference of experiment 4 from the previous 3 experiments is the clap from first 40% to 60% of the time line. Therefore, a detailed look inside this event below shows that most control group members found clap in unit 4-1 will

Table 2. Zone eye tracking distribution by experiment.

	Zone 0	Zone 1	Zone 2	Zone 3	Zone 4	Zone 5
ASD Group:						
Experiment 1	0.2661	0.0187	0.2684	0.1648	0.2667	0.0150
Experiment 2	0.3543	0.0271	0.2030	0.1473	0.2390	0.0291
Experiment 3	0.3647	0.0439	0.1637	0.1711	0.2233	0.0330
Experiment 4	0.4087	0.0182	0.2397	0.1388	0.1716	0.0228
Experiment 5	0.4137	0.0204	0.2086	0.1469	0.1940	0.0162
CTRL Group:						
Experiment 1	0.0139	0.0084	0.3814	0.1757	0.4138	0.0065
Experiment 2	0.0233	0.0141	0.3514	0.1757	0.4197	0.0156
Experiment 3	0.0222	0.0221	0.3049	0.2683	0.3604	0.0218
Experiment 4	0.0217	0.0117	0.3047	0.1635	0.4846	0.0136
Experiment 5	0.0596	0.0168	0.3095	0.1696	0.4234	0.0209

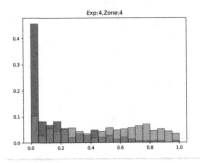

Fig. 5. Group distribution polarization at Zone 4 in Experiment 4, ASD in blue, CTRL in orange. (Color figure online)

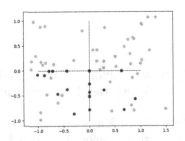

Fig. 6. Individual scatter, x-axis is percentage on zone 4 (+) or on zone 2 (−) in first 0–60% time line at experiment 4 unit 1, y-axis is percentage on zone 4 (+) or on zone 2 (−) in first 0–35% time line at experiment 4 unit 2.

percept another clap at unit 4-2, while no any member from ASD group could percept this and turn to see it.

Obviously, clap in unit 22 as a novel biological motion stimuli, after 21 units without it, greatly attracted control group's attention. 80% of sample group for training, 20% for test. Therefore, very simple linear SVM was taken into the data process as below (Fig. 7).

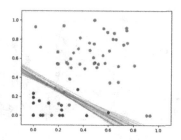

Fig. 7. Linear SVM for individual scatter, x-axis as zone 4% in unit 22, y-axis as zone 4% in unit 23, ASD in blue and CTRL in orange. (Color figure online)

Averaged by random, times $= 1000$, auc $= 0.95$, confusion: $[[9\ 1],[0\ 4]]$ (Fig. 8).

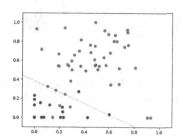

Fig. 8. Linear SVM for individual scatter after 1000 time average by random, x-axis as zone 4% in unit 22, y-axis as zone 4% in unit 23, ASD in blue and CTRL in orange. (Color figure online)

Comparison with the work by Sifre et al. [45]. With the method of Sifre et al. to process the same data set of this sample group, the perception of ASD children older than 2 years was not so good, as shown below (Fig. 9).

EXP 1, confusion matrix: $[[171\ 158], [86\ 61]]$, AUC $= 0.4673614126501664$;
EXP 2, confusion matrix: $[[183\ 146], [83\ 64]]$, AUC $= 0.49580257634968883$;
EXP 4, confusion matrix: $[[207\ 122], [83\ 64]]$, AUC $= 0.5322767404834274$;
EXP 5, confusion matrix: $[[190\ 139], [78\ 67]]$, AUC $= 0.5197882821507179$;
Unit 22, confusion matrix: $[[27\ 20], [12\ 9]]$, AUC $= 0.5015197568389058$;
Unit 23, confusion matrix: $[[39\ 8], [10\ 11]]$, AUC $= 0.6767983789260384$.

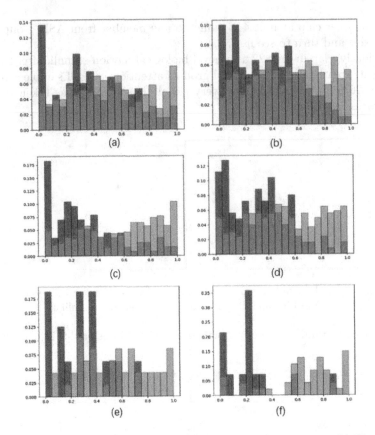

Fig. 9. Upright person Eye tracking distribution in (a) Experiment 1, (b) Experiment 2, (c) Experiment 4, (d) Experiment 5, (e) Unit 22, (f) Unit 23.

5   Result

Insistence on Sameness (IoS) is the hallmark feature of ASD [46]. It is estimated that more than one-third of individuals in the autism spectrum exhibit some form of IoS, including repetitive thoughts and actions, rigid behavior, reliance on routine procedures, resistance to change, and persistent adherence to rituals Wait. DSM-5 emphasizes the importance of IoS as a phenotypic attribute of ASD, and incorporates IoS into the diagnostic criteria of the disease. We can establish a link between predictive disorder and IoS. Studies have shown that the unpredictability of the environment is closely related to anxiety, and predictability is the basic regulator of anxiety, because even without any related disgusting consequences, the reduced ability to predict events will enhance the anxiety response. When anxiety rises, it can cause ritual behavior. Rituals and insistence on identity may be the result of anxiety caused by unpredictability and a way to reduce anxiety.

Based on our previous research work on ASD [47–52], we had the first 21 experimental units create a stereotype for the test group that the point-light upright person just walked. In the 22nd experimental unit, a new clapping plot suddenly appeared, which would arouse the attention of the control group and predict whether there will also be a clapping plot in the 23rd experimental unit, while ASD will produce corresponding discomfort and avoid to look at that, reflecting the lower tolerance for unpredictability than the control group.

6 Conclusion

For children over 2 years old with compensation mechanism developed, it's not easy to percept ASD from sample group just by simple upright or inverted stimuli with different behaviors and simple average in time and space. While the feature like IoS of ASD children and the better ability of perception of control group could be considered to design novel biological motion stimuli with time-series information as plot, like the sudden clap after relatively long period regular walking, to trigger different reactions from ASD group and control group as high-dimensionality features for better performance in ASD screening. For eye-tracking data processing, display area zoning and encoding makes it possible to get higher resolution spatial information for better classification than simple average by side.

References

1. Kim, Y.S., et al.: Prevalence of autism spectrum disorders in a total population sample. Am. J. Psychiatry, **168**(9), 904–912 (2011)
2. Fombonne, E., Quirke, S., Hagen, A.: Epidemiology of pervasive developmental disorders. Autism Spectr. Disorders, 99–111 (2011)
3. CDC: Prevalence of autism spectrum disorders: Autism and developmental disabilities monitoring network, six sites, United States, 2000. MMWR Surveill. Summaires, **56**(1), 12–28 (2007)
4. Brugha, T.S.: The Psychiatry of Adult Autism and Asperger Syndrome: A Practical Guide. Oxford University Press, Oxford (2018)
5. Happé, F.G., Mansour, H., Barrett, P., Brown, T., Abbott, P., Charlton, R.A.: Demographic and cognitive profile of individuals seeking a diagnosis of autism spectrum disorder in adulthood. J. Autism Dev. Disord. **46**(11), 3469–3480 (2016)
6. Barger, B.D., Campbell, J.M., McDonough, J.D.: Prevalence and onset of regression within autism spectrum disorders: a meta-analytic review. J. Autism Dev. Disord. **43**(4), 817–828 (2013)
7. Li, C., Xu, X.: Early screening and diagnosis for ASD children in China. Pediatr. Med. **2**(July) (2019)
8. Sheldrick, R.C., Maye, M.P., Carter, A.S.: Age at first identification of autism spectrum disorder: an analysis of two US surveys. J. Am. Acad. Child Adolesc. Psychiatry **56**(4), 313–320 (2017)
9. Chawarska, K., Paul, R., Klin, A., Hannigen, S., Dichtel, L.E., Volkmar, F.: Parental recognition of developmental problems in toddlers with autism spectrum disorders. J. Autism Dev. Disord. **37**(1), 62–72 (2007). https://doi.org/10.1007/s10803-006-0330-8

10. Begeer, S., et al.: Sex differences in the timing of identification among children and adults with autism spectrum disorders. J. Autism Dev. Disord. **43**(5), 1151–1156 (2013). https://doi.org/10.1007/s10803-012-1656-z

11. Dworzynski, K., Ronald, A., Bolton, P., Happé, F.: How different are girls and boys above and below the diagnostic threshold for autism spectrum disorders? J. Am. Acad. Child Adolesc. Psychiatry **51**(8), 788–797 (2012)

12. Russell, G., Steer, C., Golding, J.: Social and demographic factors that influence the diagnosis of autistic spectrum disorders. Soc. Psychiatry Psychiatr. Epidemiol. **46**(12), 1283–1293 (2011). https://doi.org/10.1007/s00127-010-0294-z

13. Woolfenden, S., Sarkozy, V., Ridley, G., Coory, M., Williams, K.: A systematic review of two outcomes in autism spectrum disorder-epilepsy and mortality. Dev. Med. Child Neurol. **54**(4), 306–312 (2012)

14. Bilder, D., et al.: Excess mortality and causes of death in autism spectrum disorders: a follow up of the 1980s Utah/UCLA autism epidemiologic study. J. Autism Dev. Disord. **43**(5), 1196–1204 (2013). https://doi.org/10.1007/s10803-012-1664-z

15. Howlin, P., Moss, P., Savage, S., Rutter, M.: Social outcomes in mid-to later adulthood among individuals diagnosed with autism and average nonverbal IQ as children. J. Am. Acad. Child Adolesc. Psychiatry, **52**(6), 572–581. e1 (2013)

16. Bishop, D.V., Snowling, M.J., Thompson, P.A., Greenhalgh, T.: CATALISE: a multinational and multidisciplinary Delphi consensus study of problems with language development. Phase 2. Terminology. J. Child Psychol. Psychiatry, **58**(10), 1068–1080 (2017)

17. Simion, F., Regolin, L., Bulf, H.: A predisposition for biological motion in the newborn baby. Proc. Natl. Acad. Sci. **105**(2), 809–813 (2008)

18. Majaranta, P., Bulling, A.: Eye tracking and eye-based human–computer interaction. In: Fairclough, S.H., Gilleade, K. (eds.) Advances in Physiological Computing. HIS, pp. 39–65. Springer, London (2014). https://doi.org/10.1007/978-1-4471-6392-3_3

19. Rayner, K.: Eye movements in reading and information processing: 20 years of research. Psychol. Bull. **124**(3), 372 (1998)

20. Karthikeyan, S., Jagadeesh, V., Shenoy, R., Ecksteinz, M., Manjunath, B.: From where and how to what we see. In: the IEEE International Conference on Computer Vision on Proceedings, pp. 625–632 (2013)

21. Hansen, D.W., Ji, Q.: In the eye of the beholder: a survey of models for eyes and gaze. IEEE Trans. Pattern Anal. Mach. Intell. **32**(3), 478–500 (2009)

22. Huey, E.B.: The Psychology and Pedagogy of Reading. The Macmillan Company, London (1908)

23. Zhu, Z., Ji, Q., Bennett, K.P.: Nonlinear eye gaze mapping function estimation via support vector regression. In:18th International Conference on Pattern Recognition (ICPR 2006), vol. 1, no. 1, pp. 1132–1135 (2006)

24. Valenti, R., Sebe, N., Gevers, T.: Combining head pose and eye location information for gaze estimation. IEEE Trans. Image Process. **21**(2), 802–815 (2011)

25. Lu, F., Sugano, Y., Okabe, T., Sato, Y.: Adaptive linear regression for appearance-based gaze estimation. IEEE Trans. Pattern Anal. Mach. Intell. **36**(10), 2033–2046 (2014)

26. Zhang, X., Sugano, Y., Fritz, M., Bulling, A.: Appearance-based gaze estimation in the wild. In: Proceedings of the IEEE Conference on Computer Vision and Pattern Recognition, pp. 4511–4520 (2015)

27. Klin, A., Jones, W., Schultz, R., Volkmar, F., Cohen, D.: Visual fixation patterns during viewing of naturalistic social situations as predictors of social competence in individuals with autism. Arch. Gener. Psychiatry, **59**(9) 809–816, 99–110 (2012, 2016)

28. Dang, Q.K., Chee, Y., Pham, D.D., Suh, Y.S.: A virtual blind cane using a line laser-based vision system and an inertial measurement unit. Sensors **16**(1), 1–18 (2016)

29. Pierce, K., Conant, D., Hazin, R., Stoner, R., Desmond, J.: Preference for geometric patterns early in life as a risk factor for autism. Arch. Gen. Psychiatry **68**(1), 101–109 (2011)

30. Osterling, J., Dawson, G.: Early recognition of children with autism: a study of first birthday home videotapes. J. Autism Dev. Disord. **24**(3), 247–257 (1994). https://doi.org/10.1007/BF02172225

31. Chawarska, K., Macari, S., Shic, F.: Decreased spontaneous attention to social scenes in 6-month-old infants later diagnosed with autism spectrum disorders. Biol. Psychiat. **74**(3), 195–203 (2013)

32. Wang, S., Xu, J., Jiang, M., Zhao, Q., Hurlemann, R., Adolphs, R.: Autism spectrum disorder, but not amygdala lesions, impairs social attention in visual search. Neuropsychologia **63**, 259–274 (2014)

33. Dawson, G., Webb, S.J., McPartland, J.: Understanding the nature of face processing impairment in autism: insights from behavioral and electrophysiological studies. Dev. Neuropsychol. **27**(3), 403–424 (2005)

34. Salva, O.R., Mayer, U., Vallortigara, G.: Roots of a social brain: developmental models of emerging animacy-detection mechanisms. Neurosci. Biobehav. Rev. **50**, 150–168 (2015)

35. Troje, N.F., Westhoff, C.: The inversion effect in biological motion perception: evidence for a "life detector"? Curr. Biol. **16**(8), 821–824 (2006)

36. Vallortigara, G., Regolin, L.: Gravity bias in the interpretation of biological motion by inexperienced chicks. Curr. Biol. **16**(8), R279–R280 (2006)

37. Johansson, G.: Visual perception of biological motion and a model for its analysis. Percept. Psychophys. **14**(2), 201–211 (1973). https://doi.org/10.3758/BF03212378

38. Hadad, B.S., Maurer, D., Lewis, T.L.: Sparing of sensitivity to biological motion but not of global motion after early visual deprivation. Dev. Sci. **15**(4), 474–481 (2012)

39. Tseng, P.-H., Cameron, I.G., Pari, G., Reynolds, J.N., Munoz, D.P., Itti, L.: High-throughput classification of clinical populations from natural viewing eye movements. J. Neurol. **260**(1) 275–284 (2013). https://doi.org/10.1007/s00415-012-6631-2

40. Wang, S., et al.: Atypical visual saliency in autism spectrum disorder quantified through model-based eye tracking. Neuron **88**(3), 604–616 (2015)

41. Jiang, M., Zhao, Q.: Learning visual attention to identify people with autism spectrum disorder. In: Proceedings of the IEEE International Conference on Computer Vision, pp. 3267–3276 (2017)

42. Shi, L., et al.: Different visual preference patterns in response to simple and complex dynamic social stimuli in preschool-aged children with autism spectrum disorders. PLoS ONE **10**(3), e0122280 (2015)

43. Rutherford, M.D., Troje, N.F.: IQ predicts biological motion perception in autism spectrum disorders. J. Autism Dev. Disorders, **42**(4), 557–565 (2012)

44. Chita-Tegmark, M.: Social attention in ASD: a review and meta-analysis of eye-tracking studies. Res. Dev. Disabil. **48**, 79–93 (2016)

45. Sifre, R., Olson, L., Gillespie, S., Klin, A., Jones, W., Shultz, S.: A longitudinal investigation of preferential attention to biological motion in 2- to 24-month-old infants. Sci. Rep. Nat. **8**(1), 2527–2536 (2018)
46. Richler, J., Bishop, S.L., Kleinke, J.R., Lord, C.: Restricted and repetitive behaviors in young children with autism spectrum disorders. J. Autism Dev. Disord. **37**, 73–85 (2007). https://doi.org/10.1007/s10803-006-0332-6
47. Fan, L., Du, Y., Zhai, G.: VR as an Adjuvant tool in ASD therapy. Sci. Technol. Rev. **36**(9), 46–56 (2018)
48. Zhai, G., Cai, J., Lin, W., Yang, X., Zhang, W.: Three dimensional scalable video adaptation via user-end perceptual quality assessment. IEEE Trans. Broadcast. **54**(3), 719–727 (2008)
49. Duan, H., Zhai, G., Min, X., Zhu, Y., Sun, W., Yang, X.: Assessment of visually induced motion sickness in immersive videos. In: Zeng, B., Huang, Q., El Saddik, A., Li, H., Jiang, S., Fan, X. (eds.) PCM 2017. LNCS, vol. 10735, pp. 662–672. Springer, Cham (2018). https://doi.org/10.1007/978-3-319-77380-3_63
50. Zhu, Y., Zhai, G., Min, X.: The prediction of head and eye movement for 360 degree images. Signal Process.: Image Commun. **69**, 15–25 (2018)
51. Duan, H., et al.: Learning to predict where the children with ASD look. In: IEEE International Conference on Image Processing (ICIP), Athens, Greece, pp. 704–708 (2018)
52. Tian, Y., Min, X., Zhai, G., Gao, Z.: Video-based early ASD detection via temporal pyramid networks. In: IEEE International Conference on Multimedia and Expo, pp. 272–277 (2019)

Virtual Reality

An Equalizing Method to Improve the Positioning Effect of a Multi-channel Headphone

Xinyan Hao$^{(\boxtimes)}$ (iD)

Communication University of China, Beijing, China
haoxy6171@sina.cn

Abstract. With the rapid development of communication technology and audio-visual multimedia technology, listeners' requirements for audio playback effects of mobile terminals continue to increase. How to use headphones to reproduce multi-channel audio sources to enhance the listening experience of listeners is one of the hot issues in the field of audio processing at this stage. In response to this problem, some researchers designed and produced a ten-unit multi-channel headphone through sound field simulation. Preliminary experimental results show that the sound image externalization effect of this headphone playback 5.0 movie surround sound signal is better than that of ordinary stereo headphones, but the positioning effect still needs to be further improved. In order to further improve the positioning effect of the multi-channel headphone, the HpTF (Headphone to Ear Cannel Transfer Function) at the entrance of the ear canal of the multi-channel headphone and under free-field condition are measured. By analyzing the spectrum difference of HpTF under these two conditions, the auricle difference characteristic frequency band is obtained. The headphone is equalized by the inverse filter which is designed by combining the auricle difference characteristic frequency band and the frequency spectrum characteristic of the HpTF under the free field condition. The subjective experimental results show that the positioning effect of the multi-channel headphone is significantly improved after the equalization processing performed by this method, improving the accuracy of the audience's judgment of the horizontal and vertical angles by 12% to 53% compared with that before the equalization.

Keywords: Multi-channel headphone · Equalization processing · HpTF · Inverse filtering

1 Introduction

With the development of 5G and multi-channel audio technology, enjoying surround sound and panoramic sound on the mobile terminal has become a new goal pursued by auditory presentation. How to better play the multi-channel audio

© Springer Nature Singapore Pte Ltd. 2021
G. Zhai et al. (Eds.): IFTC 2020, CCIS 1390, pp. 387–401, 2021.
https://doi.org/10.1007/978-981-16-1194-0_33

signals through headphones is the focus of current research. Existing studies have shown [1,2] that the application of multi-channel audio technology on the headphone is still immature, and there is still a lot of research space in enhancing the spatial sense, dynamic effects, and externalization effects of headphone playback. At present, most of the researches on enhancing the spatial positioning cues of headphones start from the sound source, using methods such as equalization, personalized processing, and dynamic processing to process the playback signal [3–5]. The research object of this article is a multi-channel headphone. The headphone enhances the spatial cues by changing the spatial orientation of the radiating unit and increasing the number of the radiating units, providing a new solution for the playback of multi-channel audio signals [6]. Existing experimental results show that the multi-channel headphones can effectively enhance the spatial sense of 5.1 movie surround sound playback. Considering that the positioning effect of the multi-channel headphone will directly affect the matching degree of the motion track of the audio object and the video object during the playback of the surround sound, it is necessary to find a method to improve the positioning effect of the multi-channel headphone.

In this paper, by measuring and analyzing the acoustic characteristics of the multi-channel headphone, the HpTF inverse filter with specific compensation requirements in different frequency bands is designed to equalize the headphone and effectively improve the positioning effect of the multi-channel headphone.

2   Multi-channel Headphone Structure

The shell structure of the multi-channel headphone is shown in Fig. 1. The diameter of the shell is 8 cm, and the sound-absorbing material is attached inside. The spatial orientation of the 5-radiation unit mounting holes are defined as shown in Fig. 2. The diameter of each mounting hole is 8mm. When a listener wears the multi-channel headphone, the center of the outer edge surface of the headphone shell approximately coincides with the center of the entrance section of the ear canal.

Fig. 1. Headphone shell with sound-absorbing material attached inside.

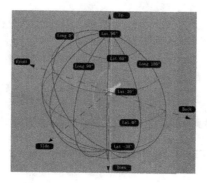

Fig. 2. Latitude and longitude map. (front unit (30°, 0°), side unit (90°, 0°), rear unit (150°, 0°).), upper unit (90°, 60°), (lower unit (90°, −60°)).

3 Measurement and Analysis of Acoustic Characteristics of Multi-channel Headphone

3.1 HpTF Measurement

As Fig. 3, 4 shows, two methods are used to measure the HpTF of the radiating units of the multi-channel headphone, and the impulse response function of HpTF is calculated by deconvolution [7]. During the measurement, the multi-channel headphone is worn on an acoustic head model with standard artificial pinna [8,9] in method 1, and the center of the diaphragm of the measuring microphone is placed at the center of the outer edge of the headphone shell in method 2. The HpTF measured by method 1 and method 2 are called "HpTF at the entrance of the ear canal" and "HpTF under the free field condition" respectively.

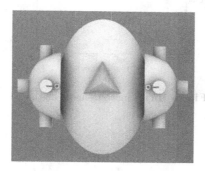

Fig. 3. HpTF measurement method 1.

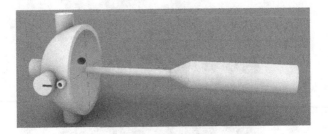

Fig. 4. HpTF measurement method 2.

Choose 5 pairs of ATH-CK7 earbuds as the radiation unit of the multi-channel headphone. The HpTF of each radiation unit under the two conditions are measured multiple times and averaged. During each measurement, the multi-channel headphone is either re-worn or replaced.

The measurement results of "HpTF at the entrance of the ear canal" and "HpTF under the free field condition" are shown in Fig. 5, 6. In order to display the HpTF of each radiating unit independently in a picture, a certain amplitude offset is added to the HpTF corresponding to S, B, U, and D respectively.It can be seen that there are obvious differences in "HpTF at the entrance of the ear canal" between different radiation units. Under the free field condition, only lateral unit have obvious differences in HpTF between other radiation units.

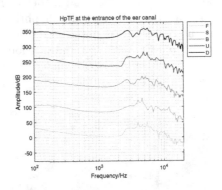

Fig. 5. HpTF measurement method 1.

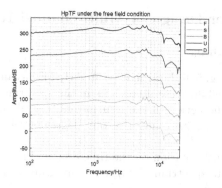

Fig. 6. HpTF measurement method 2.

3.2   Analysis of Auricle Difference Characteristic Frequency Band

The filtering effect of the auricle on sound waves is an important factor in auditory positioning. Inspired by the directional frequency band proposed by Blauert [10], this paper proposes the auricle difference characteristic frequency band for the multi-channel headphone, that is, the frequency band where the radiating unit and the human ear are coupled. The logarithmic spectrum of "HpTF at the entrance of the ear canal" is subtracted from the logarithmic spectrum of "HpTF under the free-field condition" to obtain the auricle difference characteristic frequency band, as shown in Fig. 7. In the figure, the increasing frequency band and the decreasing frequency band of the auricle difference characteristic frequency band are framed by a black dashed line and marked with a plus sign and a minus sign respectively. It can be seen that the increasing frequency band and the decreasing frequency band of each radiation units are basically the same below 1 kHz; there are common increasing frequency band at 3.5 kHz–5 kHz, 7 kHz–8 kHz, and 10 kHz–12 kHz; and common decreasing frequency band at 6 kHz–7 kHz, 9 kHz–10 kHz, and 15 kHz–17 kHz.

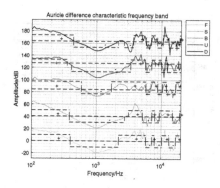

Fig. 7. Auricle difference characteristic frequency band

4   Inverse Filter Design of Multi-channel Headphone

4.1   HpTF Smoothing

It can be seen from Fig. 5, 6 that the measured HpTF has an excessively detailed spectrum structure, while these differences in the spectrum structure are indistinguishable under the action of the human auditory filter. In order to ensure that the designed inverse filter has a certain degree of robustness, the HpTF is first smoothed.

Perform FFT transformation on the time-domain impulse response function of HpTF to obtain its spectrum $X(f_0)$, and substitute it into Eq. (1) to obtain the smoothed spectrum [11].

$$|Y(f_0)| = \sqrt{\frac{\int_0^{\frac{Fs}{2}} |X(f_0)|^2 |H(f, f_0)|^2 \, df}{\int_0^{\frac{Fs}{2}} |H(f, f_0)|^2 \, df}} \tag{1}$$

Figure 8, 9 shows the comparison of the HpTF before and after smoothing. It can be seen that the spectrum structure of HpTF has a certain degree of smoothing.

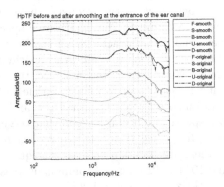

Fig. 8. Comparison of HpTF before and after smoothing at the entrance of the ear canal

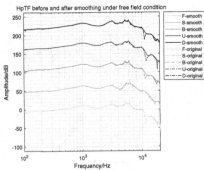

Fig. 9. Comparison of HpTF before and after smoothing under free field condition

4.2   Inverse Filter Design

In this paper, based on the principle of least squares, the frequency response of the inverse filter is solved by minimizing the cost function value [11]. Figure 10 shows the frequency domain inverse filter structure 1.

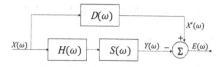

Fig. 10. Frequency domain inverse filter structure 1

Where: $X(\omega)$ is Input signal frequency response, $D(\omega)$ is Objective function frequency response, $X'(\omega)$ is Output signal target frequency response, $H(\omega)$ is Inverse filter frequency response, $S(\omega)$ is Headphone playback system frequency response, $Y(\omega)$ is Output signal frequency response, $E(\omega)$ is Error signal frequency response.

It can be seen that the cost function $J(\omega)$ is:

$$J(\omega) = E(\omega)E^*(\omega) \tag{2}$$

where:

$$E(\omega) = X'(\omega) - X(\omega)H(\omega)S(\omega) \tag{3}$$

$$X'(\omega) = X(\omega)D(\omega) \tag{4}$$

Solve the derivative of $J(\omega)$ with respect to ω and set it to zero, and get the inverse filter frequency response $H(\omega)$ as:

$$H(\omega) = \frac{S^*(\omega)D(\omega)}{|S(\omega)|^2} \tag{5}$$

Figure 11 shows the inverse filter structure 2 with a regularized function link.

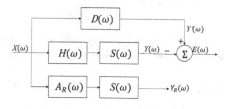

Fig. 11. Frequency domain least squares inverse filter structure 2

Where: $A_R(\omega)$ is regular function frequency response, $Y_R(\omega)$ is regularized output signal frequency response.

In the inverse filter structure 2, it is assumed that $S(\omega)$ is non-minimum phase. Set $D(\omega)$ to $e^{-j\omega N}$, so that $Y'(\omega)$ is the pure delay of N points of $X(\omega)$, ensuring the causal stability of the calculation results. The value of N in this article is 0.36Fs (Fs is the sampling frequency of the replay signal).

In structure 2, the cost function $J(\omega)$ is:

$$J(\omega) = \frac{1}{2}E(\omega)E^*(\omega) + \beta\frac{1}{2}Y_R(\omega)Y_R^*(\omega) \tag{6}$$

Where: $\beta(>0)$ is Regular coefficient,

$$E(\omega) = X'(\omega) - X(\omega)H(\omega)S(\omega) \tag{7}$$

$$X'(\omega) = e^{-j\omega N}X(\omega) \tag{8}$$

$$Y_R(\omega) = X(\omega)A_R(\omega)S(\omega) \tag{9}$$

Solve the derivative of $J(\omega)$ with respect to ω and set it to zero, and get the inverse filter frequency response $H(\omega)$ as:

$$H(\omega) = \frac{S^*(\omega)e^{-j\omega N}}{|S(\omega)|^2 + \beta|A_R(\omega)|^2} \tag{10}$$

It can be seen from Eq. (10) that the regular coefficient β and the regular function $A_R(\omega)$ form the regular term $\beta|A_R(\omega)|^2$ in the inverse filter. When $\beta|A_R(\omega)|^2 \ll |S(\omega)|^2$, the effect of the regular term is small, and $H(\omega)$ is the inverse of $S(\omega)$. When $\beta|A_R(\omega)|^2$ is close to $|S(\omega)|^2$, the effect of the regular term begins to manifest, and the compensation degree of $H(\omega)$ to $S(\omega)$ varies with the size of $\beta|A_R(\omega)|^2$. Therefore, by controlling the weight of $\beta|A_R(\omega)|^2$ at different frequencies, the compensation amount of the inverse filter at different frequencies can be adjusted.

Substituting Eq. (10) into Eq. (5), the expression of $D(\omega)$ can be obtained as shown in Eq. (11):

$$D(\omega) = \frac{e^{-j\omega N}}{1 + \beta\frac{|A_R(\omega)|^2}{|S(\omega)|^2}} \tag{11}$$

To ensure that the inverse filter is causally achievable, through Hilbert transform, the phase-frequency response function $\varphi_{min(\omega)}$ of $D(\omega)$ is obtained as:

$$\varphi_{min(\omega)} = -imag(Hilbert(\ln(|D(\omega)|))) \tag{12}$$

Substituting Eq. (11, 12) into Eq. 5 to obtain the frequency response $H(\omega)$ of the inverse filter is:

$$H(\omega) = \frac{S^*(\omega)e^{-j\omega N}e^{j\varphi_{min(\omega)}}}{|S(\omega)|^2 + \beta|A_R(\omega)|^2} \tag{13}$$

Here, in order to retain the personalized spectrum characteristics produced by the coupling between the headphone and the ear of the listener, the "HpTF under the smoothed free field condition" is selected as $S(\omega)$.

It can be seen from Fig. 9 that the smoothed HpTF under the free field condition have large roll-off frequency bands 200 Hz and above 10 kHz. The inverse filter needs to be incompletely compensated these frequency bands to avoid overloading the radiating unit. In the frequency band between 200–10 kHz, including the common auricle difference characteristic frequency band analyzed above. The inverse filter needs to perform additional gain compensation or attenuation to enhance the positioning cues brought by the coupling of the auricle and the headphone. In other frequency bands, the inverse filters directly perform full compensation.

Set the weight value of the regular function $A_R(\omega)$ on the fully compensated frequency band to 0, and 1 to the remaining frequency bands. As shown in Fig. 12.

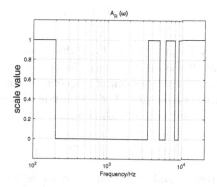

Fig. 12. Regular function scale value graph

When $A_R(\omega)$ is 1, the proportion of the regular term in Eq. 13 is determined by the regular coefficient β. Because an inverse filter is needed to personalize the compensation of the roll-off frequency band and the common auricle difference characteristic frequency band, this paper proposes to replace the regular coefficient constant β with the regular coefficient function $\beta(\omega)$, and assign different β values to the regular terms on different frequency bands.

First, let:

$$\beta(\omega)\,|A_R(\omega)|^2 = k(\omega)|S(\omega)|^2 \tag{14}$$

Incorporating Eq. 14 into Eq. 13, the frequency response of the inverse filter is shown in Eq. 15:

$$H(\omega) = \frac{e^{-j\omega N}e^{j\varphi_{\min(\omega)}}}{(1 + k(\omega))S(\omega)} \tag{15}$$

Solve the logarithmic spectrum of $H(\omega)$ as:

$$20 \log_{10} H(\omega) = -20 \log_{10}(1 + k(\omega)) - 20 \log_{10} S(\omega) \qquad (16)$$

The logarithmic spectrum of frequency response of $S(\omega)$ after inverse filtering is:

$$20 \log_{10} S'(\omega) = -20 \log_{10}(1 + k(\omega)) \qquad (17)$$

From Eq. 17, we find that the size of $20 \log_{10} S'(\omega)$ depends on $k(\omega)$. The $k(\omega)$ corresponding to the roll-off frequency band and the increasing and decreasing frequency band in the common auricle difference characteristic frequency band are calculated below.

Roll-off Frequency Band. Set the compensation gain of the inverse filter in the roll-off frequency band to 1/3 of the full compensation gain, and get:

$$k(\omega) = S(\omega)^{\frac{1}{3}} - 1 \qquad (18)$$

Increasing Frequency Band. Let the logarithmic spectrum envelope of $S'(\omega)$ be in the shape of a quadratic function with the opening facing downwards, the frequency of the envelope apex is the center frequency of the increasing frequency band, and set the amplitude to 6 dB. The amplitude of the start frequency and the cut-off frequency of the band is 0 dB, and get:

$$k(\omega) = 10^{\frac{6(\omega - \omega_H)(\omega - \omega_L)}{5(\omega_H - \omega_L)^2}} - 1 \qquad (19)$$

Where: ω_H is increase band stop frequency, ω_L is increase band start frequency.

Decreasing Frequency Band. Let the logarithmic spectrum envelope of $S'(\omega)$ be in the shape of a quadratic function with the opening facing upwards, the frequency of the valley point is the center frequency of the decreasing frequency band, and set the amplitude to -6 dB. The amplitude of the start frequency and the cut-off frequency of the band is 0 dB, and get:

$$k(\omega) = 10^{\frac{-6(\omega - \omega_H)(\omega - \omega_L)}{5(\omega_H - \omega_L)^2}} - 1 \qquad (20)$$

Where: ω_H is decrease band stop frequency, ω_L is decrease band start frequency.

In summary:

$$
k(\omega) = \begin{cases} S(\omega)^{\frac{1}{3}} - 1 & \frac{\omega}{2\pi} \in (0, 200), (10000, 20000); \\ 10^{\frac{6(\omega-\omega_H)(\omega-\omega_L)}{5(\omega_H-\omega_L)^2}} - 1 & \frac{\omega}{2\pi} \in (3500, 5000), (7000, 8000); \\ 10^{\frac{-6(\omega-\omega_H)(\omega-\omega_L)}{5(\omega_H-\omega_L)^2}} - 1 & \frac{\omega}{2\pi} \in (6000, 7000), (9000, 10000); \\ 0 & \frac{\omega}{2\pi} \in others \end{cases} \tag{21}
$$

Substitute Eq. 21 into Eq. 15 to get the frequency response $H(\omega)$ of the inverse filter.

Figure 13 take the left "S unit" as an example, and shows the frequency response of "HpTF under free field condition" after smoothing, the calculated inverse filter, and the HpTF after filtering.

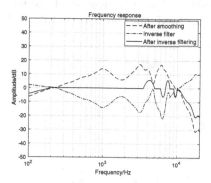

Fig. 13. Smoothed HpTF frequency response, inverse filter frequency response, filted HpTF frequency response

5   Multi-channel Headphone Positioning Effect Analysis Before and After Equalization Processing

5.1   Subjective Experiment Design

The experimental signals for the multi-channel headphone before equalization processing is 28 virtual sound signals. The virtual sound signals are made by convolving white noise with HRTF whose horizontal angles are $0°$, $30°$, $60°$, $90°$, $120°$, $150°$, $180°$ and vertical angles are $-40°$, $0°$, $40°$, $80°$. Then, convolve these virtual sound signals with the inverse filter impulse responses of each radiation unit to obtain the experimental signals for the multi-channel headphone after the equalization processing.

The experimental signals before and after the equalization processing are respectively fed to the radiation units for playback. During the experiment, listeners are required to determine the horizontal and vertical angles of the signal. The horizontal and vertical angles are forcibly selected from the angles above. A total of 20 subjects participated the experiment.

5.2   Subjective Experimental Results

Before the equalization processing, the correct rate of the horizontal angle judgment of the radiating units of the multi-channel headphone in different spatial orientations is shown in Fig. 14. It can be seen from the figure that the correct rate of judging the horizontal angle of the three orthogonal directions of 0°, 90°, and 180° by the multi-channel headphone is higher than that of other oblique directions. After the equalization processing, the correct rate of the horizontal angle judgment of the radiating units in different spatial orientations of the multi-channel headphone is shown in Fig. 15. Calculate the difference between the horizontal angle judgment accuracy rate after equalization processing and before equalization processing, and obtain the histogram of the increase value of the horizontal angle judgment accuracy rate of the multi-channel headphone, as shown in Fig. 16. It can be seen from Fig. 16 that after equalization processing, the accuracy of the horizontal angle judgment of the multi-channel headphone has been significantly improved, and the increase value is between 0.16 and 0.53.

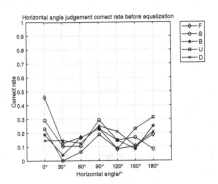

Fig. 14. Line chart of the correct rate of horizontal angle judgment before equalization processing

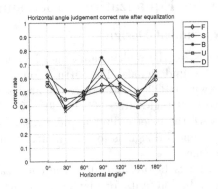

Fig. 15. Line chart of the correct rate of horizontal angle judgment after equalization processing

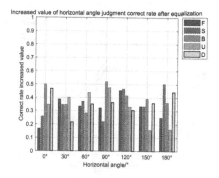

Fig. 16. Histogram of the increase value of the horizontal angle judgment accuracy after equalization processing

Before the equalization processing, the correct rate of the vertical angle judgment of the radiating units of the multi-channel headphone in different spatial orientations is shown in Fig. 17. It can be seen from the figure that the multi-channel headphone has the highest accuracy in judging the 0° vertical angle; the accuracy of judging the vertical angles of 40°, 80°, and −40° decreases sequentially. After the equalization processing, the correct rate of the vertical angle judgment of the radiating units of the multi-channel headphone in different spatial orientations is shown in Fig. 18. Calculate the difference in the accuracy of the vertical angle judgment after the equalization processing and before the equalization processing, and obtain the histogram of the vertical angle judgment accuracy increase value, as shown in Fig. 19. It can be seen from Fig. 19 that after equalization processing, the accuracy of the vertical angle judgment of the multi-channel headphone has been significantly improved, and the increase value is between 0.12 and 0.52.

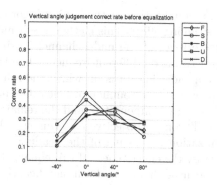

Fig. 17. Line chart of vertical angle judgment accuracy before equalization processing

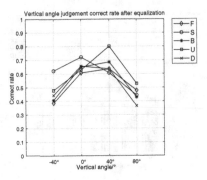

Fig. 18. Line chart of vertical angle judgment accuracy after equalization processing

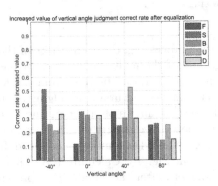

Fig. 19. Histogram of the increase value of the vertical angle judgment accuracy after equalization processing

6   Conclusion

This article proposes an equalization method suitable for enhancing the multi-channel headphone positioning effect. This method needs measuring and analyzing the acoustic characteristics of the multi-channel headphone, and performs specific equalization processing on different frequency bands of the HpTF of different spatial orientation radiating units, in which the roll-off frequency bands are incompletely compensated, the common auricle difference characteristic frequency bands are additionally compensated, and the remaining frequency bands are fully compensated. Through subjective experiments, the positioning effect before and after equalization processing of the headphone are compared. The experimental results verify the effectiveness of this equalization method that the positioning effect of the headphone has been significantly improved after the equalization processing though this method. In future research, the method proposed in this article can also be used for equalization processing for multi-channel headphones with other shell structures.

References

1. Zacharov, N., Lorho, G.: Subjective evaluation of virtual home theatre sound systems for loudspeakers and headphones (2004)
2. Melchior, F., Pike, C.: An assessment of virtual surround sound systems for headphone listening of 5.1 multichannel audio. In: 134th Convention of the Audio Engineering Society (2013)
3. Zhang, M., Tan, K.C., Er, M.H.: A refined algorithm of 3-D sound synthesis. In: Fourth International Conference on Signal Processing
4. Park, M.H., Choi, S.I., Kim, S.H., Bae, K.S.: Improvement of front-back sound localization characteristics in headphone-based 3D sound generation. In: International Conference on Advanced Communication Technology (2005)
5. Chengyun, Z., Bosun, X.: A dynamic binaural playback method of 5.1 surround sound. Appl. Acoust. (4), 283–287 (2016)
6. Huan, W.: Structure design and effect analysis of multi-channel headphone. Ph.D. thesis, Communication University of China (2019)
7. Muller, S., Massarani, P.: Transfer-function measurement with sweeps. J. Audio Eng. Soc. Audio Eng. Soc. 49(6), 443–471 (2001)
8. Na, Q., Li, L., Wei, Z.: Measurement and classification of auricles in Chinese adults. Appl. Acoust. 29(005), 518–522 (2010)
9. Blauert, J.: Sound localization in the median plane (frequency function of sound localization in median plane measured psychoacoustically at both ears with narrow band signals). Acustica, 22(4), 205–213 (1970)
10. Kohlrausch, A.G.: The perceptual (ir)relevance of hrtf magnitude and phase spectra (2001)
11. Bouchard, M., Norcross, S.G., Soulodre, G.A.: Inverse filtering design using a minimal-phase target function from regularization (2001)

Light Field Reconstruction with Arbitrary Angular Resolution Using a Deep Coarse-To-Fine Framework

Ran Li, Li Fang[✉], Long Ye, Wei Zhong, and Qin Zhang

Key Laboratory of Media Audio and Video (Communication University of China),
Ministry of Education, Beijing 100024, China
{ranli801,lifang8902,yelong,wzhong,zhangqin}@cuc.edu.cn

Abstract. Densely-sampled light fields (LFs) are favorable for numerous applications like 3D scene reconstruction, virtual reality, et al., while the acquisition is costly. Most of the current view synthesis approaches need to sample the input LFs in a special or regular pattern, which makes the actual acquisition difficult. In this article, a new coarse-to-fine deep learning framework is presented to reconstruct densely-sampled LFs with arbitrary angular resolution. Concretely, a rough reconstruction based on meta-learning is performed on each epipolar plane image (EPI) to achieve arbitrary proportion of upsampling, followed by a refinement with 3D convolutional neural networks (CNNs) on stacked EPIs. Both modules are differentiable so that the network is end-to-end trainable. In addition, these two steps are performed on 3D volumes extracted from LF data first horizontally, and then vertically, forming a pseudo-4DCNN which can synthesize 4D LFs from a group of sparse input views effectively. The key advantage is to efficiently synthesize LFs with arbitrary angular resolution using a single model. The presented approach compares superiorly against various state-of-the-art methods on various challenging scenes.

Keywords: Light field · Super resolution · Image-based rendering · View synthesis · Convolutional neural network

1 Introduction

The light field (LF) is a high-dimensional function describing the spatial propagation of light rays [1, 2] and contains abundant scene visual information, which facilitate a variety of applications like post-capture refocusing [3] and 3D reconstruction [4], depth inference [5], and virtual reality [6]. In order to render novel views without ghost effects, most applications require the LF to be densely sampled for sufficient information [7].

The densely-sampled LF is very attractive for applications involve scene visual content, but it brings great challenges to the acquisition. For example, the camera array

This work is supported by the National Natural Science Foundation of China under Grant Nos. 62001432 and 61971383, the CETC funding, and the Fundamental Research Funds for the Central Universities under Grant No. YLSZ180226.

© Springer Nature Singapore Pte Ltd. 2021
G. Zhai et al. (Eds.): IFTC 2020, CCIS 1390, pp. 402–414, 2021.
https://doi.org/10.1007/978-981-16-1194-0_34

system [8] needs a large amount of cameras and the cost is expensive; the computer-controlled gantry [9] or hand-held camera [10] are limited to static scenes and time-consuming. Commercial LF cameras can capture light rays from real-world scenes and encode both intensity and direction information [11, 12]. However, a compromise between angular resolution and spatial resolution has to be made owing to the limitation of the sensor resolution.

Instead of capturing densely-sample LFs with bulky hardware, many view synthesis methods have been developed to synthesize the required views from the given small set of images. Previous works either estimate the scene depth as ancillary information [13, 14], or use sparsity in the transformation domain as specific prior knowledge to do intensive reconstruction [15–18]. The first category relies heavily on the depth estimation, which often fails in closed areas as well as in areas that are specular or glossy. The second category is sampling and continuous reconstruction based on the plenoptic function. In these mothed, depth information is not used as supplementary mapping, but suffer from either aliasing or blurring problem when inputting LF has extremely low sampling. Lately, some learning-based approach have been proposed [19–22]. However, most of them require retraining for different interpolation rates, which brings difficulties to actual acquisition.

In this article, a new coarse-to-fine deep learning framework is presented to reconstruct a densely-sampled LF from a sparsely-sampled one with arbitrary angular resolution. Concretely, the proposed framework is composed of two modules, one is for coarse epipolar plane image (EPI) restoration and the other is for efficient LF refinement. Both modules are differentiable so that the network is end-to-end trainable. Specifically, inspired by [23], the first module independently restores each EPI using meta-learning strategy to yield intermediate EPIs with target high resolution. As for the refinement part, an encoder-like view 3D convolutional neural networks (CNNs) on stacked EPIs are used to recover high-frequency details. These two parts are performed on 3D EPI volumes extracted from LF data first horizontally, and then vertically, forming a pseudo-4DCNN which can take full advantage of 4D LF data while avoiding heavy computational complexity. Moreover, since the meta-learning strategy can accept different upsampling rates and yield a coarsely recovered LF with desired resolution, the proposed system is able to upsample with different rates using only one model. We also present experiments for evaluating the performance of the proposed approach on various datasets.

The rest of this article is arranged as follows. Latest developments of view synthesis and LF reconstruction are introduced in Sec. 2. Our presented approach is described in Sect. 3. The performance evaluation is given in Sect. 4. Finally, Sect. 5 summarizes of this paper.

2 Related Work

Many researchers have studied the problems of using a small set of sparsely-sampled images to reconstruct a complete densely-sampled LF. Depending on whether depth information is explicitly used, these works can be categorized as depth-dependent view synthesis and depth-independent LF reconstruction.

2.1 View Synthesis with Depth Map

View synthesis with depth map methods usually consist of three steps to synthesize the novel view of the scene [24]. First the disparities between input views are estimated, then the input views are warped to the target view according to these disparities, and finally the warped images are combined somehow to obtain the desired novel views. Kalantari et al. [19] first introduced deep learning technology to such task. Their approach successively uses two networks first estimate the depth map and then predict colors. Srinivasan et al. [25] first used a CNN to estimate the 4D ray depth and synthesize a Lambertian LF accordingly from a single 2D RGB image, and then used another CNN to predict the remining occluded or non-Lambertian parts, resulting in a 4D RGBD LF. Flynn et al. [14] mapped input views to a plane-sweep volume of the same perspective through homography transform, and then fused them together through two parallel CNNs to average the color of each depth plane with the learned weights. Zhou et al. [26] and Mildenhall et al. [27] proposed to infer RGB images stack as well as their opacity using trained CNNs, and then generate novel views using homography transform and alpha composition. The quality of these view synthesis methods largely depends on the precision of depth map. However, inaccurate depth estimation usually occurs within textureless, occluded and reflective regions.

2.2 LF Reconstruction Without Depth Map

LF reconstruction without depth map approaches can be regarded as angular dimension upsampling without explicitly use the depth information of the scene. Lin et al. [28] proved that using linear interpolation can only generate aliasing-free novel views when the parallax between adjacent views in a LF is less than single pixel. Some methods have studied LF restoration with particular sampling patterns. Levin et al. [29] synthesized new views from a group of images sampled on a circular path by using prior knowledge of dimensionality. Shi et al. [16] restored the complete LF in the Fourier domain by sparsity analysis, where only the boundary viewpoints or diagonal viewpoints are sampled. These methods are far from practical application due to the difficulty in capturing input views in specific mode.

Lately, several learning-based approaches have also been proposed for depthless reconstruction. Yoon et al. [31] introduced a learning-based system, where inter-mediate views are generated by two adjacent views. However, only 2X upsampling novel views can be generated. Wu et al. [21] proposed a "blur-restoration-deblur" approach to learn angular superresolution on 2D EPIs. Wu et al. [30] further discussed the problem of either blurring or aliasing, and presented a Laplacian Pyramid EPI network to predict both low-frequency scale and high-frequency details to solve the compromise issue. However, all these studies cannot take full advantage of the potential of the LF data. Wang et al. [32, 33] trained a pseudo-4DCNN that works on 3D EPI volumes, but their network only works with a fixed interpolating rate.

3   The Presented Method

3.1   4-D LF Representation

A 4D LF is usually denoted as $L(x, y, u, v)$, which uses the intersections of light rays with two parallel planes to record light rays, called the two-plane representation (see Fig. 1). Each light ray travels from the spatial coordinates (x, y) on the focal plane then to the angular coordinates (u, v) on the camera plane. Therefore, a 4D LF is regarded as a 2D image array with $N \times M$ images sampled on a 2D angular grid, of which each image is of spatial resolution $W \times H$.

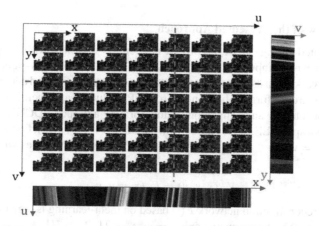

Fig. 1. A 4D light field $L(x, y, u, v)$ visualization. The horizontal EPI is a 2D (x, u) slice $L(x, y_0, u, v_0)$ by positioning $y = v_0$ and $v = v_0$ (highlighted in red), and the vertical EPI (y, v) by positioning $x = x_0$ and $u = u_0$ (highlighted in blue). (Color figure online)

As shown in Fig. 1, by fixing x in spatial domain and u in angular domain (or y and v), we can get an EPI map denoted as $E_{x_0,u_0}(y, v)$ (or $E_{y_0,v_0}(x, u)$), which is a 2D slice of the 4D LF. A 3D volume $V_{v_0}(x, y, u)$ (or $V_{u_0}(x, y, v)$) can be produced if we stack EPIs from a row (or a column) views by fixing $v = v_0$ (or $u = u_0$), as shown in Fig. 2. In EPIs, lines with different slopes visualize points of different depths in the scene, which represents the relative motion between the spot and the camera. EPI has a highly clear structure compared with conventional photo images.

The goal of LF reconstruction is to recover a densely-sampled LFs with a resolution of $W \times H \times N \times M$ from a sparse one with a resolution of $W \times H \times n \times m$. Our framework combines 2D meta-learning based superresolution and 3D CNNs to first recover all 3D row volumes and then all 3D column volumes, building a pseudo-4DCNN for densely-sampled LF reconstruction. In this way, we can take full advantage of the 4D LF data as well as preventing heavy computational complexity. The presented framework will be comprehensively introduced in the next section.

Fig. 2. 3D row volume $V_{v_0}(x, y, u)$ of light field abstracted by fixing $v = v_0$.

3.2 Overview of the Presented Approach

As demonstrated in Fig. 3, we propose a new end-to-end network to apply a direct mapping between the input undersampled LF and the output densely-sampled LF. Our proposed network consists of two parts: arbitrary rate interpolation and detail refinement. The two parts are performed first on 3D row EPI volumes and then 3D column EPI volumes, connected by an angular conversion, forming a pseudo-4DCNN.

Given input sparse LF $L_{in}(x, y, u, v)$ with the size of (W, H, n, m), first we set angular coordinates $v = v_0, v_0 \in \{1, 2, ..., m\}$ to abstract 3D row EPI volumes with the size of (H, W, n)

$$V_{v_0}(x, y, u) = L_{in}(x, y, u, v_0) \tag{1}$$

A coarse reconstruction network $F(\cdot)$ based on meta-learning is performed on each EPI in $V_{v_0}(x, y, u)$ by fixing spatial axis $y = y_0, y_0 \in \{1, 2, ..., H\}$. As

$$E_{y_0,v_0}(x, u) = V_{v_0}(x, y_0, u) \tag{2}$$

$V_{v_0}(x, y, u)$ are interpolated as $V_{v_0}(x, y, u) \uparrow$ with the size of (W, H, N), where the upsampling factor is $f = N/n$ which is arbitrary

$$V_{v_0}(x, y_0, u) \uparrow = F\big(E_{y_0,v_0}(x, u), f\big) \tag{3}$$

Then an encoder-like network $Nr(\cdot)$ is followed to restore high-frequency details of $V_{v_0}(x, y, u) \uparrow$, forming the intermediate LF with the size of (W, H, N, m).

$$L_{inter}(x, y, u, v_0) = Nr\big(V_{v_0}(x, y, u) \uparrow\big) \tag{4}$$

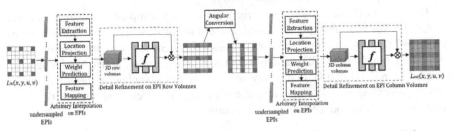

Fig. 3. The flow chart of the devised framework for restoring a densely-sampled LF from an undersampled one, taking 3×3 to 7×7 as instance.

Next, an angular conversion is performed to transfer the angular dimension from v to u. Similar operations are followed by fixing $u = u_0, u_0 \in \{1, 2, ..., N\}$ to get 3D column EPI volumes with the size of (W, H, m)

$$V_{u_0}(x, y, v) = L_{inter}(x, y, u_0, v) \tag{5}$$

which is also arbitrarily interpolated by the coarse reconstruction network $F(\cdot)$ to obtain $V_{u_0}(x, y, v) \uparrow$ with the size of (H, W, N)

$$E_{x_0, u_0}(y, v) = V_{u_0}(u_0, y, v) \tag{6}$$

$$V_{u_0}(x_0, y, v) \uparrow = F\left(E_{x_0, u_0}(y, v), f\right) \tag{7}$$

Finally, detail refinement network $Nc(\cdot)$ yields the output LF $L_{out}(x, y, u, v)$ with the size of (W, H, N, M)

$$L_{out}(x, y, u_0, v) = Nc\left(V_{u_0}(x, y, v) \uparrow\right) \tag{8}$$

3.3 Arbitrary Interpolation on EPIs

3D volumes $V_{v_0}(x, y, u)$ and $V_{u_0}(x, y, v)$ have two spatial axes and one angular axis as shown in Fig. 2. Take $V_{v_0}(x, y, u)$ for instance, this 3D volume can be considered as H stacked EPIs with the size of (W, n). And $V_{v_0}(x, y, u) \uparrow$ passed by reconstruction network $F(\cdot)$ can be regarded as H stacked EPIs with the size of (W, N), where $f = N/n$ is interpolation factor. We use the meta-learning-based network proposed in [23] to enable arbitrary f. Specifically, a feature learning module is settled to extract features from the low-resolution (LR) EPI, then the meta upsampling module dynamically predicted the weights of the upsampling filters by taking the interpolation factor as input and use these weights to generate the high-resolution (HR) EPI of arbitrary size. We modify the network to perform interpolation only on the angular dimension in EPI. Taking $E_{y_0, v_0}(x, u)$ as example, first we extract features of the low-resolution EPI, denoted $feature(H, n)$, then we use location projection for each pixel (W, N) on the HR EPI to find the corresponding pixel (W, n) on the LR EPI as

$$(W, n) = T(W, N) = \left(W, \left\lfloor \frac{N}{f} \right\rfloor\right) \tag{9}$$

where T is the transformation function, and $\lfloor \rfloor$ is floor function. The location coordinates through a fully connected network to learn the number and parameters of convolution kernels as

$$weight(H, N) = \varphi(V_{WN}; \theta) \tag{10}$$

$$V_{WN} = \left(W, \frac{N}{f} - \left\lfloor \frac{N}{f} \right\rfloor, \frac{1}{f}\right) \tag{11}$$

Finally, the feature mapping step maps *feature*(W, n) with *weight*(W, N) to get the final HR EPI as

$$\phi(feature(W, n), weight(W, N)) = feature(W, n)weight(W, N) \qquad (12)$$

where $\phi(\cdot)$ represents the feature mapping, and the matrix product is selected as the mapping function. In practice, we parallelly processed EPIs by setting y dimension in $V_{v_0}(x, y, u)$ and x dimension in $V_{u_0}(x, y, v)$ as batch size channel in $F(\cdot)$.

3.4 Detail Refinement on EPI Volum

It is challenging to directly operate on 4D LF due to the high computational complexity, and individually process EPIs cannot take full advantage of the 4D data. Inspired by [32], an encoder-like view refinement network is built to process stacked EPIs, which employs 3D CNNs and residual learning [34], making sure that both the angular and spatial information can be correlated and high-frequency details of the 3D volumes can be recovered.

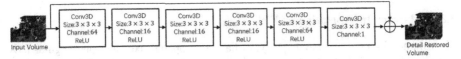

Fig. 4. Structure of the refinement network on 3D volumes. ReLU is added after every Conv3D layers except the last one. The summation of the prediction residual and the input is used as the output detail recovery volume.

The proposed networks $Nr(\cdot)$ and $Nc(\cdot)$ are of the same structure as shown in Fig. 4. Both networks consist of an encoder and a decoder, where both of them are totally symmetric with 3D convolution layers. The first layer consists of 64 channels with a $3 \times 3 \times 3$ kernel, where each kernel works on 3 neighboring EPIs. Analogously, the second layer comprises 16 channels with the kernel $3 \times 3 \times 3$. The last layer also comprises 16 channels with the kernel $3 \times 3 \times 3$. The stride of each layer is 1 and the activation is ReLU, i.e., $\sigma(x) = max(0, x)$, excepting for the last one. The summation of the prediction residual and the input 3D EPI volume is used as the network output. The input of each convolution layer is properly padded before feeding, making sure the spatial size of the output keep the same.

3.5 Edge Sensitive Loss Function

We design the presented approach to recover the 4D LF by inpainting all EPIs. Because the EPI is formed by a lot of lines, we proposed a loss function including three terms to enhance the edge pixels in the EPI.

The first term minimizes the weighted average over the overall MSE between the reconstructed L_{out} and the ground truth L_{gt} to provide a global optimization, formulated as,

$$E_s = \frac{1}{2N^2} \sum_{u_0=1}^{N} \sum_{v_0=1}^{N} \omega_{u_0,v_0} \left\| L_{gt}(u_0, v_0) - L_{out}(u_0, v_0) \right\|^2 \quad (13)$$

where ω_{u_0,v_0} denotes the prior sensitive weights introduced in [32]. Specifically, as shown in Fig. 3, generated views after the $Nr(\cdot)$ are predicted from the input views, while some of those generated after the $Nc(\cdot)$ obtain priori information broadcast from earlier generated views, consequently we use larger weights on later generated views, attaching more importance to their errors. As per the order that views are synthesized and the amount of obtained priori information, we divide the generated views into four parts and their MSE against the ground truth are added with different weights. The weight ω_{u_0,v_0} for the generated view at (u_0, v_0) is specifically given as

$$\omega_{u_0,v_0} = \begin{cases} 0.1, u_0 \in \left[1:f:N\right], v_0 \in \left[1:f:M\right] \\ 1, u_0 \in \left[1:f:N\right], v_0 \notin \left[1:f:M\right] \\ 1, u_0 \notin \left[1:f:N\right], v_0 \in \left[1:f:M\right] \\ 2, u_0 \notin \left[1:f:N\right], v_0 \notin \left[1:f:M\right] \end{cases} \quad (14)$$

As demonstrated in Fig. 1, EPI is composed of lines with different slopes, and has a very well-defined structure. To improve the EPI edge pixels, we use the MAE of the gradients (obtained by Sobel operator) of all output EPIs against the ground truth, denoted as Er and Ec respectively.

$$Er = \frac{1}{WN} \sum_{x_0=1}^{W} \sum_{u_0=1}^{N} \left\| \nabla L_{gt}(x_0, u_0) - \nabla L_{out}(x_0, u_0) \right\|_1 \quad (15)$$

$$Ec = \frac{1}{HM} \sum_{y_0=1}^{H} \sum_{v_0=1}^{M} \left\| \nabla L_{gt}(y_0, v_0) - \nabla L_{out}(y_0, v_0) \right\|_1 \quad (16)$$

where ∇ is the gradient operator. Both horizontal and vertical Sobel operator are used to enhance edge details.

The whole edge enhancement loss function is organized as

$$E = \lambda_1 E_s + \lambda_2 E_r + \lambda_3 E_c \quad (17)$$

Empirically, $\lambda_1, \lambda_2, \lambda_3$ are set to 1, 9 and 9 relatively.

4 Experiments and Results

4.1 Datasets and Training Details

We used real-world LF image datasets from Stanford Lytro LF Archive [35] and Kalantari et al. [19] as well as synthetic LF image datasets offered by the 4D light field benchmark

[36, 37] for training and test of the proposed framework. Concretely, we use 100 real-world scenes and 20 synthetic scenes for training. 70 real-world scenes from 3 datasets are utilized for test, that is 30scenes [19], Occlusions [35] and Reflective [35], which are captured by a Lytro Illum camera. As for synthetic scenes test, 4 scenes from the HCI dataset [36] and 5 scenes from the old HCI dataset [37] were used. Only the center 7×7 views are of each original LF data were cropped as ground truth. The input undersampled LFs are obtained by down sampling the ground truth to 2×2 and 3×3. For each LF data, we divided each view of the training data into 48×48 tiny patches with the stride of 20.

We process the data in RGB color space. The framework is implemented with PyTorch. The optimizer for end-to-end training is ADAM optimizer with $\beta_1 = 0.9$ and $\beta_2 = 0.999$. The batch size is 64. The initially learning rate is 10^{-4} and then decreased to one-tenth per 10 epochs until the convergence is verified. The arbitrary interpolation network was pre-trained with model provided by [23]. We use zero-mean Gaussian distribution with standard deviation of 0.01 to initialize the 3D CNN filters. In addition, all biases are initialized as zero.

4.2 Real-World Scenes

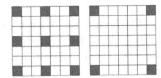

Fig. 5. Illustration of sampling patterns.

First, we reconstructed 7×7 LFs from both 3×3 and 2×2 sparse inputs to test the presented approach on real-world scenes, as demonstrated in Fig. 5. The result of comparative methods [19–21, 32] were procured by running the codes open-sourced by the corresponding authors. Mean value of PSNR and SSIM over entire views were employed for quantitative measurement of the quality of the restored densely-sampled LFs.

As to task 3×3 to 7×7, we compared with the approaches by Wu et al. [20], Wang et al. [32] and Wang et al. [33]. As shown in Table1, the performance of the presented framework surpasses those of the comparative methods on every dataset: with 2.675 dB superiority over Wu et al. [20], 0.511 dB over Wang et al. [32] and 0.376 dB over Wang et al. [33] in PSNR; and with 0.004 superiority over Wu et al. [20] and 0.034 over Wang et al. [33] in SSIM.

As to task 2×2 to 7×7, four corner views were used as input. We compared with other approaches (see Table 2), except the approach by Wang et al. [32] due to their method only accepts 3×3 inputs. The presented approach yields the best results. Two complex outdoor scenes containing discontinuous depth and occlusions, Rock and Flower2, were selected for visualization. The comparison of the reconstruction results with Kalantari et al. [19] are given in Fig. 6.

Table 1. Comparisons in PSNR and SSIM of our method compared with the state-of-the-art in 3×3 to 7×7 task on real-world scenes.

Approaches	Wu [20]	Wang [32]	Wang [33]	Ours
Occlusions16	38.862/0.985	–	34.690/0.923	**39.124/0.989**
Reflective29	46.101/0.993	–	39.934/0.959	**47.203/0.995**
30scenes	41.025/0.988	43.280/0.992	43.822/**0.993**	**43.833**/0.993
Average	41.116/0.988	43.280/0.992	43.415/0.990	**43.791/0.993**

Table 2. Comparisons in PSNR and SSIM of our method compared with the state-of-the-art in 2×2 to 7×7 task on real-world scenes.

Approaches	Kalantari [19]	Wu [20]	Wu [21]	Ours
Occlusions	37.250/0.972	32.727/0.924	34.416/0.955	**38.170/0.980**
Reflective	38.091/0.953	34.760/0.930	36.381/0.944	**38.261/0.957**
30scenes	41.402/0.982	33.662/0.918	39.171/0.975	**42.151/0.988**
Average	38.590/0.969	33.551/0.924	36.235/0.957	**39.252/0.976**

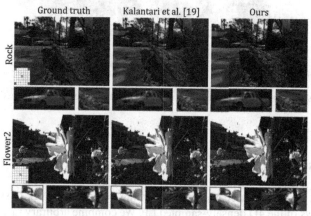

Fig. 6. Visual comparison between Kalantari et al. [19] and the presented framework in real-world scenes.

4.3 Synthetic Scenes

As to experiments on synthetic scenes, 9 synthetic LF images were used with angular resolution of 9×9. 4 of them are from the HCI [36] dataset and the rest are from the old HCI [37] dataset. The center 7×7 views were cropped as ground truth, and 4 corner views are used as input. Table 3 displays the quantitative results of our approach on two datasets against other approaches. Our proposed method provides 1.84 dB reconstruction advantage over the second best among others in terms of PSNR and 0.026 advantage in terms of SSIM. Fig. 7 shows some of the visual comparison with the second best algorithm.

Table 3. Comparisons in PSNR and SSIM of our method compared with the most advanced methods in 2 × 2 to 7 × 7 task on synthetic scenes.

Approaches	Kalantari [19]	Wu [20]	Wu [21]	Ours
HCI	32.852/0.909	26.640/0.744	31.842/0.898	**35.144/0.950**
HCI old	38.581/0.944	31.431/0.850	37.613/0.942	**40.060/0.957**
Average	36.035/0.928	29.302/0.803	35.048/0.922	**37.875/0.954**

Fig. 7. Visual comparison of Kalantari et al. [19] and our method on synthetic scenes.

5   Conclusion

In this article, we present a coarse-to-fine learning-based framework to straightly generate new views of the 4D densely-sampled LF. We combine arbitrary rate interpolation network for coarse EPI restoration and 3DCNNs for 3D EPI volume detail refinement, and forming a pseudo-4DCNN which can take full advantage of the 4D LF data while avoiding heavy computational complexity. Our framework first reconstructs an intermediate LF by recovering 3D row EPI volumes, then works on 3D column EPI volumes to obtain the final densely-sampled LF. In addition, meta learning is utilized to upsample EPIs in the coarse reconstruction network, which enables arbitrary interpolation rate with one model. All modules in our approach are differentiable, leading to an end-to-end trainable network. Experimental results prove that our framework surpasses other state-of-the-art approaches on both real-world and synthetic LF images.

References

1. Levoy, M., Hanrahan, P.: Light field rendering. In: Computer Graphics (1996)
2. Ihrke, I., et al.: Principles of light field imaging: briefly revisiting 25 years of research. IEEE Signal Process. Mag. **33**(5), 59–69 (2016)
3. Fiss, J., et al.: Refocusing plenoptic images using depth-adaptive splatting. In: ICCP. IEEE (2014)
4. Kim, C., et al.: Scene reconstruction from high spatio-angular resolution light fields. ACM Trans. Graph. **32**(4), 1–12 (2013)
5. Chen, J., et al.: Accurate light field depth estimation with superpixel regularization over partially occluded regions. IEEE Trans. Image Process. **27**(10), 4889–4900 (2018)
6. Huang, F.C., et al.: The light field stereoscope: immersive computer graphics via factored near-eye light field displays with focus cues. ACM Trans. Graph. **34**(4), 60 (2015)
7. Chai, J., Tong, X., Chan, S., et al.: Plenoptic sampling. In: Proceedings of ACM SIGGRAPH 2000 (2000)
8. Wilburn, B., et al.: High performance imaging using large camera arrays. ACM Trans. Graph. **24**(3), 765–776 (2005)
9. Gortler, S.J., Grzeszczuk, R., Szeliski, R., et al.: The lumigraph. In: Association for Computing Machinery SIGGRAPH Computer Graphics, p. 96 (2001)
10. Davis, A., et al.: Unstructured light fields. In: Computer Graphics Forum. Wiley (2012)
11. Lytro illum. https://lightfield-forum.com/lytro/
12. Raytrix. https://lightfield-forum.com/raytrix/
13. Penner, E., et al.: Soft 3D reconstruction for view synthesis. ACM Trans. Graph. **36**(6), 235.1–235.11 (2017)
14. Flynn, J., et al.: Deep stereo: learning to predict new views from the world's imagery. In: 2016 IEEE Conference on Computer Vision and Pattern Recognition (CVPR). IEEE (2016)
15. Marwah, K., et al.: Compressive light field photography using overcomplete dictionaries and optimized projections. ACM Trans. Graph. (TOG) **32**(4), 46.1–46.12 (2013)
16. Shi, L., et al.: Light field reconstruction using sparsity in the continuous fourier domain. ACM Trans. Graph. **34**(1), 1–13 (2014)
17. Vagharshakyan, S., et al.: Light field reconstruction using Shearlet transform. IEEE Trans. Pattern Anal. Mach. Intell. **PP**(1), 133–147 (2018)
18. Vagharshakyan, S., Bregovic, R., Gotchev, A.: Light field reconstruction using Shearlet transform. IEEE Trans. Pattern Anal. Mach. Intell. **40**(1), 133–147 (2018)
19. Kalantari, N.K., et al.: Learning-based view synthesis for light field cameras. ACM Trans. Graph. **35**(6), 193 (2016)
20. Wu, G., et al.: Light Field Reconstruction Using Convolutional Network on EPI and Extended Applications. IEEE Trans. Pattern Anal. Mach. Intell. **41**, 1681–1694 (2018)
21. Wu, G., et al.: Learning sheared EPI structure for light field reconstruction. IEEE Trans. Image Process. **28**, 3261–3273 (2019)
22. Yoon, Y., et al.: Learning a deep convolutional network for light-field image super-resolution. In: ICCV. IEEE (2015)
23. Hu, X., et al.: Meta-SR: a magnification-arbitrary network for super-resolution. In: 2019 IEEE/CVF CVPR (2020)
24. Chaurasia, G., et al.: Depth synthesis and local warps for plausible image-based navigation. ACM Trans. Graph. **32**(3), 1–2 (2013)
25. Srinivasan, P.P., et al.: Learning to synthesize a 4D RGBD light field from a single image. In: ICCV. IEEE (2017)
26. Zhou, T., et al.: Stereo magnification: learning view synthesis using multiplane images. ACM Trans. Graph., 1–12 (2018)

27. Mildenhall, B., et al.: Local light field fusion. ACM Trans. Graph., 1–14 (2019)
28. Lin, Z., et al.: A geometric analysis of light field rendering: special issue on research at microsoft corporation. Int. J. Comput. Vis. **58**(2), 121–138 (2004). https://doi.org/10.1023/B:VISI.0000015916.91741.27
29. Levin, A., et al.: Linear view synthesis using a dimensionality gap light field prior. In: CVPR. IEEE (2010)
30. Wu, G., et al.: Lapepi-Net: a Laplacian pyramid EPI structure for learning-based dense light field reconstruction (2019)
31. Yoon, Y., Jeon, Hae-Gon., Yoo, D., Lee, Joon-Young., Kweon, I.: Light-field image super-resolution using convolutional neural network. IEEE Signal Process. Lett. **24**(6), 848–852 (2017)
32. Wang, Y., Liu, F., Wang, Z., Hou, G., Sun, Z., Tan, T.: End-to-end view synthesis for light field imaging with pseudo 4DCNN. In: Ferrari, V., Hebert, M., Sminchisescu, C., Weiss, Y. (eds.) ECCV 2018. LNCS, vol. 11206, pp. 340–355. Springer, Cham (2018). https://doi.org/10.1007/978-3-030-01216-8_21
33. Wang, Y., et al.: High-fidelity view synthesis for light field imaging with extended pseudo 4DCNN. IEEE Trans. Comput. Imaging **6**, 830–842 (2020)
34. He, K., Zhang, X., Ren, S., et al.: Deep residual learning for image recognition. In: CVPR. IEEE (2016)
35. Raj, A.S., et al.: Stanford lytro light field archive. https://lightfields.stanford.edu/
36. Honauer, K., Johannsen, O., Kondermann, D., Goldluecke, B.: A dataset and evaluation methodology for depth estimation on 4D light fields. In: Lai, S.-H., Lepetit, V., Nishino, K., Sato, Y. (eds.) ACCV 2016. LNCS, vol. 10113, pp. 19–34. Springer, Cham (2017). https://doi.org/10.1007/978-3-319-54187-7_2
37. Wanner, S., et al.: Datasets and benchmarks for densely sampled 4D light fields. The Eurographics Association (2013)

Light Field Image Depth Estimation Method Based on Super-Resolution Cooperative Reconstruction

Ming Yang, Shigang Wang$^{(\boxtimes)}$, Xuejun Wang$^{(\boxtimes)}$, Jian Wei, and Yan Zhao

College of Communication Engineering, Jilin University,
Nanhu Road No. 5372, Changchun 130012, China
wangshigang@vip.sina.com, xjwang@jlu.edu.cn

Abstract. In order to improve image resolution in depth estimation, this paper proposes a method of simultaneous super-resolution reconstruction and light field image depth estimation. In this paper, the SRCNN super-resolution algorithm was used for the super-resolution reconstruction of two intermediate images in the depth estimation process, to improve the resolution of the final output image. In the proposed method, the SRCNN algorithm is used in the depth estimation map $f(x)$ of the input picture pixels firstly, and then the algorithm is used for the second time in the confidence reduction process of the occlusion boundary area, so that the super-resolution reconstruction and the depth of the image proceed simultaneously. Over above two steps processing, the observable improvement of the detail information of the enlarged image can be noted through the senses, and the objective evaluation index—PSNR is also significantly improved.

1 Introduction

Depth estimation is an active research area in the field of stereo vision and light field display. Since depth information is instrumental in understanding three-dimensional scenes, it plays an extremely necessary role in the field of integrated imaging. Three-dimensional reconstruction is a key step in integrated imaging; the generation of depth maps and the effects of depth maps directly affect the results of three-dimensional reconstruction.

In order to make depth maps more effective and facilitate subsequent research, many researchers have developed various methods to make depth estimation results more accurate. Since depth information has a strong relationship with the relative positions of the objects in the light field image, the problem of occlusion between objects brings challenges to the estimation of the depth.

This work was supported by a grant from the National Natural Science Foundation of China (No. 61631009); supported by the national key research and development plan of the 13th five-year plan (No. 2017YFB0404800); supported by 'The Fundamental Research Funds for the Central Universities' under the grant No. 2017TD-19.

G. Zhai et al. (Eds.): IFTC 2020, CCIS 1390, pp. 415–428, 2021.
https://doi.org/10.1007/978-981-16-1194-0_35

Jia et al. proposed a depth perception method that combines omnidirectional images with structured light coding [5], which solves the effect of occlusion between objects to a certain extent, and can also obtain relatively complete object depth information in larger scenes. Chen et al. focused on the regularized confidence map and texture edge weights, and analyzed the geometric sources of depth uncertainty caused by partial occlusion boundary regions (POBR) [1].

In addition to the effects of occlusion, the clarity of the depth map is also a key factor in considering image quality. Especially in three-dimensional imaging technology, the demand for high-resolution depth images is gradually increasing. Therefore, effectively and directly improving the resolution of depth images has become another issue that needs to be addressed urgently. Image super-resolution reconstruction is a classic problem. With the rapid development of artificial intelligence technology, convolutional neural networks are gradually being applied in this area. The SRCNN is the first end-to-end super-resolution algorithm that uses the CNN structure (that is, based on deep learning). The entire algorithm is implemented with a deep learning method, and its effect is better than the traditional multi-module integration method. While focusing on the regularized confidence map and texture edge weights, the proposed method uses the SRCNN algorithm to perform super-resolution reconstruction of the depth map, which further improves the resolution of the generated depth image. When the image is enlarged, the boundary details of the object are not lost and blurred, and the original image detail information is retained.

Compared to traditional methods, the innovations of this paper are as follows: In this paper, the SRCNN super-resolution algorithm was used to improve the resolution of the depth map, and in the process of depth estimation, the SRCNN algorithm was used for several intermediate images, so that the depth estimation and super-resolution are performed simultaneously, instead of postprocessing the depth map. The PSNR of the depth map generated by the method is significantly enhanced.

2   Related Work

Many researchers have studied the occlusion boundary of the depth map, and improved the effect of the depth map. Li et al. proposed a depth estimation algorithm based on frequency descriptors. It is recommended to perform occlusion recognition and edge direction extraction in the frequency domain for space debris, from the central sub-aperture image to improve the depth accuracy [7]. Ikeoka et al. proposed a new method using a tilted lens optical system, which can obtain the depth value of each pixel from the sharpness ratio of two tilted optical images; they used a neural network to calculate the depth from the blur value and y coordinate value to reduce the error [4]. Zhang et al. proposed a system based on the joint fusion of stereo and Kinect data to achieve high-resolution depth estimation. The estimated depth map is guided by color image depth trimming and is based on 2D polynomials. The filtering of regression (LPR) has been studied further to improve image resolution [11] Hambarde et al. proposed a two-stream depth confrontation network for single-image depth estimation in RGB images, and also designed a feature map sharing architecture. Shared feature maps can enhance residual learning to estimate the depth of the scene, and can improve the robustness of the proposed network [3]. Mun et al. proposed a light field depth estimation method based on a convolutional residual network, which deals with the discontinuity problem in the depth map, by calculating the depth cost map in the residual network [8]. Lee et al. used the color shift feature of MCA to provide a camera-based full depth map estimation. Their method can not only estimate the entire depth map, but can also correct misaligned images using a single camera equipped with MCA to generate realistic color images [6]. Senoh et al. proposed a high-quality fast depth estimation method based on non-iterative edge adaptive local cost optimization, which estimates the depth image by evaluating the cost function involving three-view matching errors and depth continuity terms [9]; the experimental results show that the speed of depth estimation has been improved. Elaraby et al. proposed a 3D object detection and recognition system with an enhanced depth estimation algorithm, which is based on Microsoft Kinect, and uses the latest deep neural network (DNN) for object detection and recognition. Compared to the traditional algorithms, the accuracy of the depth map has been improved [2].

3   Using the SILC Algorithm to Obtain Precise Boundary Information

Because of the mutual occlusion between objects in the light field image, the accurate analysis of the partially occlusion boundary region (POBR) has become the key to depth estimation. In order to improve resolution while estimating the depth, we must obtain more accurate boundary information of the occluded area firstly. The super pixel algorithm combines pixels into meaningful atomic regions. After segmentation, the boundaries of each region coincide with the boundaries of the objects in the image, and will not be affected by occlusion. The super-pixel algorithm merges the occlusion information of the occluded object, and obtains the accurate occlusion information of the object boundary area. In this study, the Simple Linear Clustering (SLIC) super pixel algorithm is used, which is faster than other general algorithms and shows the best boundary characteristics.

By default, the algorithm has only one parameter: the number k of super pixels, with generally the same size. The clustering process of the whole algorithm starts from the initialization step, that is, k initial cluster centers $C_i = [l_i, a_i, b_i, x_i, y_i]^T$ are sampled in a regular network with an interval of S pixels. The interval of the network is $S = \sqrt{\dfrac{N}{K}}$ so that the size of the super pixels produced can be roughly the same. In order to not locate the super pixel at the boundary, the center is moved to the seed position corresponding to the lowest gradient position in the 3×3 neighborhood. In the next step, every pixel is related to the nearest cluster center where the search area and its position overlap, as shown in Fig. 1. This step speeds up the algorithm, because the limitation on the size of the search area reduces the number of distance calculations. This advantage can only be achieved by introducing the measurement distance d, which determines the nearest cluster center of every pixel. Since the expected spatial range of the super pixel is an area of approximate size $S \times S$, a search for similar pixels is performed in the area $2S \times 2S$ around the center of the super pixel.

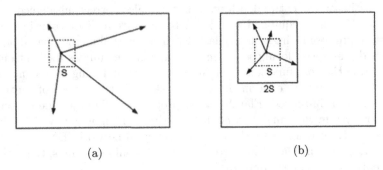

(a)   (b)

Fig. 1. Reducing the search area of super pixels. (a) In the algorithm with mean k, the calculated distance from each cluster center to each pixel in the image. (b) The SLIC algorithm only calculates the distance from each cluster center to the pixels in the $2S \times 2S$ area.

It should be noted that the desired super pixel size is only $S \times S$, represented by the smaller square. This method not only reduces the distance calculation, but also makes the complexity of the SILC independent of the number of super pixels.

When each pixel has been associated with the nearest cluster center, the cluster center is adjusted to the average vector of all pixels belonging to the cluster $[l, a, b, x, y]^T$, and the $L2$ norm is used to calculate the residual error B between the positions of the previous cluster center and the new cluster center. Next, multiple allocation steps are iterated and the steps are updated, with a general image requiring about 10 iterations. Finally, connectivity is implemented by reallocating disjoint pixels to nearby super pixels.

4   SRCNN Network

For improving the resolution of depth images, this paper uses super-resolution algorithms. The task of super-resolution is to convert the low-resolution input image into a high-resolution image, which is in the same vein as image denoising and image deblurring. Super resolution is concerned with filling in new pixels in large images obtained from smaller ones. The SRCNN is the first end-to-end super-resolution algorithm that uses CNN structure (based on deep learning). The general outline is: first, the preprocessing of the input image is done, and the bicubic algorithm is used to enlarge the input low-resolution image to the target size. Next, the goal of the algorithm is to process the relatively fuzzy and low-resolution input image through the convolutional network, to obtain a super-resolution image, making it as similar as possible to the original high-resolution image.

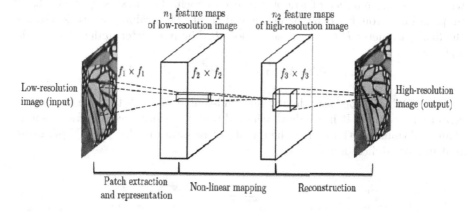

Fig. 2. SRCNN network structure

The network structure of the SRCNN is relatively simple. As shown in Fig. 2, the entire convolutional network has three convolutional layers, without pooling and fully connected layers. The algorithm could be summarized as follows:

1. Convolution operations are performed on low-resolution images to generate n_1-dimensional feature maps.
2. A convolution operation is performed on the n_1-dimensional feature map to generate n_2-dimensional feature maps.
3. Convolution of n_2-dimensional feature maps is performed to generate super-resolution images.

These convolutional layers correspond to three processing flows respectively:

1. Image feature extraction: multiple patch image blocks are extracted from low-resolution images. Each block is represented by a convolution operation as a multi-dimensional vector, and all feature vectors form the feature maps.
2. Nonlinear mapping: the n_1-dimensional feature matrix is turned into another n_2-dimensional feature matrix through convolution, to achieve nonlinear mapping.
3. Reconstruction: It is equivalent to the process of deconvolution, which restores the feature matrix of dimension n_2 to a super-resolution image.

The optimized parameters of the training model are the convolution kernel (W) and bias (b) corresponding to the three-layer convolution layer, with parameters $P = \{W_1, W_2, W_3, b_1, b_2, b_3\}$. The target loss function for training has to minimize the pixel-based mean square error between the super-resolution image $F(Y; P)$ and the original high-resolution image X, which is defined as follows:

$$L(\Theta) = \frac{1}{m} \sum_{i=1}^{m} \|F(Y_i; \Theta) - X_i\|^2 \qquad (1)$$

where m is the number of samples in each epoch. The next step is the back propagation through stochastic gradient descent. The training network obtains the final parameter P to minimize the loss L. The parameter update formula is as follows:

$$\Delta_{i+1} = 0.9 \cdot \Delta_i + \eta \cdot \frac{\partial L}{\partial W_i^l}, W_{i+1}^l = W_i^l + \Delta_{i+1} \qquad (2)$$

The SRCNN proposes a lightweight end-to-end network to solve the super-resolution problem. It has indeed achieved better performance and faster speed than traditional methods. For the quality of restoration, the SRCNN performs best in most indicators.

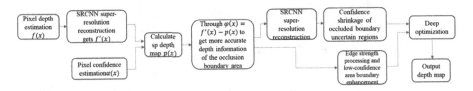

Fig. 3. Algorithm flow chart of this paper

5   Algorithm Flow

5.1   Initial Pixel Depth Estimation and Determination of Confidence Map

The overall flow chart of the proposed algorithm is shown in Fig. 3. The input of the proposed algorithm can be an $n \times n$ (n is an odd number) multi-viewpoint image. First, the multi-viewpoint image is synthesized into a normal 2D image, and then the following operations are performed on this image: the depth $f(x)$ of its pixels is calculated, and its confidence level $\alpha(x)$ is estimated pixel by pixel. The process of matching depth can be regarded as comparing the changes of pixel intensity in different directions along the epipolar plane image, calculating the angle variance along the possible directions; the direction that produces the smallest variance is the best, and its slope represents the depth of the scene. For the depth f' corresponding to a given slope, the formula for calculating the angle variance is:

$$\sigma_{f'}(x_n)^2 = \frac{1}{N_u - 1} \sum_{u'} \left[L\left(x_n + u'\left(1 - \frac{f_0}{f'}\right), u'\right) - \bar{L}_{f'}(x_n) \right]^2. \qquad (3)$$

According to this formula, the initial depth is obtained by solving the following formulae:

$$f(x) = \arg\min_{f'} C_{f'}(x), \tag{4}$$

$$C_d(x) = \sum_{x' \in W_\sigma} e^{\dfrac{-[L(X',0) - L(x,0)]^2}{2\eta^2}} \sigma_d(x), \tag{5}$$

where, η is the bilateral filter parameter, which is used to control the contribution of adjacent pixels to the intensity similarity of x. For each depth $f(x)$, the confidence level of depth estimation can be obtained according to the following formula:

$$\alpha(x) = N\left\{ \frac{\mathrm{mean}_{f'} C_{f'}(x)}{\min_{f''} C_{f''}(x)} \right\} \tag{6}$$

5.2　Application of SRCNNN Super-Resolution Algorithm

Next, we use the SRCNN super-resolution algorithm for reconstructing $f(x)$, the steps are outlined as follows:

1. The depth map $f(x)$ is zoomed to the target size using bi-cubic difference (such as zooming in twice, thrice, and so on). In this study, the zooming was done 4 times, at this time it is still called the zoomed in to the target size the image is "a low-resolution image".
2. The Y channel is reconstructed in the $YCrCb$ color space.
3. Low-resolution images are taken as inputs into a three-layer convolutional neural network. The size of the convolution kernel of the first convolution layer is 9×9, the number of convolution kernels is 64, and 64 feature maps form the output. The size of the convolution kernel of the second convolution layer is 1×1, the number of convolution kernels is 32, and 32 feature maps form the output. The size of the convolution kernel of the third convolution layer is 5×5, the number of convolution kernels is 1, and the output of 1 feature map is the final reconstructed high-resolution image. We define the output image as $f'(x)$.

5.3　Confidence Reduction of Occluded Boundary Uncertain Regions

Since the depth information at the occlusion boundary of the object is often not very accurate, and the depth map $p(x)$ obtained by the sp algorithm and super-resolution processing can reflect more accurate depth information, the result of the following formula can describe the occlusion boundary area more accurately:

$$\varphi(x) = f(x) - p(x). \tag{7}$$

Based on this equation, the contraction function $\xi_{oc}(x)$ is defined to describe the original confidence map $\alpha(x)$ of the occlusion boundary:

$$\xi_{oc}(x) = \begin{cases} \dfrac{2}{1 + e^{-\varphi(x)}} & \varphi(x) < 0, \\ 1 & \varphi(x) \geq 0. \end{cases} \tag{8}$$

After obtaining $\xi_{oc}(x)$, the SRCNN super-resolution algorithm is used for reconstructing $\xi_{oc}(x)$, as described in Sect. 5.2 to reconstruct its high-resolution image, and the output result is denoted by $\xi'_{oc}(x)$. At the same time, the initial confidence level $\alpha(x)$ on the initial depth estimate is shrunk according to the following formula:

$$\xi_{var}(x) = \begin{cases} \dfrac{2}{1 + e^{(L_d(x) - \Lambda_v)}} & L_d(x) > \Lambda_v, \\ 1 & L_d(x) < \Lambda_v. \end{cases} \tag{9}$$

where, $L_d(x)$ is the spatial variance of the occluded local area, and Λ_v is the threshold of variance. Finally, an accurate confidence map is obtained, denoted by $\hat{\alpha}(x)$:

$$\hat{\alpha}(x) = \alpha(x) \cdot \xi'_{oc}(x) \cdot \xi_{var}(x) \tag{10}$$

5.4   Edge Intensity Processing and Edge Enhancement on Low-Confidence Regions

Next, in order to make the edge of the object in the depth map more accurately coincide with the edge of the original image, the following operation is introduced:

$$\eta_{oc}(x) = \begin{cases} 1 + \gamma_1 \cos\left(\dfrac{\pi}{2}\xi_{oc}(x)\right) & \varphi(x) < 0, \\ 1 & \varphi(x) \geq 0. \end{cases} \tag{11}$$

where, $\gamma_1 \in [1, +\infty)$ is the coefficient that controls edge enhancement. The larger γ_1 is, the higher is the contrast of the occluded edge, and unwanted noise appears. Here, γ_1 is set to 5. Subsequently, the edge weight should be added to the region with extremely low confidence, so that the depth discontinuity is reduced:

$$\eta_{conf}(x) = \begin{cases} 1 + \gamma_2 \cos\left(\dfrac{\pi}{2}\alpha(x)\right) & \alpha(x) < \Lambda_c, \\ 1 & \alpha(x) \geq \Lambda_c. \end{cases} \tag{12}$$

where, Λ_c is the threshold of the low-confidence area, and the coefficient $\gamma_2 \in [1, +\infty)$ controls the degree of edge reinforcement. In this paper, Λ_c is set to 0.1 and γ_2 is set to 2.

5.5   In-Depth Optimization

This study combines the label confidence map and the strength weight of the border into the global regularization framework:

$$\left[\min_{\hat{f}(x)} \sum_x \hat{\alpha}(x)\|\hat{f}(x) - f(x)\|^2\right] + \mu \sum_x \sum_{y \in \Omega_x} \frac{\|\hat{f}(x) - \hat{f}(y)\|^2}{|I(x) - I(y)| \cdot \eta_{oc}(x) \cdot \eta_{conf}(x)} \tag{13}$$

where, the first term is the fidelity term re-weighted using the accurate confidence map $\hat{a}(x)$, the second term is the smoothness term enhanced with $\eta_{oc}(x) \cdot \eta_{conf}(x)$ for edge strength, μ is the control parameter of smoothness and fidelity constraints, and x represents the four views closest to the center view. Equation (13) is a least-squares problem. For large system of linear equations, the problem can be solved efficiently [10]. Confidence and edge strength operations are very important for low-complexity weighted least-squares models, especially for occluded boundary regions to produce good depth estimation effects. Therefore, with the application of the algorithm, the object edge information of the final depth map will be more accurate, and the image will be clearer.

6   Experimental Results

Sixteen 4×4 light field cameras with a resolution of 1280×1024 were used in the laboratory to take pictures of volunteers. The 16 cameras were distributed on the same sphere, and the volunteers stood on a stage. The overall assembly diagram of the light field camera is shown in Fig. 4, and the 16 viewpoint images obtained are shown in Fig. 5.

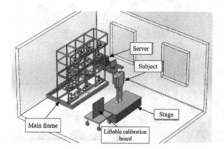

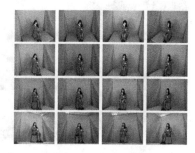

Fig. 4. Overall assembly diagram of the light field

Fig. 5. 16 multi-viewpoint images taken camera array

A total of 9 3×3 multi-view images were selected from 16 multi-view images, as the input of this experiment, and the output image was the depth map of the light field image. Since the input provides more viewpoints, the synthesized image contains more information about the scene. Compared to a single image input, the depth image output in the experiment has more accurate depth information in each part of the image, and the boundary of the object is clearer. Figure 6 shows the experimental results of this study, the results before applying the SRCNN algorithm, and the experimental results of a single image input.

Next, an $n \times n$ (n is an odd number) multi-viewpoint image was used in the 4D light field data set as input, that is, after clicking Run, all the $n \times n$ multi-viewpoint images of a scene were selected in the folder at the same time, and the output image was the light field image depth map, as shown. The following

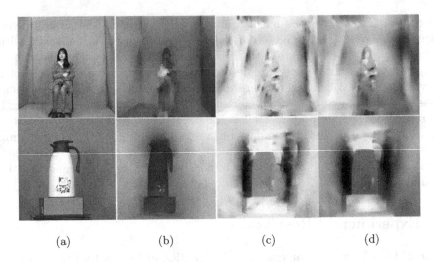

Fig. 6. (a) Light field image. (b) The depth image obtained when a single image is used as input. (c) Multi-viewpoint image input and the depth image obtained without the application of the SRCNN algorithm. (d) Multi-viewpoint image input and the depth image obtained by application of the SRCNN algorithm twice.

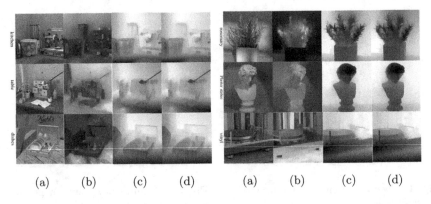

Fig. 7. (a) Light field image. (b) The depth image obtained when a single image is used as input. (c) Multi-viewpoint image input and the depth image obtained without the application of the SRCNN algorithm. (d) Multi-viewpoint image input and the depth image obtained by application of the SRCNN algorithm twice.

figure shows the experimental results of this study, the results before applying the SRCNN algorithm and the experimental results of a single image input.

It can be seen from Fig. 7 that, compared to a single image input, multi-viewpoint inputs are more conducive to depth estimation and reflect more details of the original image. As the super-resolution algorithm focuses on retaining the boundary details of the original image after zooming in, Fig. 8 and Fig. 9 show the difference in the boundary details of the object before and after the application of the SRCNN algorithm, once the image is enlarged by a certain integer multiple.

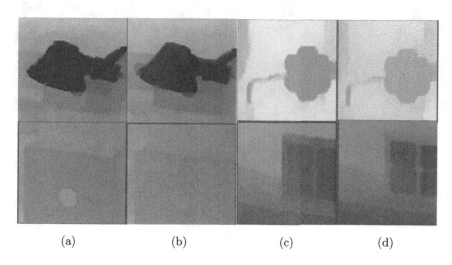

(a)   (b)   (c)   (d)

Fig. 8. After the picture is enlarged by a certain integer multiple, the difference in the boundary details of the object before and after the application of the SRCNN algorithm. (a) and (c) show the boundary details of objects before the application of the SRCNN algorithm. (b) and (d) show the boundary details of the objects processed with the SRCNN algorithm.

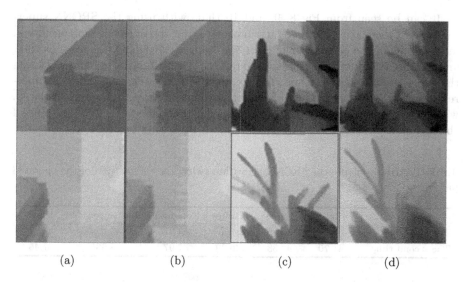

(a)   (b)   (c)   (d)

Fig. 9. After the picture is enlarged by a certain integer multiple, the difference in the boundary details of the object before and after the application of the SRCNN algorithm. (a) and (c) show the boundary details of objects before the application of the SRCNN algorithm. (b) and (d) show the boundary details of the objects processed with the SRCNN algorithm.

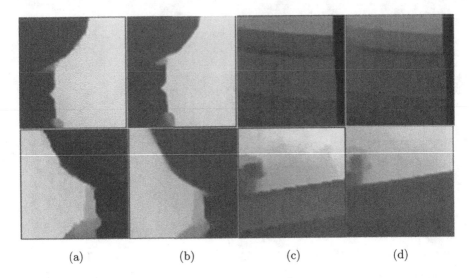

| (a) | (b) | (c) | (d) |

Fig. 10. After the picture is enlarged by a certain multiple, the difference in the boundary details of the object before and after the application of the SRCNN algorithm. (a) and (c) show the boundary details of objects before the application of the SRCNN algorithm. (b) and (d) show the boundary details of the objects processed by the SRCNN algorithm.

It can be seen from Fig. 8, 9, and 10 that, with using the SRCNN super-resolution processing, the boundary information of the object is more accurate, more details of the original image can be retained, the edge lines are smoother, and aliasing is reduced. In addition, to quantitatively analyze the effect of using the super-resolution algorithms, the commonly used evaluation index of super-resolution-PSNR is used. The PSNR of the two intermediate images is calculated, where the algorithm is applied. The following table shows the PSNR value of the operated picture after adding the SRCNN algorithm twice.

Table 1. After applying the SRCNN algorithm twice, the PSNR (dB) of the operated picture.

	Kitchen	Table	Dishes	Rosemary	Plaster statue	Vinyl
The first time	57.28	57.89	57.47	57.97	59.98	57.07
The second time	41.70	43.33	46.39	57.97	38.66	37.45

From the data in Table 1, it can be seen that the PSNR of the picture has been significantly improved after the algorithm is used twice, and the PSNR of the two operations on the experimental picture is approximately 40 dB, which shows that the application of super-resolution reconstruction of the intermediate picture twice has the desired effect. In addition, the standard depth map of the light field image in the data set was obtained, the RMSE was calculated between the image before and after the application of the algorithm and the standard depth map, and the comparison results of which, are shown in Table 2.

Table 2. Before and after applying the SRCNN algorithm, the root mean square error (rmse) between the image and the standard depth map.

	Kitchen	Table	Dishes	Rosemary	Plaster statue	Vinyl
Before adding algorithm	3.47%	2.75%	18.58%	6.20%	15.00%	5.26%
After adding algorithm	3.31%	2.67%	18.04%	5.26%	13.68%	5.12%

It can be seen from the data in Table 2 that the RMSE of the depth map and the standard depth map obtained after applying the algorithm is reduced to a certain extent, compared to when the algorithm was not applied. This shows that the details of the depth map obtained after applying the algorithm is closer to the standard depth image. After the effects of the two algorithm processes are superimposed, the resolution of the final depth map generated in this study is a substantial improvement. Compared to the image before processing, the enlarged image can retain more image detail information.

7   Conclusion

To improve image resolution in depth estimation, this paper uses the SRCNN super-resolution algorithm to obtain the super-resolution reconstruction of the two intermediate images in the depth estimation process, which improves the resolution of the final output image. In this method, the SRCNN algorithm is first used in the depth estimation map $f(x)$ of the pixels of the input picture; the second time, the algorithm is used in the confidence reduction process of the occlusion boundary area, so that the super-resolution reconstruction and the depth estimation of the image are done at the same time. After two applications of the algorithm, the improvement of the detail information can be observed by the senses once the image is enlarged, and the PSNR of the objective evaluation index is also significantly improved.

References

1. Chen, J., Hou, J., Ni, Y., Chau, L.P.: Accurate light field depth estimation with superpixel regularization over partially occluded regions. IEEE Trans. Image Process. **27**(10), 4889–4900 (2018)
2. Elaraby, A.F., Hamdy, A., Rehan, M.: A kinect-based 3D object detection and recognition system with enhanced depth estimation algorithm. In: 2018 IEEE 9th Annual Information Technology, Electronics and Mobile Communication Conference (IEMCON), pp. 247–252. IEEE (2018)

3. Hambarde, P., Dudhane, A., Murala, S.: Single image depth estimation using deep adversarial training. In: 2019 IEEE International Conference on Image Processing (ICIP), pp. 989–993. IEEE (2019)
4. Ikeoka, H., Hamamoto, T.: Depth estimation from tilted optics blur by using neural network. In: 2018 International Workshop on Advanced Image Technology (IWAIT), pp. 1–4. IEEE (2018)
5. Jia, T., Wang, B., Zhou, Z., Meng, H.: Scene depth perception based on omnidirectional structured light. IEEE Trans. Image Process. **25**(9), 4369–4378 (2016)
6. Lee, S., Lee, J., Hayes, M.H., Katsaggelos, A.K., Paik, J.: Single camera-based full depth map estimation using color shifting property of a multiple color-filter aperture. In: 2012 IEEE International Conference on Acoustics, Speech and Signal Processing (ICASSP), pp. 801–804. IEEE (2012)
7. Li, J., Jin, X.: Frequency descriptor based light field depth estimation. In: 2019 IEEE Visual Communications and Image Processing (VCIP), pp. 1–4. IEEE (2019)
8. Mun, J.H., Ho, Y.S.: Depth estimation from light field images via convolutional residual network. In: 2018 Asia-Pacific Signal and Information Processing Association Annual Summit and Conference (APSIPA ASC), pp. 1495–1498. IEEE (2018)
9. Senoh, T., Wakunami, K., Sasaki, H., Oi, R., Yamamoto, K.: Fast depth estimation using non-iterative local optimization for super multi-view images. In: 2015 IEEE Global Conference on Signal and Information Processing (GlobalSIP), pp. 1042–1046. IEEE (2015)
10. Strutz, T.: Data Fitting and Uncertainty: A Practical Introduction to Weighted Least Squares and Beyond. Springer Vieweg, Wiesbaden (2010)
11. Zhang, S., Wang, C., Chan, S.: A new high resolution depth map estimation system using stereo vision and depth sensing device. In: 2013 IEEE 9th International Colloquium on Signal Processing and its Applications, pp. 49–53. IEEE (2013)

Light Field Stitching Based on Mesh Deformation

Chao Xue, Yilei Chen, Ping An$^{(\boxtimes)}$, and Yongfang Wang

School of Communication and Information Engineering, Shanghai University,
Shanghai 200444, China
anping@shu.edu.cn

Abstract. Light field is a potential technology which can help us get richer information from the world. However, light field is limited by the field of view (FOV). Stitching multiple light fields is a solution to raising FOV of light field. In this paper we present a method that can keep the angular consistency when stitching the light fields. We first use the traditional two-dimensionall (2D) image stitching method to stitch the central sub-aperture images (SAI). We can obtain the disparity maps of the light fields, and get the disparities on two directions. Then the disparity maps can help us get a group of control points to guide the mesh grids in the SAIs to deform and warp them to a new panorama. We evaluate the stitched light field by its epipolar plane image (EPI) and the ability of refocusing. The experimental results show that our method can stitch 4D light field effectively and keep the consistency of spatial and angular domain.

Keywords: Light field stitching · Mesh deformation · Energy function

1 Introduction

Light field contains information such as light intensity, position, direction and so on. It contains both position and direction information in space. In short, it covers all the information in the propagation of rays. In recent years, the research of light field has made rapid progress. We can use camera array or microlens array which is also called plenoptic camera to capture light field images. Due to the size and cost, the most popular light field acquisition equipment is microlens array, and the portable cameras of Lytro [1], Raytrix [2] have been commercially used, which is expected to make greater progress in the future.

One of the demerits of plenoptic camera is that the FOV is not wide enough. For example, commercial Lytro Illum's FOV is only 43.5° horizontally and 62° vertically. If we want to apply light field to other areas like Virtual Reality (VR), we need widener FOV [3–5]. One of the methods to expand the field of view is to improve the hardware, but the cost is too high, so we use multiple light fields

Supported by the National Natural Science Foundation of China, under Grants 61828105, 62020106011, and 62001279.

G. Zhai et al. (Eds.): IFTC 2020, CCIS 1390, pp. 429–438, 2021.
https://doi.org/10.1007/978-981-16-1194-0_36

from different views to increase the FOV of light field. If we directly use the traditional 2D image stitching algorithm on SAIs of the light fields, we may achieve good stitching result for each pair of corresponding SAIs, but the consistency of angular domain is hard to maintain. In order to maintain the characteristics of light field, some researchers build ray models, trying to stitch light field from ray space. Guo et al. [6] establish the relationship between different light fields by using ray-space motion matrix to stitch light fields. Johansen et al. [7] used Plücker-type coordinates to obtain the relationship between the rays in two light fields, so as to calibrate the two light fields. However, If the sampling frequency of the input light field is too small, ghosting effect will be inevitable, so the quality of the stitched light field will be low. Mesh deformation is a method which is usually used in traditional image stitching. It can effectively solve the problem of ghosting effect caused by different depths. Based on this technique, Zhang et al. [8] applied this to the stitching of stereo images and achieved good effect. Wang et al. [9] use As-Projective-As-Possible Image Stitching with Moving DLT (APAP) method to align the light fields, and they divided the light fields into 4D meshes and warped the meshes to the panorama. But limited by APAP, the result may distort the object in the light field. This makes us believe that applying it to the light field is also a feasible solution.

In this paper, we first use the state-of-art 2D image stitching method [10] to stitch the center SAIs. Then we get the target disparity maps of the light fields, and get the disparitys on two directions. We use disparity maps to map the anchor points on panorama stitched by center SAIs to each SAI as control points. Then, these control points are used to guide the mesh deformation of each corresponding pair of SAIs of the two light fields, and finally the whole light field is stitched. Experimental results show that our proposed method can maintain the consistency of angular domain effectively while the image quality of the SAIs can be also guaranteed.

2   Proposed Method

In this section, we will give an overview of our light field stitching algorithm and show how it works.

We first explain why the methods like [11] and [12] are not adopted in this paper, i.e. propagating the 2D homography matrix defined in center SAIs consistently to all other corresponding SAIs. As shown in Fig. 1, it can be obtained:

$$H_1 = H_{0_{c1}}^{-1} \cdot H_c \cdot H_{1_{c1}} \tag{1}$$

where H_1 represents the transformation between the corresponding SAIs of the light fields and H_c represents the transformation between the center SAIs of two light fields, $H_{0_{c1}}$ and $H_{1_{c1}}$ are the transformations between the SAI I_{u_1,v_1} and the center SAI I_{u_c,v_c} in the two light fields respectively. Assuming that $H_{0_{c1}}$ is equal to $H_{1_{c1}}$, then Eq (1) is rewritten as:

$$H_1 = H_{c1}^{-1} \cdot H_c \cdot H_{c1} \tag{2}$$

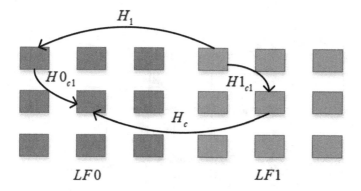

Fig. 1. Align the entire light field using the center SAIs stitching parameters.

We can see that H_1 is only similar to H_c , but they are not the same. It means that traditional 2D stitching method is not suitable for light field.

2.1 Center SAIs Stitching

The stitching of the center SAIs is the first step of our method. We expect the performance of the stitching can stay parallax-tolerant, so we choose [10] to stitch the center SAIs. [10] uses a local distortion model and uses meshes to guide the deformation of each image. In addition to good alignment and minimal local distortion, it also adds global similarity to the energy function. The energy function constrains the distortion of each image to make it similar to the global similarity transformation. The selection of similarity transformation improves the naturalness of the result. This method also selects the appropriate scale and rotation for each image.

2.2 Getting Control Points

Figure 2 is the panorama stitched by center SAIs of two light fields. As Fig. 2 shows, the blue points and red points can be obtained by method [10]. They are calculated by the mesh deformation algorithm in [10]. The blue points are deformed form the left center SAI, and the red ones deform from the right SAI. The green points are the grid vertices divided by the panorama which is stitched by the center SAIs. We label the blue and red grids as $\{g_{i,j}\}$, where i denotes the index of the blue grid or the red grid , and j denotes the labels of the two light fields. The homography matrix corresponding to each grid is denoted as $H_{i,j}$ which has been calculated in [10]. For each green point, we can find the blue or red grid where it is located, and use the homography matrix corresponding to the grid to inversely warping it to the original center SAIs. As is shown in Fig. 3, the green points in (a) are the control points in a SAI of the left light field and the green points in (b) are control points in a SAI with the same angular coordinate as (a) of the right light field. They are calculated by the grid vertexes

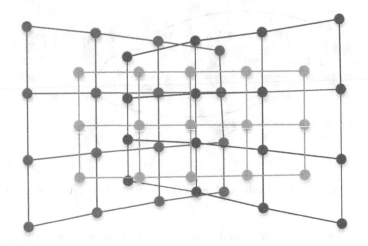

Fig. 2. Panorama stitched by the center SAIs

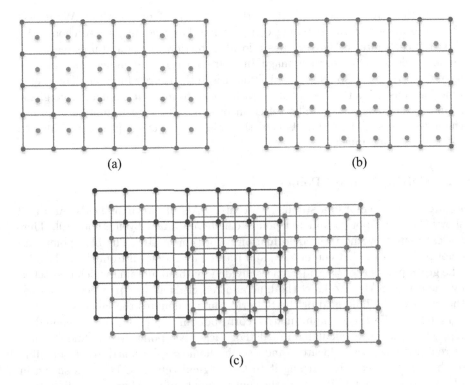

Fig. 3. The method we use to deform the mesh grids (Color figure online)

in the center panorama which is denoted by green points in Fig. 2. we denote the control points in a SAI as $p_{u,v,i,j}$. Through the disparity map, it can be written as:

$$p_{u,v,i,j} = H_{i,j}c_{i,j} + (u - v)d_{i,j}^x + (v - v_c)d_{i,j}^y \qquad (3)$$

where u_c and v_c are the angular coordinates of the center SAIs. $c_{i,j}$ is the grid vertex which is located in the $\{g_{i,j}\}$ in the panorama stitched by the center SAIs of the light fields. $d_{i,j}^x$ and $d_{i,j}^y$ are respectively the disparities of adjacent SAI on the x direction and y direction in two light fields. Then $p_{u,v,i,j}$ can be used as control points to guide the mesh deformation.

2.3 Mesh Deformation

There are many methods using control points to deform meshes, such as [13–16]. We also adopt a similar method to divide the corresponding SAIs into uniform meshes of the same size, and then guide these meshes to deform through the control points on the corresponding SAIs. Finally, this kind of problem will be deduced to a least square problem. After this step, we can keep the angular consistency of panoramas without destroying the image quality.

Disparity Term. We expect that after the grid of each SAI is deformed, the parallax on the center SAI can be maintained as much as possible, so that the scene in the stitched light field can conform to the correct depth information, thereby improving the angle consistency of the stitched light field. We define the disparity energy term below.

$$E_d = \sum_{p_{i,j,k}} \| \sum_k w_{i,j,k}\hat{v}_{i,j,k} - c_{i,j} - \hat{d}_{i,j} \|^2 \qquad (4)$$

$$\hat{d_{i,j}} = [(u - u_c)d_{i,j}^x, (v - v_c)d_{i,j}^y] \qquad (5)$$

We find the grid cell where the control point $\{p_{u,v,i,j}\}$ .is located, and obtain the weight which is represented by the inverse bilinear interpolation of the vertexes of this grid. $\hat{d}_{i,j}$ is the disparity vector of control point $\{p_{u,v,i,j}\}$. We assume that the disparity on the panorama approximates that on the center SAI, so we directly use $\hat{d}_{i,j}$ to align the SAIs.

Similarity Term. This item is used to regularize and propagate alignment constraints from overlapping areas to non-overlapping areas. Our choice for this item is to ensure that each quadrilateral undergoes a similarity transformation to keep the shape of the mesh. We choose to use the Laplacian mesh deformation method to keep the deformed mesh shape as consistent as possible. The Laplacian coordinates contain the local feature information of the surface. This form of coordinate has important applications in mesh deformation, mesh smoothing, and mesh denoising. We define the similarity energy term below.

$$E_s = \sum_{\hat{v}_{i,j}} \| \hat{v}_{i,j} - \sum_k \hat{w}_{i,j,k}\hat{v}_{i,j,k} - \delta_{i,j} \|^2 \tag{6}$$

$$\hat{w_{i,j,k}} = \frac{1}{d} \tag{7}$$

$$\delta_{i,j} = \hat{v}_{i,j} - \sum_k \hat{w}_{i,j,k}\hat{v}_{i,j,k} \tag{8}$$

Since we use simple Laplacian mesh deformation, $\hat{w}_{i,j,k}$ is set as the degree of the node of the mesh grid and $\delta_{i,j}$ denotes the Laplacian coordinates of the grid vertex of the SAIs to be stitched. At last we combine the above energy terms and the following linear least squares problem can be obtained.

$$E = E_d + \lambda E_s \tag{9}$$

where λ is the weight with default value of 1. Sparse linear solver can be used to solve the energy minimization problem. The matrix can be written as:

$$WV = d \tag{10}$$

$$W = \begin{bmatrix} \hat{w}_{1,1,1} & 0 & \hat{w}_{1,1,2} & \cdots & 0 \cdots & \hat{w}_{1,1,3} & 0 & \hat{w}_{1,1,4} & 0 & \cdots \\ 0 & \hat{w}_{1,1,1} & 0 & \hat{w}_{1,1,2} & 0 \cdots & 0 & \hat{w}_{1,1,3} & 0 & \hat{w}_{1,1,4} \cdots \\ 0 & & & & \vdots & & & & \\ & & & & 0 & & & & \\ w_{1,1,1} & 0 & w_{1,1,2} & \cdots & 0 \cdots & w_{1,1,3} & 0 & w_{1,1,4} & 0 & \cdots \\ 0 & w_{1,1,1} & 0 & w_{1,1,2} & 0 \cdots & 0 & w_{1,1,3} & 0 & w_{1,1,4} \cdots \\ & & & & \vdots & & & & \end{bmatrix} \tag{11}$$

$$V = \begin{bmatrix} \hat{v}^x_{1,1} \\ \hat{v}^y_{1,1} \\ \hat{v}^x_{2,1} \\ \hat{v}^y_{2,1} \end{bmatrix} \quad d = \begin{bmatrix} \delta^x_{1,1} \\ \delta^y_{1,1} \\ \vdots \\ c^x_{1,1} + \hat{d}^x_{1,1} \\ c^y_{1,1} + \hat{d}^y_{1,1} \\ \vdots \end{bmatrix} \tag{12}$$

We can use direct linear transformation to solve this problem. As is shown in Fig. 3(c), the red points and the yellow points calculated by our algorithm are respectively the grid vertexes of SAI of the left light field and the right light field. The blue points are the grid vertexes of the panorama of center SAI. The red and yellow points can be warped to a new panorama that maintain proper disparity with the blue meshes in the panorama stitched by the center SAIs.

Fig. 4. Center SAI thumbnails of the test light field scene.

2.4   Seam-Cutting for the SAIs

To maintain the consistency of the angular domain of the light field while seamlessly stitching the light field, we also need to improve the traditional graph cutting algorithm.Generally speaking, we use 4D graph cut to find the seams of images in light field stitching. But 4D graph cut often brings the problem of excessive calculation. For example, the light field we test in our experiment has 8×8 SAIs and each SAI is at a resolution of 541×376. If the overlap is half of the SAI's size, the graph we build will introduce 6.5 million nodes. It will cost our too time to cut the graph, so we should change the energy function in the graph cut to the following formula. In this paper, we adopt the improved two-dimensional graph cut method in [17].

$$E = \sum_p E_d(l_p) + \sum_{p,q \in N} E_s(l_p, l_q) \tag{13}$$

where p is the point in the overlapping area of the SAIs and l_p is a binary label used to distinguish which image is this pixel comes from. It is used to punish pixels located outside the overlapping area so that the pixels in these areas can maintain their original labels, and what makes it improve the quality of the stitched light field is the second term:

$$E_{s_{u,v}}(I_p, I_q) = \alpha \frac{(| I_{0_{u,v}}(p) - I_{1_{u,v}}(p) | + | I_{0_{u,v}}(q) - I_{1_{u,v}}(q) |)}{| G^d_{0_{u,v}}(p) | + | G^d_{1_{u,v}}(p) | + | G^d_{0_{u,v}}(q) | + | G^d_{1_{u,v}}(q) |}$$
$$+ (1 - \alpha) \frac{\sum_{u_0 \neq u, v_0 \neq v} | I_{0_{u_0,v_0}}(p) - I_{1_{u_0,v_0}}(p) | + | I_{0_{u_0,v_0}}(q) - I_{1_{u_0,v_0}}(q) |}{U \cdot V - 1} \tag{14}$$

where α is set as 0.84. This method considers the image quality of panoramic image and the angular consistency of SAI, reduce the number of nodes in the image and reduce the calculation time. Where $G^d(p)$ and $G^d(q)$ are the gradients of points p and q in the direction of p to q respectively.

3   Experimental Results

In this section, our method is evaluated on the light field dataset provided by [9]. During the shooting, the camera focuses on infinity. As is shown in Fig. 4, we

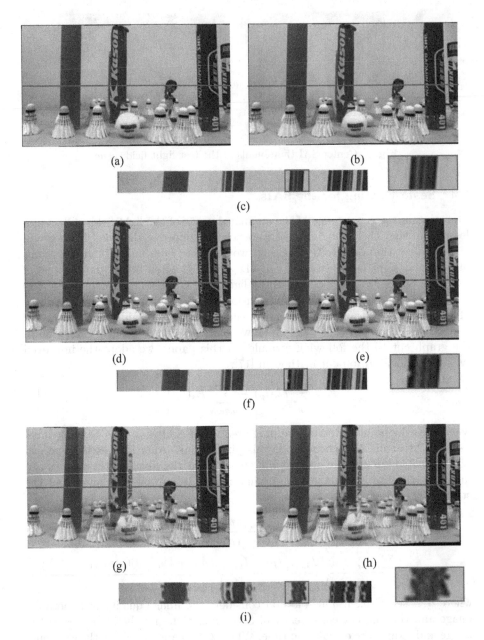

Fig. 5. Comparison of the EPIs and SAIs stitched by different alignment and graph cut methods (a) the leftmost SAI with modified graph cut; (b) the rightmost SAI with modified graph cut; (c) the EPI with modified graph cut of $y^* = 197$; (d) the leftmost SAI with traditional graph cut; (e) the rightmost SAI with traditional graph cut; (f) the EPI with traditional graph cut of $y^* = 197$; (g) the leftmost SAI by NISwGSP; (h) the rightmost SAI by NISwGSP (i) the EPI by NISwGSP of $y^* = 197$.

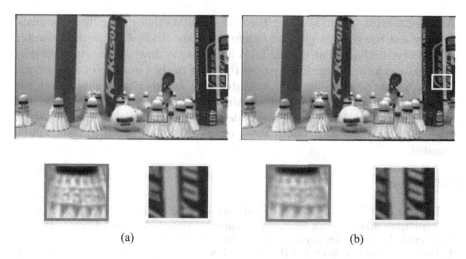

(a)   (b)

Fig. 6. The refocusing ability of the Light field stitched by our method. (a) Focusing at the badminton; (b) Focusing at the text.

select a representative light field scene as object, which contains two light fields of overlapping areas. Because of the severe vignetting, we choose 8 × SAI for every light field and discard the boundary image. In Fig. 5, we compare the left most SAI in the sixth row of the light field image with the SAI on the far right. As is shown in Fig. 5(c), since the modified graph cut can make the seam pass through the region which minimizes the inconsistency on the cutting boundary [17], it can effectively avoid the cutting in the area prone to mutation, and maintain the consistency of seam in spatial domain. Then we compare the modified graph cut whitch we use in this paper with the traditional two-dimensional graph cut on the SAI under the same coordinate. As shown in the Fig. 5(c) and (f), when we pay attention to the part of the EPIs in the red box, we can find that using traditional 2D graph cut will destroy the consistency of angular domain. It is obvious that there's a gap in the leftmost part of the lines in the red box because the seam found by the traditional graph cut goes through the face region where the change is remarkable, and some SAIs may mutate. (g) and (h) is the stitching result by the method that stitch each pair of Corresponding SAIs with traditional graphcut. It is obvious for us to find the artifact in the panoramas and the EPI of this method can't maintain consistent.

Figure 6 shows the refocusing effect of the stitched light field. Figure 6(a) focuses on the badminton in the green box, while Fig. 6(b) focuses on the text in the yellow box. It indicates that we can stitch the light fields correctly and the light fields stitched by us still has the ability of refocusing.

4   Conclusions

This paper presents a light field stitching algorithm based on mesh deformation. First, we use the classical 2D image stitching algorithm to stitch the center

SAI of light fields. Second, we get the control points though the disparity map. Then we use the control points to align two light fields. Our method doesn't use previous methods that use modified homography matrix to align lightfields. We directly deform the grid vertexes of the SAIs to the positions of a panorama that can minimize the angular inconsistency. The experiment shows that the stitched light field can not only maintain image quality, but also preserve the angular consistency. But our algorithm depends on the quality of disparity map. If the disparity map estimation is less accurate, the effect of our method will be degraded.

References

1. LYTRO ILLUM – LYTRO SUPPORT ARTICLES. http://lightfield-forum.com/lytro/lytro-archive/lytro-illum-lytro-support-articles/. Accessed 4 Nov 2018
2. Raytrix. https://www.raytrix.de/. Accessed 4 Oct 2017
3. Huang, J., Chen, Z.:6-DOF VR videos with a single 360-camera. In: Virtual Reality, pp. 37–44. IEEE(2017)
4. Overbexk, R., Erikson, D.: The making of welcome to light fields VR. In: International Conference on Multimedia and Expo, pp. 1–6. IEEE(2018)
5. Milliron, T., Szczupak, C.: Hallelujah: he world's first lytro VR experience. In: SIGGRAPH VR Village, pp. 1–2. ACM (2017)
6. Guo, X., Yu, Z., Kang, B., Lin, H., Yu, J.: Enhancing light fields through ray-space stitching. IEEE Trans. Vis. Comput. Graph. **22**(7), 1852–1861 (2016)
7. Guo, M., Zhu, H., Zhou, G., Wang, Q.: Dense light field reconstruction from sparse sampling using residual network. In: Jawahar, C.V., Li, H., Mori, G., Schindler, K. (eds.) ACCV 2018, Part VI. LNCS, vol. 11366, pp. 50–65. Springer, Cham (2019). https://doi.org/10.1007/978-3-030-20876-9_4
8. Zhang, F., Liu, F.: Casual stereoscopic panorama stitching. In: Conference on Computer Vision and Pattern Recognition, pp. 2585–2589. IEEE(2018)
9. Wang, P., Jin, X.: Light field stitching for parallax tolerance. In: International Conference on Image Processing, pp. 2002–2010. IEEE (2018)
10. Chen, Y.-S., Chuang, Y.-Y.: Natural image stitching with the global similarity prior. In: Leibe, B., Matas, J., Sebe, N., Welling, M. (eds.) ECCV 2016, Part V. LNCS, vol. 9909, pp. 186–201. Springer, Cham (2016). https://doi.org/10.1007/978-3-319-46454-1_12
11. Oliveira, A., Birtes, C.: Lenslet light field panorama creation: a sub-aperture image stitching approach. In: European Signal Processing Conference, pp. 236–240. EURASIP (2018)
12. Lv, J., Dai, F.: Panoramic light field video acquisition. In: International Conference on Multimedia and Expo, pp. 1–6. IEEE (2018)
13. Lang, M., Hornung, A., Wang, O., Poulakos, S., Smolic, A., Gross, M.: Nonlinear disparity mapping for stereoscopic 3D. ACM Trans. Graph. **29**(4), 1–10 (2010)
14. Zaragoza, J., Chin, T.: As projective-as-possible image stitching with moving DLT. In: Computer Vision and Pattern Recognition, pp. 1285–1298. IEEE (2014)
15. Zhang, F., Liu, F.: Parallax-tolerant image stitching. In: Conference on Computer Vision and Pattern Recognition, pp. 3262–3269. IEEE (2014)
16. Luo, S., Shen, I., Chen, B., Cheng, W., Chuang, Y.: Perspective-aware warping for seamless stereoscopic image cloning. Trans. Graph. **31**(6), 1–8 (2012)
17. Chen, Y., An, P.: Modified baseline for light field stitching. In: Visual Communications and Image Processing, pp. 1–4. IEEE (2019)

Integral Image Generation Based on Improved BVH Ray Tracing

Tianshu Li[1], Shigang Wang[1(✉)], Hongbin Cheng[2], Jian Wei[1], and Yan Zhao[1]

[1] College of Communication Engineering, Jilin University, Changchun 130012, China
wangshigang@vip.sina.com
[2] Changchun Cedar Electronics Technology Co., Ltd., Changchun 130103, China

Abstract. As the next generation of 3D display technology, integral imaging is widely concerned because of its wide applications, easy storage and high comfort. Nevertheless, its content generation process has always been balanced between rendering quality and operation efficiency. In this paper, a method of integral imaging element image (EI) array generation is proposed. By combining actual acquisition with computer virtual generation, an ideal camera array is established and ray tracing is applied to perform high quality image rendering for large real object models, and the bounding volume hierarchy (BVH) structure is improved for acceleration. The experimental results show that this method improves the rendering efficiency. Using a high-density small-pitch LED display with a high-transmittance lens array display platform to display stereo images, a continuous parallax effect can be seen, and there is no pseudoscopic problem. It provides a reference for the follow-up research work.

Keywords: Integral imaging · Ray tracing · Bounding volume hierarchy (BVH) · Camera array · Lens array · Elemental image(EI) array

1 Introduction

With the continuous update of display devices, intergenerational upgrades of storage devices, and continuous expansion of communication bandwidth, people are gradually no longer satisfied with traditional viewing devices and two-dimensional viewing methods, and the need for exploration of next-generation display methods is becoming more and more urgent. At present, there are some mature next-generation display methods on the market, such as VR, AR, glasses-type 3D display and immersive experience devices with non-display devices. It's known that people's pursuit of 3D display is gradually clear. However, all of them are currently limited in one way or another, which makes less effective in

Supported by National Key Research and Development Program of China (NO. 2017YFB0404800), National Natural Science Foundation of China (No. 61631009) and "the Fundamental Research Funds for the Central Universities" under the grant (No. 2017TD-19).

© Springer Nature Singapore Pte Ltd. 2021
G. Zhai et al. (Eds.): IFTC 2020, CCIS 1390, pp. 439–450, 2021.
https://doi.org/10.1007/978-981-16-1194-0_37

a wider range of scenarios. Therefore, the research of simple and easy-to-use 3D technology is particularly important.

The current 3D display technology can be divided into two categories: parallax stereo display technology and true 3D stereo display technology. VR display and glasses-type 3D display mentioned above belong to parallax stereo display technology. Their principle is that images containing parallax that conform to the object observed by both eyes are transmitted to the left and right eyes respectively, and the human brain will merge them into stereo images according to experience. According to the convergence effect, there is a certain deviation between the focus position of the human eye when actually seeing the image and the position of the processed stereo image in the human brain, which is contrary to the daily experience of viewing the object, that is, the convergence effect will cause the viewer to have different degrees of vertigo. Moreover, VR display technology requires head-mounted glasses. The distance between human eyes and the display screen is too close, which may easily lead to visual fatigue and damage to eyes. Therefore, true 3D display technology has become a more potential development direction. Currently, true 3D display has several main branches: holographic display, volume display, integrated imaging display. Holographic display is to use the principle of light interference to record the 3D information of an object under the reference action of a coherent light source, and then illuminate the hologram with a laser, and use the principle of light diffraction to display the 3D image of the object. It is difficult to popularize to the general public because of its high requirement for coherence of light source and stability of imaging system. Volume display is a 2D image projection on a dynamic display screen, which uses the temporary retention of human vision to achieve 3D display. It is complex to display equipment, and its size is limited. In contrast, the integrated imaging stereoscopic display as a passive imaging system has low requirements for the acquisition process, and the image storage format is the same as that of traditional 2D images. The display only needs to rely on the lens array placed in front of the display screen. It is in line with people's pursuit of next-generation display technology, and its research prospects are broad and have practical significance.

Since Lippmann proposed the integrated imaging stereo display [9] in 1908 and won the Nobel Prize, the development and application of integrated imaging technology have continued to emerge. In the 1970s, high-resolution photosensitive devices such as CCD cameras gradually replaced traditional films, realizing high-speed acquisition and storage of image information, and integrated imaging technology also entered a stage of rapid development. The researchers use a camera array shooting at the same time to record a element image array of the real sceney [5]. But with the continuous improvement of display resolution, the scale of the camera array is also increasing. In order to reduce the scale of camera array, some scholars proposed the method of combining depth camera with computer virtual viewpoint generation [6]. With the upgrading of data processing capability of computer, the generation method of computer-generated integral imaging (CGII) has attracted much attention in recent years [8]. However, CGII also has many problems, such as the method of independent rendering within camera arrays for large scenes and high resolution images with slow rendering times [12]. Besides, ray tracing algorithms that produce high-quality rendered images are also becoming increasingly popular [1]. However, since every pixel has to do intersection operation between ray and object points, researchers have made a lot of efforts to optimize the ray tracing technology, and proposed many 3D scene management methods, such as Oct-tree and KD-tree based on spatial division [7], and the bounding volume hierarchy (BVH) structure of partitioning from the perspective of objects [2].

In this paper, a improved BVH-based raytracing integarl image acquisition method is proposed. In the second part, the principle of improved BVH-based raytracing technology is explained in Sect. 2, including integral imaging principle, raytracing principle and improved BVH structure establishment. Section 3 provides the experiments and the results. Finally, a brief summary is given in Sect. 4.

2   Principle of EI Array Generation

Integral imaging is a true 3D display technology that uses microlens array to record and reproduce 3D space scenes. The acquisition and display process is symmetric (see Fig. 1).

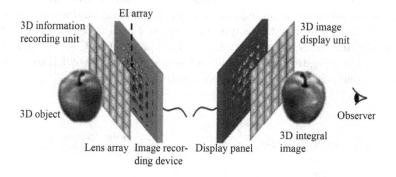

Fig. 1. Principle of integral imaging.

During the recording process, the light reflected from the 3D object illuminated by the general light source passes through the lens array and images on the image recording device, which is the EI array. It is easy to know that a point P on the object will be recorded by different stereoscopic metamagic images through different lenses. During the display process, the display panel emits light which passes through the lens array and converges in the space by crossing to restore the recorded 3D image. If the image recording unit and display unit object, lens, like the location of the plane relationship completely symmetrical, because of the observer relative record device between the location and the objects and between objects are on the contrary, it will appear depth inversion problem, is to move to the left shows the observer to the right will appear. In order to avoid the depth inversion problem, virtual mode display is adopted in this paper, so that the orientation of the object relative to the recording plane and the object relative to the observer are consistent.

The above is a traditional EI array generation technique, which is limited by the size of lens array and can only record small and close objects [10]. With the improvement of the convenience of CCD cameras, researchers gradually replaced lens arrays with camera arrays to record information of a wider range of light fields. However, due to the high cost of camera array and the difficulty of synchronous debugging, computer-generated integral imaging (CGII) techniques is easier to realize [4] and getting faster and faster. In order to increase the practical significance of 3D display, this paper adopts a EI array generation technology which combines real photography and computational generation. The 3d model of real scene modeling is taken by computer in virtual environment, which is not completely divorced from reality and easy to operate.

2.1   Principle of Raytracing

CGII can be used in a variety of ways, such as using a camera module with 3D software such as 3dsMax, Autodesk Maya, Blender, etc. The advantage is that it is easy to set up and adjust the camera array with the help of the properties given by the software. The disadvantage is that the software's built-in camera simulates the mapping optical path and imaging characteristics of real cameras, making it difficult to adjust the camera's optical center, image plane, focal length and other parameters freely. This paper uses C++ programming method in Linux system to implementation the generation of EI array, which can give the acquisition system the maximum degree of freedom.

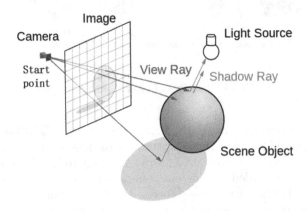

Fig. 2. Principle of raytracing.

Ray tracing is an image rendering method (see Fig. 2). A light ray from a light source shines on an object and bounces off the surface of the object into the camera's image. If the light emitted by the light source is analyzed forward, a large number of light rays do not intersect with the object or reflect through the object and do not enter the camera to participate in the imaging, so the calculation efficiency is low. Therefore, according to the reversible property of the optical path, the camera is used as the starting point to track back the light in a specific direction, find the nearest intersection point between the light and the object, and assign its color value to the pixel points through which the light passes, then an image of the scene can be drawn, effectively reducing the rendering time.

Ray tracing algorithm mainly includes three parts: ray generation, which calculates the starting point and direction of the ray pointing to each pixel point based on the geometric parameters of the camera; geting intersection between ray and object, for each ray, find the collision point with the object, find the nearest object point that intersects with the ray, if not, illuminate to the background; render processing, Calculate the color of the pixels to be recorded based on the result of the intersection of the rays.

2.2   Principle of Improved BVH

Ray-tracing renders images of high quality, but with it comes the problem of rendering too slowly. Because if each ray traverses the position and point coordinates in the whole 3D scene, it will take a lot of time to do the intersection operation. In order to make the rendering process faster, it is necessary to find an appropriate hierarchical structure for quickly determining the region in the space. Obviously not all light fellowship with a certain object, then naturally there is no need to traverse all the triangle faces of 3D objects, so using a bounding box around the object, with the object of triangle faces computing intersection before judging whether light fellowship with bounding box, the bounding box to intersection than object is simple, do not need to request a specific point, just need to find whether intersected, if even the bounding box and light no intersections occur, then obviously not with the object of triangle faces intersection. In addition, the topological relationship between bounding boxes should be established. A big box should be built between the two boxes. The judgment on the big box should be made first. This structure is called BVH, and it's to build bounding boxes for objects parallel to the X, Y, and Z axes which named axis-aligned bounding box (AABB), it is composed of the intersection of three pairs of planes, not an arbitrarily rotating bounding box. We take 2D AABB as an example, so there are only two pairs of x and Y planes (see Fig. 3), and the 3D case can be infer similarly.

First of all, as shown in the picture above the left, the ray with x plane intersection, will enter the intersection of the small as t_{min}, after go out the intersection of the large as t_{max}, then calculated the among light and two points of intersection of y plane also notes for another group of t_{min}, t_{max}, we get the light with a pair of x plane intersection, with a pair of y plane intersection, only

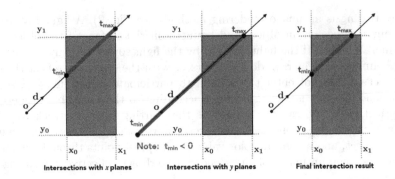

Fig. 3. Principle of BVH.

when the light into all the plane you truly into the box, so for each pair of flat t_{min}, t_{max} do the following operations:

$$t_{enter} = max\{t_{min}\}, \ t_{exit} = min\{t_{max}\} \tag{1}$$

where t_{enter} and t_{exit} correspond to the above two conditions respectively, and corresponding to the 2D example, the two real intersection points with the bounding box are finally obtained, as shown in the right result figure. When $t_{enter} < t_{exit}$, the line where the light is located must have been in the box for some time, and there must also be intersection points. However, the light is not a straight line, but a ray. In addition to ensuring that the line where the light is located stays in the box for some time, the actual physical meaning should be considered as if $t_{exit} < 0$, then the box is behind the ray, no intersection here; if $t_{exit} \geq 0$ and $t_{enter} < 0$, the ray's origin is in the box, there are intersections. In summary, ray and AABB intersect only if $t_{enter} < t_{exit}$ and $t_{exit} \geq 0$.

After understanding the principle and construction method of bounding box, we can divide the space into multiple layers of bounding box. There are many different ways of dividing space, uniform spatial partitions (Grids)BSP-treeKd-tree [3], surface area heuristic (SAH) [13]. The most significant difference between BVH and the previous methods is that the division is no longer based on space, but from the point of view of objects, that is, triangular faces. First of all find out the whole scene bounding box as a root node, then find the appropriate division point of the triangle face in the bounding box. In this paper, the root node of BVH is divided into four leaf nodes, in this way, the render efficiency will be improved. The bounding boxes overlap, but a triangular face is stored only in a unique box. The next step is repeated recursively for all subspaces.

3   Experiments and Results

The specific process of acquiring EI array based on improved BVH ray tracing includes the following steps (see Fig. 4):

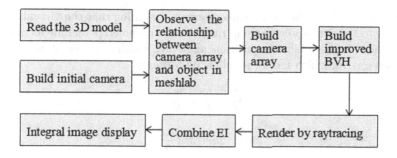

Fig. 4. Experimental flow chart.

Read the 3D object model. The actual object is photographed by the camera sequence and the .ply file is obtained through the 3D reconstruction algorithm. The model contains 442864 triangular faces and 221355 vertices. The .ply model file header is extracted, the point cloud coordinates, the number of triangles and the color information are read, and it is used for ray tracing to assign color value to the pixel. Using C++ language, an ideal 24 * 24 camera array is established in a virtual environment, which conforms to the pinhole imaging rules. The initial position of the camera optical center is set as the origin of the world coordinate system. Given the rotation angle and translation of the camera around each coordinate axis, the rotation matrix and translation matrix under the camera coordinate system are obtained as follows.

$$R(\theta x) = \begin{bmatrix} 1 & 0 & 0 & 0 \\ 0 & cos\theta x & -sin\theta x & 0 \\ 0 & sin\theta x & cos\theta x & 0 \\ 0 & 0 & 0 & 1 \end{bmatrix} \tag{2}$$

$$R(\theta y) = \begin{bmatrix} cos\theta y & 0 & sin\theta y & 0 \\ 0 & 1 & 0 & 0 \\ -sin\theta y & 0 & cos\theta y & 0 \\ 0 & 0 & 0 & 1 \end{bmatrix} \tag{3}$$

$$R(\theta z) = \begin{bmatrix} cos\theta z & -sin\theta z & 0 & 0 \\ sin\theta z & cos\theta z & 0 & 0 \\ 0 & 0 & 1 & 0 \\ 0 & 0 & 0 & 1 \end{bmatrix} \tag{4}$$

$$T = \begin{bmatrix} I & u \\ 0 & 1 \end{bmatrix} \tag{5}$$

where θx, θy and θz are the rotation angles of the camera around the coordinate axis, the translation vector $u = (tx, ty, tz)'$, and I is the 3 * 3 identity matrix. The origin of the camera coordinate system is the optical center of the camera.

The coordinate column vector is left multiplied by the rotation and translation matrix to obtain the camera's position coordinates in the world coordinate system and establish the initial camera array. Assuming that the virtual camera conforms to the small-hole imaging rule, camera parameters include focal length f of camera lens, camera acquisition angle θc, width and height w and h of camera negative, which meet the following formula:

$$\frac{f}{z} = \frac{w}{h} = \frac{w_m}{h_m} \tag{6}$$

$$\theta c = 2arctan(\frac{w_m}{2z}) \tag{7}$$

where z is the distance between the optical center of the camera and the center of the object, w_m and h_m are the width and height of the object bounding box respectively.

Each camera in the initial camera array is written into .ply file with negative as the bottom and focal length as the height, and a four-pyramid model is established instead of an ideal camera. The 3D object model and the camera array model are displayed in the 3D software Mashlab (see Fig. 5). The position of the optical center of the virtual camera array in the world coordinate system is calculated based on the standard that the sub-image captured by the object can cover the maximum range of the sub-image array.

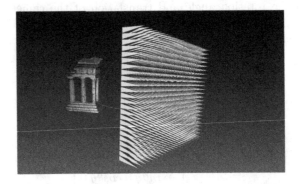

Fig. 5. 3D object model and camera array model.

Next, shooting the EI array based on the original point and ray direction obtained above. The parameters obtained by the formula 2–7 are used to set the virtual camera array to determine the optical center of each camera and its negative position in the world coordinate system, that is, the original position of the tracing ray. BVH was defined, and the number of leaf nodes in each root node was 4. Each triangular face in the model was classified until all objects were divided.

Using ray-tracing algorithm, for each camera, the ray beam for ray-tracing is established starting from its optical center and directed to the pixels on its film. For each ray, step by step along the direction of its emission to determine whether the ray intersects with the object's bounding box. If it intersects, the RGB value of the leaf node is assigned to the pixel point; if it does not intersect, it must not intersect with the object point in the bounding box, and set the pixel to 0. Repeat the operations of creating light and finding intersections, and use OpenMP to perform multi-threaded calculations on the loop that generates the integral image to improve the calculation speed. In this paper, it took 937.714 s to generate the EI array. Compared with the general BVH algorithm 1373.718 s and 4203.69 s without the using of hierarchical structure, the rendering efficiency was improved by 0.46 times and 3.48 times, respectively, as shown in the Table 1.

Table 1. Integrated imaging rendering time using different methods.

Method	Improved BVH	General BVH	Without BVH
Speed	937.714s	1373.718s	4203.69s

Because of the virtual ideal camera established by C++ programming conforming to the principle of small hole imaging, it is an inverted real image when compared with the object. Each EI is flipped 180° to get a positive virtual image, no depth reversal effect when displaying. EIs are combined according to the arrangement relation of corresponding camera to obtain EI array (see Fig. 6).

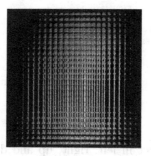

Fig. 6. The generated EI array.

Put 2D EI array displayed on the integrated imaging 3D display platform (see Fig. 7). The LED display panel is research and development by Hidayat company manufacturing high density small spacing of LED display, lens array with high light transmittance of a integrated acrylic module, can gain higher brightness [11] and low requirements for viewing environment.

The display panel and lens position of the display platform and other parameters are shown in the Table 2. On the parameter platform, the focal length of the lens array is fc, and the distance between the lens array and the display screen is g. When $g < fc$, the lens becomes virtual image, which is the virtual

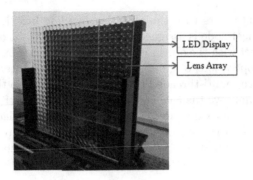

Fig. 7. Integrated imaging 3D display platform.

mode. The integrated imaging display platform is set to the virtual image display mode, the EI array on the display screen passes through the lens array to display the stereo image corresponding to the 3D object.

Table 2. Integrated imaging display platform parameters.

LED display parameters	Display resolution	384 * 384
	Pixel spacing (horizontal/vertical)	1.25 mm
	Display size	120 mm * 120 mm
Lena array parameters	Number of lens	24 * 24
	Focal length (fc)	6 mm
	Radius of lens	20 mm
	Distance between lens and display plane (g)	4.8 mm

Record the display effect in left, right, up and down four viewpoints. The display effect of left and right, up and down four directions is compared (see Fig. 8). It can be seen that on the left viewpoint, the spacing between the two the far left pillarson of the temple is larger (red squares); on the right viewpoint, the most the right side of the two pillars of the spacing of larger (blue squares). And the temple becomes narrower as a whole looks, because the right viewpoint is the narrow side of the temple. By comparing the upper and lower views, it can be seen that the angle of the eaves (red lines) and the edge of the steps (blue lines) changes along with the perspective relationship. When the viewpoint is on the top, the angle is relatively small; when the viewpoint is on the bottom, the angle is larger and tends to be flat.

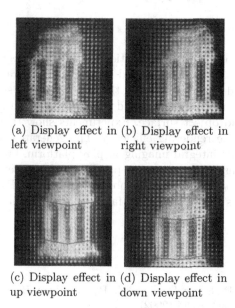

(a) Display effect in (b) Display effect in
left viewpoint   right viewpoint

(c) Display effect in (d) Display effect in
up viewpoint   down viewpoint

Fig. 8. Display effect in left, right, up and down viewpoints (Color figure online).

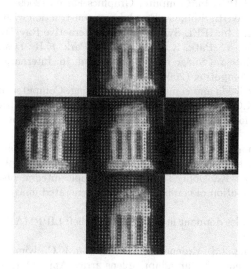

Fig. 9. Integrated imaging 3D display effect.

Comparing them by position with the display effect of the central viewpoint, the parallax gradient can be seen (see Fig. 9). And the information that can be seen when actually observing the object is obtained in each viewpoint, without pseudoscopic problem.

4 Conclusion

This paper studies an EI array generation method in integral imaging, which units the large scene 3D model collected in reality, useing ray tracing to obtain high-quality rendered images, and using the improved BVH structure to manage the point cloud information of the model to speed up the intersection operation between ray and object surface. Experiments show that this method can effectively improve the rendering efficiency. The generated integral image was displayed on the LED integral imaging display platform. From the perspective of display effect, there was continuous parallax and no pseudoscopic problem. This paper aims at a single complex object experiment. For multiple objects and the whole scenes full of triangular faces, the acceleration effect remains to be studied.

References

1. Akeley, K., Kirk, D., Seiler, L., Slusallek, P., Grantham, B.: When will ray-tracing replace rasterization?. ACM (2002)
2. Lauterbach, C., Garland, M., Sengupta, S., Luebke, D., Manocha, D.: Fast BVH construction on GPUs. In: Computer Graphics Forum (2009)
3. Hunt, W., Mark, W.R., Stoll, G.: Fast kd-tree construction with an adaptive error-bounded heuristic. In: IEEE Symposium on Interactive Ray Tracing (2008)
4. Lee, B.N.R., Cho, Y., Park, K.S., Min, S.W., Park, K.R.: Design and implementation of a fast integral image rendering method. In: International Conference on Entertainment Computing (2006)
5. Levoy, M.: Light fields and computational imaging. Computer 39(8), 46–55 (2006)
6. Li, G., Kwon, K.C., Shin, G.H., Jeong, J.S., Kim, N.: Simplified integral imaging pickup method for real objects using a depth camera. J. Opt. Soc. Korea 16(4), 381–385 (2012)
7. Li-Qiong, L., Jun-Song, B., De-An, L.: Integrated point cloud storage structure based on Octree and KDtree. In: Computer Systems and Applications (2012)
8. Liao, H., Nomura, K., Dohi, T.: Autostereoscopic integral photography imaging using pixel distribution of computer graphics generated image. In: ACM Siggraph (2005)
9. Epreuves reversibles donnant la sensation du relief: LIPPMAN, G. J. De Physique 7, 821–825 (1908)
10. Song, M.H., Jeong, J.S., Erdenebat, M.U., Kwon, K.C., Kim, N., Yoo, K.H.: Integral imaging system using an adaptive lens array. Appl. Opt. 55(23), 6399 (2016)
11. Wu, W., Wang, S., Zhong, C., Piao, M., Zhao, Y.: Integral imaging with full parallax based on mini led display unit. IEEE Access 7, 1 (2019)
12. Yanaka, K.: Integral photography using hexagonal fly's eye lens and fractional view. In: Proceedings of Spie Stereoscopic Displays and Virtual Reality Systems, San Jose Ca (2008)
13. Zhao, S., Cao, Y., Guo, Y., Chen, S., Chen, L.: A fast spatial partition method in bounding volume hierarchy

Author Index

Printed in the United States
by Baker & Taylor Publisher Services